Family Maps
of
Dunn County, Wisconsin
Deluxe Edition

With Homesteads, Roads, Waterways, Towns, Cemeteries, Railroads, and More

Family Maps of Dunn County, Wisconsin

Deluxe Edition

With Homesteads, Roads, Waterways, Towns, Cemeteries, Railroads, and More

by Gregory A. Boyd, J.D.

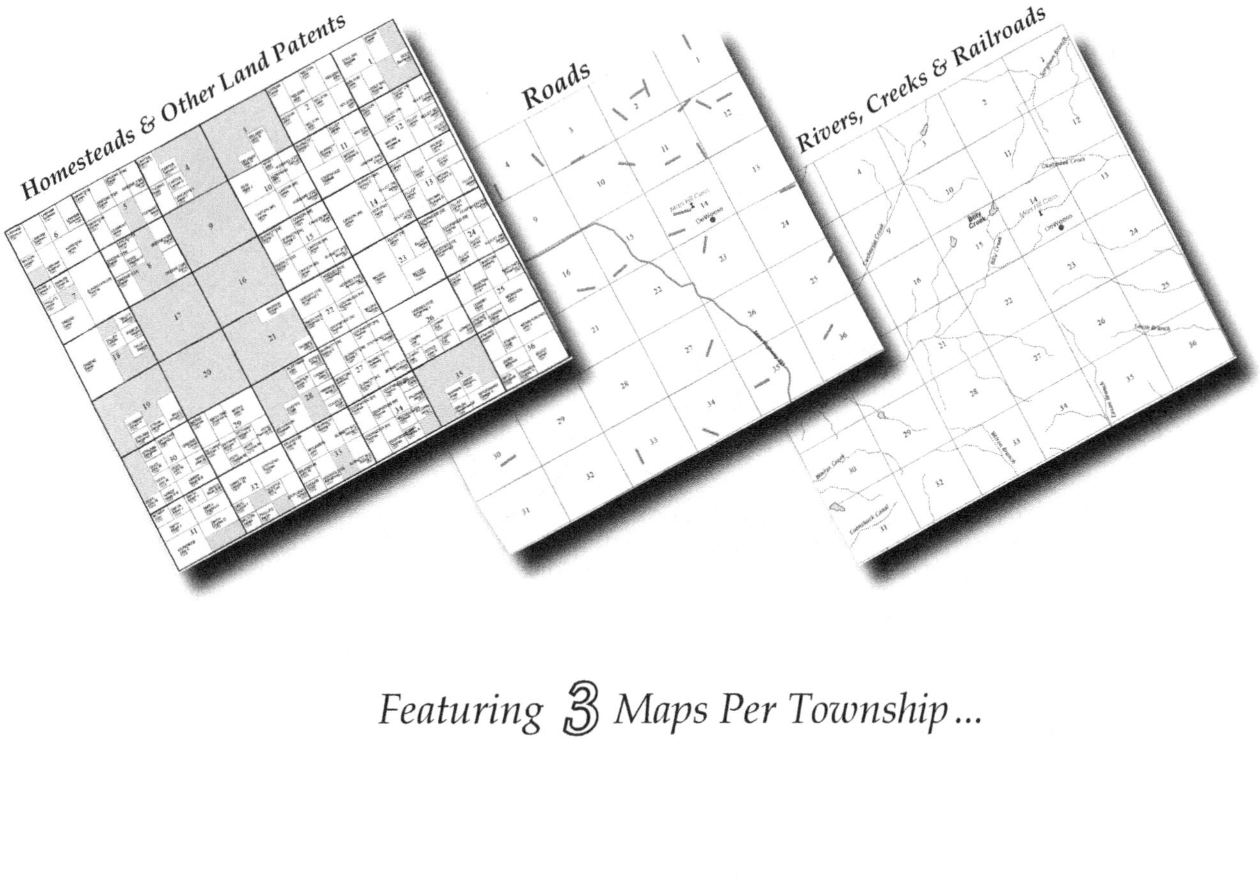

Featuring 3 Maps Per Township...

Arphax Publishing Co.
www.arphax.com

Family Maps of Dunn County, Wisconsin, Deluxe Edition: With Homesteads, Roads, Waterways, Towns, Cemeteries, Railroads, and More.
by Gregory A. Boyd, J.D.

ISBN 1-4203-1542-0

Printed in the United States of America

Published by Arphax Publishing Co., 2210 Research Park Blvd., Norman, Oklahoma, USA 73069
www.arphax.com

First Edition

ATTENTION HISTORICAL & GENEALOGICAL SOCIETIES, UNIVERSITIES, COLLEGES, CORPORATIONS, FAMILY REUNION COORDINATORS, AND PROFESSIONAL ORGANIZATIONS: Quantity discounts are available on bulk purchases of this book. For information, please contact Arphax Publishing Co., at the address listed above, or at (405) 366-6181, or visit our web-site at www.arphax.com and contact us through the "Bulk Sales" link.

—LEGAL—

The contents of this book rely on data published by the United States Government and its various agencies and departments, including but not limited to the General Land Office–Bureau of Land Management, the Department of the Interior, and the U.S. Census Bureau. The author has relied on said government agencies or re-sellers of its data, but makes no guarantee of the data's accuracy or of its representation herein, neither in its text nor maps. Said maps have been proportioned and scaled in a manner reflecting the author's primary goal—to make patentee names readable. This book will assist in the discovery of possible relationships between people, places, locales, rivers, streams, cemeteries, etc., but "proving" those relationships or exact geographic locations of any of the elements contained in the maps will require the use of other source material, which could include, but not be limited to: land patents, surveys, the patentees' applications, professionally drawn road-maps, etc.

Neither the author nor publisher makes any claim that the contents herein represent a complete or accurate record of the data it presents and disclaims any liability for reader's use of the book's contents. Many circumstances exist where human, computer, or data delivery errors could cause records to have been missed or to be inaccurately represented herein. Neither the author nor publisher shall assume any liability whatsoever for errors, inaccuracies, omissions or other inconsistencies herein.

This book is dedicated to my wonderful family:

Vicki, Jordan, & Amy Boyd

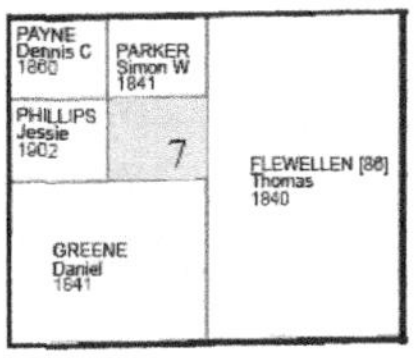

Contents

Preface....1
How to Use this Book - A Graphical Summary....2
How to Use This Book....3

- Part I -

The Big Picture

Map **A** - Where Dunn County, Wisconsin Lies Within the State....11
Map **B** - Dunn County, Wisconsin and Surrounding Counties....12
Map **C** - Congressional Townships of Dunn County, Wisconsin....13
Map **D** - Cities & Towns of Dunn County, Wisconsin....14
Map **E** - Cemeteries of Dunn County, Wisconsin....16
Surnames in Dunn County, Wisconsin Patents....18
Surname/Township Index....25

- Part II -

Township Map Groups

(each Map Group contains a Patent Index, Patent Map, Road Map, & Historical Map)

Map Group **1** - Township 31-North Range 14-West....66
Map Group **2** - Township 31-North Range 13-West....78
Map Group **3** - Township 31-North Range 12-West....88
Map Group **4** - Township 31-North Range 11-West....98
Map Group **5** - Township 30-North Range 14-West....108
Map Group **6** - Township 30-North Range 13-West....120
Map Group **7** - Township 30-North Range 12-West....130
Map Group **8** - Township 30-North Range 11-West....140
Map Group **9** - Township 29-North Range 14-West....152
Map Group **10** - Township 29-North Range 13-West....162
Map Group **11** - Township 29-North Range 12-West....172
Map Group **12** - Township 29-North Range 11-West....182
Map Group **13** - Township 28-North Range 14-West....192
Map Group **14** - Township 28-North Range 13-West....200
Map Group **15** - Township 28-North Range 12-West....212
Map Group **16** - Township 28-North Range 11-West....224
Map Group **17** - Township 27-North Range 14-West....234
Map Group **18** - Township 27-North Range 13-West....242
Map Group **19** - Township 27-North Range 12-West....252

Map Group **20** - Township 27-North Range 11-West 262
Map Group **21** - Township 26-North Range 14-West 274
Map Group **22** - Township 26-North Range 13-West 284
Map Group **23** - Township 26-North Range 12-West 296
Map Group **24** - Township 26-North Range 11-West 310

Appendices

Appendix A - Congressional Authority for Land Patents 324
Appendix B - Section Parts (Aliquot Parts) 325
Appendix C - Multi-Patentee Groups in Dunn County 329

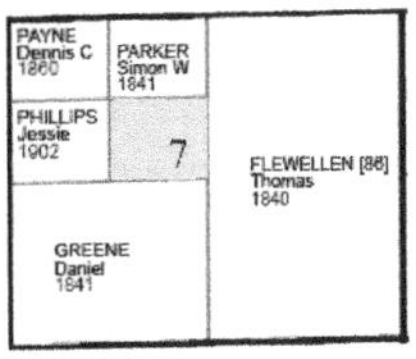

Preface

The quest for the discovery of my ancestors' origins, migrations, beliefs, and life-ways has brought me rewards that I could never have imagined. The *Family Maps* series of books is my first effort to share with historical and genealogical researchers, some of the tools that I have developed to achieve my research goals. I firmly believe that this effort will allow many people to reap the same sorts of treasures that I have.

Our Federal government's General Land Office of the Bureau of Land Management (the "GLO") has given genealogists and historians an incredible gift by virtue of its enormous database housed on its web-site at glorecords.blm.gov. Here, you can search for and find millions of parcels of land purchased by our ancestors in about thirty states.

This GLO web-site is one of the best FREE on-line tools available to family researchers. But, it is not for the faint of heart, nor is it for those unwilling or unable to to sift through and analyze the thousands of records that exist for most counties.

My immediate goal with this series is to spare you the hundreds of hours of work that it would take you to map the Land Patents for this county. Every Dunn County homestead or land patent that I have gleaned from public GLO databases is mapped here. Consequently, I can usually show you in an instant, where your ancestor's land is located, as well as the names of nearby land-owners.

Originally, that was my primary goal. But after speaking to other genealogists, it became clear that there was much more that they wanted. Taking their advice set me back almost a full year, but I think you will agree it was worth the wait. Because now, you can learn so much more.

Now, this book answers these sorts of questions:

- Are there any variant spellings for surnames that I have missed in searching GLO records?
- Where is my family's traditional home-place?
- What cemeteries are near Grandma's house?
- My Granddad used to swim in such-and-such-Creek—where is that?
- How close is this little community to that one?
- Are there any other people with the same surname who bought land in the county?
- How about cousins and in-laws—did they buy land in the area?

And these are just for starters!

The rules for using the *Family Maps* books are simple, but the strategies for success are many. Some techniques are apparent on first use, but many are gained with time and experience. Please take the time to notice the roads, cemeteries, creek-names, family names, and unique first-names throughout the whole county. You cannot imagine what YOU might be the first to discover.

I hope to learn that many of you have answered age-old research questions within these pages or that you have discovered relationships previously not even considered. When these sorts of things happen to you, will you please let me hear about it? I would like nothing better. My contact information can always be found at www.arphax.com.

One more thing: please read the "How To Use This Book" chapter; it starts on the next page. This will give you the very best chance to find the treasures that lie within these pages.

My family and I wish you the very best of luck, both in life, and in your research. Greg Boyd

How to Use This Book - A Graphical Summary

Part I

"The Big Picture"

Map A ▸ *Counties in the State*
Map B ▸ *Surrounding Counties*
Map C ▸ *Congressional Townships (Map Groups) in the County*
Map D ▸ *Cities & Towns in the County*
Map E ▸ *Cemeteries in the County*
Surnames in the County ▸ *Number of Land-Parcels for Each Surname*
Surname/Township Index ▸ Directs you to Township Map Groups in Part II

The Surname/Township Index can direct you to any number of **Township Map Groups**

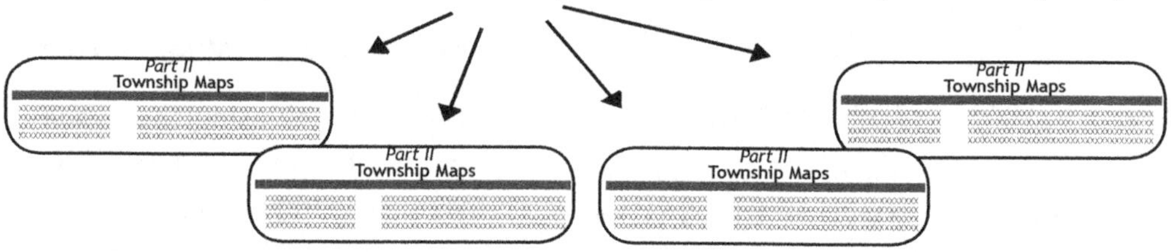

Part II

Township Map Groups

(1 for each Township in the County)

Each Township Map Group contains all four of of the following tools . . .

Land Patent Index ▸ *Every-name Index of Patents Mapped in this Township*
Land Patent Map ▸ *Map of Patents as listed in above Index*
Road Map ▸ *Map of Roads, City-centers, and Cemeteries in the Township*
Historical Map ▸ *Map of Railroads, Lakes, Rivers, Creeks, City-Centers, and Cemeteries*

Appendices

Appendix A ▸ *Congressional Authority enabling Patents within our Maps*
Appendix B ▸ *Section-Parts / Aliquot Parts (a comprehensive list)*
Appendix C ▸ *Multi-patentee Groups (Individuals within Buying Groups)*

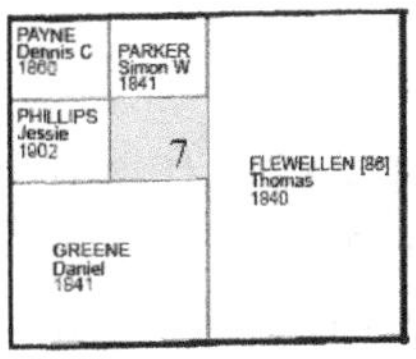

How to Use This Book

The two "Parts" of this *Family Maps* volume seek to answer two different types of questions. Part I deals with broad questions like: what counties surround Dunn County, are there any ASHCRAFTs in Dunn County, and if so, in which Townships or Maps can I find them? Ultimately, though, Part I should point you to a particular Township Map Group in Part II.

Part II concerns itself with details like: where exactly is this family's land, who else bought land in the area, and what roads and streams run through the land, or are located nearby. The Chart on the opposite page, and the remainder of this chapter attempt to convey to you the particulars of these two "parts", as well as how best to use them to achieve your research goals.

Part I
"The Big Picture"

Within Part I, you will find five "Big Picture" maps and two county-wide surname tools.

These include:

- Map A - Where Dunn County lies within the state
- Map B - Counties that surround Dunn County
- Map C - Congressional Townships of Dunn County (+ Map Group Numbers)
- Map D - Cities & Towns of Dunn County (with Index)
- Map E - Cemeteries of Dunn County (with Index)
- Surnames in Dunn County Patents (with Parcel-counts for each surname)
- Surname/Township Index (with Parcel-counts for each surname by Township)

The five "Big-Picture" Maps are fairly self-explanatory, yet should not be overlooked. This is particularly true of Maps "C", "D", and "E", all of which show Dunn County and its Congressional Townships (and their assigned Map Group Numbers).

Let me briefly explain this concept of Map Group Numbers. These are a device completely of our own invention. They were created to help you quickly locate maps without having to remember the full legal name of the various Congressional Townships. It is simply easier to remember "Map Group 1" than a legal name like: "Township 9-North Range 6-West, 5th Principal Meridian." But the fact is that the TRUE legal name for these Townships IS terribly important. These are the designations that others will be familiar with and you will need to accurately record them in your notes. This is why both Map Group numbers AND legal descriptions of Townships are almost always displayed together.

Map "C" will be your first intoduction to "Map Group Numbers", and that is all it contains: legal Township descriptions and their assigned Map Group Numbers. Once you get further into your research, and more immersed in the details, you will likely want to refer back to Map "C" from time to time, in order to regain your bearings on just where in the county you are researching.

Remember, township boundaries are a completely artificial device, created to standardize land descriptions. But do not let them become a boundary in your mind when choosing which townships to research. Your relative's in-laws, children, cousins, siblings, and mamas and papas, might just as easily have lived in the township next to the one your grandfather lived in—rather than in the one where he actually lived. So Map "C" can be your guide to which other Townships/ Map Groups you likewise ought to analyze.

Of course, the same holds true for County lines; this is the purpose behind Map "B". It shows you surrounding counties that you may want to consider for further reserarch.

Map "D", the Cities and Towns map, is the first map with an index. Map "E" is the second (Cemeteries). Both, Maps "D" and "E" give you broad views of City (or Cemetery) locations in the County. But they go much further by pointing you toward pertinent Township Map Groups so you can locate the patents, roads, and waterways located near a particular city or cemetery.

Once you are familiar with these *Family Maps* volumes and the county you are researching, the "Surnames In Dunn County" chapter (or its sister chapter in other volumes) is where you'll likely start your future research sessions. Here, you can quickly scan its few pages and see if anyone in the county possesses the surnames you are researching. The "Surnames in Dunn County" list shows only two things: surnames and the number of parcels of land we have located for that surname in Dunn County. But whether or not you immediately locate the surnames you are researching, please do not go any further without taking a few moments to scan ALL the surnames in these very few pages.

You cannot imagine how many lost ancestors are waiting to be found by someone willing to take just a little longer to scan the "Surnames In Dunn County" list. Misspellings and typographical errors abound in most any index of this sort. Don't miss out on finding your Kinard that was written Rynard or Cox that was written Lox. If it looks funny or wrong, it very often is. And one of those little errors may well be your relative.

Now, armed with a surname and the knowledge that it has one or more entries in this book, you are ready for the "Surname/Township Index." Unlike the "Surnames In Dunn County", which has only one line per Surname, the "Surname/Township Index" contains one line-item for each Township Map Group in which each surname is found. In other words, each line represents a different Township Map Group that you will need to review.

Specifically, each line of the Surname/Township Index contains the following four columns of information:

1. Surname
2. Township Map Group Number (these Map Groups are found in Part II)
3. Parcels of Land (number of them with the given Surname within the Township)
4. Meridian/Township/Range (the legal description for this Township Map Group)

The key column here is that of the Township Map Group Number. While you should definitely record the Meridian, Township, and Range, you can do that later. Right now, you need to dig a little deeper. That Map Group Number tells you where in Part II that you need to start digging.

But before you leave the "Surname/Township Index", do the same thing that you did with the "Surnames in Dunn County" list: take a moment to scan the pages of the Index and see if there are similarly spelled or misspelled surnames that deserve your attention. Here again, is an easy opportunity to discover grossly misspelled family names with very little effort. Now you are ready to turn to . . .

Part II
"Township Map Groups"

You will normally arrive here in Part II after being directed to do so by one or more "Map Group Numbers" in the Surname/Township Index of Part I.

Each Map Group represents a set of four tools dedicated to a single Congressional Township that is either wholly or partially within the county. If you are trying to learn all that you can about a particular family or their land, then these tools should usually be viewed in the order they are presented.

These four tools include:

1. a Land Patent Index
2. a Land Patent Map
3. a Road Map, and
4. an Historical Map

As I mentioned earlier, each grouping of this sort is assigned a Map Group Number. So, let's now move on to a discussion of the four tools that make up one of these Township Map Groups.

Land Patent Index

Each Township Map Group's Index begins with a title, something along these lines:

MAP GROUP 1: Index to Land Patents
Township 16-North Range 5-West (2nd PM)

The Index contains seven (7) columns. They are:

1. ID (a unique ID number for this Individual and a corresponding Parcel of land in this Township)
2. Individual in Patent (name)
3. Sec. (Section), and
4. Sec. Part (Section Part, or Aliquot Part)
5. Date Issued (Patent)
6. Other Counties (often means multiple counties were mentioned in GLO records, or the section lies within multiple counties).
7. For More Info . . . (points to other places within this index or elsewhere in the book where you can find more information)

While most of the seven columns are self-explanatory, I will take a few moments to explain the "Sec. Part." and "For More Info" columns.

The "Sec. Part" column refers to what surveryors and other land professionals refer to as an Aliquot Part. The origins and use of such a term mean little to a non-surveyor, and I have chosen to simply call these sub-sections of land what they are: a "Section Part". No matter what we call them, what we are referring to are things like a quarter-section or half-section or quarter-quarter-section. See Appendix "B" for most of the "Section Parts" you will come across (and many you will not) and what size land-parcel they represent.

The "For More Info" column of the Index may seem like a small appendage to each line, but please recognize quickly that this is not so. And to understand the various items you might find here, you need to become familiar with the Legend that appears at the top of each Land Patent Index.

Here is a sample of the Legend . . .

LEGEND

"For More Info . . . " column

A = Authority (Legislative Act, See Appendix "A")
B = Block or Lot (location in Section unknown)
C = Cancelled Patent
F = Fractional Section
G = Group (Multi-Patentee Patent, see Appendix "C")
V = Overlaps another Parcel
R = Re-Issued (Parcel patented more than once)

Most parcels of land will have only one or two of these items in their "For More Info" columns, but when that is not the case, there is often some valuable information to be gained from further investigation. Below, I will explain what each of these items means to you you as a researcher.

A = Authority
(Legislative Act, See Appendix "A")

All Federal Land Patents were issued because some branch of our government (usually the U.S. Congress) passed a law making such a transfer of title possible. And therefore every patent within these pages will have an "A" item next to it in the index. The number after the "A" indicates which item in Appendix "A" holds the citation to the particular law which authorized the transfer of land to the public. As it stands, most of the Public Land data compiled and released by our government, and which serves as the basis for the patents mapped here, concerns itself with "Cash Sale" homesteads. So in some Counties, the law which authorized cash sales will be the primary, if not the only, entry in the Appendix.

B = Block or Lot (location in Section unknown)

A "B" designation in the Index is a tip-off that the EXACT location of the patent within the map is not apparent from the legal description. This Patent will nonetheless be noted within the proper

Section along with any other Lots purchased in the Section. Given the scope of this project (many states and many Counties are being mapped), trying to locate all relevant plats for Lots (if they even exist) and accurately mapping them would have taken one person several lifetimes. But since our primary goal from the onset has been to establish relationships between neighbors and families, very little is lost to this goal since we can still observe who all lived in which Section.

C = Cancelled Patent

A Cancelled Patent is just that: cancelled. Whether the original Patentee forfeited his or her patent due to fraud, a technicality, non-payment, or whatever, the fact remains that it is significant to know who received patents for what parcels and when. A cancellation may be evidence that the Patentee never physically re-located to the land, but does not in itself prove that point. Further evidence would be required to prove that. *See also*, Re-issued Patents, *below*.

F = Fractional Section

A Fractional Section is one that contains less than 640 acres, almost always because of a body of water. The exact size and shape of land-parcels contained in such sections may not be ascertainable, but we map them nonetheless. Just keep in mind that we are not mapping an actual parcel to scale in such instances. Another point to consider is that we have located some fractional sections that are not so designated by the Bureau of Land Management in their data. This means that not all fractional sections have been so identified in our indexes.

G = Group
(Multi-Patentee Patent, see Appendix "C")

A "G" designation means that the Patent was issued to a GROUP of people (Multi-patentees). The "G" will always be followed by a number. Some such groups were quite large and it was impractical if not impossible to display each individual in our maps without unduly affecting readability. EACH person in the group is named in the Index, but they won't all be found on the Map. You will find the name of the first person in such a Group on the map with the Group number next to it, enclosed in [square brackets].

To find all the members of the Group you can either scan the Index for all people with the same Group Number or you can simply refer to Appendix "C" where all members of the Group are listed next to their number.

V = Overlaps another Parcel

An Overlap is one where PART of a parcel of land gets issued on more than one patent. For genealogical purposes, both transfers of title are important and both Patentees are mapped. If the ENTIRE parcel of land is re-issued, that is what we call it, a Re-Issued Patent (*see below*). The number after the "V" indicates the ID for the overlapping Patent(s) contained within the same Index. Like Re-Issued and Cancelled Patents, Overlaps may cause a map-reader to be confused at first, but for genealogical purposes, all of these parties' relationships to the underlying land is important, and therefore, we map them.

R = Re-Issued (Parcel patented more than once)

The label, "Re-issued Patent" describes Patents which were issued more than once for land with the EXACT SAME LEGAL DESCRIPTION. Whether the original patent was cancelled or not, there were a good many parcels which were patented more than once. The number after the "R" indicates the ID for the other Patent contained within the same Index that was for the same land. A quick glance at the map itself within the relevant Section will be the quickest way to find the other Patentee to whom the Parcel was transferred. They should both be mapped in the same general area.

I have gone to some length describing all sorts of anomalies either in the underlying data or in their representation on the maps and indexes in this book. Most of this will bore the most ardent reseracher, but I do this with all due respect to those researchers who will inevitably (and rightfully) ask: *"Why isn't so-and-so's name on the exact spot that the index says it should be?"*

In most cases it will be due to the existence of a Multi-Patentee Patent, a Re-issued Patent, a Cancelled Patent, or Overlapping Parcels named in separate Patents. I don't pretend that this discussion will answer every question along these lines, but I hope it will at least convince you of the complexity of the subject.

Not to despair, this book's companion web-site will offer a way to further explain "odd-ball" or errant data. Each book (County) will have its own web-page or pages to discuss such situations. You can go to www.arphax.com to find the relevant web-page for Dunn County.

Land Patent Map

On the first two-page spread following each Township's Index to Land Patents, you'll find the corresponding Land Patent Map. And here lies the real heart of our work. For the first time anywhere, researchers will be able to observe and analyze, on a grand scale, most of the original land-owners for an area AND see them mapped in proximity to each one another.

We encourage you to make vigorous use of the accompanying Index described above, but then later, to abandon it, and just stare at these maps for a while. This is a great way to catch misspellings or to find collateral kin you'd not known were in the area.

Each Land Patent Map represents one Congressional Township containing approximately 36-square miles. Each of these square miles is labeled by an accompanying Section Number (1 through 36, in most cases). Keep in mind, that this book concerns itself solely with Dunn County's patents. Townships which creep into one or more other counties will not be shown in their entirety in any one book. You will need to consult other books, as they become available, in order to view other countys' patents, cities, cemeteries, etc.

But getting back to Dunn County: each Land Patent Map contains a Statistical Chart that looks like the following:

Township Statistics

Parcels Mapped	:	173
Number of Patents	:	163
Number of Individuals	:	152
Patentees Identified	:	151
Number of Surnames	:	137
Multi-Patentee Parcels	:	4
Oldest Patent Date	:	11/27/1820
Most Recent Patent	:	9/28/1917
Block/Lot Parcels	:	0
Parcels Re-Issued	:	3
Parcels that Overlap	:	8
Cities and Towns	:	6
Cemeteries	:	6

This information may be of more use to a social statistician or historian than a genealogist, but I think all three will find it interesting.

Most of the statistics are self-explanatory, and what is not, was described in the above discussion of the Index's Legend, but I do want to mention a few of them that may affect your understanding of the Land Patent Maps.

First of all, Patents often contain more than one Parcel of land, so it is common for there to be more Parcels than Patents. Also, the Number of Individuals will more often than not, not match the number of Patentees. A Patentee is literally the person or PERSONS named in a patent. So, a Patent may have a multi-person Patentee or a single-person patentee. Nonetheless, we account for all these individuals in our indexes.

On the lower-righthand side of the Patent Map is a Legend which describes various features in the map, including Section Boundaries, Patent (land) Boundaries, Lots (numbered), and Multi-Patentee Group Numbers. You'll also find a "Helpful Hints" Box that will assist you.

One important note: though the vast majority of Patents mapped in this series will prove to be reasonably accurate representations of their actual locations, we cannot claim this for patents lying along state and county lines, or waterways, or that have been platted (lots).

Shifting boundaries and sparse legal descriptions in the GLO data make this a reality that we have nonetheless tried to overcome by estimating these patents' locations the best that we can.

Road Map

On the two-page spread following each Patent Map you will find a Road Map covering the exact same area (the same Congressional Township).

For me, fully exploring the past means that every once in a while I must leave the library and travel to the actual locations where my ancestors once walked and worked the land. Our Township Road Maps are a great place to begin such a quest.

Keep in mind that the scaling and proportion of these maps was chosen in order to squeeze hundreds of people-names, road-names, and place-names into tinier spaces than you would traditionally see. These are not professional road-maps, and like any secondary genealogical source, should be looked upon as an entry-way to original sources—in this case, original patents and applications, professionally produced maps and surveys, etc.

Both our Road Maps and Historical Maps contain cemeteries and city-centers, along with a listing of these on the left-hand side of the map. I should note that I am showing you city center-points, rather than city-limit boundaries, because in many instances, this will represent a place where settlement began. This may be a good time to mention that many cemeteries are located on private property, Always check with a local historical or genealogical society to see if a particular cemetery is publicly accessible (if it is not obviously so). As a final point, look for your surnames among the road-names. You will often be surprised by what you find.

Historical Map

The third and final map in each Map Group is our attempt to display what each Township might have looked like before the advent of modern roads. In frontier times, people were usually more determined to settle near rivers and creeks than they were near roads, which were often few and far between. As was the case with the Road Map, we've included the same cemeteries and city-centers. We've also included railroads, many of which came along before most roads.

While some may claim "Historical Map" to be a bit of a misnomer for this tool, we settled for this label simply because it was almost as accurate as saying "Railroads, Lakes, Rivers, Cities, and Cemeteries," and it is much easier to remember.

In Closing . . .

By way of example, here is *A Really Good Way to Use a Township Map Group.* First, find the person you are researching in the Township's Index to Land Patents, which will direct you to the proper Section and parcel on the Patent Map. But before leaving the Index, scan all the patents within it, looking for other names of interest. Now, turn to the Patent Map and locate your parcels of land. Pay special attention to the names of patent-holders who own land surrounding your person of interest. Next, turn the page and look at the same Section(s) on the Road Map. Note which roads are closest to your parcels and also the names of nearby towns and cemeteries. Using other resources, you may be able to learn of kin who have been buried here, plus, you may choose to visit these cemeteries the next time you are in the area.

Finally, turn to the Historical Map. Look once more at the same Sections where you found your research subject's land. Note the nearby streams, creeks, and other geographical features. You may be surprised to find family names were used to name them, or you may see a name you haven't heard mentioned in years and years—and a new research possibility is born.

Many more techniques for using these *Family Maps* volumes will no doubt be discovered. If from time to time, you will navigate to Dunn County's web-page at www.arphax.com (use the "Research" link), you can learn new tricks as they become known (or you can share ones you have employed). But for now, you are ready to get started. So, go, and good luck.

– Part I –

The Big Picture

Map A - Where Dunn County, Wisconsin Lies Within the State

Legend

- State Boundary
- County Boundaries
- Dunn County, Wisconsin

Helpful Hints

1. We start with Map "A" which simply shows us where within the State this county lies.
2. Map "B" zooms in further to help us more easily identify surrounding Counties.
3. Map "C" zooms in even further to reveal the Congressional Townships that either lie within or intersect Dunn County.

Map B - Dunn County, Wisconsin and Surrounding Counties

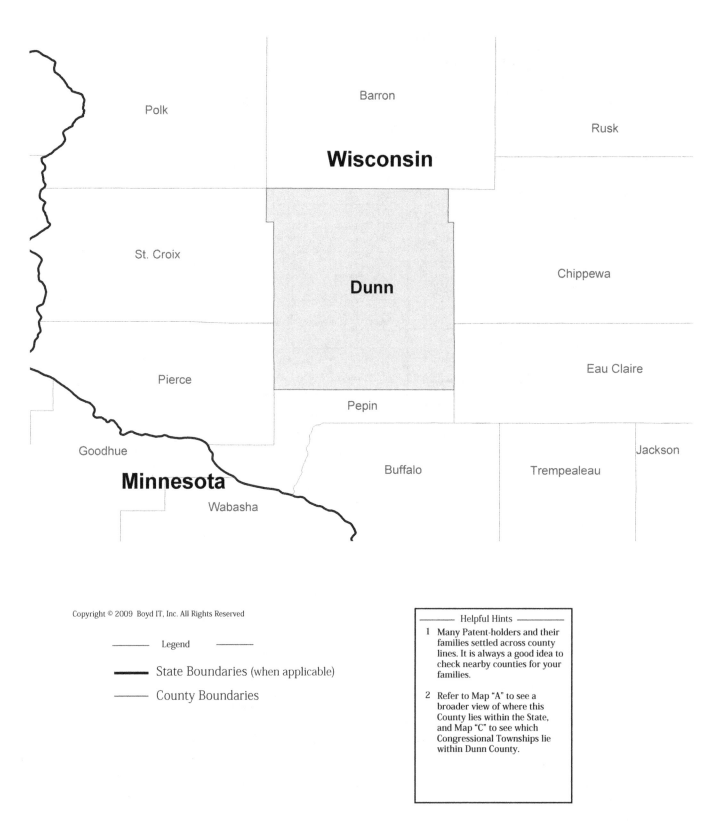

Legend

- State Boundaries (when applicable)
- County Boundaries

Helpful Hints

1. Many Patent-holders and their families settled across county lines. It is always a good idea to check nearby counties for your families.
2. Refer to Map "A" to see a broader view of where this County lies within the State, and Map "C" to see which Congressional Townships lie within Dunn County.

Map C - Congressional Townships of Dunn County, Wisconsin

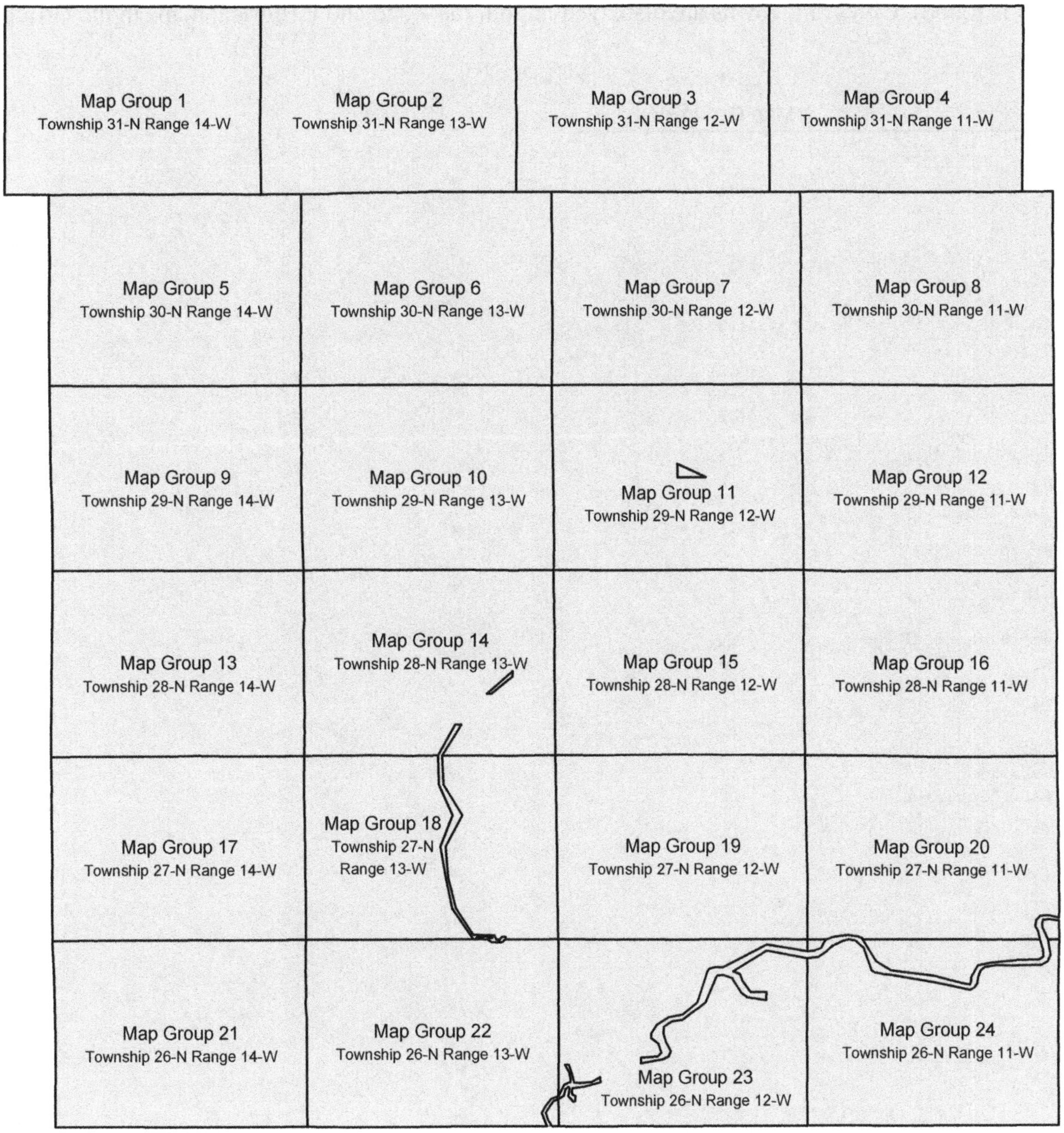
Map Group 1
Township 31-N Range 14-W
Map Group 2
Township 31-N Range 13-W
Map Group 3
Township 31-N Range 12-W
Map Group 4
Township 31-N Range 11-W
Map Group 5
Township 30-N Range 14-W
Map Group 6
Township 30-N Range 13-W
Map Group 7
Township 30-N Range 12-W
Map Group 8
Township 30-N Range 11-W
Map Group 9
Township 29-N Range 14-W
Map Group 10
Township 29-N Range 13-W
Map Group 11
Township 29-N Range 12-W
Map Group 12
Township 29-N Range 11-W
Map Group 13
Township 28-N Range 14-W
Map Group 14
Township 28-N Range 13-W
Map Group 15
Township 28-N Range 12-W
Map Group 16
Township 28-N Range 11-W
Map Group 17
Township 27-N Range 14-W
Map Group 18
Township 27-N
Range 13-W
Map Group 19
Township 27-N Range 12-W
Map Group 20
Township 27-N Range 11-W
Map Group 21
Township 26-N Range 14-W
Map Group 22
Township 26-N Range 13-W
Map Group 23
Township 26-N Range 12-W
Map Group 24
Township 26-N Range 11-W

Legend

Dunn County, Wisconsin

Congressional Townships

Helpful Hints

1 Many Patent-holders and their families settled across county lines. It is always a good idea to check nearby counties for your families (See Map "B").

2 Refer to Map "A" to see a broader view of where this county lies within the State, and Map "B" for a view of the counties surrounding Dunn County.

Map D Index: Cities & Towns of Dunn County, Wisconsin

The following represents the Cities and Towns of Dunn County (along with the corresponding Map Group in which each is found). Cities and Towns are displayed in both the Road and Historical maps in the Group.

City/Town	Map Group No.
Baxter	6
Boyceville	5
Caryville	24
Cedar Falls	15
Colfax	12
Comfort	17
Connorsville	1
Downing	5
Downsville	18
Dunnville	22
Eau Galle	22
Elk Mound	16
Falls City	20
Hatchville	13
Huber Mobile Home Park	14
Irvington	18
Knapp	9
Menominee	14
Menomonie Junction	14
Meridean	23
North Menomonie	14
Norton	11
Old Tyrone (historical)	23
Red Cedar	23
Ridgeland	3
Rock Falls	24
Rusk	15
Sand Creek	4
Tainter Lake	11
Welch Point (historical)	22
Weston	17
Wheeler	6

Map D - Cities & Towns of Dunn County, Wisconsin

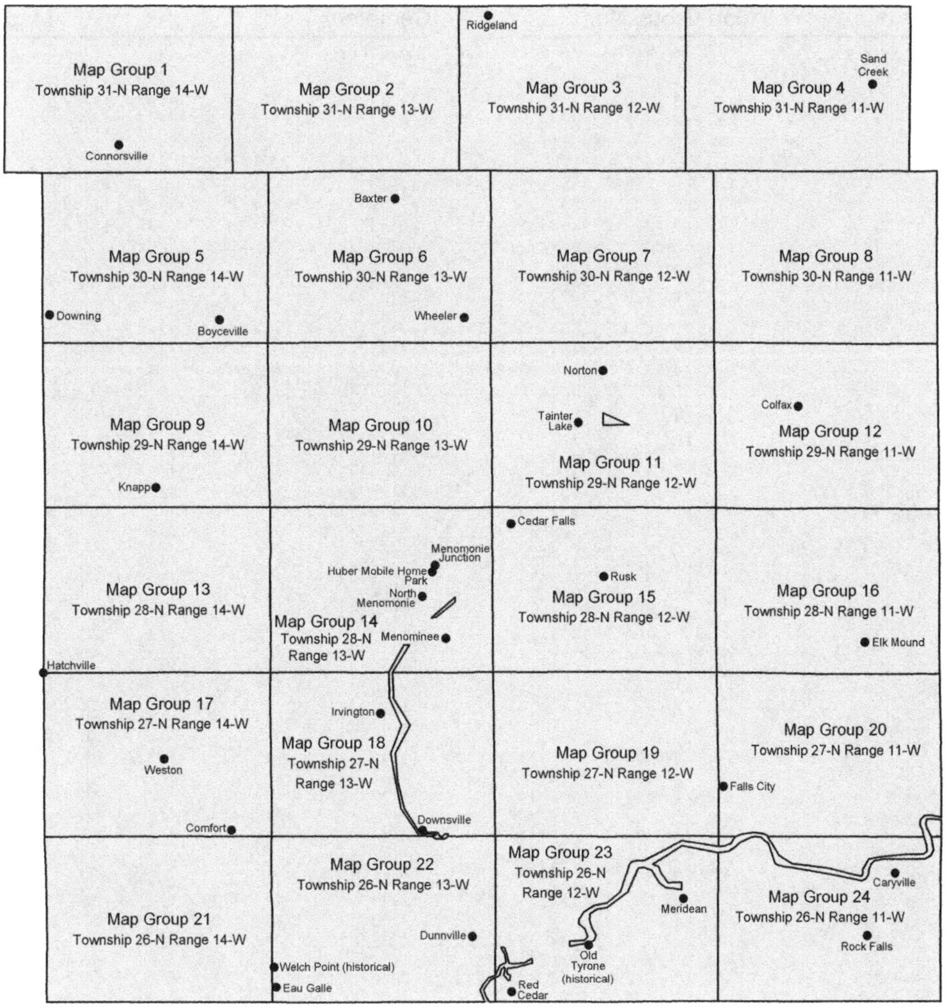
Map Group 1
Township 31-N Range 14-W
Connorsville
Map Group 2
Township 31-N Range 13-W
Ridgeland
Map Group 3
Township 31-N Range 12-W
Sand Creek
Map Group 4
Township 31-N Range 11-W
Map Group 5
Township 30-N Range 14-W
Downing
Boyceville
Baxter
Map Group 6
Township 30-N Range 13-W
Wheeler
Map Group 7
Township 30-N Range 12-W
Map Group 8
Township 30-N Range 11-W
Map Group 9
Township 29-N Range 14-W
Knapp
Map Group 10
Township 29-N Range 13-W
Norton
Tainter Lake
Map Group 11
Township 29-N Range 12-W
Colfax
Map Group 12
Township 29-N Range 11-W
Map Group 13
Township 28-N Range 14-W
Hatchville
Menomonie Junction
Huber Mobile Home Park
North Menomonie
Map Group 14
Township 28-N Range 13-W
Menominee
Cedar Falls
Rusk
Map Group 15
Township 28-N Range 12-W
Map Group 16
Township 28-N Range 11-W
Elk Mound
Map Group 17
Township 27-N Range 14-W
Weston
Comfort
Irvington
Map Group 18
Township 27-N
Range 13-W
Downsville
Map Group 19
Township 27-N Range 12-W
Map Group 20
Township 27-N Range 11-W
Falls City
Map Group 21
Township 26-N Range 14-W
Map Group 22
Township 26-N Range 13-W
Dunnville
Welch Point (historical)
Eau Galle
Map Group 23
Township 26-N
Range 12-W
Meridean
Old Tyrone (historical)
Red Cedar
Caryville
Map Group 24
Township 26-N Range 11-W
Rock Falls

Legend

Dunn County, Wisconsin

Congressional Townships

Helpful Hints

1 Cities and towns are marked only at their center-points as published by the USGS and/or NationalAtlas.gov. This often enables us to more closely approximate where these might have existed when first settled.

2 To see more specifically where these Cities & Towns are located within the county, refer to both the Road and Historical maps in the Map-Group referred to above. See also, the Map "D" Index on the opposite page.

Map E Index: Cemeteries of Dunn County, Wisconsin

The following represents many of the Cemeteries of Dunn County, along with the corresponding Township Map Group in which each is found. Cemeteries are displayed in both the Road and Historical maps in the Map Groups referred to below.

Cemetery	Map Group No.
Cedar Falls Cem.	15
Clearview Cem.	22
Evergreen Cem.	12
Evergreen Cem.	14
Evergreen Cem.	16
Evergreen Cem.	22
Falls City Cem.	20
Ford Cem.	14
Forest Center Cem.	19
Forest Hill Cem.	9
Fossum Cem.	24
Froens Cem.	19
Grandview Cem.	18
Halverson Cem.	14
Hay River Cem.	6
Highland Cem.	14
Hill Grove Cem.	12
Iron Creek Cem.	19
Irving Creek Cem.	18
Little Elk Creek Cem.	19
Lower Running Valley Cem.	12
Lower Weston Cem.	17
Lucas Cem.	13
Mamre Cem.	14
Mound Cem.	5
Myron Cem.	4
New Haven Cem.	1
Oak Grove Cem.	2
Otter Creek Cem.	7
Our Saviors Cem.	4
Our Saviors Cem.	6
Peace Cem.	18
Peru Cem.	23
Peterson Cem.	24
Pleasant Valley Cem.	23
Popple Creek Cem.	8
Potters Field Cem.	15
Pownell Cem.	22
Ridge Road Cem.	14
Riverview Cem.	18
Rock Creek Cem.	24
Rosehill Cem.	22
Saint Henrys Cem.	21
Saint John Cem.	19
Saint Johns Cem.	18
Saint Joseph Cem.	20
Saint Josephs Cem.	14
Saint Pauls Cem.	18
Sand Hill Cem.	24
Sherman Cem.	10
Spring Brook Cem.	20
Teegarden Cem.	13
Tiffany Cem.	5
Tollebu Cem.	3
Tramway Cem.	14
Upper Popple Creek Cem.	7
Vanceburg Cem.	2
Waneka Cem.	20
Weber Valley Cem.	21
Zion Cem.	4

Map E - Cemeteries of Dunn County, Wisconsin

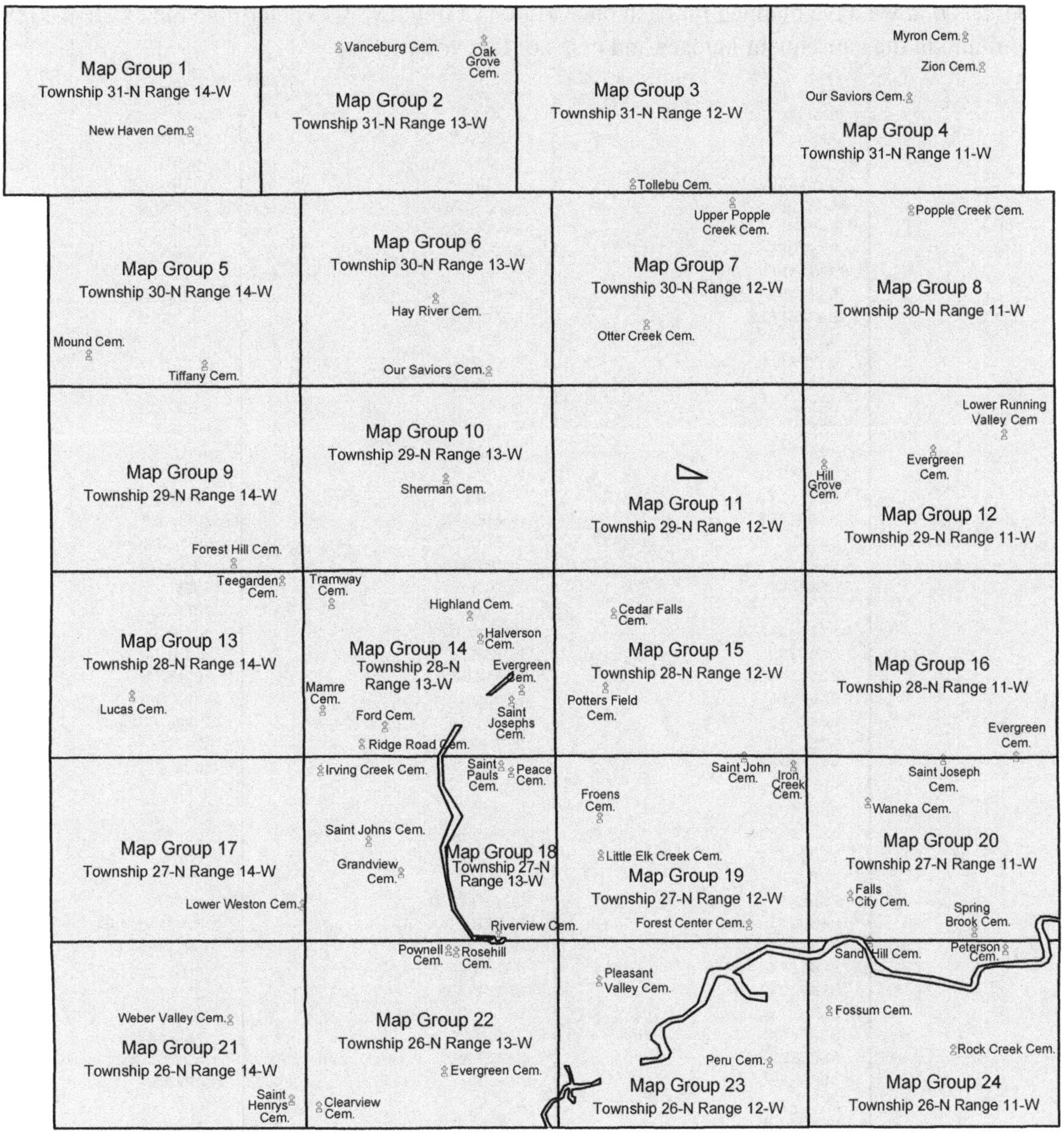
Map Group 1
Township 31-N Range 14-W
New Haven Cem.
Vanceburg Cem.
Oak Grove Cem.
Map Group 2
Township 31-N Range 13-W
Map Group 3
Township 31-N Range 12-W
Tollebu Cem.
Myron Cem.
Zion Cem.
Our Saviors Cem.
Map Group 4
Township 31-N Range 11-W
Map Group 5
Township 30-N Range 14-W
Mound Cem.
Tiffany Cem.
Map Group 6
Township 30-N Range 13-W
Hay River Cem.
Our Saviors Cem.
Upper Popple Creek Cem.
Map Group 7
Township 30-N Range 12-W
Otter Creek Cem.
Popple Creek Cem.
Map Group 8
Township 30-N Range 11-W
Map Group 9
Township 29-N Range 14-W
Forest Hill Cem.
Map Group 10
Township 29-N Range 13-W
Sherman Cem.
Map Group 11
Township 29-N Range 12-W
Lower Running Valley Cem
Evergreen Cem.
Hill Grove Cem.
Map Group 12
Township 29-N Range 11-W
Teegarden Cem.
Map Group 13
Township 28-N Range 14-W
Lucas Cem.
Tramway Cem.
Highland Cem.
Halverson Cem.
Map Group 14
Township 28-N Range 13-W
Evergreen Cem.
Mamre Cem.
Ford Cem.
Saint Josephs Cem.
Ridge Road Cem.
Cedar Falls Cem.
Map Group 15
Township 28-N Range 12-W
Potters Field Cem.
Map Group 16
Township 28-N Range 11-W
Evergreen Cem.
Irving Creek Cem.
Saint Pauls Cem.
Peace Cem.
Saint Johns Cem.
Grandview Cem.
Map Group 18
Township 27-N Range 13-W
Riverview Cem.
Map Group 17
Township 27-N Range 14-W
Lower Weston Cem.
Saint John Cem.
Iron Creek Cem.
Froens Cem.
Little Elk Creek Cem.
Map Group 19
Township 27-N Range 12-W
Forest Center Cem.
Saint Joseph Cem.
Waneka Cem.
Map Group 20
Township 27-N Range 11-W
Falls City Cem.
Spring Brook Cem.
Sand Hill Cem.
Peterson Cem.
Pownell Cem.
Rosehill Cem.
Pleasant Valley Cem.
Weber Valley Cem.
Map Group 21
Township 26-N Range 14-W
Saint Henrys Cem.
Map Group 22
Township 26-N Range 13-W
Evergreen Cem.
Clearview Cem.
Peru Cem.
Map Group 23
Township 26-N Range 12-W
Fossum Cem.
Rock Creek Cem.
Map Group 24
Township 26-N Range 11-W

Legend

Dunn County, Wisconsin

Congressional Townships

Helpful Hints

1 Cemeteries are marked at locations as published by the USGS and/or NationalAtlas.gov.

2 To see more specifically where these Cemeteries are located, refer to the Road & Historical maps in the Map-Group referred to above. See also, the Map "E" Index on the opposite page to make sure you don't miss any of the Cemeteries located within this Congressional township.

Surnames in Dunn County, Wisconsin Patents

The following list represents the surnames that we have located in Dunn County, Wisconsin Patents and the number of parcels that we have mapped for each one. Here is a quick way to determine the existence (or not) of Patents to be found in the subsequent indexes and maps of this volume.

Surname	# of Land Parcels
AAMOT	4
AASEN	2
ABBOTT	1
ACKERT	3
ACKLEY	8
ADAMS	10
AH-KE-NE-BOI-WE	1
AIKEN	1
ALBURTUS	1
ALDEN	2
ALDERMAN	3
ALDRICK	1
ALEXANDER	2
ALFARO	1
ALLEN	9
ALLESTAD	2
ALLISON	4
ALLISTAD	1
ALLRAM	1
AMBLE	1
AMES	13
AMICK	1
AMORY	7
AMUNDSEN	4
AMUNDSON	2
ANACKER	1
ANDERSEN	6
ANDERSON	69
ANDREASEN	3
ANDRESS	1
ANDREWS	8
ANDRUS	1
ANNIS	1
ARMSTRONG	1
ARNESON	4
ARNOLD	1
ASLAKSEN	4
ATWOOD	3
AUGENSEN	2
AUKNEY	1
AUSSMAN	4
AUSTIN	9
AVERY	3
AZRO	1
BABBENDORF	1
BABBITT	1
BABCOCK	9
BACHLER	1
BAGG	1
BAILEY	16
BAKER	11
BALAND	2
BALCOM	3
BALDRIDGE	3
BALDWIN	10
BALIS	2
BANKS	3
BANNISTER	1
BARBER	1
BARKER	2
BARNARD	20
BARNE	2
BARNES	2
BARNUM	3
BARTHOLOMEW	3
BARTLETT	3
BARTON	14
BARUM	2
BASFORD	1
BASKIN	2
BASKINS	1
BATCHELDER	1
BATES	3
BAXTER	3
BEADLE	2
BEAL	2
BEALE	1
BEATTIE	1
BECKER	4
BECKWITH	13
BEDDINGER	4
BEDELL	1
BEEBE	1
BEEMAN	1
BEGUHN	7
BEISSWANGER	1
BELDEN	3
BELDING	1
BELKNAP	1
BELL	1
BELLACH	1
BELLEMAN	2
BENAVIDES	2
BENDIKSDATTER	2
BENDIXSON	1
BENJAMIN	1
BENNER	1
BENNET	2
BENNETT	12
BENTON	7
BENTSEN	1
BENTSON	3
BERG	4
BERGELAND	1
BERGEMANN	8
BERGERSON	1
BERGET	2
BERNTZON	3
BESSE	1
BEST	13
BETTS	2
BEYER	6
BIGFORD	1
BILLILNGS	2
BILLINGS	15
BILSE	2
BINDINGER	2
BIRD	2
BIRKEL	1
BISHOP	5
BISS	2
BISSINGER	2
BJORNSON	1
BLACK	1
BLAIR	8
BLAKELY	7
BLANCHARD	1
BLANK	3
BLATCHFORD	2
BLODGETT	6
BLOOM	1
BLUM	1
BOA	1
BOARDMAN	2
BOCK	1
BODETT	2
BOGGESS	8
BOHN	2
BOLLE	1
BOLLES	10
BOND	3
BONNELL	2
BONNEVALD	1
BONNEY	1
BOOKS	1
BOOTH	6
BOOTON	1
BORCHERT	1
BOREE	1
BORLAND	2
BORSEN	1
BORTLE	1
BOTTOM	2
BOTUME	2
BOURN	1
BOUSE	1
BOWDISH	1
BOWERS	1
BOWMAN	4
BOYINGTON	1
BOYLE	2
BOYNTON	1
BRAATEN	4
BRADFORD	1
BRADLEY	3
BRADWAY	8
BRAINARD	2
BRAKER	1
BRANCH	3
BRANKIN	1
BRATLEY	1
BRAYNARD	2
BRECK	2
BREDESEN	3
BREEZEE	2
BRENNAN	2
BRENT	2
BREWER	7
BREWSTER	2
BRIDGHAM	1
BRIGGS	2
BRIGHT	3
BRILL	3
BRINGERUD	3
BRONKEN	3
BRONN	1
BRONSTAD	2
BROVEN	1
BROWN	25
BROWNLEE	4
BRUNELLE	5
BRUNK	2
BRUSH	2
BRYANT	3
BUCHANAN	2
BUCKLEY	2
BUDD	3
BUELL	3
BULL	1
BULLOCK	4
BULMAN	2
BUNT	2
BURCH	3
BURDETT	8
BURDICK	3
BURGERT	1
BURGESS	1
BURN	1
BURNES	4
BURNETT	1
BURNHAM	1
BURNS	2
BURNSON	2
BURT	6
BURTON	1
BURY	2
BUSE	1
BUSH	2
BUSHNELL	2
BUSHY	2
BUSSCHENDORF	2
BUTTER	1
BUTTERFIELD	9
BUXTON	1
CADY	2
CAIN	2
CALHOUN	2
CALHOUNE	1
CALLAGHAN	1
CAMERON	2
CAMP	3
CAMPBELL	7
CANEY	2
CANFIELD	5
CANTRELL	2
CAPEN	2
CARD	5
CAREY	4
CARLETON	1
CARLISLE	1
CARMAN	1
CARPENTER	5
CARRINGTON	1
CARSON	27
CARTWRIGHT	1
CARVER	1
CASCADEN	1
CASSADY	1

Surname	# of Land Parcels
CAVANAGH	1
CAW	1
CERNAK	2
CERS	3
CHAMBERLIN	6
CHAMBERS	4
CHAMPLIN	1
CHANCE	1
CHANDLER	2
CHAPIN	2
CHAPMAN	1
CHASE	16
CHENEY	5
CHICKERING	1
CHRISTENSEN	1
CHRISTIANSEN	2
CHRISTIANSON	2
CHRISTIE	1
CHRISTOFFER	2
CHRISTOFFERSEN	2
CHRISTOFFERSON	2
CHRISTOFORSEN	1
CHRISTOPHERSEN	1
CHRISTOPHERSON	3
CHRISTOPHUSEN	3
CHUBBUCK	2
CHURCH	4
CHURCHILL	1
CLACK	2
CLAIR	3
CLAPP	1
CLARK	36
CLEAVE	1
CLEAVELAND	4
CLEMENS	2
CLINE	1
CLINTON	6
CLOSS	1
CLYNGENPEEL	1
CO	50
COBB	1
COBURN	1
COCHRAN	2
COCKBURN	1
COEN	3
COLBURN	8
COLE	17
COLLAR	2
COLLINS	1
COLOMY	2
COMFORT	1
COMPANY	3
CONE	4
CONNER	1
COOK	10
COOMBS	2
COON	3
COONS	1
COOPER	3
COPELAND	7
COREY	4
CORMICAN	1
CORNISH	2
CORNWELL	2
CORWITH	7
COUN	2
COUZENS	1
COVELL	1
CRAGIN	4
CRAIG	1
CRAMER	7
CRANDAL	1
CRANDALL	3
CRANDELL	1
CRANSTON	2
CRATSENBERG	2
CREASER	2
CREGO	1
CRIPPEN	2
CRIST	1
CROCKETT	1
CROPSEY	1
CROSBY	10
CROSSMAN	3
CRYE	3
CULBERT	1
CULBERTSON	1
CULLMAN	1
CULP	4
CUMMINGS	6
CUNNINGHAM	4
CURRAN	1
CURRY	3
CURTIS	8
CURTISS	2
CUSSETAH-MICCO	3
CUTCHEON	2
CUTHING	1
CUTLER	2
CUTTING	5
DAHL	6
DAHLBAK	1
DAHLEN	1
DALRIMPLE	1
DALTON	2
DAMMAN	1
DANIELS	3
DANIELSON	2
DANTIN	1
DARLING	3
DARLINTON	5
DARNELL	1
DARRIN	1
DARROW	4
DAVIS	12
DAVISON	1
DAY	7
DE LONG	2
DE WOLF	1
DEAN	6
DEARBORN	2
DEARY	1
DECKER	3
DEFREES	12
DEGRAW	1
DELANNAY	1
DELONG	3
DEMOE	3
DENNIS	1
DENSMORE	1
DEPEW	1
DEVLE	1
DEXTER	13
DICKEY	1
DICKSON	4
DIX	13
DOANE	1
DODGE	13
DOEKENDORFF	2
DONALDSON	2
DOOLITTLE	2
DORR	3
DORRY	3
DOWD	4
DOWNER	8
DOWNING	2
DOWNS	19
DOXTER	2
DOYLE	2
DRAKE	15
DREW	1
DREWS	1
DREXLER	1
DRINKER	1
DRINKWINE	2
DRURY	3
DUELL	1
DUFFEY	2
DUNCAN	3
DUNKLEE	2
DUNN	1
DUNNIGAN	1
DYER	6
DYKINS	1
EARGOOD	2
EASTWOOD	2
EATON	36
EAVANS	2
EDMONDS	2
EDWARDS	47
EGELAND	3
EIDAHL	2
EIDE	2
EIKA	3
ELDERD	2
ELDERT	2
ELEVESON	2
ELIASEN	1
ELLEFSEN	2
ELLEFSON	1
ELLIOTT	50
ELLIS	4
ELTING	6
EMENS	2
EMERY	1
ENGEBRETSON	1
ENNERSEN	2
ERICKSEN	2
ERICKSON	1
ERIKSON	1
ESTIS	1
ETHEREDGE	1
EVANS	6
EVELAND	1
EVENS	2
EVENSON	1
EVERETT	1
EVERNAN	4
EWER	3
EWERS	1
EYTCHESON	11
FAIRBANKS	1
FAIRCHILD	2
FALES	6
FALKNER	2
FALLIS	1
FALTENBERY	1
FARNHAM	3
FARRINGTON	3
FAUCHTER	1
FAYERWEATHER	1
FEAZEL	2
FEEKS	1
FEENEY	1
FELLOWS	2
FERGUSON	2
FHUHRER	1
FIELDS	1
FIELDSTAD	1
FIGENSKAN	1
FILLEY	2
FINCH	1
FINDLEY	3
FINEGAN	3
FINEOUT	2
FINLEY	1
FISCHER	2
FISK	6
FITCH	7
FITZGERALD	2
FIXICO	1
FJELDSTED	3
FLAGLER	4
FLANDERS	2
FLEMING	2
FLETCHER	4
FLINN	2
FLINT	3
FLOOD	1
FLUENT	1
FLUG	4
FOGG	3
FOGLE	2
FOLJAMBE	1
FOOTE	1
FORA	1
FORD	2
FORDAHL	2
FORGERSON	1
FORSLID	3
FOSLID	3
FOSTER	2
FOWLER	4
FOX	5
FRAMMI	2
FRAMY	1
FRANK	1
FREDRICKSEN	1
FREESTONE	8
FRENCH	69
FRION	1
FRYE	2
FUHLROTT	2
FULLER	7
FUNK	3
FURBUR	3
GAGE	2
GALE	1
GALLAGER	1
GALLATI	1
GALLAWAY	1
GANE	2
GARDNER	4
GAREHART	5
GARRETT	1
GAUVIN	4
GEAR	1
GEBHART	3
GENTRY	2
GEORGE	3

Surname	# of Land Parcels
GERMAN	2
GEROY	3
GIBBS	7
GIBERSON	2
GIBSON	19
GIFFORD	1
GILBERT	11
GILBERTSEN	1
GILBRANSON	1
GILLESPIE	1
GILLIS	1
GILMAN	1
GLEASON	1
GLENN	2
GLENNY	3
GLUTH	3
GOBEL	3
GODELL	2
GODFREY	3
GOERCKE	3
GOETZINGER	1
GOFF	5
GOLDSMITH	2
GOODELL	7
GOODRICH	7
GOODSON	1
GORDON	1
GOSS	19
GRABHEIR	2
GRANGER	10
GRANT	3
GRANUM	4
GRAY	16
GREEN	7
GREENWEIG	2
GREGERSON	4
GREWT	1
GRIFFIN	3
GRINNELL	1
GRINSET	2
GRIPPEN	3
GRIZZELL	1
GROTHE	1
GROVER	3
GRUMPRY	1
GRUTT	1
GULAKSON	2
GUNDERSON	3
GUNDT	1
GUNNUFSEN	2
HAALTEN	3
HADLEY	1
HAERLE	4
HAGAR	3
HAGEN	4
HAIGHT	4
HALE	1
HALFERTY	1
HALFORTY	1
HALL	7
HALSTEAD	3
HALSTED	2
HALVERSEN	2
HALVORSEN	4
HALVORSON	3
HAMILTON	2
HAMME	1
HAMMER	1
HAMMOND	1
HANCHETT	1

Surname	# of Land Parcels
HANCOCK	2
HANKE	1
HANNEMEYER	1
HANSEN	10
HANSON	16
HARBIT	2
HARDAGE	3
HARDING	1
HARKNESS	1
HARLE	5
HARLEY	6
HARLY	1
HARM	2
HARMAN	2
HARMEN	1
HARMON	3
HARMS	2
HARNISH	1
HARPER	1
HARRIGAN	3
HARRINGTON	24
HARRIS	2
HARRISON	6
HARROLD	4
HARSH	2
HARSTAD	2
HARTKOPP	2
HARTMAN	1
HARVEY	1
HASHMAN	3
HAUGE	3
HAUGEN	1
HAVENSTICK	2
HAVERLAND	3
HAVILAND	1
HAWES	5
HAWS	2
HAY	1
HAYNES	2
HAYS	1
HAYWARD	3
HEASLY	2
HEBERLIG	1
HELGERSON	1
HELGESON	6
HENDRIKSON	2
HENEGAN	2
HENRIKSON	3
HENRY	1
HERMANN	3
HERRIMAN	5
HERRON	4
HILAND	1
HILL	17
HINMAN	1
HINTGEN	3
HINTZ	1
HJERSSO	3
HOADLEY	1
HOAG	1
HOBART	1
HOBBS	3
HODGDON	30
HODGE	1
HODGES	3
HOFF	1
HOFFMAN	3
HOFFMANN	1
HOGUELAND	2
HOILAND	1

Surname	# of Land Parcels
HOLBROOK	10
HOLCOMB	1
HOLM	4
HOLMAN	3
HOLTE	1
HOLVORSON	1
HOOKS	1
HOPE	3
HOPKINS	5
HORNER	1
HORSTAD	1
HORSTMANN	1
HORTWICK	2
HOUSE	1
HOUSER	3
HOVER	2
HOVEY	2
HOVLAND	3
HOWARD	6
HOWE	3
HOYT	3
HUBBARD	12
HUBER	1
HUDSPETH	1
HUFFTLE	2
HUG	1
HUGHES	5
HUGHS	1
HULL	6
HUMISTON	1
HUMPHREY	4
HUNT	3
HUSH	1
HUSTED	2
HUTCHINSON	6
HUTCHISON	2
HUYSSEN	3
HYDE	1
HYNS	2
INABNET	2
INABNIT	1
INFINGER	1
INGEBRETSEN	2
INGERSOLL	4
INGLE	2
IRVINE	8
ISAKSON	1
ISENHOOD	2
ISRAELSON	2
IVERSON	3
JACKSON	2
JACOBSEN	2
JACOBSON	4
JACOT	1
JAMERSON	2
JAMES	2
JAMRISKA	1
JARCKE	1
JARGER	1
JENONSON	1
JENSEN	4
JENSON	1
JERMAN	5
JERVY	1
JEWETT	18
JOHANESON	1
JOHANNESSEN	3
JOHANSEN	2
JOHANSON	2
JOHN	3

Surname	# of Land Parcels
JOHNS	2
JOHNSEN	1
JOHNSON	59
JOHNSTON	2
JONES	8
JONSEN	1
JONSON	2
JORDAN	3
JORNSON	2
JOYCE	1
JUMP	4
JUNOR	1
KAH-TE-NEEW-O-HO-PAZ-	1
KAISER	3
KALB	1
KALLENBACK	1
KALLENBAK	1
KARLEN	1
KAYE	3
KECK	4
KEEFE	1
KEEN	7
KEENER	1
KEHL	1
KEISER	3
KELKENBERG	1
KELLEY	7
KELLOGG	1
KELLY	1
KENNEDY	1
KENT	6
KERNES	4
KERR	1
KESLER	1
KEY	2
KIDDER	2
KIECKHOEFER	50
KIGHTLINGER	3
KIGWIN	1
KIMBALL	13
KING	4
KINGMAN	1
KINNEY	1
KINNIARD	1
KIRK	2
KIRKLAND	1
KIRSCHER	1
KITE	3
KITTELSEN	2
KLAUER	1
KNAPP	138
KNIGHT	7
KNOPPS	3
KNOTT	3
KNOX	1
KNUDSEN	10
KNUDSON	6
KNUDTSON	1
KOBB	2
KOHN	1
KOLB	2
KOPP	2
KOTTKE	1
KOWING	7
KRAMER	2
KRAMPERT	1
KRANSZ	1
KRAUS	2
KRAUSE	7
KRAUSER	2

Surname	# of Land Parcels	Surname	# of Land Parcels	Surname	# of Land Parcels	Surname	# of Land Parcels
KREUGER	1	LOWE	1	MCGREW	1	MUENCH	1
KRINGLE	1	LOWERY	3	MCINTYRE	9	MULHERON	1
KUNCLER	1	LOWRY	3	MCKAHAN	3	MULKS	7
KYES	1	LUCAS	7	MCKAHUN	1	MULLER	2
KYLE	6	LUND	2	MCKELHEER	3	MULVANY	1
LA FORGE	2	LYMAN	4	MCKIE	1	MUMER	2
LABEREE	2	LYNCH	1	MCLAIN	3	MURK	1
LACKEY	1	LYON	1	MCLENNAN	1	MURPHY	4
LACY	3	LYTLE	3	MCLEOD	2	MURRAY	1
LAFORGE	6	MACAULAY	2	MCLESKEY	2	MYERS	1
LAINE	2	MACAULEY	5	MCMAHON	1	NAMEJUNAS	1
LAMB	2	MACK	1	MCMANNAS	1	NARSEE	3
LAMMER	1	MACKEY	3	MCMANNUS	1	NELSON	14
LAMPHARE	1	MAGILTON	1	MCMANUS	1	NEMBARGER	1
LAMPMAN	2	MAHANY	1	MCMASTERS	2	NERESON	1
LANDON	9	MALHUS	1	MCMILLAN	1	NERISEN	2
LANDRUM	2	MALINDA	3	MCMURCHY	5	NERISON	4
LANDT	1	MALLEAN	1	MCMURRY	1	NESSET	3
LANE	2	MALONEY	1	MCNELIS	1	NEVIN	2
LANGBERG	3	MANCHESTER	2	MCNELLIS	1	NEWCOMB	1
LANGDAL	1	MANLEY	3	MCPHERSON	4	NEWELL	10
LANGDELL	2	MANNING	2	MCROBERT	1	NEWHALL	15
LARKHAM	1	MANS	1	MEAD	14	NEWMAN	4
LARRABEE	1	MANSFIELD	21	MEE-CHIT-E-NEE	1	NEWSOM	1
LARSEN	6	MARBURY	1	MEGGETT	2	NEWVILLE	1
LARSON	27	MARCH	9	MELLEN	1	NICHOLS	5
LARSONS	3	MARISTAD	2	MERCIER	1	NICOLS	1
LASH	2	MARK	1	MEREDETH	1	NIELSEN	2
LATHROP	5	MARKHAM	1	MERRILL	1	NILSEN	2
LAUDON	1	MARLETT	5	MESSELT	1	NILSON	3
LAWRENCE	1	MARR	1	MESSENGER	2	NOBLE	1
LAWTON	3	MARSH	2	MEYERS	1	NOER	3
LAYNE	1	MARSHALL	5	MICKELSON	2	NOGLE	2
LEACH	2	MARSTON	2	MIESTER	3	NOIS	1
LEAVENWORTH	1	MARTIN	13	MIKKELSEN	1	NOREM	3
LECLERCQ	1	MARTINSON	2	MIKKELSON	5	NORRISH	4
LEE	16	MARVIN	4	MILES	2	NORTHSTREAM	1
LEMON	2	MASON	4	MILLER	12	NORTON	4
LENTZ	2	MASONER	1	MILLIRON	1	NOWLEN	2
LEONARD	5	MASSEE	3	MILLS	11	NOYES	1
LESURE	1	MASSEY	5	MINER	4	NULPH	2
LETTEER	1	MATHERS	2	MITTELSTADT	2	NYE	2
LEWELLEN	1	MATHEWS	8	MOE	2	OBERLANDER	1
LEWIS	9	MATTESON	3	MOEN	3	OBRIEN	3
LIBBEY	1	MATTHEWS	3	MONFORT	2	OCONNELL	1
LIE	2	MATTISON	2	MONROE	1	OCONNOR	8
LIGHTBOURN	4	MAUKSTAD	1	MONTAGUE	3	OFLANEGAN	3
LIND	1	MAVES	1	MONTEITH	10	OLESEN	4
LININGER	1	MAVITY	2	MONTGOMERY	2	OLESON	23
LINK	1	MAYBEE	1	MOODY	3	OLIN	3
LIPOISKY	2	MCADOO	1	MOONEY	1	OLIVER	4
LIPPEL	2	MCALLISTER	3	MOOR	5	OLMSTEAD	2
LITTLE	5	MCARTHUR	1	MOORE	23	OLSEN	15
LIVERSON	1	MCAULEY	1	MOREHOUSE	2	OLSON	32
LIVINGSTON	2	MCBRIDE	2	MORFEY	1	OLSTAD	3
LOCKE	2	MCCART	2	MORGAN	7	OMALLEY	3
LOCKWOOD	6	MCCARTNEY	1	MORK	2	OMDAHL	1
LOE	3	MCCARTY	4	MORRICE	1	OMDAHLE	1
LOFTHUS	2	MCCOLLUM	1	MORRISON	7	OMDOLL	3
LOFTHUUS	3	MCCORKLE	6	MORSE	2	OMTVEDT	1
LOGSLETT	2	MCCORMICK	1	MORTON	6	ONDERDONK	2
LOGSLID	1	MCCULLOCH	5	MOSHER	1	ONEY	2
LOHFINK	2	MCCULLOUGH	1	MOSSNER	1	ORDEMAN	1
LONG	1	MCDONALD	4	MOSTELLER	1	ORDEMANN	3
LONGDO	2	MCDORMAN	1	MOULTON	1	ORME	4
LORD	3	MCELWAIN	1	MOUNTCASTLE	2	OSMER	2
LOTT	3	MCELWAINE	2	MOWLAN	2	OTIS	1
LOUSTED	1	MCGEOGH	2	MOYER	2	OTTUM	1
LOW	2	MCGILTON	1	MOYES	1	OVITT	1
LOWBER	2	MCGINNIS	2	MUDGE	2	OWEN	6

Surname	# of Land Parcels
PACHL	1
PADDLEFORD	2
PAGE	4
PAINE	3
PAIRO	3
PALEN	6
PALMER	3
PARK	2
PARKER	5
PATTEN	2
PAUL	2
PAULSON	3
PAYNE	4
PEARSON	2
PEASE	2
PECK	1
PEDERSEN	2
PEDERSON	2
PEET	1
PEISCH	1
PELT	1
PENNOCK	3
PENNOYER	1
PE-QUAH-KO-NAH	1
PEROT	3
PERRY	3
PETERSON	7
PETTIS	3
PHELPS	2
PHERNETTON	2
PHILLIPS	8
PHILPOTT	1
PICKARD	1
PICKERING	1
PIERCE	4
PIERSON	1
PIPPINGER	1
PIRKL	1
PITZRICK	1
PLAISTED	4
PLANT	20
PLATT	4
POISKE	1
POLLY	4
PONTOW	1
POOLER	4
PORTER	5
POST	2
POTE	3
POTETE	1
POWELL	15
POWERS	1
PRATT	1
PREMBLE	2
PRESCOTT	2
PRESTON	5
PRETY	1
PRICKETT	2
PRILL	1
PRIRCE	2
PROPER	1
PROPHET	6
PROSSER	2
PRUITT	2
PUTNAM	13
PUTNAN	2
PUTNEY	1
PYE	1
QUADERER	1
QUARLES	1

Surname	# of Land Parcels
QUIGGLE	3
QUINN	2
RACKWITZ	1
RAIMER	1
RAMSEY	5
RAND	9
RANDALL	3
RANDELL	1
RANDS	1
RANNEY	4
RAPELYE	1
RASMUSEN	2
RASMUSON	1
RASSBACH	3
RAUENBUEHLER	1
RAY	2
RAYBURN	2
REED	8
REICHARD	3
REID	1
REINCKE	1
REINECKE	1
REINKE	1
REKLEAN	1
REMINGTON	12
RENDELSBACHER	3
REPINE	1
RETZ	1
REYMERT	1
REYMOND	2
REYNOLDS	11
RICE	3
RICHARDS	2
RICHMOND	5
RICKER	2
RIDDELL	2
RIDER	1
RIEMER	1
RIGGS	50
RING	2
RIPLEY	5
RISS	1
RITER	3
RITTENHOUSE	9
RITTER	4
ROACH	4
ROBBE	1
ROBBINS	2
ROBERTS	7
ROBERTSON	3
ROBISON	2
ROCK	4
ROEMHILD	2
ROGERS	1
ROLEFF	2
ROLSTAD	1
ROMSAAS	4
RONENG	1
RONGSTAD	2
RORK	10
ROSE	1
ROSEYCRANCE	1
ROSS	1
ROSSON	2
ROSTANO	3
ROSWELL	1
ROTH	2
ROWE	3
RUE	2
RULE	1

Surname	# of Land Parcels
RUMRILL	2
RUMSEY	3
RUNKLE	2
RUNNING	3
RUNNION	1
RURICHT	1
RUSH	2
RYDER	2
SABIN	2
SAGSTUEN	1
SAHLIE	2
SAHLKE	1
SALESBURY	2
SAMPIRE	1
SAMPSON	4
SANDERS	1
SANDERSON	3
SANGER	4
SAVILLE	1
SAXTON	4
SCANLAN	5
SCHAAF	1
SCHAEFER	3
SCHAFNER	2
SCHAMBERGER	1
SCHECKEL	1
SCHELHAD	1
SCHIEBE	1
SCHLOUGH	4
SCHLUCH	1
SCHLUCK	2
SCHMITT	5
SCHOLL	6
SCHRIER	1
SCHROEDER	1
SCHROETER	3
SCHUBEL	3
SCHULSTAD	3
SCHUTTS	2
SCOTT	3
SEABERT	2
SEAMAN	2
SECOR	2
SEE	4
SEEDS	2
SEEVER	4
SEGUR	1
SEILER	1
SELLERS	3
SEMMINGSEN	3
SEMMINGSON	3
SENG	2
SERVIS	2
SEVALDSON	1
SEVERSON	7
SEVERTSON	1
SEXTON	4
SEYMOUR	1
SHAANE	1
SHADBOLT	2
SHAFER	7
SHAFFER	1
SHAFFNER	1
SHANKLIN	2
SHARPLES	3
SHAW	7
SHAY	1
SHELTON	2
SHEPARD	7
SHEPHARD	3

Surname	# of Land Parcels
SHERBURN	1
SHERBURNE	14
SHERLOCK	1
SHERMAN	2
SHIELDS	3
SHIELLS	3
SHILTS	1
SHIPMAN	2
SHO-CHETTES	1
SHUGERT	2
SHULTZ	5
SHUMAKER	1
SIBBET	1
SICKLES	1
SIEBERT	2
SIEDENBERG	2
SIEFERT	2
SIM-IS-HOYA	1
SIMONS	1
SINGERHAUS	1
SINGERHOUSE	1
SINTZ	1
SIPPEL	4
SIPPLE	1
SISCHO	3
SISSON	1
SKEEL	1
SKINNER	4
SKJERLY	2
SLAGEL	2
SLAGLE	4
SLICK	5
SLOCUM	3
SLOVER	3
SLY	4
SLYE	1
SMEAD	3
SMITH	36
SNELL	3
SNYDER	10
SOLBERG	3
SOLI	2
SOLIE	1
SOMMERKORN	1
SONNENBURG	1
SOPER	2
SORENSEN	4
SORENSON	4
SORKNESS	1
SOUTHGATE	1
SPAFFORD	13
SPALDING	3
SPENCE	3
SPOONER	3
SPRAGUE	6
STAMPS	2
STANLEY	4
STANSBERRY	1
STANSBERY	1
STAPLES	3
STARKWEATHER	3
STEARNS	4
STEBBINS	2
STEEL	2
STEEN	1
STEENBARGER	1
STEINMAN	1
STENERSEN	3
STENERSON	1
STEPHENS	1

Surname	# of Land Parcels
STEPPACHER	2
STEVENS	6
STEVES	5
STEWART	1
STICKNEY	4
STILES	11
STILLEY	4
STINGLUFF	1
STINSON	1
STOCKMAN	2
STODDARD	3
STONE	2
STOUT	87
STRATTON	3
STROBRIDGE	2
STROTHER	1
STROUD	1
STUART	1
STUBBS	3
STUDABAKER	4
STUDLEY	6
STURTEVANT	1
SUCKOW	1
SUKOW	1
SUMMERS	1
SUNDERLIN	1
SUSEY	1
SUTLIFF	6
SVENOMSON	2
SVENUNGSON	2
SWAN	5
SWARTS	1
SWARTWOOD	1
SWEENY	1
SWEET	2
SWENSON	5
SWIGER	1
SWISHER	7
SYLTE	4
SYVERSEN	4
TABOR	1
TAINTER	93
TALMAGE	1
TANDE	1
TANTON	1
TAPLIN	3
TAYLOR	23
TEEGARDEN	2
TEEL	2
TEIGENSKAU	2
TERRILL	2
THANE	2
THAYER	1
THIBODO	1
THOMAS	13
THOMPSON	32
THORESEN	2
THORN	1
THORSEN	3
THORSON	2
THUE	3
TIBBETTS	2
TIFFANY	1
TILLESEN	1
TILLESON	8
TIMMERMAN	1
TIZEN	3
TOBEY	2
TOEL	11
TOLASON	1

Surname	# of Land Parcels
TOLEDANO	2
TOLEFSON	1
TOLLEVSON	1
TOLLOFSON	3
TOMLINSON	3
TORGERSON	2
TORGUSSEN	2
TORKELSON	4
TOTMAN	1
TOWNSEND	2
TRASHER	2
TRASK	8
TRAVIS	1
TREFETHREN	3
TRIGG	2
TRONSEN	1
TROSVIG	4
TUBBS	10
TURNER	4
TUTTLE	12
TUVENG	1
TWEITEN	2
TYLER	1
ULRICH	1
UMBARGER	2
UNDERHILL	2
URSINUS	1
UTTER	1
VAIL	3
VAN ALLEN	1
VAN PELT	1
VAN RIPER	2
VAN SLIKE	2
VAN VETCHTEN	1
VAN WOERT	4
VANCE	6
VANDERHOEF	2
VARBLE	2
VARNEY	2
VASEY	4
VAUGHAN	5
VEDDER	1
VIBBERTS	4
VIETS	1
VOEGT	2
VOORIS	2
VROMAN	1
VROOMAN	2
WACHTER	2
WADE	2
WAGNER	4
WAGONER	1
WAINZIRL	1
WAIT	5
WA-KE-MA-WET	1
WALKER	16
WALLACE	1
WARD	2
WARE	3
WARREN	2
WASHBURN	5
WASHBURNE	1
WATERSTON	1
WATKINS	2
WATSON	3
WATTERMAN	2
WEAVER	3
WEBB	12
WEBER	7
WEBERT	1

Surname	# of Land Parcels
WEBSTER	4
WEILLER	1
WEIMAN	1
WELCH	1
WELLS	2
WELTON	1
WENNES	3
WERNER	3
WEST	6
WESTERMEYER	1
WESTON	7
WETHERBY	5
WHALEY	1
WHEELER	5
WHINERY	2
WHIPPLE	3
WHISLER	3
WHITE	13
WHITEFORD	1
WHITELEY	3
WHITEMAN	2
WHITLLESEY	1
WHITTLESEY	6
WICHSER	3
WICKS	1
WIEMAN	1
WIEMANN	2
WIGEN	1
WIGGINS	9
WIGHT	1
WILBUR	1
WILKINS	6
WILLEY	1
WILLIAMS	12
WILLIAMSON	2
WILLIFORD	1
WILLOCK-HOYE	1
WILSON	155
WILSTACH	6
WILSTACK	7
WINSLOW	2
WISCONSIN	24
WISEMAN	1
WITT	4
WOLD	4
WOOD	11
WOODHOUSE	1
WOODHULL	1
WOODMAN	9
WOODS	8
WOODWARD	27
WOODWORTH	2
WRIGHT	6
WYLIE	2
WYMAN	1
YAPLE	1
YARDLEY	2
YEAMAN	2
YODER	2
YOKES	2
YOUNG	8
ZIBBLE	1
ZIELIE	2
ZIMERMAN	2
ZUEHLKE	1

Surname/Township Index

This Index allows you to determine which *Township Map Group(s)* contain individuals with the following surnames. Each *Map Group* has a corresponding full-name index of all individuals who obtained patents for land within its Congressional township's borders. After each index you will find the Patent Map to which it refers, and just thereafter, you can view the township's Road Map and Historical Map, with the latter map displaying streams, railroads, and more.

So, once you find your Surname here, proceed to the Index at the beginning of the **Map Group** indicated below.

Surname	Map Group	Parcels of Land	Meridian/Township/Range		
AAMOT	**12**	4	4th PM - 1831 MN/WI	29-N	11-W
AASEN	**3**	2	4th PM - 1831 MN/WI	31-N	12-W
ABBOTT	**7**	1	4th PM - 1831 MN/WI	30-N	12-W
ACKERT	**10**	3	4th PM - 1831 MN/WI	29-N	13-W
ACKLEY	**23**	5	4th PM - 1831 MN/WI	26-N	12-W
" "	**22**	3	4th PM - 1831 MN/WI	26-N	13-W
ADAMS	**10**	6	4th PM - 1831 MN/WI	29-N	13-W
" "	**5**	2	4th PM - 1831 MN/WI	30-N	14-W
" "	**24**	1	4th PM - 1831 MN/WI	26-N	11-W
" "	**22**	1	4th PM - 1831 MN/WI	26-N	13-W
AH-KE-NE-BOI-WE	**19**	1	4th PM - 1831 MN/WI	27-N	12-W
AIKEN	**22**	1	4th PM - 1831 MN/WI	26-N	13-W
ALBURTUS	**24**	1	4th PM - 1831 MN/WI	26-N	11-W
ALDEN	**14**	2	4th PM - 1831 MN/WI	28-N	13-W
ALDERMAN	**24**	3	4th PM - 1831 MN/WI	26-N	11-W
ALDRICK	**15**	1	4th PM - 1831 MN/WI	28-N	12-W
ALEXANDER	**2**	2	4th PM - 1831 MN/WI	31-N	13-W
ALFARO	**16**	1	4th PM - 1831 MN/WI	28-N	11-W
ALLEN	**15**	3	4th PM - 1831 MN/WI	28-N	12-W
" "	**24**	2	4th PM - 1831 MN/WI	26-N	11-W
" "	**22**	1	4th PM - 1831 MN/WI	26-N	13-W
" "	**20**	1	4th PM - 1831 MN/WI	27-N	11-W
" "	**19**	1	4th PM - 1831 MN/WI	27-N	12-W
" "	**1**	1	4th PM - 1831 MN/WI	31-N	14-W
ALLESTAD	**8**	2	4th PM - 1831 MN/WI	30-N	11-W
ALLISON	**1**	4	4th PM - 1831 MN/WI	31-N	14-W
ALLISTAD	**8**	1	4th PM - 1831 MN/WI	30-N	11-W
ALLRAM	**2**	1	4th PM - 1831 MN/WI	31-N	13-W
AMBLE	**16**	1	4th PM - 1831 MN/WI	28-N	11-W
AMES	**22**	13	4th PM - 1831 MN/WI	26-N	13-W
AMICK	**13**	1	4th PM - 1831 MN/WI	28-N	14-W
AMORY	**5**	4	4th PM - 1831 MN/WI	30-N	14-W
" "	**16**	2	4th PM - 1831 MN/WI	28-N	11-W
" "	**24**	1	4th PM - 1831 MN/WI	26-N	11-W
AMUNDSEN	**4**	4	4th PM - 1831 MN/WI	31-N	11-W
AMUNDSON	**3**	2	4th PM - 1831 MN/WI	31-N	12-W
ANACKER	**5**	1	4th PM - 1831 MN/WI	30-N	14-W
ANDERSEN	**2**	3	4th PM - 1831 MN/WI	31-N	13-W
" "	**7**	2	4th PM - 1831 MN/WI	30-N	12-W
" "	**12**	1	4th PM - 1831 MN/WI	29-N	11-W
ANDERSON	**4**	16	4th PM - 1831 MN/WI	31-N	11-W
" "	**8**	13	4th PM - 1831 MN/WI	30-N	11-W
" "	**16**	11	4th PM - 1831 MN/WI	28-N	11-W
" "	**7**	7	4th PM - 1831 MN/WI	30-N	12-W

Surname	Map Group	Parcels of Land	Meridian/Township/Range		
ANDERSON (Cont'd)	3	7	4th PM - 1831 MN/WI	31-N	12-W
" "	12	5	4th PM - 1831 MN/WI	29-N	11-W
" "	24	3	4th PM - 1831 MN/WI	26-N	11-W
" "	23	1	4th PM - 1831 MN/WI	26-N	12-W
" "	22	1	4th PM - 1831 MN/WI	26-N	13-W
" "	20	1	4th PM - 1831 MN/WI	27-N	11-W
" "	19	1	4th PM - 1831 MN/WI	27-N	12-W
" "	15	1	4th PM - 1831 MN/WI	28-N	12-W
" "	9	1	4th PM - 1831 MN/WI	29-N	14-W
" "	6	1	4th PM - 1831 MN/WI	30-N	13-W
ANDREASEN	8	3	4th PM - 1831 MN/WI	30-N	11-W
ANDRESS	5	1	4th PM - 1831 MN/WI	30-N	14-W
ANDREWS	9	3	4th PM - 1831 MN/WI	29-N	14-W
" "	14	2	4th PM - 1831 MN/WI	28-N	13-W
" "	8	2	4th PM - 1831 MN/WI	30-N	11-W
" "	10	1	4th PM - 1831 MN/WI	29-N	13-W
ANDRUS	2	1	4th PM - 1831 MN/WI	31-N	13-W
ANNIS	9	1	4th PM - 1831 MN/WI	29-N	14-W
ARMSTRONG	20	1	4th PM - 1831 MN/WI	27-N	11-W
ARNESON	12	2	4th PM - 1831 MN/WI	29-N	11-W
" "	16	1	4th PM - 1831 MN/WI	28-N	11-W
" "	8	1	4th PM - 1831 MN/WI	30-N	11-W
ARNOLD	24	1	4th PM - 1831 MN/WI	26-N	11-W
ASLAKSEN	3	3	4th PM - 1831 MN/WI	31-N	12-W
" "	18	1	4th PM - 1831 MN/WI	27-N	13-W
ATWOOD	12	2	4th PM - 1831 MN/WI	29-N	11-W
" "	19	1	4th PM - 1831 MN/WI	27-N	12-W
AUGENSEN	4	2	4th PM - 1831 MN/WI	31-N	11-W
AUKNEY	11	1	4th PM - 1831 MN/WI	29-N	12-W
AUSSMAN	20	4	4th PM - 1831 MN/WI	27-N	11-W
AUSTIN	13	5	4th PM - 1831 MN/WI	28-N	14-W
" "	23	2	4th PM - 1831 MN/WI	26-N	12-W
" "	21	1	4th PM - 1831 MN/WI	26-N	14-W
" "	9	1	4th PM - 1831 MN/WI	29-N	14-W
AVERY	18	2	4th PM - 1831 MN/WI	27-N	13-W
" "	24	1	4th PM - 1831 MN/WI	26-N	11-W
AZRO	20	1	4th PM - 1831 MN/WI	27-N	11-W
BABBENDORF	15	1	4th PM - 1831 MN/WI	28-N	12-W
BABBITT	1	1	4th PM - 1831 MN/WI	31-N	14-W
BABCOCK	24	7	4th PM - 1831 MN/WI	26-N	11-W
" "	9	2	4th PM - 1831 MN/WI	29-N	14-W
BACHLER	9	1	4th PM - 1831 MN/WI	29-N	14-W
BAGG	20	1	4th PM - 1831 MN/WI	27-N	11-W
BAILEY	9	8	4th PM - 1831 MN/WI	29-N	14-W
" "	23	3	4th PM - 1831 MN/WI	26-N	12-W
" "	21	2	4th PM - 1831 MN/WI	26-N	14-W
" "	6	2	4th PM - 1831 MN/WI	30-N	13-W
" "	10	1	4th PM - 1831 MN/WI	29-N	13-W
BAKER	4	7	4th PM - 1831 MN/WI	31-N	11-W
" "	21	2	4th PM - 1831 MN/WI	26-N	14-W
" "	11	2	4th PM - 1831 MN/WI	29-N	12-W
BALAND	3	2	4th PM - 1831 MN/WI	31-N	12-W
BALCOM	16	3	4th PM - 1831 MN/WI	28-N	11-W
BALDRIDGE	3	3	4th PM - 1831 MN/WI	31-N	12-W
BALDWIN	12	7	4th PM - 1831 MN/WI	29-N	11-W
" "	3	1	4th PM - 1831 MN/WI	31-N	12-W
" "	2	1	4th PM - 1831 MN/WI	31-N	13-W
" "	1	1	4th PM - 1831 MN/WI	31-N	14-W
BALIS	10	2	4th PM - 1831 MN/WI	29-N	13-W
BANKS	14	2	4th PM - 1831 MN/WI	28-N	13-W

Surname	Map Group	Parcels of Land	Meridian/Township/Range		
BANKS (Cont'd)	**5**	1	4th PM - 1831 MN/WI	30-N	14-W
BANNISTER	**18**	1	4th PM - 1831 MN/WI	27-N	13-W
BARBER	**10**	1	4th PM - 1831 MN/WI	29-N	13-W
BARKER	**15**	2	4th PM - 1831 MN/WI	28-N	12-W
BARNARD	**15**	12	4th PM - 1831 MN/WI	28-N	12-W
" "	**22**	2	4th PM - 1831 MN/WI	26-N	13-W
" "	**13**	2	4th PM - 1831 MN/WI	28-N	14-W
" "	**10**	2	4th PM - 1831 MN/WI	29-N	13-W
" "	**19**	1	4th PM - 1831 MN/WI	27-N	12-W
" "	**11**	1	4th PM - 1831 MN/WI	29-N	12-W
BARNE	**23**	2	4th PM - 1831 MN/WI	26-N	12-W
BARNES	**20**	2	4th PM - 1831 MN/WI	27-N	11-W
BARNUM	**23**	3	4th PM - 1831 MN/WI	26-N	12-W
BARTHOLOMEW	**10**	3	4th PM - 1831 MN/WI	29-N	13-W
BARTLETT	**15**	2	4th PM - 1831 MN/WI	28-N	12-W
" "	**8**	1	4th PM - 1831 MN/WI	30-N	11-W
BARTON	**5**	11	4th PM - 1831 MN/WI	30-N	14-W
" "	**6**	2	4th PM - 1831 MN/WI	30-N	13-W
" "	**14**	1	4th PM - 1831 MN/WI	28-N	13-W
BARUM	**12**	2	4th PM - 1831 MN/WI	29-N	11-W
BASFORD	**24**	1	4th PM - 1831 MN/WI	26-N	11-W
BASKIN	**22**	2	4th PM - 1831 MN/WI	26-N	13-W
BASKINS	**22**	1	4th PM - 1831 MN/WI	26-N	13-W
BATCHELDER	**11**	1	4th PM - 1831 MN/WI	29-N	12-W
BATES	**23**	3	4th PM - 1831 MN/WI	26-N	12-W
BAXTER	**12**	2	4th PM - 1831 MN/WI	29-N	11-W
" "	**15**	1	4th PM - 1831 MN/WI	28-N	12-W
BEADLE	**20**	2	4th PM - 1831 MN/WI	27-N	11-W
BEAL	**2**	2	4th PM - 1831 MN/WI	31-N	13-W
BEALE	**11**	1	4th PM - 1831 MN/WI	29-N	12-W
BEATTIE	**11**	1	4th PM - 1831 MN/WI	29-N	12-W
BECKER	**7**	4	4th PM - 1831 MN/WI	30-N	12-W
BECKWITH	**18**	7	4th PM - 1831 MN/WI	27-N	13-W
" "	**19**	3	4th PM - 1831 MN/WI	27-N	12-W
" "	**22**	2	4th PM - 1831 MN/WI	26-N	13-W
" "	**10**	1	4th PM - 1831 MN/WI	29-N	13-W
BEDDINGER	**18**	2	4th PM - 1831 MN/WI	27-N	13-W
" "	**15**	2	4th PM - 1831 MN/WI	28-N	12-W
BEDELL	**6**	1	4th PM - 1831 MN/WI	30-N	13-W
BEEBE	**9**	1	4th PM - 1831 MN/WI	29-N	14-W
BEEMAN	**24**	1	4th PM - 1831 MN/WI	26-N	11-W
BEGUHN	**16**	4	4th PM - 1831 MN/WI	28-N	11-W
" "	**15**	3	4th PM - 1831 MN/WI	28-N	12-W
BEISSWANGER	**2**	1	4th PM - 1831 MN/WI	31-N	13-W
BELDEN	**20**	3	4th PM - 1831 MN/WI	27-N	11-W
BELDING	**10**	1	4th PM - 1831 MN/WI	29-N	13-W
BELKNAP	**4**	1	4th PM - 1831 MN/WI	31-N	11-W
BELL	**12**	1	4th PM - 1831 MN/WI	29-N	11-W
BELLACH	**18**	1	4th PM - 1831 MN/WI	27-N	13-W
BELLEMAN	**2**	2	4th PM - 1831 MN/WI	31-N	13-W
BENAVIDES	**12**	2	4th PM - 1831 MN/WI	29-N	11-W
BENDIKSDATTER	**3**	2	4th PM - 1831 MN/WI	31-N	12-W
BENDIXSON	**3**	1	4th PM - 1831 MN/WI	31-N	12-W
BENJAMIN	**2**	1	4th PM - 1831 MN/WI	31-N	13-W
BENNER	**1**	1	4th PM - 1831 MN/WI	31-N	14-W
BENNET	**23**	2	4th PM - 1831 MN/WI	26-N	12-W
BENNETT	**23**	2	4th PM - 1831 MN/WI	26-N	12-W
" "	**21**	2	4th PM - 1831 MN/WI	26-N	14-W
" "	**19**	2	4th PM - 1831 MN/WI	27-N	12-W
" "	**24**	1	4th PM - 1831 MN/WI	26-N	11-W

Surname	Map Group	Parcels of Land	Meridian/Township/Range		
BENNETT (Cont'd)	**15**	1	4th PM - 1831 MN/WI	28-N	12-W
" "	**8**	1	4th PM - 1831 MN/WI	30-N	11-W
" "	**6**	1	4th PM - 1831 MN/WI	30-N	13-W
" "	**5**	1	4th PM - 1831 MN/WI	30-N	14-W
" "	**4**	1	4th PM - 1831 MN/WI	31-N	11-W
BENTON	**8**	4	4th PM - 1831 MN/WI	30-N	11-W
" "	**21**	2	4th PM - 1831 MN/WI	26-N	14-W
" "	**22**	1	4th PM - 1831 MN/WI	26-N	13-W
BENTSEN	**16**	1	4th PM - 1831 MN/WI	28-N	11-W
BENTSON	**4**	3	4th PM - 1831 MN/WI	31-N	11-W
BERG	**8**	4	4th PM - 1831 MN/WI	30-N	11-W
BERGELAND	**3**	1	4th PM - 1831 MN/WI	31-N	12-W
BERGEMANN	**21**	8	4th PM - 1831 MN/WI	26-N	14-W
BERGERSON	**8**	1	4th PM - 1831 MN/WI	30-N	11-W
BERGET	**3**	2	4th PM - 1831 MN/WI	31-N	12-W
BERNTZON	**12**	2	4th PM - 1831 MN/WI	29-N	11-W
" "	**8**	1	4th PM - 1831 MN/WI	30-N	11-W
BESSE	**5**	1	4th PM - 1831 MN/WI	30-N	14-W
BEST	**5**	8	4th PM - 1831 MN/WI	30-N	14-W
" "	**1**	5	4th PM - 1831 MN/WI	31-N	14-W
BETTS	**23**	2	4th PM - 1831 MN/WI	26-N	12-W
BEYER	**15**	5	4th PM - 1831 MN/WI	28-N	12-W
" "	**16**	1	4th PM - 1831 MN/WI	28-N	11-W
BIGFORD	**14**	1	4th PM - 1831 MN/WI	28-N	13-W
BILLILNGS	**23**	2	4th PM - 1831 MN/WI	26-N	12-W
BILLINGS	**23**	10	4th PM - 1831 MN/WI	26-N	12-W
" "	**19**	2	4th PM - 1831 MN/WI	27-N	12-W
" "	**18**	2	4th PM - 1831 MN/WI	27-N	13-W
" "	**22**	1	4th PM - 1831 MN/WI	26-N	13-W
BILSE	**2**	2	4th PM - 1831 MN/WI	31-N	13-W
BINDINGER	**21**	2	4th PM - 1831 MN/WI	26-N	14-W
BIRD	**18**	2	4th PM - 1831 MN/WI	27-N	13-W
BIRKEL	**22**	1	4th PM - 1831 MN/WI	26-N	13-W
BISHOP	**18**	2	4th PM - 1831 MN/WI	27-N	13-W
" "	**23**	1	4th PM - 1831 MN/WI	26-N	12-W
" "	**21**	1	4th PM - 1831 MN/WI	26-N	14-W
" "	**19**	1	4th PM - 1831 MN/WI	27-N	12-W
BISS	**1**	2	4th PM - 1831 MN/WI	31-N	14-W
BISSINGER	**24**	2	4th PM - 1831 MN/WI	26-N	11-W
BJORNSON	**8**	1	4th PM - 1831 MN/WI	30-N	11-W
BLACK	**18**	1	4th PM - 1831 MN/WI	27-N	13-W
BLAIR	**7**	5	4th PM - 1831 MN/WI	30-N	12-W
" "	**21**	2	4th PM - 1831 MN/WI	26-N	14-W
" "	**19**	1	4th PM - 1831 MN/WI	27-N	12-W
BLAKELY	**10**	4	4th PM - 1831 MN/WI	29-N	13-W
" "	**5**	3	4th PM - 1831 MN/WI	30-N	14-W
BLANCHARD	**10**	1	4th PM - 1831 MN/WI	29-N	13-W
BLANK	**18**	3	4th PM - 1831 MN/WI	27-N	13-W
BLATCHFORD	**8**	2	4th PM - 1831 MN/WI	30-N	11-W
BLODGETT	**20**	2	4th PM - 1831 MN/WI	27-N	11-W
" "	**11**	2	4th PM - 1831 MN/WI	29-N	12-W
" "	**13**	1	4th PM - 1831 MN/WI	28-N	14-W
" "	**5**	1	4th PM - 1831 MN/WI	30-N	14-W
BLOOM	**19**	1	4th PM - 1831 MN/WI	27-N	12-W
BLUM	**19**	1	4th PM - 1831 MN/WI	27-N	12-W
BOA	**21**	1	4th PM - 1831 MN/WI	26-N	14-W
BOARDMAN	**2**	1	4th PM - 1831 MN/WI	31-N	13-W
" "	**1**	1	4th PM - 1831 MN/WI	31-N	14-W
BOCK	**21**	1	4th PM - 1831 MN/WI	26-N	14-W
BODETT	**5**	2	4th PM - 1831 MN/WI	30-N	14-W

Surname	Map Group	Parcels of Land	Meridian/Township/Range		
BOGGESS	**5**	8	4th PM - 1831 MN/WI	30-N	14-W
BOHN	**22**	2	4th PM - 1831 MN/WI	26-N	13-W
BOLLE	**18**	1	4th PM - 1831 MN/WI	27-N	13-W
BOLLES	**24**	10	4th PM - 1831 MN/WI	26-N	11-W
BOND	**1**	3	4th PM - 1831 MN/WI	31-N	14-W
BONNELL	**10**	2	4th PM - 1831 MN/WI	29-N	13-W
BONNEVALD	**18**	1	4th PM - 1831 MN/WI	27-N	13-W
BONNEY	**16**	1	4th PM - 1831 MN/WI	28-N	11-W
BOOKS	**24**	1	4th PM - 1831 MN/WI	26-N	11-W
BOOTH	**23**	6	4th PM - 1831 MN/WI	26-N	12-W
BOOTON	**3**	1	4th PM - 1831 MN/WI	31-N	12-W
BORCHERT	**21**	1	4th PM - 1831 MN/WI	26-N	14-W
BOREE	**4**	1	4th PM - 1831 MN/WI	31-N	11-W
BORLAND	**15**	1	4th PM - 1831 MN/WI	28-N	12-W
" "	**14**	1	4th PM - 1831 MN/WI	28-N	13-W
BORSEN	**2**	1	4th PM - 1831 MN/WI	31-N	13-W
BORTLE	**3**	1	4th PM - 1831 MN/WI	31-N	12-W
BOTTOM	**8**	2	4th PM - 1831 MN/WI	30-N	11-W
BOTUME	**8**	2	4th PM - 1831 MN/WI	30-N	11-W
BOURN	**9**	1	4th PM - 1831 MN/WI	29-N	14-W
BOUSE	**15**	1	4th PM - 1831 MN/WI	28-N	12-W
BOWDISH	**18**	1	4th PM - 1831 MN/WI	27-N	13-W
BOWERS	**22**	1	4th PM - 1831 MN/WI	26-N	13-W
BOWMAN	**23**	4	4th PM - 1831 MN/WI	26-N	12-W
BOYINGTON	**21**	1	4th PM - 1831 MN/WI	26-N	14-W
BOYLE	**22**	1	4th PM - 1831 MN/WI	26-N	13-W
" "	**21**	1	4th PM - 1831 MN/WI	26-N	14-W
BOYNTON	**14**	1	4th PM - 1831 MN/WI	28-N	13-W
BRAATEN	**12**	4	4th PM - 1831 MN/WI	29-N	11-W
BRADFORD	**11**	1	4th PM - 1831 MN/WI	29-N	12-W
BRADLEY	**4**	3	4th PM - 1831 MN/WI	31-N	11-W
BRADWAY	**10**	4	4th PM - 1831 MN/WI	29-N	13-W
" "	**6**	4	4th PM - 1831 MN/WI	30-N	13-W
BRAINARD	**16**	2	4th PM - 1831 MN/WI	28-N	11-W
BRAKER	**22**	1	4th PM - 1831 MN/WI	26-N	13-W
BRANCH	**21**	3	4th PM - 1831 MN/WI	26-N	14-W
BRANKIN	**8**	1	4th PM - 1831 MN/WI	30-N	11-W
BRATLEY	**7**	1	4th PM - 1831 MN/WI	30-N	12-W
BRAYNARD	**20**	1	4th PM - 1831 MN/WI	27-N	11-W
" "	**16**	1	4th PM - 1831 MN/WI	28-N	11-W
BRECK	**22**	2	4th PM - 1831 MN/WI	26-N	13-W
BREDESEN	**8**	3	4th PM - 1831 MN/WI	30-N	11-W
BREEZEE	**11**	2	4th PM - 1831 MN/WI	29-N	12-W
BRENNAN	**23**	1	4th PM - 1831 MN/WI	26-N	12-W
" "	**20**	1	4th PM - 1831 MN/WI	27-N	11-W
BRENT	**8**	2	4th PM - 1831 MN/WI	30-N	11-W
BREWER	**3**	3	4th PM - 1831 MN/WI	31-N	12-W
" "	**5**	2	4th PM - 1831 MN/WI	30-N	14-W
" "	**4**	1	4th PM - 1831 MN/WI	31-N	11-W
" "	**1**	1	4th PM - 1831 MN/WI	31-N	14-W
BREWSTER	**5**	2	4th PM - 1831 MN/WI	30-N	14-W
BRIDGHAM	**22**	1	4th PM - 1831 MN/WI	26-N	13-W
BRIGGS	**18**	1	4th PM - 1831 MN/WI	27-N	13-W
" "	**9**	1	4th PM - 1831 MN/WI	29-N	14-W
BRIGHT	**13**	2	4th PM - 1831 MN/WI	28-N	14-W
" "	**22**	1	4th PM - 1831 MN/WI	26-N	13-W
BRILL	**24**	3	4th PM - 1831 MN/WI	26-N	11-W
BRINGERUD	**3**	3	4th PM - 1831 MN/WI	31-N	12-W
BRONKEN	**8**	3	4th PM - 1831 MN/WI	30-N	11-W
BRONN	**16**	1	4th PM - 1831 MN/WI	28-N	11-W

Surname	Map Group	Parcels of Land	Meridian/Township/Range		
BRONSTAD	12	2	4th PM - 1831 MN/WI	29-N	11-W
BROVEN	18	1	4th PM - 1831 MN/WI	27-N	13-W
BROWN	5	7	4th PM - 1831 MN/WI	30-N	14-W
" "	10	4	4th PM - 1831 MN/WI	29-N	13-W
" "	1	3	4th PM - 1831 MN/WI	31-N	14-W
" "	24	2	4th PM - 1831 MN/WI	26-N	11-W
" "	21	2	4th PM - 1831 MN/WI	26-N	14-W
" "	20	2	4th PM - 1831 MN/WI	27-N	11-W
" "	19	1	4th PM - 1831 MN/WI	27-N	12-W
" "	15	1	4th PM - 1831 MN/WI	28-N	12-W
" "	6	1	4th PM - 1831 MN/WI	30-N	13-W
" "	3	1	4th PM - 1831 MN/WI	31-N	12-W
BROWNLEE	21	3	4th PM - 1831 MN/WI	26-N	14-W
" "	7	1	4th PM - 1831 MN/WI	30-N	12-W
BRUNELLE	15	3	4th PM - 1831 MN/WI	28-N	12-W
" "	18	2	4th PM - 1831 MN/WI	27-N	13-W
BRUNK	14	2	4th PM - 1831 MN/WI	28-N	13-W
BRUSH	24	2	4th PM - 1831 MN/WI	26-N	11-W
BRYANT	11	2	4th PM - 1831 MN/WI	29-N	12-W
" "	21	1	4th PM - 1831 MN/WI	26-N	14-W
BUCHANAN	21	2	4th PM - 1831 MN/WI	26-N	14-W
BUCKLEY	14	1	4th PM - 1831 MN/WI	28-N	13-W
" "	11	1	4th PM - 1831 MN/WI	29-N	12-W
BUDD	6	3	4th PM - 1831 MN/WI	30-N	13-W
BUELL	8	3	4th PM - 1831 MN/WI	30-N	11-W
BULL	12	1	4th PM - 1831 MN/WI	29-N	11-W
BULLOCK	23	2	4th PM - 1831 MN/WI	26-N	12-W
" "	6	2	4th PM - 1831 MN/WI	30-N	13-W
BULMAN	1	2	4th PM - 1831 MN/WI	31-N	14-W
BUNT	14	2	4th PM - 1831 MN/WI	28-N	13-W
BURCH	7	2	4th PM - 1831 MN/WI	30-N	12-W
" "	14	1	4th PM - 1831 MN/WI	28-N	13-W
BURDETT	20	8	4th PM - 1831 MN/WI	27-N	11-W
BURDICK	21	3	4th PM - 1831 MN/WI	26-N	14-W
BURGERT	14	1	4th PM - 1831 MN/WI	28-N	13-W
BURGESS	20	1	4th PM - 1831 MN/WI	27-N	11-W
BURN	14	1	4th PM - 1831 MN/WI	28-N	13-W
BURNES	16	4	4th PM - 1831 MN/WI	28-N	11-W
BURNETT	16	1	4th PM - 1831 MN/WI	28-N	11-W
BURNHAM	15	1	4th PM - 1831 MN/WI	28-N	12-W
BURNS	24	1	4th PM - 1831 MN/WI	26-N	11-W
" "	20	1	4th PM - 1831 MN/WI	27-N	11-W
BURNSON	8	2	4th PM - 1831 MN/WI	30-N	11-W
BURT	10	4	4th PM - 1831 MN/WI	29-N	13-W
" "	20	1	4th PM - 1831 MN/WI	27-N	11-W
" "	15	1	4th PM - 1831 MN/WI	28-N	12-W
BURTON	15	1	4th PM - 1831 MN/WI	28-N	12-W
BURY	20	2	4th PM - 1831 MN/WI	27-N	11-W
BUSE	18	1	4th PM - 1831 MN/WI	27-N	13-W
BUSH	10	2	4th PM - 1831 MN/WI	29-N	13-W
BUSHNELL	6	2	4th PM - 1831 MN/WI	30-N	13-W
BUSHY	9	2	4th PM - 1831 MN/WI	29-N	14-W
BUSSCHENDORF	16	2	4th PM - 1831 MN/WI	28-N	11-W
BUTTER	24	1	4th PM - 1831 MN/WI	26-N	11-W
BUTTERFIELD	2	4	4th PM - 1831 MN/WI	31-N	13-W
" "	6	3	4th PM - 1831 MN/WI	30-N	13-W
" "	11	1	4th PM - 1831 MN/WI	29-N	12-W
" "	10	1	4th PM - 1831 MN/WI	29-N	13-W
BUXTON	21	1	4th PM - 1831 MN/WI	26-N	14-W
CADY	20	2	4th PM - 1831 MN/WI	27-N	11-W

Surname	Map Group	Parcels of Land	Meridian/Township/Range		
CAIN	**24**	2	4th PM - 1831 MN/WI	26-N	11-W
CALHOUN	**6**	2	4th PM - 1831 MN/WI	30-N	13-W
CALHOUNE	**7**	1	4th PM - 1831 MN/WI	30-N	12-W
CALLAGHAN	**21**	1	4th PM - 1831 MN/WI	26-N	14-W
CAMERON	**15**	2	4th PM - 1831 MN/WI	28-N	12-W
CAMP	**24**	3	4th PM - 1831 MN/WI	26-N	11-W
CAMPBELL	**24**	3	4th PM - 1831 MN/WI	26-N	11-W
" "	**23**	2	4th PM - 1831 MN/WI	26-N	12-W
" "	**20**	2	4th PM - 1831 MN/WI	27-N	11-W
CANEY	**24**	2	4th PM - 1831 MN/WI	26-N	11-W
CANFIELD	**19**	3	4th PM - 1831 MN/WI	27-N	12-W
" "	**20**	1	4th PM - 1831 MN/WI	27-N	11-W
" "	**18**	1	4th PM - 1831 MN/WI	27-N	13-W
CANTRELL	**22**	2	4th PM - 1831 MN/WI	26-N	13-W
CAPEN	**21**	2	4th PM - 1831 MN/WI	26-N	14-W
CARD	**7**	4	4th PM - 1831 MN/WI	30-N	12-W
" "	**4**	1	4th PM - 1831 MN/WI	31-N	11-W
CAREY	**20**	2	4th PM - 1831 MN/WI	27-N	11-W
" "	**8**	1	4th PM - 1831 MN/WI	30-N	11-W
" "	**7**	1	4th PM - 1831 MN/WI	30-N	12-W
CARLETON	**16**	1	4th PM - 1831 MN/WI	28-N	11-W
CARLISLE	**21**	1	4th PM - 1831 MN/WI	26-N	14-W
CARMAN	**1**	1	4th PM - 1831 MN/WI	31-N	14-W
CARPENTER	**24**	2	4th PM - 1831 MN/WI	26-N	11-W
" "	**7**	2	4th PM - 1831 MN/WI	30-N	12-W
" "	**23**	1	4th PM - 1831 MN/WI	26-N	12-W
CARRINGTON	**20**	1	4th PM - 1831 MN/WI	27-N	11-W
CARSON	**22**	14	4th PM - 1831 MN/WI	26-N	13-W
" "	**21**	7	4th PM - 1831 MN/WI	26-N	14-W
" "	**17**	6	4th PM - 1831 MN/WI	27-N	14-W
CARTWRIGHT	**16**	1	4th PM - 1831 MN/WI	28-N	11-W
CARVER	**1**	1	4th PM - 1831 MN/WI	31-N	14-W
CASCADEN	**21**	1	4th PM - 1831 MN/WI	26-N	14-W
CASSADY	**19**	1	4th PM - 1831 MN/WI	27-N	12-W
CAVANAGH	**22**	1	4th PM - 1831 MN/WI	26-N	13-W
CAW	**10**	1	4th PM - 1831 MN/WI	29-N	13-W
CERNAK	**6**	2	4th PM - 1831 MN/WI	30-N	13-W
CERS	**4**	3	4th PM - 1831 MN/WI	31-N	11-W
CHAMBERLIN	**24**	4	4th PM - 1831 MN/WI	26-N	11-W
" "	**10**	2	4th PM - 1831 MN/WI	29-N	13-W
CHAMBERS	**20**	2	4th PM - 1831 MN/WI	27-N	11-W
" "	**15**	2	4th PM - 1831 MN/WI	28-N	12-W
CHAMPLIN	**7**	1	4th PM - 1831 MN/WI	30-N	12-W
CHANCE	**14**	1	4th PM - 1831 MN/WI	28-N	13-W
CHANDLER	**10**	2	4th PM - 1831 MN/WI	29-N	13-W
CHAPIN	**5**	2	4th PM - 1831 MN/WI	30-N	14-W
CHAPMAN	**16**	1	4th PM - 1831 MN/WI	28-N	11-W
CHASE	**1**	12	4th PM - 1831 MN/WI	31-N	14-W
" "	**24**	1	4th PM - 1831 MN/WI	26-N	11-W
" "	**23**	1	4th PM - 1831 MN/WI	26-N	12-W
" "	**20**	1	4th PM - 1831 MN/WI	27-N	11-W
" "	**12**	1	4th PM - 1831 MN/WI	29-N	11-W
CHENEY	**23**	4	4th PM - 1831 MN/WI	26-N	12-W
" "	**9**	1	4th PM - 1831 MN/WI	29-N	14-W
CHICKERING	**18**	1	4th PM - 1831 MN/WI	27-N	13-W
CHRISTENSEN	**16**	1	4th PM - 1831 MN/WI	28-N	11-W
CHRISTIANSEN	**7**	2	4th PM - 1831 MN/WI	30-N	12-W
CHRISTIANSON	**18**	1	4th PM - 1831 MN/WI	27-N	13-W
" "	**16**	1	4th PM - 1831 MN/WI	28-N	11-W
CHRISTIE	**5**	1	4th PM - 1831 MN/WI	30-N	14-W

Surname	Map Group	Parcels of Land	Meridian/Township/Range		
CHRISTOFFER	**16**	2	4th PM - 1831 MN/WI	28-N	11-W
CHRISTOFFERSEN	**16**	2	4th PM - 1831 MN/WI	28-N	11-W
CHRISTOFFERSON	**3**	2	4th PM - 1831 MN/WI	31-N	12-W
CHRISTOFORSEN	**9**	1	4th PM - 1831 MN/WI	29-N	14-W
CHRISTOPHERSEN	**16**	1	4th PM - 1831 MN/WI	28-N	11-W
CHRISTOPHERSON	**16**	3	4th PM - 1831 MN/WI	28-N	11-W
CHRISTOPHUSEN	**4**	3	4th PM - 1831 MN/WI	31-N	11-W
CHUBBUCK	**2**	2	4th PM - 1831 MN/WI	31-N	13-W
CHURCH	**14**	2	4th PM - 1831 MN/WI	28-N	13-W
" "	**11**	1	4th PM - 1831 MN/WI	29-N	12-W
" "	**10**	1	4th PM - 1831 MN/WI	29-N	13-W
CHURCHILL	**9**	1	4th PM - 1831 MN/WI	29-N	14-W
CLACK	**15**	2	4th PM - 1831 MN/WI	28-N	12-W
CLAIR	**24**	3	4th PM - 1831 MN/WI	26-N	11-W
CLAPP	**22**	1	4th PM - 1831 MN/WI	26-N	13-W
CLARK	**4**	6	4th PM - 1831 MN/WI	31-N	11-W
" "	**1**	6	4th PM - 1831 MN/WI	31-N	14-W
" "	**24**	5	4th PM - 1831 MN/WI	26-N	11-W
" "	**8**	5	4th PM - 1831 MN/WI	30-N	11-W
" "	**2**	3	4th PM - 1831 MN/WI	31-N	13-W
" "	**16**	2	4th PM - 1831 MN/WI	28-N	11-W
" "	**13**	2	4th PM - 1831 MN/WI	28-N	14-W
" "	**12**	2	4th PM - 1831 MN/WI	29-N	11-W
" "	**10**	2	4th PM - 1831 MN/WI	29-N	13-W
" "	**6**	2	4th PM - 1831 MN/WI	30-N	13-W
" "	**9**	1	4th PM - 1831 MN/WI	29-N	14-W
CLEAVE	**24**	1	4th PM - 1831 MN/WI	26-N	11-W
CLEAVELAND	**23**	4	4th PM - 1831 MN/WI	26-N	12-W
CLEMENS	**18**	2	4th PM - 1831 MN/WI	27-N	13-W
CLINE	**21**	1	4th PM - 1831 MN/WI	26-N	14-W
CLINTON	**23**	6	4th PM - 1831 MN/WI	26-N	12-W
CLOSS	**12**	1	4th PM - 1831 MN/WI	29-N	11-W
CO	**5**	29	4th PM - 1831 MN/WI	30-N	14-W
""	**1**	21	4th PM - 1831 MN/WI	31-N	14-W
COBB	**5**	1	4th PM - 1831 MN/WI	30-N	14-W
COBURN	**22**	1	4th PM - 1831 MN/WI	26-N	13-W
COCHRAN	**5**	1	4th PM - 1831 MN/WI	30-N	14-W
" "	**2**	1	4th PM - 1831 MN/WI	31-N	13-W
COCKBURN	**21**	1	4th PM - 1831 MN/WI	26-N	14-W
COEN	**9**	3	4th PM - 1831 MN/WI	29-N	14-W
COLBURN	**22**	8	4th PM - 1831 MN/WI	26-N	13-W
COLE	**12**	9	4th PM - 1831 MN/WI	29-N	11-W
" "	**23**	4	4th PM - 1831 MN/WI	26-N	12-W
" "	**9**	2	4th PM - 1831 MN/WI	29-N	14-W
" "	**18**	1	4th PM - 1831 MN/WI	27-N	13-W
" "	**15**	1	4th PM - 1831 MN/WI	28-N	12-W
COLLAR	**10**	2	4th PM - 1831 MN/WI	29-N	13-W
COLLINS	**15**	1	4th PM - 1831 MN/WI	28-N	12-W
COLOMY	**14**	2	4th PM - 1831 MN/WI	28-N	13-W
COMFORT	**10**	1	4th PM - 1831 MN/WI	29-N	13-W
COMPANY	**2**	2	4th PM - 1831 MN/WI	31-N	13-W
" "	**11**	1	4th PM - 1831 MN/WI	29-N	12-W
CONE	**24**	3	4th PM - 1831 MN/WI	26-N	11-W
" "	**11**	1	4th PM - 1831 MN/WI	29-N	12-W
CONNER	**1**	1	4th PM - 1831 MN/WI	31-N	14-W
COOK	**8**	3	4th PM - 1831 MN/WI	30-N	11-W
" "	**4**	3	4th PM - 1831 MN/WI	31-N	11-W
" "	**15**	1	4th PM - 1831 MN/WI	28-N	12-W
" "	**11**	1	4th PM - 1831 MN/WI	29-N	12-W
" "	**10**	1	4th PM - 1831 MN/WI	29-N	13-W

Surname	Map Group	Parcels of Land	Meridian/Township/Range		
COOK (Cont'd)	**9**	1	4th PM - 1831 MN/WI	29-N	14-W
COOMBS	**11**	2	4th PM - 1831 MN/WI	29-N	12-W
COON	**24**	3	4th PM - 1831 MN/WI	26-N	11-W
COONS	**24**	1	4th PM - 1831 MN/WI	26-N	11-W
COOPER	**8**	2	4th PM - 1831 MN/WI	30-N	11-W
" "	**2**	1	4th PM - 1831 MN/WI	31-N	13-W
COPELAND	**22**	5	4th PM - 1831 MN/WI	26-N	13-W
" "	**23**	2	4th PM - 1831 MN/WI	26-N	12-W
COREY	**8**	4	4th PM - 1831 MN/WI	30-N	11-W
CORMICAN	**18**	1	4th PM - 1831 MN/WI	27-N	13-W
CORNISH	**5**	2	4th PM - 1831 MN/WI	30-N	14-W
CORNWELL	**6**	2	4th PM - 1831 MN/WI	30-N	13-W
CORWITH	**24**	4	4th PM - 1831 MN/WI	26-N	11-W
" "	**23**	2	4th PM - 1831 MN/WI	26-N	12-W
" "	**20**	1	4th PM - 1831 MN/WI	27-N	11-W
COUN	**20**	2	4th PM - 1831 MN/WI	27-N	11-W
COUZENS	**23**	1	4th PM - 1831 MN/WI	26-N	12-W
COVELL	**22**	1	4th PM - 1831 MN/WI	26-N	13-W
CRAGIN	**23**	2	4th PM - 1831 MN/WI	26-N	12-W
" "	**10**	2	4th PM - 1831 MN/WI	29-N	13-W
CRAIG	**8**	1	4th PM - 1831 MN/WI	30-N	11-W
CRAMER	**23**	6	4th PM - 1831 MN/WI	26-N	12-W
" "	**24**	1	4th PM - 1831 MN/WI	26-N	11-W
CRANDAL	**21**	1	4th PM - 1831 MN/WI	26-N	14-W
CRANDALL	**24**	2	4th PM - 1831 MN/WI	26-N	11-W
" "	**23**	1	4th PM - 1831 MN/WI	26-N	12-W
CRANDELL	**9**	1	4th PM - 1831 MN/WI	29-N	14-W
CRANSTON	**20**	2	4th PM - 1831 MN/WI	27-N	11-W
CRATSENBERG	**23**	2	4th PM - 1831 MN/WI	26-N	12-W
CREASER	**23**	1	4th PM - 1831 MN/WI	26-N	12-W
" "	**18**	1	4th PM - 1831 MN/WI	27-N	13-W
CREGO	**20**	1	4th PM - 1831 MN/WI	27-N	11-W
CRIPPEN	**14**	2	4th PM - 1831 MN/WI	28-N	13-W
CRIST	**18**	1	4th PM - 1831 MN/WI	27-N	13-W
CROCKETT	**2**	1	4th PM - 1831 MN/WI	31-N	13-W
CROPSEY	**22**	1	4th PM - 1831 MN/WI	26-N	13-W
CROSBY	**10**	7	4th PM - 1831 MN/WI	29-N	13-W
" "	**7**	2	4th PM - 1831 MN/WI	30-N	12-W
" "	**22**	1	4th PM - 1831 MN/WI	26-N	13-W
CROSSMAN	**8**	2	4th PM - 1831 MN/WI	30-N	11-W
" "	**20**	1	4th PM - 1831 MN/WI	27-N	11-W
CRYE	**9**	3	4th PM - 1831 MN/WI	29-N	14-W
CULBERT	**5**	1	4th PM - 1831 MN/WI	30-N	14-W
CULBERTSON	**5**	1	4th PM - 1831 MN/WI	30-N	14-W
CULLMAN	**21**	1	4th PM - 1831 MN/WI	26-N	14-W
CULP	**5**	4	4th PM - 1831 MN/WI	30-N	14-W
CUMMINGS	**23**	3	4th PM - 1831 MN/WI	26-N	12-W
" "	**24**	2	4th PM - 1831 MN/WI	26-N	11-W
" "	**17**	1	4th PM - 1831 MN/WI	27-N	14-W
CUNNINGHAM	**22**	2	4th PM - 1831 MN/WI	26-N	13-W
" "	**9**	2	4th PM - 1831 MN/WI	29-N	14-W
CURRAN	**19**	1	4th PM - 1831 MN/WI	27-N	12-W
CURRY	**5**	3	4th PM - 1831 MN/WI	30-N	14-W
CURTIS	**22**	3	4th PM - 1831 MN/WI	26-N	13-W
" "	**20**	3	4th PM - 1831 MN/WI	27-N	11-W
" "	**24**	2	4th PM - 1831 MN/WI	26-N	11-W
CURTISS	**23**	2	4th PM - 1831 MN/WI	26-N	12-W
CUSSETAH-MICCO	**1**	3	4th PM - 1831 MN/WI	31-N	14-W
CUTCHEON	**12**	2	4th PM - 1831 MN/WI	29-N	11-W
CUTHING	**8**	1	4th PM - 1831 MN/WI	30-N	11-W

Surname	Map Group	Parcels of Land	Meridian/Township/Range		
CUTLER	**8**	2	4th PM - 1831 MN/WI	30-N	11-W
CUTTING	**8**	5	4th PM - 1831 MN/WI	30-N	11-W
DAHL	**7**	4	4th PM - 1831 MN/WI	30-N	12-W
" "	**12**	1	4th PM - 1831 MN/WI	29-N	11-W
" "	**8**	1	4th PM - 1831 MN/WI	30-N	11-W
DAHLBAK	**7**	1	4th PM - 1831 MN/WI	30-N	12-W
DAHLEN	**16**	1	4th PM - 1831 MN/WI	28-N	11-W
DALRIMPLE	**19**	1	4th PM - 1831 MN/WI	27-N	12-W
DALTON	**4**	2	4th PM - 1831 MN/WI	31-N	11-W
DAMMAN	**3**	1	4th PM - 1831 MN/WI	31-N	12-W
DANIELS	**10**	2	4th PM - 1831 MN/WI	29-N	13-W
" "	**13**	1	4th PM - 1831 MN/WI	28-N	14-W
DANIELSON	**8**	2	4th PM - 1831 MN/WI	30-N	11-W
DANTIN	**24**	1	4th PM - 1831 MN/WI	26-N	11-W
DARLING	**10**	2	4th PM - 1831 MN/WI	29-N	13-W
" "	**14**	1	4th PM - 1831 MN/WI	28-N	13-W
DARLINTON	**23**	4	4th PM - 1831 MN/WI	26-N	12-W
" "	**19**	1	4th PM - 1831 MN/WI	27-N	12-W
DARNELL	**12**	1	4th PM - 1831 MN/WI	29-N	11-W
DARRIN	**16**	1	4th PM - 1831 MN/WI	28-N	11-W
DARROW	**4**	4	4th PM - 1831 MN/WI	31-N	11-W
DAVIS	**11**	2	4th PM - 1831 MN/WI	29-N	12-W
" "	**10**	2	4th PM - 1831 MN/WI	29-N	13-W
" "	**7**	2	4th PM - 1831 MN/WI	30-N	12-W
" "	**5**	2	4th PM - 1831 MN/WI	30-N	14-W
" "	**20**	1	4th PM - 1831 MN/WI	27-N	11-W
" "	**19**	1	4th PM - 1831 MN/WI	27-N	12-W
" "	**18**	1	4th PM - 1831 MN/WI	27-N	13-W
" "	**14**	1	4th PM - 1831 MN/WI	28-N	13-W
DAVISON	**21**	1	4th PM - 1831 MN/WI	26-N	14-W
DAY	**6**	4	4th PM - 1831 MN/WI	30-N	13-W
" "	**2**	2	4th PM - 1831 MN/WI	31-N	13-W
" "	**24**	1	4th PM - 1831 MN/WI	26-N	11-W
DE LONG	**21**	2	4th PM - 1831 MN/WI	26-N	14-W
DE WOLF	**19**	1	4th PM - 1831 MN/WI	27-N	12-W
DEAN	**8**	3	4th PM - 1831 MN/WI	30-N	11-W
" "	**18**	2	4th PM - 1831 MN/WI	27-N	13-W
" "	**4**	1	4th PM - 1831 MN/WI	31-N	11-W
DEARBORN	**10**	2	4th PM - 1831 MN/WI	29-N	13-W
DEARY	**15**	1	4th PM - 1831 MN/WI	28-N	12-W
DECKER	**17**	2	4th PM - 1831 MN/WI	27-N	14-W
" "	**12**	1	4th PM - 1831 MN/WI	29-N	11-W
DEFREES	**22**	9	4th PM - 1831 MN/WI	26-N	13-W
" "	**21**	3	4th PM - 1831 MN/WI	26-N	14-W
DEGRAW	**20**	1	4th PM - 1831 MN/WI	27-N	11-W
DELANNAY	**9**	1	4th PM - 1831 MN/WI	29-N	14-W
DELONG	**21**	2	4th PM - 1831 MN/WI	26-N	14-W
" "	**22**	1	4th PM - 1831 MN/WI	26-N	13-W
DEMOE	**10**	3	4th PM - 1831 MN/WI	29-N	13-W
DENNIS	**8**	1	4th PM - 1831 MN/WI	30-N	11-W
DENSMORE	**16**	1	4th PM - 1831 MN/WI	28-N	11-W
DEPEW	**14**	1	4th PM - 1831 MN/WI	28-N	13-W
DEVLE	**8**	1	4th PM - 1831 MN/WI	30-N	11-W
DEXTER	**19**	9	4th PM - 1831 MN/WI	27-N	12-W
" "	**18**	3	4th PM - 1831 MN/WI	27-N	13-W
" "	**20**	1	4th PM - 1831 MN/WI	27-N	11-W
DICKEY	**18**	1	4th PM - 1831 MN/WI	27-N	13-W
DICKSON	**21**	3	4th PM - 1831 MN/WI	26-N	14-W
" "	**20**	1	4th PM - 1831 MN/WI	27-N	11-W
DIX	**20**	9	4th PM - 1831 MN/WI	27-N	11-W

Surname	Map Group	Parcels of Land	Meridian/Township/Range		
DIX (Cont'd)	**15**	4	4th PM - 1831 MN/WI	28-N	12-W
DOANE	**18**	1	4th PM - 1831 MN/WI	27-N	13-W
DODGE	**20**	5	4th PM - 1831 MN/WI	27-N	11-W
" "	**8**	5	4th PM - 1831 MN/WI	30-N	11-W
" "	**16**	2	4th PM - 1831 MN/WI	28-N	11-W
" "	**10**	1	4th PM - 1831 MN/WI	29-N	13-W
DOEKENDORFF	**22**	2	4th PM - 1831 MN/WI	26-N	13-W
DONALDSON	**4**	2	4th PM - 1831 MN/WI	31-N	11-W
DOOLITTLE	**18**	2	4th PM - 1831 MN/WI	27-N	13-W
DORR	**12**	3	4th PM - 1831 MN/WI	29-N	11-W
DORRY	**20**	3	4th PM - 1831 MN/WI	27-N	11-W
DOWD	**23**	4	4th PM - 1831 MN/WI	26-N	12-W
DOWNER	**24**	7	4th PM - 1831 MN/WI	26-N	11-W
" "	**11**	1	4th PM - 1831 MN/WI	29-N	12-W
DOWNING	**7**	2	4th PM - 1831 MN/WI	30-N	12-W
DOWNS	**22**	10	4th PM - 1831 MN/WI	26-N	13-W
" "	**21**	6	4th PM - 1831 MN/WI	26-N	14-W
" "	**17**	2	4th PM - 1831 MN/WI	27-N	14-W
" "	**18**	1	4th PM - 1831 MN/WI	27-N	13-W
DOXTER	**24**	2	4th PM - 1831 MN/WI	26-N	11-W
DOYLE	**2**	2	4th PM - 1831 MN/WI	31-N	13-W
DRAKE	**22**	12	4th PM - 1831 MN/WI	26-N	13-W
" "	**6**	2	4th PM - 1831 MN/WI	30-N	13-W
" "	**18**	1	4th PM - 1831 MN/WI	27-N	13-W
DREW	**12**	1	4th PM - 1831 MN/WI	29-N	11-W
DREWS	**18**	1	4th PM - 1831 MN/WI	27-N	13-W
DREXLER	**14**	1	4th PM - 1831 MN/WI	28-N	13-W
DRINKER	**5**	1	4th PM - 1831 MN/WI	30-N	14-W
DRINKWINE	**24**	2	4th PM - 1831 MN/WI	26-N	11-W
DRURY	**20**	3	4th PM - 1831 MN/WI	27-N	11-W
DUELL	**7**	1	4th PM - 1831 MN/WI	30-N	12-W
DUFFEY	**13**	2	4th PM - 1831 MN/WI	28-N	14-W
DUNCAN	**7**	3	4th PM - 1831 MN/WI	30-N	12-W
DUNKLEE	**12**	2	4th PM - 1831 MN/WI	29-N	11-W
DUNN	**23**	1	4th PM - 1831 MN/WI	26-N	12-W
DUNNIGAN	**9**	1	4th PM - 1831 MN/WI	29-N	14-W
DYER	**12**	4	4th PM - 1831 MN/WI	29-N	11-W
" "	**15**	2	4th PM - 1831 MN/WI	28-N	12-W
DYKINS	**18**	1	4th PM - 1831 MN/WI	27-N	13-W
EARGOOD	**22**	1	4th PM - 1831 MN/WI	26-N	13-W
" "	**13**	1	4th PM - 1831 MN/WI	28-N	14-W
EASTWOOD	**10**	1	4th PM - 1831 MN/WI	29-N	13-W
" "	**6**	1	4th PM - 1831 MN/WI	30-N	13-W
EATON	**22**	12	4th PM - 1831 MN/WI	26-N	13-W
" "	**21**	6	4th PM - 1831 MN/WI	26-N	14-W
" "	**17**	6	4th PM - 1831 MN/WI	27-N	14-W
" "	**24**	5	4th PM - 1831 MN/WI	26-N	11-W
" "	**18**	2	4th PM - 1831 MN/WI	27-N	13-W
" "	**12**	2	4th PM - 1831 MN/WI	29-N	11-W
" "	**20**	1	4th PM - 1831 MN/WI	27-N	11-W
" "	**14**	1	4th PM - 1831 MN/WI	28-N	13-W
" "	**11**	1	4th PM - 1831 MN/WI	29-N	12-W
EAVANS	**8**	2	4th PM - 1831 MN/WI	30-N	11-W
EDMONDS	**7**	2	4th PM - 1831 MN/WI	30-N	12-W
EDWARDS	**24**	31	4th PM - 1831 MN/WI	26-N	11-W
" "	**23**	16	4th PM - 1831 MN/WI	26-N	12-W
EGELAND	**4**	3	4th PM - 1831 MN/WI	31-N	11-W
EIDAHL	**1**	2	4th PM - 1831 MN/WI	31-N	14-W
EIDE	**19**	2	4th PM - 1831 MN/WI	27-N	12-W
EIKA	**4**	3	4th PM - 1831 MN/WI	31-N	11-W

Surname	Map Group	Parcels of Land	Meridian/Township/Range		
ELDERD	**15**	2	4th PM - 1831 MN/WI	28-N	12-W
ELDERT	**23**	2	4th PM - 1831 MN/WI	26-N	12-W
ELEVESON	**3**	2	4th PM - 1831 MN/WI	31-N	12-W
ELIASEN	**3**	1	4th PM - 1831 MN/WI	31-N	12-W
ELLEFSEN	**7**	2	4th PM - 1831 MN/WI	30-N	12-W
ELLEFSON	**3**	1	4th PM - 1831 MN/WI	31-N	12-W
ELLIOTT	**5**	29	4th PM - 1831 MN/WI	30-N	14-W
" "	**1**	21	4th PM - 1831 MN/WI	31-N	14-W
ELLIS	**24**	2	4th PM - 1831 MN/WI	26-N	11-W
" "	**10**	2	4th PM - 1831 MN/WI	29-N	13-W
ELTING	**24**	6	4th PM - 1831 MN/WI	26-N	11-W
EMENS	**23**	1	4th PM - 1831 MN/WI	26-N	12-W
" "	**19**	1	4th PM - 1831 MN/WI	27-N	12-W
EMERY	**2**	1	4th PM - 1831 MN/WI	31-N	13-W
ENGEBRETSON	**16**	1	4th PM - 1831 MN/WI	28-N	11-W
ENNERSEN	**19**	2	4th PM - 1831 MN/WI	27-N	12-W
ERICKSEN	**19**	2	4th PM - 1831 MN/WI	27-N	12-W
ERICKSON	**19**	1	4th PM - 1831 MN/WI	27-N	12-W
ERIKSON	**18**	1	4th PM - 1831 MN/WI	27-N	13-W
ESTIS	**24**	1	4th PM - 1831 MN/WI	26-N	11-W
ETHEREDGE	**16**	1	4th PM - 1831 MN/WI	28-N	11-W
EVANS	**23**	2	4th PM - 1831 MN/WI	26-N	12-W
" "	**7**	2	4th PM - 1831 MN/WI	30-N	12-W
" "	**18**	1	4th PM - 1831 MN/WI	27-N	13-W
" "	**16**	1	4th PM - 1831 MN/WI	28-N	11-W
EVELAND	**18**	1	4th PM - 1831 MN/WI	27-N	13-W
EVENS	**16**	2	4th PM - 1831 MN/WI	28-N	11-W
EVENSON	**14**	1	4th PM - 1831 MN/WI	28-N	13-W
EVERETT	**5**	1	4th PM - 1831 MN/WI	30-N	14-W
EVERNAN	**14**	4	4th PM - 1831 MN/WI	28-N	13-W
EWER	**24**	2	4th PM - 1831 MN/WI	26-N	11-W
" "	**23**	1	4th PM - 1831 MN/WI	26-N	12-W
EWERS	**23**	1	4th PM - 1831 MN/WI	26-N	12-W
EYTCHESON	**15**	5	4th PM - 1831 MN/WI	28-N	12-W
" "	**11**	4	4th PM - 1831 MN/WI	29-N	12-W
" "	**6**	2	4th PM - 1831 MN/WI	30-N	13-W
FAIRBANKS	**8**	1	4th PM - 1831 MN/WI	30-N	11-W
FAIRCHILD	**18**	2	4th PM - 1831 MN/WI	27-N	13-W
FALES	**23**	4	4th PM - 1831 MN/WI	26-N	12-W
" "	**24**	2	4th PM - 1831 MN/WI	26-N	11-W
FALKNER	**24**	2	4th PM - 1831 MN/WI	26-N	11-W
FALLIS	**1**	1	4th PM - 1831 MN/WI	31-N	14-W
FALTENBERY	**22**	1	4th PM - 1831 MN/WI	26-N	13-W
FARNHAM	**20**	2	4th PM - 1831 MN/WI	27-N	11-W
" "	**13**	1	4th PM - 1831 MN/WI	28-N	14-W
FARRINGTON	**5**	2	4th PM - 1831 MN/WI	30-N	14-W
" "	**1**	1	4th PM - 1831 MN/WI	31-N	14-W
FAUCHTER	**13**	1	4th PM - 1831 MN/WI	28-N	14-W
FAYERWEATHER	**22**	1	4th PM - 1831 MN/WI	26-N	13-W
FEAZEL	**21**	2	4th PM - 1831 MN/WI	26-N	14-W
FEEKS	**23**	1	4th PM - 1831 MN/WI	26-N	12-W
FEENEY	**6**	1	4th PM - 1831 MN/WI	30-N	13-W
FELLOWS	**12**	2	4th PM - 1831 MN/WI	29-N	11-W
FERGUSON	**11**	2	4th PM - 1831 MN/WI	29-N	12-W
FHUHRER	**22**	1	4th PM - 1831 MN/WI	26-N	13-W
FIELDS	**22**	1	4th PM - 1831 MN/WI	26-N	13-W
FIELDSTAD	**12**	1	4th PM - 1831 MN/WI	29-N	11-W
FIGENSKAN	**8**	1	4th PM - 1831 MN/WI	30-N	11-W
FILLEY	**23**	2	4th PM - 1831 MN/WI	26-N	12-W
FINCH	**24**	1	4th PM - 1831 MN/WI	26-N	11-W

Surname	Map Group	Parcels of Land	Meridian/Township/Range		
FINDLEY	**15**	3	4th PM - 1831 MN/WI	28-N	12-W
FINEGAN	**6**	3	4th PM - 1831 MN/WI	30-N	13-W
FINEOUT	**11**	1	4th PM - 1831 MN/WI	29-N	12-W
" "	**10**	1	4th PM - 1831 MN/WI	29-N	13-W
FINLEY	**3**	1	4th PM - 1831 MN/WI	31-N	12-W
FISCHER	**18**	2	4th PM - 1831 MN/WI	27-N	13-W
FISK	**22**	6	4th PM - 1831 MN/WI	26-N	13-W
FITCH	**22**	5	4th PM - 1831 MN/WI	26-N	13-W
" "	**21**	2	4th PM - 1831 MN/WI	26-N	14-W
FITZGERALD	**18**	2	4th PM - 1831 MN/WI	27-N	13-W
FIXICO	**5**	1	4th PM - 1831 MN/WI	30-N	14-W
FJELDSTED	**12**	3	4th PM - 1831 MN/WI	29-N	11-W
FLAGLER	**23**	4	4th PM - 1831 MN/WI	26-N	12-W
FLANDERS	**19**	2	4th PM - 1831 MN/WI	27-N	12-W
FLEMING	**23**	2	4th PM - 1831 MN/WI	26-N	12-W
FLETCHER	**21**	4	4th PM - 1831 MN/WI	26-N	14-W
FLINN	**3**	2	4th PM - 1831 MN/WI	31-N	12-W
FLINT	**6**	2	4th PM - 1831 MN/WI	30-N	13-W
" "	**24**	1	4th PM - 1831 MN/WI	26-N	11-W
FLOOD	**19**	1	4th PM - 1831 MN/WI	27-N	12-W
FLUENT	**4**	1	4th PM - 1831 MN/WI	31-N	11-W
FLUG	**7**	3	4th PM - 1831 MN/WI	30-N	12-W
" "	**3**	1	4th PM - 1831 MN/WI	31-N	12-W
FOGG	**6**	3	4th PM - 1831 MN/WI	30-N	13-W
FOGLE	**8**	2	4th PM - 1831 MN/WI	30-N	11-W
FOLJAMBE	**10**	1	4th PM - 1831 MN/WI	29-N	13-W
FOOTE	**16**	1	4th PM - 1831 MN/WI	28-N	11-W
FORA	**21**	1	4th PM - 1831 MN/WI	26-N	14-W
FORD	**24**	1	4th PM - 1831 MN/WI	26-N	11-W
" "	**14**	1	4th PM - 1831 MN/WI	28-N	13-W
FORDAHL	**3**	2	4th PM - 1831 MN/WI	31-N	12-W
FORGERSON	**23**	1	4th PM - 1831 MN/WI	26-N	12-W
FORSLID	**12**	3	4th PM - 1831 MN/WI	29-N	11-W
FOSLID	**12**	3	4th PM - 1831 MN/WI	29-N	11-W
FOSTER	**13**	2	4th PM - 1831 MN/WI	28-N	14-W
FOWLER	**15**	2	4th PM - 1831 MN/WI	28-N	12-W
" "	**20**	1	4th PM - 1831 MN/WI	27-N	11-W
" "	**19**	1	4th PM - 1831 MN/WI	27-N	12-W
FOX	**8**	3	4th PM - 1831 MN/WI	30-N	11-W
" "	**23**	2	4th PM - 1831 MN/WI	26-N	12-W
FRAMMI	**7**	2	4th PM - 1831 MN/WI	30-N	12-W
FRAMY	**8**	1	4th PM - 1831 MN/WI	30-N	11-W
FRANK	**22**	1	4th PM - 1831 MN/WI	26-N	13-W
FREDRICKSEN	**4**	1	4th PM - 1831 MN/WI	31-N	11-W
FREESTONE	**7**	7	4th PM - 1831 MN/WI	30-N	12-W
" "	**13**	1	4th PM - 1831 MN/WI	28-N	14-W
FRENCH	**15**	21	4th PM - 1831 MN/WI	28-N	12-W
" "	**18**	20	4th PM - 1831 MN/WI	27-N	13-W
" "	**14**	16	4th PM - 1831 MN/WI	28-N	13-W
" "	**19**	4	4th PM - 1831 MN/WI	27-N	12-W
" "	**22**	2	4th PM - 1831 MN/WI	26-N	13-W
" "	**1**	2	4th PM - 1831 MN/WI	31-N	14-W
" "	**23**	1	4th PM - 1831 MN/WI	26-N	12-W
" "	**21**	1	4th PM - 1831 MN/WI	26-N	14-W
" "	**11**	1	4th PM - 1831 MN/WI	29-N	12-W
" "	**10**	1	4th PM - 1831 MN/WI	29-N	13-W
FRION	**20**	1	4th PM - 1831 MN/WI	27-N	11-W
FRYE	**10**	1	4th PM - 1831 MN/WI	29-N	13-W
" "	**9**	1	4th PM - 1831 MN/WI	29-N	14-W
FUHLROTT	**22**	2	4th PM - 1831 MN/WI	26-N	13-W

Surname	Map Group	Parcels of Land	Meridian/Township/Range		
FULLER	**19**	5	4th PM - 1831 MN/WI	27-N	12-W
" "	**20**	1	4th PM - 1831 MN/WI	27-N	11-W
" "	**17**	1	4th PM - 1831 MN/WI	27-N	14-W
FUNK	**15**	3	4th PM - 1831 MN/WI	28-N	12-W
FURBUR	**10**	3	4th PM - 1831 MN/WI	29-N	13-W
GAGE	**12**	2	4th PM - 1831 MN/WI	29-N	11-W
GALE	**8**	1	4th PM - 1831 MN/WI	30-N	11-W
GALLAGER	**19**	1	4th PM - 1831 MN/WI	27-N	12-W
GALLATI	**2**	1	4th PM - 1831 MN/WI	31-N	13-W
GALLAWAY	**18**	1	4th PM - 1831 MN/WI	27-N	13-W
GANE	**22**	2	4th PM - 1831 MN/WI	26-N	13-W
GARDNER	**22**	2	4th PM - 1831 MN/WI	26-N	13-W
" "	**10**	1	4th PM - 1831 MN/WI	29-N	13-W
" "	**3**	1	4th PM - 1831 MN/WI	31-N	12-W
GAREHART	**14**	5	4th PM - 1831 MN/WI	28-N	13-W
GARRETT	**18**	1	4th PM - 1831 MN/WI	27-N	13-W
GAUVIN	**20**	2	4th PM - 1831 MN/WI	27-N	11-W
" "	**19**	2	4th PM - 1831 MN/WI	27-N	12-W
GEAR	**9**	1	4th PM - 1831 MN/WI	29-N	14-W
GEBHART	**14**	3	4th PM - 1831 MN/WI	28-N	13-W
GENTRY	**22**	2	4th PM - 1831 MN/WI	26-N	13-W
GEORGE	**2**	2	4th PM - 1831 MN/WI	31-N	13-W
" "	**23**	1	4th PM - 1831 MN/WI	26-N	12-W
GERMAN	**14**	2	4th PM - 1831 MN/WI	28-N	13-W
GEROY	**7**	3	4th PM - 1831 MN/WI	30-N	12-W
GIBBS	**24**	7	4th PM - 1831 MN/WI	26-N	11-W
GIBERSON	**18**	2	4th PM - 1831 MN/WI	27-N	13-W
GIBSON	**24**	6	4th PM - 1831 MN/WI	26-N	11-W
" "	**20**	6	4th PM - 1831 MN/WI	27-N	11-W
" "	**22**	3	4th PM - 1831 MN/WI	26-N	13-W
" "	**13**	2	4th PM - 1831 MN/WI	28-N	14-W
" "	**19**	1	4th PM - 1831 MN/WI	27-N	12-W
" "	**5**	1	4th PM - 1831 MN/WI	30-N	14-W
GIFFORD	**19**	1	4th PM - 1831 MN/WI	27-N	12-W
GILBERT	**14**	5	4th PM - 1831 MN/WI	28-N	13-W
" "	**18**	3	4th PM - 1831 MN/WI	27-N	13-W
" "	**13**	3	4th PM - 1831 MN/WI	28-N	14-W
GILBERTSEN	**12**	1	4th PM - 1831 MN/WI	29-N	11-W
GILBRANSON	**16**	1	4th PM - 1831 MN/WI	28-N	11-W
GILLESPIE	**1**	1	4th PM - 1831 MN/WI	31-N	14-W
GILLIS	**7**	1	4th PM - 1831 MN/WI	30-N	12-W
GILMAN	**4**	1	4th PM - 1831 MN/WI	31-N	11-W
GLEASON	**20**	1	4th PM - 1831 MN/WI	27-N	11-W
GLENN	**22**	2	4th PM - 1831 MN/WI	26-N	13-W
GLENNY	**1**	3	4th PM - 1831 MN/WI	31-N	14-W
GLUTH	**6**	3	4th PM - 1831 MN/WI	30-N	13-W
GOBEL	**22**	3	4th PM - 1831 MN/WI	26-N	13-W
GODELL	**10**	2	4th PM - 1831 MN/WI	29-N	13-W
GODFREY	**23**	3	4th PM - 1831 MN/WI	26-N	12-W
GOERCKE	**19**	2	4th PM - 1831 MN/WI	27-N	12-W
" "	**23**	1	4th PM - 1831 MN/WI	26-N	12-W
GOETZINGER	**7**	1	4th PM - 1831 MN/WI	30-N	12-W
GOFF	**5**	5	4th PM - 1831 MN/WI	30-N	14-W
GOLDSMITH	**8**	2	4th PM - 1831 MN/WI	30-N	11-W
GOODELL	**6**	4	4th PM - 1831 MN/WI	30-N	13-W
" "	**7**	2	4th PM - 1831 MN/WI	30-N	12-W
" "	**10**	1	4th PM - 1831 MN/WI	29-N	13-W
GOODRICH	**24**	4	4th PM - 1831 MN/WI	26-N	11-W
" "	**6**	3	4th PM - 1831 MN/WI	30-N	13-W
GOODSON	**4**	1	4th PM - 1831 MN/WI	31-N	11-W

Surname	Map Group	Parcels of Land	Meridian/Township/Range		
GORDON	**21**	1	4th PM - 1831 MN/WI	26-N	14-W
GOSS	**22**	13	4th PM - 1831 MN/WI	26-N	13-W
" "	**6**	3	4th PM - 1831 MN/WI	30-N	13-W
" "	**5**	2	4th PM - 1831 MN/WI	30-N	14-W
" "	**23**	1	4th PM - 1831 MN/WI	26-N	12-W
GRABHEIR	**19**	1	4th PM - 1831 MN/WI	27-N	12-W
" "	**15**	1	4th PM - 1831 MN/WI	28-N	12-W
GRANGER	**9**	6	4th PM - 1831 MN/WI	29-N	14-W
" "	**8**	2	4th PM - 1831 MN/WI	30-N	11-W
" "	**22**	1	4th PM - 1831 MN/WI	26-N	13-W
" "	**10**	1	4th PM - 1831 MN/WI	29-N	13-W
GRANT	**16**	3	4th PM - 1831 MN/WI	28-N	11-W
GRANUM	**4**	4	4th PM - 1831 MN/WI	31-N	11-W
GRAY	**22**	4	4th PM - 1831 MN/WI	26-N	13-W
" "	**14**	4	4th PM - 1831 MN/WI	28-N	13-W
" "	**23**	2	4th PM - 1831 MN/WI	26-N	12-W
" "	**6**	2	4th PM - 1831 MN/WI	30-N	13-W
" "	**24**	1	4th PM - 1831 MN/WI	26-N	11-W
" "	**20**	1	4th PM - 1831 MN/WI	27-N	11-W
" "	**19**	1	4th PM - 1831 MN/WI	27-N	12-W
" "	**15**	1	4th PM - 1831 MN/WI	28-N	12-W
GREEN	**23**	2	4th PM - 1831 MN/WI	26-N	12-W
" "	**10**	2	4th PM - 1831 MN/WI	29-N	13-W
" "	**22**	1	4th PM - 1831 MN/WI	26-N	13-W
" "	**21**	1	4th PM - 1831 MN/WI	26-N	14-W
" "	**18**	1	4th PM - 1831 MN/WI	27-N	13-W
GREENWEIG	**2**	2	4th PM - 1831 MN/WI	31-N	13-W
GREGERSON	**3**	3	4th PM - 1831 MN/WI	31-N	12-W
" "	**7**	1	4th PM - 1831 MN/WI	30-N	12-W
GREWT	**10**	1	4th PM - 1831 MN/WI	29-N	13-W
GRIFFIN	**20**	3	4th PM - 1831 MN/WI	27-N	11-W
GRINNELL	**1**	1	4th PM - 1831 MN/WI	31-N	14-W
GRINSET	**8**	2	4th PM - 1831 MN/WI	30-N	11-W
GRIPPEN	**22**	3	4th PM - 1831 MN/WI	26-N	13-W
GRIZZELL	**2**	1	4th PM - 1831 MN/WI	31-N	13-W
GROTHE	**6**	1	4th PM - 1831 MN/WI	30-N	13-W
GROVER	**15**	3	4th PM - 1831 MN/WI	28-N	12-W
GRUMPRY	**21**	1	4th PM - 1831 MN/WI	26-N	14-W
GRUTT	**6**	1	4th PM - 1831 MN/WI	30-N	13-W
GULAKSON	**12**	2	4th PM - 1831 MN/WI	29-N	11-W
GUNDERSON	**12**	1	4th PM - 1831 MN/WI	29-N	11-W
" "	**4**	1	4th PM - 1831 MN/WI	31-N	11-W
" "	**3**	1	4th PM - 1831 MN/WI	31-N	12-W
GUNDT	**4**	1	4th PM - 1831 MN/WI	31-N	11-W
GUNNUFSEN	**12**	2	4th PM - 1831 MN/WI	29-N	11-W
HAALTEN	**2**	3	4th PM - 1831 MN/WI	31-N	13-W
HADLEY	**1**	1	4th PM - 1831 MN/WI	31-N	14-W
HAERLE	**19**	4	4th PM - 1831 MN/WI	27-N	12-W
HAGAR	**6**	3	4th PM - 1831 MN/WI	30-N	13-W
HAGEN	**3**	3	4th PM - 1831 MN/WI	31-N	12-W
" "	**19**	1	4th PM - 1831 MN/WI	27-N	12-W
HAIGHT	**20**	4	4th PM - 1831 MN/WI	27-N	11-W
HALE	**7**	1	4th PM - 1831 MN/WI	30-N	12-W
HALFERTY	**15**	1	4th PM - 1831 MN/WI	28-N	12-W
HALFORTY	**15**	1	4th PM - 1831 MN/WI	28-N	12-W
HALL	**7**	2	4th PM - 1831 MN/WI	30-N	12-W
" "	**6**	2	4th PM - 1831 MN/WI	30-N	13-W
" "	**14**	1	4th PM - 1831 MN/WI	28-N	13-W
" "	**13**	1	4th PM - 1831 MN/WI	28-N	14-W
" "	**5**	1	4th PM - 1831 MN/WI	30-N	14-W

Surname	Map Group	Parcels of Land	Meridian/Township/Range		
HALSTEAD	**23**	3	4th PM - 1831 MN/WI	26-N	12-W
HALSTED	**8**	2	4th PM - 1831 MN/WI	30-N	11-W
HALVERSEN	**12**	2	4th PM - 1831 MN/WI	29-N	11-W
HALVORSEN	**16**	3	4th PM - 1831 MN/WI	28-N	11-W
" "	**14**	1	4th PM - 1831 MN/WI	28-N	13-W
HALVORSON	**2**	2	4th PM - 1831 MN/WI	31-N	13-W
" "	**11**	1	4th PM - 1831 MN/WI	29-N	12-W
HAMILTON	**16**	2	4th PM - 1831 MN/WI	28-N	11-W
HAMME	**4**	1	4th PM - 1831 MN/WI	31-N	11-W
HAMMER	**4**	1	4th PM - 1831 MN/WI	31-N	11-W
HAMMOND	**19**	1	4th PM - 1831 MN/WI	27-N	12-W
HANCHETT	**23**	1	4th PM - 1831 MN/WI	26-N	12-W
HANCOCK	**15**	2	4th PM - 1831 MN/WI	28-N	12-W
HANKE	**11**	1	4th PM - 1831 MN/WI	29-N	12-W
HANNEMEYER	**22**	1	4th PM - 1831 MN/WI	26-N	13-W
HANSEN	**4**	6	4th PM - 1831 MN/WI	31-N	11-W
" "	**19**	2	4th PM - 1831 MN/WI	27-N	12-W
" "	**21**	1	4th PM - 1831 MN/WI	26-N	14-W
" "	**12**	1	4th PM - 1831 MN/WI	29-N	11-W
HANSON	**16**	4	4th PM - 1831 MN/WI	28-N	11-W
" "	**12**	4	4th PM - 1831 MN/WI	29-N	11-W
" "	**4**	4	4th PM - 1831 MN/WI	31-N	11-W
" "	**2**	3	4th PM - 1831 MN/WI	31-N	13-W
" "	**19**	1	4th PM - 1831 MN/WI	27-N	12-W
HARBIT	**14**	1	4th PM - 1831 MN/WI	28-N	13-W
" "	**6**	1	4th PM - 1831 MN/WI	30-N	13-W
HARDAGE	**1**	3	4th PM - 1831 MN/WI	31-N	14-W
HARDING	**2**	1	4th PM - 1831 MN/WI	31-N	13-W
HARKNESS	**15**	1	4th PM - 1831 MN/WI	28-N	12-W
HARLE	**19**	5	4th PM - 1831 MN/WI	27-N	12-W
HARLEY	**19**	6	4th PM - 1831 MN/WI	27-N	12-W
HARLY	**20**	1	4th PM - 1831 MN/WI	27-N	11-W
HARM	**19**	2	4th PM - 1831 MN/WI	27-N	12-W
HARMAN	**10**	1	4th PM - 1831 MN/WI	29-N	13-W
" "	**1**	1	4th PM - 1831 MN/WI	31-N	14-W
HARMEN	**2**	1	4th PM - 1831 MN/WI	31-N	13-W
HARMON	**24**	2	4th PM - 1831 MN/WI	26-N	11-W
" "	**2**	1	4th PM - 1831 MN/WI	31-N	13-W
HARMS	**14**	2	4th PM - 1831 MN/WI	28-N	13-W
HARNISH	**19**	1	4th PM - 1831 MN/WI	27-N	12-W
HARPER	**18**	1	4th PM - 1831 MN/WI	27-N	13-W
HARRIGAN	**22**	3	4th PM - 1831 MN/WI	26-N	13-W
HARRINGTON	**15**	11	4th PM - 1831 MN/WI	28-N	12-W
" "	**10**	5	4th PM - 1831 MN/WI	29-N	13-W
" "	**11**	4	4th PM - 1831 MN/WI	29-N	12-W
" "	**20**	3	4th PM - 1831 MN/WI	27-N	11-W
" "	**9**	1	4th PM - 1831 MN/WI	29-N	14-W
HARRIS	**15**	1	4th PM - 1831 MN/WI	28-N	12-W
" "	**13**	1	4th PM - 1831 MN/WI	28-N	14-W
HARRISON	**19**	4	4th PM - 1831 MN/WI	27-N	12-W
" "	**11**	1	4th PM - 1831 MN/WI	29-N	12-W
" "	**2**	1	4th PM - 1831 MN/WI	31-N	13-W
HARROLD	**14**	2	4th PM - 1831 MN/WI	28-N	13-W
" "	**9**	2	4th PM - 1831 MN/WI	29-N	14-W
HARSH	**12**	2	4th PM - 1831 MN/WI	29-N	11-W
HARSTAD	**4**	2	4th PM - 1831 MN/WI	31-N	11-W
HARTKOPP	**22**	2	4th PM - 1831 MN/WI	26-N	13-W
HARTMAN	**15**	1	4th PM - 1831 MN/WI	28-N	12-W
HARVEY	**5**	1	4th PM - 1831 MN/WI	30-N	14-W
HASHMAN	**20**	3	4th PM - 1831 MN/WI	27-N	11-W

Surname	Map Group	Parcels of Land	Meridian/Township/Range		
HAUGE	**8**	3	4th PM - 1831 MN/WI	30-N	11-W
HAUGEN	**8**	1	4th PM - 1831 MN/WI	30-N	11-W
HAVENSTICK	**5**	2	4th PM - 1831 MN/WI	30-N	14-W
HAVERLAND	**14**	3	4th PM - 1831 MN/WI	28-N	13-W
HAVILAND	**14**	1	4th PM - 1831 MN/WI	28-N	13-W
HAWES	**24**	5	4th PM - 1831 MN/WI	26-N	11-W
HAWS	**24**	2	4th PM - 1831 MN/WI	26-N	11-W
HAY	**15**	1	4th PM - 1831 MN/WI	28-N	12-W
HAYNES	**11**	2	4th PM - 1831 MN/WI	29-N	12-W
HAYS	**9**	1	4th PM - 1831 MN/WI	29-N	14-W
HAYWARD	**24**	3	4th PM - 1831 MN/WI	26-N	11-W
HEASLY	**15**	2	4th PM - 1831 MN/WI	28-N	12-W
HEBERLIG	**19**	1	4th PM - 1831 MN/WI	27-N	12-W
HELGERSON	**8**	1	4th PM - 1831 MN/WI	30-N	11-W
HELGESON	**3**	5	4th PM - 1831 MN/WI	31-N	12-W
" "	**1**	1	4th PM - 1831 MN/WI	31-N	14-W
HENDRIKSON	**3**	2	4th PM - 1831 MN/WI	31-N	12-W
HENEGAN	**18**	2	4th PM - 1831 MN/WI	27-N	13-W
HENRIKSON	**19**	3	4th PM - 1831 MN/WI	27-N	12-W
HENRY	**4**	1	4th PM - 1831 MN/WI	31-N	11-W
HERMANN	**22**	3	4th PM - 1831 MN/WI	26-N	13-W
HERRIMAN	**5**	5	4th PM - 1831 MN/WI	30-N	14-W
HERRON	**24**	3	4th PM - 1831 MN/WI	26-N	11-W
" "	**18**	1	4th PM - 1831 MN/WI	27-N	13-W
HILAND	**4**	1	4th PM - 1831 MN/WI	31-N	11-W
HILL	**23**	11	4th PM - 1831 MN/WI	26-N	12-W
" "	**12**	4	4th PM - 1831 MN/WI	29-N	11-W
" "	**11**	1	4th PM - 1831 MN/WI	29-N	12-W
" "	**10**	1	4th PM - 1831 MN/WI	29-N	13-W
HINMAN	**5**	1	4th PM - 1831 MN/WI	30-N	14-W
HINTGEN	**16**	3	4th PM - 1831 MN/WI	28-N	11-W
HINTZ	**19**	1	4th PM - 1831 MN/WI	27-N	12-W
HJERSSO	**4**	3	4th PM - 1831 MN/WI	31-N	11-W
HOADLEY	**23**	1	4th PM - 1831 MN/WI	26-N	12-W
HOAG	**6**	1	4th PM - 1831 MN/WI	30-N	13-W
HOBART	**24**	1	4th PM - 1831 MN/WI	26-N	11-W
HOBBS	**22**	2	4th PM - 1831 MN/WI	26-N	13-W
" "	**21**	1	4th PM - 1831 MN/WI	26-N	14-W
HODGDON	**23**	15	4th PM - 1831 MN/WI	26-N	12-W
" "	**21**	15	4th PM - 1831 MN/WI	26-N	14-W
HODGE	**6**	1	4th PM - 1831 MN/WI	30-N	13-W
HODGES	**2**	2	4th PM - 1831 MN/WI	31-N	13-W
" "	**24**	1	4th PM - 1831 MN/WI	26-N	11-W
HOFF	**2**	1	4th PM - 1831 MN/WI	31-N	13-W
HOFFMAN	**2**	3	4th PM - 1831 MN/WI	31-N	13-W
HOFFMANN	**3**	1	4th PM - 1831 MN/WI	31-N	12-W
HOGUELAND	**19**	2	4th PM - 1831 MN/WI	27-N	12-W
HOILAND	**4**	1	4th PM - 1831 MN/WI	31-N	11-W
HOLBROOK	**22**	7	4th PM - 1831 MN/WI	26-N	13-W
" "	**21**	2	4th PM - 1831 MN/WI	26-N	14-W
" "	**16**	1	4th PM - 1831 MN/WI	28-N	11-W
HOLCOMB	**20**	1	4th PM - 1831 MN/WI	27-N	11-W
HOLM	**8**	4	4th PM - 1831 MN/WI	30-N	11-W
HOLMAN	**22**	2	4th PM - 1831 MN/WI	26-N	13-W
" "	**17**	1	4th PM - 1831 MN/WI	27-N	14-W
HOLTE	**7**	1	4th PM - 1831 MN/WI	30-N	12-W
HOLVORSON	**23**	1	4th PM - 1831 MN/WI	26-N	12-W
HOOKS	**12**	1	4th PM - 1831 MN/WI	29-N	11-W
HOPE	**24**	3	4th PM - 1831 MN/WI	26-N	11-W
HOPKINS	**24**	3	4th PM - 1831 MN/WI	26-N	11-W

Surname	Map Group	Parcels of Land	Meridian/Township/Range		
HOPKINS (Cont'd)	**23**	2	4th PM - 1831 MN/WI	26-N	12-W
HORNER	**18**	1	4th PM - 1831 MN/WI	27-N	13-W
HORSTAD	**15**	1	4th PM - 1831 MN/WI	28-N	12-W
HORSTMANN	**23**	1	4th PM - 1831 MN/WI	26-N	12-W
HORTWICK	**23**	2	4th PM - 1831 MN/WI	26-N	12-W
HOUSE	**14**	1	4th PM - 1831 MN/WI	28-N	13-W
HOUSER	**23**	3	4th PM - 1831 MN/WI	26-N	12-W
HOVER	**10**	2	4th PM - 1831 MN/WI	29-N	13-W
HOVEY	**8**	2	4th PM - 1831 MN/WI	30-N	11-W
HOVLAND	**4**	3	4th PM - 1831 MN/WI	31-N	11-W
HOWARD	**12**	6	4th PM - 1831 MN/WI	29-N	11-W
HOWE	**16**	3	4th PM - 1831 MN/WI	28-N	11-W
HOYT	**20**	2	4th PM - 1831 MN/WI	27-N	11-W
" "	**21**	1	4th PM - 1831 MN/WI	26-N	14-W
HUBBARD	**23**	10	4th PM - 1831 MN/WI	26-N	12-W
" "	**24**	2	4th PM - 1831 MN/WI	26-N	11-W
HUBER	**10**	1	4th PM - 1831 MN/WI	29-N	13-W
HUDSPETH	**21**	1	4th PM - 1831 MN/WI	26-N	14-W
HUFFTLE	**20**	2	4th PM - 1831 MN/WI	27-N	11-W
HUG	**22**	1	4th PM - 1831 MN/WI	26-N	13-W
HUGHES	**6**	3	4th PM - 1831 MN/WI	30-N	13-W
" "	**18**	2	4th PM - 1831 MN/WI	27-N	13-W
HUGHS	**21**	1	4th PM - 1831 MN/WI	26-N	14-W
HULL	**10**	4	4th PM - 1831 MN/WI	29-N	13-W
" "	**20**	1	4th PM - 1831 MN/WI	27-N	11-W
" "	**18**	1	4th PM - 1831 MN/WI	27-N	13-W
HUMISTON	**15**	1	4th PM - 1831 MN/WI	28-N	12-W
HUMPHREY	**22**	2	4th PM - 1831 MN/WI	26-N	13-W
" "	**9**	2	4th PM - 1831 MN/WI	29-N	14-W
HUNT	**23**	3	4th PM - 1831 MN/WI	26-N	12-W
HUSH	**21**	1	4th PM - 1831 MN/WI	26-N	14-W
HUSTED	**24**	2	4th PM - 1831 MN/WI	26-N	11-W
HUTCHINSON	**10**	3	4th PM - 1831 MN/WI	29-N	13-W
" "	**11**	1	4th PM - 1831 MN/WI	29-N	12-W
" "	**6**	1	4th PM - 1831 MN/WI	30-N	13-W
" "	**1**	1	4th PM - 1831 MN/WI	31-N	14-W
HUTCHISON	**20**	2	4th PM - 1831 MN/WI	27-N	11-W
HUYSSEN	**24**	3	4th PM - 1831 MN/WI	26-N	11-W
HYDE	**5**	1	4th PM - 1831 MN/WI	30-N	14-W
HYNS	**18**	2	4th PM - 1831 MN/WI	27-N	13-W
INABNET	**2**	2	4th PM - 1831 MN/WI	31-N	13-W
INABNIT	**2**	1	4th PM - 1831 MN/WI	31-N	13-W
INFINGER	**12**	1	4th PM - 1831 MN/WI	29-N	11-W
INGEBRETSEN	**12**	2	4th PM - 1831 MN/WI	29-N	11-W
INGERSOLL	**24**	2	4th PM - 1831 MN/WI	26-N	11-W
" "	**20**	2	4th PM - 1831 MN/WI	27-N	11-W
INGLE	**14**	2	4th PM - 1831 MN/WI	28-N	13-W
IRVINE	**18**	8	4th PM - 1831 MN/WI	27-N	13-W
ISAKSON	**8**	1	4th PM - 1831 MN/WI	30-N	11-W
ISENHOOD	**15**	2	4th PM - 1831 MN/WI	28-N	12-W
ISRAELSON	**12**	2	4th PM - 1831 MN/WI	29-N	11-W
IVERSON	**11**	3	4th PM - 1831 MN/WI	29-N	12-W
JACKSON	**4**	2	4th PM - 1831 MN/WI	31-N	11-W
JACOBSEN	**8**	2	4th PM - 1831 MN/WI	30-N	11-W
JACOBSON	**12**	3	4th PM - 1831 MN/WI	29-N	11-W
" "	**8**	1	4th PM - 1831 MN/WI	30-N	11-W
JACOT	**1**	1	4th PM - 1831 MN/WI	31-N	14-W
JAMERSON	**24**	2	4th PM - 1831 MN/WI	26-N	11-W
JAMES	**15**	1	4th PM - 1831 MN/WI	28-N	12-W
" "	**1**	1	4th PM - 1831 MN/WI	31-N	14-W

Surname	Map Group	Parcels of Land	Meridian/Township/Range		
JAMRISKA	**5**	1	4th PM - 1831 MN/WI	30-N	14-W
JARCKE	**5**	1	4th PM - 1831 MN/WI	30-N	14-W
JARGER	**13**	1	4th PM - 1831 MN/WI	28-N	14-W
JENONSON	**5**	1	4th PM - 1831 MN/WI	30-N	14-W
JENSEN	**6**	3	4th PM - 1831 MN/WI	30-N	13-W
" "	**16**	1	4th PM - 1831 MN/WI	28-N	11-W
JENSON	**21**	1	4th PM - 1831 MN/WI	26-N	14-W
JERMAN	**24**	3	4th PM - 1831 MN/WI	26-N	11-W
" "	**20**	2	4th PM - 1831 MN/WI	27-N	11-W
JERVY	**9**	1	4th PM - 1831 MN/WI	29-N	14-W
JEWETT	**1**	18	4th PM - 1831 MN/WI	31-N	14-W
JOHANESON	**19**	1	4th PM - 1831 MN/WI	27-N	12-W
JOHANNESSEN	**16**	3	4th PM - 1831 MN/WI	28-N	11-W
JOHANSEN	**4**	2	4th PM - 1831 MN/WI	31-N	11-W
JOHANSON	**8**	2	4th PM - 1831 MN/WI	30-N	11-W
JOHN	**1**	3	4th PM - 1831 MN/WI	31-N	14-W
JOHNS	**12**	2	4th PM - 1831 MN/WI	29-N	11-W
JOHNSEN	**16**	1	4th PM - 1831 MN/WI	28-N	11-W
JOHNSON	**16**	15	4th PM - 1831 MN/WI	28-N	11-W
" "	**4**	12	4th PM - 1831 MN/WI	31-N	11-W
" "	**8**	5	4th PM - 1831 MN/WI	30-N	11-W
" "	**19**	4	4th PM - 1831 MN/WI	27-N	12-W
" "	**14**	4	4th PM - 1831 MN/WI	28-N	13-W
" "	**12**	3	4th PM - 1831 MN/WI	29-N	11-W
" "	**11**	3	4th PM - 1831 MN/WI	29-N	12-W
" "	**10**	3	4th PM - 1831 MN/WI	29-N	13-W
" "	**7**	3	4th PM - 1831 MN/WI	30-N	12-W
" "	**24**	2	4th PM - 1831 MN/WI	26-N	11-W
" "	**5**	2	4th PM - 1831 MN/WI	30-N	14-W
" "	**20**	1	4th PM - 1831 MN/WI	27-N	11-W
" "	**17**	1	4th PM - 1831 MN/WI	27-N	14-W
" "	**2**	1	4th PM - 1831 MN/WI	31-N	13-W
JOHNSTON	**22**	2	4th PM - 1831 MN/WI	26-N	13-W
JONES	**2**	3	4th PM - 1831 MN/WI	31-N	13-W
" "	**23**	2	4th PM - 1831 MN/WI	26-N	12-W
" "	**10**	2	4th PM - 1831 MN/WI	29-N	13-W
" "	**5**	1	4th PM - 1831 MN/WI	30-N	14-W
JONSEN	**16**	1	4th PM - 1831 MN/WI	28-N	11-W
JONSON	**16**	2	4th PM - 1831 MN/WI	28-N	11-W
JORDAN	**22**	3	4th PM - 1831 MN/WI	26-N	13-W
JORNSON	**8**	2	4th PM - 1831 MN/WI	30-N	11-W
JOYCE	**23**	1	4th PM - 1831 MN/WI	26-N	12-W
JUMP	**8**	4	4th PM - 1831 MN/WI	30-N	11-W
JUNOR	**21**	1	4th PM - 1831 MN/WI	26-N	14-W
KAH-TE-NEEW-O-HO-PAZ-SHAY	**24**	1	4th PM - 1831 MN/WI	26-N	11-W
KAISER	**2**	3	4th PM - 1831 MN/WI	31-N	13-W
KALB	**1**	1	4th PM - 1831 MN/WI	31-N	14-W
KALLENBACK	**2**	1	4th PM - 1831 MN/WI	31-N	13-W
KALLENBAK	**2**	1	4th PM - 1831 MN/WI	31-N	13-W
KARLEN	**9**	1	4th PM - 1831 MN/WI	29-N	14-W
KAYE	**5**	3	4th PM - 1831 MN/WI	30-N	14-W
KECK	**9**	4	4th PM - 1831 MN/WI	29-N	14-W
KEEFE	**22**	1	4th PM - 1831 MN/WI	26-N	13-W
KEEN	**6**	7	4th PM - 1831 MN/WI	30-N	13-W
KEENER	**24**	1	4th PM - 1831 MN/WI	26-N	11-W
KEHL	**19**	1	4th PM - 1831 MN/WI	27-N	12-W
KEISER	**2**	3	4th PM - 1831 MN/WI	31-N	13-W
KELKENBERG	**16**	1	4th PM - 1831 MN/WI	28-N	11-W
KELLEY	**14**	3	4th PM - 1831 MN/WI	28-N	13-W
" "	**23**	1	4th PM - 1831 MN/WI	26-N	12-W

Surname	Map Group	Parcels of Land	Meridian/Township/Range		
KELLEY (Cont'd)	**15**	1	4th PM - 1831 MN/WI	28-N	12-W
" "	**13**	1	4th PM - 1831 MN/WI	28-N	14-W
" "	**9**	1	4th PM - 1831 MN/WI	29-N	14-W
KELLOGG	**18**	1	4th PM - 1831 MN/WI	27-N	13-W
KELLY	**21**	1	4th PM - 1831 MN/WI	26-N	14-W
KENNEDY	**21**	1	4th PM - 1831 MN/WI	26-N	14-W
KENT	**16**	2	4th PM - 1831 MN/WI	28-N	11-W
" "	**10**	2	4th PM - 1831 MN/WI	29-N	13-W
" "	**22**	1	4th PM - 1831 MN/WI	26-N	13-W
" "	**15**	1	4th PM - 1831 MN/WI	28-N	12-W
KERNES	**21**	4	4th PM - 1831 MN/WI	26-N	14-W
KERR	**14**	1	4th PM - 1831 MN/WI	28-N	13-W
KESLER	**9**	1	4th PM - 1831 MN/WI	29-N	14-W
KEY	**18**	2	4th PM - 1831 MN/WI	27-N	13-W
KIDDER	**15**	2	4th PM - 1831 MN/WI	28-N	12-W
KIECKHOEFER	**5**	29	4th PM - 1831 MN/WI	30-N	14-W
" "	**1**	21	4th PM - 1831 MN/WI	31-N	14-W
KIGHTLINGER	**24**	3	4th PM - 1831 MN/WI	26-N	11-W
KIGWIN	**24**	1	4th PM - 1831 MN/WI	26-N	11-W
KIMBALL	**24**	3	4th PM - 1831 MN/WI	26-N	11-W
" "	**7**	3	4th PM - 1831 MN/WI	30-N	12-W
" "	**21**	2	4th PM - 1831 MN/WI	26-N	14-W
" "	**20**	2	4th PM - 1831 MN/WI	27-N	11-W
" "	**15**	2	4th PM - 1831 MN/WI	28-N	12-W
" "	**14**	1	4th PM - 1831 MN/WI	28-N	13-W
KING	**10**	2	4th PM - 1831 MN/WI	29-N	13-W
" "	**18**	1	4th PM - 1831 MN/WI	27-N	13-W
" "	**6**	1	4th PM - 1831 MN/WI	30-N	13-W
KINGMAN	**18**	1	4th PM - 1831 MN/WI	27-N	13-W
KINNEY	**12**	1	4th PM - 1831 MN/WI	29-N	11-W
KINNIARD	**1**	1	4th PM - 1831 MN/WI	31-N	14-W
KIRK	**21**	2	4th PM - 1831 MN/WI	26-N	14-W
KIRKLAND	**19**	1	4th PM - 1831 MN/WI	27-N	12-W
KIRSCHER	**22**	1	4th PM - 1831 MN/WI	26-N	13-W
KITE	**21**	3	4th PM - 1831 MN/WI	26-N	14-W
KITTELSEN	**18**	2	4th PM - 1831 MN/WI	27-N	13-W
KLAUER	**10**	1	4th PM - 1831 MN/WI	29-N	13-W
KNAPP	**14**	42	4th PM - 1831 MN/WI	28-N	13-W
" "	**22**	20	4th PM - 1831 MN/WI	26-N	13-W
" "	**1**	19	4th PM - 1831 MN/WI	31-N	14-W
" "	**2**	15	4th PM - 1831 MN/WI	31-N	13-W
" "	**12**	9	4th PM - 1831 MN/WI	29-N	11-W
" "	**7**	8	4th PM - 1831 MN/WI	30-N	12-W
" "	**15**	6	4th PM - 1831 MN/WI	28-N	12-W
" "	**23**	5	4th PM - 1831 MN/WI	26-N	12-W
" "	**6**	3	4th PM - 1831 MN/WI	30-N	13-W
" "	**18**	2	4th PM - 1831 MN/WI	27-N	13-W
" "	**10**	2	4th PM - 1831 MN/WI	29-N	13-W
" "	**8**	2	4th PM - 1831 MN/WI	30-N	11-W
" "	**5**	2	4th PM - 1831 MN/WI	30-N	14-W
" "	**9**	1	4th PM - 1831 MN/WI	29-N	14-W
" "	**4**	1	4th PM - 1831 MN/WI	31-N	11-W
" "	**3**	1	4th PM - 1831 MN/WI	31-N	12-W
KNIGHT	**8**	5	4th PM - 1831 MN/WI	30-N	11-W
" "	**4**	2	4th PM - 1831 MN/WI	31-N	11-W
KNOPPS	**14**	3	4th PM - 1831 MN/WI	28-N	13-W
KNOTT	**10**	3	4th PM - 1831 MN/WI	29-N	13-W
KNOX	**8**	1	4th PM - 1831 MN/WI	30-N	11-W
KNUDSEN	**12**	4	4th PM - 1831 MN/WI	29-N	11-W
" "	**8**	3	4th PM - 1831 MN/WI	30-N	11-W

Surname	Map Group	Parcels of Land	Meridian/Township/Range		
KNUDSEN (Cont'd)	3	2	4th PM - 1831 MN/WI	31-N	12-W
" "	7	1	4th PM - 1831 MN/WI	30-N	12-W
KNUDSON	4	5	4th PM - 1831 MN/WI	31-N	11-W
" "	8	1	4th PM - 1831 MN/WI	30-N	11-W
KNUDTSON	12	1	4th PM - 1831 MN/WI	29-N	11-W
KOBB	20	2	4th PM - 1831 MN/WI	27-N	11-W
KOHN	11	1	4th PM - 1831 MN/WI	29-N	12-W
KOLB	5	2	4th PM - 1831 MN/WI	30-N	14-W
KOPP	24	2	4th PM - 1831 MN/WI	26-N	11-W
KOTTKE	2	1	4th PM - 1831 MN/WI	31-N	13-W
KOWING	5	7	4th PM - 1831 MN/WI	30-N	14-W
KRAMER	15	2	4th PM - 1831 MN/WI	28-N	12-W
KRAMPERT	6	1	4th PM - 1831 MN/WI	30-N	13-W
KRANSZ	21	1	4th PM - 1831 MN/WI	26-N	14-W
KRAUS	16	2	4th PM - 1831 MN/WI	28-N	11-W
KRAUSE	8	5	4th PM - 1831 MN/WI	30-N	11-W
" "	7	2	4th PM - 1831 MN/WI	30-N	12-W
KRAUSER	4	2	4th PM - 1831 MN/WI	31-N	11-W
KREUGER	10	1	4th PM - 1831 MN/WI	29-N	13-W
KRINGLE	3	1	4th PM - 1831 MN/WI	31-N	12-W
KUNCLER	15	1	4th PM - 1831 MN/WI	28-N	12-W
KYES	1	1	4th PM - 1831 MN/WI	31-N	14-W
KYLE	22	6	4th PM - 1831 MN/WI	26-N	13-W
LA FORGE	12	1	4th PM - 1831 MN/WI	29-N	11-W
" "	4	1	4th PM - 1831 MN/WI	31-N	11-W
LABEREE	16	2	4th PM - 1831 MN/WI	28-N	11-W
LACKEY	5	1	4th PM - 1831 MN/WI	30-N	14-W
LACY	5	2	4th PM - 1831 MN/WI	30-N	14-W
" "	20	1	4th PM - 1831 MN/WI	27-N	11-W
LAFORGE	12	3	4th PM - 1831 MN/WI	29-N	11-W
" "	8	3	4th PM - 1831 MN/WI	30-N	11-W
LAINE	5	2	4th PM - 1831 MN/WI	30-N	14-W
LAMB	24	1	4th PM - 1831 MN/WI	26-N	11-W
" "	5	1	4th PM - 1831 MN/WI	30-N	14-W
LAMMER	18	1	4th PM - 1831 MN/WI	27-N	13-W
LAMPHARE	21	1	4th PM - 1831 MN/WI	26-N	14-W
LAMPMAN	16	2	4th PM - 1831 MN/WI	28-N	11-W
LANDON	24	6	4th PM - 1831 MN/WI	26-N	11-W
" "	20	2	4th PM - 1831 MN/WI	27-N	11-W
" "	15	1	4th PM - 1831 MN/WI	28-N	12-W
LANDRUM	14	2	4th PM - 1831 MN/WI	28-N	13-W
LANDT	2	1	4th PM - 1831 MN/WI	31-N	13-W
LANE	21	1	4th PM - 1831 MN/WI	26-N	14-W
" "	20	1	4th PM - 1831 MN/WI	27-N	11-W
LANGBERG	12	3	4th PM - 1831 MN/WI	29-N	11-W
LANGDAL	16	1	4th PM - 1831 MN/WI	28-N	11-W
LANGDELL	20	1	4th PM - 1831 MN/WI	27-N	11-W
" "	16	1	4th PM - 1831 MN/WI	28-N	11-W
LARKHAM	18	1	4th PM - 1831 MN/WI	27-N	13-W
LARRABEE	13	1	4th PM - 1831 MN/WI	28-N	14-W
LARSEN	4	3	4th PM - 1831 MN/WI	31-N	11-W
" "	12	2	4th PM - 1831 MN/WI	29-N	11-W
" "	16	1	4th PM - 1831 MN/WI	28-N	11-W
LARSON	4	9	4th PM - 1831 MN/WI	31-N	11-W
" "	8	5	4th PM - 1831 MN/WI	30-N	11-W
" "	3	4	4th PM - 1831 MN/WI	31-N	12-W
" "	2	3	4th PM - 1831 MN/WI	31-N	13-W
" "	23	2	4th PM - 1831 MN/WI	26-N	12-W
" "	22	1	4th PM - 1831 MN/WI	26-N	13-W
" "	12	1	4th PM - 1831 MN/WI	29-N	11-W

Surname	Map Group	Parcels of Land	Meridian/Township/Range		
LARSON (Cont'd)	10	1	4th PM - 1831 MN/WI	29-N	13-W
" "	6	1	4th PM - 1831 MN/WI	30-N	13-W
LARSONS	2	3	4th PM - 1831 MN/WI	31-N	13-W
LASH	19	2	4th PM - 1831 MN/WI	27-N	12-W
LATHROP	23	4	4th PM - 1831 MN/WI	26-N	12-W
" "	24	1	4th PM - 1831 MN/WI	26-N	11-W
LAUDON	15	1	4th PM - 1831 MN/WI	28-N	12-W
LAWRENCE	21	1	4th PM - 1831 MN/WI	26-N	14-W
LAWTON	5	3	4th PM - 1831 MN/WI	30-N	14-W
LAYNE	21	1	4th PM - 1831 MN/WI	26-N	14-W
LEACH	11	2	4th PM - 1831 MN/WI	29-N	12-W
LEAVENWORTH	12	1	4th PM - 1831 MN/WI	29-N	11-W
LECLERCQ	18	1	4th PM - 1831 MN/WI	27-N	13-W
LEE	3	6	4th PM - 1831 MN/WI	31-N	12-W
" "	20	5	4th PM - 1831 MN/WI	27-N	11-W
" "	7	2	4th PM - 1831 MN/WI	30-N	12-W
" "	19	1	4th PM - 1831 MN/WI	27-N	12-W
" "	16	1	4th PM - 1831 MN/WI	28-N	11-W
" "	8	1	4th PM - 1831 MN/WI	30-N	11-W
LEMON	22	1	4th PM - 1831 MN/WI	26-N	13-W
" "	21	1	4th PM - 1831 MN/WI	26-N	14-W
LENTZ	19	1	4th PM - 1831 MN/WI	27-N	12-W
" "	15	1	4th PM - 1831 MN/WI	28-N	12-W
LEONARD	12	3	4th PM - 1831 MN/WI	29-N	11-W
" "	19	1	4th PM - 1831 MN/WI	27-N	12-W
" "	7	1	4th PM - 1831 MN/WI	30-N	12-W
LESURE	20	1	4th PM - 1831 MN/WI	27-N	11-W
LETTEER	4	1	4th PM - 1831 MN/WI	31-N	11-W
LEWELLEN	10	1	4th PM - 1831 MN/WI	29-N	13-W
LEWIS	24	3	4th PM - 1831 MN/WI	26-N	11-W
" "	23	3	4th PM - 1831 MN/WI	26-N	12-W
" "	6	3	4th PM - 1831 MN/WI	30-N	13-W
LIBBEY	23	1	4th PM - 1831 MN/WI	26-N	12-W
LIE	7	2	4th PM - 1831 MN/WI	30-N	12-W
LIGHTBOURN	6	3	4th PM - 1831 MN/WI	30-N	13-W
" "	5	1	4th PM - 1831 MN/WI	30-N	14-W
LIND	3	1	4th PM - 1831 MN/WI	31-N	12-W
LININGER	9	1	4th PM - 1831 MN/WI	29-N	14-W
LINK	19	1	4th PM - 1831 MN/WI	27-N	12-W
LIPOISKY	6	2	4th PM - 1831 MN/WI	30-N	13-W
LIPPEL	16	2	4th PM - 1831 MN/WI	28-N	11-W
LITTLE	12	4	4th PM - 1831 MN/WI	29-N	11-W
" "	18	1	4th PM - 1831 MN/WI	27-N	13-W
LIVERSON	14	1	4th PM - 1831 MN/WI	28-N	13-W
LIVINGSTON	20	1	4th PM - 1831 MN/WI	27-N	11-W
" "	8	1	4th PM - 1831 MN/WI	30-N	11-W
LOCKE	24	1	4th PM - 1831 MN/WI	26-N	11-W
" "	23	1	4th PM - 1831 MN/WI	26-N	12-W
LOCKWOOD	23	4	4th PM - 1831 MN/WI	26-N	12-W
" "	10	2	4th PM - 1831 MN/WI	29-N	13-W
LOE	2	2	4th PM - 1831 MN/WI	31-N	13-W
" "	3	1	4th PM - 1831 MN/WI	31-N	12-W
LOFTHUS	4	2	4th PM - 1831 MN/WI	31-N	11-W
LOFTHUUS	3	3	4th PM - 1831 MN/WI	31-N	12-W
LOGSLETT	8	2	4th PM - 1831 MN/WI	30-N	11-W
LOGSLID	4	1	4th PM - 1831 MN/WI	31-N	11-W
LOHFINK	2	2	4th PM - 1831 MN/WI	31-N	13-W
LONG	1	1	4th PM - 1831 MN/WI	31-N	14-W
LONGDO	4	2	4th PM - 1831 MN/WI	31-N	11-W
LORD	6	2	4th PM - 1831 MN/WI	30-N	13-W

Surname	Map Group	Parcels of Land	Meridian/Township/Range		
LORD (Cont'd)	**1**	1	4th PM - 1831 MN/WI	31-N	14-W
LOTT	**23**	2	4th PM - 1831 MN/WI	26-N	12-W
" "	**24**	1	4th PM - 1831 MN/WI	26-N	11-W
LOUSTED	**11**	1	4th PM - 1831 MN/WI	29-N	12-W
LOW	**22**	2	4th PM - 1831 MN/WI	26-N	13-W
LOWBER	**16**	2	4th PM - 1831 MN/WI	28-N	11-W
LOWE	**18**	1	4th PM - 1831 MN/WI	27-N	13-W
LOWERY	**12**	2	4th PM - 1831 MN/WI	29-N	11-W
" "	**11**	1	4th PM - 1831 MN/WI	29-N	12-W
LOWRY	**11**	3	4th PM - 1831 MN/WI	29-N	12-W
LUCAS	**23**	3	4th PM - 1831 MN/WI	26-N	12-W
" "	**24**	1	4th PM - 1831 MN/WI	26-N	11-W
" "	**20**	1	4th PM - 1831 MN/WI	27-N	11-W
" "	**19**	1	4th PM - 1831 MN/WI	27-N	12-W
" "	**5**	1	4th PM - 1831 MN/WI	30-N	14-W
LUND	**15**	1	4th PM - 1831 MN/WI	28-N	12-W
" "	**4**	1	4th PM - 1831 MN/WI	31-N	11-W
LYMAN	**5**	3	4th PM - 1831 MN/WI	30-N	14-W
" "	**16**	1	4th PM - 1831 MN/WI	28-N	11-W
LYNCH	**4**	1	4th PM - 1831 MN/WI	31-N	11-W
LYON	**15**	1	4th PM - 1831 MN/WI	28-N	12-W
LYTLE	**23**	2	4th PM - 1831 MN/WI	26-N	12-W
" "	**24**	1	4th PM - 1831 MN/WI	26-N	11-W
MACAULAY	**22**	2	4th PM - 1831 MN/WI	26-N	13-W
MACAULEY	**23**	3	4th PM - 1831 MN/WI	26-N	12-W
" "	**22**	2	4th PM - 1831 MN/WI	26-N	13-W
MACK	**14**	1	4th PM - 1831 MN/WI	28-N	13-W
MACKEY	**18**	3	4th PM - 1831 MN/WI	27-N	13-W
MAGILTON	**21**	1	4th PM - 1831 MN/WI	26-N	14-W
MAHANY	**5**	1	4th PM - 1831 MN/WI	30-N	14-W
MALHUS	**11**	1	4th PM - 1831 MN/WI	29-N	12-W
MALINDA	**1**	3	4th PM - 1831 MN/WI	31-N	14-W
MALLEAN	**9**	1	4th PM - 1831 MN/WI	29-N	14-W
MALONEY	**22**	1	4th PM - 1831 MN/WI	26-N	13-W
MANCHESTER	**4**	2	4th PM - 1831 MN/WI	31-N	11-W
MANLEY	**22**	2	4th PM - 1831 MN/WI	26-N	13-W
" "	**13**	1	4th PM - 1831 MN/WI	28-N	14-W
MANNING	**24**	1	4th PM - 1831 MN/WI	26-N	11-W
" "	**21**	1	4th PM - 1831 MN/WI	26-N	14-W
MANS	**22**	1	4th PM - 1831 MN/WI	26-N	13-W
MANSFIELD	**16**	13	4th PM - 1831 MN/WI	28-N	11-W
" "	**20**	5	4th PM - 1831 MN/WI	27-N	11-W
" "	**8**	3	4th PM - 1831 MN/WI	30-N	11-W
MARBURY	**2**	1	4th PM - 1831 MN/WI	31-N	13-W
MARCH	**1**	9	4th PM - 1831 MN/WI	31-N	14-W
MARISTAD	**8**	2	4th PM - 1831 MN/WI	30-N	11-W
MARK	**14**	1	4th PM - 1831 MN/WI	28-N	13-W
MARKHAM	**14**	1	4th PM - 1831 MN/WI	28-N	13-W
MARLETT	**5**	4	4th PM - 1831 MN/WI	30-N	14-W
" "	**1**	1	4th PM - 1831 MN/WI	31-N	14-W
MARR	**22**	1	4th PM - 1831 MN/WI	26-N	13-W
MARSH	**4**	2	4th PM - 1831 MN/WI	31-N	11-W
MARSHALL	**23**	3	4th PM - 1831 MN/WI	26-N	12-W
" "	**16**	2	4th PM - 1831 MN/WI	28-N	11-W
MARSTON	**23**	2	4th PM - 1831 MN/WI	26-N	12-W
MARTIN	**8**	3	4th PM - 1831 MN/WI	30-N	11-W
" "	**23**	2	4th PM - 1831 MN/WI	26-N	12-W
" "	**21**	2	4th PM - 1831 MN/WI	26-N	14-W
" "	**11**	2	4th PM - 1831 MN/WI	29-N	12-W
" "	**6**	2	4th PM - 1831 MN/WI	30-N	13-W

Surname	Map Group	Parcels of Land	Meridian/Township/Range		
MARTIN (Cont'd)	**7**	1	4th PM - 1831 MN/WI	30-N	12-W
" "	**2**	1	4th PM - 1831 MN/WI	31-N	13-W
MARTINSON	**8**	2	4th PM - 1831 MN/WI	30-N	11-W
MARVIN	**24**	4	4th PM - 1831 MN/WI	26-N	11-W
MASON	**8**	4	4th PM - 1831 MN/WI	30-N	11-W
MASONER	**19**	1	4th PM - 1831 MN/WI	27-N	12-W
MASSEE	**23**	3	4th PM - 1831 MN/WI	26-N	12-W
MASSEY	**23**	3	4th PM - 1831 MN/WI	26-N	12-W
" "	**19**	2	4th PM - 1831 MN/WI	27-N	12-W
MATHERS	**23**	2	4th PM - 1831 MN/WI	26-N	12-W
MATHEWS	**12**	7	4th PM - 1831 MN/WI	29-N	11-W
" "	**11**	1	4th PM - 1831 MN/WI	29-N	12-W
MATTESON	**7**	3	4th PM - 1831 MN/WI	30-N	12-W
MATTHEWS	**11**	3	4th PM - 1831 MN/WI	29-N	12-W
MATTISON	**6**	2	4th PM - 1831 MN/WI	30-N	13-W
MAUKSTAD	**8**	1	4th PM - 1831 MN/WI	30-N	11-W
MAVES	**16**	1	4th PM - 1831 MN/WI	28-N	11-W
MAVITY	**7**	2	4th PM - 1831 MN/WI	30-N	12-W
MAYBEE	**21**	1	4th PM - 1831 MN/WI	26-N	14-W
MCADOO	**20**	1	4th PM - 1831 MN/WI	27-N	11-W
MCALLISTER	**9**	3	4th PM - 1831 MN/WI	29-N	14-W
MCARTHUR	**10**	1	4th PM - 1831 MN/WI	29-N	13-W
MCAULEY	**22**	1	4th PM - 1831 MN/WI	26-N	13-W
MCBRIDE	**22**	2	4th PM - 1831 MN/WI	26-N	13-W
MCCART	**24**	2	4th PM - 1831 MN/WI	26-N	11-W
MCCARTNEY	**17**	1	4th PM - 1831 MN/WI	27-N	14-W
MCCARTY	**4**	3	4th PM - 1831 MN/WI	31-N	11-W
" "	**17**	1	4th PM - 1831 MN/WI	27-N	14-W
MCCOLLUM	**24**	1	4th PM - 1831 MN/WI	26-N	11-W
MCCORKLE	**23**	5	4th PM - 1831 MN/WI	26-N	12-W
" "	**22**	1	4th PM - 1831 MN/WI	26-N	13-W
MCCORMICK	**10**	1	4th PM - 1831 MN/WI	29-N	13-W
MCCULLOCH	**7**	3	4th PM - 1831 MN/WI	30-N	12-W
" "	**9**	2	4th PM - 1831 MN/WI	29-N	14-W
MCCULLOUGH	**10**	1	4th PM - 1831 MN/WI	29-N	13-W
MCDONALD	**12**	3	4th PM - 1831 MN/WI	29-N	11-W
" "	**16**	1	4th PM - 1831 MN/WI	28-N	11-W
MCDORMAN	**9**	1	4th PM - 1831 MN/WI	29-N	14-W
MCELWAIN	**11**	1	4th PM - 1831 MN/WI	29-N	12-W
MCELWAINE	**12**	2	4th PM - 1831 MN/WI	29-N	11-W
MCGEOGH	**23**	2	4th PM - 1831 MN/WI	26-N	12-W
MCGILTON	**21**	1	4th PM - 1831 MN/WI	26-N	14-W
MCGINNIS	**21**	1	4th PM - 1831 MN/WI	26-N	14-W
" "	**14**	1	4th PM - 1831 MN/WI	28-N	13-W
MCGREW	**16**	1	4th PM - 1831 MN/WI	28-N	11-W
MCINTYRE	**6**	8	4th PM - 1831 MN/WI	30-N	13-W
" "	**2**	1	4th PM - 1831 MN/WI	31-N	13-W
MCKAHAN	**15**	3	4th PM - 1831 MN/WI	28-N	12-W
MCKAHUN	**15**	1	4th PM - 1831 MN/WI	28-N	12-W
MCKELHEER	**1**	3	4th PM - 1831 MN/WI	31-N	14-W
MCKIE	**4**	1	4th PM - 1831 MN/WI	31-N	11-W
MCLAIN	**22**	3	4th PM - 1831 MN/WI	26-N	13-W
MCLENNAN	**11**	1	4th PM - 1831 MN/WI	29-N	12-W
MCLEOD	**5**	2	4th PM - 1831 MN/WI	30-N	14-W
MCLESKEY	**5**	2	4th PM - 1831 MN/WI	30-N	14-W
MCMAHON	**13**	1	4th PM - 1831 MN/WI	28-N	14-W
MCMANNAS	**13**	1	4th PM - 1831 MN/WI	28-N	14-W
MCMANNUS	**5**	1	4th PM - 1831 MN/WI	30-N	14-W
MCMANUS	**13**	1	4th PM - 1831 MN/WI	28-N	14-W
MCMASTERS	**4**	2	4th PM - 1831 MN/WI	31-N	11-W

Surname	Map Group	Parcels of Land	Meridian/Township/Range		
MCMILLAN	**22**	1	4th PM - 1831 MN/WI	26-N	13-W
MCMURCHY	**6**	5	4th PM - 1831 MN/WI	30-N	13-W
MCMURRY	**15**	1	4th PM - 1831 MN/WI	28-N	12-W
MCNELIS	**20**	1	4th PM - 1831 MN/WI	27-N	11-W
MCNELLIS	**20**	1	4th PM - 1831 MN/WI	27-N	11-W
MCPHERSON	**6**	3	4th PM - 1831 MN/WI	30-N	13-W
" "	**7**	1	4th PM - 1831 MN/WI	30-N	12-W
MCROBERT	**21**	1	4th PM - 1831 MN/WI	26-N	14-W
MEAD	**24**	12	4th PM - 1831 MN/WI	26-N	11-W
" "	**10**	2	4th PM - 1831 MN/WI	29-N	13-W
MEE-CHIT-E-NEE	**19**	1	4th PM - 1831 MN/WI	27-N	12-W
MEGGETT	**24**	2	4th PM - 1831 MN/WI	26-N	11-W
MELLEN	**21**	1	4th PM - 1831 MN/WI	26-N	14-W
MERCIER	**14**	1	4th PM - 1831 MN/WI	28-N	13-W
MEREDETH	**19**	1	4th PM - 1831 MN/WI	27-N	12-W
MERRILL	**18**	1	4th PM - 1831 MN/WI	27-N	13-W
MESSELT	**7**	1	4th PM - 1831 MN/WI	30-N	12-W
MESSENGER	**15**	1	4th PM - 1831 MN/WI	28-N	12-W
" "	**3**	1	4th PM - 1831 MN/WI	31-N	12-W
MEYERS	**9**	1	4th PM - 1831 MN/WI	29-N	14-W
MICKELSON	**3**	1	4th PM - 1831 MN/WI	31-N	12-W
MIESTER	**15**	3	4th PM - 1831 MN/WI	28-N	12-W
MIKKELSEN	**6**	1	4th PM - 1831 MN/WI	30-N	13-W
MIKKELSON	**6**	4	4th PM - 1831 MN/WI	30-N	13-W
" "	**2**	1	4th PM - 1831 MN/WI	31-N	13-W
MILES	**6**	2	4th PM - 1831 MN/WI	30-N	13-W
MILLER	**4**	7	4th PM - 1831 MN/WI	31-N	11-W
" "	**9**	2	4th PM - 1831 MN/WI	29-N	14-W
" "	**15**	1	4th PM - 1831 MN/WI	28-N	12-W
" "	**14**	1	4th PM - 1831 MN/WI	28-N	13-W
" "	**5**	1	4th PM - 1831 MN/WI	30-N	14-W
MILLIRON	**9**	1	4th PM - 1831 MN/WI	29-N	14-W
MILLS	**5**	6	4th PM - 1831 MN/WI	30-N	14-W
" "	**21**	5	4th PM - 1831 MN/WI	26-N	14-W
MINER	**20**	4	4th PM - 1831 MN/WI	27-N	11-W
MITTELSTADT	**4**	2	4th PM - 1831 MN/WI	31-N	11-W
MOE	**11**	2	4th PM - 1831 MN/WI	29-N	12-W
MOEN	**3**	3	4th PM - 1831 MN/WI	31-N	12-W
MONFORT	**23**	2	4th PM - 1831 MN/WI	26-N	12-W
MONROE	**7**	1	4th PM - 1831 MN/WI	30-N	12-W
MONTAGUE	**23**	3	4th PM - 1831 MN/WI	26-N	12-W
MONTEITH	**12**	7	4th PM - 1831 MN/WI	29-N	11-W
" "	**1**	3	4th PM - 1831 MN/WI	31-N	14-W
MONTGOMERY	**22**	1	4th PM - 1831 MN/WI	26-N	13-W
" "	**6**	1	4th PM - 1831 MN/WI	30-N	13-W
MOODY	**21**	3	4th PM - 1831 MN/WI	26-N	14-W
MOONEY	**14**	1	4th PM - 1831 MN/WI	28-N	13-W
MOOR	**20**	3	4th PM - 1831 MN/WI	27-N	11-W
" "	**16**	2	4th PM - 1831 MN/WI	28-N	11-W
MOORE	**11**	8	4th PM - 1831 MN/WI	29-N	12-W
" "	**24**	5	4th PM - 1831 MN/WI	26-N	11-W
" "	**16**	5	4th PM - 1831 MN/WI	28-N	11-W
" "	**17**	2	4th PM - 1831 MN/WI	27-N	14-W
" "	**20**	1	4th PM - 1831 MN/WI	27-N	11-W
" "	**10**	1	4th PM - 1831 MN/WI	29-N	13-W
" "	**9**	1	4th PM - 1831 MN/WI	29-N	14-W
MOREHOUSE	**20**	2	4th PM - 1831 MN/WI	27-N	11-W
MORFEY	**22**	1	4th PM - 1831 MN/WI	26-N	13-W
MORGAN	**14**	3	4th PM - 1831 MN/WI	28-N	13-W
" "	**11**	3	4th PM - 1831 MN/WI	29-N	12-W

Surname	Map Group	Parcels of Land	Meridian/Township/Range		
MORGAN (Cont'd)	**17**	1	4th PM - 1831 MN/WI	27-N	14-W
MORK	**3**	2	4th PM - 1831 MN/WI	31-N	12-W
MORRICE	**2**	1	4th PM - 1831 MN/WI	31-N	13-W
MORRISON	**23**	3	4th PM - 1831 MN/WI	26-N	12-W
" "	**22**	3	4th PM - 1831 MN/WI	26-N	13-W
" "	**5**	1	4th PM - 1831 MN/WI	30-N	14-W
MORSE	**19**	2	4th PM - 1831 MN/WI	27-N	12-W
MORTON	**21**	5	4th PM - 1831 MN/WI	26-N	14-W
" "	**19**	1	4th PM - 1831 MN/WI	27-N	12-W
MOSHER	**24**	1	4th PM - 1831 MN/WI	26-N	11-W
MOSSNER	**1**	1	4th PM - 1831 MN/WI	31-N	14-W
MOSTELLER	**15**	1	4th PM - 1831 MN/WI	28-N	12-W
MOULTON	**24**	1	4th PM - 1831 MN/WI	26-N	11-W
MOUNTCASTLE	**14**	2	4th PM - 1831 MN/WI	28-N	13-W
MOWLAN	**6**	2	4th PM - 1831 MN/WI	30-N	13-W
MOYER	**23**	1	4th PM - 1831 MN/WI	26-N	12-W
" "	**9**	1	4th PM - 1831 MN/WI	29-N	14-W
MOYES	**15**	1	4th PM - 1831 MN/WI	28-N	12-W
MUDGE	**10**	2	4th PM - 1831 MN/WI	29-N	13-W
MUENCH	**8**	1	4th PM - 1831 MN/WI	30-N	11-W
MULHERON	**21**	1	4th PM - 1831 MN/WI	26-N	14-W
MULKS	**19**	5	4th PM - 1831 MN/WI	27-N	12-W
" "	**20**	2	4th PM - 1831 MN/WI	27-N	11-W
MULLER	**3**	2	4th PM - 1831 MN/WI	31-N	12-W
MULVANY	**9**	1	4th PM - 1831 MN/WI	29-N	14-W
MUMER	**16**	2	4th PM - 1831 MN/WI	28-N	11-W
MURK	**15**	1	4th PM - 1831 MN/WI	28-N	12-W
MURPHY	**23**	2	4th PM - 1831 MN/WI	26-N	12-W
" "	**21**	1	4th PM - 1831 MN/WI	26-N	14-W
" "	**3**	1	4th PM - 1831 MN/WI	31-N	12-W
MURRAY	**18**	1	4th PM - 1831 MN/WI	27-N	13-W
MYERS	**22**	1	4th PM - 1831 MN/WI	26-N	13-W
NAMEJUNAS	**20**	1	4th PM - 1831 MN/WI	27-N	11-W
NARSEE	**1**	3	4th PM - 1831 MN/WI	31-N	14-W
NELSON	**4**	7	4th PM - 1831 MN/WI	31-N	11-W
" "	**16**	4	4th PM - 1831 MN/WI	28-N	11-W
" "	**18**	2	4th PM - 1831 MN/WI	27-N	13-W
" "	**21**	1	4th PM - 1831 MN/WI	26-N	14-W
NEMBARGER	**9**	1	4th PM - 1831 MN/WI	29-N	14-W
NERESON	**4**	1	4th PM - 1831 MN/WI	31-N	11-W
NERISEN	**4**	2	4th PM - 1831 MN/WI	31-N	11-W
NERISON	**4**	4	4th PM - 1831 MN/WI	31-N	11-W
NESSET	**8**	3	4th PM - 1831 MN/WI	30-N	11-W
NEVIN	**20**	2	4th PM - 1831 MN/WI	27-N	11-W
NEWCOMB	**12**	1	4th PM - 1831 MN/WI	29-N	11-W
NEWELL	**15**	6	4th PM - 1831 MN/WI	28-N	12-W
" "	**11**	3	4th PM - 1831 MN/WI	29-N	12-W
" "	**14**	1	4th PM - 1831 MN/WI	28-N	13-W
NEWHALL	**15**	10	4th PM - 1831 MN/WI	28-N	12-W
" "	**14**	3	4th PM - 1831 MN/WI	28-N	13-W
" "	**11**	2	4th PM - 1831 MN/WI	29-N	12-W
NEWMAN	**23**	2	4th PM - 1831 MN/WI	26-N	12-W
" "	**11**	2	4th PM - 1831 MN/WI	29-N	12-W
NEWSOM	**15**	1	4th PM - 1831 MN/WI	28-N	12-W
NEWVILLE	**23**	1	4th PM - 1831 MN/WI	26-N	12-W
NICHOLS	**23**	2	4th PM - 1831 MN/WI	26-N	12-W
" "	**20**	1	4th PM - 1831 MN/WI	27-N	11-W
" "	**15**	1	4th PM - 1831 MN/WI	28-N	12-W
" "	**5**	1	4th PM - 1831 MN/WI	30-N	14-W
NICOLS	**5**	1	4th PM - 1831 MN/WI	30-N	14-W

Surname	Map Group	Parcels of Land	Meridian/Township/Range		
NIELSEN	**16**	1	4th PM - 1831 MN/WI	28-N	11-W
" "	**2**	1	4th PM - 1831 MN/WI	31-N	13-W
NILSEN	**12**	2	4th PM - 1831 MN/WI	29-N	11-W
NILSON	**8**	2	4th PM - 1831 MN/WI	30-N	11-W
" "	**3**	1	4th PM - 1831 MN/WI	31-N	12-W
NOBLE	**10**	1	4th PM - 1831 MN/WI	29-N	13-W
NOER	**8**	3	4th PM - 1831 MN/WI	30-N	11-W
NOGLE	**10**	2	4th PM - 1831 MN/WI	29-N	13-W
NOIS	**20**	1	4th PM - 1831 MN/WI	27-N	11-W
NOREM	**16**	3	4th PM - 1831 MN/WI	28-N	11-W
NORRISH	**24**	4	4th PM - 1831 MN/WI	26-N	11-W
NORTHSTREAM	**8**	1	4th PM - 1831 MN/WI	30-N	11-W
NORTON	**24**	3	4th PM - 1831 MN/WI	26-N	11-W
" "	**16**	1	4th PM - 1831 MN/WI	28-N	11-W
NOWLEN	**15**	2	4th PM - 1831 MN/WI	28-N	12-W
NOYES	**15**	1	4th PM - 1831 MN/WI	28-N	12-W
NULPH	**22**	1	4th PM - 1831 MN/WI	26-N	13-W
" "	**10**	1	4th PM - 1831 MN/WI	29-N	13-W
NYE	**22**	1	4th PM - 1831 MN/WI	26-N	13-W
" "	**11**	1	4th PM - 1831 MN/WI	29-N	12-W
OBERLANDER	**13**	1	4th PM - 1831 MN/WI	28-N	14-W
OBRIEN	**15**	3	4th PM - 1831 MN/WI	28-N	12-W
OCONNELL	**6**	1	4th PM - 1831 MN/WI	30-N	13-W
OCONNOR	**1**	8	4th PM - 1831 MN/WI	31-N	14-W
OFLANEGAN	**14**	3	4th PM - 1831 MN/WI	28-N	13-W
OLESEN	**12**	3	4th PM - 1831 MN/WI	29-N	11-W
" "	**2**	1	4th PM - 1831 MN/WI	31-N	13-W
OLESON	**8**	6	4th PM - 1831 MN/WI	30-N	11-W
" "	**4**	6	4th PM - 1831 MN/WI	31-N	11-W
" "	**12**	4	4th PM - 1831 MN/WI	29-N	11-W
" "	**16**	3	4th PM - 1831 MN/WI	28-N	11-W
" "	**7**	3	4th PM - 1831 MN/WI	30-N	12-W
" "	**11**	1	4th PM - 1831 MN/WI	29-N	12-W
OLIN	**9**	3	4th PM - 1831 MN/WI	29-N	14-W
OLIVER	**7**	3	4th PM - 1831 MN/WI	30-N	12-W
" "	**1**	1	4th PM - 1831 MN/WI	31-N	14-W
OLMSTEAD	**15**	2	4th PM - 1831 MN/WI	28-N	12-W
OLSEN	**4**	7	4th PM - 1831 MN/WI	31-N	11-W
" "	**12**	3	4th PM - 1831 MN/WI	29-N	11-W
" "	**3**	3	4th PM - 1831 MN/WI	31-N	12-W
" "	**8**	2	4th PM - 1831 MN/WI	30-N	11-W
OLSON	**8**	8	4th PM - 1831 MN/WI	30-N	11-W
" "	**12**	6	4th PM - 1831 MN/WI	29-N	11-W
" "	**4**	5	4th PM - 1831 MN/WI	31-N	11-W
" "	**23**	4	4th PM - 1831 MN/WI	26-N	12-W
" "	**19**	3	4th PM - 1831 MN/WI	27-N	12-W
" "	**18**	2	4th PM - 1831 MN/WI	27-N	13-W
" "	**14**	2	4th PM - 1831 MN/WI	28-N	13-W
" "	**16**	1	4th PM - 1831 MN/WI	28-N	11-W
" "	**9**	1	4th PM - 1831 MN/WI	29-N	14-W
OLSTAD	**3**	3	4th PM - 1831 MN/WI	31-N	12-W
OMALLEY	**5**	3	4th PM - 1831 MN/WI	30-N	14-W
OMDAHL	**10**	1	4th PM - 1831 MN/WI	29-N	13-W
OMDAHLE	**10**	1	4th PM - 1831 MN/WI	29-N	13-W
OMDOLL	**14**	3	4th PM - 1831 MN/WI	28-N	13-W
OMTVEDT	**8**	1	4th PM - 1831 MN/WI	30-N	11-W
ONDERDONK	**23**	2	4th PM - 1831 MN/WI	26-N	12-W
ONEY	**6**	2	4th PM - 1831 MN/WI	30-N	13-W
ORDEMAN	**19**	1	4th PM - 1831 MN/WI	27-N	12-W
ORDEMANN	**19**	3	4th PM - 1831 MN/WI	27-N	12-W

Surname	Map Group	Parcels of Land	Meridian/Township/Range		
ORME	**8**	4	4th PM - 1831 MN/WI	30-N	11-W
OSMER	**21**	2	4th PM - 1831 MN/WI	26-N	14-W
OTIS	**21**	1	4th PM - 1831 MN/WI	26-N	14-W
OTTUM	**18**	1	4th PM - 1831 MN/WI	27-N	13-W
OVITT	**20**	1	4th PM - 1831 MN/WI	27-N	11-W
OWEN	**20**	3	4th PM - 1831 MN/WI	27-N	11-W
" "	**19**	2	4th PM - 1831 MN/WI	27-N	12-W
" "	**10**	1	4th PM - 1831 MN/WI	29-N	13-W
PACHL	**15**	1	4th PM - 1831 MN/WI	28-N	12-W
PADDLEFORD	**11**	1	4th PM - 1831 MN/WI	29-N	12-W
" "	**10**	1	4th PM - 1831 MN/WI	29-N	13-W
PAGE	**23**	3	4th PM - 1831 MN/WI	26-N	12-W
" "	**10**	1	4th PM - 1831 MN/WI	29-N	13-W
PAINE	**22**	2	4th PM - 1831 MN/WI	26-N	13-W
" "	**11**	1	4th PM - 1831 MN/WI	29-N	12-W
PAIRO	**8**	3	4th PM - 1831 MN/WI	30-N	11-W
PALEN	**23**	6	4th PM - 1831 MN/WI	26-N	12-W
PALMER	**15**	2	4th PM - 1831 MN/WI	28-N	12-W
" "	**21**	1	4th PM - 1831 MN/WI	26-N	14-W
PARK	**14**	2	4th PM - 1831 MN/WI	28-N	13-W
PARKER	**16**	3	4th PM - 1831 MN/WI	28-N	11-W
" "	**19**	1	4th PM - 1831 MN/WI	27-N	12-W
" "	**10**	1	4th PM - 1831 MN/WI	29-N	13-W
PATTEN	**20**	2	4th PM - 1831 MN/WI	27-N	11-W
PAUL	**12**	2	4th PM - 1831 MN/WI	29-N	11-W
PAULSON	**8**	3	4th PM - 1831 MN/WI	30-N	11-W
PAYNE	**19**	2	4th PM - 1831 MN/WI	27-N	12-W
" "	**15**	2	4th PM - 1831 MN/WI	28-N	12-W
PEARSON	**20**	2	4th PM - 1831 MN/WI	27-N	11-W
PEASE	**21**	1	4th PM - 1831 MN/WI	26-N	14-W
" "	**13**	1	4th PM - 1831 MN/WI	28-N	14-W
PECK	**9**	1	4th PM - 1831 MN/WI	29-N	14-W
PEDERSEN	**16**	1	4th PM - 1831 MN/WI	28-N	11-W
" "	**10**	1	4th PM - 1831 MN/WI	29-N	13-W
PEDERSON	**2**	2	4th PM - 1831 MN/WI	31-N	13-W
PEET	**18**	1	4th PM - 1831 MN/WI	27-N	13-W
PEISCH	**20**	1	4th PM - 1831 MN/WI	27-N	11-W
PELT	**12**	1	4th PM - 1831 MN/WI	29-N	11-W
PENNOCK	**22**	2	4th PM - 1831 MN/WI	26-N	13-W
" "	**20**	1	4th PM - 1831 MN/WI	27-N	11-W
PENNOYER	**16**	1	4th PM - 1831 MN/WI	28-N	11-W
PE-QUAH-KO-NAH	**24**	1	4th PM - 1831 MN/WI	26-N	11-W
PEROT	**6**	3	4th PM - 1831 MN/WI	30-N	13-W
PERRY	**24**	2	4th PM - 1831 MN/WI	26-N	11-W
" "	**18**	1	4th PM - 1831 MN/WI	27-N	13-W
PETERSON	**12**	2	4th PM - 1831 MN/WI	29-N	11-W
" "	**8**	2	4th PM - 1831 MN/WI	30-N	11-W
" "	**24**	1	4th PM - 1831 MN/WI	26-N	11-W
" "	**4**	1	4th PM - 1831 MN/WI	31-N	11-W
" "	**2**	1	4th PM - 1831 MN/WI	31-N	13-W
PETTIS	**21**	3	4th PM - 1831 MN/WI	26-N	14-W
PHELPS	**21**	1	4th PM - 1831 MN/WI	26-N	14-W
" "	**12**	1	4th PM - 1831 MN/WI	29-N	11-W
PHERNETTON	**9**	2	4th PM - 1831 MN/WI	29-N	14-W
PHILLIPS	**2**	3	4th PM - 1831 MN/WI	31-N	13-W
" "	**24**	2	4th PM - 1831 MN/WI	26-N	11-W
" "	**21**	1	4th PM - 1831 MN/WI	26-N	14-W
" "	**17**	1	4th PM - 1831 MN/WI	27-N	14-W
" "	**15**	1	4th PM - 1831 MN/WI	28-N	12-W
PHILPOTT	**15**	1	4th PM - 1831 MN/WI	28-N	12-W

Surname	Map Group	Parcels of Land	Meridian/Township/Range		
PICKARD	1	1	4th PM - 1831 MN/WI	31-N	14-W
PICKERING	22	1	4th PM - 1831 MN/WI	26-N	13-W
PIERCE	10	3	4th PM - 1831 MN/WI	29-N	13-W
" "	23	1	4th PM - 1831 MN/WI	26-N	12-W
PIERSON	23	1	4th PM - 1831 MN/WI	26-N	12-W
PIPPINGER	9	1	4th PM - 1831 MN/WI	29-N	14-W
PIRKL	21	1	4th PM - 1831 MN/WI	26-N	14-W
PITZRICK	9	1	4th PM - 1831 MN/WI	29-N	14-W
PLAISTED	24	4	4th PM - 1831 MN/WI	26-N	11-W
PLANT	2	18	4th PM - 1831 MN/WI	31-N	13-W
" "	1	2	4th PM - 1831 MN/WI	31-N	14-W
PLATT	5	4	4th PM - 1831 MN/WI	30-N	14-W
POISKE	7	1	4th PM - 1831 MN/WI	30-N	12-W
POLLY	14	4	4th PM - 1831 MN/WI	28-N	13-W
PONTOW	18	1	4th PM - 1831 MN/WI	27-N	13-W
POOLER	12	4	4th PM - 1831 MN/WI	29-N	11-W
PORTER	18	3	4th PM - 1831 MN/WI	27-N	13-W
" "	5	2	4th PM - 1831 MN/WI	30-N	14-W
POST	17	1	4th PM - 1831 MN/WI	27-N	14-W
" "	16	1	4th PM - 1831 MN/WI	28-N	11-W
POTE	22	3	4th PM - 1831 MN/WI	26-N	13-W
POTETE	22	1	4th PM - 1831 MN/WI	26-N	13-W
POWELL	5	15	4th PM - 1831 MN/WI	30-N	14-W
POWERS	15	1	4th PM - 1831 MN/WI	28-N	12-W
PRATT	14	1	4th PM - 1831 MN/WI	28-N	13-W
PREMBLE	5	2	4th PM - 1831 MN/WI	30-N	14-W
PRESCOTT	24	2	4th PM - 1831 MN/WI	26-N	11-W
PRESTON	23	4	4th PM - 1831 MN/WI	26-N	12-W
" "	5	1	4th PM - 1831 MN/WI	30-N	14-W
PRETY	15	1	4th PM - 1831 MN/WI	28-N	12-W
PRICKETT	23	2	4th PM - 1831 MN/WI	26-N	12-W
PRILL	3	1	4th PM - 1831 MN/WI	31-N	12-W
PRIRCE	11	2	4th PM - 1831 MN/WI	29-N	12-W
PROPER	10	1	4th PM - 1831 MN/WI	29-N	13-W
PROPHET	14	3	4th PM - 1831 MN/WI	28-N	13-W
" "	13	2	4th PM - 1831 MN/WI	28-N	14-W
" "	15	1	4th PM - 1831 MN/WI	28-N	12-W
PROSSER	19	2	4th PM - 1831 MN/WI	27-N	12-W
PRUITT	14	2	4th PM - 1831 MN/WI	28-N	13-W
PUTNAM	20	8	4th PM - 1831 MN/WI	27-N	11-W
" "	16	5	4th PM - 1831 MN/WI	28-N	11-W
PUTNAN	20	2	4th PM - 1831 MN/WI	27-N	11-W
PUTNEY	6	1	4th PM - 1831 MN/WI	30-N	13-W
PYE	22	1	4th PM - 1831 MN/WI	26-N	13-W
QUADERER	2	1	4th PM - 1831 MN/WI	31-N	13-W
QUARLES	5	1	4th PM - 1831 MN/WI	30-N	14-W
QUIGGLE	24	3	4th PM - 1831 MN/WI	26-N	11-W
QUINN	9	2	4th PM - 1831 MN/WI	29-N	14-W
RACKWITZ	19	1	4th PM - 1831 MN/WI	27-N	12-W
RAIMER	15	1	4th PM - 1831 MN/WI	28-N	12-W
RAMSEY	20	3	4th PM - 1831 MN/WI	27-N	11-W
" "	21	2	4th PM - 1831 MN/WI	26-N	14-W
RAND	21	5	4th PM - 1831 MN/WI	26-N	14-W
" "	22	2	4th PM - 1831 MN/WI	26-N	13-W
" "	17	2	4th PM - 1831 MN/WI	27-N	14-W
RANDALL	2	2	4th PM - 1831 MN/WI	31-N	13-W
" "	20	1	4th PM - 1831 MN/WI	27-N	11-W
RANDELL	20	1	4th PM - 1831 MN/WI	27-N	11-W
RANDS	21	1	4th PM - 1831 MN/WI	26-N	14-W
RANNEY	24	3	4th PM - 1831 MN/WI	26-N	11-W

Surname	Map Group	Parcels of Land	Meridian/Township/Range		
RANNEY (Cont'd)	**20**	1	4th PM - 1831 MN/WI	27-N	11-W
RAPELYE	**8**	1	4th PM - 1831 MN/WI	30-N	11-W
RASMUSEN	**4**	2	4th PM - 1831 MN/WI	31-N	11-W
RASMUSON	**4**	1	4th PM - 1831 MN/WI	31-N	11-W
RASSBACH	**2**	3	4th PM - 1831 MN/WI	31-N	13-W
RAUENBUEHLER	**21**	1	4th PM - 1831 MN/WI	26-N	14-W
RAY	**24**	2	4th PM - 1831 MN/WI	26-N	11-W
RAYBURN	**22**	2	4th PM - 1831 MN/WI	26-N	13-W
REED	**16**	3	4th PM - 1831 MN/WI	28-N	11-W
" "	**13**	3	4th PM - 1831 MN/WI	28-N	14-W
" "	**5**	1	4th PM - 1831 MN/WI	30-N	14-W
" "	**1**	1	4th PM - 1831 MN/WI	31-N	14-W
REICHARD	**20**	3	4th PM - 1831 MN/WI	27-N	11-W
REINCKE	**15**	1	4th PM - 1831 MN/WI	28-N	12-W
REINECKE	**19**	1	4th PM - 1831 MN/WI	27-N	12-W
REINKE	**19**	1	4th PM - 1831 MN/WI	27-N	12-W
REKLEAN	**16**	1	4th PM - 1831 MN/WI	28-N	11-W
REMINGTON	**20**	8	4th PM - 1831 MN/WI	27-N	11-W
" "	**23**	3	4th PM - 1831 MN/WI	26-N	12-W
" "	**19**	1	4th PM - 1831 MN/WI	27-N	12-W
RENDELSBACHER	**14**	3	4th PM - 1831 MN/WI	28-N	13-W
REPINE	**20**	1	4th PM - 1831 MN/WI	27-N	11-W
RETZ	**6**	1	4th PM - 1831 MN/WI	30-N	13-W
REYMERT	**15**	1	4th PM - 1831 MN/WI	28-N	12-W
REYMOND	**15**	2	4th PM - 1831 MN/WI	28-N	12-W
REYNOLDS	**23**	5	4th PM - 1831 MN/WI	26-N	12-W
" "	**19**	3	4th PM - 1831 MN/WI	27-N	12-W
" "	**24**	2	4th PM - 1831 MN/WI	26-N	11-W
" "	**22**	1	4th PM - 1831 MN/WI	26-N	13-W
RICE	**18**	1	4th PM - 1831 MN/WI	27-N	13-W
" "	**14**	1	4th PM - 1831 MN/WI	28-N	13-W
" "	**7**	1	4th PM - 1831 MN/WI	30-N	12-W
RICHARDS	**18**	2	4th PM - 1831 MN/WI	27-N	13-W
RICHMOND	**5**	5	4th PM - 1831 MN/WI	30-N	14-W
RICKER	**20**	2	4th PM - 1831 MN/WI	27-N	11-W
RIDDELL	**24**	2	4th PM - 1831 MN/WI	26-N	11-W
RIDER	**19**	1	4th PM - 1831 MN/WI	27-N	12-W
RIEMER	**8**	1	4th PM - 1831 MN/WI	30-N	11-W
RIGGS	**5**	29	4th PM - 1831 MN/WI	30-N	14-W
" "	**1**	21	4th PM - 1831 MN/WI	31-N	14-W
RING	**1**	2	4th PM - 1831 MN/WI	31-N	14-W
RIPLEY	**19**	2	4th PM - 1831 MN/WI	27-N	12-W
" "	**22**	1	4th PM - 1831 MN/WI	26-N	13-W
" "	**20**	1	4th PM - 1831 MN/WI	27-N	11-W
" "	**15**	1	4th PM - 1831 MN/WI	28-N	12-W
RISS	**22**	1	4th PM - 1831 MN/WI	26-N	13-W
RITER	**15**	3	4th PM - 1831 MN/WI	28-N	12-W
RITTENHOUSE	**11**	8	4th PM - 1831 MN/WI	29-N	12-W
" "	**15**	1	4th PM - 1831 MN/WI	28-N	12-W
RITTER	**20**	3	4th PM - 1831 MN/WI	27-N	11-W
" "	**19**	1	4th PM - 1831 MN/WI	27-N	12-W
ROACH	**10**	4	4th PM - 1831 MN/WI	29-N	13-W
ROBBE	**16**	1	4th PM - 1831 MN/WI	28-N	11-W
ROBBINS	**24**	2	4th PM - 1831 MN/WI	26-N	11-W
ROBERTS	**24**	2	4th PM - 1831 MN/WI	26-N	11-W
" "	**21**	2	4th PM - 1831 MN/WI	26-N	14-W
" "	**1**	2	4th PM - 1831 MN/WI	31-N	14-W
" "	**20**	1	4th PM - 1831 MN/WI	27-N	11-W
ROBERTSON	**24**	3	4th PM - 1831 MN/WI	26-N	11-W
ROBISON	**20**	2	4th PM - 1831 MN/WI	27-N	11-W

Surname	Map Group	Parcels of Land	Meridian/Township/Range		
ROCK	**24**	2	4th PM - 1831 MN/WI	26-N	11-W
" "	**20**	2	4th PM - 1831 MN/WI	27-N	11-W
ROEMHILD	**2**	2	4th PM - 1831 MN/WI	31-N	13-W
ROGERS	**5**	1	4th PM - 1831 MN/WI	30-N	14-W
ROLEFF	**16**	2	4th PM - 1831 MN/WI	28-N	11-W
ROLSTAD	**3**	1	4th PM - 1831 MN/WI	31-N	12-W
ROMSAAS	**7**	4	4th PM - 1831 MN/WI	30-N	12-W
RONENG	**7**	1	4th PM - 1831 MN/WI	30-N	12-W
RONGSTAD	**8**	2	4th PM - 1831 MN/WI	30-N	11-W
RORK	**23**	6	4th PM - 1831 MN/WI	26-N	12-W
" "	**24**	2	4th PM - 1831 MN/WI	26-N	11-W
" "	**20**	2	4th PM - 1831 MN/WI	27-N	11-W
ROSE	**20**	1	4th PM - 1831 MN/WI	27-N	11-W
ROSEYCRANCE	**21**	1	4th PM - 1831 MN/WI	26-N	14-W
ROSS	**9**	1	4th PM - 1831 MN/WI	29-N	14-W
ROSSON	**21**	2	4th PM - 1831 MN/WI	26-N	14-W
ROSTANO	**7**	3	4th PM - 1831 MN/WI	30-N	12-W
ROSWELL	**11**	1	4th PM - 1831 MN/WI	29-N	12-W
ROTH	**13**	2	4th PM - 1831 MN/WI	28-N	14-W
ROWE	**15**	2	4th PM - 1831 MN/WI	28-N	12-W
" "	**18**	1	4th PM - 1831 MN/WI	27-N	13-W
RUE	**19**	2	4th PM - 1831 MN/WI	27-N	12-W
RULE	**4**	1	4th PM - 1831 MN/WI	31-N	11-W
RUMRILL	**20**	2	4th PM - 1831 MN/WI	27-N	11-W
RUMSEY	**19**	3	4th PM - 1831 MN/WI	27-N	12-W
RUNKLE	**4**	2	4th PM - 1831 MN/WI	31-N	11-W
RUNNING	**12**	3	4th PM - 1831 MN/WI	29-N	11-W
RUNNION	**14**	1	4th PM - 1831 MN/WI	28-N	13-W
RURICHT	**15**	1	4th PM - 1831 MN/WI	28-N	12-W
RUSH	**2**	2	4th PM - 1831 MN/WI	31-N	13-W
RYDER	**5**	2	4th PM - 1831 MN/WI	30-N	14-W
SABIN	**10**	2	4th PM - 1831 MN/WI	29-N	13-W
SAGSTUEN	**4**	1	4th PM - 1831 MN/WI	31-N	11-W
SAHLIE	**10**	2	4th PM - 1831 MN/WI	29-N	13-W
SAHLKE	**10**	1	4th PM - 1831 MN/WI	29-N	13-W
SALESBURY	**14**	2	4th PM - 1831 MN/WI	28-N	13-W
SAMPIRE	**2**	1	4th PM - 1831 MN/WI	31-N	13-W
SAMPSON	**18**	2	4th PM - 1831 MN/WI	27-N	13-W
" "	**4**	2	4th PM - 1831 MN/WI	31-N	11-W
SANDERS	**1**	1	4th PM - 1831 MN/WI	31-N	14-W
SANDERSON	**18**	3	4th PM - 1831 MN/WI	27-N	13-W
SANGER	**22**	2	4th PM - 1831 MN/WI	26-N	13-W
" "	**12**	2	4th PM - 1831 MN/WI	29-N	11-W
SAVILLE	**18**	1	4th PM - 1831 MN/WI	27-N	13-W
SAXTON	**23**	4	4th PM - 1831 MN/WI	26-N	12-W
SCANLAN	**18**	5	4th PM - 1831 MN/WI	27-N	13-W
SCHAAF	**20**	1	4th PM - 1831 MN/WI	27-N	11-W
SCHAEFER	**19**	3	4th PM - 1831 MN/WI	27-N	12-W
SCHAFNER	**21**	2	4th PM - 1831 MN/WI	26-N	14-W
SCHAMBERGER	**18**	1	4th PM - 1831 MN/WI	27-N	13-W
SCHECKEL	**22**	1	4th PM - 1831 MN/WI	26-N	13-W
SCHELHAD	**15**	1	4th PM - 1831 MN/WI	28-N	12-W
SCHIEBE	**16**	1	4th PM - 1831 MN/WI	28-N	11-W
SCHLOUGH	**2**	4	4th PM - 1831 MN/WI	31-N	13-W
SCHLUCH	**6**	1	4th PM - 1831 MN/WI	30-N	13-W
SCHLUCK	**2**	2	4th PM - 1831 MN/WI	31-N	13-W
SCHMITT	**21**	4	4th PM - 1831 MN/WI	26-N	14-W
" "	**22**	1	4th PM - 1831 MN/WI	26-N	13-W
SCHOLL	**3**	6	4th PM - 1831 MN/WI	31-N	12-W
SCHRIER	**9**	1	4th PM - 1831 MN/WI	29-N	14-W

Surname	Map Group	Parcels of Land	Meridian/Township/Range		
SCHROEDER	**11**	1	4th PM - 1831 MN/WI	29-N	12-W
SCHROETER	**21**	3	4th PM - 1831 MN/WI	26-N	14-W
SCHUBEL	**5**	3	4th PM - 1831 MN/WI	30-N	14-W
SCHULSTAD	**8**	3	4th PM - 1831 MN/WI	30-N	11-W
SCHUTTS	**9**	2	4th PM - 1831 MN/WI	29-N	14-W
SCOTT	**21**	1	4th PM - 1831 MN/WI	26-N	14-W
" "	**6**	1	4th PM - 1831 MN/WI	30-N	13-W
" "	**2**	1	4th PM - 1831 MN/WI	31-N	13-W
SEABERT	**14**	2	4th PM - 1831 MN/WI	28-N	13-W
SEAMAN	**16**	2	4th PM - 1831 MN/WI	28-N	11-W
SECOR	**23**	2	4th PM - 1831 MN/WI	26-N	12-W
SEE	**8**	4	4th PM - 1831 MN/WI	30-N	11-W
SEEDS	**12**	2	4th PM - 1831 MN/WI	29-N	11-W
SEEVER	**8**	2	4th PM - 1831 MN/WI	30-N	11-W
" "	**4**	2	4th PM - 1831 MN/WI	31-N	11-W
SEGUR	**22**	1	4th PM - 1831 MN/WI	26-N	13-W
SEILER	**22**	1	4th PM - 1831 MN/WI	26-N	13-W
SELLERS	**6**	2	4th PM - 1831 MN/WI	30-N	13-W
" "	**24**	1	4th PM - 1831 MN/WI	26-N	11-W
SEMMINGSEN	**8**	3	4th PM - 1831 MN/WI	30-N	11-W
SEMMINGSON	**12**	2	4th PM - 1831 MN/WI	29-N	11-W
" "	**8**	1	4th PM - 1831 MN/WI	30-N	11-W
SENG	**21**	2	4th PM - 1831 MN/WI	26-N	14-W
SERVIS	**5**	2	4th PM - 1831 MN/WI	30-N	14-W
SEVALDSON	**23**	1	4th PM - 1831 MN/WI	26-N	12-W
SEVERSON	**19**	3	4th PM - 1831 MN/WI	27-N	12-W
" "	**16**	3	4th PM - 1831 MN/WI	28-N	11-W
" "	**18**	1	4th PM - 1831 MN/WI	27-N	13-W
SEVERTSON	**8**	1	4th PM - 1831 MN/WI	30-N	11-W
SEXTON	**23**	3	4th PM - 1831 MN/WI	26-N	12-W
" "	**15**	1	4th PM - 1831 MN/WI	28-N	12-W
SEYMOUR	**20**	1	4th PM - 1831 MN/WI	27-N	11-W
SHAANE	**4**	1	4th PM - 1831 MN/WI	31-N	11-W
SHADBOLT	**6**	2	4th PM - 1831 MN/WI	30-N	13-W
SHAFER	**24**	4	4th PM - 1831 MN/WI	26-N	11-W
" "	**18**	1	4th PM - 1831 MN/WI	27-N	13-W
" "	**10**	1	4th PM - 1831 MN/WI	29-N	13-W
" "	**6**	1	4th PM - 1831 MN/WI	30-N	13-W
SHAFFER	**21**	1	4th PM - 1831 MN/WI	26-N	14-W
SHAFFNER	**21**	1	4th PM - 1831 MN/WI	26-N	14-W
SHANKLIN	**23**	2	4th PM - 1831 MN/WI	26-N	12-W
SHARPLES	**6**	2	4th PM - 1831 MN/WI	30-N	13-W
" "	**7**	1	4th PM - 1831 MN/WI	30-N	12-W
SHAW	**23**	3	4th PM - 1831 MN/WI	26-N	12-W
" "	**16**	3	4th PM - 1831 MN/WI	28-N	11-W
" "	**2**	1	4th PM - 1831 MN/WI	31-N	13-W
SHAY	**24**	1	4th PM - 1831 MN/WI	26-N	11-W
SHELTON	**3**	2	4th PM - 1831 MN/WI	31-N	12-W
SHEPARD	**15**	4	4th PM - 1831 MN/WI	28-N	12-W
" "	**6**	2	4th PM - 1831 MN/WI	30-N	13-W
" "	**14**	1	4th PM - 1831 MN/WI	28-N	13-W
SHEPHARD	**15**	2	4th PM - 1831 MN/WI	28-N	12-W
" "	**18**	1	4th PM - 1831 MN/WI	27-N	13-W
SHERBURN	**14**	1	4th PM - 1831 MN/WI	28-N	13-W
SHERBURNE	**15**	13	4th PM - 1831 MN/WI	28-N	12-W
" "	**14**	1	4th PM - 1831 MN/WI	28-N	13-W
SHERLOCK	**18**	1	4th PM - 1831 MN/WI	27-N	13-W
SHERMAN	**23**	1	4th PM - 1831 MN/WI	26-N	12-W
" "	**20**	1	4th PM - 1831 MN/WI	27-N	11-W
SHIELDS	**10**	2	4th PM - 1831 MN/WI	29-N	13-W

Surname	Map Group	Parcels of Land	Meridian/Township/Range		
SHIELDS (Cont'd)	**20**	1	4th PM - 1831 MN/WI	27-N	11-W
SHIELLS	**20**	3	4th PM - 1831 MN/WI	27-N	11-W
SHILTS	**9**	1	4th PM - 1831 MN/WI	29-N	14-W
SHIPMAN	**23**	2	4th PM - 1831 MN/WI	26-N	12-W
SHO-CHETTES	**24**	1	4th PM - 1831 MN/WI	26-N	11-W
SHUGERT	**23**	2	4th PM - 1831 MN/WI	26-N	12-W
SHULTZ	**6**	5	4th PM - 1831 MN/WI	30-N	13-W
SHUMAKER	**15**	1	4th PM - 1831 MN/WI	28-N	12-W
SIBBET	**2**	1	4th PM - 1831 MN/WI	31-N	13-W
SICKLES	**15**	1	4th PM - 1831 MN/WI	28-N	12-W
SIEBERT	**2**	2	4th PM - 1831 MN/WI	31-N	13-W
SIEDENBERG	**16**	2	4th PM - 1831 MN/WI	28-N	11-W
SIEFERT	**14**	2	4th PM - 1831 MN/WI	28-N	13-W
SIM-IS-HOYA	**1**	1	4th PM - 1831 MN/WI	31-N	14-W
SIMONS	**13**	1	4th PM - 1831 MN/WI	28-N	14-W
SINGERHAUS	**18**	1	4th PM - 1831 MN/WI	27-N	13-W
SINGERHOUSE	**18**	1	4th PM - 1831 MN/WI	27-N	13-W
SINTZ	**21**	1	4th PM - 1831 MN/WI	26-N	14-W
SIPPEL	**19**	2	4th PM - 1831 MN/WI	27-N	12-W
" "	**20**	1	4th PM - 1831 MN/WI	27-N	11-W
" "	**16**	1	4th PM - 1831 MN/WI	28-N	11-W
SIPPLE	**20**	1	4th PM - 1831 MN/WI	27-N	11-W
SISCHO	**7**	3	4th PM - 1831 MN/WI	30-N	12-W
SISSON	**7**	1	4th PM - 1831 MN/WI	30-N	12-W
SKEEL	**20**	1	4th PM - 1831 MN/WI	27-N	11-W
SKINNER	**20**	4	4th PM - 1831 MN/WI	27-N	11-W
SKJERLY	**3**	2	4th PM - 1831 MN/WI	31-N	12-W
SLAGEL	**21**	2	4th PM - 1831 MN/WI	26-N	14-W
SLAGLE	**21**	4	4th PM - 1831 MN/WI	26-N	14-W
SLICK	**20**	3	4th PM - 1831 MN/WI	27-N	11-W
" "	**10**	2	4th PM - 1831 MN/WI	29-N	13-W
SLOCUM	**9**	3	4th PM - 1831 MN/WI	29-N	14-W
SLOVER	**9**	2	4th PM - 1831 MN/WI	29-N	14-W
" "	**24**	1	4th PM - 1831 MN/WI	26-N	11-W
SLY	**1**	3	4th PM - 1831 MN/WI	31-N	14-W
" "	**20**	1	4th PM - 1831 MN/WI	27-N	11-W
SLYE	**16**	1	4th PM - 1831 MN/WI	28-N	11-W
SMEAD	**23**	3	4th PM - 1831 MN/WI	26-N	12-W
SMITH	**2**	7	4th PM - 1831 MN/WI	31-N	13-W
" "	**22**	5	4th PM - 1831 MN/WI	26-N	13-W
" "	**20**	4	4th PM - 1831 MN/WI	27-N	11-W
" "	**18**	4	4th PM - 1831 MN/WI	27-N	13-W
" "	**9**	4	4th PM - 1831 MN/WI	29-N	14-W
" "	**23**	3	4th PM - 1831 MN/WI	26-N	12-W
" "	**21**	3	4th PM - 1831 MN/WI	26-N	14-W
" "	**24**	2	4th PM - 1831 MN/WI	26-N	11-W
" "	**15**	2	4th PM - 1831 MN/WI	28-N	12-W
" "	**14**	1	4th PM - 1831 MN/WI	28-N	13-W
" "	**6**	1	4th PM - 1831 MN/WI	30-N	13-W
SNELL	**22**	3	4th PM - 1831 MN/WI	26-N	13-W
SNYDER	**7**	6	4th PM - 1831 MN/WI	30-N	12-W
" "	**8**	2	4th PM - 1831 MN/WI	30-N	11-W
" "	**18**	1	4th PM - 1831 MN/WI	27-N	13-W
" "	**2**	1	4th PM - 1831 MN/WI	31-N	13-W
SOLBERG	**12**	3	4th PM - 1831 MN/WI	29-N	11-W
SOLI	**12**	2	4th PM - 1831 MN/WI	29-N	11-W
SOLIE	**19**	1	4th PM - 1831 MN/WI	27-N	12-W
SOMMERKORN	**16**	1	4th PM - 1831 MN/WI	28-N	11-W
SONNENBURG	**8**	1	4th PM - 1831 MN/WI	30-N	11-W
SOPER	**11**	2	4th PM - 1831 MN/WI	29-N	12-W

Surname	Map Group	Parcels of Land	Meridian/Township/Range		
SORENSEN	**16**	4	4th PM - 1831 MN/WI	28-N	11-W
SORENSON	**16**	4	4th PM - 1831 MN/WI	28-N	11-W
SORKNESS	**8**	1	4th PM - 1831 MN/WI	30-N	11-W
SOUTHGATE	**16**	1	4th PM - 1831 MN/WI	28-N	11-W
SPAFFORD	**16**	7	4th PM - 1831 MN/WI	28-N	11-W
" "	**20**	2	4th PM - 1831 MN/WI	27-N	11-W
" "	**4**	2	4th PM - 1831 MN/WI	31-N	11-W
" "	**19**	1	4th PM - 1831 MN/WI	27-N	12-W
" "	**15**	1	4th PM - 1831 MN/WI	28-N	12-W
SPALDING	**22**	2	4th PM - 1831 MN/WI	26-N	13-W
" "	**20**	1	4th PM - 1831 MN/WI	27-N	11-W
SPENCE	**24**	3	4th PM - 1831 MN/WI	26-N	11-W
SPOONER	**16**	3	4th PM - 1831 MN/WI	28-N	11-W
SPRAGUE	**15**	4	4th PM - 1831 MN/WI	28-N	12-W
" "	**14**	2	4th PM - 1831 MN/WI	28-N	13-W
STAMPS	**1**	2	4th PM - 1831 MN/WI	31-N	14-W
STANLEY	**19**	2	4th PM - 1831 MN/WI	27-N	12-W
" "	**16**	2	4th PM - 1831 MN/WI	28-N	11-W
STANSBERRY	**2**	1	4th PM - 1831 MN/WI	31-N	13-W
STANSBERY	**2**	1	4th PM - 1831 MN/WI	31-N	13-W
STAPLES	**12**	3	4th PM - 1831 MN/WI	29-N	11-W
STARKWEATHER	**22**	3	4th PM - 1831 MN/WI	26-N	13-W
STEARNS	**23**	4	4th PM - 1831 MN/WI	26-N	12-W
STEBBINS	**16**	2	4th PM - 1831 MN/WI	28-N	11-W
STEEL	**23**	2	4th PM - 1831 MN/WI	26-N	12-W
STEEN	**5**	1	4th PM - 1831 MN/WI	30-N	14-W
STEENBARGER	**12**	1	4th PM - 1831 MN/WI	29-N	11-W
STEINMAN	**18**	1	4th PM - 1831 MN/WI	27-N	13-W
STENERSEN	**4**	3	4th PM - 1831 MN/WI	31-N	11-W
STENERSON	**3**	1	4th PM - 1831 MN/WI	31-N	12-W
STEPHENS	**19**	1	4th PM - 1831 MN/WI	27-N	12-W
STEPPACHER	**24**	2	4th PM - 1831 MN/WI	26-N	11-W
STEVENS	**23**	4	4th PM - 1831 MN/WI	26-N	12-W
" "	**13**	1	4th PM - 1831 MN/WI	28-N	14-W
" "	**6**	1	4th PM - 1831 MN/WI	30-N	13-W
STEVES	**23**	5	4th PM - 1831 MN/WI	26-N	12-W
STEWART	**15**	1	4th PM - 1831 MN/WI	28-N	12-W
STICKNEY	**5**	3	4th PM - 1831 MN/WI	30-N	14-W
" "	**6**	1	4th PM - 1831 MN/WI	30-N	13-W
STILES	**10**	8	4th PM - 1831 MN/WI	29-N	13-W
" "	**14**	3	4th PM - 1831 MN/WI	28-N	13-W
STILLEY	**8**	4	4th PM - 1831 MN/WI	30-N	11-W
STINGLUFF	**12**	1	4th PM - 1831 MN/WI	29-N	11-W
STINSON	**22**	1	4th PM - 1831 MN/WI	26-N	13-W
STOCKMAN	**18**	2	4th PM - 1831 MN/WI	27-N	13-W
STODDARD	**7**	2	4th PM - 1831 MN/WI	30-N	12-W
" "	**9**	1	4th PM - 1831 MN/WI	29-N	14-W
STONE	**24**	1	4th PM - 1831 MN/WI	26-N	11-W
" "	**20**	1	4th PM - 1831 MN/WI	27-N	11-W
STOUT	**14**	36	4th PM - 1831 MN/WI	28-N	13-W
" "	**2**	14	4th PM - 1831 MN/WI	31-N	13-W
" "	**1**	13	4th PM - 1831 MN/WI	31-N	14-W
" "	**22**	12	4th PM - 1831 MN/WI	26-N	13-W
" "	**23**	4	4th PM - 1831 MN/WI	26-N	12-W
" "	**18**	2	4th PM - 1831 MN/WI	27-N	13-W
" "	**15**	2	4th PM - 1831 MN/WI	28-N	12-W
" "	**8**	2	4th PM - 1831 MN/WI	30-N	11-W
" "	**5**	2	4th PM - 1831 MN/WI	30-N	14-W
STRATTON	**18**	3	4th PM - 1831 MN/WI	27-N	13-W
STROBRIDGE	**2**	2	4th PM - 1831 MN/WI	31-N	13-W

Surname	Map Group	Parcels of Land	Meridian/Township/Range		
STROTHER	**14**	1	4th PM - 1831 MN/WI	28-N	13-W
STROUD	**12**	1	4th PM - 1831 MN/WI	29-N	11-W
STUART	**1**	1	4th PM - 1831 MN/WI	31-N	14-W
STUBBS	**6**	2	4th PM - 1831 MN/WI	30-N	13-W
" "	**2**	1	4th PM - 1831 MN/WI	31-N	13-W
STUDABAKER	**10**	2	4th PM - 1831 MN/WI	29-N	13-W
" "	**6**	2	4th PM - 1831 MN/WI	30-N	13-W
STUDLEY	**12**	6	4th PM - 1831 MN/WI	29-N	11-W
STURTEVANT	**10**	1	4th PM - 1831 MN/WI	29-N	13-W
SUCKOW	**11**	1	4th PM - 1831 MN/WI	29-N	12-W
SUKOW	**14**	1	4th PM - 1831 MN/WI	28-N	13-W
SUMMERS	**1**	1	4th PM - 1831 MN/WI	31-N	14-W
SUNDERLIN	**22**	1	4th PM - 1831 MN/WI	26-N	13-W
SUSEY	**1**	1	4th PM - 1831 MN/WI	31-N	14-W
SUTLIFF	**5**	6	4th PM - 1831 MN/WI	30-N	14-W
SVENOMSON	**7**	2	4th PM - 1831 MN/WI	30-N	12-W
SVENUNGSON	**7**	1	4th PM - 1831 MN/WI	30-N	12-W
" "	**4**	1	4th PM - 1831 MN/WI	31-N	11-W
SWAN	**24**	3	4th PM - 1831 MN/WI	26-N	11-W
" "	**2**	2	4th PM - 1831 MN/WI	31-N	13-W
SWARTS	**1**	1	4th PM - 1831 MN/WI	31-N	14-W
SWARTWOOD	**1**	1	4th PM - 1831 MN/WI	31-N	14-W
SWEENY	**15**	1	4th PM - 1831 MN/WI	28-N	12-W
SWEET	**14**	2	4th PM - 1831 MN/WI	28-N	13-W
SWENSON	**6**	4	4th PM - 1831 MN/WI	30-N	13-W
" "	**24**	1	4th PM - 1831 MN/WI	26-N	11-W
SWIGER	**21**	1	4th PM - 1831 MN/WI	26-N	14-W
SWISHER	**18**	5	4th PM - 1831 MN/WI	27-N	13-W
" "	**20**	2	4th PM - 1831 MN/WI	27-N	11-W
SYLTE	**4**	4	4th PM - 1831 MN/WI	31-N	11-W
SYVERSEN	**12**	2	4th PM - 1831 MN/WI	29-N	11-W
" "	**4**	2	4th PM - 1831 MN/WI	31-N	11-W
TABOR	**6**	1	4th PM - 1831 MN/WI	30-N	13-W
TAINTER	**14**	36	4th PM - 1831 MN/WI	28-N	13-W
" "	**2**	14	4th PM - 1831 MN/WI	31-N	13-W
" "	**1**	13	4th PM - 1831 MN/WI	31-N	14-W
" "	**22**	12	4th PM - 1831 MN/WI	26-N	13-W
" "	**23**	4	4th PM - 1831 MN/WI	26-N	12-W
" "	**20**	3	4th PM - 1831 MN/WI	27-N	11-W
" "	**18**	2	4th PM - 1831 MN/WI	27-N	13-W
" "	**15**	2	4th PM - 1831 MN/WI	28-N	12-W
" "	**8**	2	4th PM - 1831 MN/WI	30-N	11-W
" "	**7**	2	4th PM - 1831 MN/WI	30-N	12-W
" "	**5**	2	4th PM - 1831 MN/WI	30-N	14-W
" "	**19**	1	4th PM - 1831 MN/WI	27-N	12-W
TALMAGE	**6**	1	4th PM - 1831 MN/WI	30-N	13-W
TANDE	**8**	1	4th PM - 1831 MN/WI	30-N	11-W
TANTON	**20**	1	4th PM - 1831 MN/WI	27-N	11-W
TAPLIN	**17**	3	4th PM - 1831 MN/WI	27-N	14-W
TAYLOR	**19**	6	4th PM - 1831 MN/WI	27-N	12-W
" "	**20**	4	4th PM - 1831 MN/WI	27-N	11-W
" "	**23**	2	4th PM - 1831 MN/WI	26-N	12-W
" "	**12**	2	4th PM - 1831 MN/WI	29-N	11-W
" "	**10**	2	4th PM - 1831 MN/WI	29-N	13-W
" "	**5**	2	4th PM - 1831 MN/WI	30-N	14-W
" "	**2**	2	4th PM - 1831 MN/WI	31-N	13-W
" "	**16**	1	4th PM - 1831 MN/WI	28-N	11-W
" "	**14**	1	4th PM - 1831 MN/WI	28-N	13-W
" "	**6**	1	4th PM - 1831 MN/WI	30-N	13-W
TEEGARDEN	**9**	2	4th PM - 1831 MN/WI	29-N	14-W

Surname	Map Group	Parcels of Land	Meridian/Township/Range		
TEEL	**20**	2	4th PM - 1831 MN/WI	27-N	11-W
TEIGENSKAU	**12**	2	4th PM - 1831 MN/WI	29-N	11-W
TERRILL	**6**	2	4th PM - 1831 MN/WI	30-N	13-W
THANE	**18**	2	4th PM - 1831 MN/WI	27-N	13-W
THAYER	**10**	1	4th PM - 1831 MN/WI	29-N	13-W
THIBODO	**15**	1	4th PM - 1831 MN/WI	28-N	12-W
THOMAS	**2**	5	4th PM - 1831 MN/WI	31-N	13-W
" "	**6**	3	4th PM - 1831 MN/WI	30-N	13-W
" "	**24**	1	4th PM - 1831 MN/WI	26-N	11-W
" "	**19**	1	4th PM - 1831 MN/WI	27-N	12-W
" "	**10**	1	4th PM - 1831 MN/WI	29-N	13-W
" "	**5**	1	4th PM - 1831 MN/WI	30-N	14-W
" "	**3**	1	4th PM - 1831 MN/WI	31-N	12-W
THOMPSON	**3**	7	4th PM - 1831 MN/WI	31-N	12-W
" "	**4**	5	4th PM - 1831 MN/WI	31-N	11-W
" "	**21**	4	4th PM - 1831 MN/WI	26-N	14-W
" "	**18**	4	4th PM - 1831 MN/WI	27-N	13-W
" "	**16**	4	4th PM - 1831 MN/WI	28-N	11-W
" "	**8**	4	4th PM - 1831 MN/WI	30-N	11-W
" "	**22**	2	4th PM - 1831 MN/WI	26-N	13-W
" "	**20**	2	4th PM - 1831 MN/WI	27-N	11-W
THORESEN	**8**	2	4th PM - 1831 MN/WI	30-N	11-W
THORN	**18**	1	4th PM - 1831 MN/WI	27-N	13-W
THORSEN	**3**	3	4th PM - 1831 MN/WI	31-N	12-W
THORSON	**3**	2	4th PM - 1831 MN/WI	31-N	12-W
THUE	**11**	3	4th PM - 1831 MN/WI	29-N	12-W
TIBBETTS	**22**	2	4th PM - 1831 MN/WI	26-N	13-W
TIFFANY	**2**	1	4th PM - 1831 MN/WI	31-N	13-W
TILLESEN	**16**	1	4th PM - 1831 MN/WI	28-N	11-W
TILLESON	**16**	8	4th PM - 1831 MN/WI	28-N	11-W
TIMMERMAN	**22**	1	4th PM - 1831 MN/WI	26-N	13-W
TIZEN	**4**	3	4th PM - 1831 MN/WI	31-N	11-W
TOBEY	**23**	2	4th PM - 1831 MN/WI	26-N	12-W
TOEL	**1**	11	4th PM - 1831 MN/WI	31-N	14-W
TOLASON	**15**	1	4th PM - 1831 MN/WI	28-N	12-W
TOLEDANO	**1**	2	4th PM - 1831 MN/WI	31-N	14-W
TOLEFSON	**16**	1	4th PM - 1831 MN/WI	28-N	11-W
TOLLEVSON	**8**	1	4th PM - 1831 MN/WI	30-N	11-W
TOLLOFSON	**8**	3	4th PM - 1831 MN/WI	30-N	11-W
TOMLINSON	**24**	3	4th PM - 1831 MN/WI	26-N	11-W
TORGERSON	**23**	1	4th PM - 1831 MN/WI	26-N	12-W
" "	**1**	1	4th PM - 1831 MN/WI	31-N	14-W
TORGUSSEN	**8**	2	4th PM - 1831 MN/WI	30-N	11-W
TORKELSON	**6**	3	4th PM - 1831 MN/WI	30-N	13-W
" "	**10**	1	4th PM - 1831 MN/WI	29-N	13-W
TOTMAN	**22**	1	4th PM - 1831 MN/WI	26-N	13-W
TOWNSEND	**24**	2	4th PM - 1831 MN/WI	26-N	11-W
TRASHER	**15**	2	4th PM - 1831 MN/WI	28-N	12-W
TRASK	**19**	4	4th PM - 1831 MN/WI	27-N	12-W
" "	**20**	2	4th PM - 1831 MN/WI	27-N	11-W
" "	**24**	1	4th PM - 1831 MN/WI	26-N	11-W
" "	**23**	1	4th PM - 1831 MN/WI	26-N	12-W
TRAVIS	**1**	1	4th PM - 1831 MN/WI	31-N	14-W
TREFETHREN	**8**	3	4th PM - 1831 MN/WI	30-N	11-W
TRIGG	**5**	2	4th PM - 1831 MN/WI	30-N	14-W
TRONSEN	**12**	1	4th PM - 1831 MN/WI	29-N	11-W
TROSVIG	**4**	4	4th PM - 1831 MN/WI	31-N	11-W
TUBBS	**20**	6	4th PM - 1831 MN/WI	27-N	11-W
" "	**23**	2	4th PM - 1831 MN/WI	26-N	12-W
" "	**19**	2	4th PM - 1831 MN/WI	27-N	12-W

Surname	Map Group	Parcels of Land	Meridian/Township/Range		
TURNER	**22**	2	4th PM - 1831 MN/WI	26-N	13-W
" "	**9**	2	4th PM - 1831 MN/WI	29-N	14-W
TUTTLE	**23**	4	4th PM - 1831 MN/WI	26-N	12-W
" "	**5**	4	4th PM - 1831 MN/WI	30-N	14-W
" "	**10**	2	4th PM - 1831 MN/WI	29-N	13-W
" "	**9**	2	4th PM - 1831 MN/WI	29-N	14-W
TUVENG	**6**	1	4th PM - 1831 MN/WI	30-N	13-W
TWEITEN	**16**	2	4th PM - 1831 MN/WI	28-N	11-W
TYLER	**15**	1	4th PM - 1831 MN/WI	28-N	12-W
ULRICH	**2**	1	4th PM - 1831 MN/WI	31-N	13-W
UMBARGER	**10**	2	4th PM - 1831 MN/WI	29-N	13-W
UNDERHILL	**24**	2	4th PM - 1831 MN/WI	26-N	11-W
URSINUS	**15**	1	4th PM - 1831 MN/WI	28-N	12-W
UTTER	**17**	1	4th PM - 1831 MN/WI	27-N	14-W
VAIL	**16**	3	4th PM - 1831 MN/WI	28-N	11-W
VAN ALLEN	**22**	1	4th PM - 1831 MN/WI	26-N	13-W
VAN PELT	**12**	1	4th PM - 1831 MN/WI	29-N	11-W
VAN RIPER	**14**	2	4th PM - 1831 MN/WI	28-N	13-W
VAN SLIKE	**6**	2	4th PM - 1831 MN/WI	30-N	13-W
VAN VETCHTEN	**18**	1	4th PM - 1831 MN/WI	27-N	13-W
VAN WOERT	**8**	4	4th PM - 1831 MN/WI	30-N	11-W
VANCE	**2**	6	4th PM - 1831 MN/WI	31-N	13-W
VANDERHOEF	**4**	2	4th PM - 1831 MN/WI	31-N	11-W
VARBLE	**1**	2	4th PM - 1831 MN/WI	31-N	14-W
VARNEY	**18**	2	4th PM - 1831 MN/WI	27-N	13-W
VASEY	**23**	2	4th PM - 1831 MN/WI	26-N	12-W
" "	**22**	2	4th PM - 1831 MN/WI	26-N	13-W
VAUGHAN	**12**	3	4th PM - 1831 MN/WI	29-N	11-W
" "	**16**	2	4th PM - 1831 MN/WI	28-N	11-W
VEDDER	**24**	1	4th PM - 1831 MN/WI	26-N	11-W
VIBBERTS	**24**	2	4th PM - 1831 MN/WI	26-N	11-W
" "	**20**	2	4th PM - 1831 MN/WI	27-N	11-W
VIETS	**24**	1	4th PM - 1831 MN/WI	26-N	11-W
VOEGT	**21**	2	4th PM - 1831 MN/WI	26-N	14-W
VOORIS	**15**	2	4th PM - 1831 MN/WI	28-N	12-W
VROMAN	**23**	1	4th PM - 1831 MN/WI	26-N	12-W
VROOMAN	**24**	2	4th PM - 1831 MN/WI	26-N	11-W
WACHTER	**5**	2	4th PM - 1831 MN/WI	30-N	14-W
WADE	**22**	1	4th PM - 1831 MN/WI	26-N	13-W
" "	**21**	1	4th PM - 1831 MN/WI	26-N	14-W
WAGNER	**6**	3	4th PM - 1831 MN/WI	30-N	13-W
" "	**15**	1	4th PM - 1831 MN/WI	28-N	12-W
WAGONER	**24**	1	4th PM - 1831 MN/WI	26-N	11-W
WAINZIRL	**21**	1	4th PM - 1831 MN/WI	26-N	14-W
WAIT	**18**	2	4th PM - 1831 MN/WI	27-N	13-W
" "	**10**	2	4th PM - 1831 MN/WI	29-N	13-W
" "	**1**	1	4th PM - 1831 MN/WI	31-N	14-W
WA-KE-MA-WET	**19**	1	4th PM - 1831 MN/WI	27-N	12-W
WALKER	**24**	5	4th PM - 1831 MN/WI	26-N	11-W
" "	**18**	4	4th PM - 1831 MN/WI	27-N	13-W
" "	**22**	2	4th PM - 1831 MN/WI	26-N	13-W
" "	**15**	2	4th PM - 1831 MN/WI	28-N	12-W
" "	**23**	1	4th PM - 1831 MN/WI	26-N	12-W
" "	**12**	1	4th PM - 1831 MN/WI	29-N	11-W
" "	**1**	1	4th PM - 1831 MN/WI	31-N	14-W
WALLACE	**18**	1	4th PM - 1831 MN/WI	27-N	13-W
WARD	**24**	1	4th PM - 1831 MN/WI	26-N	11-W
" "	**5**	1	4th PM - 1831 MN/WI	30-N	14-W
WARE	**20**	3	4th PM - 1831 MN/WI	27-N	11-W
WARREN	**18**	1	4th PM - 1831 MN/WI	27-N	13-W

Surname	Map Group	Parcels of Land	Meridian/Township/Range		
WARREN (Cont'd)	**7**	1	4th PM - 1831 MN/WI	30-N	12-W
WASHBURN	**2**	5	4th PM - 1831 MN/WI	31-N	13-W
WASHBURNE	**22**	1	4th PM - 1831 MN/WI	26-N	13-W
WATERSTON	**19**	1	4th PM - 1831 MN/WI	27-N	12-W
WATKINS	**15**	2	4th PM - 1831 MN/WI	28-N	12-W
WATSON	**24**	2	4th PM - 1831 MN/WI	26-N	11-W
" "	**21**	1	4th PM - 1831 MN/WI	26-N	14-W
WATTERMAN	**24**	2	4th PM - 1831 MN/WI	26-N	11-W
WEAVER	**7**	3	4th PM - 1831 MN/WI	30-N	12-W
WEBB	**24**	6	4th PM - 1831 MN/WI	26-N	11-W
" "	**22**	3	4th PM - 1831 MN/WI	26-N	13-W
" "	**20**	3	4th PM - 1831 MN/WI	27-N	11-W
WEBER	**21**	7	4th PM - 1831 MN/WI	26-N	14-W
WEBERT	**16**	1	4th PM - 1831 MN/WI	28-N	11-W
WEBSTER	**6**	2	4th PM - 1831 MN/WI	30-N	13-W
" "	**17**	1	4th PM - 1831 MN/WI	27-N	14-W
" "	**10**	1	4th PM - 1831 MN/WI	29-N	13-W
WEILLER	**16**	1	4th PM - 1831 MN/WI	28-N	11-W
WEIMAN	**11**	1	4th PM - 1831 MN/WI	29-N	12-W
WELCH	**22**	1	4th PM - 1831 MN/WI	26-N	13-W
WELLS	**23**	2	4th PM - 1831 MN/WI	26-N	12-W
WELTON	**6**	1	4th PM - 1831 MN/WI	30-N	13-W
WENNES	**6**	3	4th PM - 1831 MN/WI	30-N	13-W
WERNER	**4**	3	4th PM - 1831 MN/WI	31-N	11-W
WEST	**1**	5	4th PM - 1831 MN/WI	31-N	14-W
" "	**18**	1	4th PM - 1831 MN/WI	27-N	13-W
WESTERMEYER	**21**	1	4th PM - 1831 MN/WI	26-N	14-W
WESTON	**24**	4	4th PM - 1831 MN/WI	26-N	11-W
" "	**18**	2	4th PM - 1831 MN/WI	27-N	13-W
" "	**3**	1	4th PM - 1831 MN/WI	31-N	12-W
WETHERBY	**9**	5	4th PM - 1831 MN/WI	29-N	14-W
WHALEY	**14**	1	4th PM - 1831 MN/WI	28-N	13-W
WHEELER	**10**	2	4th PM - 1831 MN/WI	29-N	13-W
" "	**23**	1	4th PM - 1831 MN/WI	26-N	12-W
" "	**18**	1	4th PM - 1831 MN/WI	27-N	13-W
" "	**15**	1	4th PM - 1831 MN/WI	28-N	12-W
WHINERY	**15**	2	4th PM - 1831 MN/WI	28-N	12-W
WHIPPLE	**24**	2	4th PM - 1831 MN/WI	26-N	11-W
" "	**5**	1	4th PM - 1831 MN/WI	30-N	14-W
WHISLER	**1**	3	4th PM - 1831 MN/WI	31-N	14-W
WHITE	**20**	5	4th PM - 1831 MN/WI	27-N	11-W
" "	**10**	4	4th PM - 1831 MN/WI	29-N	13-W
" "	**15**	3	4th PM - 1831 MN/WI	28-N	12-W
" "	**14**	1	4th PM - 1831 MN/WI	28-N	13-W
WHITEFORD	**13**	1	4th PM - 1831 MN/WI	28-N	14-W
WHITELEY	**20**	3	4th PM - 1831 MN/WI	27-N	11-W
WHITEMAN	**5**	2	4th PM - 1831 MN/WI	30-N	14-W
WHITLLESEY	**24**	1	4th PM - 1831 MN/WI	26-N	11-W
WHITTLESEY	**24**	6	4th PM - 1831 MN/WI	26-N	11-W
WICHSER	**14**	3	4th PM - 1831 MN/WI	28-N	13-W
WICKS	**16**	1	4th PM - 1831 MN/WI	28-N	11-W
WIEMAN	**11**	1	4th PM - 1831 MN/WI	29-N	12-W
WIEMANN	**11**	2	4th PM - 1831 MN/WI	29-N	12-W
WIGEN	**3**	1	4th PM - 1831 MN/WI	31-N	12-W
WIGGINS	**20**	6	4th PM - 1831 MN/WI	27-N	11-W
" "	**19**	2	4th PM - 1831 MN/WI	27-N	12-W
" "	**23**	1	4th PM - 1831 MN/WI	26-N	12-W
WIGHT	**12**	1	4th PM - 1831 MN/WI	29-N	11-W
WILBUR	**9**	1	4th PM - 1831 MN/WI	29-N	14-W
WILKINS	**24**	4	4th PM - 1831 MN/WI	26-N	11-W

Surname	Map Group	Parcels of Land	Meridian/Township/Range		
WILKINS (Cont'd)	**23**	2	4th PM - 1831 MN/WI	26-N	12-W
WILLEY	**22**	1	4th PM - 1831 MN/WI	26-N	13-W
WILLIAMS	**20**	6	4th PM - 1831 MN/WI	27-N	11-W
" "	**21**	2	4th PM - 1831 MN/WI	26-N	14-W
" "	**5**	2	4th PM - 1831 MN/WI	30-N	14-W
" "	**10**	1	4th PM - 1831 MN/WI	29-N	13-W
" "	**6**	1	4th PM - 1831 MN/WI	30-N	13-W
WILLIAMSON	**15**	1	4th PM - 1831 MN/WI	28-N	12-W
" "	**8**	1	4th PM - 1831 MN/WI	30-N	11-W
WILLIFORD	**24**	1	4th PM - 1831 MN/WI	26-N	11-W
WILLOCK-HOYE	**1**	1	4th PM - 1831 MN/WI	31-N	14-W
WILSON	**14**	52	4th PM - 1831 MN/WI	28-N	13-W
" "	**22**	16	4th PM - 1831 MN/WI	26-N	13-W
" "	**2**	15	4th PM - 1831 MN/WI	31-N	13-W
" "	**1**	13	4th PM - 1831 MN/WI	31-N	14-W
" "	**5**	10	4th PM - 1831 MN/WI	30-N	14-W
" "	**18**	9	4th PM - 1831 MN/WI	27-N	13-W
" "	**11**	8	4th PM - 1831 MN/WI	29-N	12-W
" "	**15**	7	4th PM - 1831 MN/WI	28-N	12-W
" "	**10**	7	4th PM - 1831 MN/WI	29-N	13-W
" "	**23**	6	4th PM - 1831 MN/WI	26-N	12-W
" "	**21**	5	4th PM - 1831 MN/WI	26-N	14-W
" "	**19**	4	4th PM - 1831 MN/WI	27-N	12-W
" "	**8**	2	4th PM - 1831 MN/WI	30-N	11-W
" "	**16**	1	4th PM - 1831 MN/WI	28-N	11-W
WILSTACH	**23**	6	4th PM - 1831 MN/WI	26-N	12-W
WILSTACK	**23**	7	4th PM - 1831 MN/WI	26-N	12-W
WINSLOW	**24**	2	4th PM - 1831 MN/WI	26-N	11-W
WISCONSIN	**24**	1	4th PM - 1831 MN/WI	26-N	11-W
" "	**23**	1	4th PM - 1831 MN/WI	26-N	12-W
" "	**22**	1	4th PM - 1831 MN/WI	26-N	13-W
" "	**21**	1	4th PM - 1831 MN/WI	26-N	14-W
" "	**20**	1	4th PM - 1831 MN/WI	27-N	11-W
" "	**19**	1	4th PM - 1831 MN/WI	27-N	12-W
" "	**18**	1	4th PM - 1831 MN/WI	27-N	13-W
" "	**17**	1	4th PM - 1831 MN/WI	27-N	14-W
" "	**16**	1	4th PM - 1831 MN/WI	28-N	11-W
" "	**15**	1	4th PM - 1831 MN/WI	28-N	12-W
" "	**14**	1	4th PM - 1831 MN/WI	28-N	13-W
" "	**13**	1	4th PM - 1831 MN/WI	28-N	14-W
" "	**12**	1	4th PM - 1831 MN/WI	29-N	11-W
" "	**11**	1	4th PM - 1831 MN/WI	29-N	12-W
" "	**10**	1	4th PM - 1831 MN/WI	29-N	13-W
" "	**9**	1	4th PM - 1831 MN/WI	29-N	14-W
" "	**8**	1	4th PM - 1831 MN/WI	30-N	11-W
" "	**7**	1	4th PM - 1831 MN/WI	30-N	12-W
" "	**6**	1	4th PM - 1831 MN/WI	30-N	13-W
" "	**5**	1	4th PM - 1831 MN/WI	30-N	14-W
" "	**4**	1	4th PM - 1831 MN/WI	31-N	11-W
" "	**3**	1	4th PM - 1831 MN/WI	31-N	12-W
" "	**2**	1	4th PM - 1831 MN/WI	31-N	13-W
" "	**1**	1	4th PM - 1831 MN/WI	31-N	14-W
WISEMAN	**4**	1	4th PM - 1831 MN/WI	31-N	11-W
WITT	**6**	4	4th PM - 1831 MN/WI	30-N	13-W
WOLD	**7**	4	4th PM - 1831 MN/WI	30-N	12-W
WOOD	**16**	3	4th PM - 1831 MN/WI	28-N	11-W
" "	**24**	2	4th PM - 1831 MN/WI	26-N	11-W
" "	**19**	2	4th PM - 1831 MN/WI	27-N	12-W
" "	**11**	2	4th PM - 1831 MN/WI	29-N	12-W
" "	**2**	2	4th PM - 1831 MN/WI	31-N	13-W

Surname	Map Group	Parcels of Land	Meridian/Township/Range		
WOODHOUSE	**22**	1	4th PM - 1831 MN/WI	26-N	13-W
WOODHULL	**19**	1	4th PM - 1831 MN/WI	27-N	12-W
WOODMAN	**20**	5	4th PM - 1831 MN/WI	27-N	11-W
" "	**2**	2	4th PM - 1831 MN/WI	31-N	13-W
" "	**22**	1	4th PM - 1831 MN/WI	26-N	13-W
" "	**15**	1	4th PM - 1831 MN/WI	28-N	12-W
WOODS	**10**	7	4th PM - 1831 MN/WI	29-N	13-W
" "	**21**	1	4th PM - 1831 MN/WI	26-N	14-W
WOODWARD	**20**	11	4th PM - 1831 MN/WI	27-N	11-W
" "	**23**	4	4th PM - 1831 MN/WI	26-N	12-W
" "	**19**	4	4th PM - 1831 MN/WI	27-N	12-W
" "	**16**	4	4th PM - 1831 MN/WI	28-N	11-W
" "	**12**	2	4th PM - 1831 MN/WI	29-N	11-W
" "	**22**	1	4th PM - 1831 MN/WI	26-N	13-W
" "	**15**	1	4th PM - 1831 MN/WI	28-N	12-W
WOODWORTH	**22**	1	4th PM - 1831 MN/WI	26-N	13-W
" "	**12**	1	4th PM - 1831 MN/WI	29-N	11-W
WRIGHT	**16**	2	4th PM - 1831 MN/WI	28-N	11-W
" "	**12**	2	4th PM - 1831 MN/WI	29-N	11-W
" "	**18**	1	4th PM - 1831 MN/WI	27-N	13-W
" "	**14**	1	4th PM - 1831 MN/WI	28-N	13-W
WYLIE	**23**	2	4th PM - 1831 MN/WI	26-N	12-W
WYMAN	**11**	1	4th PM - 1831 MN/WI	29-N	12-W
YAPLE	**11**	1	4th PM - 1831 MN/WI	29-N	12-W
YARDLEY	**2**	2	4th PM - 1831 MN/WI	31-N	13-W
YEAMAN	**16**	2	4th PM - 1831 MN/WI	28-N	11-W
YODER	**9**	2	4th PM - 1831 MN/WI	29-N	14-W
YOKES	**16**	2	4th PM - 1831 MN/WI	28-N	11-W
YOUNG	**18**	5	4th PM - 1831 MN/WI	27-N	13-W
" "	**20**	1	4th PM - 1831 MN/WI	27-N	11-W
" "	**19**	1	4th PM - 1831 MN/WI	27-N	12-W
" "	**15**	1	4th PM - 1831 MN/WI	28-N	12-W
ZIBBLE	**21**	1	4th PM - 1831 MN/WI	26-N	14-W
ZIELIE	**23**	2	4th PM - 1831 MN/WI	26-N	12-W
ZIMERMAN	**15**	2	4th PM - 1831 MN/WI	28-N	12-W
ZUEHLKE	**11**	1	4th PM - 1831 MN/WI	29-N	12-W

– Part II –

Township Map Groups

Map Group 1: Index to Land Patents

Township 31-North Range 14-West (4th PM - 1831 MN/WI)

After you locate an individual in this Index, take note of the Section and Section Part then proceed to the Land Patent map on the pages immediately following. You should have no difficulty locating the corresponding parcel of land.

The "For More Info" Column will lead you to more information about the underlying Patents. See the *Legend* at right, and the "How to Use this Book" chapter, for more information.

LEGEND

"For More Info . . . " column

A = Authority (Legislative Act, See Appendix "A")
B = Block or Lot (location in Section unknown)
C = Cancelled Patent
F = Fractional Section
G = Group (Multi-Patentee Patent, see Appendix "C")
V = Overlaps another Parcel
R = Re-Issued (Parcel patented more than once)

(A & G items require you to look in the Appendixes referred to above. All other Letter-designations followed by a number require you to locate line-items in this index that possess the ID number found after the letter).

ID	Individual in Patent	Sec.	Sec. Part	Date Issued	Other Counties	For More Info . . .
67	ALLEN, Gilbert	28	SWSE	1881-09-17		A6
80	ALLISON, John	28	E½NW	1860-07-16		A5
81	" "	28	W½NE	1860-07-16		A5
82	" "	8	NE	1860-07-16		A5
83	" "	8	SE	1860-07-16		A5 G6
84	BABBITT, John	20	NE	1882-04-10		A6
68	BALDWIN, H J	30	NWNW	1888-08-06		A2 F
73	BENNER, Henry	28	W½NW	1882-04-10		A6
2	BEST, Alexander H	32	W½SW	1878-06-24		A6
7	BEST, Charles M	8	S½SW	1886-04-10		A6
25	BEST, Edward T	32	E½SE	1877-03-20		A6
129	BEST, S T	24	NE	1878-11-30		A6
148	BEST, William H	32	SESW	1888-11-15		A2
77	BISS, James	28	E½NE	1873-01-10		A6
78	" "	28	E½SE	1873-01-10		A6
9	BOARDMAN, Darius T	24	NW	1885-07-27		A6
26	BOND, Elizabeth A	30	E½NW	1878-06-24		A6 G156 F
27	" "	30	NWSW	1878-06-24		A6 G156 F
28	" "	30	SWNW	1878-06-24		A6 G156 F
126	BREWER, Philo	14	SE	1875-01-15		A6
17	BROWN, Che-par-nee	6	N½SE	1863-10-10		A5 G285
18	" "	6	NESW	1863-10-10		A5 G285
19	" "	6	SWSE	1863-10-10		A5 G285
121	BULMAN, Nathaniel	18	E½NW	1881-09-17		A6 F
122	" "	18	SWNW	1881-09-17		A6 F
86	CARMAN, John H	24	SE	1878-06-24		A6
79	CARVER, James S	10	NW	1885-05-20		A6
36	CHASE, Jonathan	21	NENW	1854-10-02		A2 G202
37	" "	21	NWNE	1854-10-02		A2 G202
38	" "	4	NENW	1854-10-02		A2 G202
39	" "	4	NWNE	1854-10-02		A2 G202
40	" "	4	NWNW	1854-10-02		A2 G202
113	" "	4	SENW	1854-10-02		A2
114	" "	4	SWNE	1854-10-02		A2
41	" "	5	NENE	1854-10-02		A2 G202
42	" "	5	SESW	1854-10-02		A2 G202
43	" "	5	SWSE	1854-10-02		A2 G202
44	" "	6	NWNW	1854-10-02		A2 G202
115	" "	6	SESE	1854-10-02		A2
8	CLARK, Clarence P	26	NWSW	1904-09-28		A6
11	CLARK, David H	36	SESW	1876-05-15		A6
12	" "	36	SWNW	1876-05-15		A6
13	" "	36	W½SW	1876-05-15		A6
69	CLARK, Elias	36	NESE	1876-05-15		A6 G75
70	" "	36	SENE	1876-05-15		A6 G75
69	CLARK, Hannah	36	NESE	1876-05-15		A6 G75

ID	Individual in Patent	Sec.	Sec. Part	Date Issued	Other Counties	For More Info . . .
70	CLARK, Hannah (Cont'd)	36	SENE	1876-05-15		A6 G75
48	CO, Riggs And	10	NE	1860-07-16		A5 G335
66	" "	18	NE	1860-07-16		A5 G339
53	" "	18	SE	1860-07-16		A5 G328
59	" "	20	NW	1860-07-16		A5 G328
46	" "	32	E½NW	1860-07-16		A5 G338
47	" "	32	NWNW	1860-07-16		A5 G338
50	" "	10	SWSE	1860-08-01		A5 G328 V51
51	" "	10	W½SE	1860-08-01		A5 G328 V50, 35
52	" "	12	NE	1860-08-01		A5 G328
54	" "	2	NESW	1860-08-01		A5 G328
55	" "	2	NWSW	1860-08-01		A5 G328
56	" "	2	S½NW	1860-08-01		A5 G328
57	" "	2	S½SW	1860-08-01		A5 G328
58	" "	2	SE	1860-08-01		A5 G328
60	" "	30	E½SE	1860-08-01		A5 G328
61	" "	30	E½SW	1860-08-01		A5 G328
62	" "	30	NWSE	1860-08-01		A5 G328
63	" "	30	SWSE	1860-08-01		A5 G328
49	" "	32	NE	1860-08-01		A5 G337
64	" "	32	NESW	1860-08-01		A5 G328
65	" "	32	W½SE	1860-08-01		A5 G328
10	CONNER, David	22	E½SE	1879-10-01		A6
20	CUSSETAH-MICCO,	4	NESE	1863-10-10		A5 G286
21	" "	4	S½SE	1863-10-10		A5 G286
22	" "	4	SENE	1863-10-10		A5 G286 R95
106	EIDAHL, John J	2	N½NE	1879-10-01		A6 F
107	" "	2	NENW	1879-10-01		A6 F
48	ELLIOTT, John	10	NE	1860-07-16		A5 G335
66	" "	18	NE	1860-07-16		A5 G339
53	" "	18	SE	1860-07-16		A5 G328
59	" "	20	NW	1860-07-16		A5 G328
46	" "	32	E½NW	1860-07-16		A5 G338
47	" "	32	NWNW	1860-07-16		A5 G338
50	" "	10	SWSE	1860-08-01		A5 G328 V51
51	" "	10	W½SE	1860-08-01		A5 G328 V50, 35
52	" "	12	NE	1860-08-01		A5 G328
54	" "	2	NESW	1860-08-01		A5 G328
55	" "	2	NWSW	1860-08-01		A5 G328
56	" "	2	S½NW	1860-08-01		A5 G328
57	" "	2	S½SW	1860-08-01		A5 G328
58	" "	2	SE	1860-08-01		A5 G328
60	" "	30	E½SE	1860-08-01		A5 G328
61	" "	30	E½SW	1860-08-01		A5 G328
62	" "	30	NWSE	1860-08-01		A5 G328
63	" "	30	SWSE	1860-08-01		A5 G328
49	" "	32	NE	1860-08-01		A5 G337
64	" "	32	NESW	1860-08-01		A5 G328
65	" "	32	W½SE	1860-08-01		A5 G328
128	FALLIS, Robert F	6	SWNW	1892-06-25		A6 F
34	FARRINGTON, Fremont D	36	S½SE	1883-02-10		A6
74	FRENCH, Homer L	10	SW	1881-09-17		A6
147	FRENCH, William E	22	SWSW	1875-10-01		A2
72	GILLESPIE, Fabian	18	SW	1860-02-01		A5 G305 F
26	GLENNY, Elizabeth A	30	E½NW	1878-06-24		A6 G156 F
27	" "	30	NWSW	1878-06-24		A6 G156 F
28	" "	30	SWNW	1878-06-24		A6 G156 F
127	GRINNELL, Ralph W	24	SW	1873-01-10		A6
125	HADLEY, Paul	34	SW	1876-11-03		A6
153	HARDAGE, Siah	4	N½SW	1860-10-01		A5 G399
154	" "	4	NWSE	1860-10-01		A5 G399
155	" "	4	SWNW	1860-10-01		A5 G399
75	HARMAN, Isaac	12	SW	1885-01-30		A6
123	HELGESON, Ole	2	NWNW	1878-06-01		A2 F
120	HUTCHINSON, Marshal	22	NE	1881-02-10		A6
4	JACOT, Augustus	20	NESE	1892-05-26		A6
117	JAMES, Joseph W	34	SWNE	1873-09-20		A6
36	JEWETT, George K	21	NENW	1854-10-02		A2 G202
37	" "	21	NWNE	1854-10-02		A2 G202
38	" "	4	NENW	1854-10-02		A2 G202
39	" "	4	NWNE	1854-10-02		A2 G202
40	" "	4	NWNW	1854-10-02		A2 G202
41	" "	5	NENE	1854-10-02		A2 G202

ID	Individual in Patent	Sec.	Sec. Part	Date Issued	Other Counties	For More Info . . .
42	JEWETT, George K (Cont'd)	5	SESW	1854-10-02		A2 G202
43	" "	5	SWSE	1854-10-02		A2 G202
44	" "	6	NWNW	1854-10-02		A2 G202
135	JEWETT, Samuel A	7	W½NW	1855-04-19		A2 C R136
130	" "	5	W½SW	1856-06-03		A7
138	" "	21	SENW	1856-06-16		A7 G203
139	" "	21	SWNE	1856-06-16		A7 G203
137	" "	5	NESW	1856-06-16		A7 G204
132	" "	6	S½SW	1856-06-16		A7
136	" "	7	W½NW	1856-06-16		A7 R135
134	" "	7	NENW	1856-10-01		A4
133	" "	6	SENW	1869-01-01		A2
131	" "	6	NWSW	1870-06-10		A2 F
20	JOHN,	4	NESE	1863-10-10		A5 G286
21	" "	4	S½SE	1863-10-10		A5 G286
22	" "	4	SENE	1863-10-10		A5 G286 R95
1	KALB, Adam	12	SE	1873-12-20		A6
48	KIECKHOEFER, A T	10	NE	1860-07-16		A5 G335
66	" "	18	NE	1860-07-16		A5 G339
53	" "	18	SE	1860-07-16		A5 G328
59	" "	20	NW	1860-07-16		A5 G328
46	" "	32	E½NW	1860-07-16		A5 G338
47	" "	32	NWNW	1860-07-16		A5 G338
50	" "	10	SWSE	1860-08-01		A5 G328 V51
51	" "	10	W½SE	1860-08-01		A5 G328 V50, 35
52	" "	12	NE	1860-08-01		A5 G328
54	" "	2	NESW	1860-08-01		A5 G328
55	" "	2	NWSW	1860-08-01		A5 G328
56	" "	2	S½NW	1860-08-01		A5 G328
57	" "	2	S½SW	1860-08-01		A5 G328
58	" "	2	SE	1860-08-01		A5 G328
60	" "	30	E½SE	1860-08-01		A5 G328
61	" "	30	E½SW	1860-08-01		A5 G328
62	" "	30	NWSE	1860-08-01		A5 G328
63	" "	30	SWSE	1860-08-01		A5 G328
49	" "	32	NE	1860-08-01		A5 G337
64	" "	32	NESW	1860-08-01		A5 G328
65	" "	32	W½SE	1860-08-01		A5 G328
23	KINNIARD, James	28	SW	1863-10-10		A5 G287
93	KNAPP, John H	17	SENE	1855-12-15		A2 G224
87	" "	20	NESW	1855-12-15		A2
88	" "	20	SESE	1855-12-15		A2
89	" "	21	N½SW	1855-12-15		A2
99	" "	21	NWSE	1855-12-15		A2 G219 V90
90	" "	21	W½SE	1855-12-15		A2 V99
91	" "	22	NWSW	1855-12-15		A2
92	" "	28	NWSE	1855-12-15		A2
94	" "	4	S½SW	1855-12-15		A2 G224
95	" "	4	SENE	1855-12-15		A2 G224 F R22
96	" "	5	SENE	1855-12-15		A2 G224
97	" "	9	NENW	1855-12-15		A2 G224
100	" "	6	NENW	1870-06-10		A2 G219 F
101	" "	8	NENW	1870-06-10		A2 G219
102	" "	8	NESW	1870-06-10		A2 G219
103	" "	8	NWSW	1870-06-10		A2 G219
105	" "	8	W½NW	1870-06-10		A2 G219
98	" "	18	NWNW	1871-04-05		A2 G219
104	" "	8	SENW	1871-04-05		A2 G219
119	KYES, Mark B	30	SWSW	1901-06-08		A6
35	LONG, George E	10	NWSE	1889-02-16		A6 V51
5	LORD, Charles D	26	NW	1873-12-20		A6 C R6
6	" "	26	NW	1874-04-01		A6 R5
17	MALINDA,	6	N½SE	1863-10-10		A5 G285
18	" "	6	NESW	1863-10-10		A5 G285
19	" "	6	SWSE	1863-10-10		A5 G285
36	MARCH, Leonard	21	NENW	1854-10-02		A2 G202
37	" "	21	NWNE	1854-10-02		A2 G202
38	" "	4	NENW	1854-10-02		A2 G202
39	" "	4	NWNE	1854-10-02		A2 G202
40	" "	4	NWNW	1854-10-02		A2 G202
41	" "	5	NENE	1854-10-02		A2 G202
42	" "	5	SESW	1854-10-02		A2 G202
43	" "	5	SWSE	1854-10-02		A2 G202

ID	Individual in Patent	Sec.	Sec. Part	Date Issued	Other Counties	For More Info . . .
44	MARCH, Leonard (Cont'd)	6	NWNW	1854-10-02		A2 G202
108	MARLETT, John	26	SWSW	1867-07-15		A2
109	MCKELHEER, John	34	E½NW	1874-07-15		A6
110	" "	34	NWNE	1874-07-15		A6
111	" "	34	NWNW	1874-07-15		A6
45	MONTEITH, George	34	SWNW	1903-06-27		A6
150	MONTEITH, William P	36	N½NE	1879-10-01		A6
151	" "	36	N½NW	1879-10-01		A6
149	MOSSNER, William	12	NW	1870-06-10		A2
153	NARSEE,	4	N½SW	1860-10-01		A5 G399
154	" "	4	NWSE	1860-10-01		A5 G399
155	" "	4	SWNW	1860-10-01		A5 G399
23	OCONNOR, Edgar	28	SW	1863-10-10		A5 G287
24	" "	30	NE	1863-10-10		A5 G288
20	" "	4	NESE	1863-10-10		A5 G286
21	" "	4	S½SE	1863-10-10		A5 G286
22	" "	4	SENE	1863-10-10		A5 G286 R95
17	" "	6	N½SE	1863-10-10		A5 G285
18	" "	6	NESW	1863-10-10		A5 G285
19	" "	6	SWSE	1863-10-10		A5 G285
48	OLIVER, Eleanor	10	NE	1860-07-16		A5 G335
83	PICKARD, Mercy	8	SE	1860-07-16		A5 G6
72	PLANT, Henry B	18	SW	1860-02-01		A5 G305 F
71	" "	19	NW	1860-02-01		A5 F
142	REED, Thomas	6	N½NE	1884-09-20		A6 F
48	RIGGS, George W	10	NE	1860-07-16		A5 G335
66	" "	18	NE	1860-07-16		A5 G339
53	" "	18	SE	1860-07-16		A5 G328
59	" "	20	NW	1860-07-16		A5 G328
46	" "	32	E½NW	1860-07-16		A5 G338
47	" "	32	NWNW	1860-07-16		A5 G338
50	" "	10	SWSE	1860-08-01		A5 G328 V51
51	" "	10	W½SE	1860-08-01		A5 G328 V50, 35
52	" "	12	NE	1860-08-01		A5 G328
54	" "	2	NESW	1860-08-01		A5 G328
55	" "	2	NWSW	1860-08-01		A5 G328
56	" "	2	S½NW	1860-08-01		A5 G328
57	" "	2	S½SW	1860-08-01		A5 G328
58	" "	2	SE	1860-08-01		A5 G328
60	" "	30	E½SE	1860-08-01		A5 G328
61	" "	30	E½SW	1860-08-01		A5 G328
62	" "	30	NWSE	1860-08-01		A5 G328
63	" "	30	SWSE	1860-08-01		A5 G328
49	" "	32	NE	1860-08-01		A5 G337
64	" "	32	NESW	1860-08-01		A5 G328
65	" "	32	W½SE	1860-08-01		A5 G328
29	RING, Elizabeth A	20	NWSW	1881-09-17		A6 G405
30	" "	20	S½SW	1881-09-17		A6 G405
31	ROBERTS, Francis	22	E½SW	1873-09-20		A6
32	" "	22	W½SE	1873-09-20		A6
49	SANDERS, Harriet H	32	NE	1860-08-01		A5 G337
23	SIM-IS-HOYA,	28	SW	1863-10-10		A5 G287
76	SLY, Ithamar	14	SW	1875-09-15		A6
112	SLY, John R	14	NE	1875-09-15		A6
116	SLY, Joseph C	14	NW	1875-09-15		A6
138	STAMPS, Sarah	21	SENW	1856-06-16		A7 G203
139	" "	21	SWNE	1856-06-16		A7 G203
93	STOUT, Henry L	17	SENE	1855-12-15		A2 G224
99	" "	21	NWSE	1855-12-15		A2 G219 V90
94	" "	4	S½SW	1855-12-15		A2 G224
95	" "	4	SENE	1855-12-15		A2 G224 F R22
96	" "	5	SENE	1855-12-15		A2 G224
97	" "	9	NENW	1855-12-15		A2 G224
100	" "	6	NENW	1870-06-10		A2 G219 F
101	" "	8	NENW	1870-06-10		A2 G219
102	" "	8	NESW	1870-06-10		A2 G219
103	" "	8	NWSW	1870-06-10		A2 G219
105	" "	8	W½NW	1870-06-10		A2 G219
98	" "	18	NWNW	1871-04-05		A2 G219
104	" "	8	SENW	1871-04-05		A2 G219
140	STUART, Samuel J	26	E½SE	1907-11-29		A2
137	SUMMERS, Mary	5	NESW	1856-06-16		A7 G204
23	SUSEY,	28	SW	1863-10-10		A5 G287

ID	Individual in Patent	Sec.	Sec. Part	Date Issued	Other Counties	For More Info . . .
85	SWARTS, John C	26	E½NE	1892-04-20		A6
152	SWARTWOOD, William	32	SWNW	1889-02-16		A6
93	TAINTER, Andrew	17	SENE	1855-12-15		A2 G224
99	" "	21	NWSE	1855-12-15		A2 G219 V90
94	" "	4	S½SW	1855-12-15		A2 G224
95	" "	4	SENE	1855-12-15		A2 G224 F R22
96	" "	5	SENE	1855-12-15		A2 G224
97	" "	9	NENW	1855-12-15		A2 G224
100	" "	6	NENW	1870-06-10		A2 G219 F
101	" "	8	NENW	1870-06-10		A2 G219
102	" "	8	NESW	1870-06-10		A2 G219
103	" "	8	NWSW	1870-06-10		A2 G219
105	" "	8	W½NW	1870-06-10		A2 G219
98	" "	18	NWNW	1871-04-05		A2 G219
104	" "	8	SENW	1871-04-05		A2 G219
153	TOEL, William	4	N½SW	1860-10-01		A5 G399
154	" "	4	NWSE	1860-10-01		A5 G399
155	" "	4	SWNW	1860-10-01		A5 G399
23	" "	28	SW	1863-10-10		A5 G287
24	" "	30	NE	1863-10-10		A5 G288
20	" "	4	NESE	1863-10-10		A5 G286
21	" "	4	S½SE	1863-10-10		A5 G286
22	" "	4	SENE	1863-10-10		A5 G286 R95
17	" "	6	N½SE	1863-10-10		A5 G285
18	" "	6	NESW	1863-10-10		A5 G285
19	" "	6	SWSE	1863-10-10		A5 G285
46	TOLEDANO, Arthur G	32	E½NW	1860-07-16		A5 G338
47	" "	32	NWNW	1860-07-16		A5 G338
124	TORGERSON, Ole	6	S½NE	1883-02-10		A6
118	TRAVIS, Leslie	22	NW	1878-06-24		A6
29	VARBLE, Elizabeth A	20	NWSW	1881-09-17		A6 G405
30	" "	20	S½SW	1881-09-17		A6 G405
33	WAIT, Fredrick	26	W½NE	1878-06-24		A6
66	WALKER, Robert D	18	NE	1860-07-16		A5 G339
14	WEST, David H	2	S½NE	1878-06-24		A6
143	WEST, Thomas	36	NESW	1873-09-20		A6
144	" "	36	NWSE	1873-09-20		A6
145	" "	36	SENW	1873-09-20		A6
146	" "	36	SWNE	1873-09-20		A6
3	WHISLER, Andrew	34	SE	1873-09-20		A6
15	WHISLER, David	26	E½SW	1875-04-01		A6
16	" "	26	W½SE	1875-04-01		A6
24	WILLOCK-HOYE,	30	NE	1863-10-10		A5 G288
93	WILSON, Thomas B	17	SENE	1855-12-15		A2 G224
99	" "	21	NWSE	1855-12-15		A2 G219 V90
94	" "	4	S½SW	1855-12-15		A2 G224
95	" "	4	SENE	1855-12-15		A2 G224 F R22
96	" "	5	SENE	1855-12-15		A2 G224
97	" "	9	NENW	1855-12-15		A2 G224
100	" "	6	NENW	1870-06-10		A2 G219 F
101	" "	8	NENW	1870-06-10		A2 G219
102	" "	8	NESW	1870-06-10		A2 G219
103	" "	8	NWSW	1870-06-10		A2 G219
105	" "	8	W½NW	1870-06-10		A2 G219
98	" "	18	NWNW	1871-04-05		A2 G219
104	" "	8	SENW	1871-04-05		A2 G219
141	WISCONSIN, State Of	16		1941-08-16		A3

Patent Map

T31-N R14-W
4th PM - 1831 MN/WI Meridian

Map Group 1

Township Statistics

Parcels Mapped	:	155
Number of Patents	:	107
Number of Individuals	:	95
Patentees Identified	:	80
Number of Surnames	:	81
Multi-Patentee Parcels	:	66
Oldest Patent Date	:	10/2/1854
Most Recent Patent	:	8/16/1941
Block/Lot Parcels	:	0
Parcels Re - Issued	:	3
Parcels that Overlap	:	5
Cities and Towns	:	1
Cemeteries	:	1

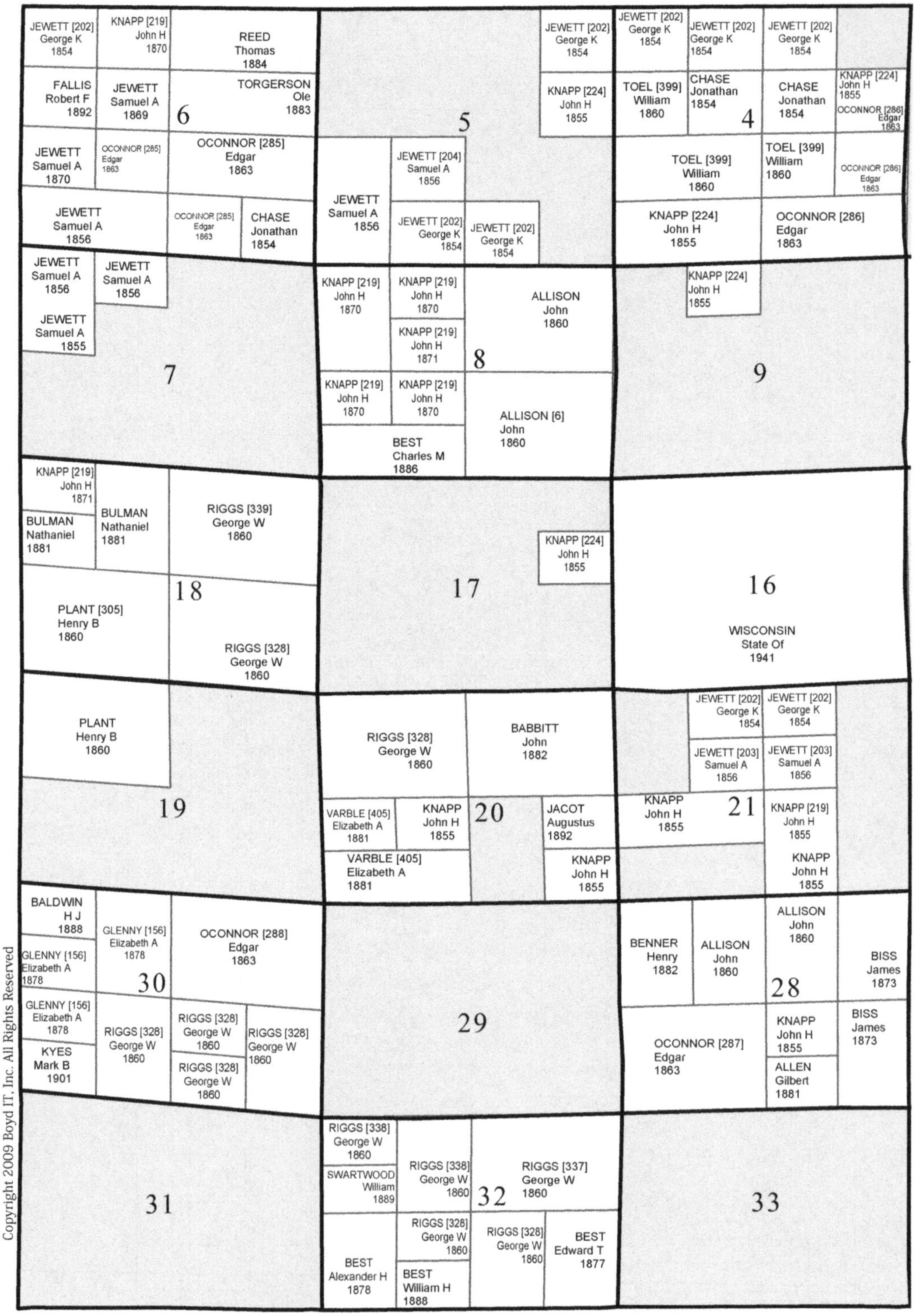

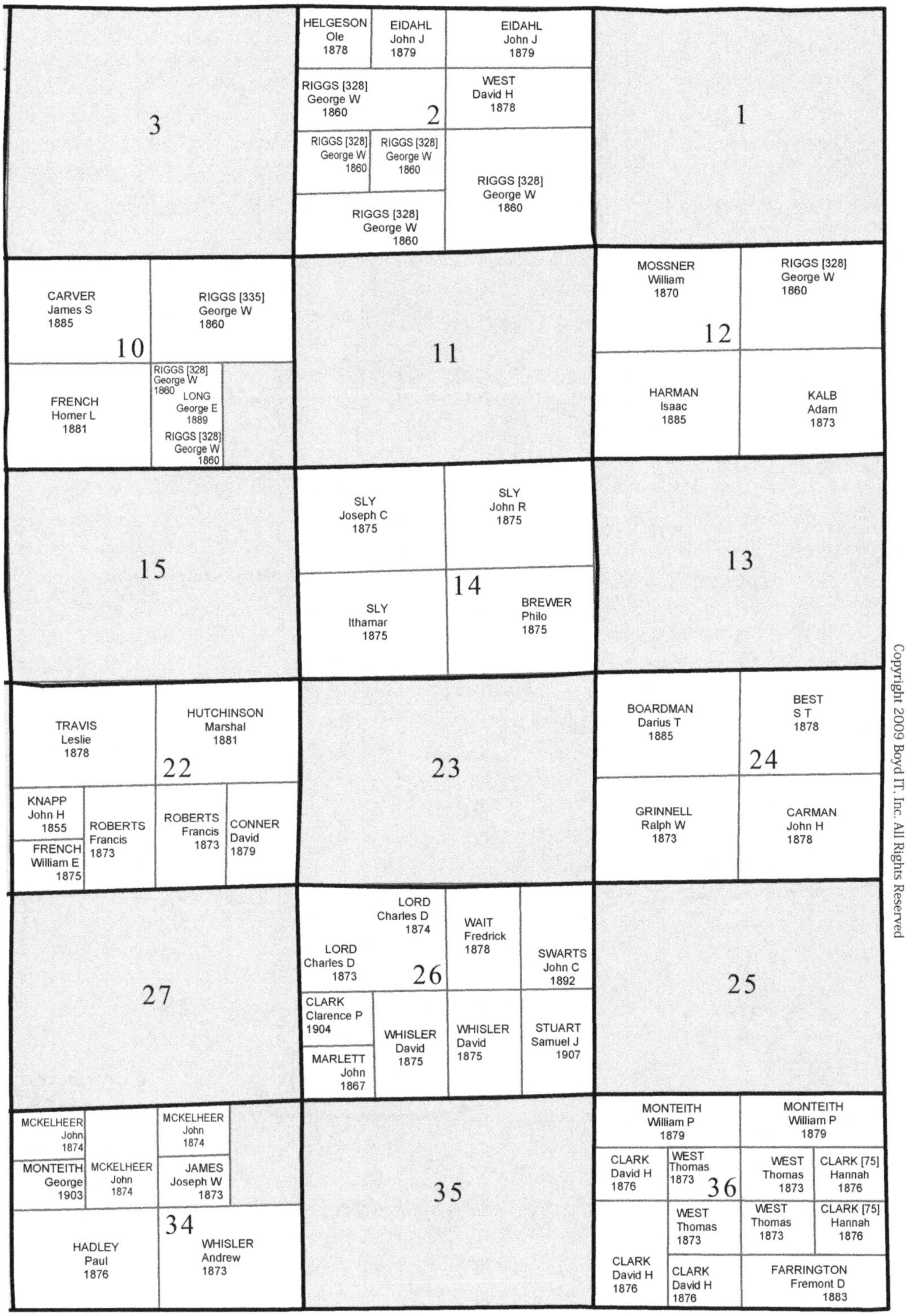
3
HELGESON Ole 1878
EIDAHL John J 1879
EIDAHL John J 1879
RIGGS [328] George W 1860
2
WEST David H 1878
RIGGS [328] George W 1860
RIGGS [328] George W 1860
RIGGS [328] George W 1860
RIGGS [328] George W 1860
1
CARVER James S 1885
RIGGS [335] George W 1860
10
FRENCH Homer L 1881
RIGGS [328] George W 1860
LONG George E 1889
RIGGS [328] George W 1860
11
MOSSNER William 1870
RIGGS [328] George W 1860
12
HARMAN Isaac 1885
KALB Adam 1873
15
SLY Joseph C 1875
SLY John R 1875
14
SLY Ithamar 1875
BREWER Philo 1875
13
TRAVIS Leslie 1878
HUTCHINSON Marshal 1881
22
KNAPP John H 1855
FRENCH William E 1875
ROBERTS Francis 1873
ROBERTS Francis 1873
CONNER David 1879
23
BOARDMAN Darius T 1885
BEST S T 1878
24
GRINNELL Ralph W 1873
CARMAN John H 1878
27
LORD Charles D 1874
LORD Charles D 1873
26
WAIT Fredrick 1878
SWARTS John C 1892
CLARK Clarence P 1904
MARLETT John 1867
WHISLER David 1875
WHISLER David 1875
STUART Samuel J 1907
25
MCKELHEER John 1874
MONTEITH George 1903
MCKELHEER John 1874
MCKELHEER John 1874
JAMES Joseph W 1873
34
HADLEY Paul 1876
WHISLER Andrew 1873
35
MONTEITH William P 1879
MONTEITH William P 1879
CLARK David H 1876
WEST Thomas 1873
36
WEST Thomas 1873
CLARK [75] Hannah 1876
WEST Thomas 1873
WEST Thomas 1873
CLARK [75] Hannah 1876
CLARK David H 1876
CLARK David H 1876
FARRINGTON Fremont D 1883

Helpful Hints

1. This Map's INDEX can be found on the preceding pages.
2. Refer to Map "C" to see where this Township lies within Dunn County, Wisconsin.
3. Numbers within square brackets [ ] denote a multi-patentee land parcel (multi-owner). Refer to Appendix "C" for a full list of members in this group.
4. Areas that look to be crowded with Patentees usually indicate multiple sales of the same parcel (Re-issues) or Overlapping parcels. See this Township's Index for an explanation of these and other circumstances that might explain "odd" groupings of Patentees on this map.

Legend

- Patent Boundary
- Section Boundary
- No Patents Found (or Outside County)
- 1., 2., 3., ... Lot Numbers (when beside a name)
- [ ] Group Number (see Appendix "C")

Scale: Section = 1 mile X 1 mile (generally, with some exceptions)

Road Map

T31-N R14-W
4th PM - 1831 MN/WI Meridian

Map Group 1

Cities & Towns

Connorsville

Cemeteries

New Haven Cemetery

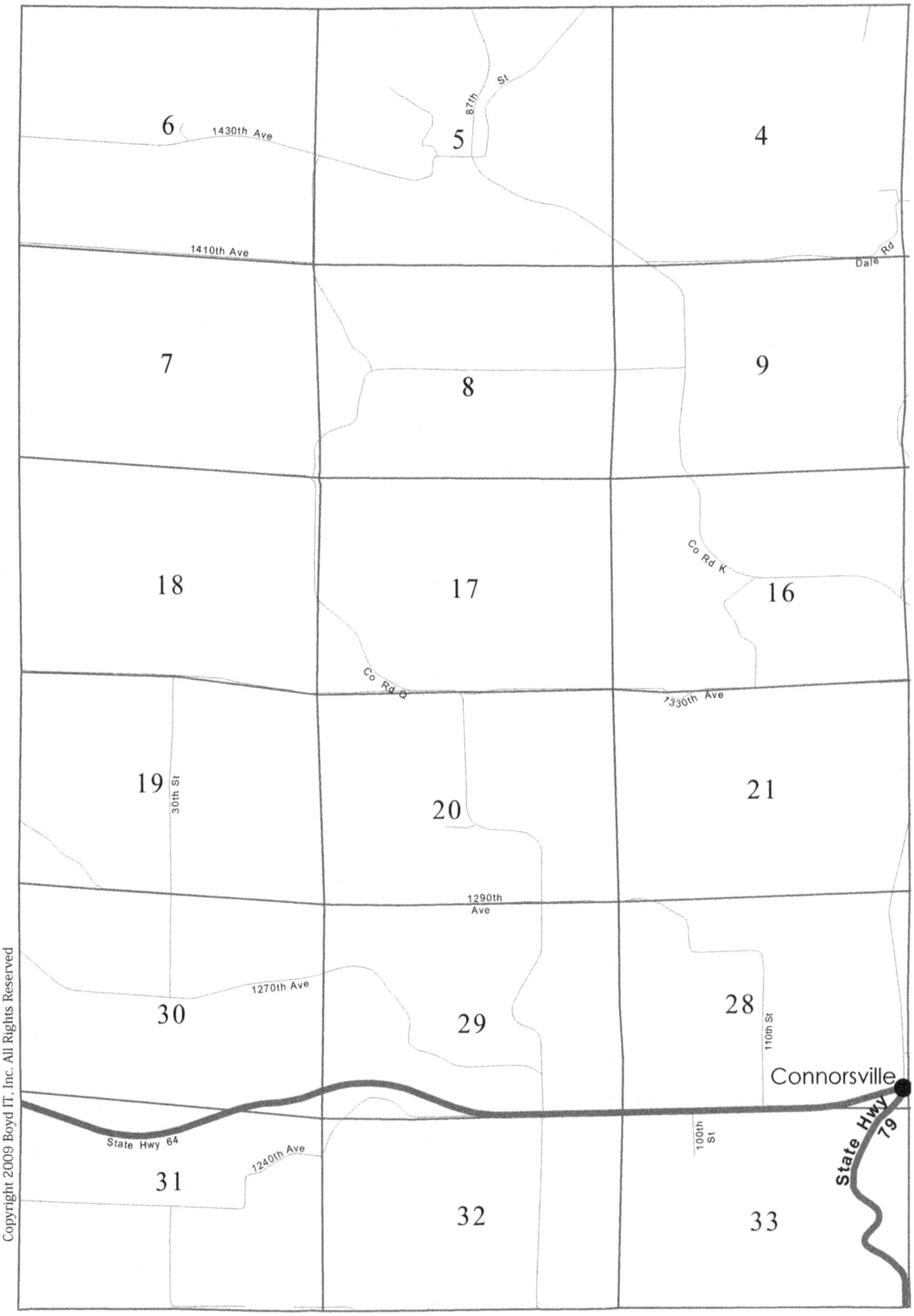
6
1430th Ave
87th St
5
4
1410th Ave
Dale Rd
7
8
9
18
17
Co Rd K
16
Co Rd Q
1330th Ave
19
30th St
20
21
1290th Ave
1270th Ave
30
29
28
110th St
Connorsville
State Hwy 64
100th St
State Hwy 79
1240th Ave
31
32
33

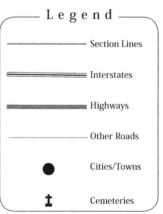

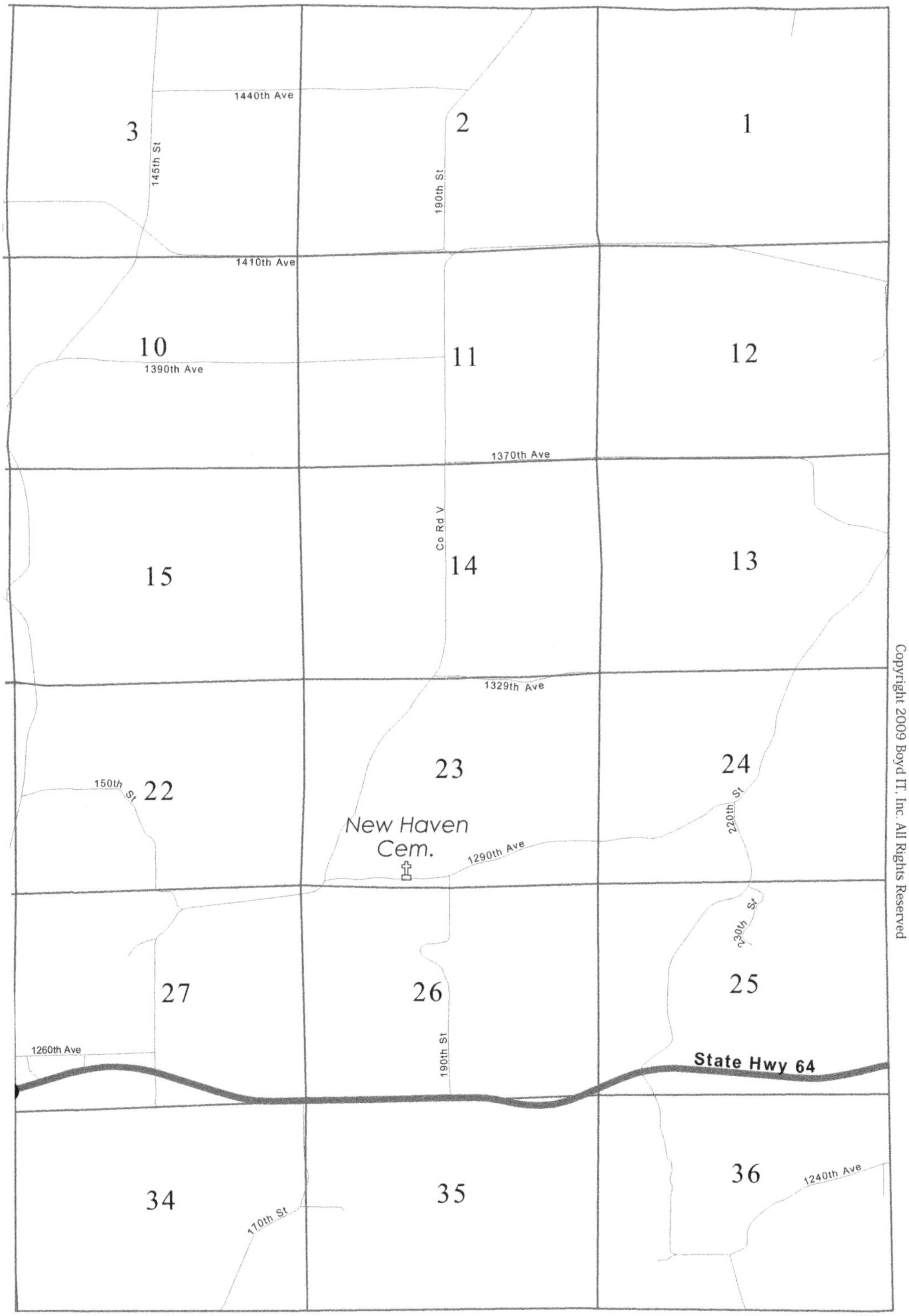

Helpful Hints

1. This road map has a number of uses, but primarily it is to help you: a) find the present location of land owned by your ancestors (at least the general area), b) find cemeteries and city-centers, and c) estimate the route/roads used by Census-takers & tax-assessors.

2. If you plan to travel to Dunn County to locate cemeteries or land parcels, please pick up a modern travel map for the area before you do. Mapping old land parcels on modern maps is not as exact a science as you might think. Just the slightest variations in public land survey coordinates, estimates of parcel boundaries, or road-map deviations can greatly alter a map's representation of how a road either does or doesn't cross a particular parcel of land.

Legend

- Section Lines
- Interstates
- Highways
- Other Roads
- Cities/Towns
- Cemeteries

Scale: Section = 1 mile X 1 mile
(generally, with some exceptions)

Historical Map

T31-N R14-W
4th PM - 1831 MN/WI Meridian

Map Group 1

Cities & Towns
Connorsville

Cemeteries
New Haven Cemetery

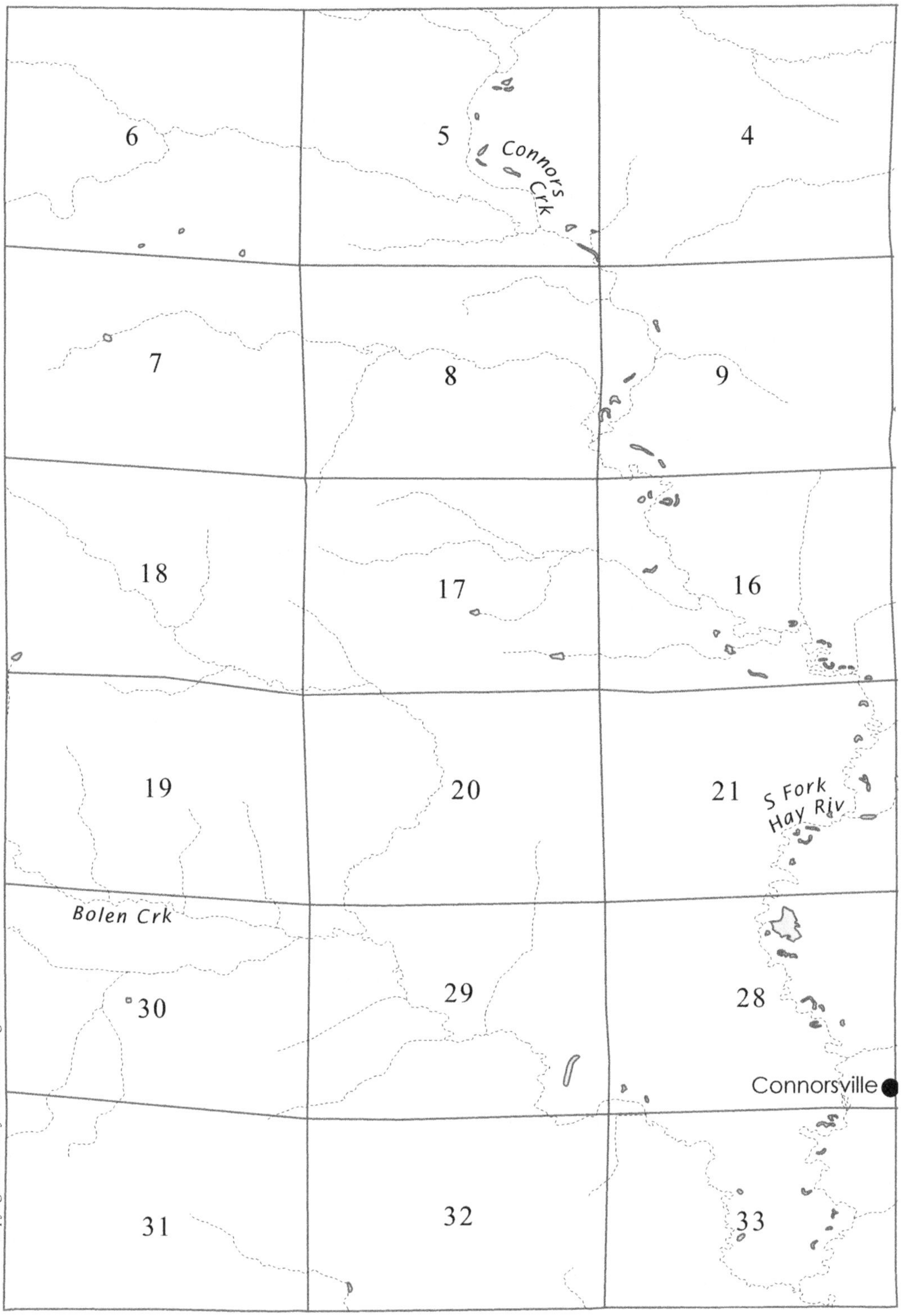

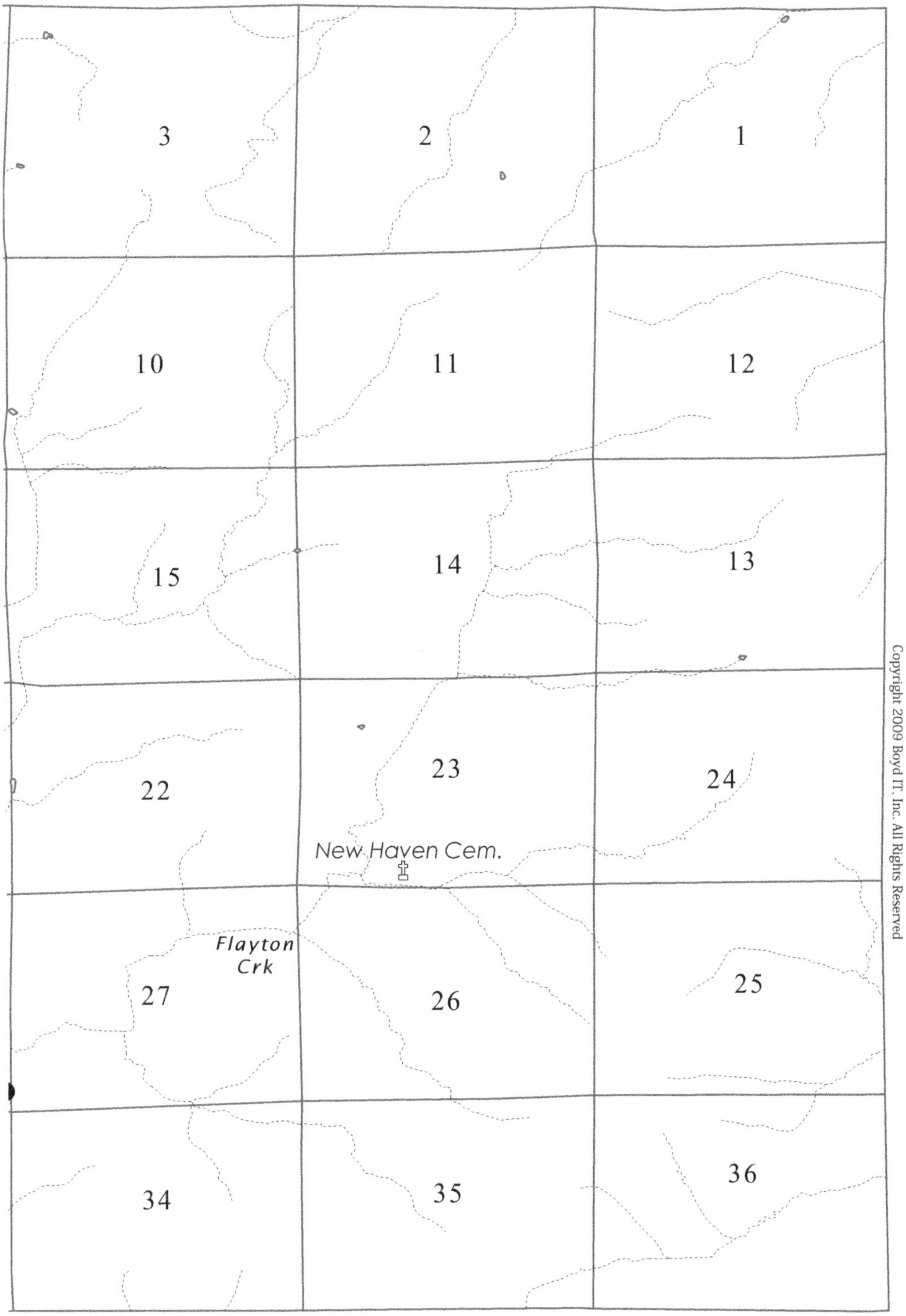
3
2
1
10
11
12
15
14
13
22
23
24
New Haven Cem.
27
Flayton Crk
26
25
34
35
36

Helpful Hints

1. This Map takes a different look at the same Congressional Township displayed in the preceding two maps. It presents features that can help you better envision the historical development of the area: a) Water-bodies (lakes & ponds), b) Water-courses (rivers, streams, etc.), c) Railroads, d) City/town center-points (where they were oftentimes located when first settled), and e) Cemeteries.
2. Using this "Historical" map in tandem with this Township's Patent Map and Road Map, may lead you to some interesting discoveries. You will often find roads, towns, cemeteries, and waterways are named after nearby landowners: sometimes those names will be the ones you are researching. See how many of these research gems you can find here in Dunn County.

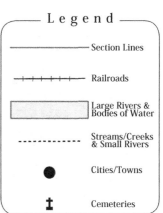

Legend

- Section Lines
- Railroads
- Large Rivers & Bodies of Water
- Streams/Creeks & Small Rivers
- Cities/Towns
- Cemeteries

Scale: Section = 1 mile X 1 mile
(there are some exceptions)

Map Group 2: Index to Land Patents

Township 31-North Range 13-West (4th PM - 1831 MN/WI)

After you locate an individual in this Index, take note of the Section and Section Part then proceed to the Land Patent map on the pages immediately following. You should have no difficulty locating the corresponding parcel of land.

The "For More Info" Column will lead you to more information about the underlying Patents. See the *Legend* at right, and the "How to Use this Book" chapter, for more information.

LEGEND

"For More Info . . . " column

A = Authority (Legislative Act, See Appendix "A")
B = Block or Lot (location in Section unknown)
C = Cancelled Patent
F = Fractional Section
G = Group (Multi-Patentee Patent, see Appendix "C")
V = Overlaps another Parcel
R = Re-Issued (Parcel patented more than once)

(A & G items require you to look in the Appendixes referred to above. All other Letter-designations followed by a number require you to locate line-items in this index that possess the ID number found after the letter).

ID	Individual in Patent	Sec.	Sec. Part	Date Issued	Other Counties	For More Info . . .
239	ALEXANDER, Rebecca	4	E½SW	1860-02-01		A5 G304
240	" "	4	W½SE	1860-02-01		A5 G304
251	ALLRAM, John	20	NW	1878-06-24		A6
302	ANDERSEN, Peter	14	SESE	1884-01-15		A6
303	" "	14	SWNE	1884-01-15		A6
304	" "	14	W½SE	1884-01-15		A6
176	ANDRUS, Charles D	36	E½NW	1884-01-15		A6
215	BALDWIN, H J	32	NESE	1889-03-21		A2
308	BEAL, Phillip	4	W½SW	1859-05-02		A2
309	" "	9	NWNW	1859-05-02		A2
211	BEISSWANGER, Gottlieb	2	NE	1873-09-20		A6 F
156	BELLEMAN, Adam	4	E½NE	1884-01-15		A6 F
157	" "	4	NESE	1884-01-15		A6
185	BENJAMIN, David	18	E½SE	1882-06-01		A6
206	BILSE, Frederick	11	NWNE	1892-08-01		A2
212	BILSE, Gottlieb J	11	SWNE	1911-06-15		A6
186	BOARDMAN, Deius T	4	SWNE	1870-06-10		A2
162	BORSEN, Anton	26	SW	1879-11-10		A6
167	BUTTERFIELD, Bela C	32	NENW	1900-03-17		A6
283	BUTTERFIELD, Lewis	32	N½NE	1886-10-21		A6
284	" "	32	SENW	1886-10-21		A6
285	" "	32	SWNE	1886-10-21		A6
241	CHUBBUCK, Ann M	14	E½NW	1860-02-01		A5 G433
242	" "	14	SWNW	1860-02-01		A5 G433
188	CLARK, Edmund A	30	N½NE	1878-11-30		A6
189	" "	30	NWSE	1878-11-30		A6
190	" "	30	SWNE	1878-11-30		A6
246	COCHRAN, James	18	E½NW	1868-02-01		A5
276	COMPANY, Knapp Stout And	24	SWSW	1884-10-04		A2
277	" "	5	SESW	1892-08-01		A2
286	COOPER, Margaret	22	NE	1859-05-02		A2
315	CROCKETT, Abigail	17	NE	1860-02-01		A5 G123
299	DAY, Nelson B	15	S½SW	1859-09-01		A5
300	" "	22	N½NW	1859-09-01		A5
180	DOYLE, William	24	E½NW	1907-05-18		A6 G172
181	" "	24	W½NE	1907-05-18	Dekalb	A6 G172
315	EMERY, Stephen	17	NE	1860-02-01		A5 G123
253	GALLATI, John	4	SESE	1905-06-30		A6
161	GEORGE, Annis	8	SENW	1884-10-04		A2
205	GEORGE, Emily L	5	NESW	1892-08-01		A2
267	GREENWEIG, Elizabeth	34	NENW	1866-04-20		A5 G222
268	" "	34	W½NE	1866-04-20		A5 G222
330	GRIZZELL, Letty	25	S½NW	1860-07-16		A5 G412
195	HAALTEN, Egbert O	14	N½NE	1890-03-29		A6
196	" "	14	NESE	1890-03-29		A6
197	" "	14	SENE	1890-03-29		A6

ID	Individual in Patent	Sec.	Sec. Part	Date Issued	Other Counties	For More Info . . .
180	HALVORSON, Christian	24	E½NW	1907-05-18		A6 G172
181	" "	24	W½NE	1907-05-18	Dekalb	A6 G172
216	HANSON, Halvor	24	N½SW	1884-01-15		A6
217	" "	24	NWSE	1884-01-15		A6
218	" "	24	SWNW	1884-01-15		A6
168	HARDING, Polly	25	NE	1860-07-16		A5 G410
250	HARMEN, Jesiah	10	NW	1879-10-01		A6
333	HARMON, William S	11	NWSW	1904-12-20		A6
270	HARRISON, John K	20	SW	1879-10-01		A6
237	HODGES, Mary B	15	SENE	1860-02-01		A5 G306
238	" "	15	W½NE	1860-02-01		A5 G306
163	HOFF, Anton H	6	S½NW	1886-01-20		A6 F
290	HOFFMAN, Mary	12	NWSW	1883-07-10		A6 G191
291	" "	12	S½SW	1883-07-10		A6 G191
292	" "	12	SWSE	1883-07-10		A6 G191
305	INABNET, Peter	6	NENE	1879-10-01		A6 F
306	" "	6	S½NE	1879-10-01		A6 F
201	INABNIT, Eliza	9	SENE	1897-02-15		A6 G197
201	INABNIT, Peter	9	SENE	1897-02-15		A6 G197
252	JOHNSON, John E	22	S½NW	1883-02-10		A6
202	JONES, Eliza Selina	9	E½SW	1860-02-01		A5 G208
203	" "	9	SWSW	1860-02-01		A5 G208
332	JONES, William	23	NESW	1859-05-02		A2
182	KAISER, Christof	12	N½SE	1873-09-20		A6
183	" "	12	NESW	1873-09-20		A6
184	" "	12	SESE	1873-09-20		A6
209	KALLENBACK, George	12	NW	1873-12-20		A6
325	KALLENBAK, Valtin	12	NE	1873-09-20		A6
290	KEISER, Jacob	12	NWSW	1883-07-10		A6 G191
291	" "	12	S½SW	1883-07-10		A6 G191
292	" "	12	SWSE	1883-07-10		A6 G191
254	KNAPP, John H	36	NESE	1854-10-02		A2
263	" "	34	NESE	1866-02-15		A2 G219
267	" "	34	NENW	1866-04-20		A5 G222
268	" "	34	W½NE	1866-04-20		A5 G222
265	" "	36	W½NW	1869-01-01		A2 G219
264	" "	34	SENE	1869-10-20		A2 G219
256	" "	26	SWSE	1871-04-05		A2 G219
257	" "	30	SESW	1871-04-05		A2 G219
258	" "	30	SWSE	1871-04-05		A2 G219
260	" "	32	SENE	1871-04-05		A2 G219
261	" "	32	SWNW	1871-04-05		A2 G219
262	" "	32	SWSW	1871-04-05		A2 G219
266	" "	6	NWNW	1871-04-20		A2 G219 F
255	" "	26	SESE	1872-12-10		A2 G218
259	" "	32	NWSE	1877-04-05		A2 G219
329	KOTTKE, Wilhelm	2	NW	1876-01-10		A6 F
328	LANDT, Warren S	32	NWNW	1873-06-20		A2
296	LARSON, Mons	22	N½SE	1874-05-06		A2
297	" "	34	NENE	1874-05-06		A2
298	" "	34	NWNW	1875-05-01		A2
219	LARSONS, Hans	2	NESW	1882-06-01		A6
220	" "	2	NWSE	1882-06-01		A6
221	" "	2	W½SW	1882-06-01		A6
159	LOE, Andrew A	24	E½NE	1883-02-10		A6
160	" "	24	E½SE	1883-02-10		A6
213	LOHFINK, Gottlieb	18	W½NW	1881-09-17		A6
214	" "	18	W½SW	1881-09-17		A6
331	MARBURY, William H	14	NESW	1858-09-03		A7 R295
198	MARTIN, Elias	36	S½SW	1880-09-01		A6
187	MCINTYRE, Dougle	32	SESW	1886-01-20		A6
271	MIKKELSON, John	36	NE	1883-02-10		A6
310	MORRICE, Rowley	26	NE	1859-05-02		A2
158	NIELSEN, Amund	26	NW	1880-09-01		A6
204	OLESEN, Ellen	10	NE	1881-09-17		A6
318	PEDERSON, Syvert	22	S½SE	1884-09-20		A6
319	" "	22	SESW	1884-09-20		A6
243	PETERSON, Ingebret	10	SE	1883-02-10		A6
165	PHILLIPS, Arthur P	30	E½SE	1899-04-22		A6
166	" "	30	SENE	1899-04-22		A6
177	PHILLIPS, Charles J	28	NW	1875-08-10		A6
224	PLANT, Henry B	14	SESW	1860-02-01		A5
225	" "	14	W½SW	1860-02-01		A5

ID	Individual in Patent	Sec.	Sec. Part	Date Issued	Other Counties	For More Info . . .
226	PLANT, Henry B (Cont'd)	15	SE	1860-02-01		A5
237	" "	15	SENE	1860-02-01		A5 G306
238	" "	15	W½NE	1860-02-01		A5 G306
227	" "	23	NW	1860-02-01		A5
239	" "	4	E½SW	1860-02-01		A5 G304
240	" "	4	W½SE	1860-02-01		A5 G304
228	" "	7	NESW	1860-02-01		A5
229	" "	7	SENW	1860-02-01		A5
230	" "	8	E½SE	1860-02-01		A5
231	" "	8	E½SW	1860-02-01		A5
232	" "	8	NENW	1860-02-01		A5
233	" "	8	NWSE	1860-02-01		A5
234	" "	8	SWSE	1860-02-01		A5
235	" "	8	W½NW	1860-02-01		A5
236	" "	8	W½SW	1860-02-01		A5
223	" "	10	SW	1884-02-20		A2
179	QUADERER, Christ	6	SE	1873-05-20		A6
199	RANDALL, Elias	30	N½NW	1891-06-08		A6 F
200	" "	30	SWNW	1891-06-08		A6 F
247	RASSBACH, Jeremiah	30	NESW	1890-03-29		A6 F
248	" "	30	SENW	1890-03-29		A6 F
249	" "	30	W½SW	1890-03-29		A6 F
172	ROEMHILD, Casper F	18	NE	1873-05-20		A6
210	ROEMHILD, George	6	SW	1872-09-25		A6
207	RUSH, Frederick	22	NESW	1860-02-01		A5
208	" "	22	W½SW	1860-02-01		A5
164	SAMPIRE, Arny	4	NWNE	1861-01-21		A2
287	SCHLOUGH, Martin	28	NWSW	1878-11-05		A2
316	SCHLOUGH, Stephen	28	E½SW	1880-09-01		A6
317	" "	28	S½SE	1880-09-01		A6
334	SCHLOUGH, William	28	SWSW	1902-05-01		A6
288	SCHLUCK, Martin	20	N½SE	1878-06-24		A6
289	" "	20	S½NE	1878-06-24		A6
275	SCOTT, John	24	NWNW	1917-02-07		A6
269	SHAW, John J	36	SESE	1876-01-20		A2
178	SIBBET, Charles	20	S½SE	1889-01-19		A6
193	SIEBERT, Edwart	18	E½SW	1876-01-10		A6
194	" "	18	W½SE	1876-01-10		A6
173	SMITH, Casper	2	NESE	1878-06-24		A6
174	" "	2	S½SE	1878-06-24		A6
175	" "	2	SESW	1878-06-24		A6
272	SMITH, John R	34	E½SW	1883-03-10		A6
273	" "	34	NWSE	1883-03-10		A6
274	" "	34	SENW	1883-03-10		A6
320	SMITH, Theodore A	28	N½NE	1883-03-10		A6
295	SNYDER, Matthias	14	NESW	1858-02-20		A7 C R331
335	STANSBERRY, William	5	NENE	1896-09-16		A6 F
336	STANSBERY, William	4	W½NW	1872-09-25		A6
263	STOUT, Henry L	34	NESE	1866-02-15		A2 G219
267	" "	34	NENW	1866-04-20		A5 G222
268	" "	34	W½NE	1866-04-20		A5 G222
265	" "	36	W½NW	1869-01-01		A2 G219
264	" "	34	SENE	1869-10-20		A2 G219
256	" "	26	SWSE	1871-04-05		A2 G219
257	" "	30	SESW	1871-04-05		A2 G219
258	" "	30	SWSE	1871-04-05		A2 G219
260	" "	32	SENE	1871-04-05		A2 G219
261	" "	32	SWNW	1871-04-05		A2 G219
262	" "	32	SWSW	1871-04-05		A2 G219
266	" "	6	NWNW	1871-04-20		A2 G219 F
255	" "	26	SESE	1872-12-10		A2 G218
259	" "	32	NWSE	1877-04-05		A2 G219
326	STROBRIDGE, W A	28	N½SE	1876-12-30		A6
327	" "	28	S½NE	1876-12-30		A6
322	STUBBS, Thomas	34	S½SE	1877-03-20		A6
244	SWAN, James A	36	N½SW	1883-07-10		A6
245	" "	36	W½SE	1883-07-10		A6
263	TAINTER, Andrew	34	NESE	1866-02-15		A2 G219
267	" "	34	NENW	1866-04-20		A5 G222
268	" "	34	W½NE	1866-04-20		A5 G222
265	" "	36	W½NW	1869-01-01		A2 G219
264	" "	34	SENE	1869-10-20		A2 G219
256	" "	26	SWSE	1871-04-05		A2 G219

ID	Individual in Patent	Sec.	Sec. Part	Date Issued	Other Counties	For More Info . . .
257	TAINTER, Andrew (Cont'd)	30	SESW	1871-04-05		A2 G219
258	" "	30	SWSE	1871-04-05		A2 G219
260	" "	32	SENE	1871-04-05		A2 G219
261	" "	32	SWNW	1871-04-05		A2 G219
262	" "	32	SWSW	1871-04-05		A2 G219
266	" "	6	NWNW	1871-04-20		A2 G219 F
255	" "	26	SESE	1872-12-10		A2 G218
259	" "	32	NWSE	1877-04-05		A2 G219
191	TAYLOR, Edmund	34	SWNW	1884-01-15		A6
192	" "	34	W½SW	1884-01-15		A6
312	THOMAS, Samuel A	9	SE	1859-05-02		A2
311	" "	9	E½NW	1859-09-01		A5
313	" "	9	SWNW	1859-09-01		A5
202	" "	9	E½SW	1860-02-01		A5 G208
203	" "	9	SWSW	1860-02-01		A5 G208
301	TIFFANY, Patris	9	NWSW	1856-04-01		A2
222	ULRICH, Hans	20	N½NE	1885-01-30		A6
279	VANCE, Levi	6	NENW	1854-07-05		A7
280	" "	6	NWNE	1854-07-05		A7
278	" "	5	SESE	1855-12-15		A2
281	" "	8	NENE	1855-12-15		A2
282	" "	8	NWNE	1859-05-02		A2
307	VANCE, Peter	8	S½NE	1859-12-10		A2
169	WASHBURN, Cadwallader C	24	SESW	1860-07-16		A5 G411
170	" "	24	SWSE	1860-07-16		A5 G411
171	" "	25	N½NW	1860-07-16		A5 G411
168	" "	25	NE	1860-07-16		A5 G410
169	WASHBURN, William D	24	SESW	1860-07-16		A5 G411
170	" "	24	SWSE	1860-07-16		A5 G411
171	" "	25	N½NW	1860-07-16		A5 G411
168	" "	25	NE	1860-07-16		A5 G410
330	" "	25	S½NW	1860-07-16		A5 G412
255	WILSON, ThOmas B	26	SESE	1872-12-10		A2 G218
321	WILSON, Thomas B	4	E½NW	1857-04-01		A2
263	" "	34	NESE	1866-02-15		A2 G219
267	" "	34	NENW	1866-04-20		A5 G222
268	" "	34	W½NE	1866-04-20		A5 G222
265	" "	36	W½NW	1869-01-01		A2 G219
264	" "	34	SENE	1869-10-20		A2 G219
256	" "	26	SWSE	1871-04-05		A2 G219
257	" "	30	SESW	1871-04-05		A2 G219
258	" "	30	SWSE	1871-04-05		A2 G219
260	" "	32	SENE	1871-04-05		A2 G219
261	" "	32	SWNW	1871-04-05		A2 G219
262	" "	32	SWSW	1871-04-05		A2 G219
266	" "	6	NWNW	1871-04-20		A2 G219 F
259	" "	32	NWSE	1877-04-05		A2 G219
314	WISCONSIN, State Of	16		1941-08-16		A3
293	WOOD, Mary Jane	25	NWSW	1860-07-16		A5
294	" "	26	N½SE	1860-07-16		A5
241	WOODMAN, Horatio	14	E½NW	1860-02-01		A5 G433
242	" "	14	SWNW	1860-02-01		A5 G433
323	YARDLEY, Thomas W	9	NENE	1860-02-01		A5
324	" "	9	W½NE	1860-02-01		A5

Patent Map

T31-N R13-W
4th PM - 1831 MN/WI Meridian

Map Group 2

Township Statistics

Parcels Mapped	:	181
Number of Patents	:	125
Number of Individuals	:	108
Patentees Identified	:	101
Number of Surnames	:	94
Multi-Patentee Parcels	:	34
Oldest Patent Date	:	7/5/1854
Most Recent Patent	:	8/16/1941
Block/Lot Parcels	:	0
Parcels Re - Issued	:	1
Parcels that Overlap	:	0
Cities and Towns	:	0
Cemeteries	:	2

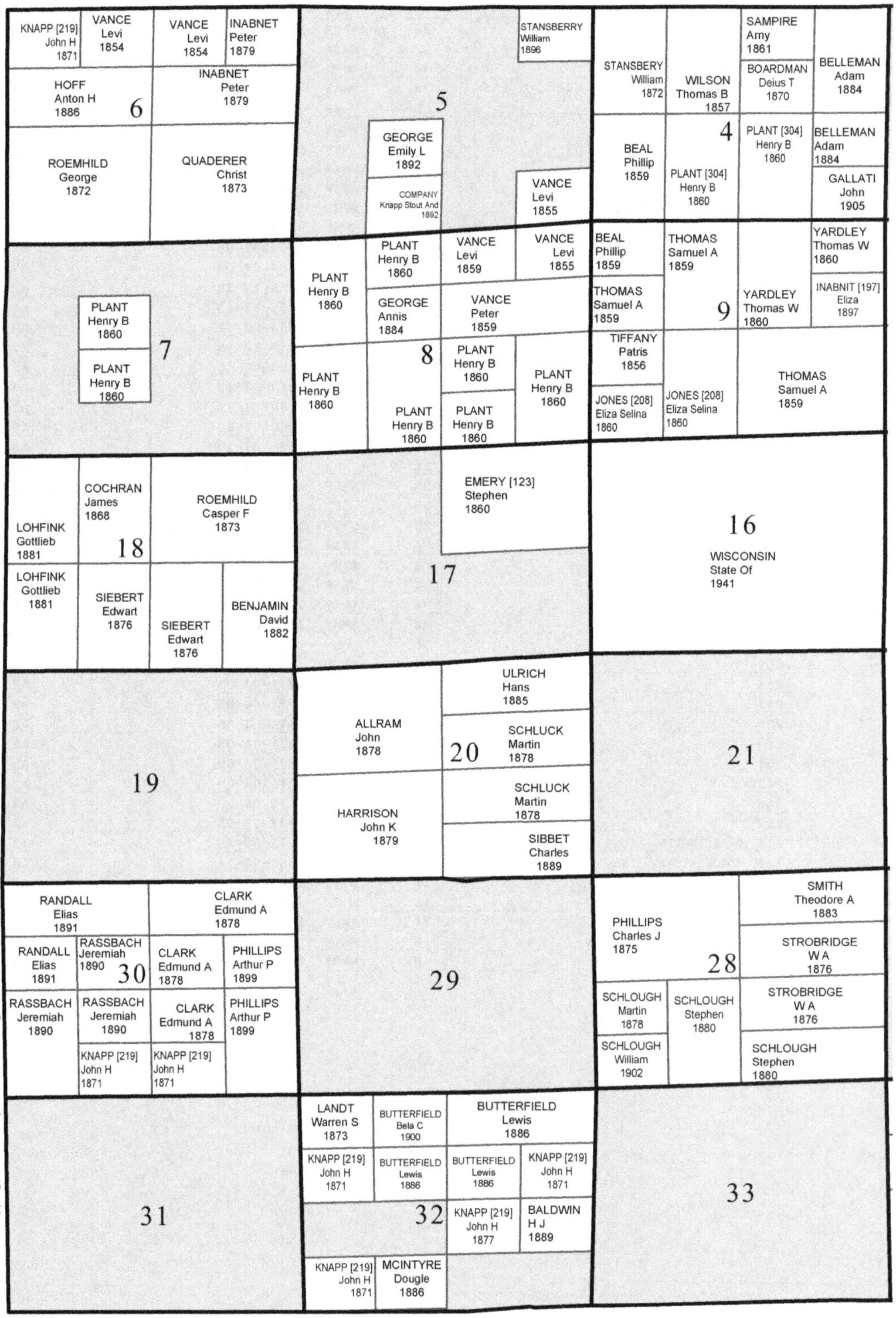
KNAPP [219] John H 1871
VANCE Levi 1854
VANCE Levi 1854
INABNET Peter 1879
HOFF Anton H 1886
6
INABNET Peter 1879
ROEMHILD George 1872
QUADERER Christ 1873
STANSBERRY William 1896
5
GEORGE Emily L 1892
COMPANY Knapp Stout And 1892
VANCE Levi 1855
STANSBERY William 1872
WILSON Thomas B 1857
SAMPIRE Amy 1861
BOARDMAN Deius T 1870
BELLEMAN Adam 1884
4
BEAL Phillip 1859
PLANT [304] Henry B 1860
PLANT [304] Henry B 1860
BELLEMAN Adam 1884
GALLATI John 1905
7
PLANT Henry B 1860
PLANT Henry B 1860
PLANT Henry B 1860
PLANT Henry B 1860
VANCE Levi 1859
VANCE Levi 1855
GEORGE Annis 1884
VANCE Peter 1859
8
PLANT Henry B 1860
PLANT Henry B 1860
PLANT Henry B 1860
PLANT Henry B 1860
PLANT Henry B 1860
PLANT Henry B 1860
BEAL Phillip 1859
THOMAS Samuel A 1859
YARDLEY Thomas W 1860
THOMAS Samuel A 1859
9
YARDLEY Thomas W 1860
INABNIT [197] Eliza 1897
TIFFANY Patris 1856
JONES [208] Eliza Selina 1860
JONES [208] Eliza Selina 1860
THOMAS Samuel A 1859
LOHFINK Gottlieb 1881
COCHRAN James 1868
18
ROEMHILD Casper F 1873
LOHFINK Gottlieb 1881
SIEBERT Edwart 1876
SIEBERT Edwart 1876
BENJAMIN David 1882
EMERY [123] Stephen 1860
17
16
WISCONSIN State Of 1941
19
ULRICH Hans 1885
ALLRAM John 1878
20
SCHLUCK Martin 1878
SCHLUCK Martin 1878
HARRISON John K 1879
SIBBET Charles 1889
21
RANDALL Elias 1891
CLARK Edmund A 1878
RANDALL Elias 1891
RASSBACH Jeremiah 1890
30
CLARK Edmund A 1878
PHILLIPS Arthur P 1899
RASSBACH Jeremiah 1890
RASSBACH Jeremiah 1890
CLARK Edmund A 1878
PHILLIPS Arthur P 1899
KNAPP [219] John H 1871
KNAPP [219] John H 1871
29
PHILLIPS Charles J 1875
SMITH Theodore A 1883
STROBRIDGE W A 1876
28
SCHLOUGH Martin 1878
SCHLOUGH Stephen 1880
STROBRIDGE W A 1876
SCHLOUGH William 1902
SCHLOUGH Stephen 1880
31
LANDT Warren S 1873
BUTTERFIELD Bela C 1900
BUTTERFIELD Lewis 1886
KNAPP [219] John H 1871
BUTTERFIELD Lewis 1886
BUTTERFIELD Lewis 1886
KNAPP [219] John H 1871
32
KNAPP [219] John H 1877
BALDWIN H J 1889
KNAPP [219] John H 1871
MCINTYRE Dougle 1886
33

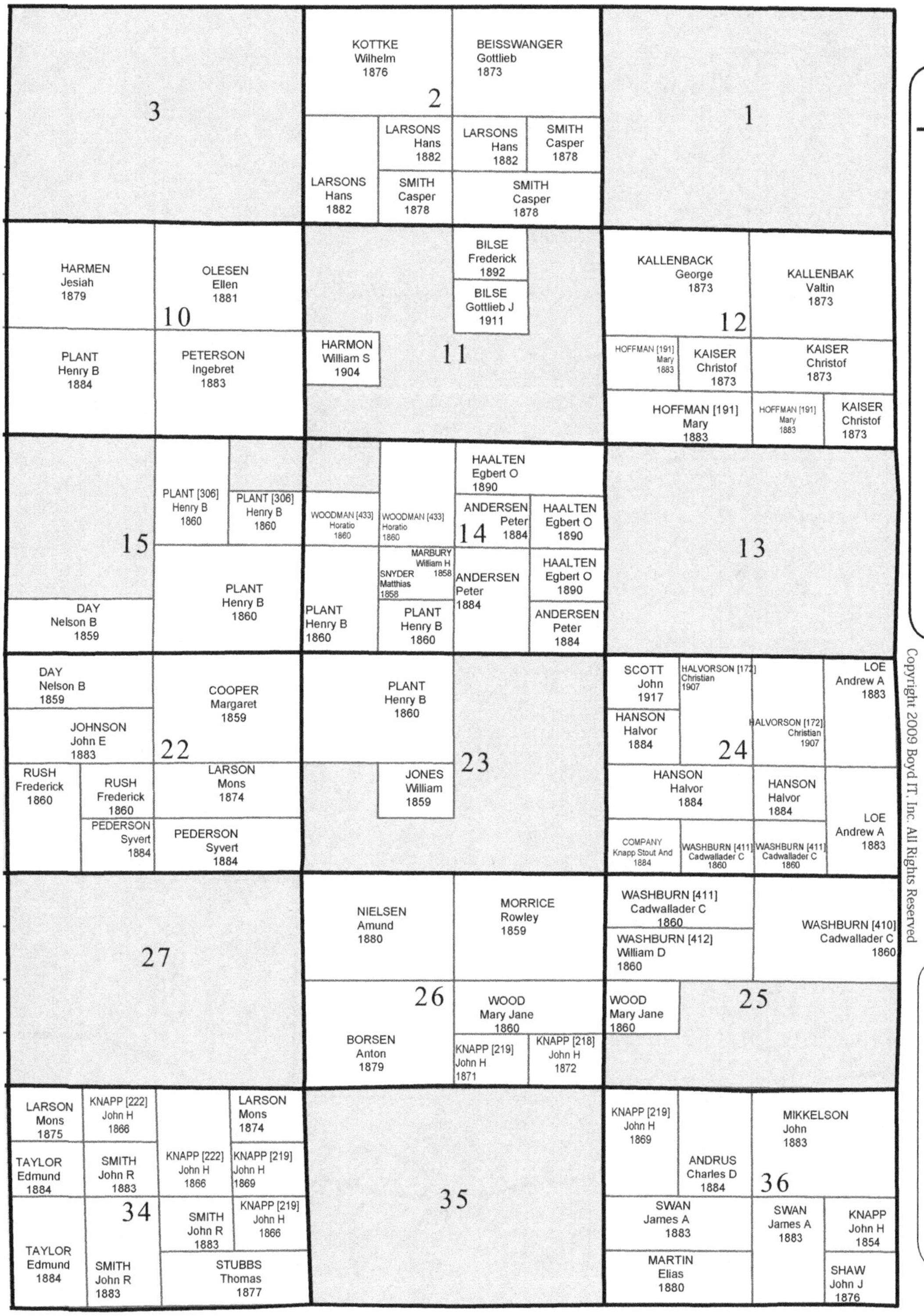
3
KOTTKE Wilhelm 1876
BEISSWANGER Gottlieb 1873
2
LARSONS Hans 1882
LARSONS Hans 1882
SMITH Casper 1878
LARSONS Hans 1882
SMITH Casper 1878
SMITH Casper 1878
1
HARMEN Jesiah 1879
OLESEN Ellen 1881
10
PLANT Henry B 1884
PETERSON Ingebret 1883
BILSE Frederick 1892
BILSE Gottlieb J 1911
HARMON William S 1904
11
KALLENBACK George 1873
KALLENBAK Valtin 1873
12
HOFFMAN [191] Mary 1883
KAISER Christof 1873
KAISER Christof 1873
HOFFMAN [191] Mary 1883
HOFFMAN [191] Mary 1883
KAISER Christof 1873
PLANT [306] Henry B 1860
PLANT [306] Henry B 1860
15
DAY Nelson B 1859
PLANT Henry B 1860
WOODMAN [433] Horatio 1860
WOODMAN [433] Horatio 1860
HAALTEN Egbert O 1890
ANDERSEN Peter 1884
HAALTEN Egbert O 1890
14
MARBURY William H
SNYDER Matthias 1858
1858
ANDERSEN Peter 1884
HAALTEN Egbert O 1890
PLANT Henry B 1860
PLANT Henry B 1860
ANDERSEN Peter 1884
13
DAY Nelson B 1859
COOPER Margaret 1859
JOHNSON John E 1883
22
RUSH Frederick 1860
RUSH Frederick 1860
LARSON Mons 1874
PEDERSON Syvert 1884
PEDERSON Syvert 1884
PLANT Henry B 1860
23
JONES William 1859
SCOTT John 1917
HALVORSON [172] Christian 1907
LOE Andrew A 1883
HANSON Halvor 1884
HALVORSON [172] Christian 1907
24
HANSON Halvor 1884
HANSON Halvor 1884
LOE Andrew A 1883
COMPANY Knapp Stout And 1884
WASHBURN [411] Cadwallader C 1860
WASHBURN [411] Cadwallader C 1860
27
NIELSEN Amund 1880
MORRICE Rowley 1859
26
BORSEN Anton 1879
WOOD Mary Jane 1860
KNAPP [219] John H 1871
KNAPP [218] John H 1872
WASHBURN [411] Cadwallader C 1860
WASHBURN [412] William D 1860
WASHBURN [410] Cadwallader C 1860
WOOD Mary Jane 1860
25
LARSON Mons 1875
KNAPP [222] John H 1866
LARSON Mons 1874
TAYLOR Edmund 1884
SMITH John R 1883
KNAPP [222] John H 1866
KNAPP [219] John H 1869
34
SMITH John R 1883
KNAPP [219] John H 1866
TAYLOR Edmund 1884
SMITH John R 1883
STUBBS Thomas 1877
35
KNAPP [219] John H 1869
ANDRUS Charles D 1884
MIKKELSON John 1883
36
SWAN James A 1883
SWAN James A 1883
KNAPP John H 1854
MARTIN Elias 1880
SHAW John J 1876

Helpful Hints

1. This Map's INDEX can be found on the preceding pages.
2. Refer to Map "C" to see where this Township lies within Dunn County, Wisconsin.
3. Numbers within square brackets [ ] denote a multi-patentee land parcel (multi-owner). Refer to Appendix "C" for a full list of members in this group.
4. Areas that look to be crowded with Patentees usually indicate multiple sales of the same parcel (Re-issues) or Overlapping parcels. See this Township's Index for an explanation of these and other circumstances that might explain "odd" groupings of Patentees on this map.

Legend

- Patent Boundary
- Section Boundary
- No Patents Found (or Outside County)
- 1., 2., 3., ... Lot Numbers (when beside a name)
- [ ] Group Number (see Appendix "C")

Scale: Section = 1 mile X 1 mile (generally, with some exceptions)

Road Map

T31-N R13-W
4th PM - 1831 MN/WI Meridian

Map Group 2

Cities & Towns

None

Cemeteries

Oak Grove Cemetery
Vanceburg Cemetery

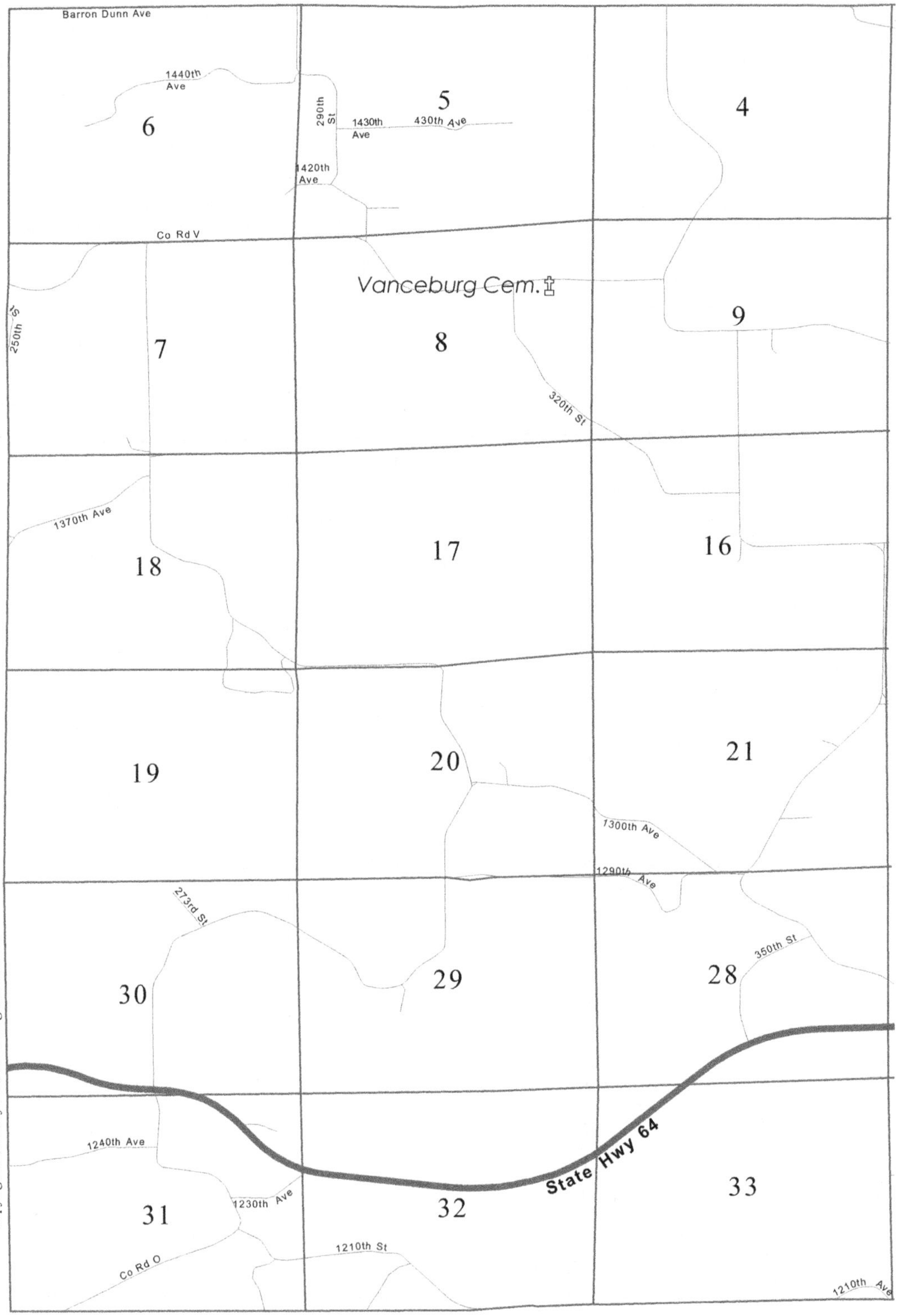

Barron Dunn Ave
1440th Ave
6
5
4
290th St
1430th Ave
430th Ave
1420th Ave
Co Rd V
Vanceburg Cem.
250th St
7
8
9
320th St
1370th Ave
18
17
16
19
20
21
1300th Ave
1290th Ave
273rd St
30
29
28
350th St
1240th Ave
1230th Ave
State Hwy 64
31
32
33
Co Rd O
1210th St
1210th Ave

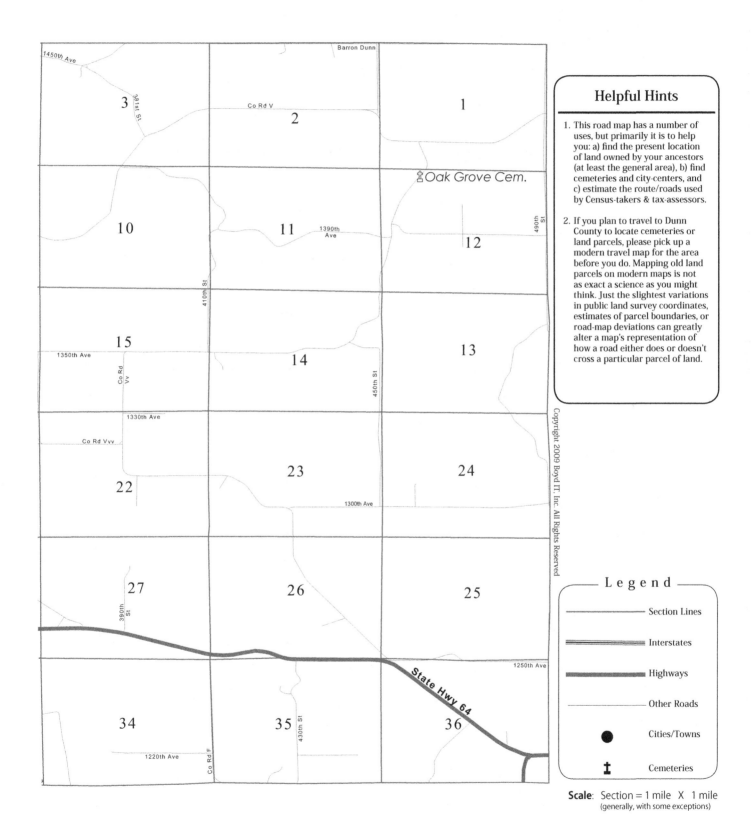

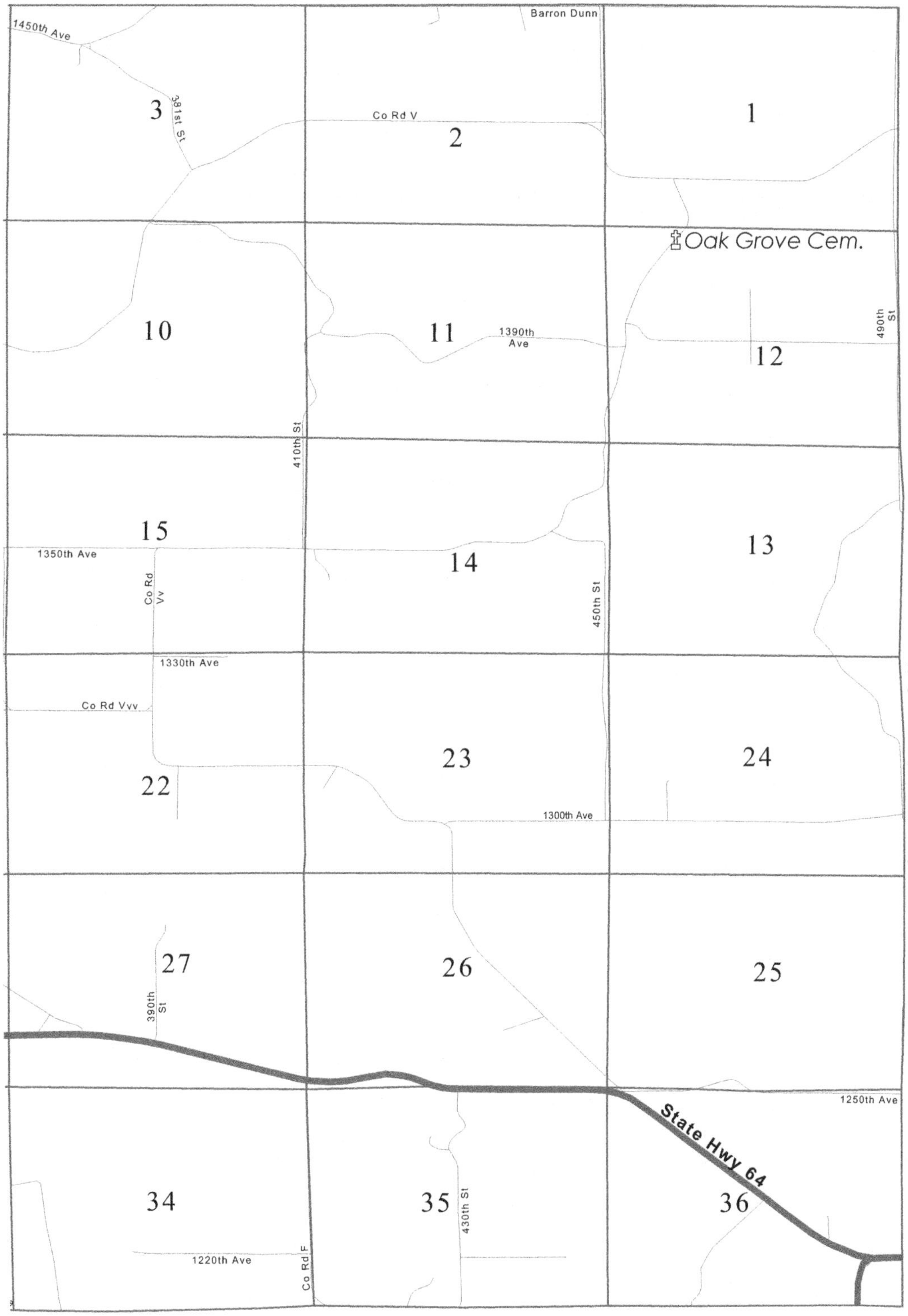

Helpful Hints

1. This road map has a number of uses, but primarily it is to help you: a) find the present location of land owned by your ancestors (at least the general area), b) find cemeteries and city-centers, and c) estimate the route/roads used by Census-takers & tax-assessors.
2. If you plan to travel to Dunn County to locate cemeteries or land parcels, please pick up a modern travel map for the area before you do. Mapping old land parcels on modern maps is not as exact a science as you might think. Just the slightest variations in public land survey coordinates, estimates of parcel boundaries, or road-map deviations can greatly alter a map's representation of how a road either does or doesn't cross a particular parcel of land.

Legend

- Section Lines
- Interstates
- Highways
- Other Roads
- Cities/Towns
- Cemeteries

Scale: Section = 1 mile X 1 mile
(generally, with some exceptions)

Historical Map

T31-N R13-W
4th PM - 1831 MN/WI Meridian

Map Group 2

Cities & Towns
None

Cemeteries
Oak Grove Cemetery
Vanceburg Cemetery

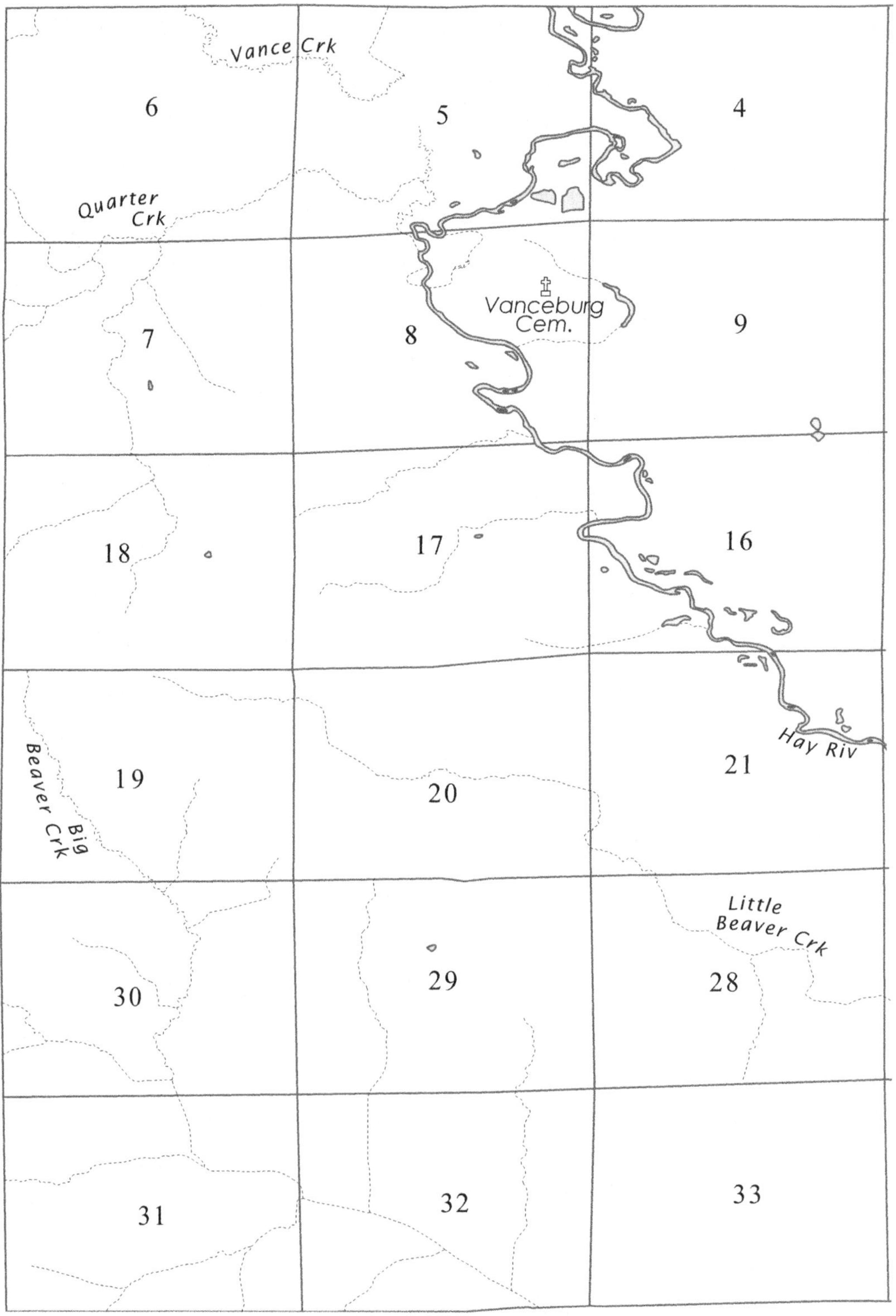

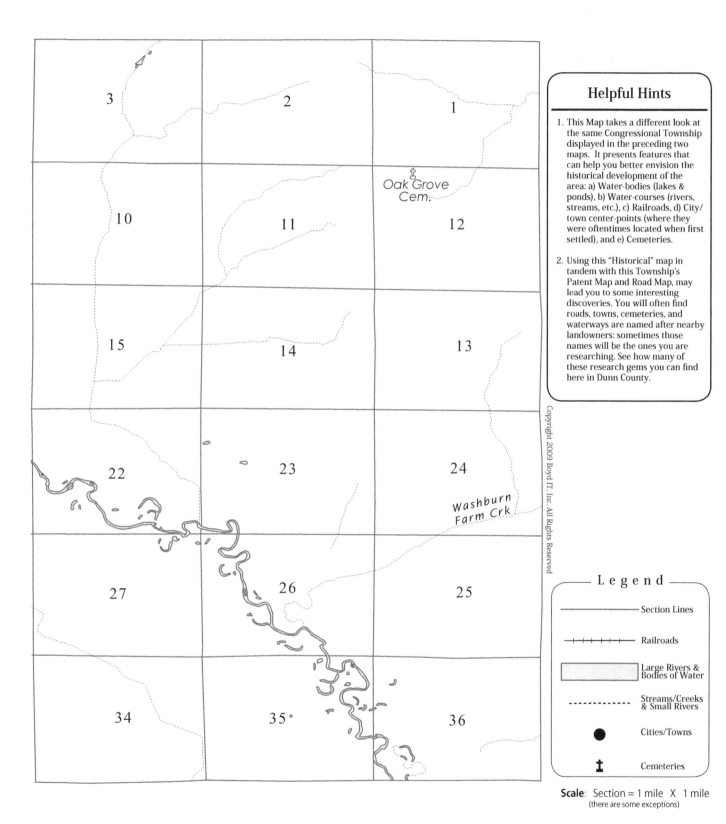

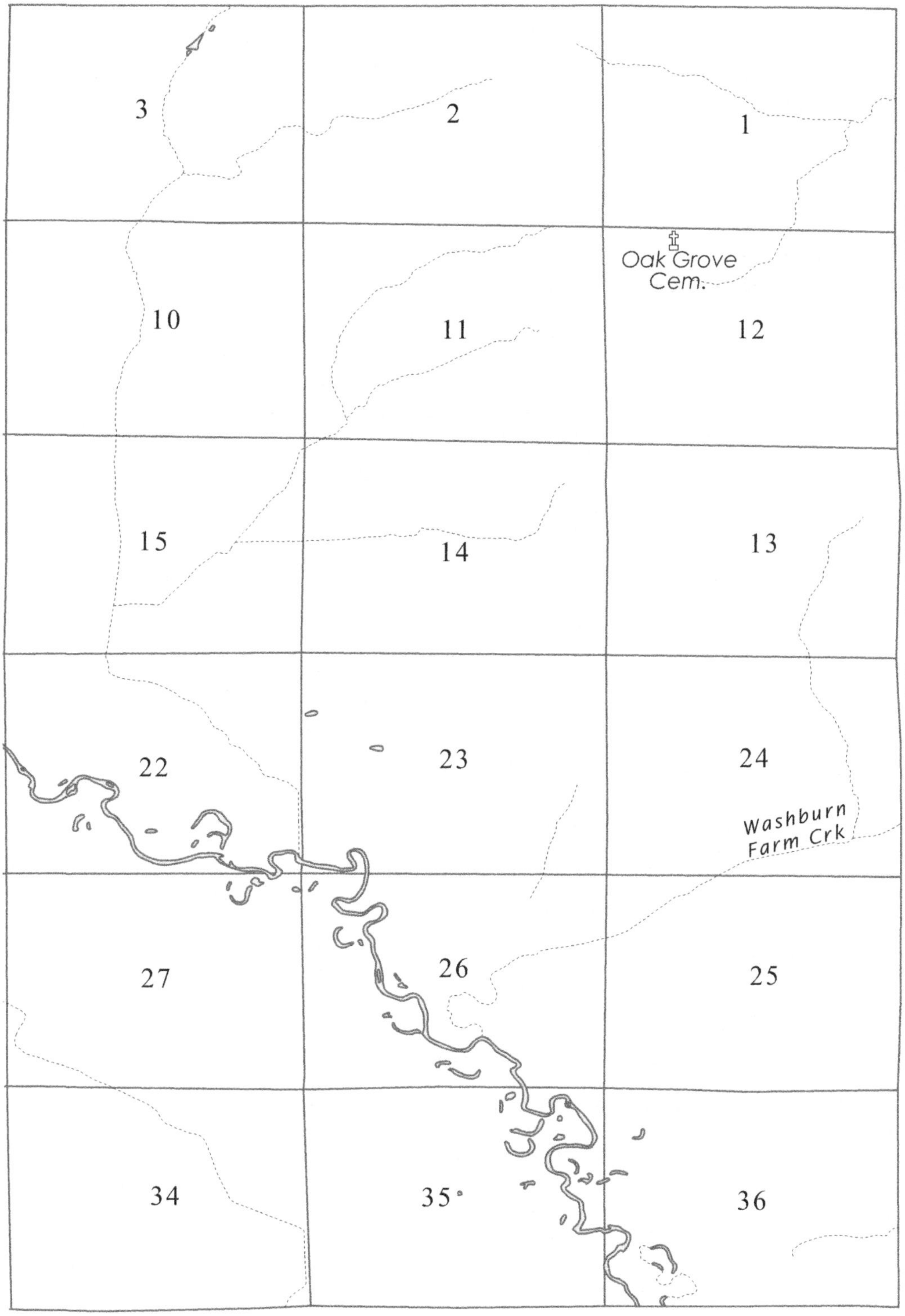

Helpful Hints

1. This Map takes a different look at the same Congressional Township displayed in the preceding two maps. It presents features that can help you better envision the historical development of the area: a) Water-bodies (lakes & ponds), b) Water-courses (rivers, streams, etc.), c) Railroads, d) City/town center-points (where they were oftentimes located when first settled), and e) Cemeteries.

2. Using this "Historical" map in tandem with this Township's Patent Map and Road Map, may lead you to some interesting discoveries. You will often find roads, towns, cemeteries, and waterways are named after nearby landowners: sometimes those names will be the ones you are researching. See how many of these research gems you can find here in Dunn County.

Legend

- Section Lines
- Railroads
- Large Rivers & Bodies of Water
- Streams/Creeks & Small Rivers
- Cities/Towns
- Cemeteries

Scale: Section = 1 mile X 1 mile
(there are some exceptions)

Map Group 3: Index to Land Patents

Township 31-North Range 12-West (4th PM - 1831 MN/WI)

After you locate an individual in this Index, take note of the Section and Section Part then proceed to the Land Patent map on the pages immediately following. You should have no difficulty locating the corresponding parcel of land.

The "For More Info" Column will lead you to more information about the underlying Patents. See the *Legend* at right, and the "How to Use this Book" chapter, for more information.

LEGEND

"For More Info . . . " column

A = Authority (Legislative Act, See Appendix "A")
B = Block or Lot (location in Section unknown)
C = Cancelled Patent
F = Fractional Section
G = Group (Multi-Patentee Patent, see Appendix "C")
V = Overlaps another Parcel
R = Re-Issued (Parcel patented more than once)

(A & G items require you to look in the Appendixes referred to above. All other Letter-designations followed by a number require you to locate line-items in this index that possess the ID number found after the letter).

ID	Individual in Patent	Sec.	Sec. Part	Date Issued	Other Counties	For More Info . . .
382	AASEN, Iver	26	E½NW	1884-01-15		A6
383	" "	26	E½SW	1884-01-15		A6
449	AMUNDSON, Silla	11	N½NE	1884-01-15		A6
450	" "	2	W½SE	1884-01-15		A6
339	ANDERSON, Andrew	2	NWSW	1892-04-29		A6
340	" "	2	S½NW	1892-04-29		A6
341	" "	2	SWNE	1892-04-29		A6
418	ANDERSON, Ole	12	NENE	1878-11-05		A2
417	" "	12	N½SE	1880-09-01		A6
419	" "	12	S½NE	1880-09-01		A6
440	ANDERSON, Peter	1	E½NE	1883-03-10		A6 F
389	ASLAKSEN, John	14	NESE	1894-06-15		A6
390	" "	14	S½SE	1894-06-15		A6
391	" "	14	SENE	1894-06-15		A6
380	BALAND, Holsten T	15	N½SW	1883-02-10		A6
463	BALAND, Torger	15	NW	1879-11-10		A6
444	BALDRIDGE, S C	36	E½SE	1890-03-29		A6
445	" "	36	SENE	1890-03-29		A6
446	" "	36	SWSE	1890-03-29		A6
379	BALDWIN, Heth W	36	SW	1883-03-10		A6
447	BENDIKSDATTER, Sigra	11	E½SE	1897-11-10		A6
448	" "	14	NENE	1897-11-10		A6
388	BENDIXSON, Jens	14	NWSE	1904-07-27		A6
343	BERGELAND, Anund E	24	NE	1893-05-10		A6
393	BERGET, John O	14	NWSW	1898-03-21		A6
394	" "	14	SWNW	1898-03-21		A6
386	BOOTON, James	3	NENW	1907-11-08		A6
359	BORTLE, David S	36	W½NW	1885-08-20		A6
361	BREWER, Gaylord I	36	E½NW	1880-09-01		A6
362	" "	36	W½NE	1880-09-01		A6
401	BREWER, Louisa F	34	NENE	1874-05-06		A2
353	BRINGERUD, Christen P	24	N½SW	1878-06-24		A6
354	" "	24	SENW	1878-06-24		A6
355	" "	24	SWSW	1878-06-24		A6
400	BROWN, Lewellyn D	6	NW	1876-11-03		A6 F
432	CHRISTOFFERSON, Otto	13	E½SW	1899-02-25		A6
433	" "	13	W½SE	1899-02-25		A6
356	DAMMAN, Cornelius P	8	SWSW	1876-12-30		A6
348	ELEVESON, Austin	1	E½NW	1885-01-30		A6 F
349	" "	1	NWNE	1885-01-30		A6 F
430	ELIASEN, Oliver	4	NE	1884-01-15		A6 F
402	ELLEFSON, Lue	1	SWNE	1902-05-01		A6
338	FINLEY, Alfred B	18	N½NE	1869-10-20		A2
437	FLINN, Patrick	2	N½NW	1882-06-30		A6
438	" "	2	NWNE	1882-06-30		A6
465	FLUG, William	28	NW	1883-02-10		A6

ID	Individual in Patent	Sec.	Sec. Part	Date Issued	Other Counties	For More Info . . .
412	FORDAHL, Ole A	30	N½SW	1884-01-15		A6 F
413	" "	30	S½NW	1884-01-15		A6 F
358	GARDNER, David A	12	SESE	1915-03-27		A6
363	GREGERSON, George Benjamin	36	NWSE	1921-06-14		A6
420	GREGERSON, Ole	2	E½NE	1897-02-15		A6
421	" "	2	E½SE	1897-02-15		A6
455	GUNDERSON, Thomas	1	W½NW	1898-03-21		A6 F
375	HAGEN, Hans K	22	E½SE	1884-01-15		A6
376	" "	22	NESW	1884-01-15		A6
377	" "	22	NWSE	1884-01-15		A6
372	HELGESON, Halvor	10	N½NE	1884-01-15		A6
373	" "	10	NWSE	1884-01-15		A6
374	" "	10	SWNE	1884-01-15		A6
422	HELGESON, Ole	10	E½SE	1878-06-24		A6
423	" "	11	S½SW	1878-06-24		A6
424	HENDRIKSON, Ole	12	NENW	1898-07-25		A6
425	" "	12	NWNE	1898-07-25		A6
464	HOFFMANN, Wilhelm	18	SESW	1896-10-16		A6
392	KNAPP, John H	19	NESE	1855-12-15		A2
461	KNUDSEN, Tom	24	NENW	1896-01-18		A6
462	" "	24	W½NW	1896-01-18		A6
367	KRINGLE, Gertrude N	4	NW	1880-09-01		A6 F
344	LARSON, Arne	12	S½SW	1883-02-10		A6
345	" "	13	W½NW	1883-02-10		A6
403	LARSON, Martin A	13	NWSW	1891-10-23		A2
456	LARSON, Tollef	14	SWSW	1884-10-04		A2
368	LEE, Gunder A	34	S½SE	1885-07-27		A6
369	" "	4	1	1885-07-27		A6
370	" "	4	2	1885-07-27		A6
385	LEE, Jacob K	28	SW	1889-02-16		A6
414	LEE, Ole A	34	N½SE	1884-01-15		A6
415	" "	34	S½NE	1884-01-15		A6
387	LIND, Jens A	30	SE	1893-03-27		A6
416	LOE, Ole A	18	SWSW	1884-10-04		A2 F
427	LOFTHUUS, Ole T	22	NWSW	1883-02-10		A6
428	" "	22	S½SW	1883-02-10		A6 F
429	" "	22	SWSE	1883-02-10		A6 F
337	MESSENGER, A J	6	NENE	1870-06-10		A2 F
406	MICKELSON, Morris	30	N½NW	1908-06-25		A6
409	MOEN, Nils O	32	E½SE	1883-07-10		A6
410	" "	32	SENE	1883-07-10		A6
411	" "	32	SWSE	1883-07-10		A6
407	MORK, Nels H	26	W½NW	1882-06-01		A6
408	" "	26	W½SW	1882-06-01		A6
395	MULLER, Konrad	18	NWSW	1891-06-08		A6
396	" "	18	SWNW	1891-06-08		A6
357	MURPHY, Dan	13	SWNE	1891-10-23		A2
378	NILSON, Hans	30	NE	1893-03-27		A6
434	OLSEN, Otto	12	SWSE	1897-04-02		A6
435	" "	13	E½NW	1897-04-02		A6
436	" "	13	NWNE	1897-04-02		A6
441	OLSTAD, Peter S	32	N½NE	1885-08-20		A6
442	" "	32	NWSE	1885-08-20		A6
443	" "	32	SWNE	1885-08-20		A6
350	PRILL, Carl	18	SESE	1896-10-07		A6
426	ROLSTAD, Ole O	34	NWNE	1903-11-10		A6
364	SCHOLL, George	18	N½SE	1876-08-23		A6
365	" "	18	S½NE	1876-08-23		A6
366	" "	18	SWSE	1879-09-04		A2
397	SCHOLL, Kunnegunde	18	N½NW	1876-12-30		A6 F
398	" "	18	NESW	1876-12-30		A6 F
399	" "	18	SENW	1876-12-30		A6 F
404	SHELTON, Michael	6	SENE	1883-07-10		A6
405	" "	6	W½NE	1883-07-10		A6 F
342	SKJERLY, Andrew	2	E½SW	1896-01-22		A6
384	SKJERLY, JOhn A	10	SENE	1910-04-14		A6
439	STENERSON, Peder	32	NW	1887-02-21		A6
360	THOMAS, Emery J	10	SWSE	1904-09-28		A6
351	THOMPSON, Charles	12	N½SW	1880-09-01		A6
352	" "	12	S½NW	1880-09-01		A6
431	THOMPSON, Oscar K	12	NWNW	1910-04-14		A6
458	THOMPSON, Tollef	11	SWSE	1883-07-10		A6
459	" "	14	N½NW	1883-07-10		A6

ID	Individual in Patent	Sec.	Sec. Part	Date Issued	Other Counties	For More Info . . .
460	THOMPSON, Tollef (Cont'd)	14	NWNE	1883-07-10		A6
457	" "	11	NWSE	1889-03-21		A2
452	THORSEN, Svend	14	E½SW	1884-09-20		A6
453	" "	14	SENW	1884-09-20		A6
454	" "	14	SWNE	1884-09-20		A6
346	THORSON, Aslak	13	E½NE	1892-04-29		A6
347	" "	13	E½SE	1892-04-29		A6
381	WESTON, Horatio N	32	SW	1882-05-10		A6
371	WIGEN, Halvor G	15	N½SE	1884-01-15		A6
451	WISCONSIN, State Of	16		1941-08-16		A3

Patent Map

T31-N R12-W
4th PM - 1831 MN/WI Meridian

Map Group 3

Township Statistics

Parcels Mapped	:	129
Number of Patents	:	79
Number of Individuals	:	76
Patentees Identified	:	76
Number of Surnames	:	62
Multi-Patentee Parcels	:	0
Oldest Patent Date	:	12/15/1855
Most Recent Patent	:	8/16/1941
Block/Lot Parcels	:	2
Parcels Re - Issued	:	0
Parcels that Overlap	:	0
Cities and Towns	:	1
Cemeteries	:	1

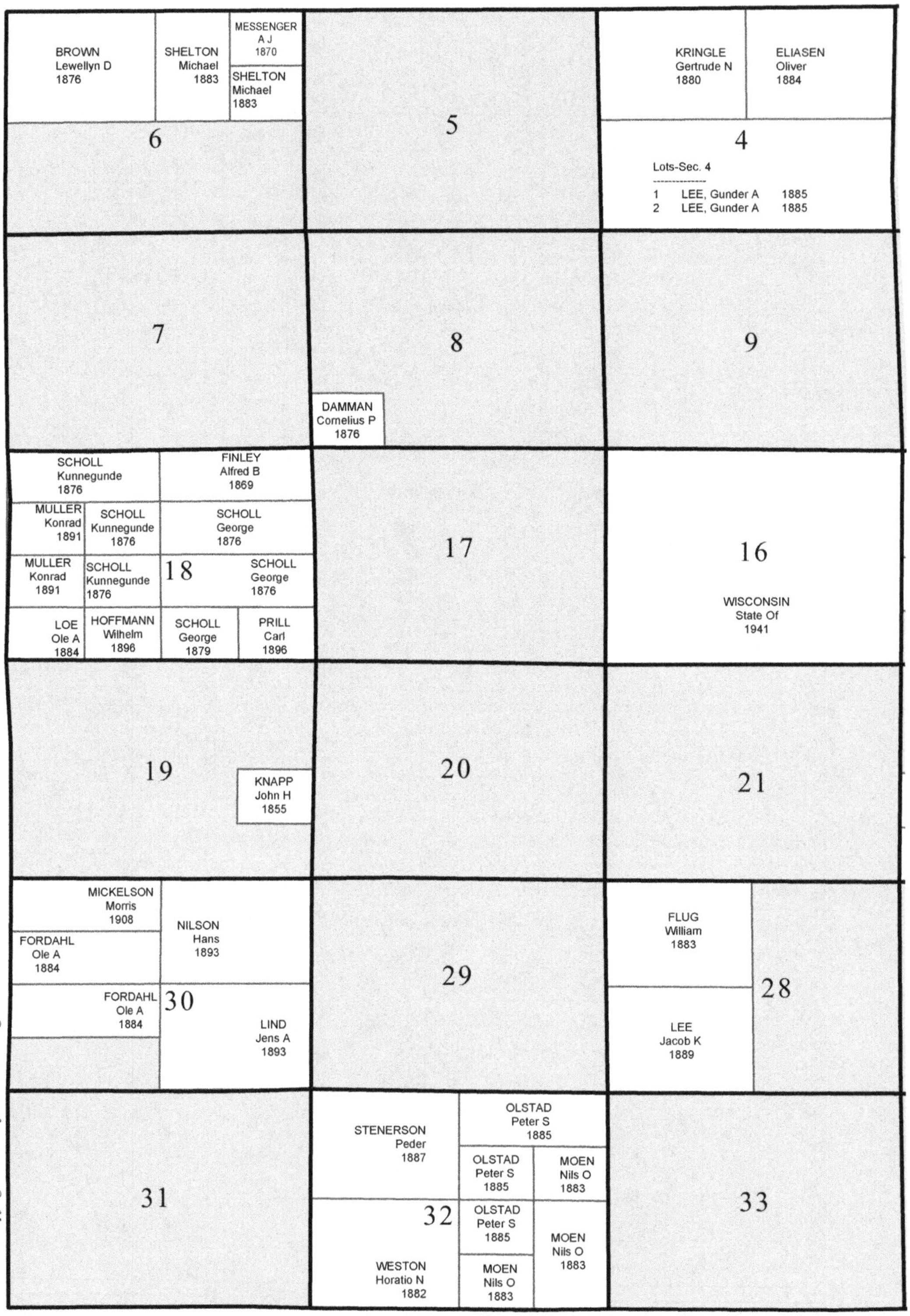
BROWN Lewellyn D 1876
SHELTON Michael 1883
MESSENGER A J 1870
SHELTON Michael 1883
6
5
KRINGLE Gertrude N 1880
ELIASEN Oliver 1884
4
Lots-Sec. 4
1 LEE, Gunder A 1885
2 LEE, Gunder A 1885
7
8
9
DAMMAN Cornelius P 1876
SCHOLL Kunnegunde 1876
FINLEY Alfred B 1869
MULLER Konrad 1891
SCHOLL Kunnegunde 1876
SCHOLL George 1876
MULLER Konrad 1891
SCHOLL Kunnegunde 1876
18
SCHOLL George 1876
LOE Ole A 1884
HOFFMANN Wilhelm 1896
SCHOLL George 1879
PRILL Carl 1896
17
16
WISCONSIN State Of 1941
19
KNAPP John H 1855
20
21
MICKELSON Morris 1908
NILSON Hans 1893
FORDAHL Ole A 1884
FORDAHL Ole A 1884
30
LIND Jens A 1893
29
FLUG William 1883
28
LEE Jacob K 1889
31
STENERSON Peder 1887
OLSTAD Peter S 1885
OLSTAD Peter S 1885
MOEN Nils O 1883
32
OLSTAD Peter S 1885
MOEN Nils O 1883
WESTON Horatio N 1882
MOEN Nils O 1883
33

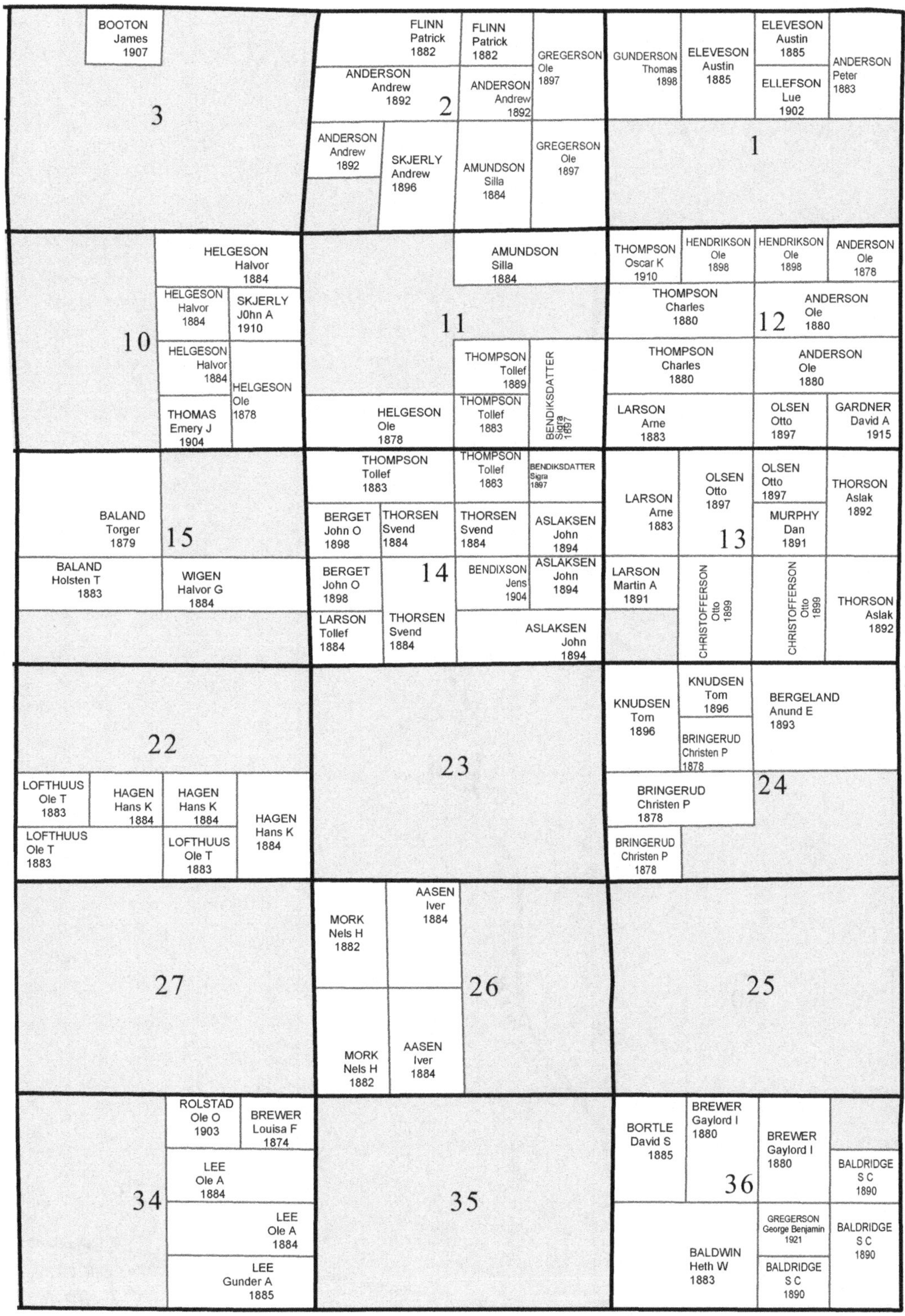
BOOTON James 1907
3
FLINN Patrick 1882
FLINN Patrick 1882
GREGERSON Ole 1897
ANDERSON Andrew 1892
2
ANDERSON Andrew 1892
ANDERSON Andrew 1892
SKJERLY Andrew 1896
AMUNDSON Silla 1884
GREGERSON Ole 1897
GUNDERSON Thomas 1898
ELEVESON Austin 1885
ELEVESON Austin 1885
ANDERSON Peter 1883
ELLEFSON Lue 1902
1
HELGESON Halvor 1884
HELGESON Halvor 1884
SKJERLY JOhn A 1910
10
HELGESON Halvor 1884
HELGESON Ole 1878
THOMAS Emery J 1904
AMUNDSON Silla 1884
11
THOMPSON Tollef 1889
BENDIKSDATTER Sigra 1897
THOMPSON Tollef 1883
HELGESON Ole 1878
THOMPSON Oscar K 1910
HENDRIKSON Ole 1898
HENDRIKSON Ole 1898
ANDERSON Ole 1878
THOMPSON Charles 1880
12
ANDERSON Ole 1880
THOMPSON Charles 1880
ANDERSON Ole 1880
LARSON Arne 1883
OLSEN Otto 1897
GARDNER David A 1915
BALAND Torger 1879
15
BALAND Holsten T 1883
WIGEN Halvor G 1884
THOMPSON Tollef 1883
THOMPSON Tollef 1883
BENDIKSDATTER Sigra 1897
BERGET John O 1898
THORSEN Svend 1884
THORSEN Svend 1884
ASLAKSEN John 1894
BERGET John O 1898
14
BENDIXSON Jens 1904
ASLAKSEN John 1894
LARSON Tollef 1884
THORSEN Svend 1884
ASLAKSEN John 1894
LARSON Arne 1883
OLSEN Otto 1897
OLSEN Otto 1897
THORSON Aslak 1892
MURPHY Dan 1891
13
LARSON Martin A 1891
CHRISTOFFERSON Otto 1899
CHRISTOFFERSON Otto 1899
THORSON Aslak 1892
22
LOFTHUUS Ole T 1883
HAGEN Hans K 1884
HAGEN Hans K 1884
HAGEN Hans K 1884
LOFTHUUS Ole T 1883
LOFTHUUS Ole T 1883
23
KNUDSEN Tom 1896
KNUDSEN Tom 1896
BERGELAND Anund E 1893
BRINGERUD Christen P 1878
BRINGERUD Christen P 1878
24
BRINGERUD Christen P 1878
27
MORK Nels H 1882
AASEN Iver 1884
26
MORK Nels H 1882
AASEN Iver 1884
25
ROLSTAD Ole O 1903
BREWER Louisa F 1874
LEE Ole A 1884
34
LEE Ole A 1884
LEE Gunder A 1885
35
BORTLE David S 1885
BREWER Gaylord I 1880
BREWER Gaylord I 1880
BALDRIDGE S C 1890
36
GREGERSON George Benjamin 1921
BALDRIDGE S C 1890
BALDWIN Heth W 1883
BALDRIDGE S C 1890

Helpful Hints

1. This Map's INDEX can be found on the preceding pages.
2. Refer to Map "C" to see where this Township lies within Dunn County, Wisconsin.
3. Numbers within square brackets [ ] denote a multi-patentee land parcel (multi-owner). Refer to Appendix "C" for a full list of members in this group.
4. Areas that look to be crowded with Patentees usually indicate multiple sales of the same parcel (Re-issues) or Overlapping parcels. See this Township's Index for an explanation of these and other circumstances that might explain "odd" groupings of Patentees on this map.

Legend

———	Patent Boundary
▬▬▬	Section Boundary
(shaded)	No Patents Found (or Outside County)
1., 2., 3., ...	Lot Numbers (when beside a name)
[ ]	Group Number (see Appendix "C")

Scale: Section = 1 mile X 1 mile
(generally, with some exceptions)

Road Map

T31-N R12-W
4th PM - 1831 MN/WI Meridian

Map Group 3

Cities & Towns
Ridgeland

Cemeteries
Tollebu Cemetery

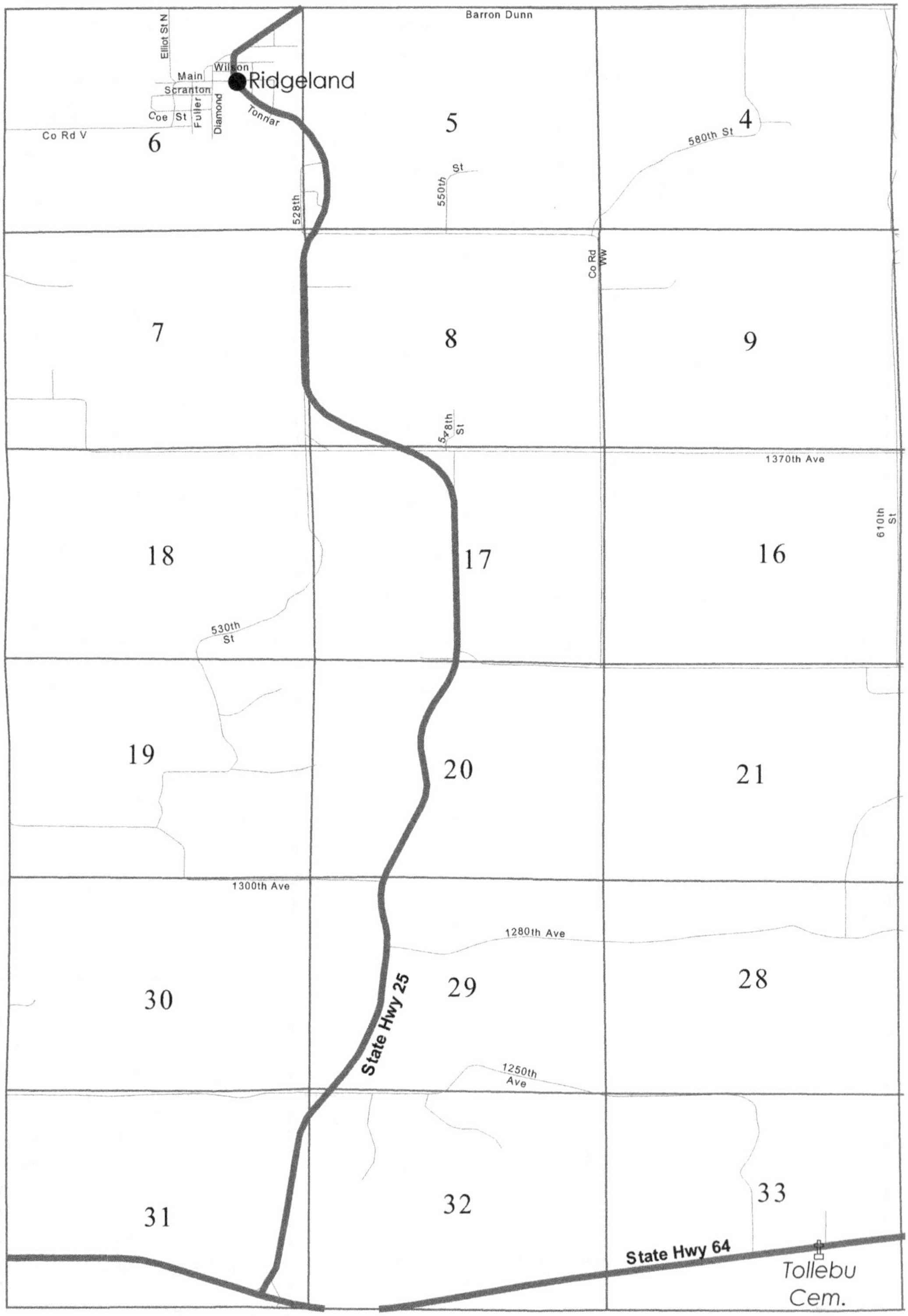
Barron Dunn
Elliot St N
Main
Wilson
Scranton
Ridgeland
Coe St
Fuller
Diamond
Tonnar
Co Rd V
528th
550th St
580th St
Co Rd WW
548th St
1370th Ave
610th St
530th St
1300th Ave
1280th Ave
State Hwy 25
1250th Ave
State Hwy 64
Tollebu Cem.
6
5
4
7
8
9
18
17
16
19
20
21
30
29
28
31
32
33

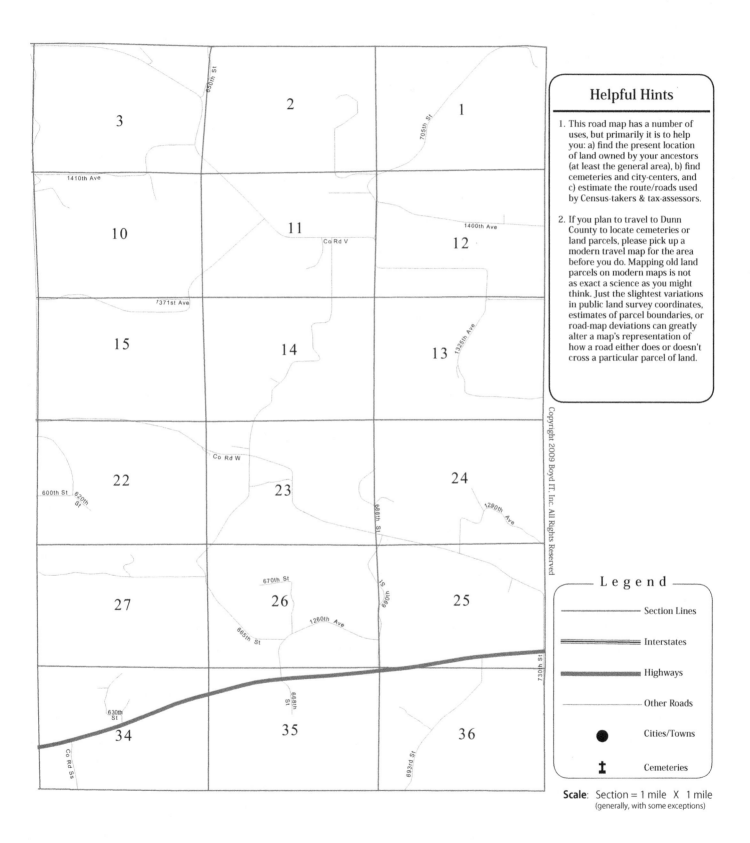

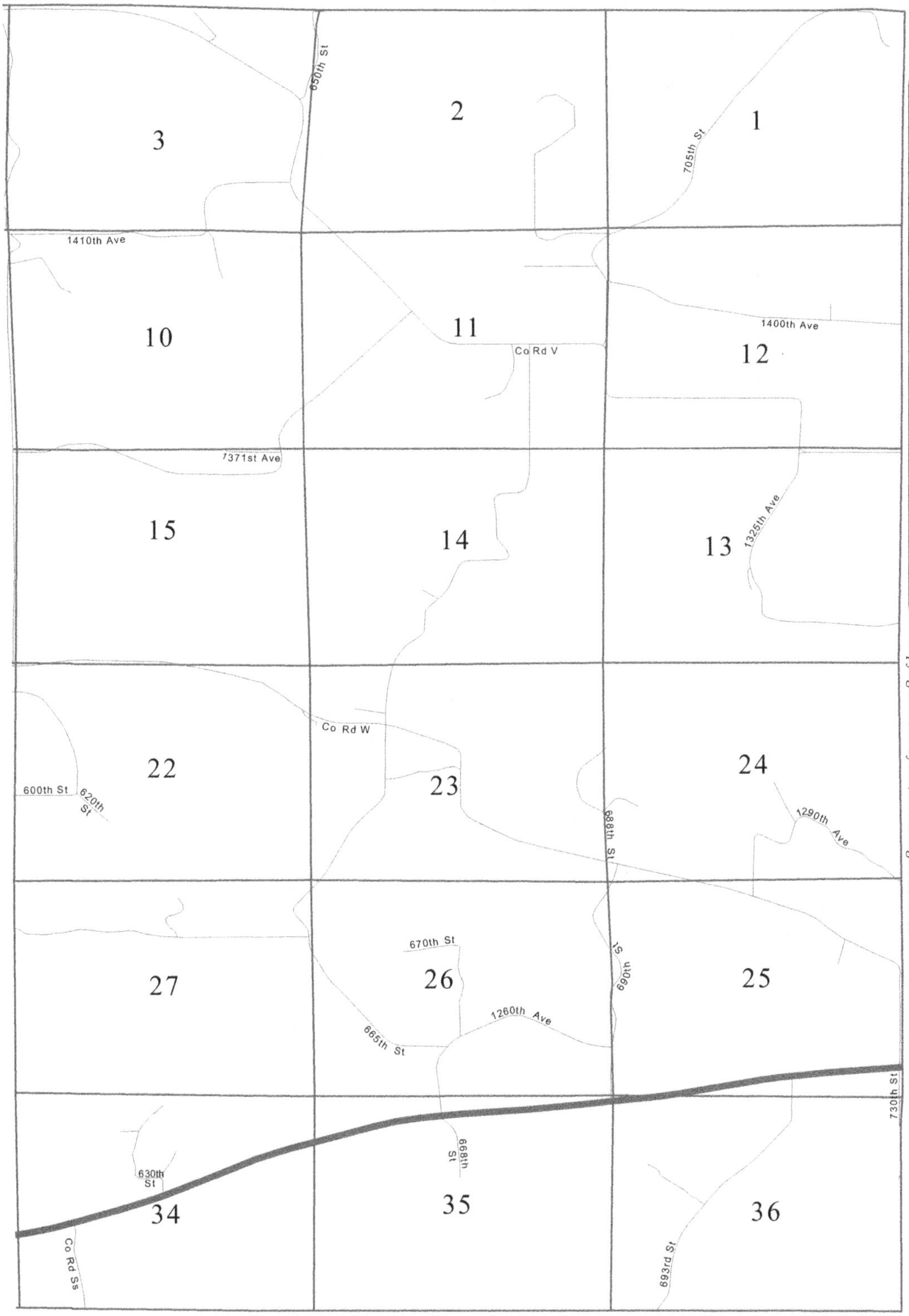

Helpful Hints

1. This road map has a number of uses, but primarily it is to help you: a) find the present location of land owned by your ancestors (at least the general area), b) find cemeteries and city-centers, and c) estimate the route/roads used by Census-takers & tax-assessors.
2. If you plan to travel to Dunn County to locate cemeteries or land parcels, please pick up a modern travel map for the area before you do. Mapping old land parcels on modern maps is not as exact a science as you might think. Just the slightest variations in public land survey coordinates, estimates of parcel boundaries, or road-map deviations can greatly alter a map's representation of how a road either does or doesn't cross a particular parcel of land.

Legend

- Section Lines
- Interstates
- Highways
- Other Roads
- Cities/Towns
- Cemeteries

Scale: Section = 1 mile X 1 mile
(generally, with some exceptions)

Historical Map

T31-N R12-W
4th PM - 1831 MN/WI Meridian

Map Group 3

Cities & Towns

Ridgeland

Cemeteries

Tollebu Cemetery

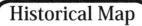

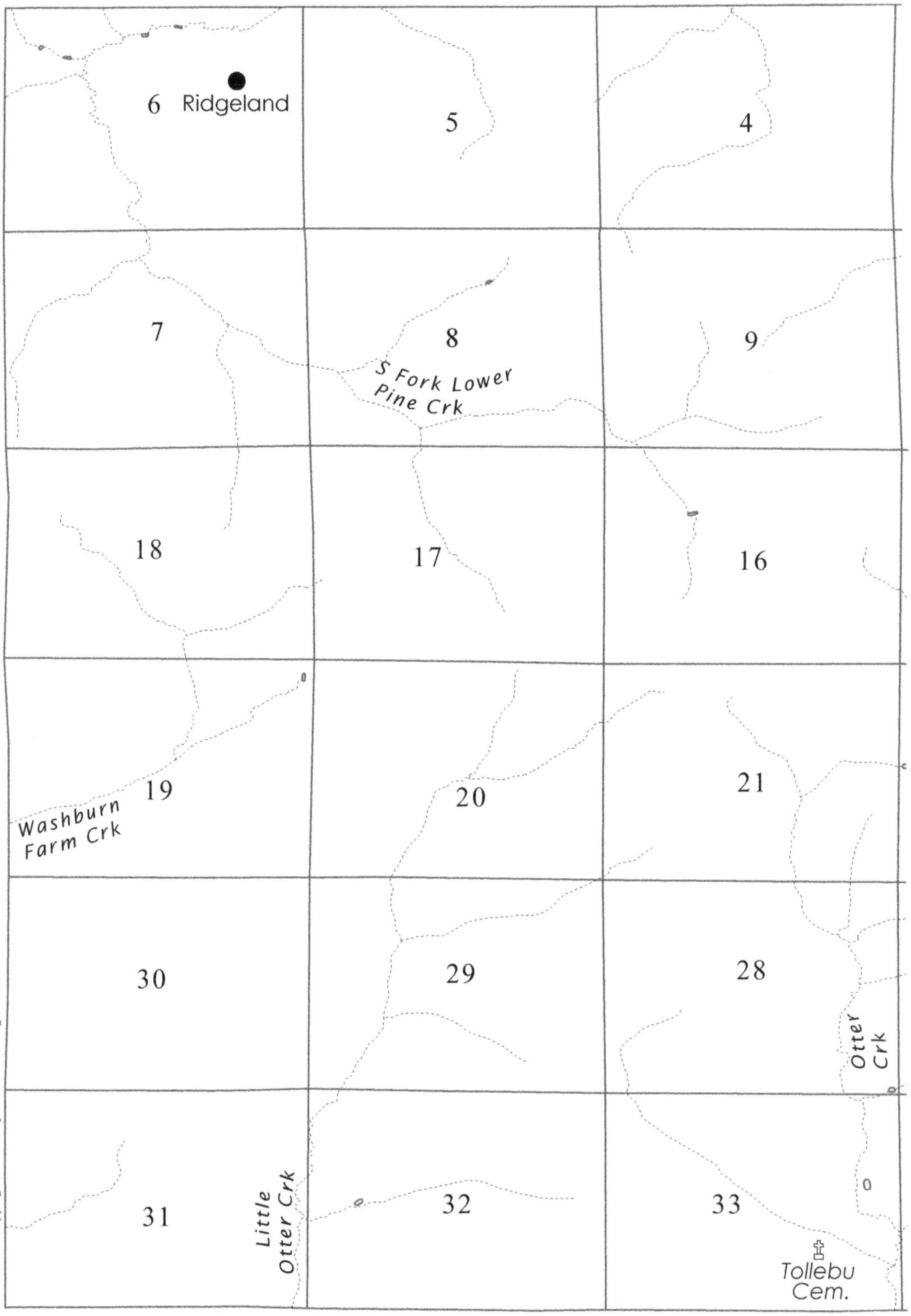
6
Ridgeland
5
4
7
8
9
S Fork Lower Pine Crk
18
17
16
19
20
21
Washburn Farm Crk
30
29
28
Otter Crk
31
32
33
Little Otter Crk
Tollebu Cem.

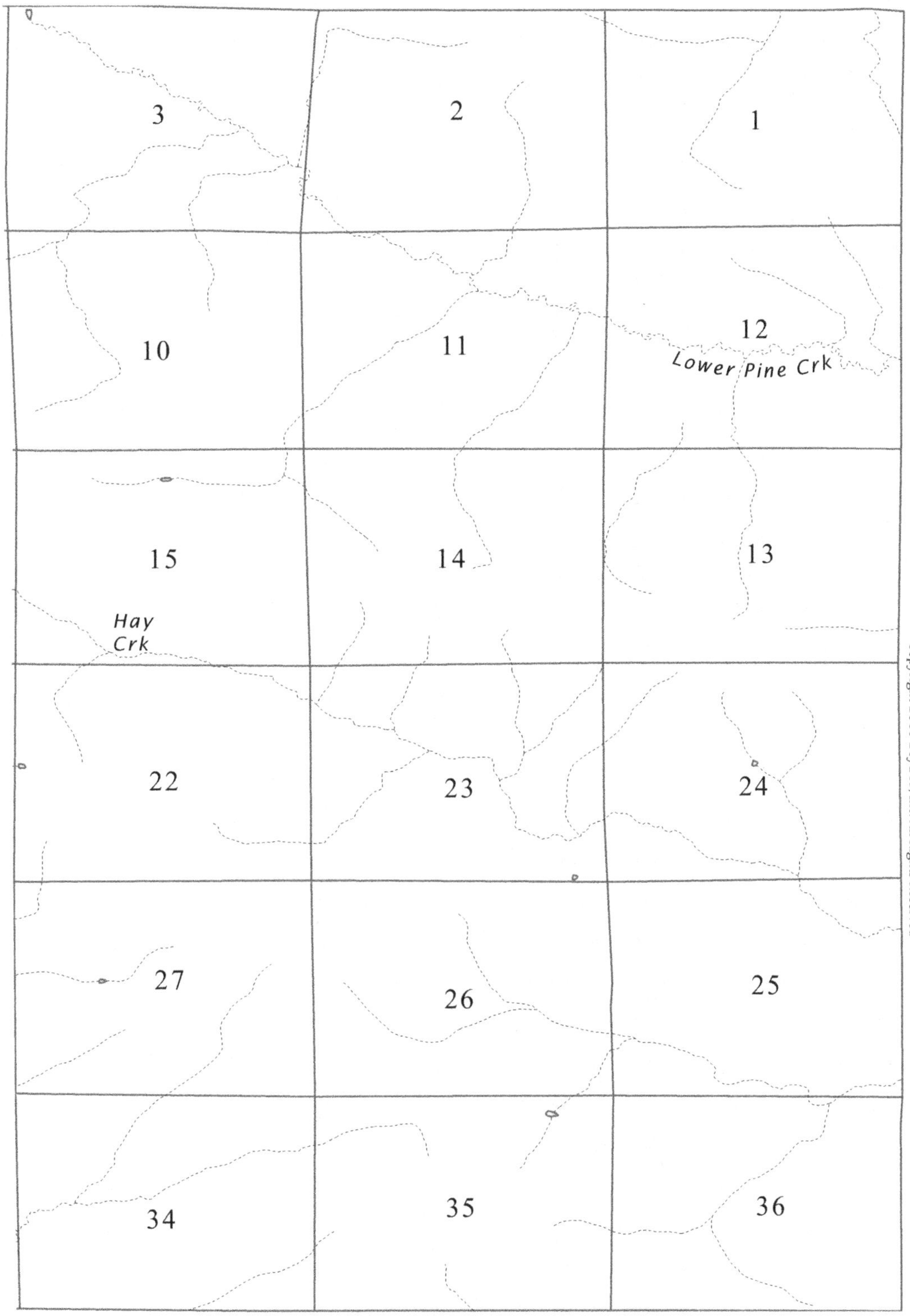
3
2
1
10
11
12
Lower Pine Crk
15
14
13
Hay Crk
22
23
24
27
26
25
34
35
36

Helpful Hints

1. This Map takes a different look at the same Congressional Township displayed in the preceding two maps. It presents features that can help you better envision the historical development of the area: a) Water-bodies (lakes & ponds), b) Water-courses (rivers, streams, etc.), c) Railroads, d) City/town center-points (where they were oftentimes located when first settled), and e) Cemeteries.

2. Using this "Historical" map in tandem with this Township's Patent Map and Road Map, may lead you to some interesting discoveries. You will often find roads, towns, cemeteries, and waterways are named after nearby landowners: sometimes those names will be the ones you are researching. See how many of these research gems you can find here in Dunn County.

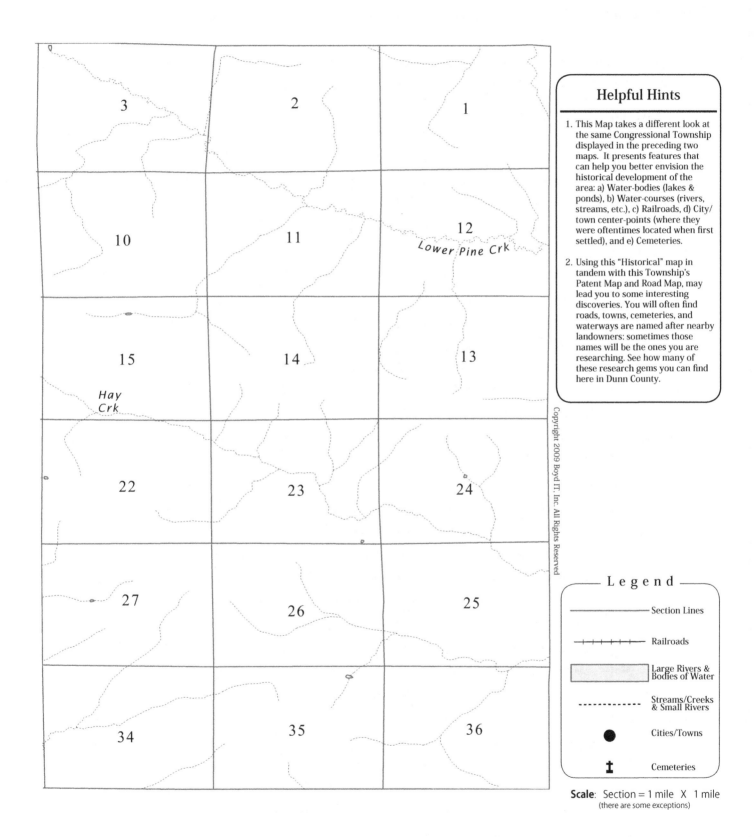

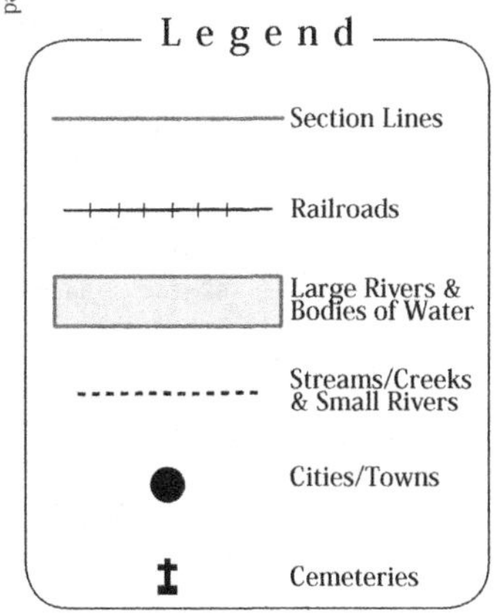
Legend
Section Lines
Railroads
Large Rivers & Bodies of Water
Streams/Creeks & Small Rivers
Cities/Towns
Cemeteries

Scale: Section = 1 mile X 1 mile
(there are some exceptions)

Map Group 4: Index to Land Patents

Township 31-North Range 11-West (4th PM - 1831 MN/WI)

After you locate an individual in this Index, take note of the Section and Section Part then proceed to the Land Patent map on the pages immediately following. You should have no difficulty locating the corresponding parcel of land.

The "For More Info" Column will lead you to more information about the underlying Patents. See the *Legend* at right, and the "How to Use this Book" chapter, for more information.

LEGEND

"For More Info . . . " column

A = Authority (Legislative Act, See Appendix "A")
B = Block or Lot (location in Section unknown)
C = Cancelled Patent
F = Fractional Section
G = Group (Multi-Patentee Patent, see Appendix "C")
V = Overlaps another Parcel
R = Re-Issued (Parcel patented more than once)

(A & G items require you to look in the Appendixes referred to above. All other Letter-designations followed by a number require you to locate line-items in this index that possess the ID number found after the letter).

ID	Individual in Patent	Sec.	Sec. Part	Date Issued	Other Counties	For More Info . . .
502	AMUNDSEN, Carl	28	SE	1880-10-01		A6
515	AMUNDSEN, Edwin	18	E½NW	1888-10-05		A6
516	" "	18	W½NE	1888-10-05		A6
601	AMUNDSEN, Martin	28	SW	1882-05-10		A6
483	ANDERSON, Andrew T	10	N½NW	1883-08-01		A6
484	" "	3	S½SW	1883-08-01		A6
493	ANDERSON, Bergith	15	E½SE	1880-11-20		A6 G206
494	" "	15	SWSE	1880-11-20		A6 G206
495	" "	22	NENE	1880-11-20		A6 G206
536	ANDERSON, Hans T	3	SWNW	1884-01-15		A6
537	" "	4	SENE	1884-01-15		A6
538	" "	4	W½NE	1884-01-15		A6
546	ANDERSON, Ingebor	10	SWSW	1884-08-09		A6
547	" "	15	NWSW	1884-08-09		A6
548	" "	15	W½NW	1884-08-09		A6
590	ANDERSON, Kgreste	6	NENW	1882-04-10		A6 G10
591	" "	6	NWNE	1882-04-10		A6 G10
623	ANDERSON, Ole	22	NW	1878-06-01		A6
643	ANDERSON, Peter	6	NWNW	1883-02-20		A6
590	ANDERSON, Thorsten	6	NENW	1882-04-10		A6 G10
591	" "	6	NWNE	1882-04-10		A6 G10
685	" "	5	SESW	1915-04-16		A6
686	AUGENSEN, Thov	7	S½SE	1882-06-01		A6
687	" "	8	W½SW	1882-06-01		A6
511	BAKER, David W	32	NW	1883-08-01		A6
517	BAKER, Elnathen	19	NENE	1893-08-28		A6
518	" "	20	N½NW	1893-08-28		A6
519	" "	20	SWNW	1893-08-28		A6
556	BAKER, James F	20	SENW	1904-03-01		A6
586	BAKER, Joseph I	32	N½NE	1888-10-05		A6
587	" "	32	SWNE	1888-10-05		A6
505	BELKNAP, Charles A	9	S½SE	1903-11-10		A6
555	BENNETT, Jacob	11	NW	1882-04-10		A6
496	BENTSON, Bernt	14	SWNW	1892-02-08		A6
497	" "	14	W½SW	1892-02-08		A6
498	" "	15	SENE	1892-02-08		A6
508	BOREE, Charles R	3	NESW	1872-04-01		A2
647	BRADLEY, Peter H	5	SWSW	1884-09-15		A6
648	" "	6	E½SE	1884-09-15		A6
649	" "	6	SENE	1884-09-15		A6
562	BREWER, John	30	NE	1873-01-10		A6
470	CARD, Amanda D	30	SE	1874-12-30		A6 G101
582	CERS, Joseph	9	N½NE	1886-08-10		A6
583	" "	9	NESE	1886-08-10		A6
584	" "	9	SENE	1886-08-10		A6
602	CHRISTOPHUSEN, Martin	10	NESE	1892-02-08		A6

ID	Individual in Patent	Sec.	Sec. Part	Date Issued	Other Counties	For More Info . . .
603	CHRISTOPHUSEN, Martin (Cont'd)	10	SENE	1892-02-08		A6
604	" "	11	W½SW	1892-02-08		A6
525	CLARK, Ezra T	29	SW	1873-01-10		A6
698	CLARK, William	25	SENE	1868-10-01		A2
691	CLARK, William B	35	NESW	1870-05-02		A6
692	" "	35	NWSE	1870-05-02		A6
693	" "	35	S½SE	1870-05-02		A6
694	CLARK, William C	25	SE	1870-06-10		A6
540	COOK, Henry D	6	NWSE	1888-10-05		A6
541	" "	6	S½NW	1888-10-05		A6
542	" "	6	SWNE	1888-10-05		A6
549	DALTON, Isaiah A	26	N½SE	1873-01-10		A6
550	" "	26	N½SW	1873-01-10		A6
467	DARROW, Alexander	33	N½SE	1873-05-15		A6
468	" "	33	SENE	1873-05-15		A6
469	" "	33	SESE	1873-05-15		A6
470	DARROW, Amanda	30	SE	1874-12-30		A6 G101
599	DEAN, Lafayette	32	S½SE	1870-10-20		A6
666	DONALDSON, Seymour	25	N½SW	1876-12-30		A6
667	" "	25	S½NW	1876-12-30		A6
688	EGELAND, Torgrim O	3	NWSW	1883-05-05		A6
689	" "	4	N½SE	1883-05-05		A6
690	" "	4	SESE	1883-05-05		A6
644	EIKA, Peter	14	SESW	1875-04-01		A6
645	" "	23	NENW	1875-04-01		A6
646	" "	23	W½NW	1875-04-01		A6
615	FLUENT, Nelson P	30	NW	1873-01-10		A6
563	FREDRICKSEN, John	34	E½NE	1886-03-30		A6
520	GILMAN, Ernest L	18	NWSE	1918-03-05		A6
585	GOODSON, Joseph	36	SE	1873-01-10		A6
526	GRANUM, Frederek A	10	S½SE	1892-05-11		A6
564	GRANUM, John	10	NWSE	1899-06-15		A6
565	" "	10	SENW	1899-06-15		A6
566	" "	10	W½NE	1899-06-15		A6
530	GUNDERSON, Gilbert	2	NE	1877-03-01		A6
699	GUNDT, William	9	N½NW	1916-05-26		A2
596	HAMME, Knudt S	8	NWNE	1890-02-14		A2
475	HAMMER, Andrew	15	SWSW	1904-12-20		A6
531	HANSEN, Halver	5	NWNW	1879-12-15		A6
532	" "	6	NENE	1879-12-15		A6
568	HANSEN, John	34	E½NW	1885-10-22		A6
569	" "	34	W½NE	1885-10-22		A6
612	HANSEN, Mathias	1	NESE	1876-11-03		A6
613	" "	1	SENE	1876-11-03		A6
476	HANSON, Andrew	1	E½SW	1874-04-10		A6
477	" "	1	S½NW	1874-04-10		A6
485	HANSON, Anton	5	NWSW	1904-09-28		A6
551	HANSON, Iver	3	E½NW	1882-05-10		A6
560	HARSTAD, Johannes J	18	N½SW	1905-03-30		A6
561	" "	18	SWNW	1910-07-14		A6
500	HENRY, Catharine	34	SE	1864-04-15		A5 G372
589	HILAND, Julius	6	SW	1896-01-18		A6
635	HJERSSO, Ole T	21	N½NW	1892-04-29		A6
636	" "	21	SENW	1892-04-29		A6
637	" "	21	SWNE	1892-04-29		A6
487	HOILAND, Arne	18	E½SE	1910-07-14		A6
662	HOVLAND, Samuel S	23	N½SW	1874-12-30		A6
663	" "	23	SENW	1874-12-30		A6
664	" "	23	SESW	1874-12-30		A6
466	JACKSON, Aaron N	22	SESW	1869-05-15		A7 G200
466	JACKSON, Andrew	22	SESW	1869-05-15		A7 G200
466	JACKSON, Berthier M	22	SESW	1869-05-15		A7 G200
499	" "	36	NE	1873-01-10		A6
466	JACKSON, Sally J	22	SESW	1869-05-15		A7 G200
558	JOHANSEN, Johan	1	W½NE	1877-04-25		A6
559	" "	1	W½SE	1877-04-25		A6
471	JOHNSON, Amon	1	SESE	1877-04-25		A2
493	JOHNSON, Bergith	15	E½SE	1880-11-20		A6 G206
494	" "	15	SWSE	1880-11-20		A6 G206
495	" "	22	NENE	1880-11-20		A6 G206
597	JOHNSON, Knute	7	E½NE	1879-12-15		A6
598	" "	7	N½SE	1879-12-15		A6
614	JOHNSON, Nary	9	SENW	1878-06-01		A2

ID	Individual in Patent	Sec.	Sec. Part	Date Issued	Other Counties	For More Info . . .
616	JOHNSON, Neri	8	SESW	1874-10-20		A2
625	JOHNSON, Ole	8	NENE	1878-11-05		A2
624	" "	8	N½SE	1883-02-20		A6
626	" "	8	SENE	1883-02-20		A6
627	" "	9	SWNW	1883-02-20		A6
567	KNAPP, John H	10	SESW	1854-10-02		A2
539	KNIGHT, Henry A	22	SWSW	1868-12-01		A2
571	KNIGHT, John	36	S½SW	1873-01-10		A6
478	KNUDSON, Andrew	14	E½NW	1888-10-05		A6
479	" "	14	NWNW	1888-10-05		A6
480	" "	15	NENE	1888-10-05		A6
629	KNUDSON, Ole	3	SE	1873-12-15		A6
628	" "	10	NENE	1875-04-15		A2
543	KRAUSER, Henry	26	S½SE	1881-09-09		A6
544	" "	26	S½SW	1881-09-09		A6
658	LA FORGE, SAMUEL	34	SW	1873-05-15		A6
609	LARSEN, Mary	21	E½NE	1884-09-20		A6
610	" "	21	NESE	1884-09-20		A6
611	" "	22	NWSW	1884-09-20		A6
521	LARSON, Even	20	N½NE	1900-03-17		A6
522	" "	20	SENE	1900-03-17		A6
523	" "	21	SWNW	1900-03-17		A6
552	LARSON, Iver	18	S½SW	1883-02-20		A6
553	" "	18	SWSE	1883-02-20		A6
554	" "	19	NWNE	1883-02-20		A6
572	LARSON, John	14	NESW	1878-06-01		A2
600	LARSON, Louis	1	N½NW	1882-08-25		A6
679	LARSON, Thom	17	SWSE	1913-02-04		A6
668	LETTEER, Sidney	35	N½NE	1891-01-24		A6
665	LOFTHUS, Samuel T	22	NESW	1900-07-12		A6
683	LOFTHUS, Thorbjoren O	22	SE	1878-06-01		A6
489	LOGSLID, Asmund G	8	W½NW	1892-04-29		A6
545	LONGDO, Henry	32	SW	1878-06-13		A6
557	LONGDO, James	34	W½NW	1889-06-20		A6
488	LUND, Arne	11	SESW	1884-09-30		A2
578	LYNCH, John W	30	SW	1880-04-30		A6
527	MANCHESTER, George	36	N½SW	1873-05-15		A6
528	" "	36	S½NW	1873-05-15		A6
656	MARSH, Samuel B	3	NWNW	1887-04-20		A6
657	" "	4	NENE	1887-04-20		A6
512	MCCARTY, Edward	21	SESE	1868-12-01		A2
513	" "	25	S½SW	1873-01-10		A6
514	" "	36	N½NW	1873-01-10		A6
588	MCKIE, Joseph	5	SE	1891-11-16		A6
506	MCMASTERS, Charles P	25	N½NW	1873-05-15		A6
507	" "	25	W½NE	1873-05-15		A6
529	MILLER, George	5	NE	1888-10-05		A6 F
652	MILLER, Robert	24	SESE	1875-03-01		A6
653	" "	24	W½SE	1875-03-01		A6
654	" "	25	NENE	1875-03-01		A6
695	MILLER, William C	5	E½NW	1890-09-11		A6
696	" "	5	NESW	1890-09-11		A6
697	" "	5	SWNW	1890-09-11		A6
503	MITTELSTADT, Carl	32	N½SE	1884-01-15		A6
504	" "	32	SENE	1884-01-15		A6
490	NELSON, Ben	12	SESE	1878-06-01		A6
491	" "	13	E½NE	1878-06-01		A6
492	" "	13	NESE	1878-06-01		A6
682	NELSON, Samuel	15	NWNE	1873-11-01		A2 G317
659	" "	12	NESE	1875-04-01		A6
660	" "	12	W½SE	1875-04-01		A6
661	" "	13	NWNE	1875-04-01		A6
573	NERESON, John	7	W½NW	1899-02-25		A6
533	NERISEN, Halvor	17	E½NW	1888-10-05		A6
534	" "	17	W½NE	1888-10-05		A6
617	NERISON, Neri	17	W½NW	1885-01-13		A6
618	" "	18	E½NE	1885-01-13		A6
630	NERISON, Ole	7	E½NW	1879-12-15		A6
631	" "	7	N½SW	1879-12-15		A6
481	OLESON, Andrew	2	SW	1874-12-30		A6
486	OLESON, Arent Martin	21	NWNE	1931-10-30		A6
524	OLESON, Ever	2	SE	1873-12-15		A6
574	OLESON, John	1	NWSW	1873-11-01		A2

ID	Individual in Patent	Sec.	Sec. Part	Date Issued	Other Counties	For More Info . . .
575	OLESON, John (Cont'd)	15	NENW	1874-01-10		A2
592	OLESON, Knud	3	NE	1874-04-10		A6
472	OLSEN, Anders	17	N½SE	1884-09-15		A6
473	" "	17	SENE	1884-09-15		A6
474	" "	17	SESE	1884-09-15		A6
535	OLSEN, Halvor	1	NENE	1883-05-05		A6
576	OLSEN, John	4	N½NW	1878-11-05		A6
702	OLSEN, William	18	NWNW	1893-07-24		A6
703	" "	7	S½SW	1893-07-24		A6
482	OLSON, Andrew	11	NESW	1869-07-20		A2
577	OLSON, John	1	SWSW	1872-11-01		A2
619	OLSON, Nils	9	N½SW	1884-09-15		A6
620	" "	9	NWSE	1884-09-15		A6
621	" "	9	SWNE	1884-09-15		A6
650	PETERSON, Peter	23	SWSW	1868-12-01		A2
680	RASMUSEN, Thomas	24	NENE	1876-03-01		A6
681	" "	24	S½NE	1876-03-01		A6
682	RASMUSON, Thomas	15	NWNE	1873-11-01		A2 G317
501	RULE, Rebecca	33	SW	1865-10-20		A5 G373
669	RUNKLE, Silas S	4	N½SW	1904-03-01		A6
670	" "	4	S½NW	1904-03-01		A6
570	SAGSTUEN, John J	17	SW	1910-04-14		A6
641	SAMPSON, Osman	4	S½SW	1904-03-01		A6
642	" "	4	SWSE	1904-03-01		A6
509	SEEVER, Chauncey	10	N½SW	1904-08-26		A6
510	" "	10	SWNW	1904-08-26		A6
651	SHAANE, Petter J	12	NE	1873-12-15		A6
500	SPAFFORD, C C	34	SE	1864-04-15		A5 G372
501	" "	33	SW	1865-10-20		A5 G373
593	STENERSEN, Knud	8	E½NW	1883-08-01		A6
594	" "	8	NESW	1883-08-01		A6
595	" "	8	SWNE	1883-08-01		A6
684	SVENUNGSON, Thorgus	19	N½NW	1885-07-13		A6
632	SYLTE, Ole O	20	NESE	1881-09-09		A6
633	" "	20	S½SE	1881-09-09		A6
634	" "	21	NWSW	1881-09-09		A6
640	SYLTE, Oscar	20	NWSE	1910-04-14		A6
605	SYVERSEN, Martin	22	SENE	1888-10-05		A6
606	" "	22	W½NE	1888-10-05		A6
622	THOMPSON, Nils	24	NWNE	1884-09-15		A6
675	THOMPSON, Steiner	15	SWNE	1873-11-01		A2
672	" "	15	E½SW	1877-03-01		A6
673	" "	15	NWSE	1877-03-01		A6
674	" "	15	SENW	1877-03-01		A6
676	TIZEN, Swen	13	SESE	1873-12-15		A6
677	" "	13	SWNE	1873-12-15		A6
678	" "	13	W½SE	1873-12-15		A6
607	TROSVIG, Martinus	21	E½SW	1874-10-01		A6
608	" "	21	W½SE	1874-10-01		A6
638	TROSVIG, Ole	20	SW	1875-09-20		A6
639	" "	20	SWNE	1877-04-25		A2
700	VANDERHOEF, William M	6	SWSE	1891-08-04		A6
701	" "	7	W½NE	1891-08-04		A6
579	WERNER, John	17	NENE	1878-06-01		A6
580	" "	8	S½SE	1878-06-01		A6
581	" "	9	SWSW	1878-06-01		A6
671	WISCONSIN, State Of	16		1941-08-16		A3
655	WISEMAN, Robert	24	NESE	1917-10-03		A2

Patent Map

T31-N R11-W
4th PM - 1831 MN/WI Meridian

Map Group 4

Township Statistics

Parcels Mapped	238
Number of Patents	144
Number of Individuals	142
Patentees Identified	137
Number of Surnames	89
Multi-Patentee Parcels	10
Oldest Patent Date	10/2/1854
Most Recent Patent	8/16/1941
Block/Lot Parcels	0
Parcels Re - Issued	0
Parcels that Overlap	0
Cities and Towns	1
Cemeteries	3

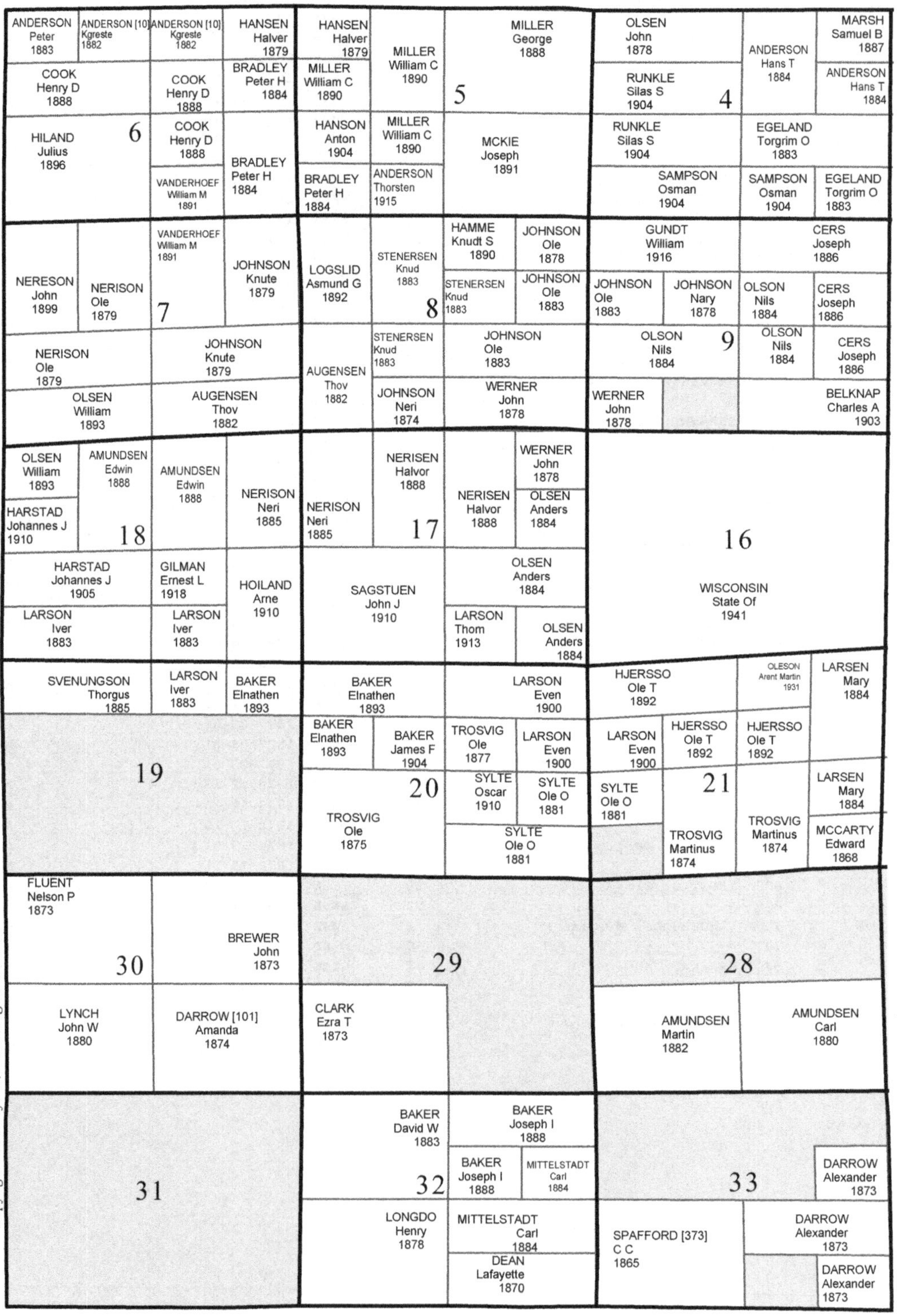

ANDERSON Peter 1883
ANDERSON [10] Kgreste 1882
ANDERSON [10] Kgreste 1882
HANSEN Halver 1879
COOK Henry D 1888
COOK Henry D 1888
BRADLEY Peter H 1884
HILAND Julius 1896
6
COOK Henry D 1888
BRADLEY Peter H 1884
VANDERHOEF William M 1891
HANSEN Halver 1879
MILLER William C 1890
MILLER William C 1890
MILLER George 1888
5
HANSON Anton 1904
MILLER William C 1890
MCKIE Joseph 1891
BRADLEY Peter H 1884
ANDERSON Thorsten 1915
OLSEN John 1878
ANDERSON Hans T 1884
MARSH Samuel B 1887
RUNKLE Silas S 1904
4
ANDERSON Hans T 1884
RUNKLE Silas S 1904
EGELAND Torgrim O 1883
SAMPSON Osman 1904
SAMPSON Osman 1904
EGELAND Torgrim O 1883
NERESON John 1899
NERISON Ole 1879
VANDERHOEF William M 1891
7
JOHNSON Knute 1879
NERISON Ole 1879
JOHNSON Knute 1879
OLSEN William 1893
AUGENSEN Thov 1882
LOGSLID Asmund G 1892
STENERSEN Knud 1883
HAMME Knudt S 1890
JOHNSON Ole 1878
STENERSEN Knud 1883
8
JOHNSON Ole 1883
AUGENSEN Thov 1882
STENERSEN Knud 1883
JOHNSON Ole 1883
JOHNSON Neri 1874
WERNER John 1878
GUNDT William 1916
CERS Joseph 1886
JOHNSON Ole 1883
JOHNSON Nary 1878
OLSON Nils 1884
CERS Joseph 1886
OLSON Nils 1884
9
OLSON Nils 1884
CERS Joseph 1886
WERNER John 1878
BELKNAP Charles A 1903
OLSEN William 1893
AMUNDSEN Edwin 1888
AMUNDSEN Edwin 1888
HARSTAD Johannes J 1910
18
NERISON Neri 1885
NERISON Neri 1885
NERISEN Halvor 1888
17
NERISEN Halvor 1888
WERNER John 1878
OLSEN Anders 1884
HARSTAD Johannes J 1905
GILMAN Ernest L 1918
HOILAND Arne 1910
LARSON Iver 1883
LARSON Iver 1883
SAGSTUEN John J 1910
OLSEN Anders 1884
LARSON Thom 1913
OLSEN Anders 1884
16
WISCONSIN State Of 1941
SVENUNGSON Thorgus 1885
LARSON Iver 1883
BAKER Elnathen 1893
19
BAKER Elnathen 1893
LARSON Even 1900
BAKER Elnathen 1893
BAKER James F 1904
TROSVIG Ole 1877
LARSON Even 1900
20
TROSVIG Ole 1875
SYLTE Oscar 1910
SYLTE Ole O 1881
SYLTE Ole O 1881
HJERSSO Ole T 1892
OLESON Arent Martin 1931
LARSEN Mary 1884
LARSON Even 1900
HJERSSO Ole T 1892
HJERSSO Ole T 1892
SYLTE Ole O 1881
21
LARSEN Mary 1884
TROSVIG Martinus 1874
TROSVIG Martinus 1874
MCCARTY Edward 1868
FLUENT Nelson P 1873
30
BREWER John 1873
LYNCH John W 1880
DARROW [101] Amanda 1874
29
CLARK Ezra T 1873
28
AMUNDSEN Martin 1882
AMUNDSEN Carl 1880
31
BAKER David W 1883
BAKER Joseph I 1888
BAKER Joseph I 1888
MITTELSTADT Carl 1884
32
LONGDO Henry 1878
MITTELSTADT Carl 1884
DEAN Lafayette 1870
33
DARROW Alexander 1873
SPAFFORD [373] C C 1865
DARROW Alexander 1873
DARROW Alexander 1873

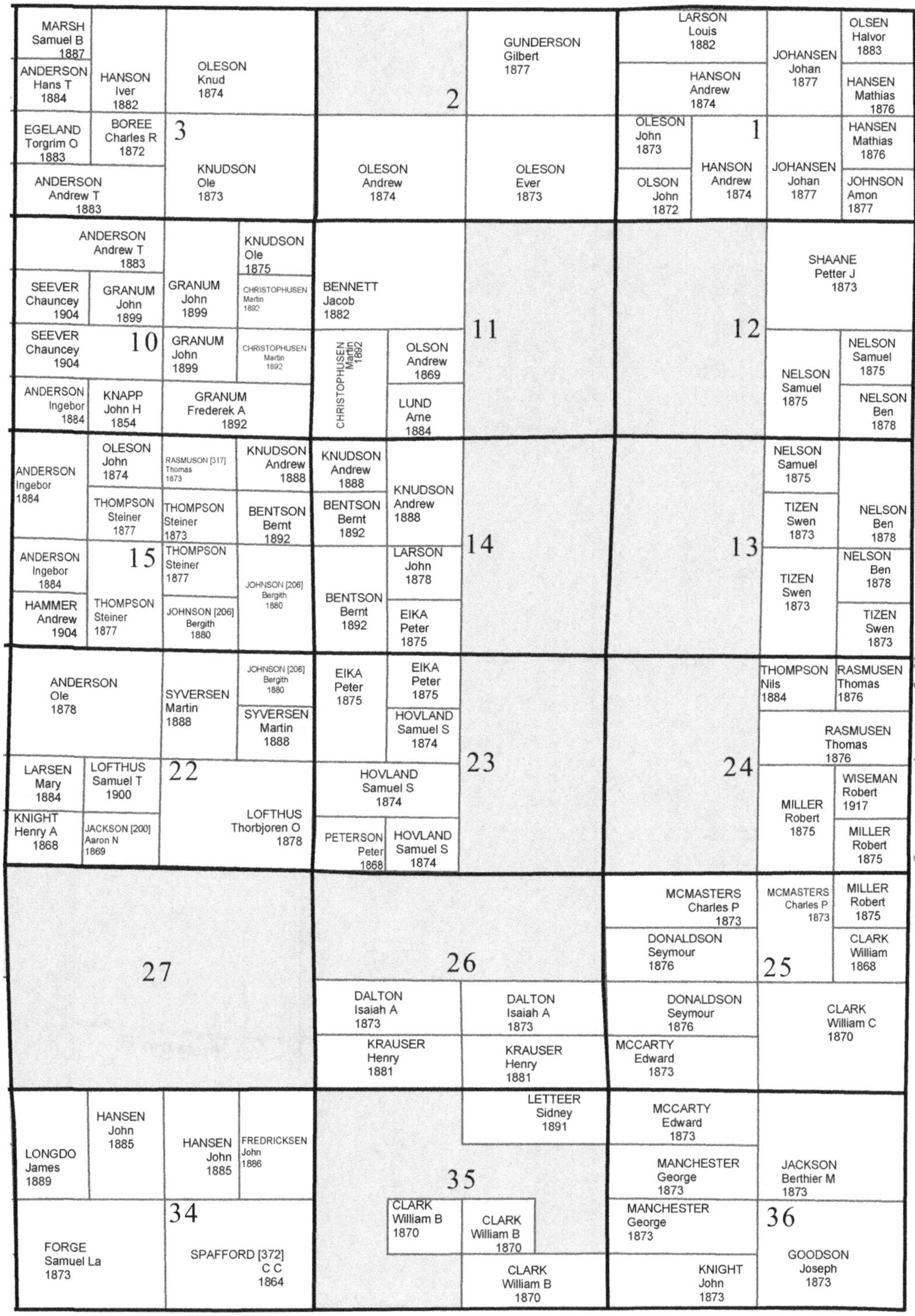
MARSH Samuel B 1887
ANDERSON Hans T 1884
HANSON Iver 1882
OLESON Knud 1874
EGELAND Torgrim O 1883
BOREE Charles R 1872
3
KNUDSON Ole 1873
ANDERSON Andrew T 1883
2
GUNDERSON Gilbert 1877
OLESON Andrew 1874
OLESON Ever 1873
LARSON Louis 1882
HANSON Andrew 1874
JOHANSEN Johan 1877
OLSEN Halvor 1883
HANSEN Mathias 1876
OLESON John 1873
1
HANSEN Mathias 1876
OLSON John 1872
HANSON Andrew 1874
JOHANSEN Johan 1877
JOHNSON Amon 1877
ANDERSON Andrew T 1883
KNUDSON Ole 1875
SEEVER Chauncey 1904
GRANUM John 1899
GRANUM John 1899
CHRISTOPHUSEN Martin 1892
SEEVER Chauncey 1904
10
GRANUM John 1899
CHRISTOPHUSEN Martin 1892
ANDERSON Ingebor 1884
KNAPP John H 1854
GRANUM Frederek A 1892
BENNETT Jacob 1882
CHRISTOPHUSEN Martin 1892
OLSON Andrew 1869
LUND Arne 1884
11
SHAANE Petter J 1873
12
NELSON Samuel 1875
NELSON Samuel 1875
NELSON Ben 1878
ANDERSON Ingebor 1884
OLESON John 1874
RASMUSON [317] Thomas 1873
KNUDSON Andrew 1888
THOMPSON Steiner 1877
THOMPSON Steiner 1873
BENTSON Bernt 1892
ANDERSON Ingebor 1884
15
THOMPSON Steiner 1877
JOHNSON [206] Bergith 1880
HAMMER Andrew 1904
THOMPSON Steiner 1877
JOHNSON [206] Bergith 1880
KNUDSON Andrew 1888
KNUDSON Andrew 1888
BENTSON Bernt 1892
LARSON John 1878
BENTSON Bernt 1892
EIKA Peter 1875
14
NELSON Samuel 1875
TIZEN Swen 1873
NELSON Ben 1878
13
TIZEN Swen 1873
NELSON Ben 1878
TIZEN Swen 1873
ANDERSON Ole 1878
SYVERSEN Martin 1888
JOHNSON [206] Bergith 1880
SYVERSEN Martin 1888
LARSEN Mary 1884
LOFTHUS Samuel T 1900
22
KNIGHT Henry A 1868
JACKSON [200] Aaron N 1869
LOFTHUS Thorbjoren O 1878
EIKA Peter 1875
EIKA Peter 1875
HOVLAND Samuel S 1874
HOVLAND Samuel S 1874
PETERSON Peter 1868
HOVLAND Samuel S 1874
23
THOMPSON Nils 1884
RASMUSEN Thomas 1876
RASMUSEN Thomas 1876
24
MILLER Robert 1875
WISEMAN Robert 1917
MILLER Robert 1875
27
26
MCMASTERS Charles P 1873
DONALDSON Seymour 1876
MCMASTERS Charles P 1873
MILLER Robert 1875
CLARK William 1868
25
DALTON Isaiah A 1873
DALTON Isaiah A 1873
KRAUSER Henry 1881
KRAUSER Henry 1881
DONALDSON Seymour 1876
MCCARTY Edward 1873
CLARK William C 1870
LONGDO James 1889
HANSEN John 1885
HANSEN John 1885
FREDRICKSEN John 1886
34
FORGE Samuel La 1873
SPAFFORD [372] C C 1864
LETTEER Sidney 1891
35
CLARK William B 1870
CLARK William B 1870
CLARK William B 1870
MCCARTY Edward 1873
MANCHESTER George 1873
MANCHESTER George 1873
KNIGHT John 1873
JACKSON Berthier M 1873
36
GOODSON Joseph 1873

Helpful Hints

1. This Map's INDEX can be found on the preceding pages.
2. Refer to Map "C" to see where this Township lies within Dunn County, Wisconsin.
3. Numbers within square brackets [ ] denote a multi-patentee land parcel (multi-owner). Refer to Appendix "C" for a full list of members in this group.
4. Areas that look to be crowded with Patentees usually indicate multiple sales of the same parcel (Re-issues) or Overlapping parcels. See this Township's Index for an explanation of these and other circumstances that might explain "odd" groupings of Patentees on this map.

Legend

- Patent Boundary
- Section Boundary
- No Patents Found (or Outside County)
- 1., 2., 3., ... Lot Numbers (when beside a name)
- [ ] Group Number (see Appendix "C")

Scale: Section = 1 mile X 1 mile (generally, with some exceptions)

Road Map

T31-N R11-W
4th PM - 1831 MN/WI Meridian

Map Group 4

Cities & Towns

Sand Creek

Cemeteries

Myron Cemetery
Our Saviors Cemetery
Zion Cemetery

6
5
4
1400th Ave
7
8
1390th Ave
9
770th St
18
17
16
19
20
836th St
21
1325th Ave
780th St
1290th Ave
760th St
30
29
28
1233rd Ave
State Hwy 64
810th St
730th St
31
32
33
820th St

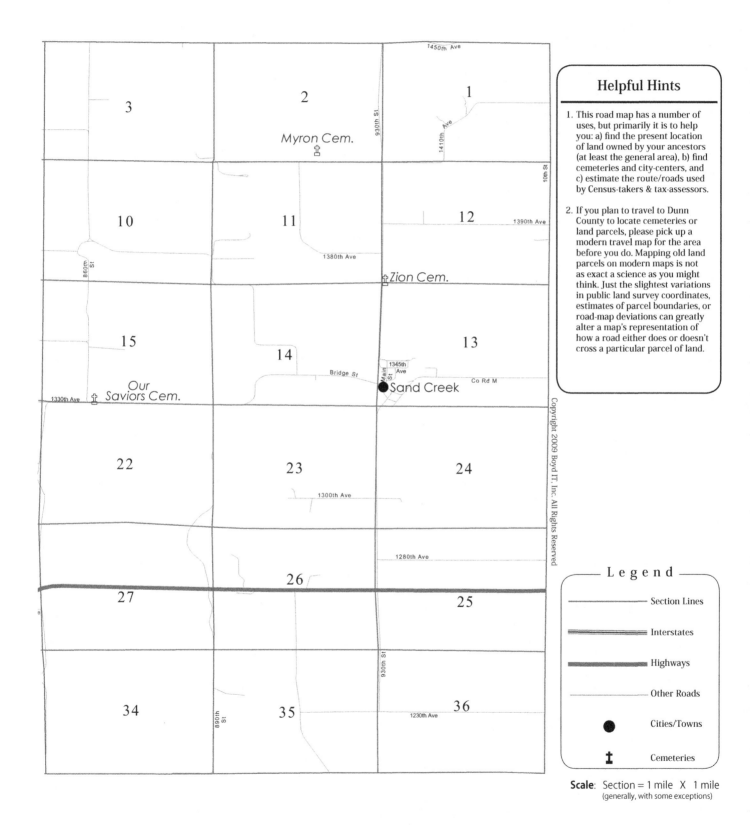

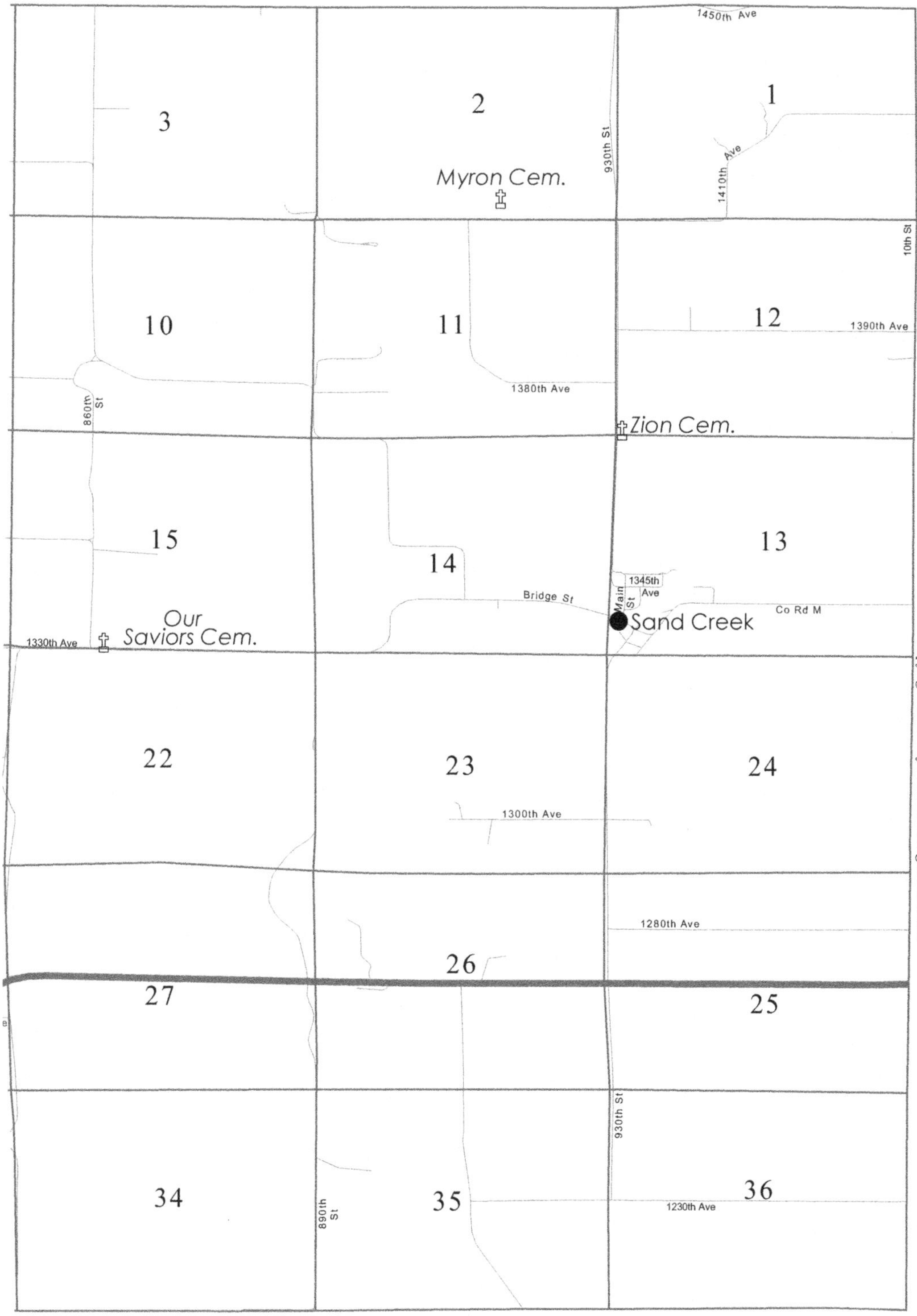

Helpful Hints

1. This road map has a number of uses, but primarily it is to help you: a) find the present location of land owned by your ancestors (at least the general area), b) find cemeteries and city-centers, and c) estimate the route/roads used by Census-takers & tax-assessors.

2. If you plan to travel to Dunn County to locate cemeteries or land parcels, please pick up a modern travel map for the area before you do. Mapping old land parcels on modern maps is not as exact a science as you might think. Just the slightest variations in public land survey coordinates, estimates of parcel boundaries, or road-map deviations can greatly alter a map's representation of how a road either does or doesn't cross a particular parcel of land.

Legend

- Section Lines
- Interstates
- Highways
- Other Roads
- Cities/Towns
- Cemeteries

Scale: Section = 1 mile X 1 mile
(generally, with some exceptions)

Historical Map

T31-N R11-W
4th PM - 1831 MN/WI Meridian

Map Group 4

Cities & Towns

Sand Creek

Cemeteries

Myron Cemetery
Our Saviors Cemetery
Zion Cemetery

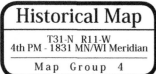

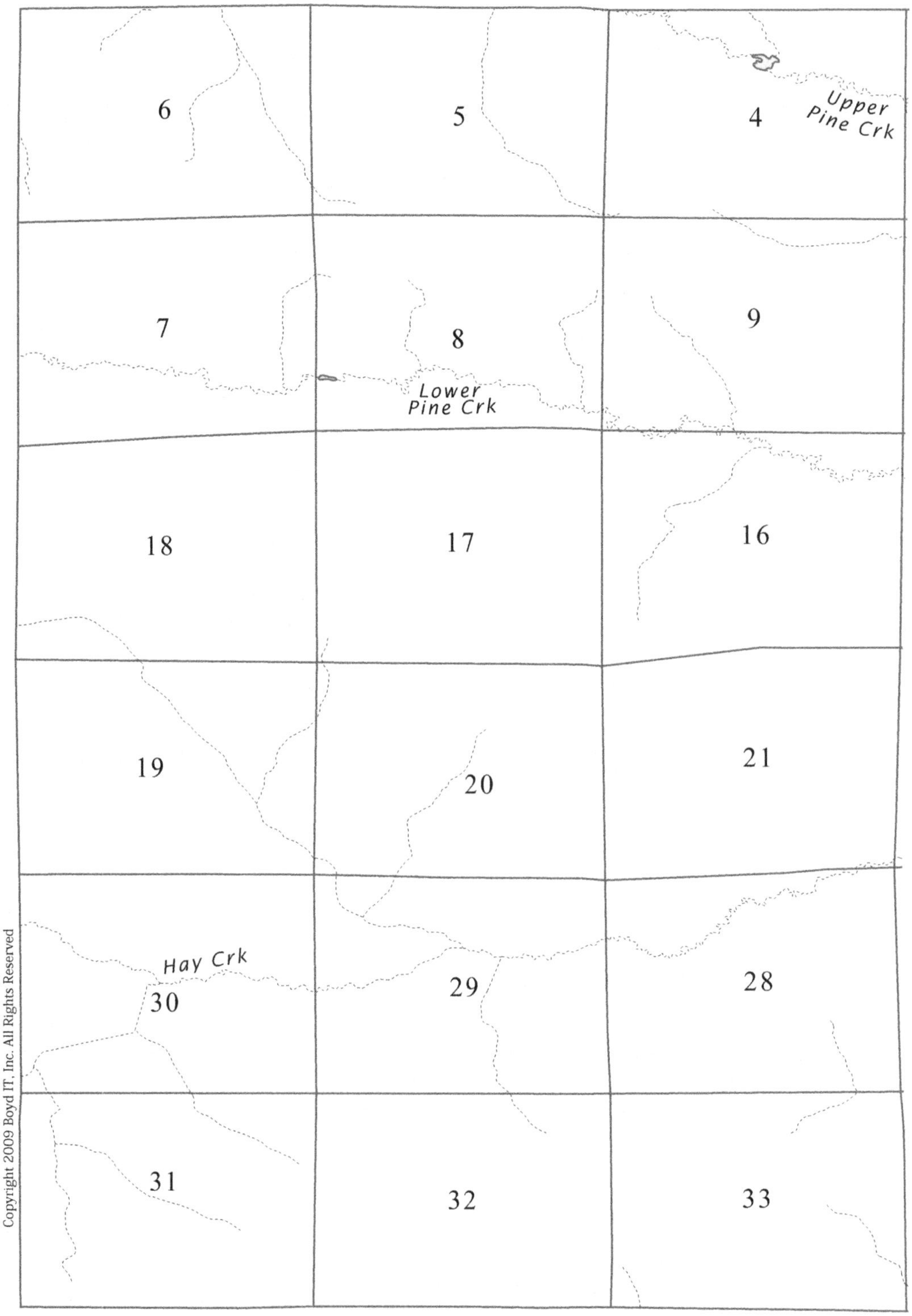
6
5
4
Upper Pine Crk
7
8
9
Lower Pine Crk
18
17
16
19
20
21
Hay Crk
30
29
28
31
32
33

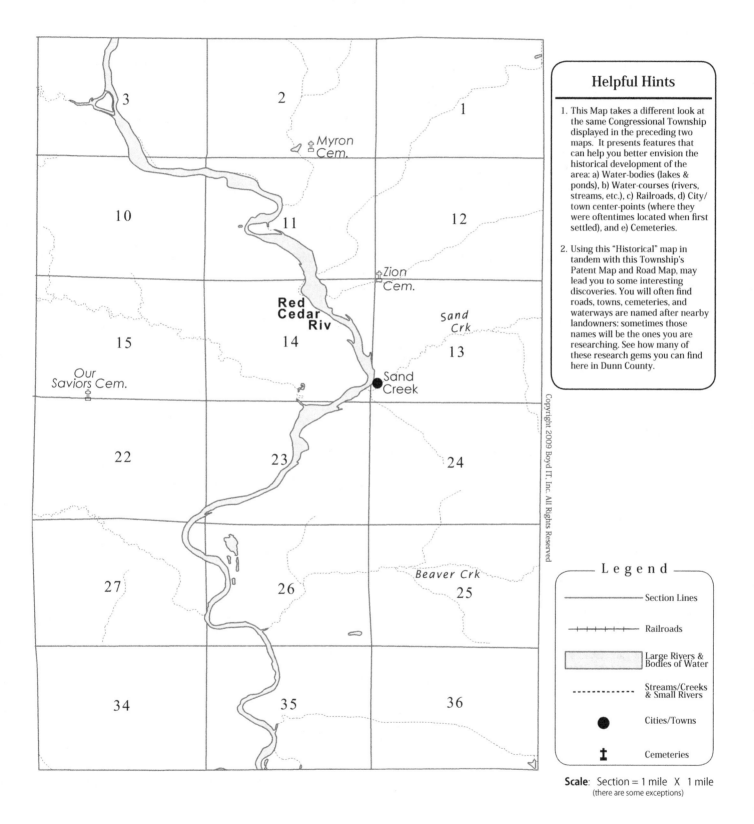

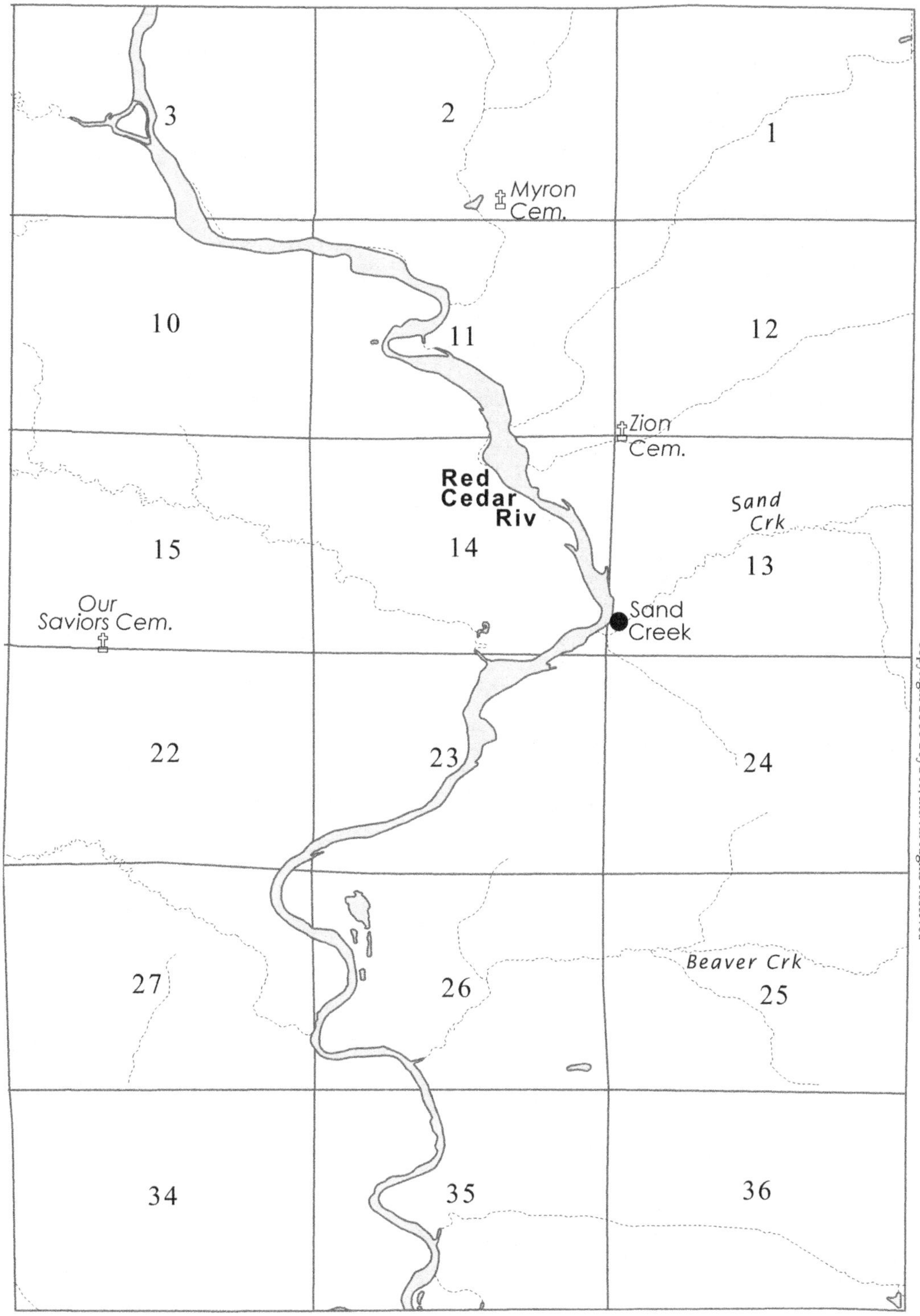
3
2
1
Myron Cem.
10
11
12
Zion Cem.
Red Cedar Riv
Sand Crk
15
14
13
Our Saviors Cem.
Sand Creek
22
23
24
27
26
Beaver Crk
25
34
35
36

Helpful Hints

1. This Map takes a different look at the same Congressional Township displayed in the preceding two maps. It presents features that can help you better envision the historical development of the area: a) Water-bodies (lakes & ponds), b) Water-courses (rivers, streams, etc.), c) Railroads, d) City/town center-points (where they were oftentimes located when first settled), and e) Cemeteries.
2. Using this "Historical" map in tandem with this Township's Patent Map and Road Map, may lead you to some interesting discoveries. You will often find roads, towns, cemeteries, and waterways are named after nearby landowners: sometimes those names will be the ones you are researching. See how many of these research gems you can find here in Dunn County.

Legend

- Section Lines
- Railroads
- Large Rivers & Bodies of Water
- Streams/Creeks & Small Rivers
- Cities/Towns
- Cemeteries

Scale: Section = 1 mile X 1 mile
(there are some exceptions)

Map Group 5: Index to Land Patents

Township 30-North Range 14-West (4th PM - 1831 MN/WI)

After you locate an individual in this Index, take note of the Section and Section Part then proceed to the Land Patent map on the pages immediately following. You should have no difficulty locating the corresponding parcel of land.

The "For More Info" Column will lead you to more information about the underlying Patents. See the *Legend* at right, and the "How to Use this Book" chapter, for more information.

LEGEND

"For More Info . . . " column

A = Authority (Legislative Act, See Appendix "A")
B = Block or Lot (location in Section unknown)
C = Cancelled Patent
F = Fractional Section
G = Group (Multi-Patentee Patent, see Appendix "C")
V = Overlaps another Parcel
R = Re-Issued (Parcel patented more than once)

(A & G items require you to look in the Appendixes referred to above. All other Letter-designations followed by a number require you to locate line-items in this index that possess the ID number found after the letter).

ID	Individual in Patent	Sec.	Sec. Part	Date Issued	Other Counties	For More Info . . .
815	ADAMS, Esther H	4	10	1859-09-01		A5 G31
816	" "	4	W½SE	1859-09-01		A5 G31
821	AMORY, James	9	NESE	1860-08-01		A5
823	" "	9	NWSE	1860-08-01		A5 G7
822	" "	9	S½NE	1860-08-01		A5
824	" "	9	S½SE	1860-08-01		A5 G7
817	ANACKER, Hartman	34	E½SW	1879-10-01		A6
818	ANDRESS, Hezekiah	32	NENW	1874-04-01		A6
833	BANKS, John	10	S½SW	1854-10-02		A2
806	BARTON, Gorham	10	NWNW	1859-09-01		A5
815	" "	4	10	1859-09-01		A5 G31
807	" "	4	11	1859-09-01		A5
808	" "	4	12	1859-09-01		A5
809	" "	4	5	1859-09-01		A5
810	" "	4	6	1859-09-01		A5
811	" "	4	N½SW	1859-09-01		A5
812	" "	4	S½SW	1859-09-01		A5
816	" "	4	W½SE	1859-09-01		A5 G31
813	" "	5	SESE	1859-09-01		A5
814	" "	9	N½NE	1859-09-01		A5
854	BENNETT, John W	21	NE	1860-08-01		A5
880	BESSE, Oliver	24	SE	1880-09-01		A6
707	BEST, Alexander H	6	2	1878-06-24		A6
738	BEST, Edward T	6	1	1877-03-20		A6
850	BEST, John N	6	10	1877-03-20		A6
851	" "	6	3	1877-03-20		A6
852	" "	6	W½SW	1877-03-20		A6
861	BEST, Lycurgus C	8	N½SW	1873-05-20		A6
862	" "	8	W½NW	1873-05-20		A6
898	BEST, Solon P	8	S½SW	1873-12-20		A6
865	BLAKELY, Martin	34	E½SE	1878-06-24		A6
873	BLAKELY, Nelson L	36	N½NE	1879-11-10		A6
874	" "	36	SENE	1879-11-10		A6
896	BLODGETT, Roswell P	12	SE	1900-03-17		A6
884	BODETT, Peter	14	E½NE	1878-06-24		A6
885	" "	14	E½SE	1878-06-24		A6
825	BOGGESS, Jeptha	27	E½SW	1860-07-16		A5
832	" "	27	SE	1860-07-16		A5 G43
826	" "	27	W½SW	1860-07-16		A5
827	" "	34	E½NE	1860-07-16		A5
830	" "	34	E½NW	1860-07-16		A5 G44
828	" "	34	NWNE	1860-07-16		A5
831	" "	34	SWNE	1860-07-16		A5 G44
829	" "	34	W½NW	1860-07-16		A5
855	BREWER, John W	6	S½SE	1872-09-25		A6
856	" "	6	SESW	1872-09-25		A6

ID	Individual in Patent	Sec.	Sec. Part	Date Issued	Other Counties	For More Info . . .
719	BREWSTER, Charles F	22	SESE	1869-08-05		A2
720	" "	22	W½SE	1869-08-05		A2
756	BROWN, George H	2	11	1892-04-20		A6
757	" "	2	12	1892-04-20		A6
758	" "	2	4	1892-04-20		A6
759	" "	2	5	1892-04-20		A6
870	BROWN, Millard F	26	NESE	1881-02-10		A6
871	BROWN, Moses	26	SESW	1871-11-20		A6
872	" "	26	W½SE	1871-11-20		A6
770	CHAPIN, George W	28	E½NW	1860-07-16		A5 G309
771	" "	28	NESW	1860-07-16		A5 G309
895	CHRISTIE, Priscilla	15	W½SW	1860-07-16		A5 G267
785	CO, Riggs And	18	E½SW	1860-07-16		A5 G328
805	" "	18	SE	1860-07-16		A5 G340
786	" "	18	SENW	1860-07-16		A5 G328
787	" "	20	E½SE	1860-07-16		A5 G328
783	" "	20	E½SW	1860-07-16		A5 G332
788	" "	20	NE	1860-07-16		A5 G328
804	" "	20	NW	1860-07-16		A5 G331
784	" "	20	NWSE	1860-07-16		A5 G332
789	" "	20	SWSE	1860-07-16		A5 G328
782	" "	22	NE	1860-07-16		A5 G334
790	" "	22	NW	1860-07-16		A5 G328
780	" "	30	E½NW	1860-07-16		A5 G336
781	" "	30	S½NE	1860-07-16		A5 G336
791	" "	32	S½SE	1860-07-16		A5 G328
801	" "	32	SW	1860-07-16		A5 G329
792	" "	6	4	1860-07-16		A5 G328
793	" "	6	5	1860-07-16		A5 G328
794	" "	6	6	1860-07-16		A5 G328
795	" "	6	7	1860-07-16		A5 G328
796	" "	6	8	1860-07-16		A5 G328
797	" "	6	9	1860-07-16		A5 G328
778	" "	6	N½SE	1860-07-16		A5 G341
779	" "	6	NESW	1860-07-16		A5 G341
798	" "	8	N½SE	1860-07-16		A5 G327
777	" "	8	S½SE	1860-07-16		A5 G333
799	" "	21	E½SW	1860-08-01		A5 G342
800	" "	21	SENW	1860-08-01		A5 G342
802	" "	21	SWNW	1860-08-01		A5 G330
803	" "	21	W½SW	1860-08-01		A5 G330
801	COBB, Sarah N	32	SW	1860-07-16		A5 G329
901	COCHRAN, Thomas C	22	SW	1860-07-16		A5
802	CORNISH, Susan W	21	SWNW	1860-08-01		A5 G330
803	" "	21	W½SW	1860-08-01		A5 G330
782	CULBERT, James W	22	NE	1860-07-16		A5 G334
743	CULBERTSON, Eli	18	NE	1875-08-10		A6
722	CULP, Cornelius	2	10	1882-05-10		A6
723	" "	2	6	1882-05-10		A6
724	" "	2	7	1882-05-10		A6
725	" "	2	8	1882-05-10		A6
780	CURRY, Elizabeth	30	E½NW	1860-07-16		A5 G336
781	" "	30	S½NE	1860-07-16		A5 G336
780	CURRY, Louisa L	30	E½NW	1860-07-16		A5 G336
781	" "	30	S½NE	1860-07-16		A5 G336
780	CURRY, Lucinda F	30	E½NW	1860-07-16		A5 G336
781	" "	30	S½NE	1860-07-16		A5 G336
750	CURRY, Lucy	26	W½NW	1860-07-16		A5 G227
863	DAVIS, Lydia D	12	E½NW	1880-09-01		A6
864	" "	12	W½NE	1880-09-01		A6
832	DRINKER, Joseph H	27	SE	1860-07-16		A5 G43
785	ELLIOTT, John	18	E½SW	1860-07-16		A5 G328
805	" "	18	SE	1860-07-16		A5 G340
786	" "	18	SENW	1860-07-16		A5 G328
787	" "	20	E½SE	1860-07-16		A5 G328
783	" "	20	E½SW	1860-07-16		A5 G332
788	" "	20	NE	1860-07-16		A5 G328
804	" "	20	NW	1860-07-16		A5 G331
784	" "	20	NWSE	1860-07-16		A5 G332
789	" "	20	SWSE	1860-07-16		A5 G328
782	" "	22	NE	1860-07-16		A5 G334
790	" "	22	NW	1860-07-16		A5 G328
780	" "	30	E½NW	1860-07-16		A5 G336

ID	Individual in Patent	Sec.	Sec. Part	Date Issued	Other Counties	For More Info . . .
781	ELLIOTT, John (Cont'd)	30	S½NE	1860-07-16		A5 G336
791	" "	32	S½SE	1860-07-16		A5 G328
801	" "	32	SW	1860-07-16		A5 G329
792	" "	6	4	1860-07-16		A5 G328
793	" "	6	5	1860-07-16		A5 G328
794	" "	6	6	1860-07-16		A5 G328
795	" "	6	7	1860-07-16		A5 G328
796	" "	6	8	1860-07-16		A5 G328
797	" "	6	9	1860-07-16		A5 G328
778	" "	6	N½SE	1860-07-16		A5 G341
779	" "	6	NESW	1860-07-16		A5 G341
798	" "	8	N½SE	1860-07-16		A5 G327
777	" "	8	S½SE	1860-07-16		A5 G333
799	" "	21	E½SW	1860-08-01		A5 G342
800	" "	21	SENW	1860-08-01		A5 G342
802	" "	21	SWNW	1860-08-01		A5 G330
803	" "	21	W½SW	1860-08-01		A5 G330
836	EVERETT, John	2	1	1905-05-02		A6
752	FARRINGTON, Fremont D	2	2	1883-02-10		A6
753	" "	2	3	1883-02-10		A6
832	FIXICO, Tallissee	27	SE	1860-07-16		A5 G43
804	GIBSON, W W	20	NW	1860-07-16		A5 G331
710	GOFF, Amos	12	NESW	1878-11-30		A6
711	" "	12	SWNW	1878-11-30		A6
712	" "	12	W½SW	1878-11-30		A6
718	GOFF, C M	14	SESW	1872-02-14		A2
744	GOFF, Elisha	23	NE	1871-08-25		A6
708	GOSS, Alfred	10	N½SW	1863-04-20		A5
709	" "	10	S½NW	1863-04-20		A5
760	HALL, George	18	NENW	1882-04-10		A6
894	HARVEY, William R	15	E½SW	1860-07-16		A5 G268
839	HAVENSTICK, Susanna	15	E½NE	1860-07-16		A5 G423
840	" "	15	SWNE	1860-07-16		A5 G423
739	HERRIMAN, Edwin	5	5	1859-05-02		A2
740	" "	5	6	1859-05-02		A2
741	" "	5	7	1859-05-02		A2
742	" "	5	8	1859-05-02		A2
819	HERRIMAN, Ira	5	NESE	1859-05-02		A2
714	HINMAN, Arthur L	4	4	1894-01-27		A2
732	HYDE, Dillon	15	SE	1860-07-16		A5 G196
860	JAMRISKA, Joseph	12	E½NE	1900-03-17		A6
908	JARCKE, Ann	36	SE	1860-10-01		A5 G307
805	JENONSON, Eunice A	18	SE	1860-07-16		A5 G340
783	JOHNSON, Hannah	20	E½SW	1860-07-16		A5 G332
784	" "	20	NWSE	1860-07-16		A5 G332
820	JONES, Isaac S	11	S½SW	1860-02-01		A5 G209
704	KAYE, Abel	23	SWSE	1871-03-15		A6
705	" "	26	SENE	1871-03-15		A6
706	" "	26	W½NE	1871-03-15		A6
785	KIECKHOEFER, A T	18	E½SW	1860-07-16		A5 G328
805	" "	18	SE	1860-07-16		A5 G340
786	" "	18	SENW	1860-07-16		A5 G328
787	" "	20	E½SE	1860-07-16		A5 G328
783	" "	20	E½SW	1860-07-16		A5 G332
788	" "	20	NE	1860-07-16		A5 G328
804	" "	20	NW	1860-07-16		A5 G331
784	" "	20	NWSE	1860-07-16		A5 G332
789	" "	20	SWSE	1860-07-16		A5 G328
782	" "	22	NE	1860-07-16		A5 G334
790	" "	22	NW	1860-07-16		A5 G328
780	" "	30	E½NW	1860-07-16		A5 G336
781	" "	30	S½NE	1860-07-16		A5 G336
791	" "	32	S½SE	1860-07-16		A5 G328
801	" "	32	SW	1860-07-16		A5 G329
792	" "	6	4	1860-07-16		A5 G328
793	" "	6	5	1860-07-16		A5 G328
794	" "	6	6	1860-07-16		A5 G328
795	" "	6	7	1860-07-16		A5 G328
796	" "	6	8	1860-07-16		A5 G328
797	" "	6	9	1860-07-16		A5 G328
778	" "	6	N½SE	1860-07-16		A5 G341
779	" "	6	NESW	1860-07-16		A5 G341
798	" "	8	N½SE	1860-07-16		A5 G327

ID	Individual in Patent	Sec.	Sec. Part	Date Issued	Other Counties	For More Info . . .
777	KIECKHOEFER, A T (Cont'd)	8	S½SE	1860-07-16		A5 G333
799	" "	21	E½SW	1860-08-01		A5 G342
800	" "	21	SENW	1860-08-01		A5 G342
802	" "	21	SWNW	1860-08-01		A5 G330
803	" "	21	W½SW	1860-08-01		A5 G330
842	KNAPP, John H	30	SWSW	1855-12-15		A2 G219
841	" "	33	NWNW	1855-12-15		A2 G224
774	KOLB, Susanna	28	S½SW	1860-07-16		A5 G310
775	" "	28	SWSE	1860-07-16		A5 G310
747	KOWING, Francis	23	W½NW	1858-08-10		A7
745	" "	14	W½SW	1860-07-16		A5
746	" "	23	E½NW	1860-07-16		A5
748	" "	25	NESW	1860-07-16		A5
749	" "	25	NWSE	1860-07-16		A5
751	" "	26	E½NW	1860-07-16		A5 G228
750	" "	26	W½NW	1860-07-16		A5 G227
875	LACKEY, Nelson	12	SESW	1889-07-01		A6
754	LACY, Garret	10	SESE	1859-09-01		A5
755	" "	10	W½SE	1859-09-01		A5
799	LAINE, Lewis	21	E½SW	1860-08-01		A5 G342
800	" "	21	SENW	1860-08-01		A5 G342
894	LAMB, Jacob C	15	E½SW	1860-07-16		A5 G268
730	LAWTON, David E	26	NESW	1873-12-20		A6
731	" "	26	W½SW	1873-12-20		A6
897	LAWTON, Sherman J	34	W½SE	1876-03-10		A6
733	LIGHTBOURN, Donald S	25	NE	1860-10-01		A5
843	LUCAS, John	24	NE	1866-08-01		A5
892	LYMAN, Elias A	3	SWSW	1860-07-16		A5 G269
893	" "	4	E½SE	1860-07-16		A5 G269
886	LYMAN, Phineas H	30	SE	1871-11-20		A6
866	MAHANY, Mary E	15	NW	1860-10-01		A5
844	MARLETT, John	4	1	1874-04-01		A6
845	" "	4	2	1874-04-01		A6
846	" "	4	3	1874-04-01		A6
847	" "	4	7	1874-04-01		A6
848	MCLEOD, John	14	NWNE	1876-05-10		A2
849	" "	24	N½NW	1879-11-10		A6
780	MCLESKEY, W L	30	E½NW	1860-07-16		A5 G336
781	" "	30	S½NE	1860-07-16		A5 G336
713	MCMANNUS, Anthony	23	SW	1860-07-16		A5
832	MILLER, Sam	27	SE	1860-07-16		A5 G43
890	MILLS, Richard	10	NENW	1860-07-16		A5
891	" "	10	W½NE	1860-07-16		A5
894	" "	15	E½SW	1860-07-16		A5 G268
895	" "	15	W½SW	1860-07-16		A5 G267
892	" "	3	SWSW	1860-07-16		A5 G269
893	" "	4	E½SE	1860-07-16		A5 G269
782	MORRISON, Elizabeth	22	NE	1860-07-16		A5 G334
721	NICHOLS, Charles W	34	W½SW	1880-09-01		A6
776	NICOLS, George W	30	E½SW	1860-08-01		A5
881	OMALLEY, Patrick F	8	E½NE	1859-09-01		A5
882	" "	9	N½SW	1859-09-01		A5
883	" "	9	NW	1859-09-01		A5
905	PLATT, William H	2	SW	1860-10-01		A5
906	" "	21	SE	1860-10-01		A5
907	" "	3	SE	1860-10-01		A5
908	" "	36	SE	1860-10-01		A5 G307
876	PORTER, Nelson	30	NWSW	1871-03-15		A6 F
877	" "	30	W½NW	1871-03-15		A6 F
761	POWELL, George May	27	NW	1860-07-16		A5
770	" "	28	E½NW	1860-07-16		A5 G309
762	" "	28	E½SE	1860-07-16		A5
763	" "	28	NE	1860-07-16		A5
771	" "	28	NESW	1860-07-16		A5 G309
764	" "	28	NWSE	1860-07-16		A5
772	" "	28	NWSW	1860-07-16		A5 G311
774	" "	28	S½SW	1860-07-16		A5 G310
775	" "	28	SWSE	1860-07-16		A5 G310
773	" "	28	W½NW	1860-07-16		A5 G311
765	" "	29	NE	1860-07-16		A5
767	" "	32	N½SE	1860-07-16		A5
769	" "	32	SWNE	1860-07-16		A5
766	" "	32	E½NE	1861-09-05		A5

ID	Individual in Patent	Sec.	Sec. Part	Date Issued	Other Counties	For More Info . . .
768	POWELL, George May (Cont'd)	32	NWNE	1861-09-05		A5
780	PREMBLE, Charles	30	E½NW	1860-07-16		A5 G336
781	" "	30	S½NE	1860-07-16		A5 G336
805	PRESTON, David	18	SE	1860-07-16		A5 G340
751	QUARLES, Nancy	26	E½NW	1860-07-16		A5 G228
729	REED, Daniel R	12	NWNW	1884-09-20		A6
867	RICHMOND, Mathias	11	NESW	1872-09-25		A6
868	" "	11	NWSE	1872-09-25		A6
869	" "	11	W½NE	1872-09-25		A6
909	RICHMOND, William	10	NESE	1877-09-26		A6
910	" "	10	SENE	1877-09-26		A6
785	RIGGS, George W	18	E½SW	1860-07-16		A5 G328
805	" "	18	SE	1860-07-16		A5 G340
786	" "	18	SENW	1860-07-16		A5 G328
787	" "	20	E½SE	1860-07-16		A5 G328
783	" "	20	E½SW	1860-07-16		A5 G332
788	" "	20	NE	1860-07-16		A5 G328
804	" "	20	NW	1860-07-16		A5 G331
784	" "	20	NWSE	1860-07-16		A5 G332
789	" "	20	SWSE	1860-07-16		A5 G328
782	" "	22	NE	1860-07-16		A5 G334
790	" "	22	NW	1860-07-16		A5 G328
780	" "	30	E½NW	1860-07-16		A5 G336
781	" "	30	S½NE	1860-07-16		A5 G336
791	" "	32	S½SE	1860-07-16		A5 G328
801	" "	32	SW	1860-07-16		A5 G329
792	" "	6	4	1860-07-16		A5 G328
793	" "	6	5	1860-07-16		A5 G328
794	" "	6	6	1860-07-16		A5 G328
795	" "	6	7	1860-07-16		A5 G328
796	" "	6	8	1860-07-16		A5 G328
797	" "	6	9	1860-07-16		A5 G328
778	" "	6	N½SE	1860-07-16		A5 G341
779	" "	6	NESW	1860-07-16		A5 G341
798	" "	8	N½SE	1860-07-16		A5 G327
777	" "	8	S½SE	1860-07-16		A5 G333
799	" "	21	E½SW	1860-08-01		A5 G342
800	" "	21	SENW	1860-08-01		A5 G342
802	" "	21	SWNW	1860-08-01		A5 G330
803	" "	21	W½SW	1860-08-01		A5 G330
820	ROGERS, Betsey	11	S½SW	1860-02-01		A5 G209
823	RYDER, Ann	9	NWSE	1860-08-01		A5 G7
824	" "	9	S½SE	1860-08-01		A5 G7
715	SCHUBEL, Augustus	36	N½SW	1890-03-29		A6
716	" "	36	SENW	1890-03-29		A6
717	" "	36	SWNE	1890-03-29		A6
772	SERVIS, Joseph L	28	NWSW	1860-07-16		A5 G311
773	" "	28	W½NW	1860-07-16		A5 G311
911	STEEN, William	10	NENE	1878-06-24		A6
902	STICKNEY, Warren H	22	NESE	1869-08-05		A2
903	" "	24	N½SW	1871-08-25		A6
904	" "	24	S½NW	1871-08-25		A6
842	STOUT, Henry L	30	SWSW	1855-12-15		A2 G219
841	" "	33	NWNW	1855-12-15		A2 G224
726	SUTLIFF, Corwin	2	9	1873-05-20		A6
727	" "	2	E½SE	1873-05-20		A6
728	" "	2	NWSE	1873-05-20		A6
878	SUTLIFF, Norman	8	E½NW	1871-08-25		A6
879	" "	8	W½NE	1871-08-25		A6
900	SUTLIFF, T C	2	SWSE	1876-01-20		A2
842	TAINTER, Andrew	30	SWSW	1855-12-15		A2 G219
841	" "	33	NWNW	1855-12-15		A2 G224
830	TAYLOR, B W	34	E½NW	1860-07-16		A5 G44
831	" "	34	SWNE	1860-07-16		A5 G44
853	THOMAS, John	36	SESW	1885-01-30		A6
834	TRIGG, John E	18	W½NW	1878-06-24		A6
835	" "	18	W½SW	1878-06-24		A6
734	TUTTLE, Durlin W	14	NESW	1859-05-02		A2
736	" "	14	SWNE	1859-05-02		A2
737	" "	14	W½SE	1859-05-02		A2
735	" "	14	NW	1859-09-01		A5
837	WACHTER, John F	4	8	1878-11-30		A6
838	" "	4	9	1878-11-30		A6

ID	Individual in Patent	Sec.	Sec. Part	Date Issued	Other Counties	For More Info . . .
732	WARD, Alice	15	SE	1860-07-16		A5 G196
805	WHIPPLE, Adaline E	18	SE	1860-07-16		A5 G340
805	WHIPPLE, William L	18	SE	1860-07-16		A5 G340
778	WHITEMAN, Anna	6	N½SE	1860-07-16		A5 G341
779	" "	6	NESW	1860-07-16		A5 G341
839	WILLIAMS, John F	15	E½NE	1860-07-16		A5 G423
840	" "	15	SWNE	1860-07-16		A5 G423
857	WILSON, Jonathan	23	N½SE	1871-03-15		A6
858	" "	23	SESE	1871-03-15		A6
859	" "	24	SWSW	1871-03-15		A6
887	WILSON, Ransom B	24	SESW	1871-03-15		A6
888	" "	25	NENW	1871-03-15		A6
889	" "	25	W½NW	1871-03-15		A6
799	WILSON, Sally	21	E½SW	1860-08-01		A5 G342
800	" "	21	SENW	1860-08-01		A5 G342
842	WILSON, Thomas B	30	SWSW	1855-12-15		A2 G219
841	" "	33	NWNW	1855-12-15		A2 G224
899	WISCONSIN, State Of	16		1941-09-25		A3

Patent Map

T30-N R14-W
4th PM - 1831 MN/WI Meridian

Map Group 5

Township Statistics

Parcels Mapped	208
Number of Patents	130
Number of Individuals	121
Patentees Identified	103
Number of Surnames	99
Multi-Patentee Parcels	55
Oldest Patent Date	10/2/1854
Most Recent Patent	9/25/1941
Block/Lot Parcels	38
Parcels Re - Issued	0
Parcels that Overlap	0
Cities and Towns	2
Cemeteries	2

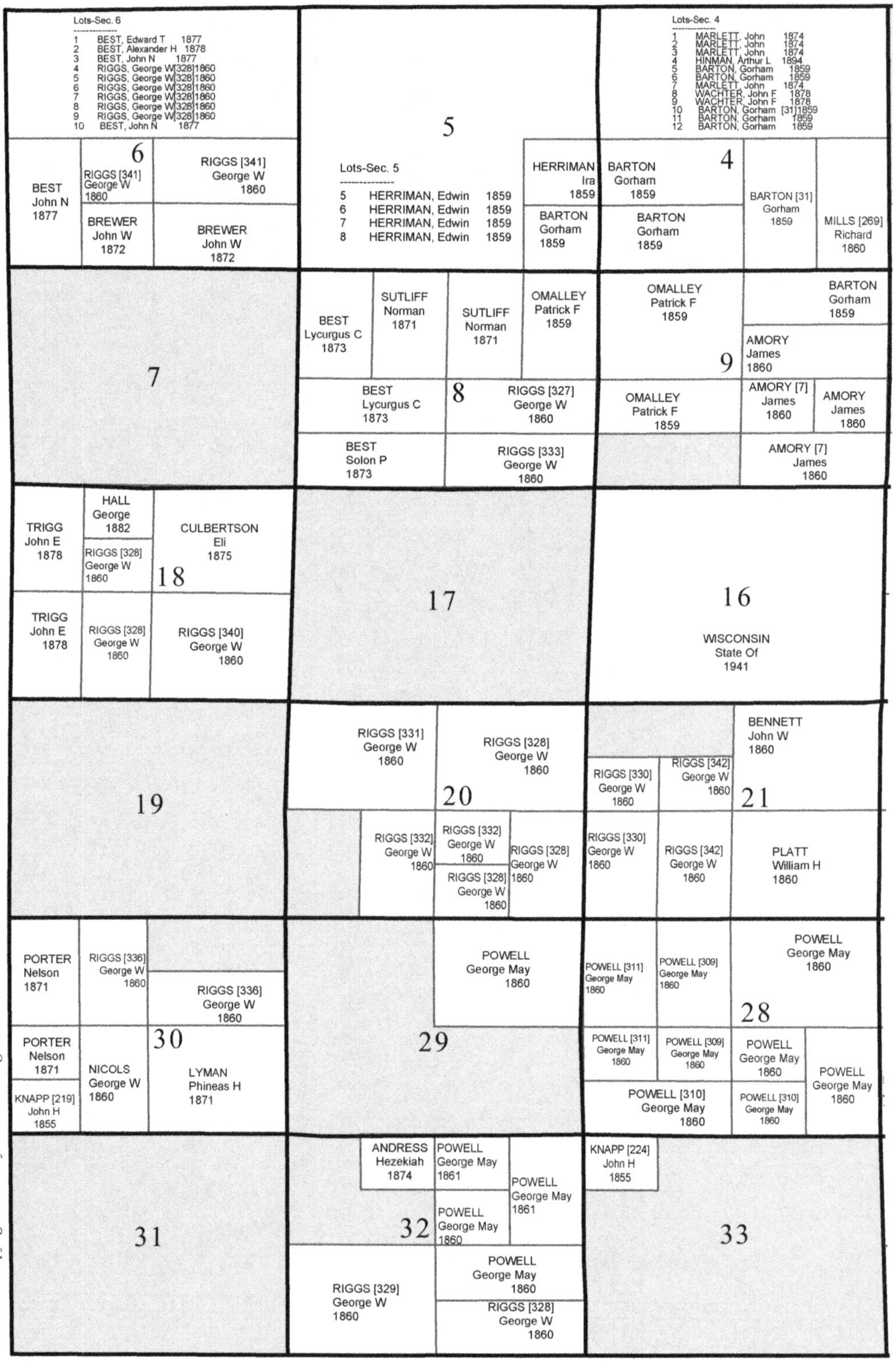
Lots-Sec. 6
1 BEST, Edward T 1877
2 BEST, Alexander H 1878
3 BEST, John N 1877
4 RIGGS, George W[328]1860
5 RIGGS, George W[328]1860
6 RIGGS, George W[328]1860
7 RIGGS, George W[328]1860
8 RIGGS, George W[328]1860
9 RIGGS, George W[328]1860
10 BEST, John N 1877
6
BEST John N 1877
RIGGS [341] George W 1860
RIGGS [341] George W 1860
BREWER John W 1872
BREWER John W 1872
5
Lots-Sec. 5
5 HERRIMAN, Edwin 1859
6 HERRIMAN, Edwin 1859
7 HERRIMAN, Edwin 1859
8 HERRIMAN, Edwin 1859
HERRIMAN Ira 1859
BARTON Gorham 1859
Lots-Sec. 4
1 MARLETT, John 1874
2 MARLETT, John 1874
3 MARLETT, John 1874
4 HINMAN, Arthur L 1894
5 BARTON, Gorham 1859
6 BARTON, Gorham 1859
7 MARLETT, John 1874
8 WACHTER, John F 1878
9 WACHTER, John F 1878
10 BARTON, Gorham [31]1859
11 BARTON, Gorham 1859
12 BARTON, Gorham 1859
4
BARTON Gorham 1859
BARTON [31] Gorham 1859
BARTON Gorham 1859
MILLS [269] Richard 1860
7
BEST Lycurgus C 1873
SUTLIFF Norman 1871
SUTLIFF Norman 1871
OMALLEY Patrick F 1859
BEST Lycurgus C 1873
8
RIGGS [327] George W 1860
BEST Solon P 1873
RIGGS [333] George W 1860
OMALLEY Patrick F 1859
BARTON Gorham 1859
AMORY James 1860
9
OMALLEY Patrick F 1859
AMORY [7] James 1860
AMORY James 1860
AMORY [7] James 1860
TRIGG John E 1878
HALL George 1882
RIGGS [328] George W 1860
CULBERTSON Eli 1875
18
TRIGG John E 1878
RIGGS [328] George W 1860
RIGGS [340] George W 1860
17
16
WISCONSIN State Of 1941
19
RIGGS [331] George W 1860
RIGGS [328] George W 1860
20
RIGGS [332] George W 1860
RIGGS [332] George W 1860
RIGGS [328] George W 1860
RIGGS [328] George W 1860
RIGGS [330] George W 1860
RIGGS [342] George W 1860
BENNETT John W 1860
21
RIGGS [330] George W 1860
RIGGS [342] George W 1860
PLATT William H 1860
PORTER Nelson 1871
RIGGS [336] George W 1860
RIGGS [336] George W 1860
30
PORTER Nelson 1871
NICOLS George W 1860
LYMAN Phineas H 1871
KNAPP [219] John H 1855
POWELL George May 1860
29
POWELL [311] George May 1860
POWELL [309] George May 1860
POWELL George May 1860
28
POWELL [311] George May 1860
POWELL [309] George May 1860
POWELL George May 1860
POWELL George May 1860
POWELL [310] George May 1860
POWELL [310] George May 1860
31
ANDRESS Hezekiah 1874
POWELL George May 1861
POWELL George May 1861
POWELL George May 1860
32
POWELL George May 1860
RIGGS [329] George W 1860
RIGGS [328] George W 1860
KNAPP [224] John H 1855
33

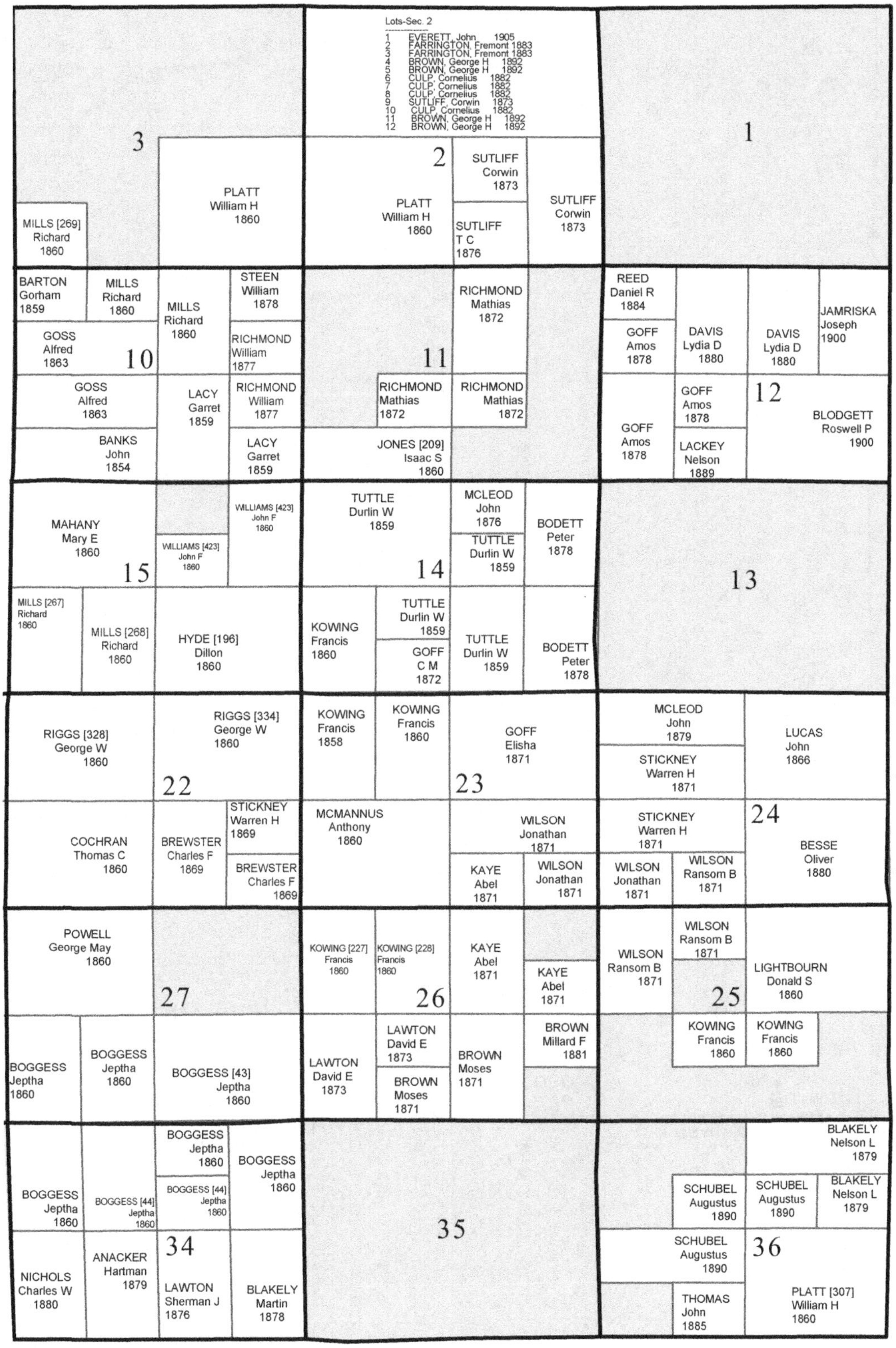
Lots-Sec. 2
1 EVERETT, John 1905
2 FARRINGTON, Fremont 1883
3 FARRINGTON, Fremont 1883
4 BROWN, George H 1892
5 BROWN, George H 1892
6 CULP, Cornelius 1882
7 CULP, Cornelius 1882
8 CULP, Cornelius 1882
9 SUTLIFF, Corwin 1873
10 CULP, Cornelius 1882
11 BROWN, George H 1892
12 BROWN, George H 1892
3
MILLS [269] Richard 1860
PLATT William H 1860
2
PLATT William H 1860
SUTLIFF Corwin 1873
SUTLIFF T C 1876
SUTLIFF Corwin 1873
1
BARTON Gorham 1859
MILLS Richard 1860
MILLS Richard 1860
STEEN William 1878
GOSS Alfred 1863
10
RICHMOND William 1877
GOSS Alfred 1863
LACY Garret 1859
RICHMOND William 1877
BANKS John 1854
LACY Garret 1859
RICHMOND Mathias 1872
11
RICHMOND Mathias 1872
RICHMOND Mathias 1872
JONES [209] Isaac S 1860
REED Daniel R 1884
GOFF Amos 1878
DAVIS Lydia D 1880
DAVIS Lydia D 1880
JAMRISKA Joseph 1900
GOFF Amos 1878
GOFF Amos 1878
12
BLODGETT Roswell P 1900
LACKEY Nelson 1889
MAHANY Mary E 1860
WILLIAMS [423] John F 1860
WILLIAMS [423] John F 1860
15
MILLS [267] Richard 1860
MILLS [268] Richard 1860
HYDE [196] Dillon 1860
TUTTLE Durlin W 1859
MCLEOD John 1876
TUTTLE Durlin W 1859
BODETT Peter 1878
14
KOWING Francis 1860
TUTTLE Durlin W 1859
GOFF C M 1872
TUTTLE Durlin W 1859
BODETT Peter 1878
13
RIGGS [328] George W 1860
RIGGS [334] George W 1860
22
COCHRAN Thomas C 1860
BREWSTER Charles F 1869
STICKNEY Warren H 1869
BREWSTER Charles F 1869
KOWING Francis 1858
KOWING Francis 1860
GOFF Elisha 1871
23
MCMANNUS Anthony 1860
WILSON Jonathan 1871
KAYE Abel 1871
WILSON Jonathan 1871
MCLEOD John 1879
STICKNEY Warren H 1871
LUCAS John 1866
STICKNEY Warren H 1871
24
BESSE Oliver 1880
WILSON Jonathan 1871
WILSON Ransom B 1871
POWELL George May 1860
27
BOGGESS Jeptha 1860
BOGGESS Jeptha 1860
BOGGESS [43] Jeptha 1860
KOWING [227] Francis 1860
KOWING [228] Francis 1860
KAYE Abel 1871
KAYE Abel 1871
26
LAWTON David E 1873
LAWTON David E 1873
BROWN Moses 1871
BROWN Moses 1871
BROWN Millard F 1881
WILSON Ransom B 1871
WILSON Ransom B 1871
LIGHTBOURN Donald S 1860
25
KOWING Francis 1860
KOWING Francis 1860
BOGGESS Jeptha 1860
BOGGESS Jeptha 1860
BOGGESS Jeptha 1860
BOGGESS [44] Jeptha 1860
BOGGESS [44] Jeptha 1860
NICHOLS Charles W 1880
ANACKER Hartman 1879
34
LAWTON Sherman J 1876
BLAKELY Martin 1878
35
BLAKELY Nelson L 1879
SCHUBEL Augustus 1890
SCHUBEL Augustus 1890
BLAKELY Nelson L 1879
SCHUBEL Augustus 1890
36
THOMAS John 1885
PLATT [307] William H 1860

Helpful Hints

1. This Map's INDEX can be found on the preceding pages.
2. Refer to Map "C" to see where this Township lies within Dunn County, Wisconsin.
3. Numbers within square brackets [ ] denote a multi-patentee land parcel (multi-owner). Refer to Appendix "C" for a full list of members in this group.
4. Areas that look to be crowded with Patentees usually indicate multiple sales of the same parcel (Re-issues) or Overlapping parcels. See this Township's Index for an explanation of these and other circumstances that might explain "odd" groupings of Patentees on this map.

Legend

Patent Boundary

Section Boundary

No Patents Found (or Outside County)

1., 2., 3., ... Lot Numbers (when beside a name)

[ ] Group Number (see Appendix "C")

Scale: Section = 1 mile X 1 mile (generally, with some exceptions)

Road Map

T30-N R14-W
4th PM - 1831 MN/WI Meridian

Map Group 5

Cities & Towns

Boyceville
Downing

Cemeteries

Mound Cemetery
Tiffany Cemetery

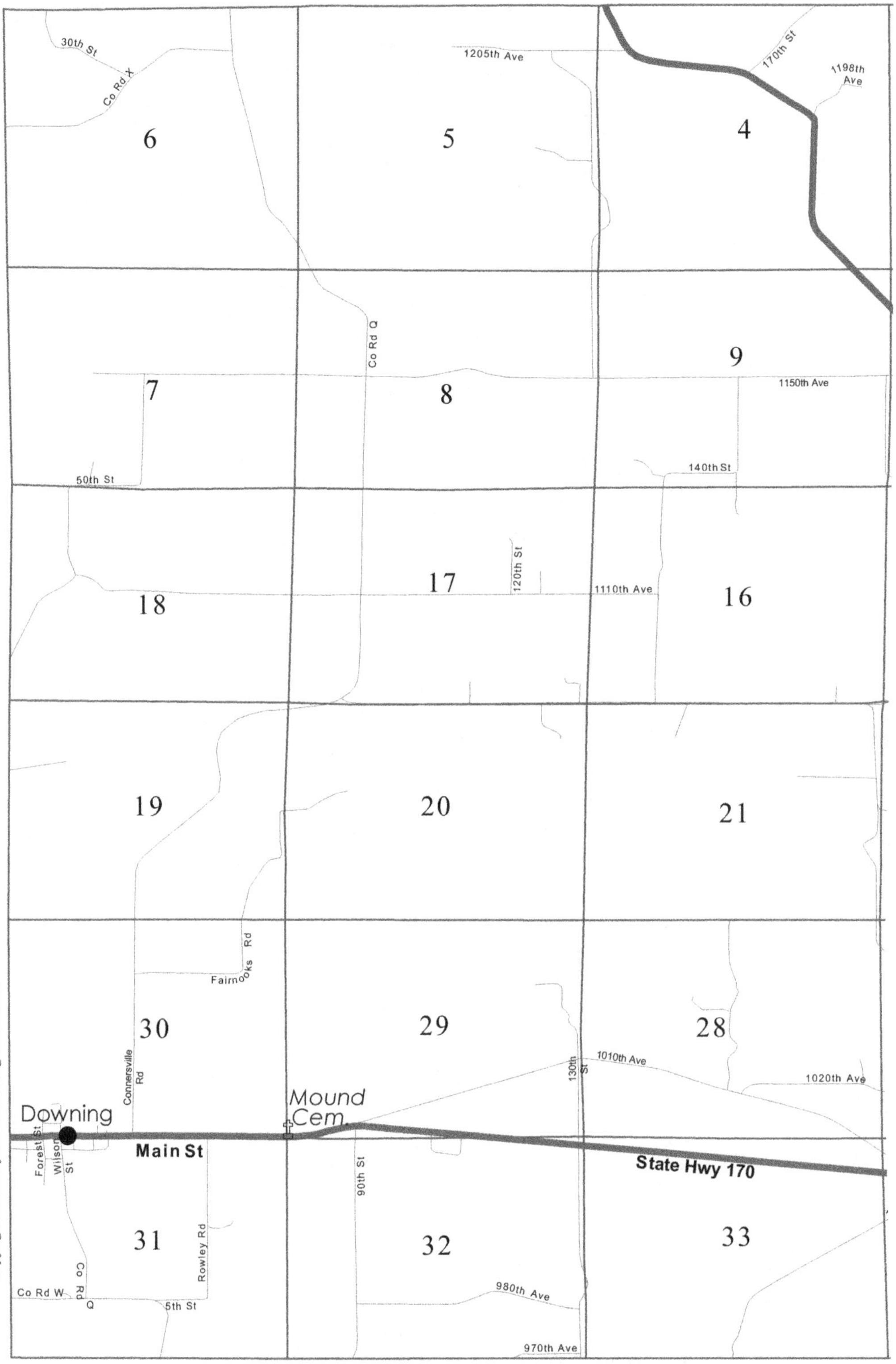
30th St
Co Rd X
1205th Ave
170th St
1198th Ave
6
5
4
Co Rd Q
9
1150th Ave
7
8
140th St
50th St
120th St
17
1110th Ave
16
18
19
20
21
Rd
Fairnooks
30
29
28
130th St
1010th Ave
1020th Ave
Connersville Rd
Mound Cem.
Downing
Forest St
Wilson St
Main St
90th St
State Hwy 170
31
Rowley Rd
32
33
Co Rd Q
Co Rd W
5th St
980th Ave
970th Ave

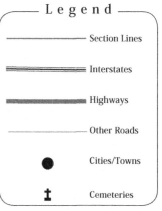

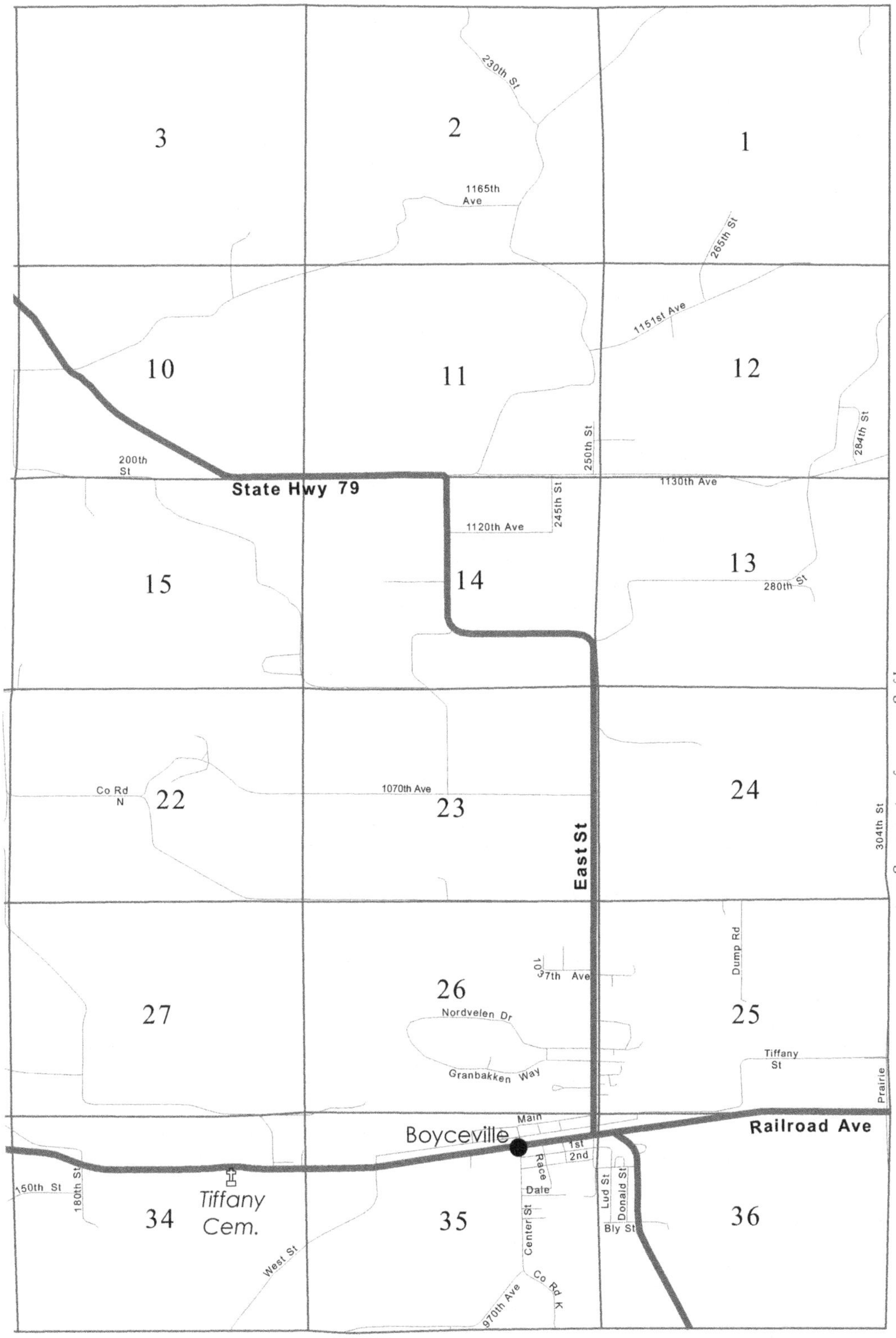

Helpful Hints

1. This road map has a number of uses, but primarily it is to help you: a) find the present location of land owned by your ancestors (at least the general area), b) find cemeteries and city-centers, and c) estimate the route/roads used by Census-takers & tax-assessors.
2. If you plan to travel to Dunn County to locate cemeteries or land parcels, please pick up a modern travel map for the area before you do. Mapping old land parcels on modern maps is not as exact a science as you might think. Just the slightest variations in public land survey coordinates, estimates of parcel boundaries, or road-map deviations can greatly alter a map's representation of how a road either does or doesn't cross a particular parcel of land.

Legend

- Section Lines
- Interstates
- Highways
- Other Roads
- Cities/Towns
- Cemeteries

Scale: Section = 1 mile X 1 mile
(generally, with some exceptions)

Historical Map

T30-N R14-W
4th PM - 1831 MN/WI Meridian

Map Group 5

Cities & Towns

Boyceville
Downing

Cemeteries

Mound Cemetery
Tiffany Cemetery

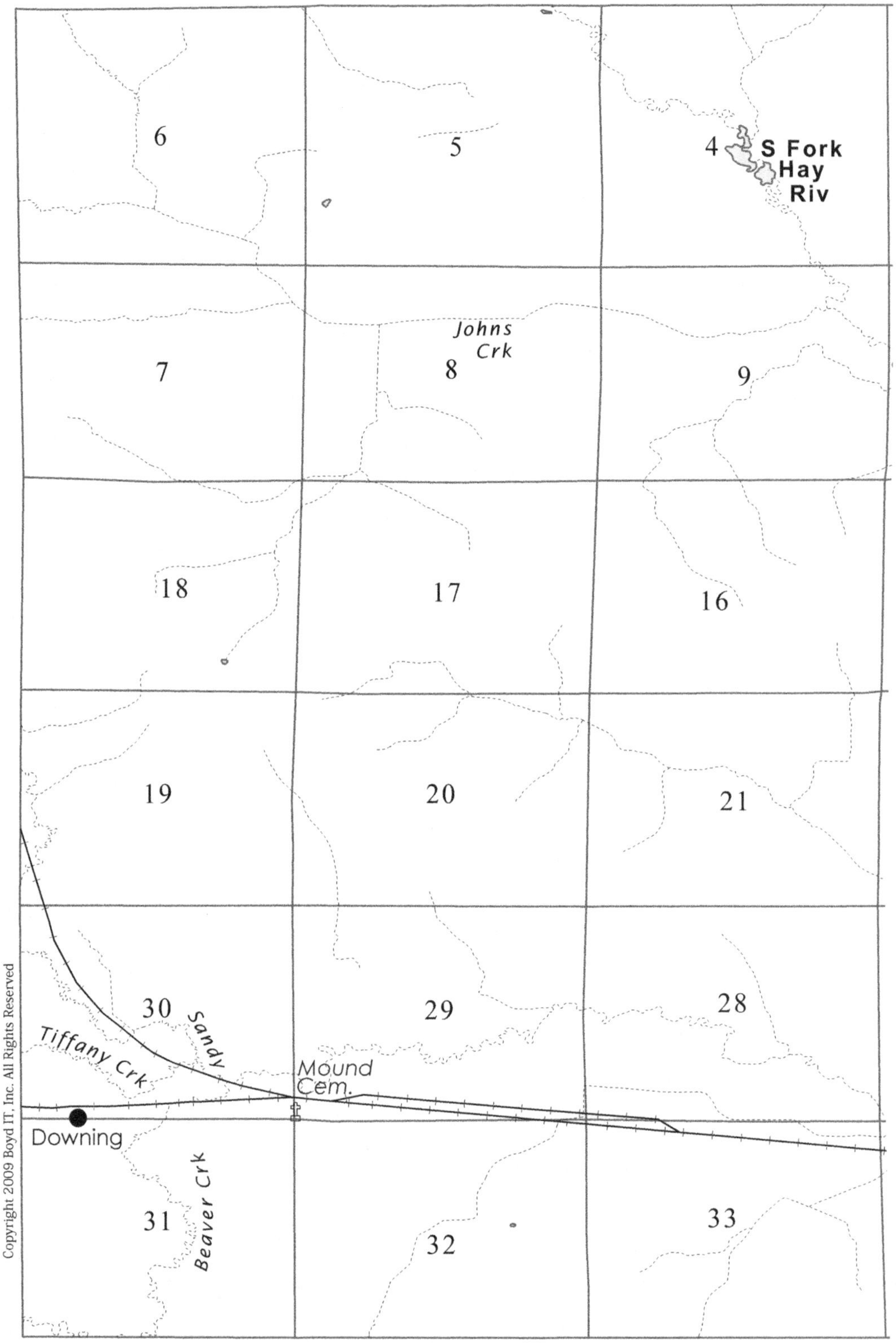

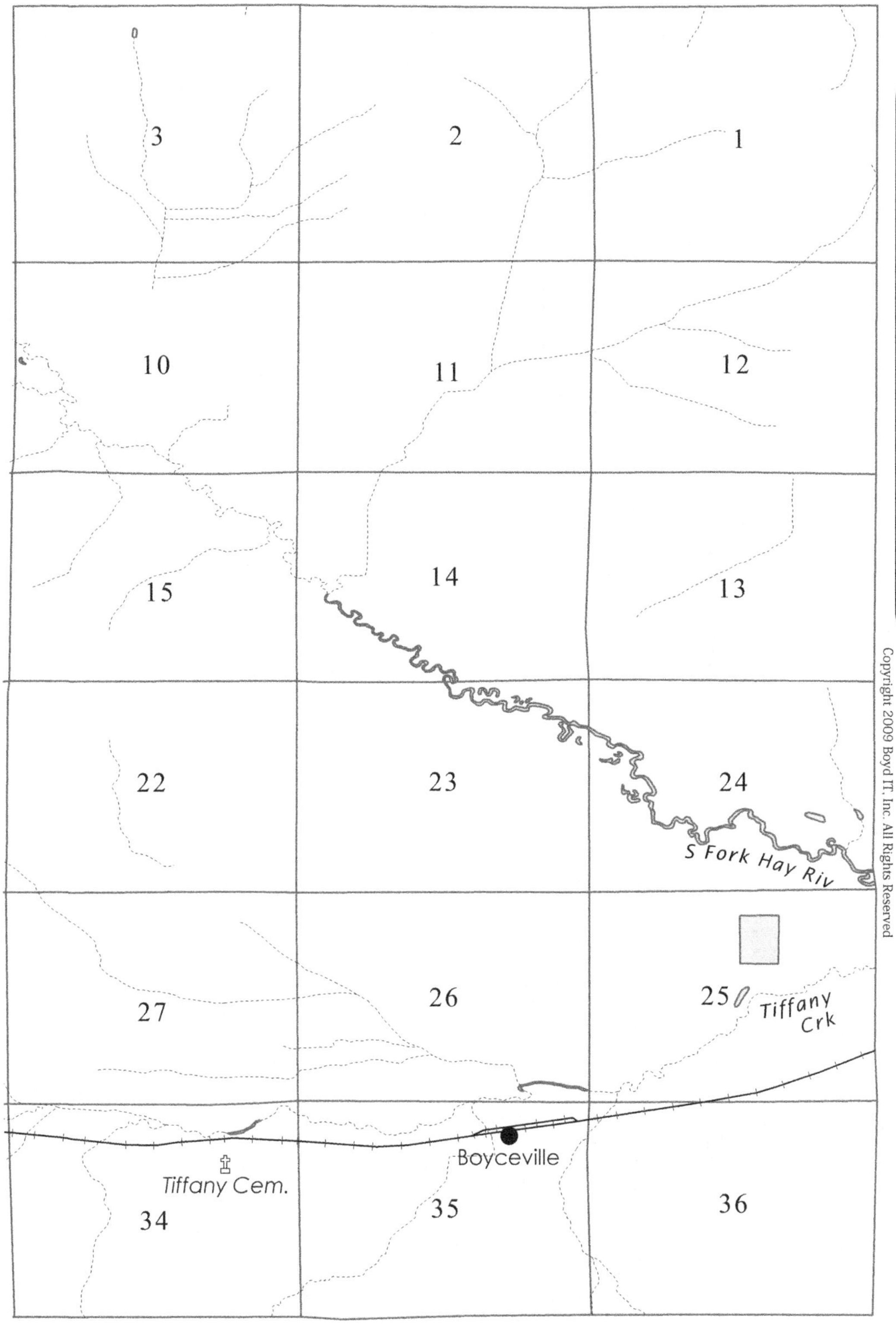
3
2
1
10
11
12
15
14
13
22
23
24
S Fork Hay Riv
27
26
25
Tiffany Crk
Tiffany Cem.
Boyceville
34
35
36

Helpful Hints

1. This Map takes a different look at the same Congressional Township displayed in the preceding two maps. It presents features that can help you better envision the historical development of the area: a) Water-bodies (lakes & ponds), b) Water-courses (rivers, streams, etc.), c) Railroads, d) City/town center-points (where they were oftentimes located when first settled), and e) Cemeteries.
2. Using this "Historical" map in tandem with this Township's Patent Map and Road Map, may lead you to some interesting discoveries. You will often find roads, towns, cemeteries, and waterways are named after nearby landowners: sometimes those names will be the ones you are researching. See how many of these research gems you can find here in Dunn County.

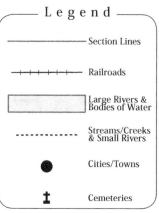

Legend

- Section Lines
- Railroads
- Large Rivers & Bodies of Water
- Streams/Creeks & Small Rivers
- Cities/Towns
- Cemeteries

Scale: Section = 1 mile X 1 mile
(there are some exceptions)

Map Group 6: Index to Land Patents

Township 30-North Range 13-West (4th PM - 1831 MN/WI)

After you locate an individual in this Index, take note of the Section and Section Part then proceed to the Land Patent map on the pages immediately following. You should have no difficulty locating the corresponding parcel of land.

The "For More Info" Column will lead you to more information about the underlying Patents. See the *Legend* at right, and the "How to Use this Book" chapter, for more information.

LEGEND

"For More Info . . . " column

A = Authority (Legislative Act, See Appendix "A")
B = Block or Lot (location in Section unknown)
C = Cancelled Patent
F = Fractional Section
G = Group (Multi-Patentee Patent, see Appendix "C")
V = Overlaps another Parcel
R = Re-Issued (Parcel patented more than once)

(A & G items require you to look in the Appendixes referred to above. All other Letter-designations followed by a number require you to locate line-items in this index that possess the ID number found after the letter).

ID	Individual in Patent	Sec.	Sec. Part	Date Issued	Other Counties	For More Info . . .
1002	ANDERSON, Johan	34	SE	1878-11-30		A6
959	BAILEY, Mary	15	S½SW	1859-09-10		A5 G212
960	" "	22	NWNW	1859-09-10		A5 G212
984	BARTON, Gorham	15	SENE	1859-09-01		A5 G32
985	" "	15	W½NE	1859-09-01		A5 G32
987	BEDELL, Hall	14	NW	1881-02-10		A6
922	BENNETT, Andrew S	24	S½SE	1862-01-07		A5
931	BRADWAY, Asa	32	N½SW	1873-12-20		A6
992	BRADWAY, Heman	32	SENE	1874-05-06		A2
1025	BRADWAY, Lewis S	32	NWSE	1889-02-16		A6
1026	" "	32	S½SE	1889-02-16		A6
937	BROWN, Benjamin F	14	SE	1889-02-16		A6
949	BUDD, Daniel S	36	SESW	1890-05-14		A6
950	" "	36	SWSE	1890-05-14		A6
951	" "	36	W½SW	1890-05-14		A6
916	BULLOCK, Alonzo	26	SESE	1873-06-20		A2
917	" "	8	SESE	1878-11-05		A2
1052	BUSHNELL, Richard C	18	S½NE	1895-07-08		A6
1053	" "	18	S½NW	1895-07-08		A6
946	BUTTERFIELD, A G	13	SWSE	1911-03-07		A2 G263
947	" "	24	NENE	1911-03-07		A2 G263
948	" "	24	NWNE	1911-03-07		A2 G263
946	BUTTERFIELD, Mattie	13	SWSE	1911-03-07		A2 G263
947	" "	24	NENE	1911-03-07		A2 G263
948	" "	24	NWNE	1911-03-07		A2 G263
1054	CALHOUN, Robert	12	N½SW	1880-11-01		A6
1055	" "	12	S½NW	1880-11-01		A6
1000	CERNAK, Jano	18	E½SE	1908-10-22		A6
1001	" "	18	NWSE	1916-10-20		A6
944	CLARK, Chester D	22	E½NW	1880-09-01		A6
945	" "	22	W½NE	1880-09-01		A6
1064	CORNWELL, Eliza	31	N½SE	1860-10-01		A5 G301
1065	" "	31	S½NE	1860-10-01		A5 G301
1022	DAY, Joseph	12	S½SW	1879-11-10		A6
946	DAY, Perry	13	SWSE	1911-03-07		A2 G263
947	" "	24	NENE	1911-03-07		A2 G263
948	" "	24	NWNE	1911-03-07		A2 G263
941	DRAKE, Charles	10	E½NW	1881-02-10		A6
942	" "	10	W½NE	1881-02-10		A6
1051	EASTWOOD, Rebecca J	22	SE	1882-09-30		A2
1034	EYTCHESON, N J	14	NESW	1875-03-10		A2
1035	" "	14	SWSW	1875-03-10		A2
1058	FEENEY, Thomas	28	N½SE	1859-12-10		A2
1047	FINEGAN, Patrick	27	E½NW	1860-03-10		A5 G130
1048	" "	27	NWSW	1860-03-10		A5 G130
1049	" "	27	SWNW	1860-03-10		A5 G130

ID	Individual in Patent	Sec.	Sec. Part	Date Issued	Other Counties	For More Info . . .
952	FLINT, David	28	S½SE	1860-08-01		A5 G132
953	" "	33	N½NE	1860-08-01		A5 G132
977	FOGG, Francis A	33	NWSE	1859-12-20		A2
976	" "	33	NESE	1860-08-01		A5
978	" "	33	S½NE	1860-08-01		A5
946	GLUTH, Louis F	13	SWSE	1911-03-07		A2 G263
947	" "	24	NENE	1911-03-07		A2 G263
948	" "	24	NWNE	1911-03-07		A2 G263
943	GOODELL, Chauncey	22	E½NE	1882-04-10		A6
1003	GOODELL, John A	10	NESW	1877-06-04		A6
1004	" "	10	SWNW	1877-06-04		A6
1005	" "	10	W½SW	1877-06-04		A6
913	GOODRICH, Allen S	24	NESW	1862-01-07		A5 G160
914	" "	24	SENW	1862-01-07		A5 G160
915	" "	24	SWNE	1862-01-07		A5 G160
913	GOSS, Alfred	24	NESW	1862-01-07		A5 G160
914	" "	24	SENW	1862-01-07		A5 G160
915	" "	24	SWNE	1862-01-07		A5 G160
957	GRAY, James B	15	N½SW	1859-09-10		A5 G213
958	" "	15	SWNW	1859-09-10		A5 G213
1041	GROTHE, Ole J	8	N½SE	1892-05-26		A6
1063	GRUTT, William	30	NWSE	1896-01-18		A6
1047	HAGAR, Margaret	27	E½NW	1860-03-10		A5 G130
1048	" "	27	NWSW	1860-03-10		A5 G130
1049	" "	27	SWNW	1860-03-10		A5 G130
934	HALL, B F	14	NWSW	1875-03-10		A2
935	" "	14	SESW	1875-03-10		A2
981	HARBIT, Francis M	32	S½SW	1884-09-20		A6
1031	HOAG, Martha	24	SESW	1883-02-10		A6
1074	HODGE, Wilson	26	N½SE	1877-04-05		A2
1027	HUGHES, Lydia	24	N½NW	1873-09-20		A6
1028	" "	24	NWSW	1873-09-20		A6
1029	" "	24	SWNW	1873-09-20		A6
999	HUTCHINSON, Elizabeth	31	N½NE	1860-07-16		A5 G272
1016	JENSEN, Jorgen	8	NESW	1880-09-01		A6
1017	" "	8	S½SW	1880-09-01		A6
1018	" "	8	SWSE	1880-09-01		A6
957	KEEN, David M	15	N½SW	1859-09-10		A5 G213
959	" "	15	S½SW	1859-09-10		A5 G212
958	" "	15	SWNW	1859-09-10		A5 G213
955	" "	21	S½NE	1859-09-10		A5
960	" "	22	NWNW	1859-09-10		A5 G212
956	" "	22	SWNW	1859-09-10		A5
954	" "	15	NWNW	1860-03-01		A2
966	KING, Dwight A	32	NESE	1884-09-20		A6
1008	KNAPP, John H	12	E½NE	1870-06-10		A2
1009	" "	12	E½SE	1870-06-10		A2
1010	" "	12	W½SE	1871-04-05		A2
1032	KRAMPERT, Meri	6	W½SE	1903-08-25		A6 G231
1033	LARSON, Mons	2	SESW	1874-05-06		A2
1019	LEWIS, Joseph C	20	E½NW	1879-10-01		A6
1020	" "	20	NESW	1879-10-01		A6
1021	" "	20	NWNE	1879-10-01		A6
1066	LIGHTBOURN, Donald S	30	NE	1860-10-01		A5 G302
1064	" "	31	N½SE	1860-10-01		A5 G301
1065	" "	31	S½NE	1860-10-01		A5 G301
961	LIPOISKY, Dort	6	4	1900-03-17		A6
962	" "	6	9	1900-03-17		A6
982	LORD, George N	18	SW	1883-02-10		A6
983	" "	18	SWSE	1883-02-10		A6
972	MARTIN, Elias	2	1	1880-09-01		A6
973	" "	2	2	1880-09-01		A6
1072	MATTISON, William T	10	E½SE	1860-10-01		A5
1073	" "	10	NWSE	1860-10-01		A5
963	MCINTYRE, Dougle	6	1	1886-01-20		A6
964	" "	6	2	1886-01-20		A6
965	" "	6	3	1886-01-20		A6
946	MCINTYRE, Janett	13	SWSE	1911-03-07		A2 G263
947	" "	24	NENE	1911-03-07		A2 G263
948	" "	24	NWNE	1911-03-07		A2 G263
1038	MCINTYRE, Niel	4	NWSW	1882-06-01		A6
1039	" "	4	S½SW	1882-06-01		A6
912	MCMURCHY, A	4	3	1884-10-04		A2

ID	Individual in Patent	Sec.	Sec. Part	Date Issued	Other Counties	For More Info . . .
927	MCMURCHY, Archibald	4	2	1886-01-20		A6
928	" "	4	5	1886-01-20		A6
929	" "	4	6	1886-01-20		A6
930	" "	4	7	1886-01-20		A6
946	MCPHERSON, D D	13	SWSE	1911-03-07		A2 G263
947	" "	24	NENE	1911-03-07		A2 G263
948	" "	24	NWNE	1911-03-07		A2 G263
991	MIKKELSEN, Hans	10	E½NE	1883-07-10		A6
923	MIKKELSON, Anthon	2	10	1883-02-10		A6
924	" "	2	7	1883-02-10		A6
925	" "	2	8	1883-02-10		A6
926	" "	2	9	1883-02-10		A6
984	MILES, Lucy	15	SENE	1859-09-01		A5 G32
985	" "	15	W½NE	1859-09-01		A5 G32
999	MONTGOMERY, James	31	N½NE	1860-07-16		A5 G272
1023	MOWLAN, Joseph	12	N½NW	1879-11-10		A6
1024	" "	12	W½NE	1879-11-10		A6
936	OCONNELL, Barney	36	NE	1875-05-15		A6
932	ONEY, Asa	34	SENW	1879-11-10		A6
933	" "	34	W½NW	1879-11-10		A6
1066	PEROT, William Henry	30	NE	1860-10-01		A5 G302
1064	" "	31	N½SE	1860-10-01		A5 G301
1065	" "	31	S½NE	1860-10-01		A5 G301
1066	PUTNEY, Persis	30	NE	1860-10-01		A5 G302
1062	RETZ, Wilhelm	30	N½NW	1880-09-01		A6 F
1032	SCHLUCH, Meri	6	W½SE	1903-08-25		A6 G231
1032	SCHLUCH, Paul	6	W½SE	1903-08-25		A6 G231
921	SCOTT, Andrew L	2	4	1902-05-01		A6
1012	SELLERS, John M	32	SENW	1860-07-16		A5
1013	" "	32	W½NW	1860-07-16		A5
1014	SHADBOLT, John W	10	SESW	1877-02-20		A6
1015	" "	10	SWSE	1877-02-20		A6
1050	SHAFER, Peter	31	N½NW	1866-02-15		A2
974	SHARPLES, Ellen	24	N½SE	1880-05-15		A6 G356
975	" "	24	SENE	1880-05-15		A6 G356
974	SHARPLES, Franklin W	24	N½SE	1880-05-15		A6 G356
975	" "	24	SENE	1880-05-15		A6 G356
1067	SHEPARD, William More	30	E½SE	1860-10-01		A5
1068	" "	30	SWSE	1860-10-01		A5
980	SHULTZ, Francis A	6	6	1874-05-06		A2
979	" "	6	5	1875-03-10		A2
1069	SHULTZ, William	6	7	1876-12-30		A6
1070	" "	6	8	1876-12-30		A6
1071	" "	6	E½SE	1876-12-30		A6
1056	SMITH, Sollomon S	6	SW	1894-03-08		A6 F
1042	STEVENS, Ole	2	SE	1882-05-10		A6
986	STICKNEY, H J	14	NE	1881-02-10		A6
1059	STUBBS, Thomas	4	1	1877-03-20		A6
1060	" "	4	8	1877-03-20		A6
1006	STUDABAKER, John F	20	NWSW	1882-06-30		A6
1007	" "	20	W½NW	1882-06-30		A6
1043	SWENSON, Ole	2	11	1880-09-01		A6
1044	" "	2	3	1880-09-01		A6
1045	" "	2	5	1880-09-01		A6
1046	" "	2	6	1880-09-01		A6
1061	TABOR, Warren O	22	SW	1882-05-10		A6
1011	TALMAGE, John H	26	NW	1882-04-10		A6
968	TAYLOR, Edmund	4	4	1884-01-15		A6
1036	TERRILL, Nathan M	18	N½NE	1893-03-27		A6
1037	" "	18	N½NW	1893-03-27		A6 F
993	THOMAS, Israel J	32	N½NE	1880-09-01		A6
994	" "	32	NENW	1880-09-01		A6
995	" "	32	SWNE	1880-09-01		A6
988	TORKELSON, Halvor	36	E½SE	1880-09-01		A6
989	" "	36	NESW	1880-09-01		A6
990	" "	36	NWSE	1880-09-01		A6
1040	TUVENG, Nils O	34	SW	1879-11-10		A6
952	VAN SLIKE, ELIZABETH	28	S½SE	1860-08-01		A5 G132
953	" "	33	N½NE	1860-08-01		A5 G132
938	WAGNER, Carl	20	N½SE	1882-06-01		A6
939	" "	20	SESE	1882-06-01		A6
940	" "	20	SWNE	1882-06-01		A6
997	WEBSTER, James H	28	S½NE	1885-01-30		A6

ID	Individual in Patent	Sec.	Sec. Part	Date Issued	Other Counties	For More Info . . .
998	WEBSTER, James H (Cont'd)	28	S½NW	1885-01-30		A6
1030	WELTON, Bennett H	36	NW	1882-06-30		A6 G416
1030	WELTON, Maria L	36	NW	1882-06-30		A6 G416
918	WENNES, Andreas A	2	12	1879-10-01		A6
919	" "	2	NESW	1879-10-01		A6
920	" "	2	W½SW	1879-10-01		A6
996	WILLIAMS, J A	8	NE	1889-02-16		A6
1057	WISCONSIN, State Of	16		1941-08-16		A3
967	WITT, Edith	8	NWNW	1910-04-14		A6
969	WITT, Edward	8	E½NW	1894-03-08		A6
970	" "	8	NWSW	1894-03-08		A6
971	" "	8	SWNW	1894-03-08		A6

Patent Map

T30-N R13-W
4th PM - 1831 MN/WI Meridian

Map Group 6

Township Statistics

Parcels Mapped	163
Number of Patents	94
Number of Individuals	104
Patentees Identified	88
Number of Surnames	91
Multi-Patentee Parcels	25
Oldest Patent Date	9/1/1859
Most Recent Patent	8/16/1941
Block/Lot Parcels	29
Parcels Re - Issued	0
Parcels that Overlap	0
Cities and Towns	2
Cemeteries	2

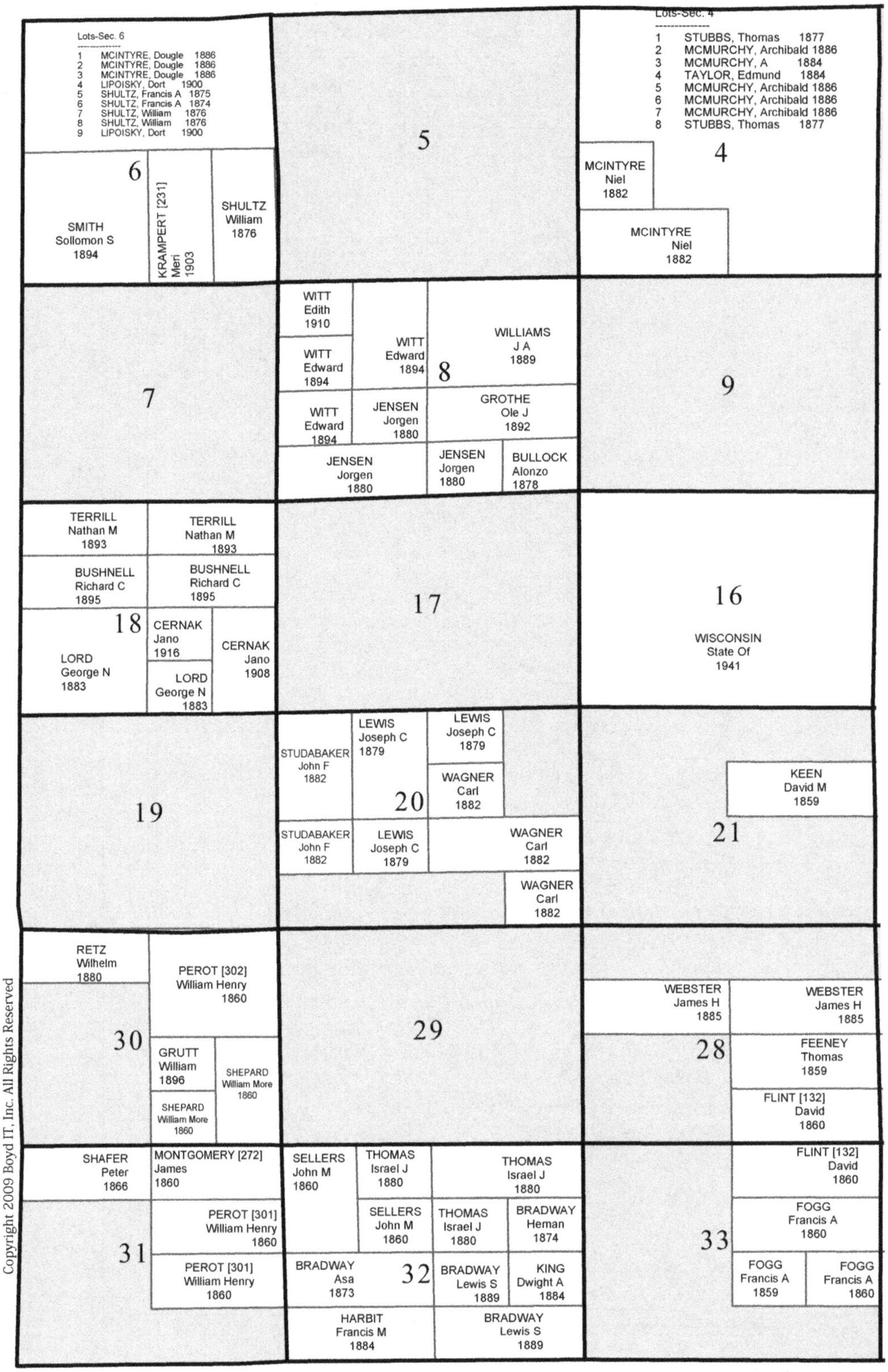
Lots-Sec. 6
1 MCINTYRE, Dougle 1886
2 MCINTYRE, Dougle 1886
3 MCINTYRE, Dougle 1886
4 LIPOISKY, Dort 1900
5 SHULTZ, Francis A 1875
6 SHULTZ, Francis A 1874
7 SHULTZ, William 1876
8 SHULTZ, William 1876
9 LIPOISKY, Dort 1900
6
SMITH Sollomon S 1894
KRAMPERT [231] Meri 1903
SHULTZ William 1876
5
Lots-Sec. 4
1 STUBBS, Thomas 1877
2 MCMURCHY, Archibald 1886
3 MCMURCHY, A 1884
4 TAYLOR, Edmund 1884
5 MCMURCHY, Archibald 1886
6 MCMURCHY, Archibald 1886
7 MCMURCHY, Archibald 1886
8 STUBBS, Thomas 1877
4
MCINTYRE Niel 1882
MCINTYRE Niel 1882
7
WITT Edith 1910
WITT Edward 1894
WITT Edward 1894
WILLIAMS J A 1889
8
WITT Edward 1894
JENSEN Jorgen 1880
GROTHE Ole J 1892
JENSEN Jorgen 1880
JENSEN Jorgen 1880
BULLOCK Alonzo 1878
9
TERRILL Nathan M 1893
TERRILL Nathan M 1893
BUSHNELL Richard C 1895
BUSHNELL Richard C 1895
18
LORD George N 1883
CERNAK Jano 1916
CERNAK Jano 1908
LORD George N 1883
17
16
WISCONSIN State Of 1941
19
STUDABAKER John F 1882
LEWIS Joseph C 1879
LEWIS Joseph C 1879
WAGNER Carl 1882
20
STUDABAKER John F 1882
LEWIS Joseph C 1879
WAGNER Carl 1882
WAGNER Carl 1882
KEEN David M 1859
21
RETZ Wilhelm 1880
PEROT [302] William Henry 1860
30
GRUTT William 1896
SHEPARD William More 1860
SHEPARD William More 1860
29
WEBSTER James H 1885
WEBSTER James H 1885
28
FEENEY Thomas 1859
FLINT [132] David 1860
SHAFER Peter 1866
MONTGOMERY [272] James 1860
PEROT [301] William Henry 1860
31
PEROT [301] William Henry 1860
SELLERS John M 1860
THOMAS Israel J 1880
THOMAS Israel J 1880
SELLERS John M 1860
THOMAS Israel J 1880
BRADWAY Heman 1874
BRADWAY Asa 1873
32
BRADWAY Lewis S 1889
KING Dwight A 1884
HARBIT Francis M 1884
BRADWAY Lewis S 1889
FLINT [132] David 1860
FOGG Francis A 1860
33
FOGG Francis A 1859
FOGG Francis A 1860

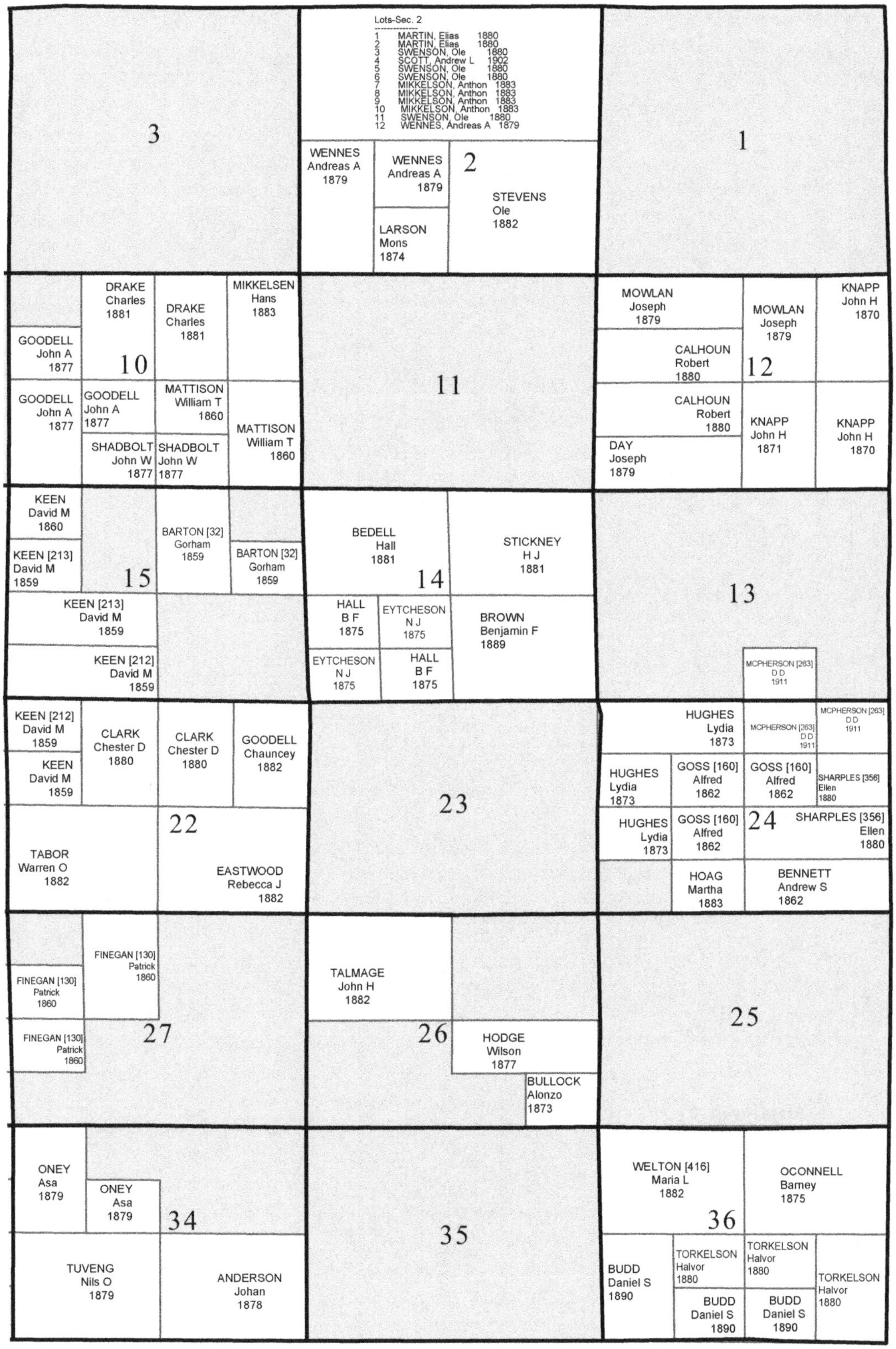
Lots-Sec. 2
1 MARTIN, Elias 1880
2 MARTIN, Elias 1880
3 SWENSON, Ole 1880
4 SCOTT, Andrew L 1902
5 SWENSON, Ole 1880
6 SWENSON, Ole 1880
7 MIKKELSON, Anthon 1883
8 MIKKELSON, Anthon 1883
9 MIKKELSON, Anthon 1883
10 MIKKELSON, Anthon 1883
11 SWENSON, Ole 1880
12 WENNES, Andreas A 1879
3
1
2
WENNES Andreas A 1879
WENNES Andreas A 1879
STEVENS Ole 1882
LARSON Mons 1874
DRAKE Charles 1881
DRAKE Charles 1881
MIKKELSEN Hans 1883
GOODELL John A 1877
10
GOODELL John A 1877
GOODELL John A 1877
MATTISON William T 1860
MATTISON William T 1860
SHADBOLT John W 1877
SHADBOLT John W 1877
11
MOWLAN Joseph 1879
MOWLAN Joseph 1879
KNAPP John H 1870
CALHOUN Robert 1880
12
CALHOUN Robert 1880
KNAPP John H 1871
KNAPP John H 1870
DAY Joseph 1879
KEEN David M 1860
KEEN [213] David M 1859
BARTON [32] Gorham 1859
BARTON [32] Gorham 1859
15
BEDELL Hall 1881
14
STICKNEY H J 1881
13
KEEN [213] David M 1859
KEEN [212] David M 1859
HALL B F 1875
EYTCHESON N J 1875
BROWN Benjamin F 1889
EYTCHESON N J 1875
HALL B F 1875
MCPHERSON [263] D D 1911
KEEN [212] David M 1859
CLARK Chester D 1880
CLARK Chester D 1880
GOODELL Chauncey 1882
KEEN David M 1859
23
HUGHES Lydia 1873
MCPHERSON [263] D D 1911
MCPHERSON [263] D D 1911
HUGHES Lydia 1873
GOSS [160] Alfred 1862
GOSS [160] Alfred 1862
SHARPLES [356] Ellen 1880
22
TABOR Warren O 1882
EASTWOOD Rebecca J 1882
HUGHES Lydia 1873
GOSS [160] Alfred 1862
24
SHARPLES [356] Ellen 1880
HOAG Martha 1883
BENNETT Andrew S 1862
FINEGAN [130] Patrick 1860
FINEGAN [130] Patrick 1860
TALMAGE John H 1882
25
FINEGAN [130] Patrick 1860
27
26
HODGE Wilson 1877
BULLOCK Alonzo 1873
ONEY Asa 1879
ONEY Asa 1879
34
35
WELTON [416] Maria L 1882
OCONNELL Barney 1875
36
TUVENG Nils O 1879
ANDERSON Johan 1878
BUDD Daniel S 1890
TORKELSON Halvor 1880
TORKELSON Halvor 1880
TORKELSON Halvor 1880
BUDD Daniel S 1890
BUDD Daniel S 1890

Helpful Hints

1. This Map's INDEX can be found on the preceding pages.
2. Refer to Map "C" to see where this Township lies within Dunn County, Wisconsin.
3. Numbers within square brackets [ ] denote a multi-patentee land parcel (multi-owner). Refer to Appendix "C" for a full list of members in this group.
4. Areas that look to be crowded with Patentees usually indicate multiple sales of the same parcel (Re-issues) or Overlapping parcels. See this Township's Index for an explanation of these and other circumstances that might explain "odd" groupings of Patentees on this map.

Legend

Patent Boundary

Section Boundary

No Patents Found (or Outside County)

1., 2., 3., ... Lot Numbers (when beside a name)

[ ] Group Number (see Appendix "C")

Scale: Section = 1 mile X 1 mile (generally, with some exceptions)

Road Map

T30-N R13-W
4th PM - 1831 MN/WI Meridian

Map Group 6

Cities & Towns

Baxter
Wheeler

Cemeteries

Hay River Cemetery
Our Saviors Cemetery

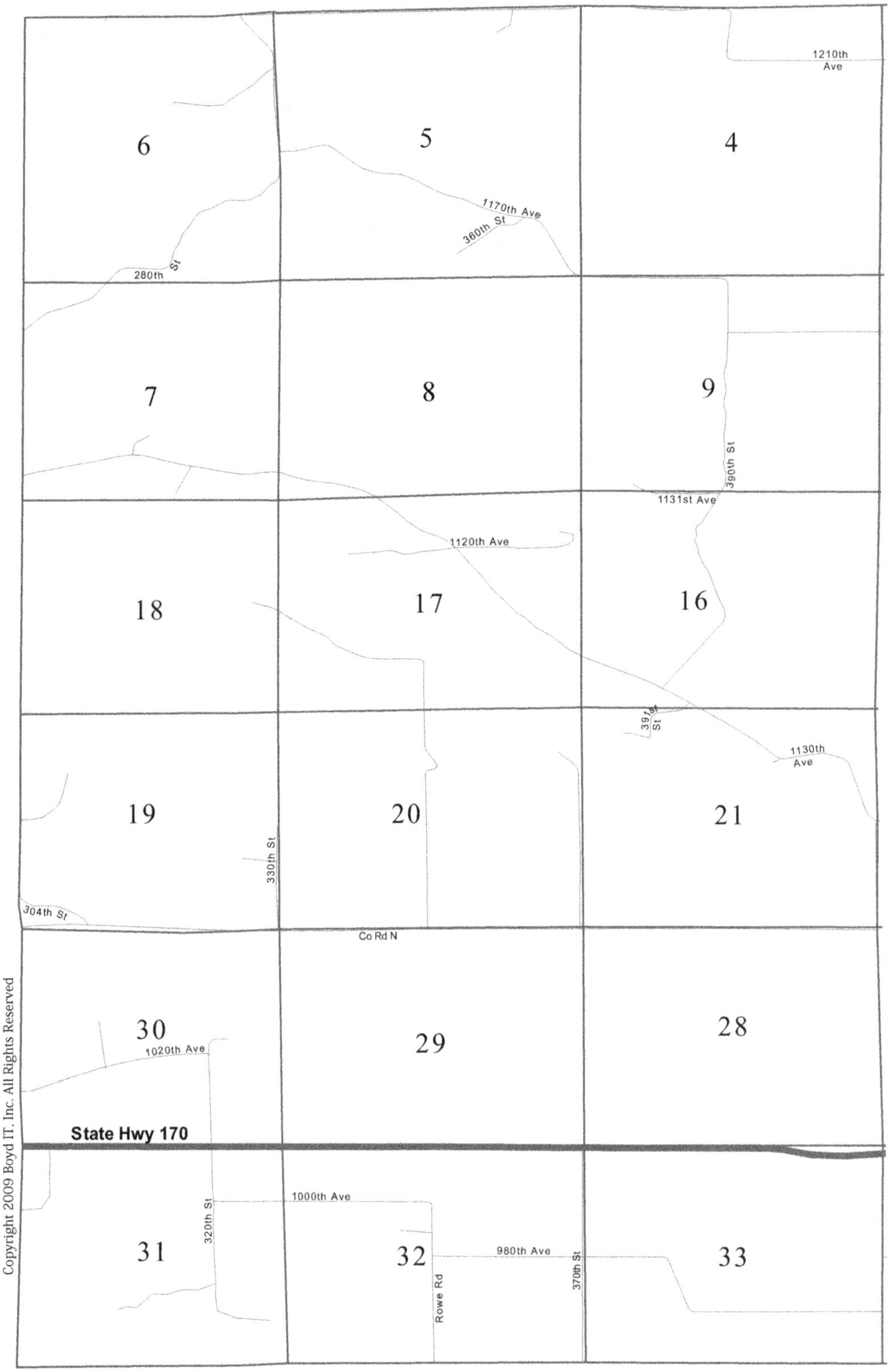

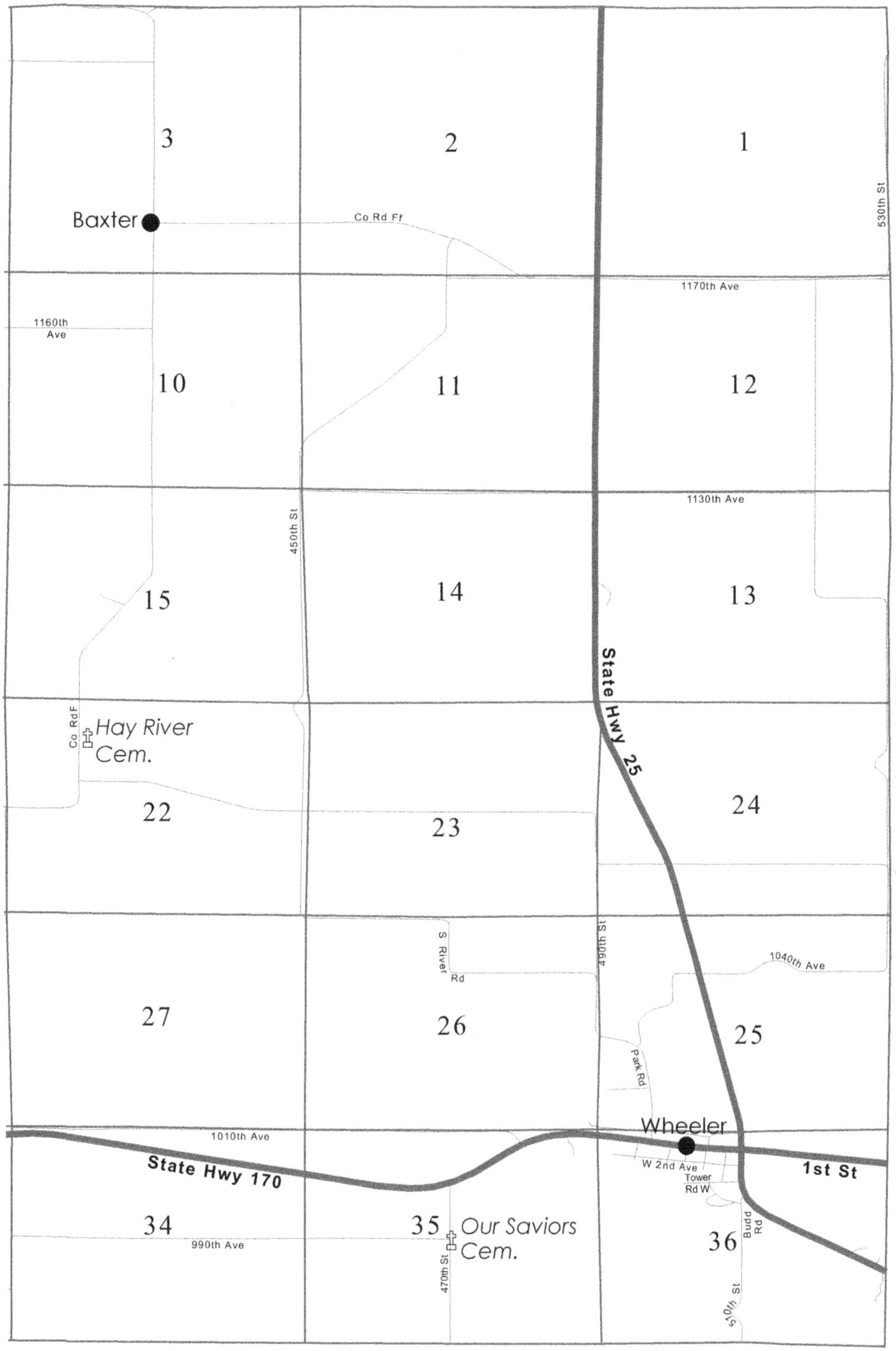

Helpful Hints

1. This road map has a number of uses, but primarily it is to help you: a) find the present location of land owned by your ancestors (at least the general area), b) find cemeteries and city-centers, and c) estimate the route/roads used by Census-takers & tax-assessors.
2. If you plan to travel to Dunn County to locate cemeteries or land parcels, please pick up a modern travel map for the area before you do. Mapping old land parcels on modern maps is not as exact a science as you might think. Just the slightest variations in public land survey coordinates, estimates of parcel boundaries, or road-map deviations can greatly alter a map's representation of how a road either does or doesn't cross a particular parcel of land.

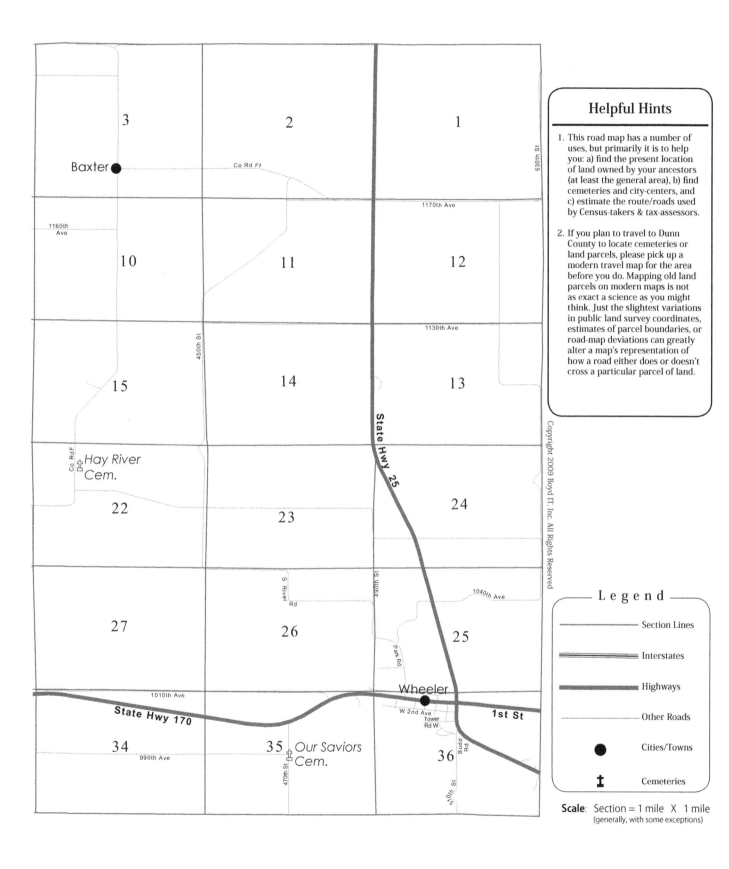

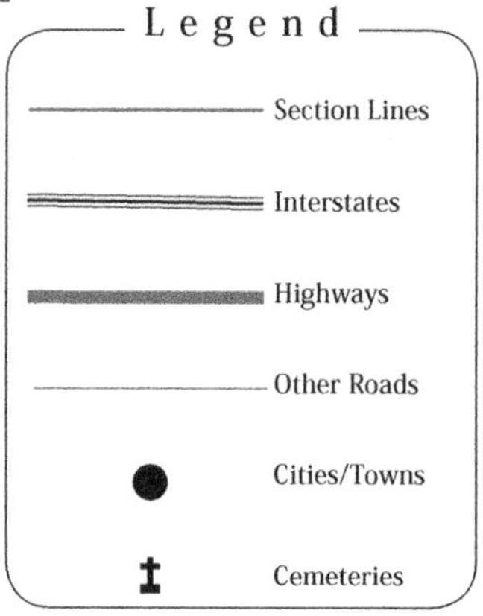
Legend
Section Lines
Interstates
Highways
Other Roads
Cities/Towns
Cemeteries

Scale: Section = 1 mile X 1 mile
(generally, with some exceptions)

Historical Map

T30-N R13-W
4th PM - 1831 MN/WI Meridian

Map Group 6

Cities & Towns
- Baxter
- Wheeler

Cemeteries
- Hay River Cemetery
- Our Saviors Cemetery

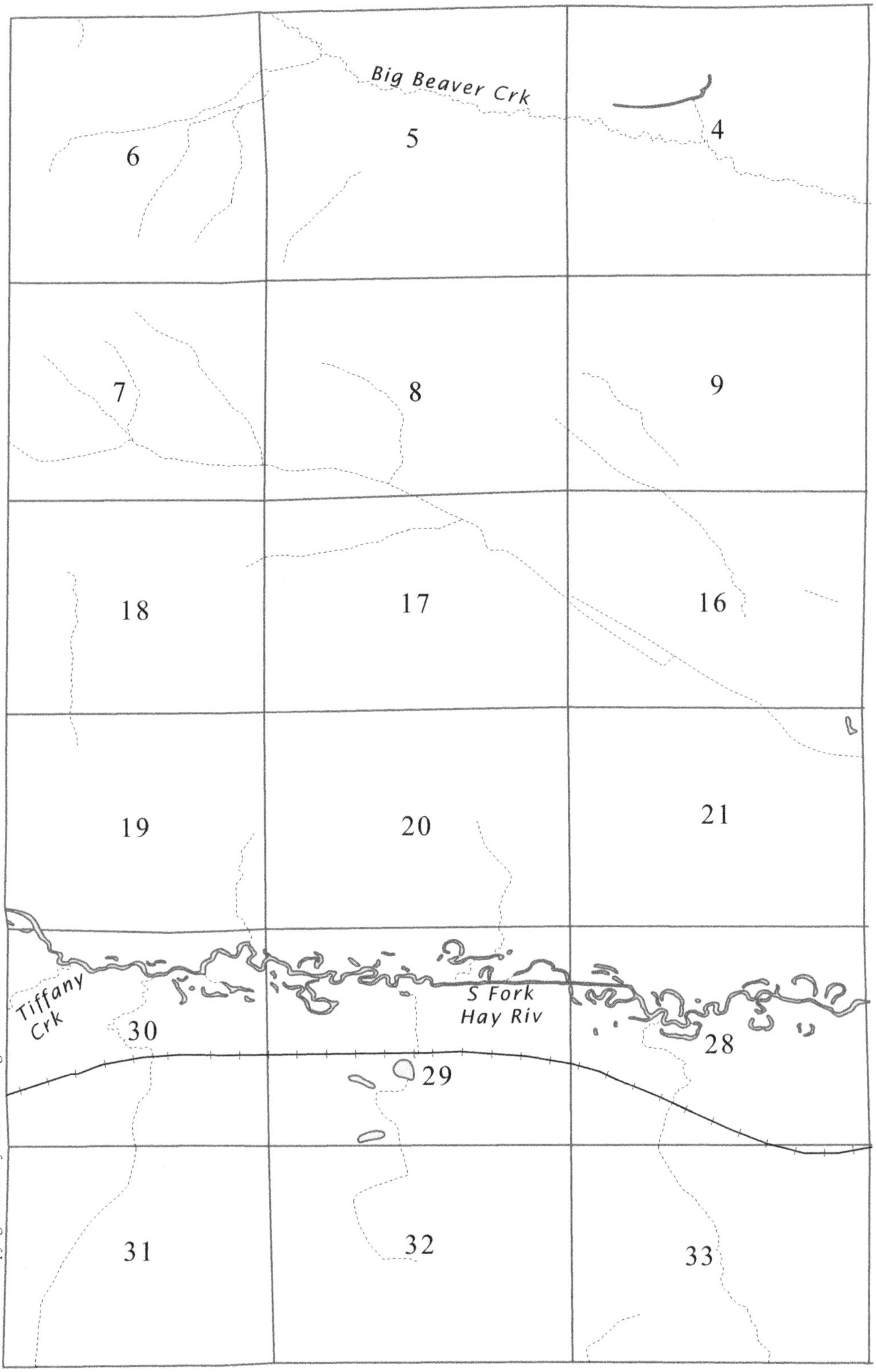

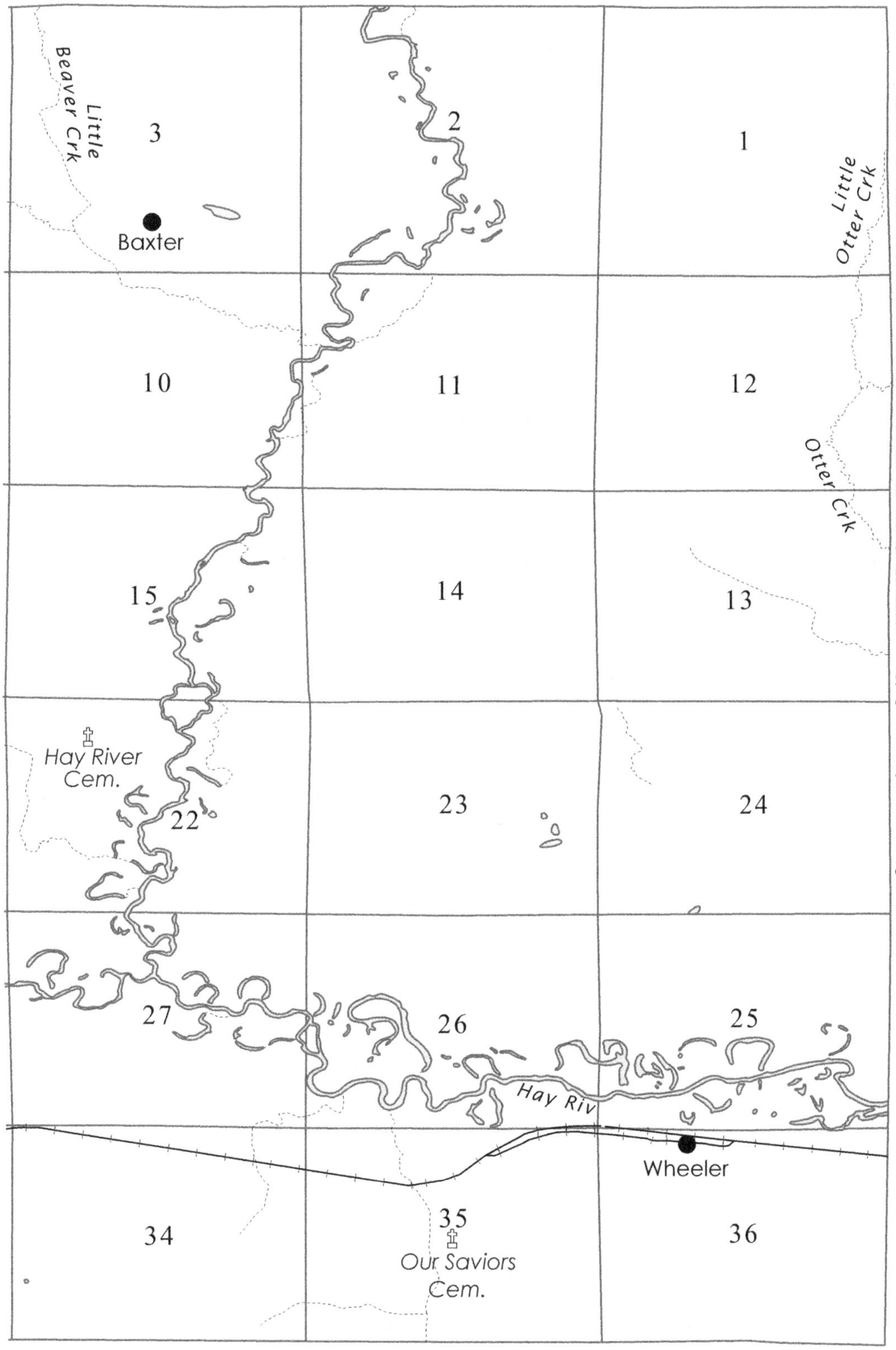

Helpful Hints

1. This Map takes a different look at the same Congressional Township displayed in the preceding two maps. It presents features that can help you better envision the historical development of the area: a) Water-bodies (lakes & ponds), b) Water-courses (rivers, streams, etc.), c) Railroads, d) City/town center-points (where they were oftentimes located when first settled), and e) Cemeteries.
2. Using this "Historical" map in tandem with this Township's Patent Map and Road Map, may lead you to some interesting discoveries. You will often find roads, towns, cemeteries, and waterways are named after nearby landowners: sometimes those names will be the ones you are researching. See how many of these research gems you can find here in Dunn County.

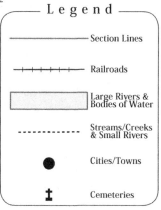

Legend

- Section Lines
- Railroads
- Large Rivers & Bodies of Water
- Streams/Creeks & Small Rivers
- Cities/Towns
- Cemeteries

Scale: Section = 1 mile X 1 mile
(there are some exceptions)

Map Group 7: Index to Land Patents

Township 30-North Range 12-West (4th PM - 1831 MN/WI)

After you locate an individual in this Index, take note of the Section and Section Part then proceed to the Land Patent map on the pages immediately following. You should have no difficulty locating the corresponding parcel of land.

The "For More Info" Column will lead you to more information about the underlying Patents. See the *Legend* at right, and the "How to Use this Book" chapter, for more information.

LEGEND

"For More Info . . . " column

A = Authority (Legislative Act, See Appendix "A")
B = Block or Lot (location in Section unknown)
C = Cancelled Patent
F = Fractional Section
G = Group (Multi-Patentee Patent, see Appendix "C")
V = Overlaps another Parcel
R = Re-Issued (Parcel patented more than once)

(A & G items require you to look in the Appendixes referred to above. All other Letter-designations followed by a number require you to locate line-items in this index that possess the ID number found after the letter).

ID	Individual in Patent	Sec.	Sec. Part	Date Issued	Other Counties	For More Info . . .
1104	ABBOTT, Charles W	32	E½NE	1884-09-20		A6
1084	ANDERSEN, Anne	26	W½NW	1880-11-01		A6 G8
1085	" "	26	W½SW	1880-11-01		A6 G8
1084	ANDERSEN, Knud	26	W½NW	1880-11-01		A6 G8
1085	" "	26	W½SW	1880-11-01		A6 G8
1177	ANDERSON, Markus	26	NESW	1882-04-10		A6
1178	" "	26	NWSE	1882-04-10		A6
1179	" "	26	SENW	1882-04-10		A6
1180	" "	26	SWNE	1882-04-10		A6
1198	ANDERSON, Sever K	24	N½SW	1900-04-26		A6
1199	" "	24	NWSE	1900-04-26		A6
1200	" "	24	SWNE	1900-04-26		A6
1075	BECKER, A D	28	W½NE	1879-11-10		A6
1076	" "	28	W½SE	1879-11-10		A6
1089	BECKER, C A	28	E½NE	1881-09-17		A6
1090	" "	28	E½SE	1881-09-17		A6
1142	BLAIR, James	6	SW	1878-06-24		A6
1210	BLAIR, Thomas	6	3	1882-05-10		A6
1211	" "	6	4	1882-05-10		A6
1212	" "	6	5	1882-05-10		A6
1213	" "	6	6	1882-05-10		A6
1129	BRATLEY, Hans A	36	SE	1898-04-25		A6
1102	BROWNLEE, Charles H	10	SW	1891-08-04		A6
1120	BURCH, George E	26	N½NE	1913-08-21		A6
1121	" "	26	NENW	1913-08-21		A6
1195	CALHOUNE, Robert	8	NESW	1889-03-21		A2
1218	CARD, Abel C	2	10	1882-04-10		A6 G61
1219	" "	2	11	1882-04-10		A6 G61
1220	" "	2	12	1882-04-10		A6 G61
1221	" "	2	NWSE	1882-04-10		A6 G61
1218	CARD, D P	2	10	1882-04-10		A6 G61
1219	" "	2	11	1882-04-10		A6 G61
1220	" "	2	12	1882-04-10		A6 G61
1221	" "	2	NWSE	1882-04-10		A6 G61
1218	CARD, William	2	10	1882-04-10		A6 G61
1219	" "	2	11	1882-04-10		A6 G61
1220	" "	2	12	1882-04-10		A6 G61
1221	" "	2	NWSE	1882-04-10		A6 G61
1140	CAREY, Jacob C	10	NE	1891-05-09		A6
1196	CARPENTER, Sarah A	18	E½NW	1891-07-27		A6
1197	" "	18	N½NE	1891-07-27		A6
1135	CHAMPLIN, Ira A	20	SW	1874-11-10		A6
1105	CHRISTIANSEN, Christian	34	E½NE	1906-08-16		A6
1106	" "	34	E½SE	1906-08-16		A6
1109	CROSBY, E F	32	N½SW	1879-11-10		A6
1110	" "	32	W½NW	1879-11-10		A6

ID	Individual in Patent	Sec.	Sec. Part	Date Issued	Other Counties	For More Info . . .
1094	DAHL, Charles E	2	2	1892-04-09		A6
1095	" "	2	3	1892-04-09		A6
1096	" "	2	6	1892-04-09		A6
1097	" "	2	7	1892-04-09		A6
1118	DAHLBAK, Esten E	4	N½SE	1886-01-20		A6
1201	DAVIS, Silas L	32	E½NW	1878-11-30		A6
1202	" "	32	W½NE	1878-11-30		A6
1103	DOWNING, Charles H	14	SE	1882-04-10		A6
1122	DOWNING, George R	14	NE	1882-05-10		A6
1098	DUELL, Charles E	30	S½SE	1878-01-25		A5 G114
1098	DUELL, Horace M	30	S½SE	1878-01-25		A5 G114
1092	DUNCAN, J H	3	NESW	1866-02-10		A7 G409
1139	" "	12	N½NE	1877-04-05		A2
1147	DUNCAN, Joel H	1	SE	1872-09-25		A6
1100	EDMONDS, Charles	20	SE	1878-11-30		A6
1222	EDMONDS, William	32	N½SE	1890-09-09		A6
1208	ELLEFSEN, Svennung	2	S½SE	1891-05-09		A6
1209	" "	2	S½SW	1891-05-09		A6
1216	EVANS, Walter F	4	10	1875-03-10		A2
1217	" "	4	9	1875-03-10		A2
1148	FLUG, John	6	10	1889-02-16		A6
1149	" "	6	11	1889-02-16		A6
1150	" "	6	9	1889-02-16		A6
1165	FRAMMI, Knud A	24	S½SE	1892-04-29		A6
1166	" "	24	SESW	1892-04-29		A6
1133	FREESTONE, Hezekiah F	22	NWSW	1883-02-10		A6
1134	" "	22	S½SW	1883-02-10		A6
1136	FREESTONE, Ira P	22	NW	1882-04-10		A6
1214	FREESTONE, Thomas	12	SWNW	1883-07-10		A6
1215	" "	12	W½SW	1883-07-10		A6
1223	FREESTONE, William	14	N½NW	1885-05-20		A6
1224	" "	14	SENW	1885-05-20		A6
1162	GEROY, Julius	14	NWSW	1889-02-16		A6
1163	" "	14	S½SW	1889-02-16		A6
1164	" "	14	SWNW	1889-02-16		A6
1101	GILLIS, Charles	28	NW	1877-06-04		A6
1141	GOETZINGER, Jacob	6	SE	1885-01-30		A6
1107	GOODELL, David	18	NESE	1885-05-20		A6
1108	" "	18	SENE	1885-05-20		A6
1119	GREGERSON, George A	2	N½SW	1901-06-08		A6
1161	HALE, John W	24	NW	1905-01-30		A6
1077	HALL, A G	18	W½SE	1877-05-15		A6
1088	HALL, Benjamin	18	SESE	1877-05-15		A6
1185	HOLTE, Ole A	4	S½SE	1912-09-12		A2
1167	JOHNSON, Lars	8	E½NW	1883-02-10		A6
1168	" "	8	NWSW	1883-02-10		A6
1169	" "	8	SWNW	1883-02-10		A6
1191	KIMBALL, Porter B	24	N½NE	1883-02-10		A6
1192	" "	24	NESE	1883-02-10		A6
1193	" "	24	SENE	1883-02-10		A6
1130	KNAPP, Henry E	18	SWNE	1875-03-10		A2
1151	KNAPP, John H	18	E½SW	1870-06-01		A2
1154	" "	22	SWSE	1870-06-01		A2
1152	" "	18	W½NW	1870-06-10		A2 F
1153	" "	18	W½SW	1871-04-05		A2
1156	" "	30	E½NE	1871-04-05		A2 G225
1157	" "	30	NESE	1871-04-05		A2 G225
1155	" "	4	W½SW	1872-02-14		A2
1093	KNUDSEN, Chal	34	NW	1882-04-10		A6
1225	KRAUSE, Willis E	34	W½NE	1896-07-31		A6
1226	" "	34	W½SE	1896-07-31		A6
1086	LEE, Anton O	4	7	1912-05-13		A6
1087	" "	4	8	1912-05-13		A6
1158	LEONARD, John J	14	NESW	1872-09-02		A2
1159	LIE, John J	36	N½NE	1891-07-14		A6
1160	" "	36	N½NW	1891-07-14		A6
1176	MARTIN, Margaretha	24	SWSW	1920-02-24		A6
1111	MATTESON, Elias	2	1	1893-05-06		A6
1112	" "	2	8	1893-05-06		A6
1113	" "	2	9	1893-05-06		A6
1137	MAVITY, Isaac L	12	E½SE	1893-12-19		A6
1138	" "	12	SENE	1893-12-19		A6
1203	MCCULLOCH, Solomon B	22	N½SE	1878-06-24		A6

ID	Individual in Patent	Sec.	Sec. Part	Date Issued	Other Counties	For More Info . . .
1204	MCCULLOCH, Solomon B (Cont'd)	22	NESW	1878-06-24		A6
1205	" "	22	SESE	1878-06-24		A6
1143	MCPHERSON, James	28	SW	1879-11-10		A6
1190	MESSELT, Peder C	8	NE	1884-01-15		A6
1092	MONROE, Dennis	3	NESW	1866-02-10		A7 G409
1114	OLESON, Engerbret	4	11	1882-06-01		A6
1115	" "	4	12	1882-06-01		A6
1116	" "	4	E½SW	1882-06-01		A6
1173	OLIVER, Lyman	36	SESW	1883-07-10		A6
1174	" "	36	SWNW	1883-07-10		A6
1175	" "	36	W½SW	1883-07-10		A6
1091	POISKE, Caroline	10	NW	1882-05-10		A6 G308
1091	POISKE, Charles	10	NW	1882-05-10		A6 G308
1194	RICE, Rachel A	8	S½SW	1886-04-10		A6
1181	ROMSAAS, Martinus T	6	1	1884-01-15		A6
1182	" "	6	2	1884-01-15		A6
1183	" "	6	7	1884-01-15		A6
1184	" "	6	8	1884-01-15		A6
1117	RONENG, Erik L	8	SE	1892-05-04		A6
1081	ROSTANO, Andrew A	36	NESW	1914-10-23		A6
1082	" "	36	S½NE	1914-10-23		A6
1083	" "	36	SENW	1914-10-23		A6
1207	SHARPLES, Henry	20	NW	1881-09-17		A6 G357
1207	SHARPLES, Susan	20	NW	1881-09-17		A6 G357
1144	SISCHO, Jesse	26	NESE	1884-01-15		A6
1145	" "	26	S½SE	1884-01-15		A6
1146	" "	26	SENE	1884-01-15		A6
1099	SISSON, Charles E	26	SESW	1905-03-30		A6
1078	SNYDER, Albert H	12	SESW	1884-09-20		A6
1079	" "	12	SWNE	1884-09-20		A6
1080	" "	12	W½SE	1884-09-20		A6
1123	SNYDER, Gilbert H	12	N½NW	1882-06-30		A6
1124	" "	12	NESW	1882-06-30		A6
1125	" "	12	SENW	1882-06-30		A6
1131	STODDARD, Henry	32	S½SE	1882-04-10		A6
1132	" "	32	S½SW	1882-04-10		A6
1126	SVENOMSON, Gunild	2	4	1892-05-04		A6
1127	" "	2	5	1892-05-04		A6
1128	SVENUNGSON, Hage	10	SE	1891-11-09		A6 G387
1128	SVENUNGSON, Torge	10	SE	1891-11-09		A6 G387
1156	TAINTER, J B	30	E½NE	1871-04-05		A2 G225
1157	" "	30	NESE	1871-04-05		A2 G225
1092	WARREN, Catharine	3	NESW	1866-02-10		A7 G409
1092	WARREN, Jacob A	3	NESW	1866-02-10		A7 G409
1092	WARREN, James	3	NESW	1866-02-10		A7 G409
1170	WEAVER, Lemuel H	1	SESW	1871-11-20		A6
1171	" "	1	W½SW	1871-11-20		A6
1172	" "	2	NESE	1871-11-20		A6
1206	WISCONSIN, State Of	16		1941-08-16		A3
1186	WOLD, Ole A	4	3	1882-05-10		A6
1187	" "	4	4	1882-05-10		A6
1188	" "	4	5	1882-05-10		A6
1189	" "	4	6	1882-05-10		A6

Patent Map

T30-N R12-W
4th PM - 1831 MN/WI Meridian

Map Group 7

Township Statistics

Parcels Mapped	:	152
Number of Patents	:	83
Number of Individuals	:	90
Patentees Identified	:	80
Number of Surnames	:	69
Multi-Patentee Parcels	:	13
Oldest Patent Date	:	2/10/1866
Most Recent Patent	:	8/16/1941
Block/Lot Parcels	:	33
Parcels Re - Issued	:	0
Parcels that Overlap	:	0
Cities and Towns	:	0
Cemeteries	:	2

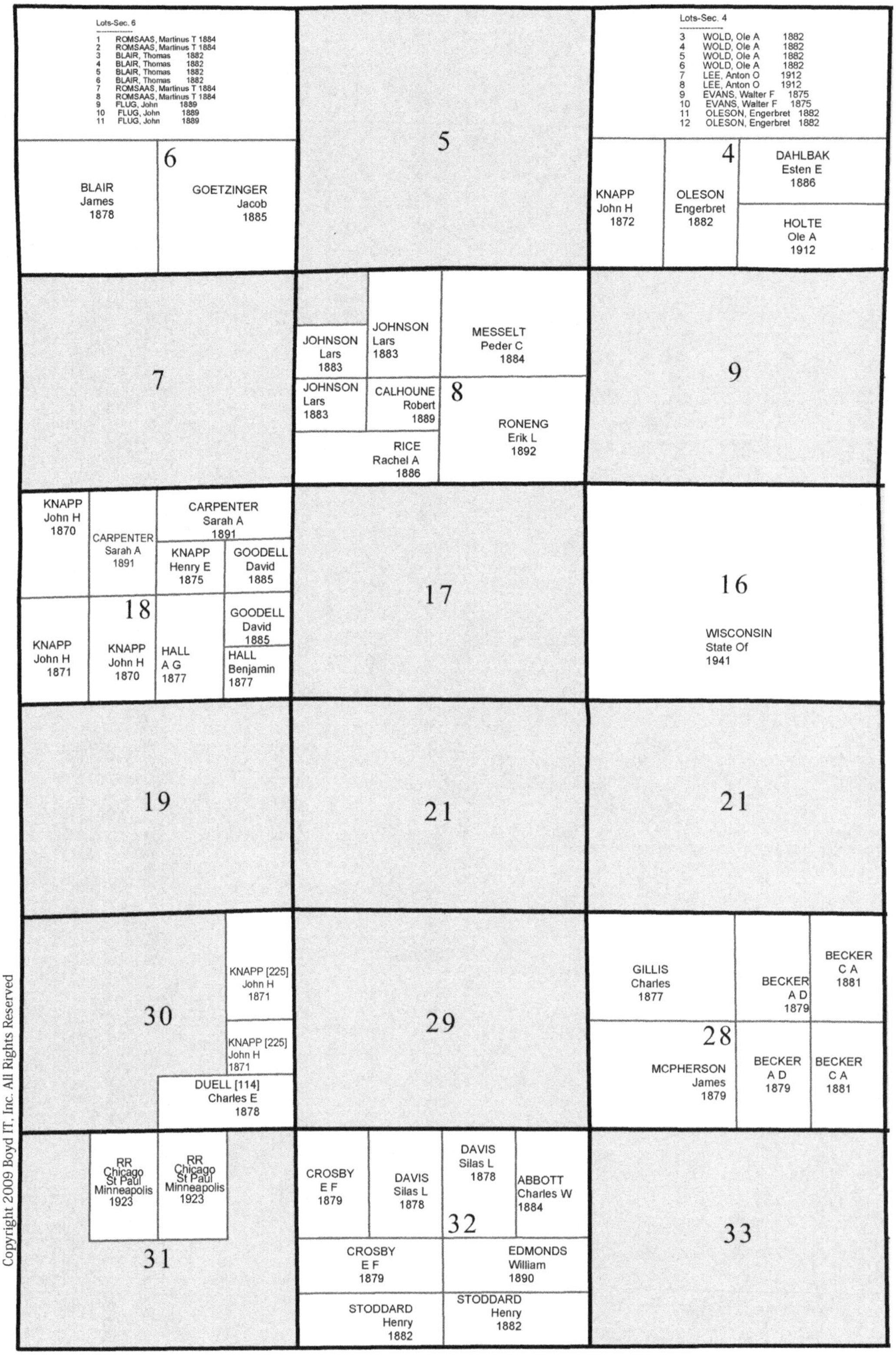

Lots-Sec. 6
1 ROMSAAS, Martinus T 1884
2 ROMSAAS, Martinus T 1884
3 BLAIR, Thomas 1882
4 BLAIR, Thomas 1882
5 BLAIR, Thomas 1882
6 BLAIR, Thomas 1882
7 ROMSAAS, Martinus T 1884
8 ROMSAAS, Martinus T 1884
9 FLUG, John 1889
10 FLUG, John 1889
11 FLUG, John 1889
6
BLAIR James 1878
GOETZINGER Jacob 1885
5
Lots-Sec. 4
3 WOLD, Ole A 1882
4 WOLD, Ole A 1882
5 WOLD, Ole A 1882
6 WOLD, Ole A 1882
7 LEE, Anton O 1912
8 LEE, Anton O 1912
9 EVANS, Walter F 1875
10 EVANS, Walter F 1875
11 OLESON, Engerbret 1882
12 OLESON, Engerbret 1882
4
KNAPP John H 1872
OLESON Engerbret 1882
DAHLBAK Esten E 1886
HOLTE Ole A 1912
7
JOHNSON Lars 1883
JOHNSON Lars 1883
MESSELT Peder C 1884
JOHNSON Lars 1883
CALHOUNE Robert 1889
8
RONENG Erik L 1892
RICE Rachel A 1886
9
KNAPP John H 1870
CARPENTER Sarah A 1891
CARPENTER Sarah A 1891
KNAPP Henry E 1875
GOODELL David 1885
18
KNAPP John H 1871
KNAPP John H 1870
HALL A G 1877
GOODELL David 1885
HALL Benjamin 1877
17
16
WISCONSIN State Of 1941
19
21
21
30
KNAPP [225] John H 1871
KNAPP [225] John H 1871
DUELL [114] Charles E 1878
29
GILLIS Charles 1877
BECKER A D 1879
BECKER C A 1881
28
MCPHERSON James 1879
BECKER A D 1879
BECKER C A 1881
RR Chicago St Paul Minneapolis 1923
RR Chicago St Paul Minneapolis 1923
31
CROSBY E F 1879
DAVIS Silas L 1878
DAVIS Silas L 1878
ABBOTT Charles W 1884
32
CROSBY E F 1879
EDMONDS William 1890
STODDARD Henry 1882
STODDARD Henry 1882
33

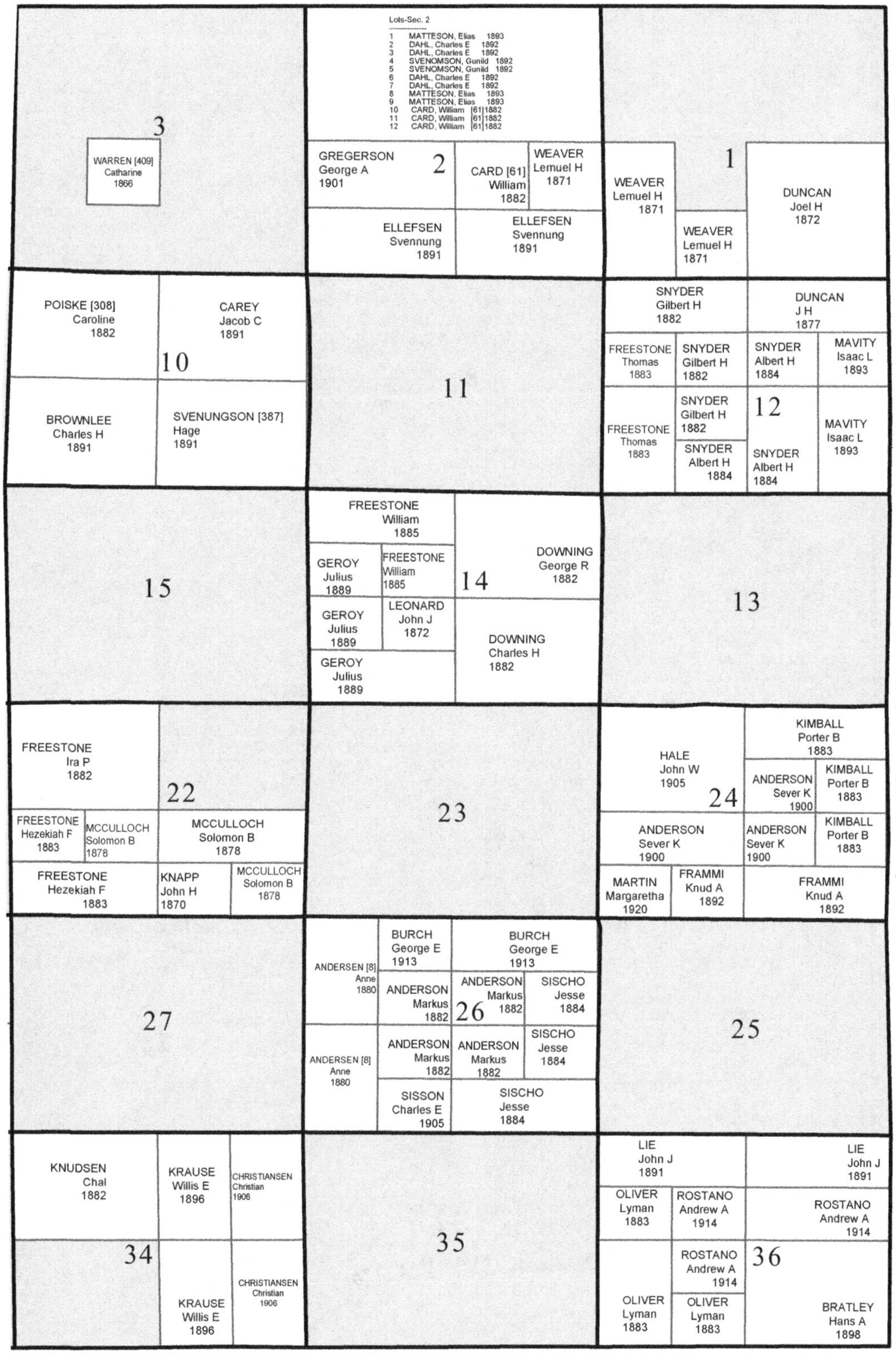
Lots-Sec. 2
1 MATTESON, Elias 1893
2 DAHL, Charles E 1892
3 DAHL, Charles E 1892
4 SVENOMSON, Gunild 1892
5 SVENOMSON, Gunild 1892
6 DAHL, Charles E 1892
7 DAHL, Charles E 1892
8 MATTESON, Elias 1893
9 MATTESON, Elias 1893
10 CARD, William [61]1882
11 CARD, William [61]1882
12 CARD, William [61]1882
3
WARREN [409] Catharine 1866
GREGERSON George A 1901
2
CARD [61] William 1882
WEAVER Lemuel H 1871
ELLEFSEN Svennung 1891
ELLEFSEN Svennung 1891
WEAVER Lemuel H 1871
1
DUNCAN Joel H 1872
WEAVER Lemuel H 1871
POISKE [308] Caroline 1882
CAREY Jacob C 1891
10
BROWNLEE Charles H 1891
SVENUNGSON [387] Hage 1891
11
SNYDER Gilbert H 1882
DUNCAN J H 1877
FREESTONE Thomas 1883
SNYDER Gilbert H 1882
SNYDER Albert H 1884
MAVITY Isaac L 1893
SNYDER Gilbert H 1882
12
FREESTONE Thomas 1883
SNYDER Albert H 1884
SNYDER Albert H 1884
MAVITY Isaac L 1893
15
FREESTONE William 1885
GEROY Julius 1889
FREESTONE William 1885
14
DOWNING George R 1882
GEROY Julius 1889
LEONARD John J 1872
GEROY Julius 1889
DOWNING Charles H 1882
13
FREESTONE Ira P 1882
22
FREESTONE Hezekiah F 1883
MCCULLOCH Solomon B 1878
MCCULLOCH Solomon B 1878
FREESTONE Hezekiah F 1883
KNAPP John H 1870
MCCULLOCH Solomon B 1878
23
HALE John W 1905
KIMBALL Porter B 1883
ANDERSON Sever K 1900
KIMBALL Porter B 1883
24
ANDERSON Sever K 1900
ANDERSON Sever K 1900
KIMBALL Porter B 1883
MARTIN Margaretha 1920
FRAMMI Knud A 1892
FRAMMI Knud A 1892
27
ANDERSEN [8] Anne 1880
BURCH George E 1913
BURCH George E 1913
ANDERSON Markus 1882
26
ANDERSON Markus 1882
SISCHO Jesse 1884
ANDERSEN [8] Anne 1880
ANDERSON Markus 1882
ANDERSON Markus 1882
SISCHO Jesse 1884
SISSON Charles E 1905
SISCHO Jesse 1884
25
KNUDSEN Chal 1882
KRAUSE Willis E 1896
CHRISTIANSEN Christian 1906
34
KRAUSE Willis E 1896
CHRISTIANSEN Christian 1906
35
LIE John J 1891
LIE John J 1891
OLIVER Lyman 1883
ROSTANO Andrew A 1914
ROSTANO Andrew A 1914
ROSTANO Andrew A 1914
36
OLIVER Lyman 1883
OLIVER Lyman 1883
BRATLEY Hans A 1898

Helpful Hints

1. This Map's INDEX can be found on the preceding pages.
2. Refer to Map "C" to see where this Township lies within Dunn County, Wisconsin.
3. Numbers within square brackets [ ] denote a multi-patentee land parcel (multi-owner). Refer to Appendix "C" for a full list of members in this group.
4. Areas that look to be crowded with Patentees usually indicate multiple sales of the same parcel (Re-issues) or Overlapping parcels. See this Township's Index for an explanation of these and other circumstances that might explain "odd" groupings of Patentees on this map.

Legend

- Patent Boundary
- Section Boundary
- No Patents Found (or Outside County)
- 1., 2., 3., ... Lot Numbers (when beside a name)
- [ ] Group Number (see Appendix "C")

Scale: Section = 1 mile X 1 mile (generally, with some exceptions)

Road Map

T30-N R12-W
4th PM - 1831 MN/WI Meridian

Map Group 7

Cities & Towns

None

Cemeteries

Otter Creek Cemetery
Upper Popple Creek Cemetery

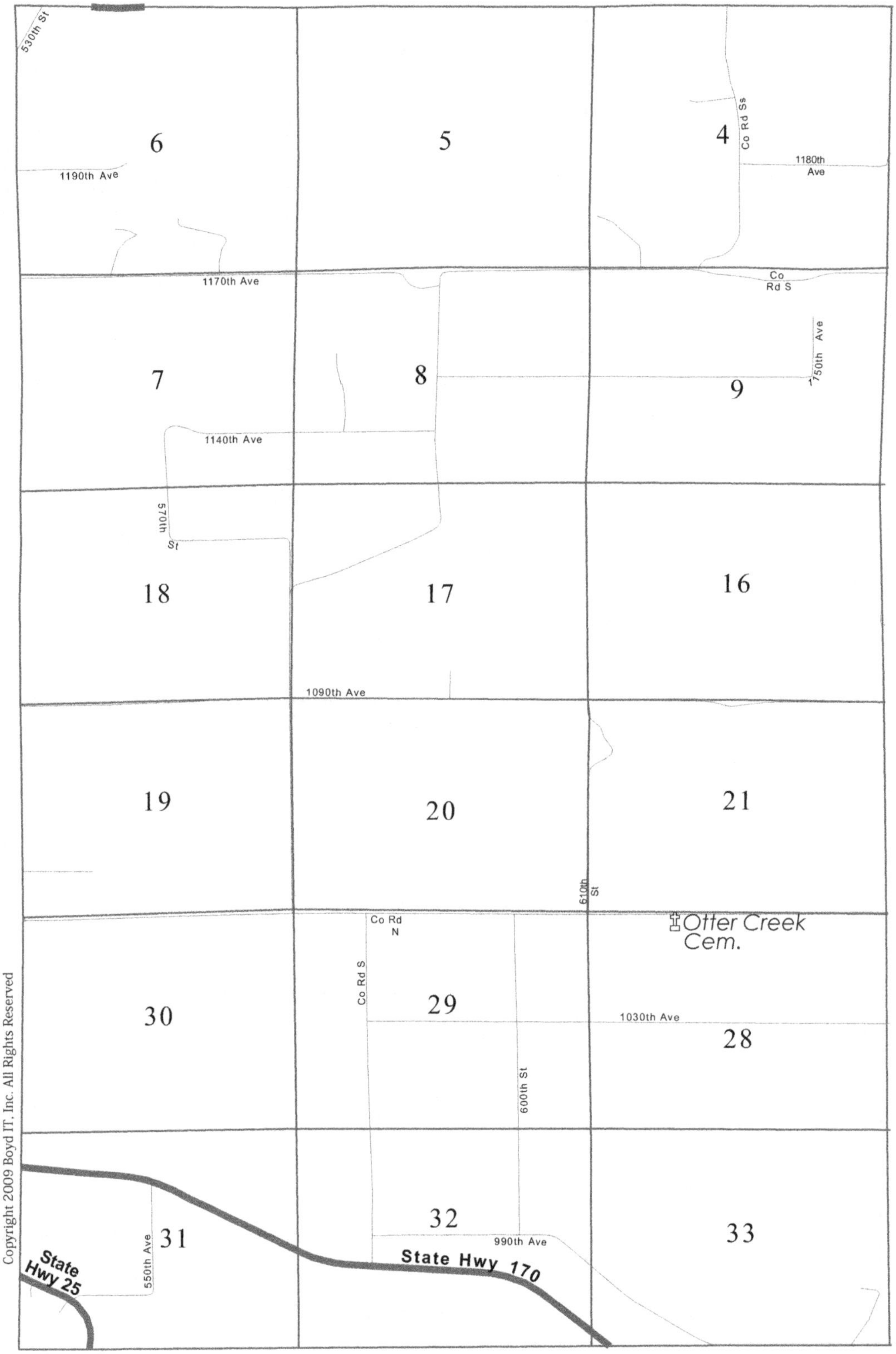

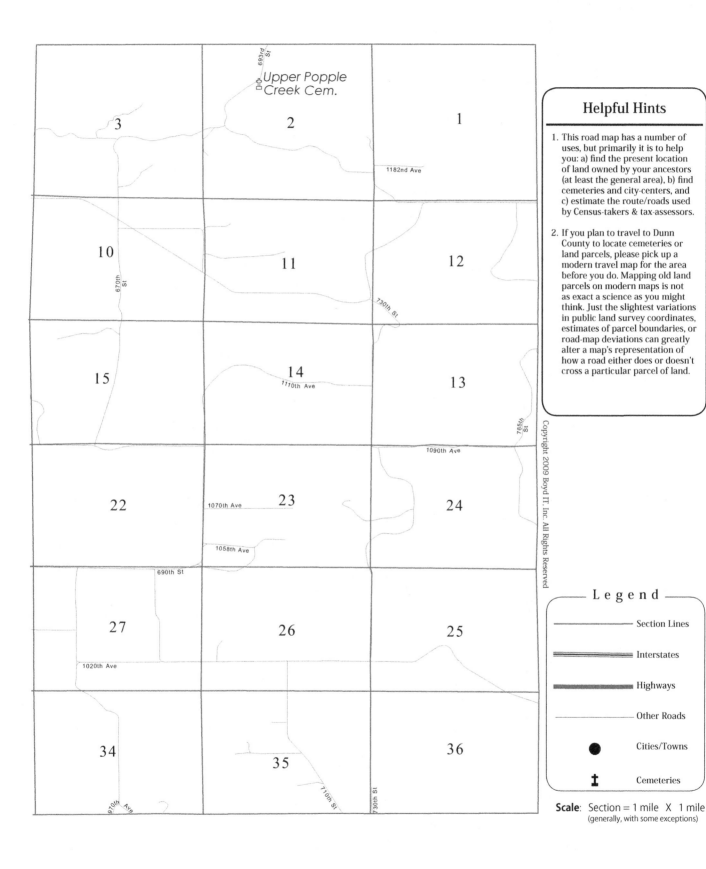

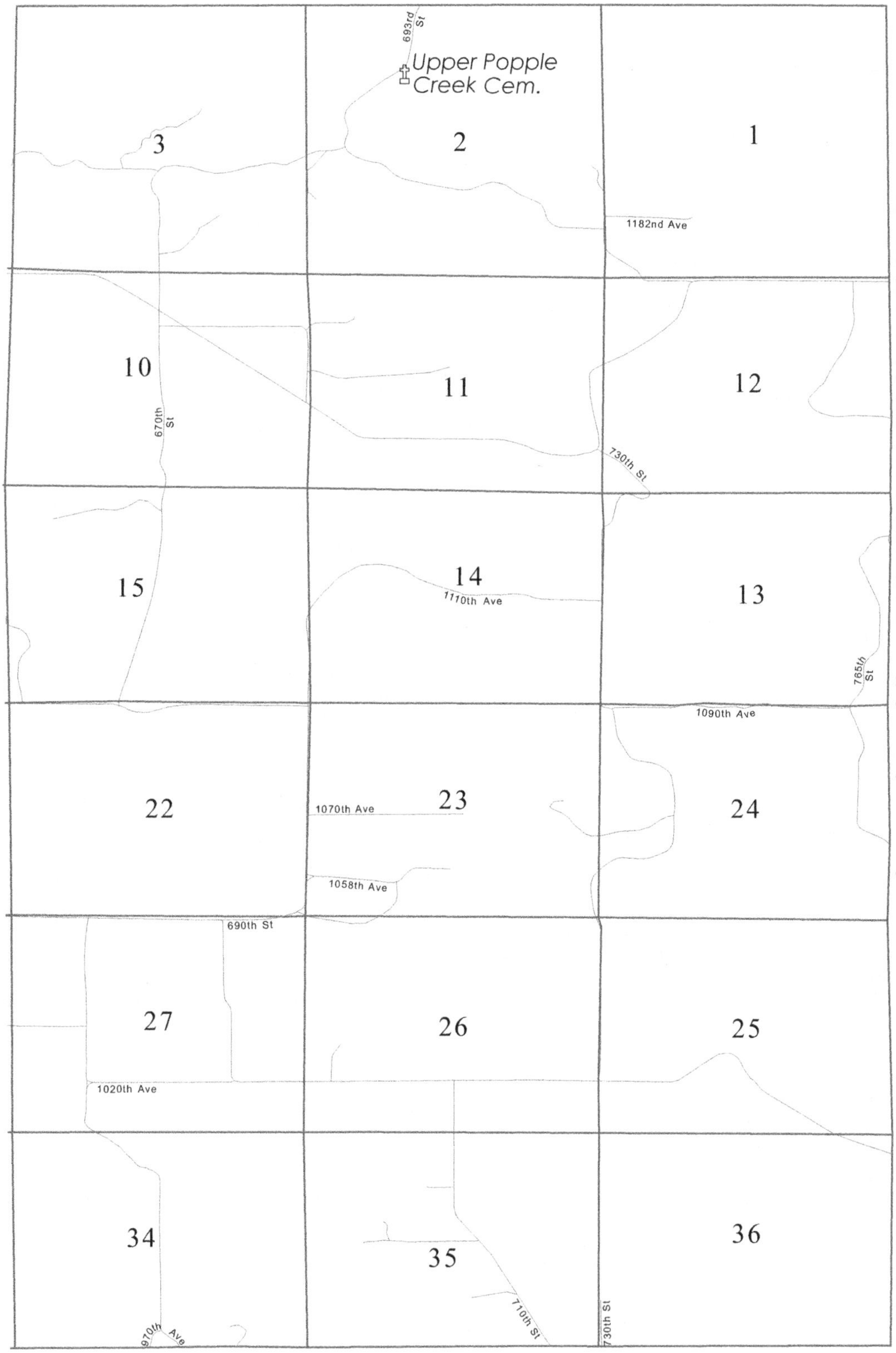

Helpful Hints

1. This road map has a number of uses, but primarily it is to help you: a) find the present location of land owned by your ancestors (at least the general area), b) find cemeteries and city-centers, and c) estimate the route/roads used by Census-takers & tax-assessors.
2. If you plan to travel to Dunn County to locate cemeteries or land parcels, please pick up a modern travel map for the area before you do. Mapping old land parcels on modern maps is not as exact a science as you might think. Just the slightest variations in public land survey coordinates, estimates of parcel boundaries, or road-map deviations can greatly alter a map's representation of how a road either does or doesn't cross a particular parcel of land.

Legend

- Section Lines
- Interstates
- Highways
- Other Roads
- Cities/Towns
- Cemeteries

Scale: Section = 1 mile X 1 mile
(generally, with some exceptions)

Historical Map

T30-N R12-W
4th PM - 1831 MN/WI Meridian

Map Group 7

Cities & Towns

None

Cemeteries

Otter Creek Cemetery
Upper Popple Creek Cemetery

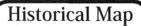

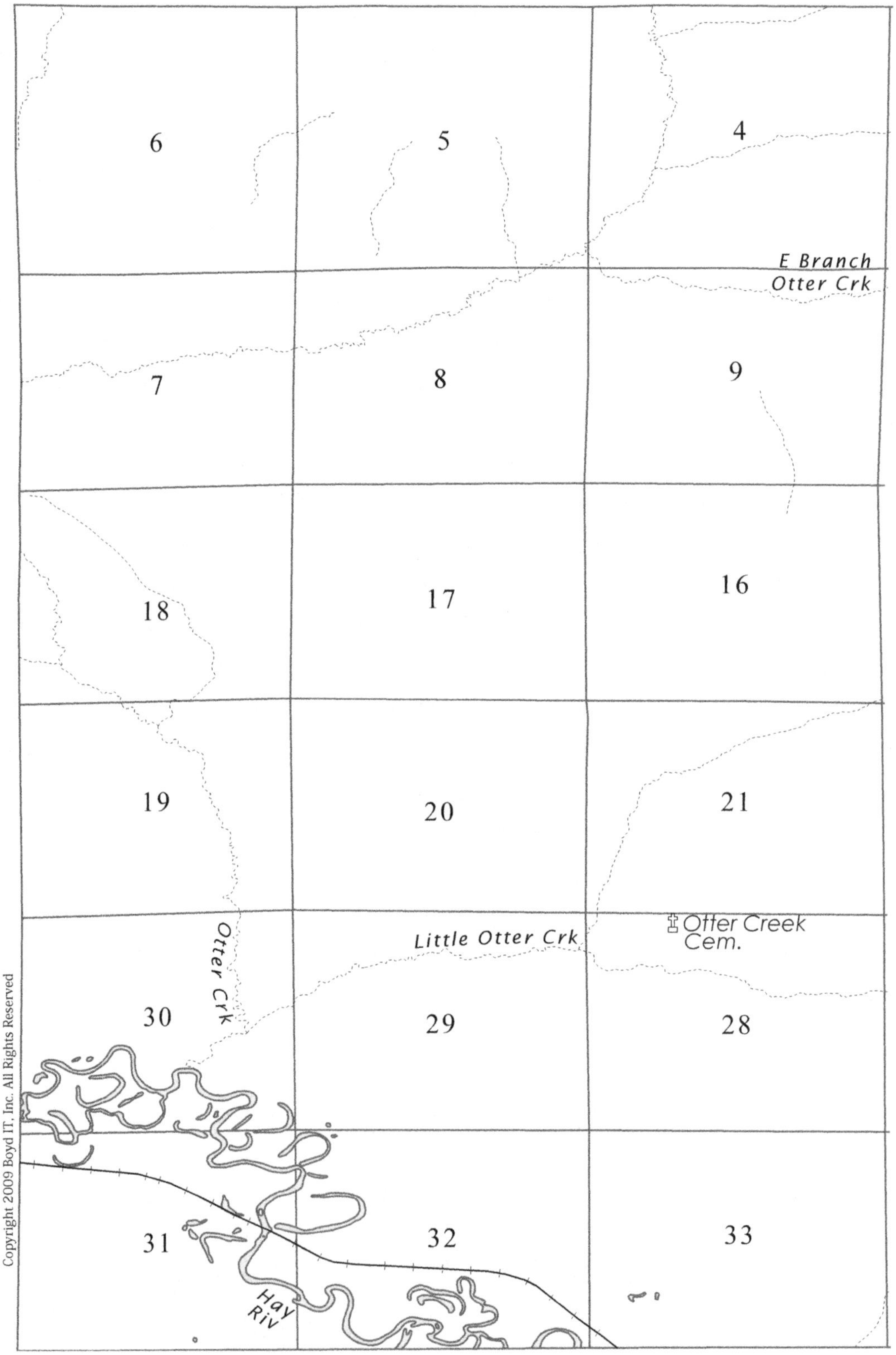
6
5
4
E Branch
Otter Crk
7
8
9
18
17
16
19
20
21
Otter Crk
Little Otter Crk
Otter Creek
Cem.
30
29
28
31
32
33
Hay
Riv

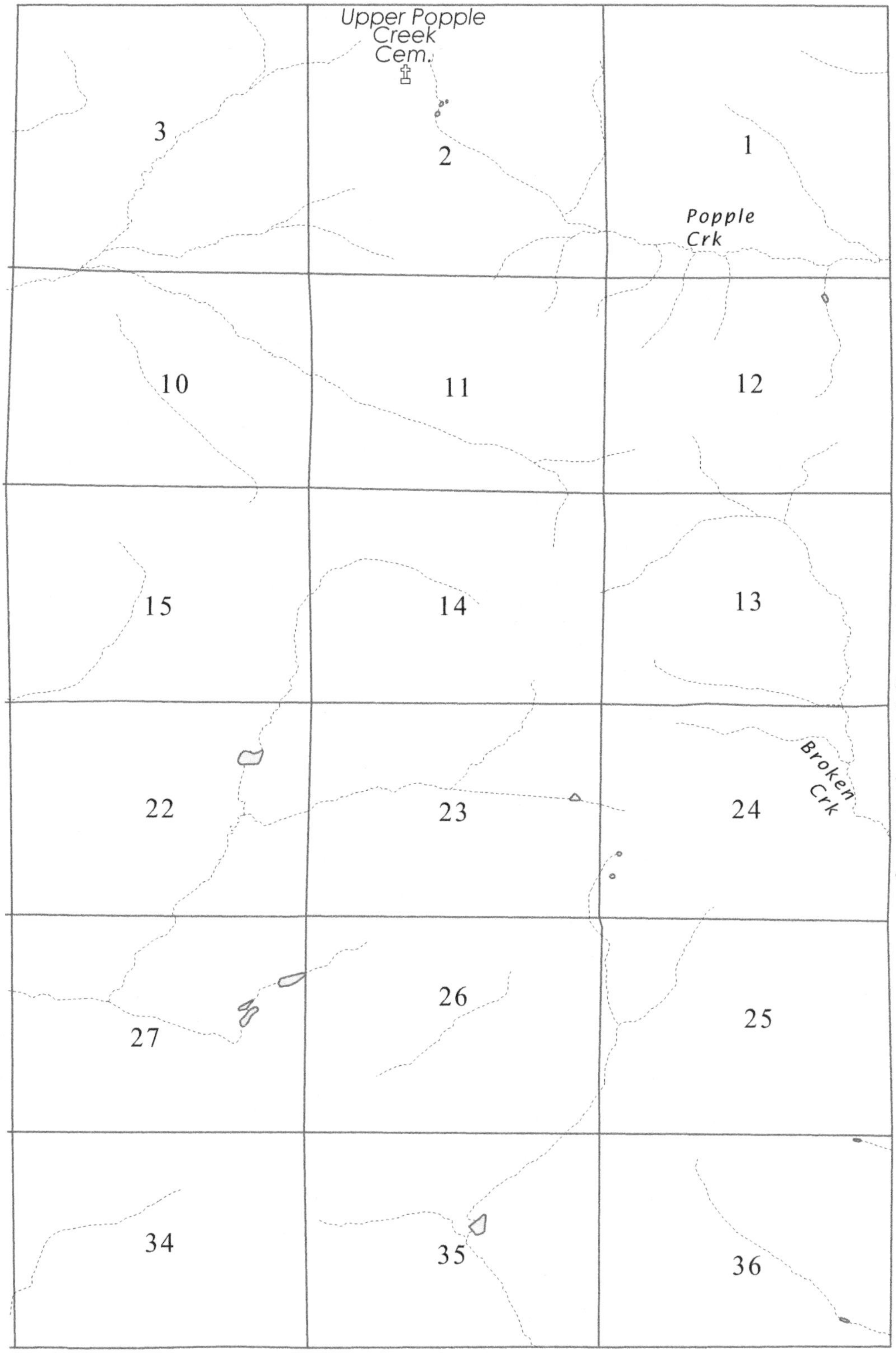

Helpful Hints

1. This Map takes a different look at the same Congressional Township displayed in the preceding two maps. It presents features that can help you better envision the historical development of the area: a) Water-bodies (lakes & ponds), b) Water-courses (rivers, streams, etc.), c) Railroads, d) City/town center-points (where they were oftentimes located when first settled), and e) Cemeteries.
2. Using this "Historical" map in tandem with this Township's Patent Map and Road Map, may lead you to some interesting discoveries. You will often find roads, towns, cemeteries, and waterways are named after nearby landowners: sometimes those names will be the ones you are researching. See how many of these research gems you can find here in Dunn County.

Legend

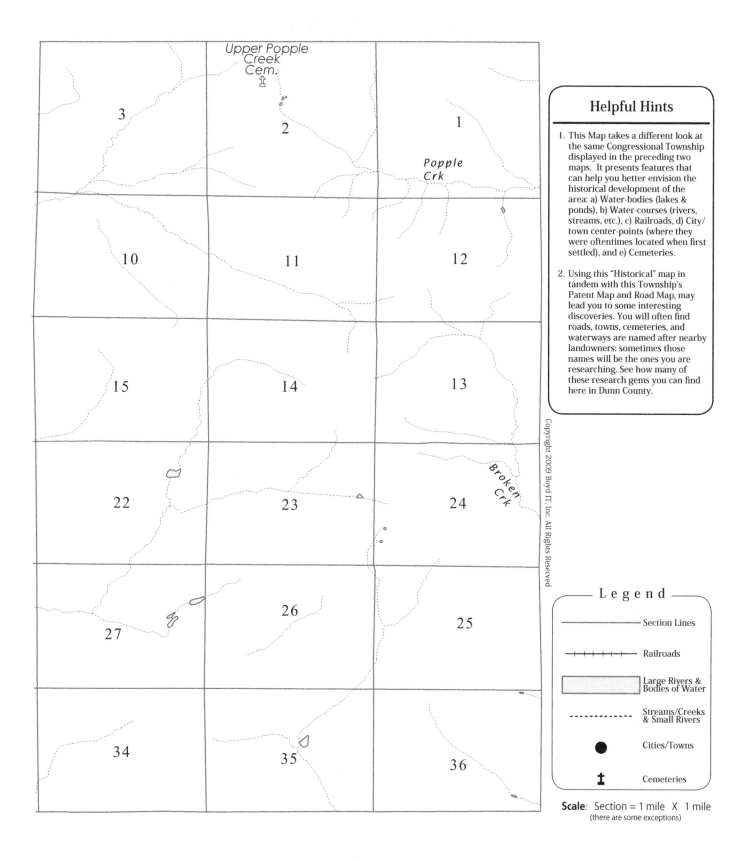

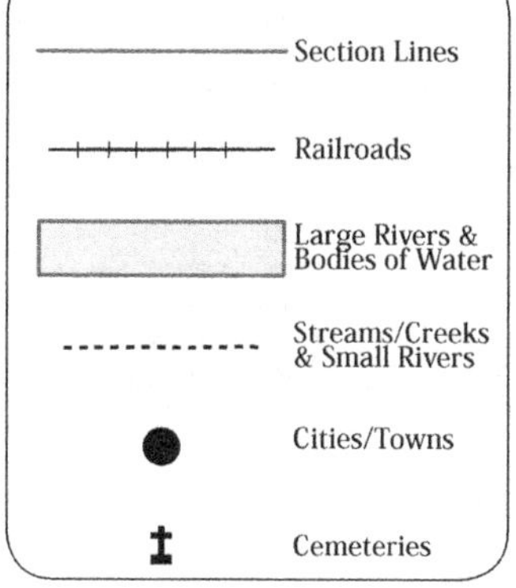
Section Lines
Railroads
Large Rivers & Bodies of Water
Streams/Creeks & Small Rivers
Cities/Towns
Cemeteries

Scale: Section = 1 mile X 1 mile
(there are some exceptions)

Map Group 8: Index to Land Patents

Township 30-North Range 11-West (4th PM - 1831 MN/WI)

After you locate an individual in this Index, take note of the Section and Section Part then proceed to the Land Patent map on the pages immediately following. You should have no difficulty locating the corresponding parcel of land.

The "For More Info" Column will lead you to more information about the underlying Patents. See the *Legend* at right, and the "How to Use this Book" chapter, for more information.

LEGEND

"For More Info . . . " column

- **A** = Authority (Legislative Act, See Appendix "A")
- **B** = Block or Lot (location in Section unknown)
- **C** = Cancelled Patent
- **F** = Fractional Section
- **G** = Group (Multi-Patentee Patent, see Appendix "C")
- **V** = Overlaps another Parcel
- **R** = Re-Issued (Parcel patented more than once)

(A & G items require you to look in the Appendixes referred to above. All other Letter-designations followed by a number require you to locate line-items in this index that possess the ID number found after the letter).

ID	Individual in Patent	Sec.	Sec. Part	Date Issued	Other Counties	For More Info . . .
1404	ALLESTAD, Ole C	26	E½SE	1880-10-01		A6
1405	" "	26	NWSE	1880-10-01		A6
1413	ALLISTAD, Ole R	26	SWSE	1885-03-16		A2
1234	ANDERSON, Anders	20	S½NW	1873-12-15		A6
1235	" "	20	W½NE	1873-12-15		A6
1233	" "	20	NENE	1874-10-20		A2
1271	ANDERSON, David	26	N½NW	1906-06-30		A6
1302	ANDERSON, Halvor N	28	W½NW	1885-07-13		A6
1303	ANDERSON, Hans	27	N½NW	1873-01-10		A6
1304	" "	27	SWNW	1873-01-10		A6
1305	" "	28	SENE	1873-01-10		A6
1435	ANDERSON, Jacob	1	SWSE	1873-05-15		A6 G12
1436	" "	12	NWSE	1873-05-15		A6 G12
1437	" "	12	W½NE	1873-05-15		A6 G12
1338	ANDERSON, John A	20	N½NW	1893-05-19		A6
1380	ANDERSON, Louis	34	E½SE	1882-04-10		A6
1435	ANDERSON, Sarah A	1	SWSE	1873-05-15		A6 G12
1436	" "	12	NWSE	1873-05-15		A6 G12
1437	" "	12	W½NE	1873-05-15		A6 G12
1321	ANDREASEN, Iver	11	E½SE	1871-09-15		A6
1322	" "	11	SESW	1871-09-15		A6
1323	" "	11	SWSE	1871-09-15		A6
1339	ANDREWS, John	33	E½SE	1864-04-15		A5
1340	" "	34	W½SW	1864-04-15		A5
1247	ARNESON, Andrew	32	NE	1875-03-01		A6
1397	BARTLETT, Monroe	8	SWSW	1891-06-08		A6
1448	BENNETT, Theodore	26	NE	1879-12-15		A6
1425	BENTON, Betsey	10	NENW	1860-11-20		A5 G396
1426	" "	10	NWNE	1860-11-20		A5 G396
1427	" "	3	SESW	1860-11-20		A5 G396
1428	" "	3	SWSE	1860-11-20		A5 G396
1332	BERG, Johannes P	22	N½SE	1889-04-13		A6
1333	" "	22	SENE	1889-04-13		A6
1334	" "	22	SWSE	1889-04-13		A6
1375	BERG, Laurits O	32	SENW	1888-05-07		A2
1385	BERGERSON, Martha	36	NENW	1906-12-17		A6
1446	BERNTZON, Staale	36	SESW	1875-03-05		A2
1268	BJORNSON, Christian	30	NENE	1885-03-16		A2
1433	BLATCHFORD, Samuel N	14	N½SE	1884-09-15		A6 V1386
1434	" "	14	SESE	1884-09-15		A6 V1386
1342	BOTTOM, John	13	W½NW	1860-09-10		A5 G46
1343	" "	14	E½NE	1860-09-10		A5 G46
1342	BOTUME, John	13	W½NW	1860-09-10		A5 G46
1343	" "	14	E½NE	1860-09-10		A5 G46
1249	BRANKIN, Andrias	22	NWNW	1866-10-10		A2
1401	BREDESEN, Niels	30	NESE	1875-11-20		A6

ID	Individual in Patent	Sec.	Sec. Part	Date Issued	Other Counties	For More Info . . .
1402	BREDESEN, Niels (Cont'd)	30	SENE	1875-11-20		A6
1403	" "	30	W½NE	1875-11-20		A6
1294	BRENT, Frederick	12	E½NE	1870-09-10		A6
1295	" "	12	E½SE	1870-09-10		A6
1244	BRONKEN, Andrew A	30	W½NW	1878-06-01		A6
1245	" "	30	W½SW	1878-06-01		A6
1416	BRONKEN, Peder S	14	SW	1879-12-15		A6
1422	BUELL, Rachel P	5	1	1873-05-15		A6
1423	" "	5	2	1873-05-15		A6
1424	" "	5	3	1873-05-15		A6
1269	BURNSON, Christian	34	E½SW	1873-12-15		A6
1270	" "	34	W½SE	1873-12-15		A6
1313	CAREY, Henry	17	NE	1860-09-10		A5
1459	CLARK, Thomas L	15	NW	1860-08-01		A5 G76
1461	CLARK, Thomas Lewis	10	SENW	1860-08-01		A5 G77
1460	" "	10	SW	1860-08-01		A5
1462	" "	10	W½NW	1860-08-01		A5 G77
1463	" "	9	SENE	1860-08-01		A5 G77
1318	COOK, Ishmael	1	8	1873-12-15		A6
1319	" "	1	9	1873-12-15		A6
1320	" "	1	E½SE	1873-12-15		A6
1228	COOPER, Abram L	18	N½SE	1891-11-16		A6
1229	" "	18	S½NE	1891-11-16		A6
1453	COREY, Thomas G	5	10	1873-01-10		A6
1454	" "	5	7	1873-01-10		A6
1455	" "	5	8	1873-01-10		A6
1456	" "	5	9	1873-01-10		A6
1293	CRAIG, Francis O	6	8	1865-11-10		A2
1383	CROSSMAN, Marcia A	10	E½NE	1862-04-26		A5 G94
1384	" "	11	NWNW	1862-04-26		A5 G94
1317	CUTHING, Hiram P	5	SE	1870-09-10		A6
1383	CUTLER, Charles	10	E½NE	1862-04-26		A5 G94
1384	" "	11	NWNW	1862-04-26		A5 G94
1383	CUTLER, Henry	10	E½NE	1862-04-26		A5 G94
1384	" "	11	NWNW	1862-04-26		A5 G94
1383	CUTLER, Mary	10	E½NE	1862-04-26		A5 G94
1384	" "	11	NWNW	1862-04-26		A5 G94
1316	CUTTING, Henry P	4	NWSE	1883-10-20		A6
1344	CUTTING, John F	4	SW	1869-09-01		A6
1429	CUTTING, Sally	5	N½SW	1864-04-15		A5 G96
1430	" "	5	SESW	1864-04-15		A5 G96
1431	" "	8	NENW	1864-04-15		A5 G96
1470	DAHL, Tobias	36	W½SW	1873-12-15		A6 G97
1345	DANIELSON, John H	32	N½SE	1910-06-02		A6
1346	" "	32	NESW	1910-06-02		A6
1372	DEAN, Lafayette	5	4	1870-10-20		A6
1399	DEAN, Nancy E	6	1	1865-07-01		A2
1398	" "	4	4	1882-06-30		A2
1331	DENNIS, James B	18	S½SE	1900-11-28		A6
1417	DEVLE, Peter A	28	SESW	1884-01-15		A6
1432	DODGE, Samuel	21	NE	1863-04-20		A5 G111
1449	DODGE, Thomas	6	10	1873-01-10		A6
1451	" "	6	9	1873-01-10		A6
1452	" "	6	N½SE	1873-01-10		A6
1450	" "	6	2	1875-10-01		A2
1285	EAVANS, Eli	34	SENW	1875-08-10		A6
1286	" "	34	SWNE	1875-08-10		A6
1341	FAIRBANKS, John B	11	NE	1860-08-01		A5 G127
1371	FIGENSKAN, Knudt G	22	N½NE	1873-12-15		A6
1265	FOGLE, Charles W	24	N½NE	1906-03-28		A6
1266	" "	24	N½NW	1906-03-28		A6
1250	FOX, Avery N	1	1	1873-01-10		A6
1251	" "	1	2	1873-01-10		A6
1252	" "	1	7	1873-01-10		A6
1246	FRAMY, Andrew A	20	NWSE	1883-03-10		A2
1341	GALE, Betsey	11	NE	1860-08-01		A5 G127
1376	GOLDSMITH, Leonard	8	E½SW	1869-09-20		A2
1377	" "	8	NWSW	1869-09-20		A2
1457	GRANGER, Thomas	33	SENE	1862-04-01		A2
1458	" "	34	SWNW	1862-04-01		A2
1349	GRINSET, John J	33	E½SW	1888-10-05		A6
1350	" "	33	W½SE	1888-10-05		A6
1314	HALSTED, Henry	1	3	1874-10-20		A2

ID	Individual in Patent	Sec.	Sec. Part	Date Issued	Other Counties	For More Info . . .
1315	HALSTED, Henry (Cont'd)	1	4	1874-10-20		A2
1258	HAUGE, Berthe M	30	E½NW	1882-04-10		A6 G182
1259	" "	30	NESW	1882-04-10		A6 G182
1260	" "	30	NWSE	1882-04-10		A6 G182
1324	HAUGEN, Iver J	2	NWSW	1891-11-16		A6
1406	HELGERSON, Ole	15	SW	1873-01-10		A6
1227	HOLM, Aagot I P	26	NESW	1910-12-01		A6
1275	HOLM, E K	26	SESW	1890-02-14		A2
1281	HOLM, Edward	26	S½NW	1892-05-11		A6
1282	" "	26	W½SW	1892-05-11		A6
1284	HOVEY, Edwin M	9	SE	1873-05-15		A6
1382	HOVEY, Luman B	4	SWSE	1866-06-15		A2
1386	ISAKSON, Martin	14	SE	1873-12-15		A6 V1433, 1434
1238	JACOBSEN, Anders	28	E½NW	1871-09-15		A6
1239	" "	28	W½NE	1871-09-15		A6
1253	JACOBSON, B C	35	E½SE	1870-05-20		A6
1255	JOHANSON, Benjamin	14	N½NW	1875-05-20		A6
1256	" "	14	NWNE	1875-05-20		A6
1298	JOHNSON, Gert	12	NENW	1885-07-13		A6
1351	JOHNSON, John	20	NESE	1884-09-30		A2
1443	JOHNSON, Seivert	10	NESE	1871-09-15		A6
1444	" "	10	SWNE	1871-09-15		A6
1445	" "	10	W½SE	1871-09-15		A6
1254	JORNSON, Ben B	34	SENE	1890-02-14		A2
1267	JORNSON, Christian B	20	SWSW	1889-05-11		A2
1277	JUMP, Edmond	5	11	1870-10-20		A6
1278	" "	5	12	1870-10-20		A6
1279	" "	5	5	1870-10-20		A6
1280	" "	5	6	1870-10-20		A6
1347	KNAPP, John H	28	NENE	1873-11-01		A2 G219
1348	" "	28	NESE	1873-11-01		A2 G219
1310	KNIGHT, Henry A	2	1	1876-03-01		A6
1311	" "	2	2	1876-03-01		A6
1312	" "	2	7	1876-03-01		A6
1352	KNIGHT, John	2	3	1873-01-10		A6
1353	" "	2	4	1873-01-10		A6
1459	KNOX, Rebecca W	15	NW	1860-08-01		A5 G76
1407	KNUDSEN, Ole	20	SENE	1871-09-15		A6
1408	" "	21	NESW	1871-09-15		A6
1409	" "	21	S½NW	1871-09-15		A6
1309	KNUDSON, Helge	29	SE	1873-12-15		A6
1367	KRAUSE, Julius	4	5	1874-12-30		A6
1368	" "	4	6	1874-12-30		A6
1369	" "	4	7	1874-12-30		A6
1370	" "	4	8	1874-12-30		A6
1381	KRAUSE, Ludwig	8	NE	1873-01-10		A6
1471	LAFORGE, William P	4	1	1873-01-10		A6
1472	" "	4	2	1873-01-10		A6
1473	" "	4	3	1873-01-10		A6
1261	LARSON, Bertie	21	N½SE	1874-12-30		A6 G236
1262	" "	21	SESW	1874-12-30		A6 G236
1263	" "	21	SWSE	1874-12-30		A6 G236
1261	LARSON, John	21	N½SE	1874-12-30		A6 G236
1262	" "	21	SESW	1874-12-30		A6 G236
1263	" "	21	SWSE	1874-12-30		A6 G236
1373	LARSON, Lars	8	N½SE	1889-05-11		A2
1410	LARSON, Ole	36	NE	1873-12-15		A6
1325	LEE, Jacob A	6	SW	1869-09-01		A6
1432	LIVINGSTON, Mehitable	21	NE	1863-04-20		A5 G111
1365	LOGSLETT, Jorgen J	32	S½SE	1896-01-22		A6
1366	" "	32	S½SW	1896-01-22		A6
1362	MANSFIELD, John W	11	E½NW	1860-08-03		A5
1363	" "	11	NESW	1860-08-03		A5
1364	" "	11	NWSE	1860-08-03		A5
1299	MARISTAD, Gunder O	32	NWSW	1883-08-01		A6
1300	" "	32	SWNW	1883-08-01		A6
1230	MARTIN, Ambrose	20	N½SW	1906-06-30		A6
1231	" "	20	SESW	1906-06-30		A6
1232	" "	20	SWSE	1906-06-30		A6
1387	MARTINSON, Martin	34	N½NE	1876-01-10		A6
1388	" "	34	N½NW	1876-01-10		A6
1439	MASON, Sarah	2	11	1873-12-15		A6
1440	" "	2	12	1873-12-15		A6

ID	Individual in Patent	Sec.	Sec. Part	Date Issued	Other Counties	For More Info . . .
1441	MASON, Sarah (Cont'd)	2	5	1873-12-15		A6
1442	" "	2	6	1873-12-15		A6
1415	MAUKSTAD, Peder O	20	SESE	1893-02-01		A2
1354	MUENCH, John	2	SWNE	1890-05-14		A6
1306	NESSET, Hans O	22	E½NW	1878-06-01		A6
1307	" "	22	SWNE	1878-06-01		A6
1308	" "	22	SWNW	1878-06-01		A6
1389	NILSON, Martin	24	NESE	1891-05-09		A6
1390	" "	24	S½NE	1891-06-08		A6
1391	NOER, Martin	12	SESW	1883-02-20		A6
1392	" "	12	SWSE	1883-02-20		A6
1393	" "	12	W½SW	1883-02-20		A6
1414	NORTHSTREAM, Oscar	30	SESW	1893-06-13		A6
1248	OLESON, Andrew	1	SESW	1865-11-10		A2
1257	OLESON, Bertha	31	E½SW	1871-09-15		A6 G289
1257	OLESON, Forger	31	E½SW	1871-09-15		A6 G289
1378	OLESON, Lewis	24	E½SW	1885-10-22		A6
1379	" "	24	S½NW	1885-10-22		A6
1394	OLESON, Matthias	24	NWSE	1875-05-20		A6
1395	" "	24	S½SE	1875-05-20		A6
1296	OLSEN, Gabriel	36	NESW	1882-05-10		A6
1297	" "	36	SENW	1882-05-10		A6
1292	OLSON, Ever	25	E½NE	1869-09-01		A6
1396	OLSON, Melvin N	22	SESE	1928-11-08		A6
1418	OLSON, Peter	12	NESW	1873-01-10		A6
1419	" "	12	NWNW	1873-01-10		A6
1420	" "	12	S½NW	1873-01-10		A6
1421	" "	8	S½SE	1875-03-05		A2
1469	OLSON, Tobias C	36	SWNW	1876-03-01		A2
1468	" "	36	NWNW	1882-06-30		A2
1374	OMTVEDT, Lars T	6	4	1898-03-21		A6
1355	ORME, John	3	1	1873-01-10		A6
1356	" "	3	2	1873-01-10		A6
1357	" "	3	7	1873-01-10		A6
1358	" "	3	8	1873-01-10		A6
1429	PAIRO, Charles W	5	N½SW	1864-04-15		A5 G96
1430	" "	5	SESW	1864-04-15		A5 G96
1431	" "	8	NENW	1864-04-15		A5 G96
1335	PAULSON, Johannes	10	SESE	1871-09-15		A6
1336	" "	11	SWNW	1871-09-15		A6
1337	" "	11	W½SW	1871-09-15		A6
1470	PETERSON, Nelson T	36	W½SW	1873-12-15		A6 G97
1412	PETERSON, Ole	15	NE	1873-01-10		A6
1438	RAPELYE, Sarah A	36	SE	1860-09-10		A5
1283	RIEMER, Edward	9	SW	1873-05-15		A6
1236	RONGSTAD, Anders J	14	S½NW	1896-08-12		A6
1237	" "	14	SWNE	1896-08-12		A6
1258	SCHULSTAD, Berthe M	30	E½NW	1882-04-10		A6 G182
1259	" "	30	NESW	1882-04-10		A6 G182
1260	" "	30	NWSE	1882-04-10		A6 G182
1272	SEE, David	5	SWSW	1873-12-15		A6
1273	" "	6	S½SE	1873-12-15		A6
1274	" "	7	NWNE	1873-12-15		A6
1326	SEE, Jacob A	6	5	1865-07-01		A2
1287	SEEVER, Elizabeth I	18	NW	1897-11-10		A6 G352 F
1359	SEEVER, John P	18	N½NE	1900-11-12		A6
1287	SEEVER, John W	18	NW	1897-11-10		A6 G352 F
1240	SEMMINGSEN, Andreas	29	S½SW	1870-09-10		A6
1241	" "	30	SESE	1870-09-10		A6
1242	" "	32	NENW	1870-09-10		A6
1243	SEMMINGSON, Andreas	32	NWNW	1866-06-15		A2
1264	SEVERTSON, Betsy	28	NWSE	1870-05-02		A2
1288	SNYDER, Eugene	8	NWNW	1880-04-30		A6
1289	" "	8	S½NW	1902-08-22		A6
1301	SONNENBURG, Gustav	18	SW	1892-05-04		A6
1276	SORKNESS, Ebert S	4	SESE	1868-12-01		A2
1474	STILLEY, William	1	5	1873-01-10		A6
1475	" "	1	6	1873-01-10		A6
1476	" "	2	8	1873-01-10		A6
1477	" "	2	9	1873-01-10		A6
1347	STOUT, Henry L	28	NENE	1873-11-01		A2 G219
1348	" "	28	NESE	1873-11-01		A2 G219
1347	TAINTER, Andrew	28	NENE	1873-11-01		A2 G219

ID	Individual in Patent	Sec.	Sec. Part	Date Issued	Other Counties	For More Info . . .
1348	TAINTER, Andrew (Cont'd)	28	NESE	1873-11-01		A2 G219
1411	TANDE, Ole Oleson	24	W½SW	1917-06-30		A2
1425	THOMPSON, Reuben	10	NENW	1860-11-20		A5 G396
1426	" "	10	NWNE	1860-11-20		A5 G396
1427	" "	3	SESW	1860-11-20		A5 G396
1428	" "	3	SWSE	1860-11-20		A5 G396
1360	THORESEN, John	2	S½SE	1880-11-20		A6
1361	" "	2	S½SW	1880-11-20		A6
1327	TOLLEVSON, Jacob	30	SWSE	1866-06-15		A2
1328	TOLLOFSON, Jacob	28	N½SW	1873-01-10		A6
1329	" "	28	SWSW	1873-01-10		A6
1330	" "	33	NWNW	1873-01-10		A6
1290	TORGUSSEN, Evend	27	S½SW	1873-01-10		A6
1291	" "	28	S½SE	1873-01-10		A6
1461	TREFETHREN, Jane	10	SENW	1860-08-01		A5 G77
1462	" "	10	W½NW	1860-08-01		A5 G77
1463	" "	9	SENE	1860-08-01		A5 G77
1464	VAN WOERT, THOMAS	6	11	1875-05-20		A6
1465	" "	6	3	1875-05-20		A6
1466	" "	6	6	1875-05-20		A6
1467	" "	6	7	1875-05-20		A6
1400	WILLIAMSON, Nere	22	SW	1873-01-10		A6
1347	WILSON, Thomas B	28	NENE	1873-11-01		A2 G219
1348	" "	28	NESE	1873-11-01		A2 G219
1447	WISCONSIN, State Of	16		1941-08-16		A3

Patent Map

T30-N R11-W
4th PM - 1831 MN/WI Meridian

Map Group 8

Township Statistics

Parcels Mapped	:	251
Number of Patents	:	144
Number of Individuals	:	155
Patentees Identified	:	137
Number of Surnames	:	117
Multi-Patentee Parcels	:	31
Oldest Patent Date	:	8/1/1860
Most Recent Patent	:	8/16/1941
Block/Lot Parcels	:	55
Parcels Re - Issued	:	0
Parcels that Overlap	:	3
Cities and Towns	:	0
Cemeteries	:	1

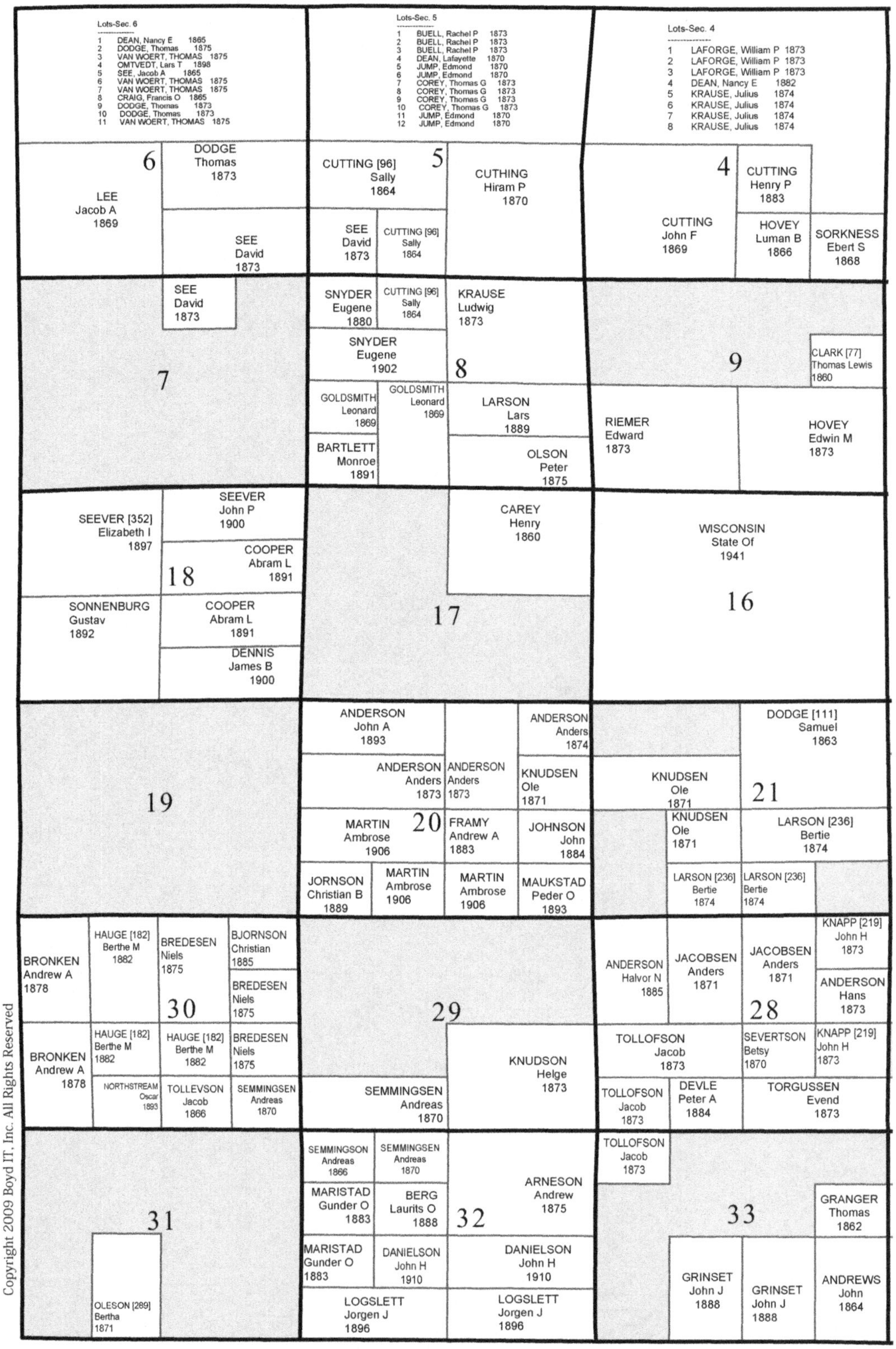

Lots-Sec. 6
1 DEAN, Nancy E 1865
2 DODGE, Thomas 1875
3 VAN WOERT, THOMAS 1875
4 OMTVEDT, Lars T 1898
5 SEE, Jacob A 1865
6 VAN WOERT, THOMAS 1875
7 VAN WOERT, THOMAS 1875
8 CRAIG, Francis O 1865
9 DODGE, Thomas 1873
10 DODGE, Thomas 1873
11 VAN WOERT, THOMAS 1875
Lots-Sec. 5
1 BUELL, Rachel P 1873
2 BUELL, Rachel P 1873
3 BUELL, Rachel P 1873
4 DEAN, Lafayette 1870
5 JUMP, Edmond 1870
6 JUMP, Edmond 1870
7 COREY, Thomas G 1873
8 COREY, Thomas G 1873
9 COREY, Thomas G 1873
10 COREY, Thomas G 1873
11 JUMP, Edmond 1870
12 JUMP, Edmond 1870
Lots-Sec. 4
1 LAFORGE, William P 1873
2 LAFORGE, William P 1873
3 LAFORGE, William P 1873
4 DEAN, Nancy E 1882
5 KRAUSE, Julius 1874
6 KRAUSE, Julius 1874
7 KRAUSE, Julius 1874
8 KRAUSE, Julius 1874
6
LEE Jacob A 1869
DODGE Thomas 1873
SEE David 1873
5
CUTTING [96] Sally 1864
CUTHING Hiram P 1870
SEE David 1873
CUTTING [96] Sally 1864
4
CUTTING Henry P 1883
CUTTING John F 1869
HOVEY Luman B 1866
SORKNESS Ebert S 1868
7
SEE David 1873
8
SNYDER Eugene 1880
CUTTING [96] Sally 1864
KRAUSE Ludwig 1873
SNYDER Eugene 1902
GOLDSMITH Leonard 1869
GOLDSMITH Leonard 1869
LARSON Lars 1889
BARTLETT Monroe 1891
OLSON Peter 1875
9
CLARK [77] Thomas Lewis 1860
RIEMER Edward 1873
HOVEY Edwin M 1873
18
SEEVER [352] Elizabeth I 1897
SEEVER John P 1900
COOPER Abram L 1891
SONNENBURG Gustav 1892
COOPER Abram L 1891
DENNIS James B 1900
17
CAREY Henry 1860
16
WISCONSIN State Of 1941
19
20
ANDERSON John A 1893
ANDERSON Anders 1874
ANDERSON Anders 1873
ANDERSON Anders 1873
KNUDSEN Ole 1871
MARTIN Ambrose 1906
FRAMY Andrew A 1883
JOHNSON John 1884
JORNSON Christian B 1889
MARTIN Ambrose 1906
MARTIN Ambrose 1906
MAUKSTAD Peder O 1893
21
DODGE [111] Samuel 1863
KNUDSEN Ole 1871
KNUDSEN Ole 1871
LARSON [236] Bertie 1874
LARSON [236] Bertie 1874
LARSON [236] Bertie 1874
30
BRONKEN Andrew A 1878
HAUGE [182] Berthe M 1882
BREDESEN Niels 1875
BJORNSON Christian 1885
BREDESEN Niels 1875
BRONKEN Andrew A 1878
HAUGE [182] Berthe M 1882
HAUGE [182] Berthe M 1882
BREDESEN Niels 1875
NORTHSTREAM Oscar 1893
TOLLEVSON Jacob 1866
SEMMINGSEN Andreas 1870
29
KNUDSON Helge 1873
SEMMINGSEN Andreas 1870
28
ANDERSON Halvor N 1885
JACOBSEN Anders 1871
JACOBSEN Anders 1871
KNAPP [219] John H 1873
ANDERSON Hans 1873
TOLLOFSON Jacob 1873
SEVERTSON Betsy 1870
KNAPP [219] John H 1873
TOLLOFSON Jacob 1873
DEVLE Peter A 1884
TORGUSSEN Evend 1873
31
OLESON [269] Bertha 1871
32
SEMMINGSON Andreas 1866
SEMMINGSEN Andreas 1870
ARNESON Andrew 1875
MARISTAD Gunder O 1883
BERG Laurits O 1888
MARISTAD Gunder O 1883
DANIELSON John H 1910
DANIELSON John H 1910
LOGSLETT Jorgen J 1896
LOGSLETT Jorgen J 1896
33
TOLLOFSON Jacob 1873
GRANGER Thomas 1862
GRINSET John J 1888
GRINSET John J 1888
ANDREWS John 1864

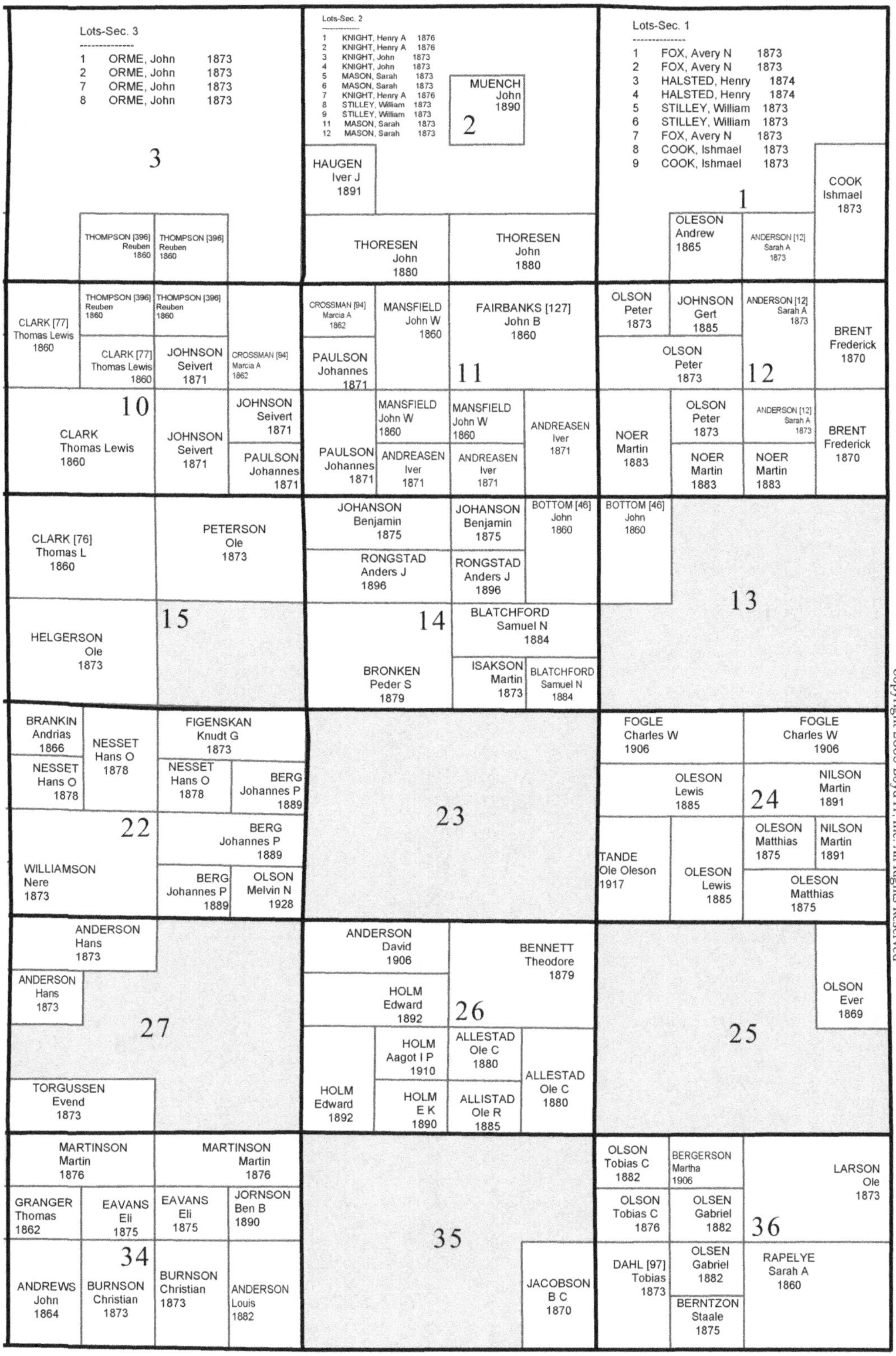
Lots-Sec. 3
1 ORME, John 1873
2 ORME, John 1873
7 ORME, John 1873
8 ORME, John 1873
3
THOMPSON [396] Reuben 1860
THOMPSON [396] Reuben 1860
Lots-Sec. 2
1 KNIGHT, Henry A 1876
2 KNIGHT, Henry A 1876
3 KNIGHT, John 1873
4 KNIGHT, John 1873
5 MASON, Sarah 1873
6 MASON, Sarah 1873
7 KNIGHT, Henry A 1876
8 STILLEY, William 1873
9 STILLEY, William 1873
11 MASON, Sarah 1873
12 MASON, Sarah 1873
MUENCH John 1890
2
HAUGEN Iver J 1891
THORESEN John 1880
THORESEN John 1880
Lots-Sec. 1
1 FOX, Avery N 1873
2 FOX, Avery N 1873
3 HALSTED, Henry 1874
4 HALSTED, Henry 1874
5 STILLEY, William 1873
6 STILLEY, William 1873
7 FOX, Avery N 1873
8 COOK, Ishmael 1873
9 COOK, Ishmael 1873
1
COOK Ishmael 1873
OLESON Andrew 1865
ANDERSON [12] Sarah A 1873
CLARK [77] Thomas Lewis 1860
THOMPSON [396] Reuben 1860
THOMPSON [396] Reuben 1860
CLARK [77] Thomas Lewis 1860
JOHNSON Seivert 1871
CROSSMAN [94] Marcia A 1862
10
CLARK Thomas Lewis 1860
JOHNSON Seivert 1871
JOHNSON Seivert 1871
PAULSON Johannes 1871
CROSSMAN [94] Marcia A 1862
MANSFIELD John W 1860
FAIRBANKS [127] John B 1860
PAULSON Johannes 1871
11
MANSFIELD John W 1860
MANSFIELD John W 1860
ANDREASEN Iver 1871
PAULSON Johannes 1871
ANDREASEN Iver 1871
ANDREASEN Iver 1871
OLSON Peter 1873
JOHNSON Gert 1885
ANDERSON [12] Sarah A 1873
BRENT Frederick 1870
OLSON Peter 1873
12
NOER Martin 1883
OLSON Peter 1873
ANDERSON [12] Sarah A 1873
BRENT Frederick 1870
NOER Martin 1883
NOER Martin 1883
CLARK [76] Thomas L 1860
PETERSON Ole 1873
HELGERSON Ole 1873
15
JOHANSON Benjamin 1875
JOHANSON Benjamin 1875
BOTTOM [46] John 1860
RONGSTAD Anders J 1896
RONGSTAD Anders J 1896
14
BLATCHFORD Samuel N 1884
BRONKEN Peder S 1879
ISAKSON Martin 1873
BLATCHFORD Samuel N 1884
BOTTOM [46] John 1860
13
BRANKIN Andrias 1866
NESSET Hans O 1878
FIGENSKAN Knudt G 1873
NESSET Hans O 1878
NESSET Hans O 1878
BERG Johannes P 1889
22
BERG Johannes P 1889
WILLIAMSON Nere 1873
BERG Johannes P 1889
OLSON Melvin N 1928
23
FOGLE Charles W 1906
FOGLE Charles W 1906
OLESON Lewis 1885
24
NILSON Martin 1891
OLESON Matthias 1875
NILSON Martin 1891
TANDE Ole Oleson 1917
OLESON Lewis 1885
OLESON Matthias 1875
ANDERSON Hans 1873
ANDERSON Hans 1873
27
TORGUSSEN Evend 1873
ANDERSON David 1906
BENNETT Theodore 1879
HOLM Edward 1892
26
HOLM Aagot I P 1910
ALLESTAD Ole C 1880
ALLESTAD Ole C 1880
HOLM Edward 1892
HOLM E K 1890
ALLISTAD Ole R 1885
25
OLSON Ever 1869
MARTINSON Martin 1876
MARTINSON Martin 1876
GRANGER Thomas 1862
EAVANS Eli 1875
EAVANS Eli 1875
JORNSON Ben B 1890
34
ANDREWS John 1864
BURNSON Christian 1873
BURNSON Christian 1873
ANDERSON Louis 1882
35
JACOBSON B C 1870
OLSON Tobias C 1882
BERGERSON Martha 1906
LARSON Ole 1873
OLSON Tobias C 1876
OLSEN Gabriel 1882
36
DAHL [97] Tobias 1873
OLSEN Gabriel 1882
RAPELYE Sarah A 1860
BERNTZON Staale 1875

Helpful Hints

1. This Map's INDEX can be found on the preceding pages.
2. Refer to Map "C" to see where this Township lies within Dunn County, Wisconsin.
3. Numbers within square brackets [ ] denote a multi-patentee land parcel (multi-owner). Refer to Appendix "C" for a full list of members in this group.
4. Areas that look to be crowded with Patentees usually indicate multiple sales of the same parcel (Re-issues) or Overlapping parcels. See this Township's Index for an explanation of these and other circumstances that might explain "odd" groupings of Patentees on this map.

Legend

- Patent Boundary
- Section Boundary
- No Patents Found (or Outside County)
- 1., 2., 3., ... Lot Numbers (when beside a name)
- [ ] Group Number (see Appendix "C")

Scale: Section = 1 mile X 1 mile (generally, with some exceptions)

Road Map

T30-N R11-W
4th PM - 1831 MN/WI Meridian

Map Group 8

Cities & Towns

None

Cemeteries

Popple Creek Cemetery

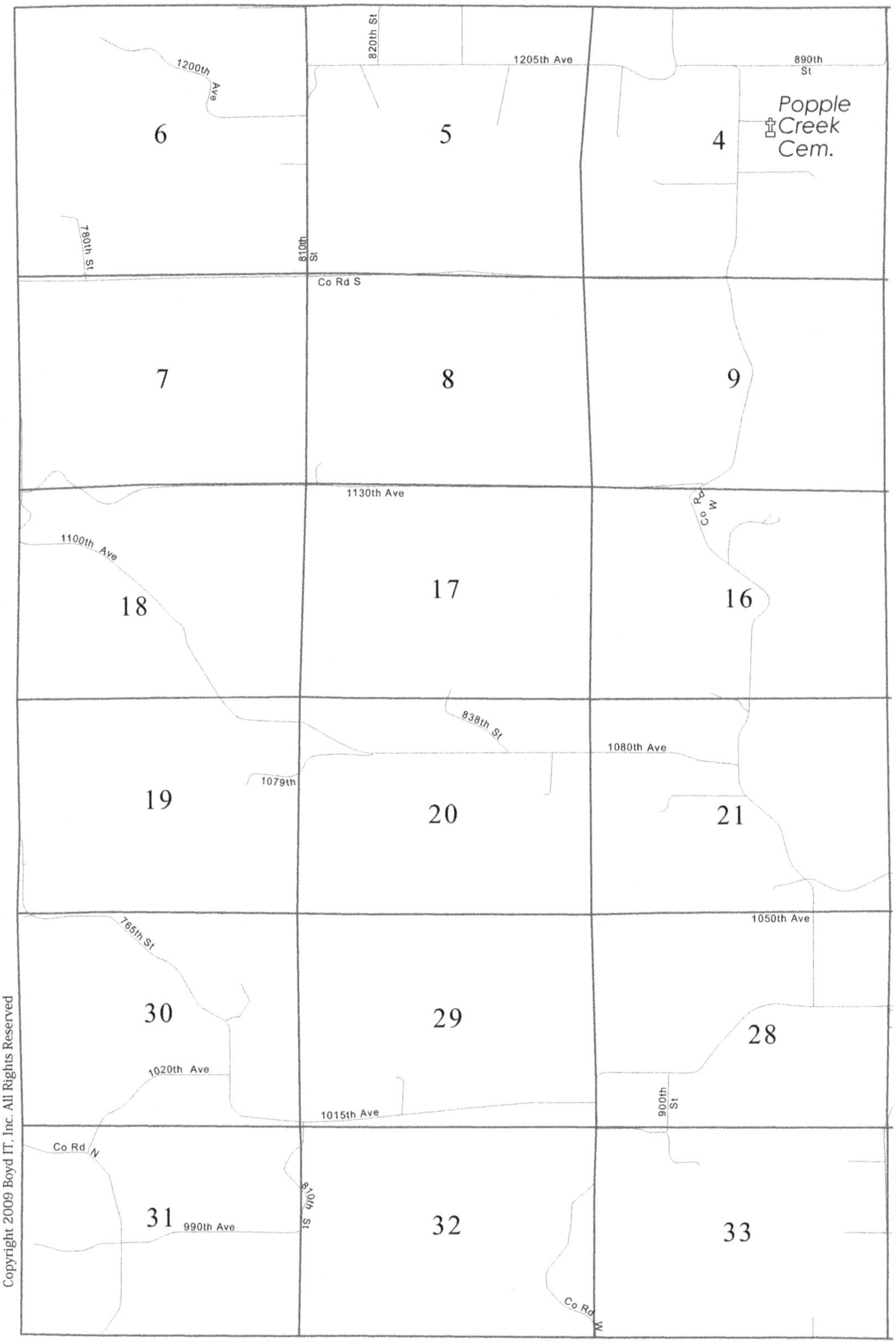

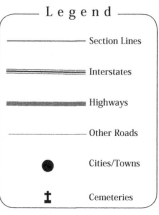

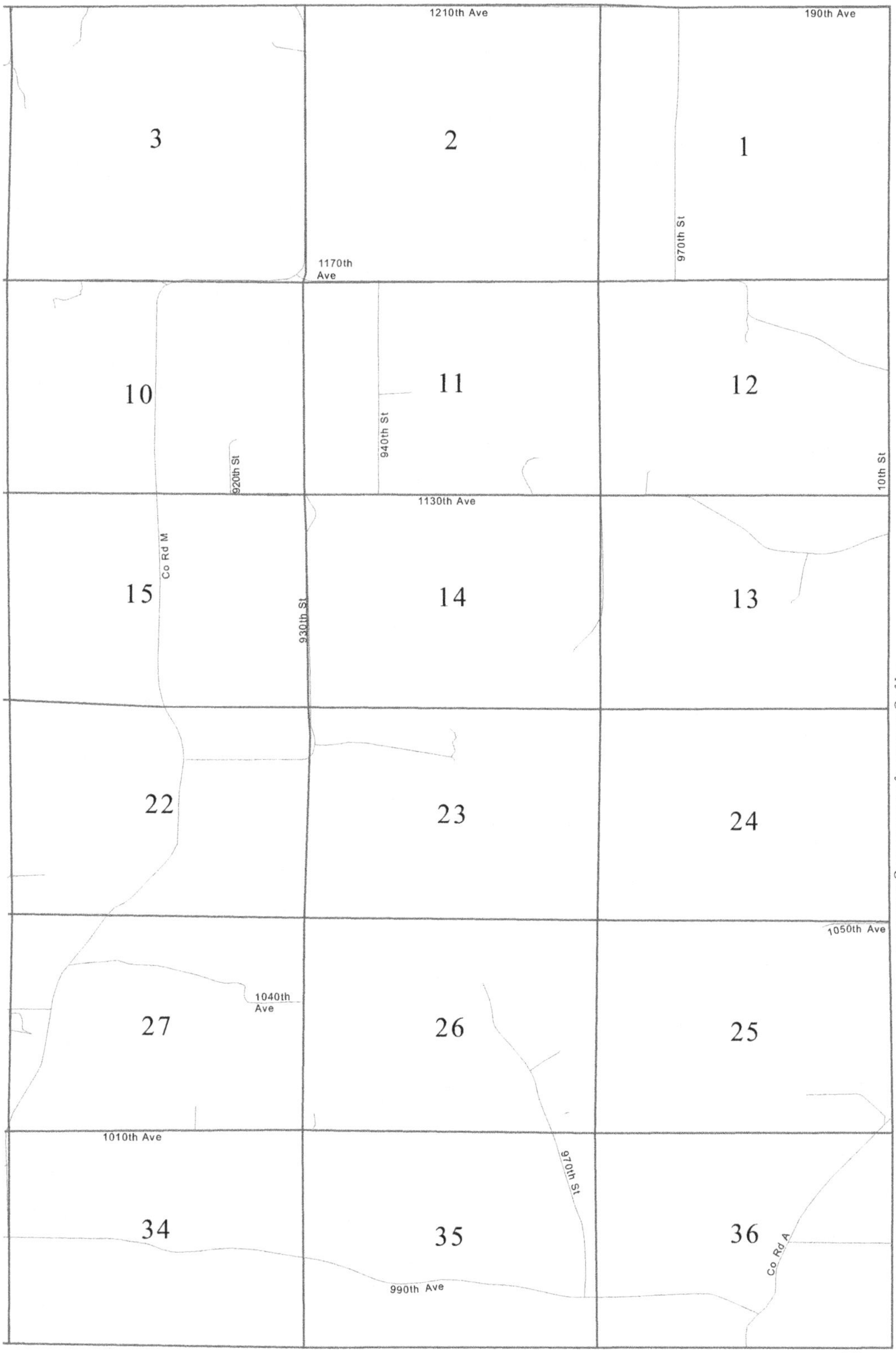
1210th Ave
190th Ave
3
2
1
970th St
1170th Ave
10
11
12
940th St
920th St
10th St
1130th Ave
Co Rd M
15
14
13
930th St
22
23
24
1050th Ave
1040th Ave
27
26
25
1010th Ave
970th St
34
35
36
Co Rd A
990th Ave

Helpful Hints

1. This road map has a number of uses, but primarily it is to help you: a) find the present location of land owned by your ancestors (at least the general area), b) find cemeteries and city-centers, and c) estimate the route/roads used by Census-takers & tax-assessors.

2. If you plan to travel to Dunn County to locate cemeteries or land parcels, please pick up a modern travel map for the area before you do. Mapping old land parcels on modern maps is not as exact a science as you might think. Just the slightest variations in public land survey coordinates, estimates of parcel boundaries, or road-map deviations can greatly alter a map's representation of how a road either does or doesn't cross a particular parcel of land.

Legend

- Section Lines
- Interstates
- Highways
- Other Roads
- Cities/Towns
- Cemeteries

Scale: Section = 1 mile X 1 mile
(generally, with some exceptions)

Historical Map

T30-N R11-W
4th PM - 1831 MN/WI Meridian

Map Group 8

Cities & Towns
None

Cemeteries
Popple Creek Cemetery

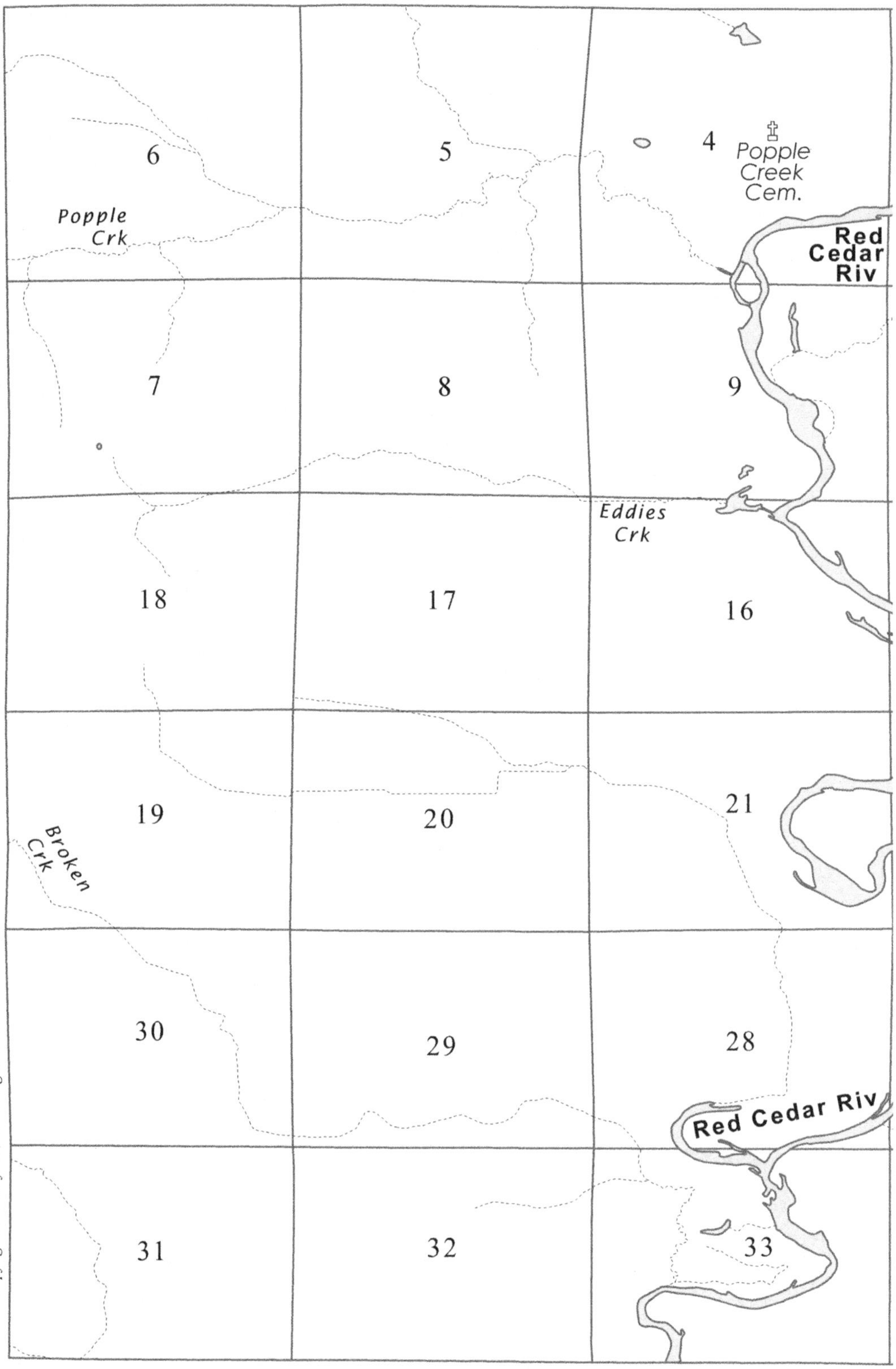

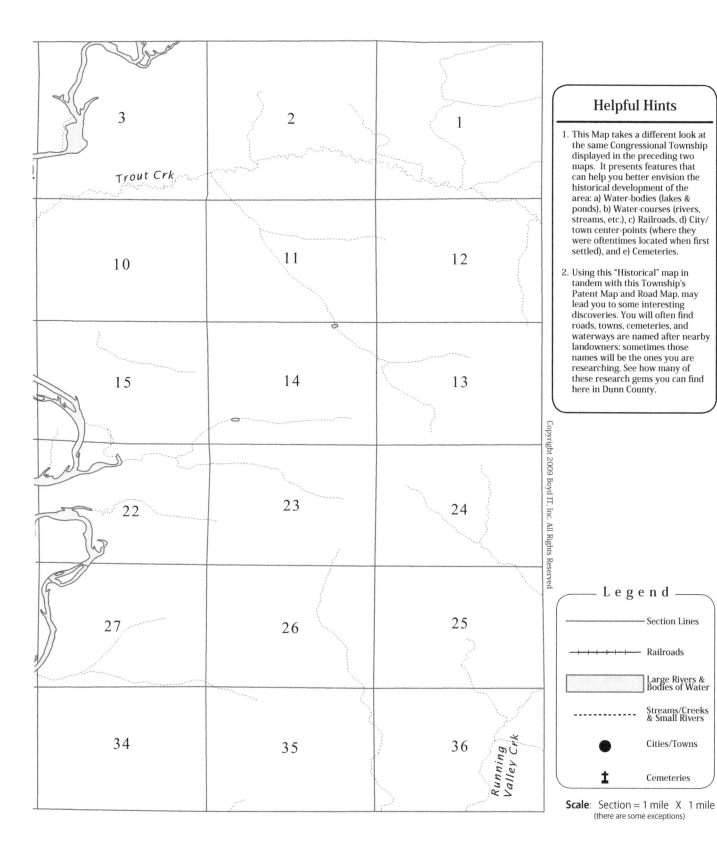

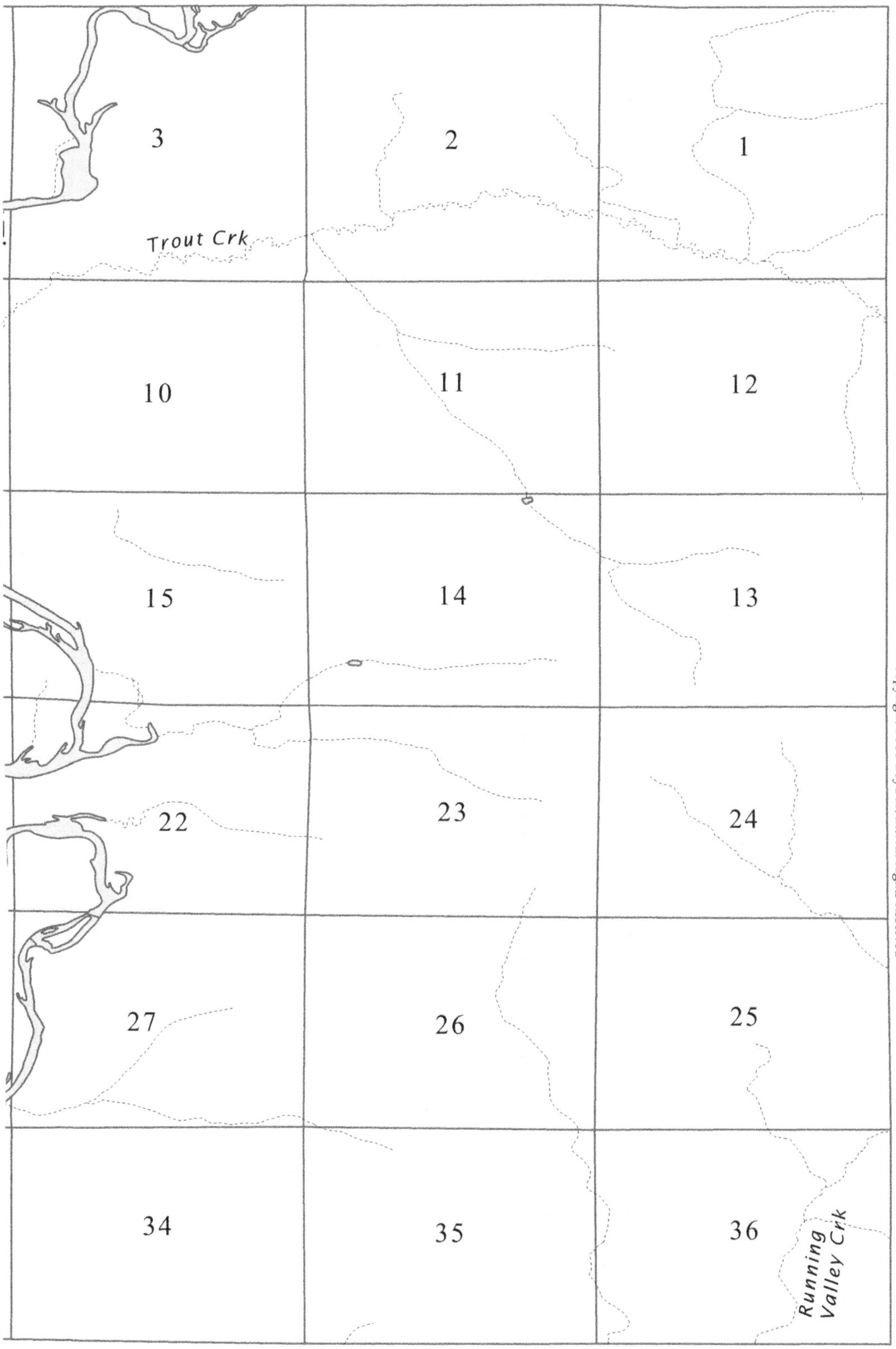

Helpful Hints

1. This Map takes a different look at the same Congressional Township displayed in the preceding two maps. It presents features that can help you better envision the historical development of the area: a) Water-bodies (lakes & ponds), b) Water-courses (rivers, streams, etc.), c) Railroads, d) City/town center-points (where they were oftentimes located when first settled), and e) Cemeteries.

2. Using this "Historical" map in tandem with this Township's Patent Map and Road Map, may lead you to some interesting discoveries. You will often find roads, towns, cemeteries, and waterways are named after nearby landowners: sometimes those names will be the ones you are researching. See how many of these research gems you can find here in Dunn County.

Legend

- Section Lines
- Railroads
- Large Rivers & Bodies of Water
- Streams/Creeks & Small Rivers
- Cities/Towns
- Cemeteries

Scale: Section = 1 mile X 1 mile
(there are some exceptions)

Map Group 9: Index to Land Patents

Township 29-North Range 14-West (4th PM - 1831 MN/WI)

After you locate an individual in this Index, take note of the Section and Section Part then proceed to the Land Patent map on the pages immediately following. You should have no difficulty locating the corresponding parcel of land.

The "For More Info" Column will lead you to more information about the underlying Patents. See the *Legend* at right, and the "How to Use this Book" chapter, for more information.

LEGEND

"For More Info . . . " column

A = Authority (Legislative Act, See Appendix "A")
B = Block or Lot (location in Section unknown)
C = Cancelled Patent
F = Fractional Section
G = Group (Multi-Patentee Patent, see Appendix "C")
V = Overlaps another Parcel
R = Re-Issued (Parcel patented more than once)

(A & G items require you to look in the Appendixes referred to above. All other Letter-designations followed by a number require you to locate line-items in this index that possess the ID number found after the letter).

ID	Individual in Patent	Sec.	Sec. Part	Date Issued	Other Counties	For More Info . . .
1503	ANDERSON, Christ	12	W½NW	1878-06-24		A6
1541	ANDREWS, John	12	N½SW	1874-07-15		A6
1542	" "	12	SENW	1874-07-15		A6
1543	" "	12	SWNE	1874-07-15		A6
1506	ANNIS, Darius	26	NE	1869-10-20		A6 V1482
1593	AUSTIN, William	6	NW	1871-03-10		A6 F
1524	BABCOCK, George W	4	E½NE	1877-02-20		A6 F
1525	" "	4	NESE	1877-02-20		A6 F
1534	BACHLER, Jakob	2	W½NW	1882-05-10		A6 F
1496	BAILEY, Burzelia	28	NW	1869-09-01		A6
1501	BAILEY, Charles W	32	N½SW	1869-09-01		A6
1502	" "	32	S½NW	1869-09-01		A6
1507	BAILEY, David	18	SW	1871-11-20		A6
1508	BAILEY, David C	32	W½SE	1872-09-25		A6
1544	BAILEY, John	32	NE	1869-10-20		A6
1549	BAILEY, John G	20	SE	1871-03-10		A6
1557	BAILEY, John Q	32	E½SE	1876-12-30		A6
1479	BEEBE, Absalom	8	SE	1872-10-01		A6
1526	BOURN, Henry C	8	N½NW	1878-11-30		A6
1495	BRIGGS, Benajor A	20	W½NW	1874-07-15		A6
1586	BUSHY, Peter	4	S½SE	1871-11-20		A6
1587	" "	4	S½SW	1871-11-20		A6
1511	CHENEY, Elbridge	34	W½SW	1885-08-20		A6
1585	CHRISTOFORSEN, Peder	20	S½NE	1878-06-24		A6
1498	CHURCHILL, Charles H	20	E½NW	1876-11-03		A6
1584	CLARK, Orson E	10	N½NW	1880-09-01		A6
1497	COEN, Charles G	30	SE	1871-11-20		A6
1571	COEN, Levi	30	NE	1870-09-10		A6
1570	" "	30	E½SW	1878-06-24		A6
1582	COLE, Omar	34	E½NE	1869-10-20		A6
1583	" "	34	E½SE	1869-10-20		A6
1499	COOK, Charles P	12	S½SW	1875-09-15		A6
1530	CRANDELL, Hiram	4	NESW	1892-08-08		A6
1532	CRYE, Isaiah	26	E½SE	1876-05-15		A6
1547	CRYE, John	10	E½NE	1872-09-25		A6
1548	" "	10	E½SE	1872-09-25		A6
1515	CUNNINGHAM, Esther H	26	NW	1870-06-10		A6 V1481, 1483
1517	CUNNINGHAM, George	18	NE	1871-11-20		A6
1569	DELANNAY, Leonidas J	22	SW	1869-10-20		A6
1536	DUNNIGAN, James	18	N½SE	1876-03-10		A6
1500	FRYE, Charles T	34	SESW	1891-08-04		A6
1505	GEAR, Columbus C	8	S½NW	1878-06-24		A6
1485	GRANGER, Amos	2	SENW	1871-08-25		A6
1486	" "	2	SWNE	1871-08-25		A6
1487	" "	2	W½SE	1871-08-25		A6
1538	GRANGER, Jedidiah W	1	SWNW	1871-08-25		A6

ID	Individual in Patent	Sec.	Sec. Part	Date Issued	Other Counties	For More Info . . .
1539	GRANGER, Jedidiah W (Cont'd)	2	E½SE	1871-08-25		A6
1540	" "	2	SENE	1871-08-25		A6
1551	HARRINGTON, John	14	SE	1869-08-05		A2
1512	HARROLD, Elijah	26	SW	1869-10-20		A6
1580	HARROLD, Miles	26	W½SE	1872-09-02		A2
1555	HAYS, John N	4	N½NW	1878-06-24		A6 F
1489	HUMPHREY, Arch K	34	E½NW	1869-09-01		A6
1490	" "	34	W½NE	1869-09-01		A6
1564	JERVY, Joseph	34	W½SE	1876-05-15		A6
1535	KARLEN, Jakob	2	NENW	1889-02-16		A6 F
1491	KECK, Archibald	36	W½NW	1871-03-15		A6
1492	" "	36	W½SW	1871-03-15		A6
1595	KECK, William	36	W½NE	1871-03-10		A6
1596	" "	36	W½SE	1871-03-10		A6
1578	KELLEY, Michael	32	S½SW	1878-11-30		A6
1579	KESLER, Michael	2	SW	1872-10-01		A6
1581	KNAPP, Miles	8	SW	1878-06-24		A6
1527	LININGER, Henry	24	SE	1870-06-10		A6
1516	MALLEAN, Fred	18	S½SE	1880-05-15		A6
1552	MCALLISTER, John	1	E½SW	1871-08-25		A6
1553	" "	1	SENW	1871-08-25		A6
1554	" "	1	SWNE	1871-08-25		A6
1558	MCCULLOCH, John Q	36	E½NE	1872-10-01		A6
1559	" "	36	E½SE	1872-10-01		A6
1597	MCDORMAN, William	20	SW	1869-10-20		A6
1545	MEYERS, John C	10	W½SE	1877-09-26		A6
1533	MILLER, Jacob D	34	W½NW	1876-11-03		A6
1588	MILLER, Philip	12	S½SE	1876-05-15		A6
1565	MILLIRON, Joseph	28	SW	1873-12-20		A6
1509	MOORE, Ebenezer	6	W½NE	1873-12-20		A6
1528	MOYER, Henry	22	NW	1870-06-10		A6
1573	MULVANY, Mathew	32	N½NW	1874-11-10		A6
1478	NEMBARGER, Abram	24	NE	1869-10-20		A6
1572	OLIN, Lewis	6	S½SE	1873-04-01		A6
1574	OLIN, Mathew	6	E½SW	1872-10-01		A6
1575	" "	6	N½SE	1873-12-20		A6
1513	OLSON, Enoch	8	NE	1871-03-15		A6 C R1514
1514	OLSON, Ereck	8	NE	1877-09-26		A6 R1513
1598	PECK, William W	24	S½SW	1877-02-20		A6
1504	PHERNETTON, Christopher	6	E½NE	1878-06-24		A6
1529	PHERNETTON, Henry	6	W½SW	1875-11-20		A6
1556	PIPPINGER, John	22	SE	1872-10-01		A6
1493	PITZRICK, August	20	N½NE	1878-06-24		A6
1510	QUINN, Edward	18	E½NW	1874-11-10		A6
1537	QUINN, James	18	W½NW	1875-11-20		A6 F
1560	ROSS, John	34	NESW	1871-04-20		A2
1521	SCHRIER, George	2	N½NE	1877-06-04		A6 F
1480	SCHUTTS, Adolph	24	S½NW	1874-11-10		A6
1494	SCHUTTS, August	24	N½NW	1874-11-10		A6
1589	SHILTS, Samuel	22	NE	1871-03-10		A6
1518	SLOCUM, George N	1	S½SE	1871-04-20		A6
1519	" "	12	NENW	1871-04-20		A6
1520	" "	12	NWNE	1871-04-20		A6
1488	SLOVER, Angeline	10	W½SW	1882-04-10		A6
1531	SLOVER, Isaac	10	E½SW	1883-07-10		A6
1481	SMITH, Alfred	26	NENW	1894-09-28		A6 V1515
1482	" "	26	NWNE	1894-09-28		A6 V1506
1483	" "	26	S½NW	1894-09-28		A6 V1515
1592	SMITH, Willard S	24	N½SW	1877-06-04		A6
1591	STODDARD, Washington	28	SE	1871-11-20		A6
1522	TEEGARDEN, George	10	S½NW	1872-10-01		A6
1523	" "	10	W½NE	1872-10-01		A6
1546	TURNER, John C	30	NW	1872-09-25		A6 F
1594	TURNER, William H	30	W½SW	1873-12-20		A6 F
1484	TUTTLE, Alfred	12	N½SE	1875-04-15		A6
1561	TUTTLE, John	12	E½NE	1873-05-20		A6
1566	WETHERBY, L P	4	NWSE	1871-11-20		A6
1567	" "	4	SENW	1871-11-20		A6
1568	" "	4	W½NE	1871-11-20		A6
1576	WETHERBY, Leonard	4	NWSW	1873-05-20		A6 G418
1577	" "	4	SWNW	1873-05-20		A6 G418
1576	WETHERBY, Matilda E	4	NWSW	1873-05-20		A6 G418
1577	" "	4	SWNW	1873-05-20		A6 G418

ID	Individual in Patent	Sec.	Sec. Part	Date Issued	Other Counties	For More Info . . .
1550	WILBUR, John H	28	NE	1871-11-20		A6
1590	WISCONSIN, State Of	16		1941-08-16		A3
1562	YODER, John	36	E½NW	1871-03-10		A6
1563	" "	36	E½SW	1871-03-10		A6

Patent Map

T29-N R14-W
4th PM - 1831 MN/WI Meridian

Map Group 9

Township Statistics

Parcels Mapped	:	121
Number of Patents	:	95
Number of Individuals	:	94
Patentees Identified	:	93
Number of Surnames	:	70
Multi-Patentee Parcels	:	2
Oldest Patent Date	:	8/5/1869
Most Recent Patent	:	8/16/1941
Block/Lot Parcels	:	0
Parcels Re - Issued	:	1
Parcels that Overlap	:	5
Cities and Towns	:	1
Cemeteries	:	1

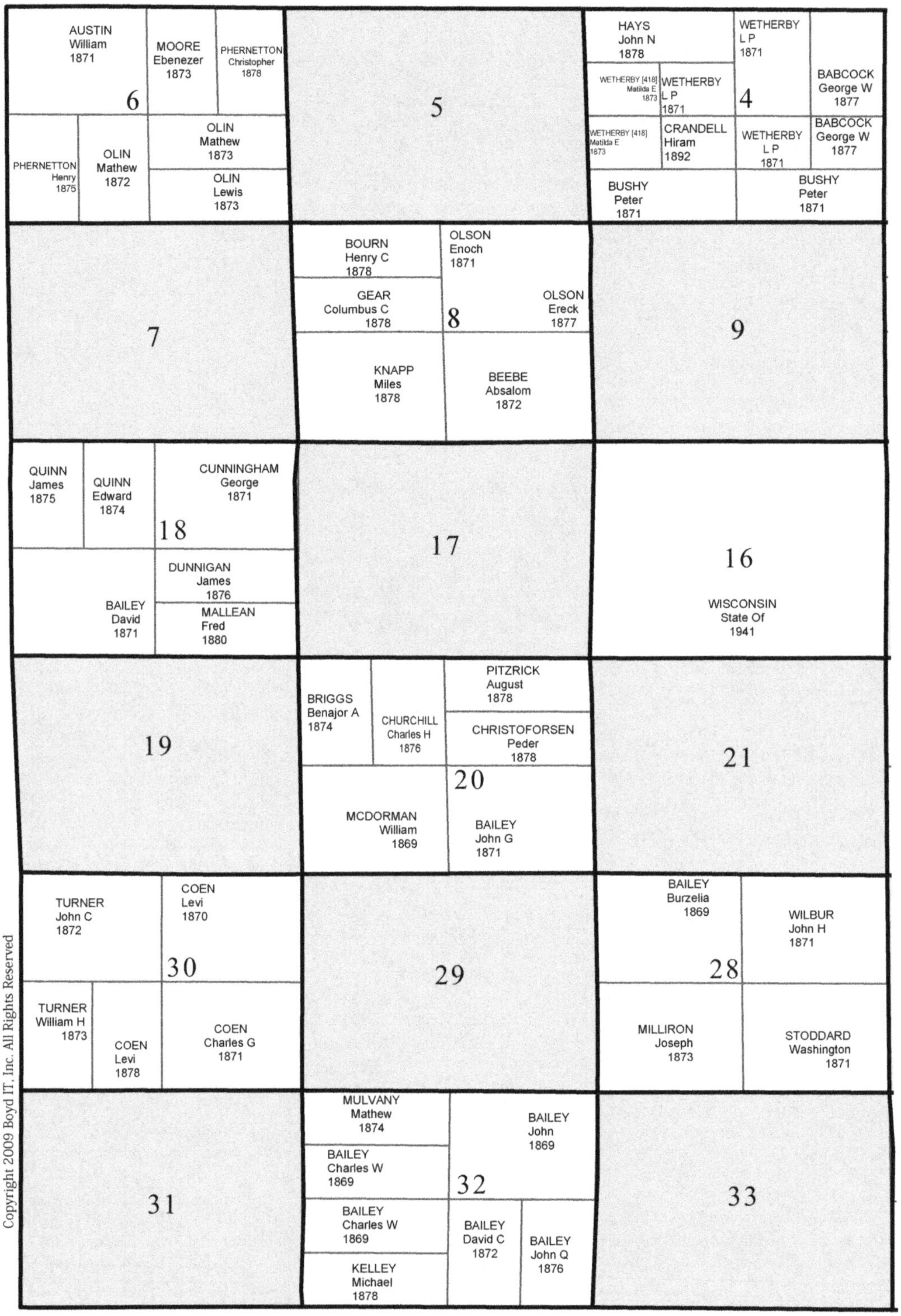
AUSTIN William 1871
MOORE Ebenezer 1873
PHERNETTON Christopher 1878
6
PHERNETTON Henry 1875
OLIN Mathew 1872
OLIN Mathew 1873
OLIN Lewis 1873
5
HAYS John N 1878
WETHERBY L P 1871
WETHERBY [418] Matilda E 1873
WETHERBY L P 1871
4
BABCOCK George W 1877
WETHERBY [418] Matilda E 1873
CRANDELL Hiram 1892
WETHERBY L P 1871
BABCOCK George W 1877
BUSHY Peter 1871
BUSHY Peter 1871
7
BOURN Henry C 1878
OLSON Enoch 1871
GEAR Columbus C 1878
8
OLSON Ereck 1877
KNAPP Miles 1878
BEEBE Absalom 1872
9
QUINN James 1875
QUINN Edward 1874
CUNNINGHAM George 1871
18
DUNNIGAN James 1876
BAILEY David 1871
MALLEAN Fred 1880
17
16
WISCONSIN State Of 1941
19
BRIGGS Benajor A 1874
CHURCHILL Charles H 1876
PITZRICK August 1878
CHRISTOFORSEN Peder 1878
20
MCDORMAN William 1869
BAILEY John G 1871
21
TURNER John C 1872
COEN Levi 1870
30
TURNER William H 1873
COEN Levi 1878
COEN Charles G 1871
29
BAILEY Burzelia 1869
WILBUR John H 1871
28
MILLIRON Joseph 1873
STODDARD Washington 1871
31
MULVANY Mathew 1874
BAILEY John 1869
BAILEY Charles W 1869
32
BAILEY Charles W 1869
BAILEY David C 1872
BAILEY John Q 1876
KELLEY Michael 1878
33

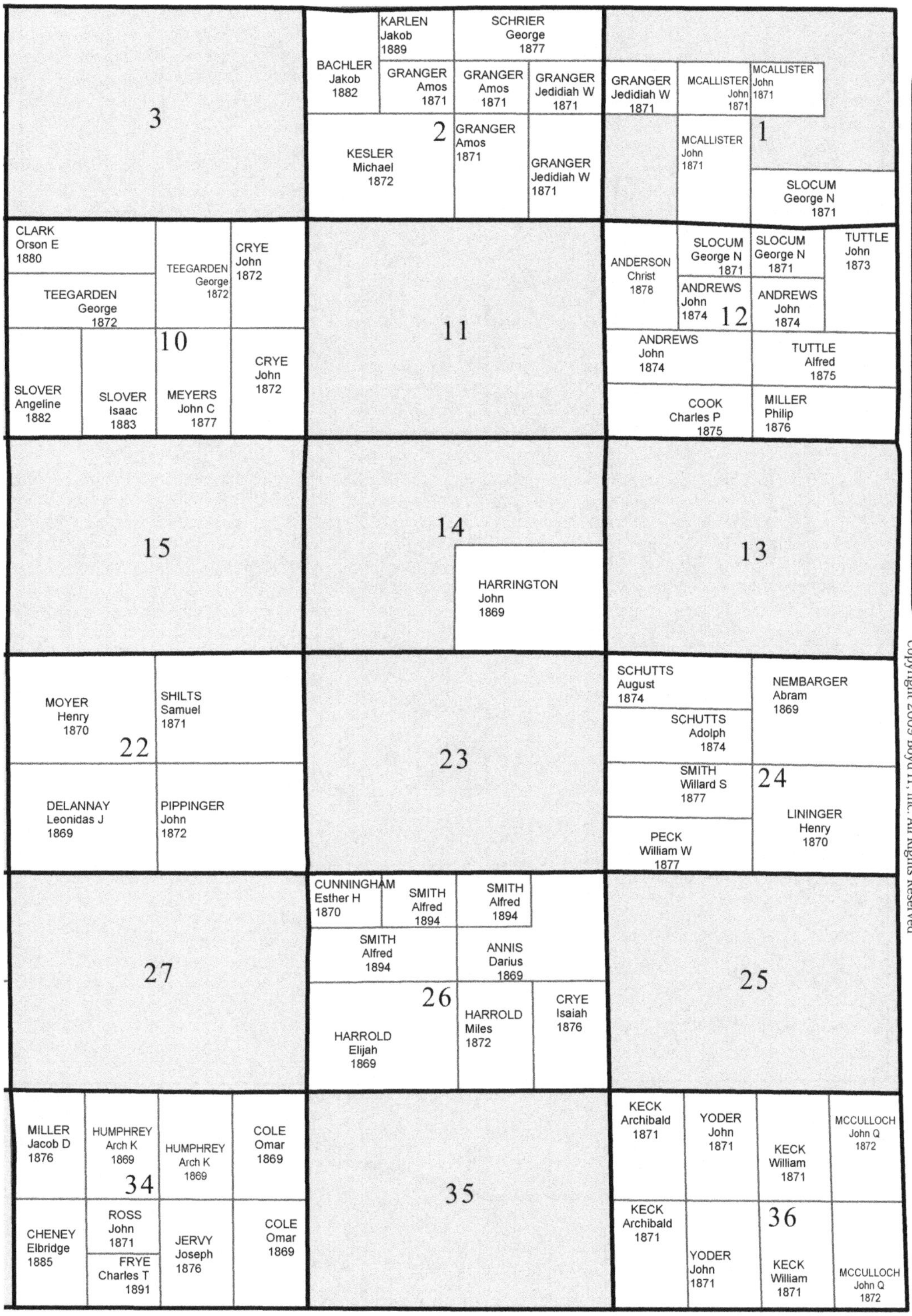
3
KARLEN Jakob 1889
SCHRIER George 1877
BACHLER Jakob 1882
GRANGER Amos 1871
GRANGER Amos 1871
GRANGER Jedidiah W 1871
KESLER Michael 1872
2
GRANGER Amos 1871
GRANGER Jedidiah W 1871
GRANGER Jedidiah W 1871
MCALLISTER John 1871
MCALLISTER John 1871
MCALLISTER John 1871
1
SLOCUM George N 1871
CLARK Orson E 1880
TEEGARDEN George 1872
CRYE John 1872
TEEGARDEN George 1872
10
SLOVER Angeline 1882
SLOVER Isaac 1883
MEYERS John C 1877
CRYE John 1872
11
ANDERSON Christ 1878
SLOCUM George N 1871
SLOCUM George N 1871
TUTTLE John 1873
ANDREWS John 1874
12
ANDREWS John 1874
ANDREWS John 1874
TUTTLE Alfred 1875
COOK Charles P 1875
MILLER Philip 1876
15
14
HARRINGTON John 1869
13
MOYER Henry 1870
SHILTS Samuel 1871
22
DELANNAY Leonidas J 1869
PIPPINGER John 1872
23
SCHUTTS August 1874
NEMBARGER Abram 1869
SCHUTTS Adolph 1874
SMITH Willard S 1877
24
PECK William W 1877
LININGER Henry 1870
27
CUNNINGHAM Esther H 1870
SMITH Alfred 1894
SMITH Alfred 1894
SMITH Alfred 1894
ANNIS Darius 1869
26
HARROLD Elijah 1869
HARROLD Miles 1872
CRYE Isaiah 1876
25
MILLER Jacob D 1876
HUMPHREY Arch K 1869
HUMPHREY Arch K 1869
COLE Omar 1869
34
CHENEY Elbridge 1885
ROSS John 1871
FRYE Charles T 1891
JERVY Joseph 1876
COLE Omar 1869
35
KECK Archibald 1871
YODER John 1871
KECK William 1871
MCCULLOCH John Q 1872
KECK Archibald 1871
36
YODER John 1871
KECK William 1871
MCCULLOCH John Q 1872

Helpful Hints

1. This Map's INDEX can be found on the preceding pages.
2. Refer to Map "C" to see where this Township lies within Dunn County, Wisconsin.
3. Numbers within square brackets [ ] denote a multi-patentee land parcel (multi-owner). Refer to Appendix "C" for a full list of members in this group.
4. Areas that look to be crowded with Patentees usually indicate multiple sales of the same parcel (Re-issues) or Overlapping parcels. See this Township's Index for an explanation of these and other circumstances that might explain "odd" groupings of Patentees on this map.

Legend

- Patent Boundary
- Section Boundary
- No Patents Found (or Outside County)
- 1., 2., 3., ... Lot Numbers (when beside a name)
- [ ] Group Number (see Appendix "C")

Scale: Section = 1 mile X 1 mile (generally, with some exceptions)

Road Map

T29-N R14-W
4th PM - 1831 MN/WI Meridian

Map Group 9

Cities & Towns

Knapp

Cemeteries

Forest Hill Cemetery

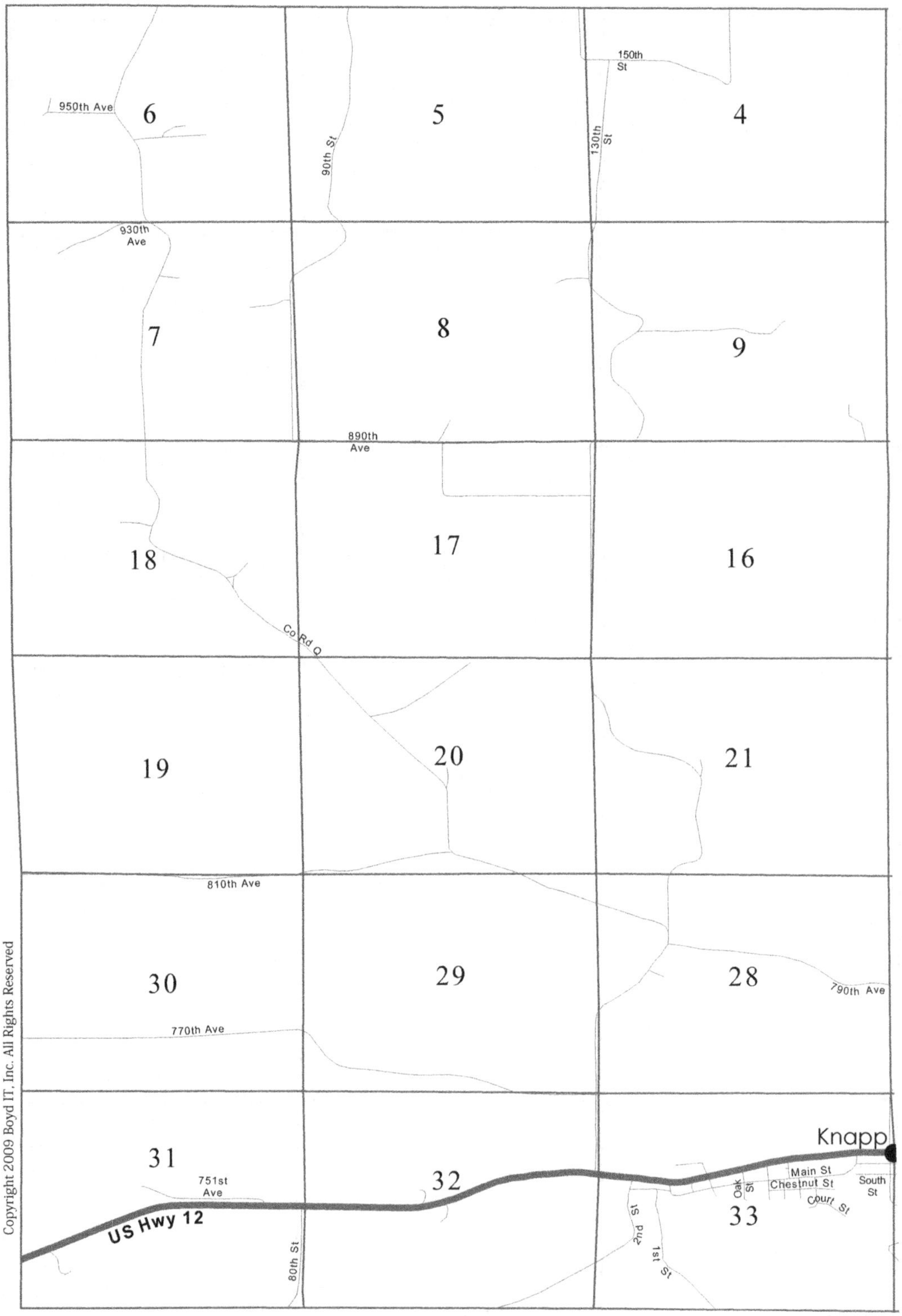

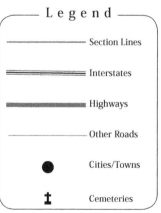

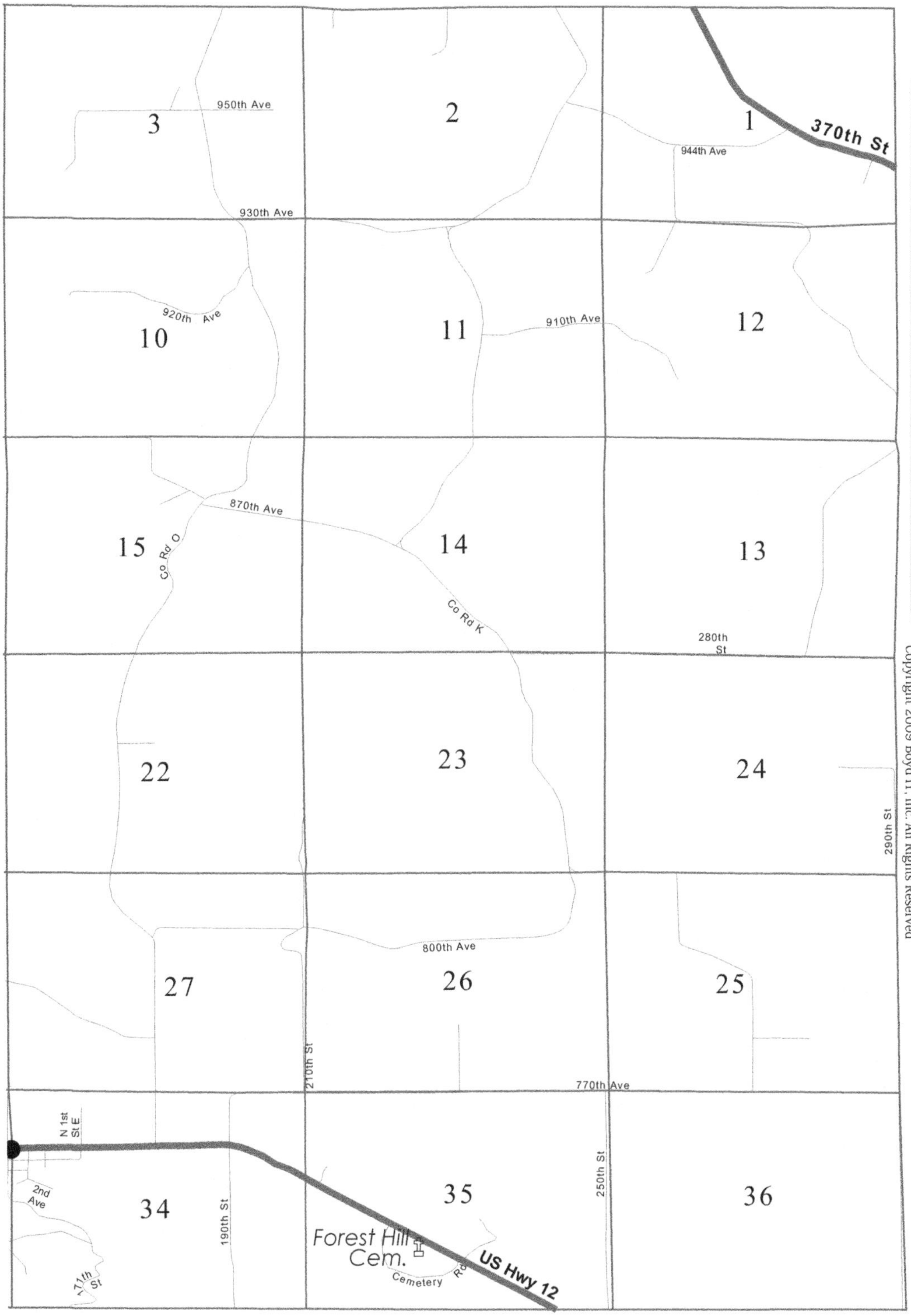

Helpful Hints

1. This road map has a number of uses, but primarily it is to help you: a) find the present location of land owned by your ancestors (at least the general area), b) find cemeteries and city-centers, and c) estimate the route/roads used by Census-takers & tax-assessors.
2. If you plan to travel to Dunn County to locate cemeteries or land parcels, please pick up a modern travel map for the area before you do. Mapping old land parcels on modern maps is not as exact a science as you might think. Just the slightest variations in public land survey coordinates, estimates of parcel boundaries, or road-map deviations can greatly alter a map's representation of how a road either does or doesn't cross a particular parcel of land.

Legend

- Section Lines
- Interstates
- Highways
- Other Roads
- Cities/Towns
- Cemeteries

Scale: Section = 1 mile X 1 mile
(generally, with some exceptions)

Historical Map

T29-N R14-W
4th PM - 1831 MN/WI Meridian

Map Group 9

Cities & Towns

Knapp

Cemeteries

Forest Hill Cemetery

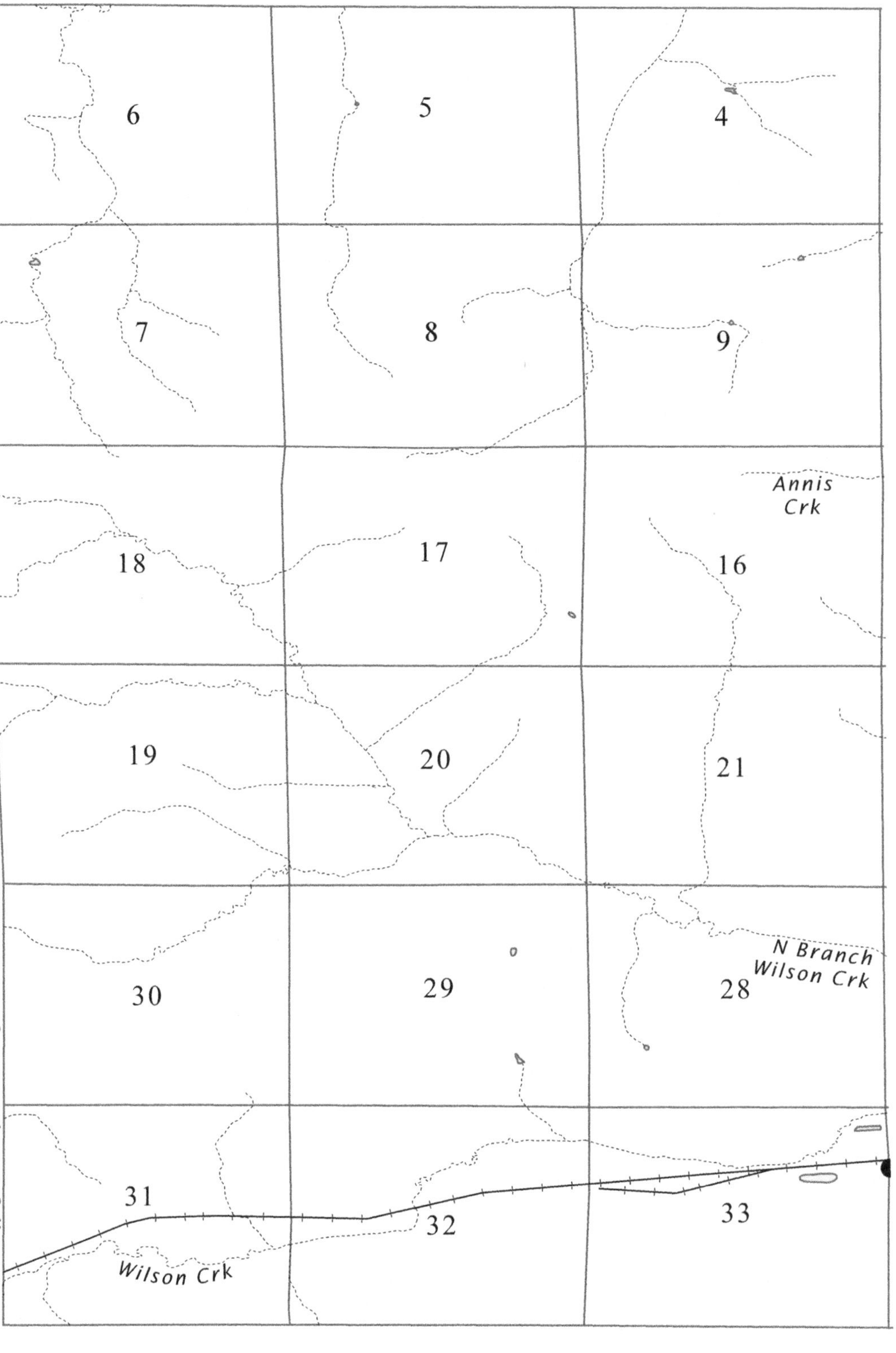
6
5
4
7
8
9
18
17
16
Annis Crk
19
20
21
30
29
28
N Branch Wilson Crk
31
32
33
Wilson Crk

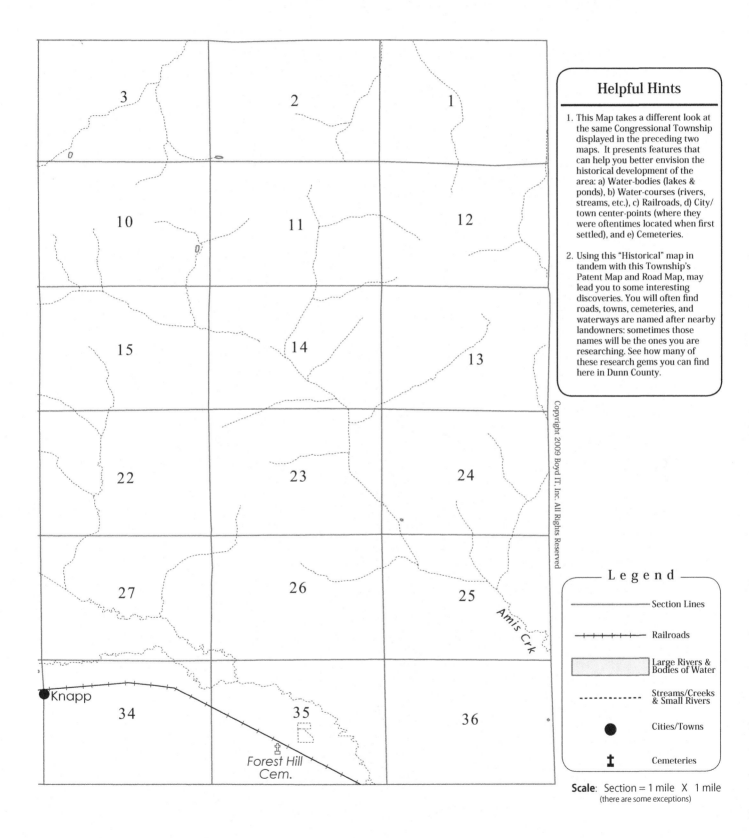

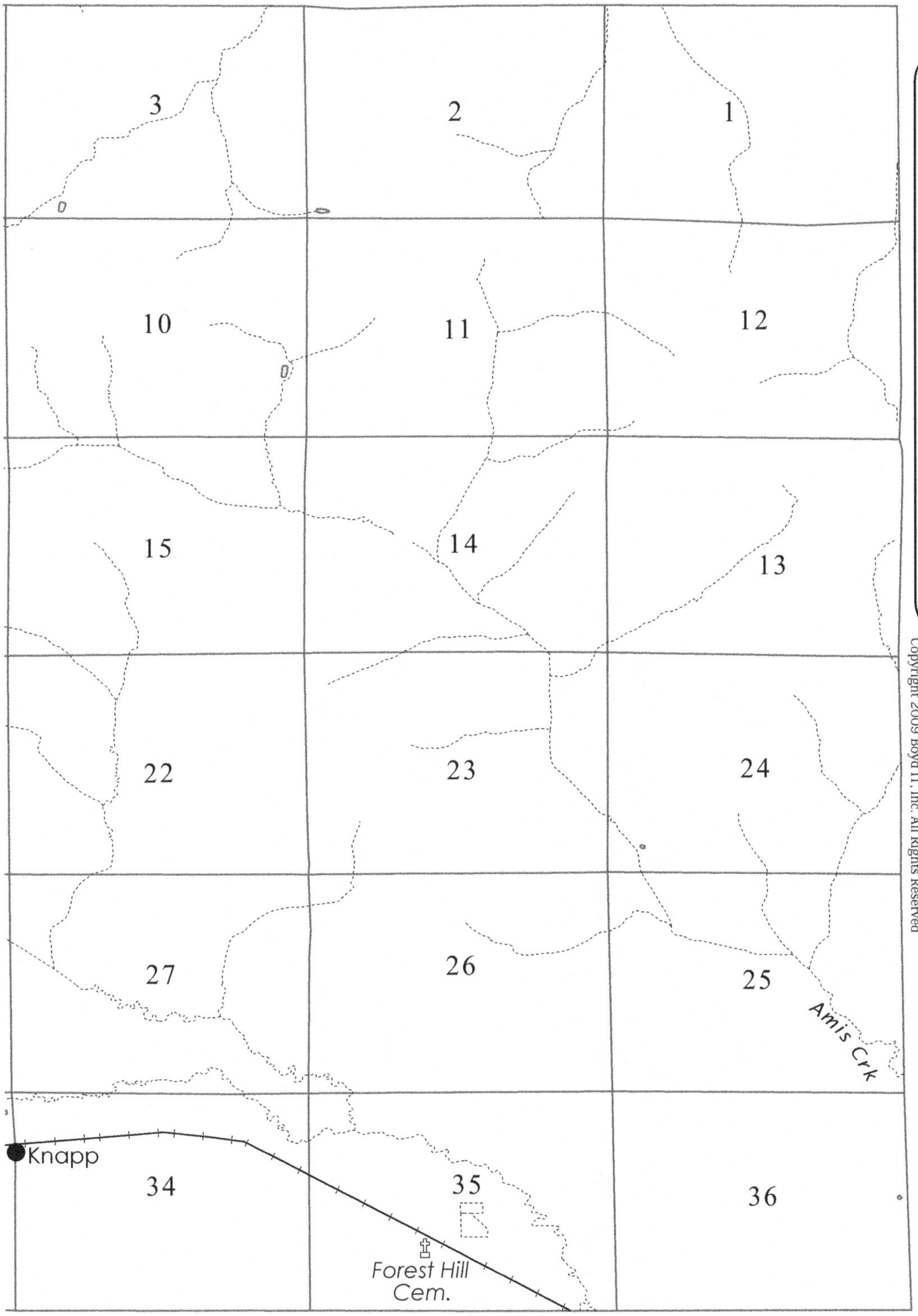

Helpful Hints

1. This Map takes a different look at the same Congressional Township displayed in the preceding two maps. It presents features that can help you better envision the historical development of the area: a) Water-bodies (lakes & ponds), b) Water-courses (rivers, streams, etc.), c) Railroads, d) City/town center-points (where they were oftentimes located when first settled), and e) Cemeteries.
2. Using this "Historical" map in tandem with this Township's Patent Map and Road Map, may lead you to some interesting discoveries. You will often find roads, towns, cemeteries, and waterways are named after nearby landowners: sometimes those names will be the ones you are researching. See how many of these research gems you can find here in Dunn County.

Legend

- Section Lines
- Railroads
- Large Rivers & Bodies of Water
- Streams/Creeks & Small Rivers
- Cities/Towns
- Cemeteries

Scale: Section = 1 mile X 1 mile
(there are some exceptions)

Map Group 10: Index to Land Patents

Township 29-North Range 13-West (4th PM - 1831 MN/WI)

After you locate an individual in this Index, take note of the Section and Section Part then proceed to the Land Patent map on the pages immediately following. You should have no difficulty locating the corresponding parcel of land.

The "For More Info" Column will lead you to more information about the underlying Patents. See the *Legend* at right, and the "How to Use this Book" chapter, for more information.

LEGEND

"For More Info . . . " column

A = Authority (Legislative Act, See Appendix "A")
B = Block or Lot (location in Section unknown)
C = Cancelled Patent
F = Fractional Section
G = Group (Multi-Patentee Patent, see Appendix "C")
V = Overlaps another Parcel
R = Re-Issued (Parcel patented more than once)

(A & G items require you to look in the Appendixes referred to above. All other Letter-designations followed by a number require you to locate line-items in this index that possess the ID number found after the letter).

ID	Individual in Patent	Sec.	Sec. Part	Date Issued	Other Counties	For More Info . . .
1668	ACKERT, George	20	NE	1873-09-20		A6
1700	ACKERT, John	21	NE	1871-04-20		A6
1708	ACKERT, John L	20	NW	1870-05-20		A6
1750	ADAMS, Nathaniel C	8	NESE	1870-09-10		A6
1751	" "	9	E½SW	1870-09-10		A6
1752	" "	9	NWSW	1870-09-10		A6
1781	ADAMS, William	17	E½NE	1870-05-20		A6
1782	" "	8	SESE	1870-05-20		A6
1783	" "	9	SWSW	1870-05-20		A6
1658	ANDREWS, England F	2	SWNE	1891-11-16		A6
1673	BAILEY, Harriet	32	NW	1869-08-05		A2
1719	BALIS, Luther	36	S½SW	1860-10-01		A5 G214
1720	" "	36	W½SE	1860-10-01		A5 G214
1666	BARBER, Gabriel	28	W½SE	1877-09-26		A6
1689	BARNARD, James M	14	NW	1863-05-20		A5
1690	" "	24	S½NE	1864-02-10		A7 G24
1624	BARTHOLOMEW, Bennett J	32	S½NE	1870-06-01		A2
1718	BARTHOLOMEW, Joseph	34	SE	1869-09-01		A6
1757	BARTHOLOMEW, Reuben S	34	SW	1869-09-01		A6
1772	BECKWITH, Seth S	36	NWNW	1859-03-03		A7
1604	BELDING, Aretus M	10	NW	1864-09-15		A5 G379
1669	BLAKELY, George H	6	E½SE	1873-12-20		A6
1670	" "	6	NESW	1873-12-20		A6
1671	" "	6	NWSE	1873-12-20		A6
1711	BLAKELY, John M	6	NE	1877-05-15		A6
1678	BLANCHARD, Henry C	28	SW	1869-09-01		A6
1627	BONNELL, C M	20	S½SE	1871-04-20		A6
1628	" "	21	S½SW	1871-04-20		A6
1618	BRADWAY, Asa	8	W½NE	1873-12-20		A6
1675	BRADWAY, Heman	6	SESW	1870-05-20		A6
1676	" "	6	SWSE	1870-05-20		A6
1677	" "	7	E½NW	1870-05-20		A6
1745	BROWN, Mitchell M	18	W½SE	1872-10-01		A6
1747	BROWN, Moses	15	NWSE	1866-02-15		A2
1746	" "	15	NESE	1866-09-01		A2
1761	BROWN, Russell G	32	SE	1871-11-20		A6
1623	BURT, Benjamin	24	W½SE	1878-11-30		A6
1767	BURT, Samuel V	26	SESW	1862-03-10		A5
1768	" "	26	SWSE	1862-03-10		A5
1769	" "	35	W½NE	1862-03-10		A5
1615	BUSH, Andrew	8	N½SW	1871-04-20		A6
1616	" "	8	S½NW	1871-04-20		A6
1667	BUTTERFIELD, George A	12	N½NE	1873-09-20		A6
1762	CAW, Samuel A	2	SWNW	1909-08-19		A6
1607	CHAMBERLIN, Edwin E	13	N½SW	1863-05-20		A5 G382
1608	" "	14	N½SE	1863-05-20		A5 G382

ID	Individual in Patent	Sec.	Sec. Part	Date Issued	Other Counties	For More Info . . .
1770	CHANDLER, Seth C	36	N½SW	1860-08-01		A5
1771	" "	36	S½NW	1860-08-01		A5
1688	CHURCH, James	13	N½NE	1860-10-01		A5
1612	CLARK, Alton L	4	NESE	1879-10-01		A6
1613	" "	4	SENE	1879-10-01		A6
1729	COLLAR, Lewis	24	S½SW	1871-08-25		A6
1730	" "	25	E½NW	1871-08-25		A6
1640	COMFORT, Daniel T	27	NE	1870-05-20		A6
1634	COOK, Charles P	18	S½NE	1875-09-15		A6
1790	CRAGIN, George A	36	NENE	1860-07-16		A5 G424
1791	" "	36	W½NE	1860-07-16		A5 G424
1649	CROSBY, Edward T	28	NW	1869-09-01		A6
1652	CROSBY, Elhanan	23	NESE	1864-10-20		A5
1653	" "	23	S½SE	1864-10-20		A5
1654	CROSBY, Elhanan W	27	NW	1864-10-20		A5 G93
1726	CROSBY, Joshua	20	N½SE	1869-09-01		A6
1727	" "	21	N½SW	1869-09-01		A6
1753	CROSBY, Nathaniel	34	NW	1869-09-01		A6
1748	DANIELS, N P	10	NESW	1876-04-01		A6
1749	" "	10	W½SW	1876-04-01		A6
1641	DARLING, David D	22	E½NW	1873-05-20		A6
1779	DARLING, Van R	22	E½SW	1873-09-20		A6
1655	DAVIS, Elias H	28	E½SE	1872-09-25		A6
1733	DAVIS, Lewis Y	22	NE	1870-05-20		A6
1621	DEARBORN, Benjamin B	23	S½SW	1872-09-25		A6
1622	" "	26	NENW	1872-09-25		A6
1721	DEMOE, Joseph	2	E½NW	1883-02-10		A6 F
1722	" "	2	NWNE	1883-02-10		A6 F
1723	" "	2	NWNW	1883-02-10		A6 F
1775	DODGE, Sydney W	22	W½NW	1873-09-20		A6
1696	EASTWOOD, Joel M	22	SESE	1884-10-04		A2
1599	ELLIS, Aaron G	4	N½NW	1882-04-10		A6 F
1600	" "	4	S½NW	1882-04-10		A6 F
1787	FINEOUT, William L	34	NE	1869-09-01		A6
1690	FOLJAMBE, Charles	24	S½NE	1864-02-10		A7 G24
1763	FRENCH, Samuel B	26	W½NE	1873-06-20		A2
1636	FRYE, Charles T	7	SW	1876-01-10		A6 F
1758	FURBUR, Roger	13	NENW	1870-05-20		A6
1759	" "	13	S½NW	1870-05-20		A6
1760	" "	13	SWNE	1870-05-20		A6
1604	GARDNER, William R	10	NW	1864-09-15		A5 G379
1625	GODELL, Betsy	25	W½NE	1871-03-15		A6 G158
1626	" "	25	W½SE	1871-03-15		A6 G158
1625	GODELL, John	25	W½NE	1871-03-15		A6 G158
1626	" "	25	W½SE	1871-03-15		A6 G158
1674	GOODELL, Harrison	36	NENW	1877-02-20		A6
1737	GRANGER, Marshall M	20	SW	1869-09-01		A6
1735	GREEN, Lucius L	8	E½NE	1871-08-25		A6
1736	" "	9	N½NW	1871-08-25		A6
1629	GREWT, Charles	6	E½NW	1882-04-10		A6 F
1687	HARMAN, Isaac	2	E½NE	1893-08-28		A6
1672	HARRINGTON, George M	17	SE	1870-09-10		A6
1703	HARRINGTON, John	25	SWNW	1866-09-01		A2
1704	" "	36	SESE	1866-09-01		A2
1702	" "	22	W½SW	1870-06-01		A2
1734	HARRINGTON, Lorinda	8	N½NW	1875-12-20		A6
1786	HILL, William	2	SE	1900-09-07		A6
1709	HOVER, John L	4	E½SW	1879-11-10		A6
1710	" "	4	W½SE	1879-11-10		A6
1679	HUBER, Henry	15	E½NW	1922-06-10		A2
1728	HULL, Julia E	11	NWSE	1865-05-05		A2
1738	HULL, Marvin	11	E½NE	1870-05-20		A6
1739	" "	11	NESE	1870-05-20		A6
1740	" "	11	SWNE	1870-05-20		A6
1630	HUTCHINSON, Charles H	22	NESE	1870-05-20		A6
1631	" "	23	N½SW	1870-05-20		A6
1632	" "	23	SWNW	1870-05-20		A6
1705	JOHNSON, John	30	N½NE	1871-08-25		A6
1706	" "	30	NENW	1871-08-25		A6
1707	" "	30	SENE	1871-08-25		A6
1656	JONES, Elizabeth	18	E½NW	1870-12-10		A6
1657	" "	18	N½NE	1870-12-10		A6
1719	KENT, Depusey	36	S½SW	1860-10-01		A5 G214

ID	Individual in Patent	Sec.	Sec. Part	Date Issued	Other Counties	For More Info . . .
1720	KENT, Depusey (Cont'd)	36	W½SE	1860-10-01		A5 G214
1719	KENT, Joseph D	36	S½SW	1860-10-01		A5 G214
1720	" "	36	W½SE	1860-10-01		A5 G214
1645	KING, Dwight A	4	N½NE	1884-09-20		A6 F
1646	" "	4	SWNE	1884-09-20		A6 F
1715	KLAUER, John P	18	W½NW	1878-11-30		A6 F
1642	KNAPP, David P	34	SESE	1862-03-10		A5 C
1643	" "	34	W½SE	1862-03-10		A5 C
1660	KNOTT, Francis	12	E½SW	1889-02-16		A6
1661	" "	12	SENW	1889-02-16		A6
1662	" "	12	SWSW	1889-02-16		A6
1780	KREUGER, William A	24	NWSW	1884-09-20		A6
1617	LARSON, Andrew	12	S½NE	1882-05-10		A6
1654	LEWELLEN, George	27	NW	1864-10-20		A5 G93
1638	LOCKWOOD, Chauncey A	9	S½NW	1881-09-17		A6
1639	" "	9	W½NE	1881-09-17		A6
1633	MCARTHUR, Charles	4	SESE	1880-09-01		A6
1701	MCCORMICK, John F	25	SW	1870-09-10		A6
1691	MCCULLOUGH, James	2	E½SW	1881-09-17		A6
1605	MEAD, Welthy	13	SESW	1863-05-20		A5 G381
1606	" "	13	W½SE	1863-05-20		A5 G381
1647	MOORE, Ebenezer	6	W½NE	1873-01-10		A6 C
1607	MUDGE, William R	13	N½SW	1863-05-20		A5 G382
1608	" "	14	N½SE	1863-05-20		A5 G382
1644	NOBLE, David P	32	N½NE	1870-06-01		A2
1712	NOGLE, John	17	W½NE	1870-05-20		A6
1713	" "	8	W½SE	1870-05-20		A6
1714	NULPH, John	32	SW	1869-09-01		A6
1765	OMDAHL, Samuel	15	SW	1870-05-20		A6 G293
1765	OMDAHLE, Samuel	15	SW	1870-05-20		A6 G293
1680	OWEN, Henry U	15	SWNE	1922-06-10		A2
1766	PADDLEFORD, Samuel T	12	S½SE	1873-12-20		A6
1651	PAGE, Edwin	2	W½SW	1881-09-17		A6
1778	PARKER, Thomas	21	SE	1871-04-20		A6
1699	PEDERSEN, Johan L	24	E½SE	1889-02-16		A6
1663	PIERCE, Franklin	26	E½SE	1869-08-05		A2
1664	" "	35	E½NE	1869-08-05		A2
1695	PIERCE, Jefferson	26	E½NE	1873-05-20		A6
1755	PROPER, Perry B	17	SW	1878-06-24		A6
1681	ROACH, Henry W	26	NESW	1870-05-20		A6
1682	" "	26	SENW	1870-05-20		A6
1683	" "	26	W½NW	1870-05-20		A6
1741	ROACH, Mary A	26	W½SW	1863-04-20		A5
1697	SABIN, Joel	30	W½NW	1876-02-10		A6 F
1698	" "	30	W½SW	1876-02-10		A6 F
1731	SAHLIE, Lewis	12	NWSW	1891-11-09		A6
1732	" "	12	SWNW	1891-11-09		A6
1754	SAHLKE, Nicholas	10	NESE	1903-08-25		A6
1756	SHAFER, Peter	21	NW	1870-05-20		A6
1635	SHIELDS, Charles	22	W½SE	1877-02-20		A6
1764	SHIELDS, Samuel H	30	SE	1869-09-01		A6
1784	SLICK, William B	4	W½SW	1871-04-20		A6
1785	" "	5	E½SE	1871-04-20		A6
1601	STILES, Aaron K	10	NE	1863-05-20		A5
1603	" "	11	NW	1863-05-20		A5 G384
1607	" "	13	N½SW	1863-05-20		A5 G382
1605	" "	13	SESW	1863-05-20		A5 G381
1606	" "	13	W½SE	1863-05-20		A5 G381
1608	" "	14	N½SE	1863-05-20		A5 G382
1602	" "	24	NWNE	1863-07-01		A7
1604	" "	10	NW	1864-09-15		A5 G379
1609	STUDABAKER, Abraham W	17	N½NW	1869-09-01		A6
1610	" "	8	S½SW	1869-09-01		A6
1603	STURTEVANT, Ann L	11	NW	1863-05-20		A5 G384
1719	TAYLOR, Hiram H	36	S½SW	1860-10-01		A5 G214
1720	" "	36	W½SE	1860-10-01		A5 G214
1654	THAYER, Linus B	27	NW	1864-10-20		A5 G93
1648	THOMAS, Edmund H	7	SE	1871-08-25		A6
1614	TORKELSON, Amund	12	N½SE	1882-05-10		A6
1717	TUTTLE, John	7	W½NW	1873-05-20		A6 F
1716	TUTTLE, John P	26	NWSE	1871-08-25		A6
1724	UMBARGER, Joseph	30	SENW	1873-12-20		A6
1725	" "	30	SWNE	1873-12-20		A6

ID	Individual in Patent	Sec.	Sec. Part	Date Issued	Other Counties	For More Info . . .
1619	WAIT, Barton	24	NESW	1882-06-30		A6
1620	" "	24	SENW	1882-06-30		A6
1650	WEBSTER, Edward	18	E½SE	1876-03-10		A6
1637	WHEELER, Charles	28	W½NE	1872-10-01		A6
1773	WHEELER, Solon S	28	E½NE	1872-10-01		A6
1659	WHITE, Eugene B	18	SW	1870-06-10		A6 F
1742	WHITE, Miles	13	E½SE	1861-07-01		A5
1743	" "	13	SENE	1861-07-01		A5
1744	" "	24	NENE	1861-07-01		A5
1690	WILLIAMS, Mary	24	S½NE	1864-02-10		A7 G24
1665	WILSON, Frederick T	30	E½SW	1878-11-30		A6
1776	WILSON, Thomas B	36	1	1857-04-01		A2
1777	" "	36	2	1857-04-01		A2
1788	WILSON, William	25	E½NE	1860-07-16		A5
1789	" "	25	E½SE	1860-07-16		A5
1790	" "	36	NENE	1860-07-16		A5 G424
1791	" "	36	W½NE	1860-07-16		A5 G424
1774	WISCONSIN, State Of	16		1941-08-16		A3
1611	WOODS, Alexander	14	NE	1871-08-25		A6
1684	WOODS, Henry W	10	SESE	1870-05-20		A6
1685	" "	11	SWSW	1870-05-20		A6
1686	" "	15	E½NE	1870-05-20		A6
1692	WOODS, James	10	SESW	1870-06-10		A6
1693	" "	10	W½SE	1870-06-10		A6
1694	" "	15	NWNE	1870-06-10		A6

Patent Map

T29-N R13-W
4th PM - 1831 MN/WI Meridian

Map Group 10

Township Statistics

Parcels Mapped	:	193
Number of Patents	:	132
Number of Individuals	:	138
Patentees Identified	:	128
Number of Surnames	:	107
Multi-Patentee Parcels	:	15
Oldest Patent Date	:	4/1/1857
Most Recent Patent	:	8/16/1941
Block/Lot Parcels	:	2
Parcels Re - Issued	:	0
Parcels that Overlap	:	0
Cities and Towns	:	0
Cemeteries	:	1

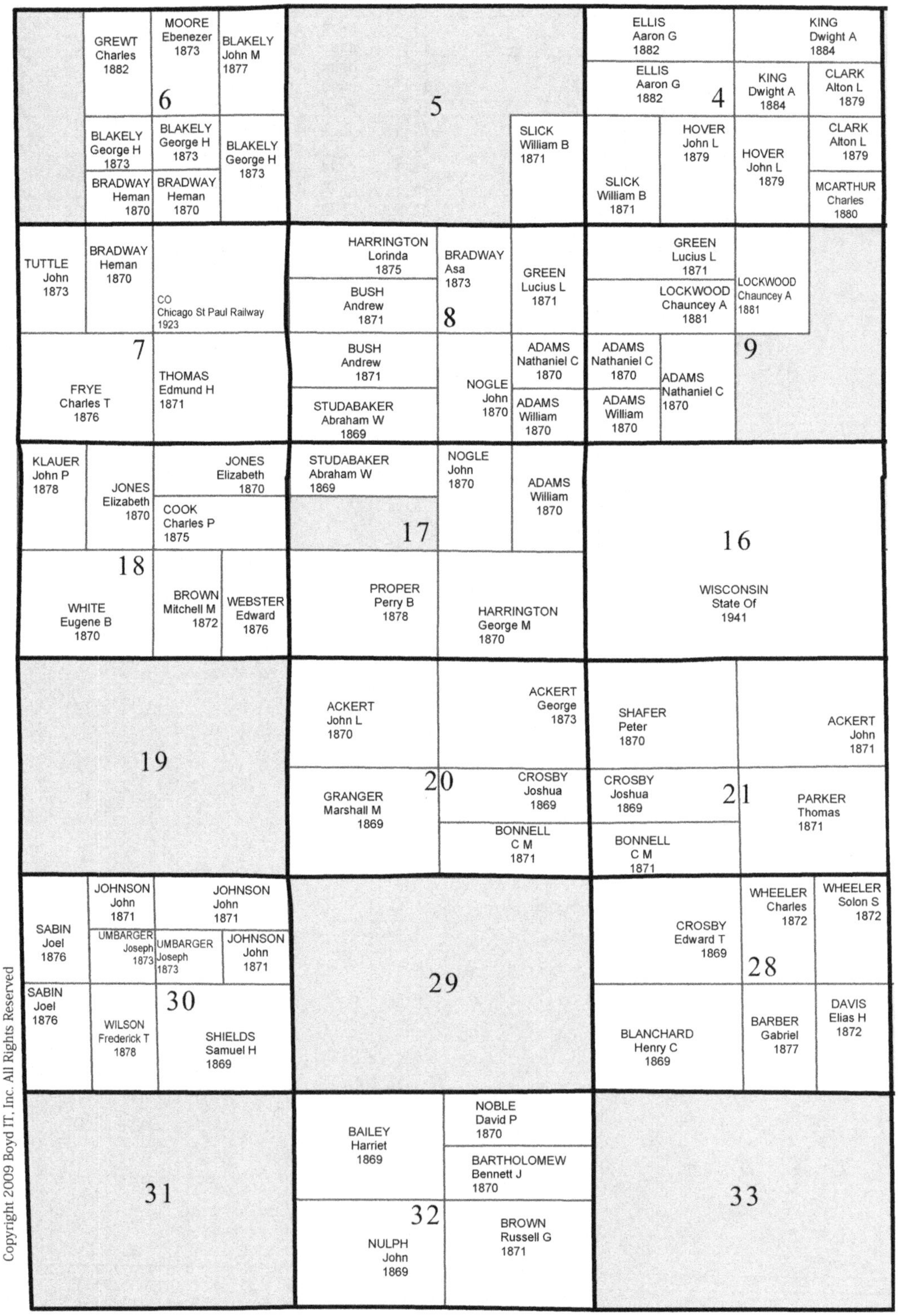
GREWT Charles 1882
MOORE Ebenezer 1873
BLAKELY John M 1877
6
BLAKELY George H 1873
BLAKELY George H 1873
BLAKELY George H 1873
BRADWAY Heman 1870
BRADWAY Heman 1870
5
ELLIS Aaron G 1882
KING Dwight A 1884
ELLIS Aaron G 1882
4
KING Dwight A 1884
CLARK Alton L 1879
SLICK William B 1871
HOVER John L 1879
HOVER John L 1879
CLARK Alton L 1879
SLICK William B 1871
MCARTHUR Charles 1880
TUTTLE John 1873
BRADWAY Heman 1870
CO Chicago St Paul Railway 1923
7
FRYE Charles T 1876
THOMAS Edmund H 1871
HARRINGTON Lorinda 1875
BRADWAY Asa 1873
GREEN Lucius L 1871
BUSH Andrew 1871
8
BUSH Andrew 1871
STUDABAKER Abraham W 1869
NOGLE John 1870
ADAMS Nathaniel C 1870
ADAMS William 1870
GREEN Lucius L 1871
LOCKWOOD Chauncey A 1881
LOCKWOOD Chauncey A 1881
ADAMS Nathaniel C 1870
ADAMS Nathaniel C 1870
ADAMS William 1870
9
KLAUER John P 1878
JONES Elizabeth 1870
JONES Elizabeth 1870
COOK Charles P 1875
18
WHITE Eugene B 1870
BROWN Mitchell M 1872
WEBSTER Edward 1876
STUDABAKER Abraham W 1869
NOGLE John 1870
ADAMS William 1870
17
PROPER Perry B 1878
HARRINGTON George M 1870
16
WISCONSIN State Of 1941
19
ACKERT John L 1870
ACKERT George 1873
20
GRANGER Marshall M 1869
CROSBY Joshua 1869
BONNELL C M 1871
SHAFER Peter 1870
ACKERT John 1871
CROSBY Joshua 1869
21
PARKER Thomas 1871
BONNELL C M 1871
SABIN Joel 1876
JOHNSON John 1871
JOHNSON John 1871
UMBARGER Joseph 1873
UMBARGER Joseph 1873
JOHNSON John 1871
SABIN Joel 1876
WILSON Frederick T 1878
30
SHIELDS Samuel H 1869
29
CROSBY Edward T 1869
WHEELER Charles 1872
WHEELER Solon S 1872
28
BLANCHARD Henry C 1869
BARBER Gabriel 1877
DAVIS Elias H 1872
31
BAILEY Harriet 1869
NOBLE David P 1870
BARTHOLOMEW Bennett J 1870
32
NULPH John 1869
BROWN Russell G 1871
33

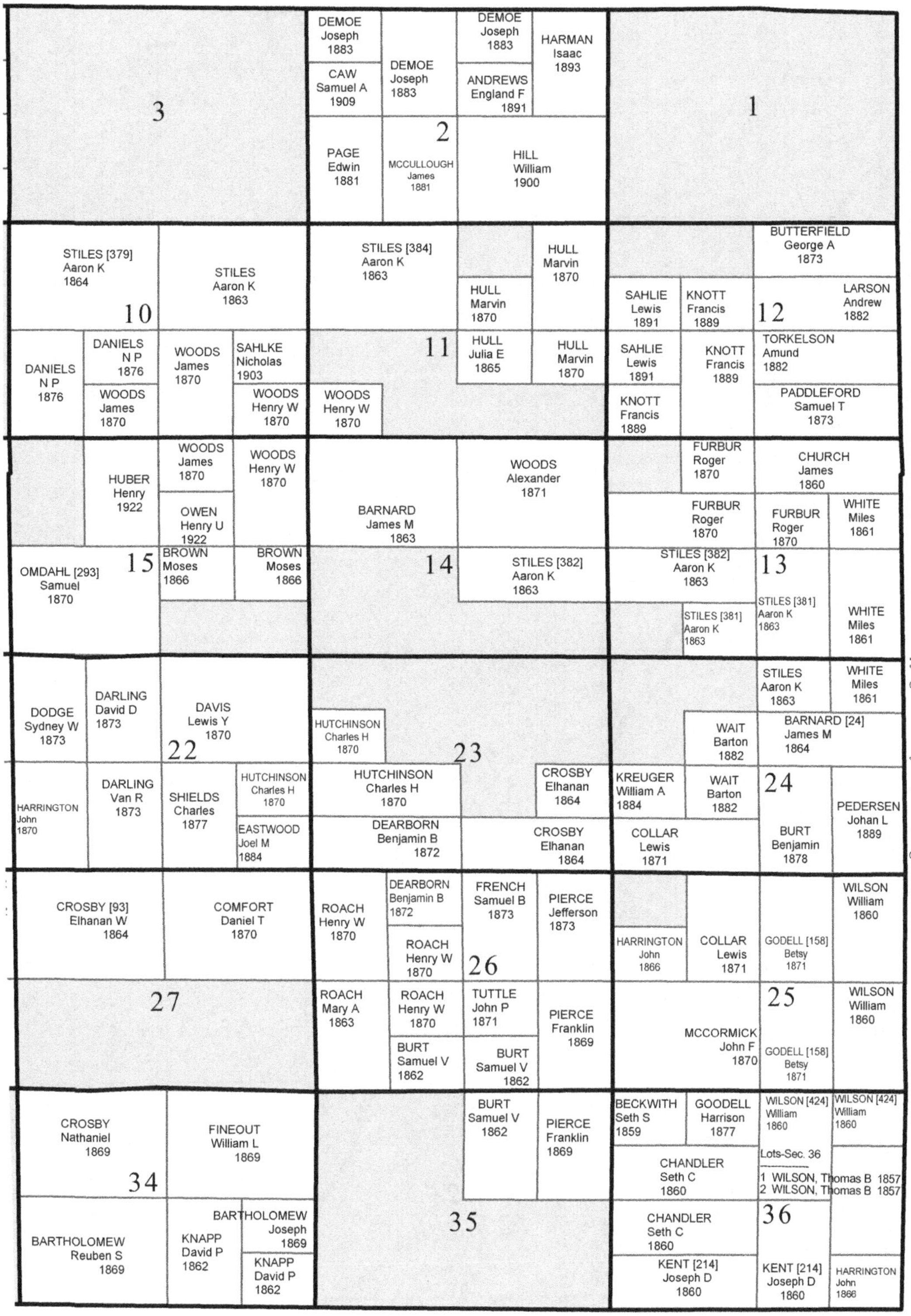

3
DEMOE Joseph 1883
CAW Samuel A 1909
DEMOE Joseph 1883
DEMOE Joseph 1883
ANDREWS England F 1891
HARMAN Isaac 1893
2
PAGE Edwin 1881
MCCULLOUGH James 1881
HILL William 1900
1
STILES [379] Aaron K 1864
10
STILES Aaron K 1863
STILES [384] Aaron K 1863
HULL Marvin 1870
HULL Marvin 1870
BUTTERFIELD George A 1873
SAHLIE Lewis 1891
KNOTT Francis 1889
12
LARSON Andrew 1882
DANIELS N P 1876
DANIELS N P 1876
WOODS James 1870
SAHLKE Nicholas 1903
11
HULL Julia E 1865
HULL Marvin 1870
SAHLIE Lewis 1891
KNOTT Francis 1889
TORKELSON Amund 1882
WOODS James 1870
WOODS Henry W 1870
WOODS Henry W 1870
KNOTT Francis 1889
PADDLEFORD Samuel T 1873
HUBER Henry 1922
WOODS James 1870
WOODS Henry W 1870
OWEN Henry U 1922
WOODS Alexander 1871
BARNARD James M 1863
FURBUR Roger 1870
CHURCH James 1860
FURBUR Roger 1870
FURBUR Roger 1870
WHITE Miles 1861
OMDAHL [293] Samuel 1870
15
BROWN Moses 1866
BROWN Moses 1866
14
STILES [382] Aaron K 1863
STILES [382] Aaron K 1863
13
STILES [381] Aaron K 1863
STILES [381] Aaron K 1863
WHITE Miles 1861
DODGE Sydney W 1873
DARLING David D 1873
DAVIS Lewis Y 1870
22
HUTCHINSON Charles H 1870
23
STILES Aaron K 1863
WHITE Miles 1861
WAIT Barton 1882
BARNARD [24] James M 1864
HARRINGTON John 1870
DARLING Van R 1873
SHIELDS Charles 1877
HUTCHINSON Charles H 1870
EASTWOOD Joel M 1884
HUTCHINSON Charles H 1870
DEARBORN Benjamin B 1872
CROSBY Elhanan 1864
CROSBY Elhanan 1864
KREUGER William A 1884
WAIT Barton 1882
24
COLLAR Lewis 1871
BURT Benjamin 1878
PEDERSEN Johan L 1889
CROSBY [93] Elhanan W 1864
COMFORT Daniel T 1870
ROACH Henry W 1870
DEARBORN Benjamin B 1872
ROACH Henry W 1870
FRENCH Samuel B 1873
26
PIERCE Jefferson 1873
HARRINGTON John 1866
COLLAR Lewis 1871
GODELL [158] Betsy 1871
WILSON William 1860
27
ROACH Mary A 1863
ROACH Henry W 1870
TUTTLE John P 1871
BURT Samuel V 1862
BURT Samuel V 1862
PIERCE Franklin 1869
MCCORMICK John F 1870
25
GODELL [158] Betsy 1871
WILSON William 1860
CROSBY Nathaniel 1869
34
FINEOUT William L 1869
BURT Samuel V 1862
PIERCE Franklin 1869
BECKWITH Seth S 1859
GOODELL Harrison 1877
WILSON [424] William 1860
WILSON [424] William 1860
CHANDLER Seth C 1860
Lots-Sec. 36
1 WILSON, Thomas B 1857
2 WILSON, Thomas B 1857
BARTHOLOMEW Reuben S 1869
KNAPP David P 1862
BARTHOLOMEW Joseph 1869
KNAPP David P 1862
35
CHANDLER Seth C 1860
36
KENT [214] Joseph D 1860
KENT [214] Joseph D 1860
HARRINGTON John 1866

Helpful Hints

1. This Map's INDEX can be found on the preceding pages.
2. Refer to Map "C" to see where this Township lies within Dunn County, Wisconsin.
3. Numbers within square brackets [ ] denote a multi-patentee land parcel (multi-owner). Refer to Appendix "C" for a full list of members in this group.
4. Areas that look to be crowded with Patentees usually indicate multiple sales of the same parcel (Re-issues) or Overlapping parcels. See this Township's Index for an explanation of these and other circumstances that might explain "odd" groupings of Patentees on this map.

Legend

- Patent Boundary
- Section Boundary
- No Patents Found (or Outside County)
- 1., 2., 3., ... Lot Numbers (when beside a name)
- [ ] Group Number (see Appendix "C")

Scale: Section = 1 mile X 1 mile (generally, with some exceptions)

Road Map

T29-N R13-W
4th PM - 1831 MN/WI Meridian

Map Group 10

Cities & Towns

None

Cemeteries

Sherman Cemetery

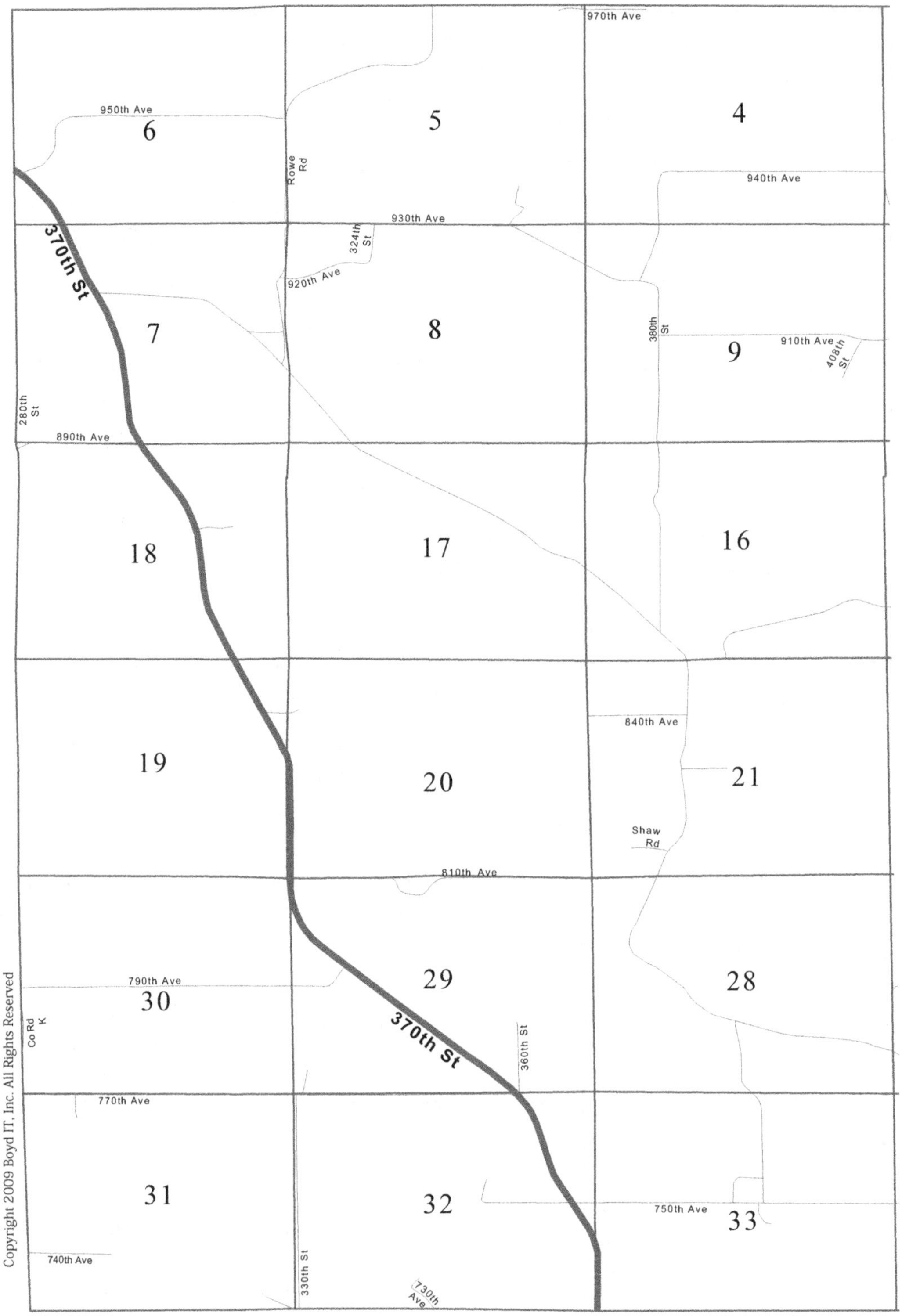

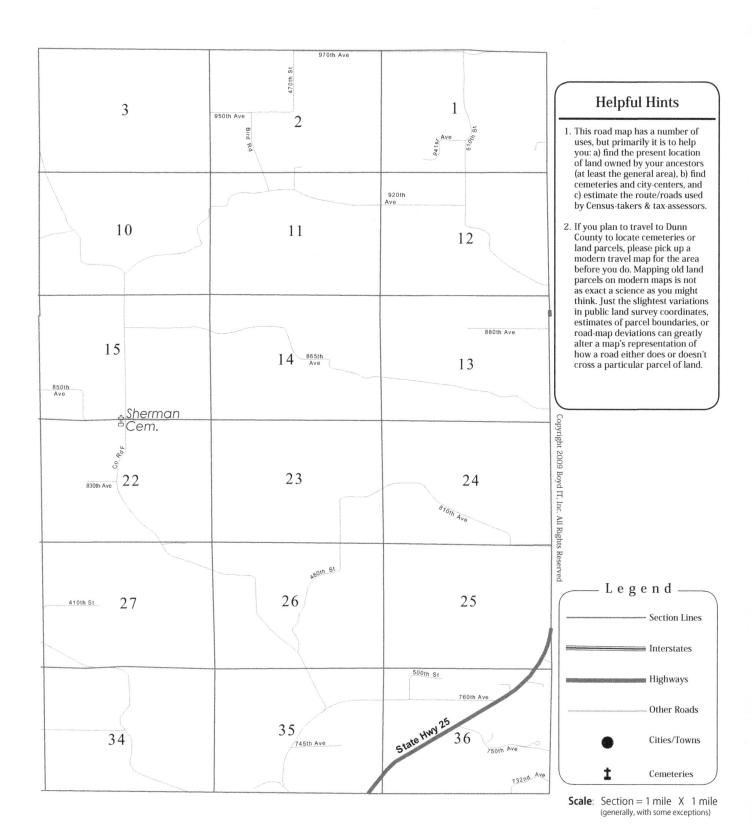

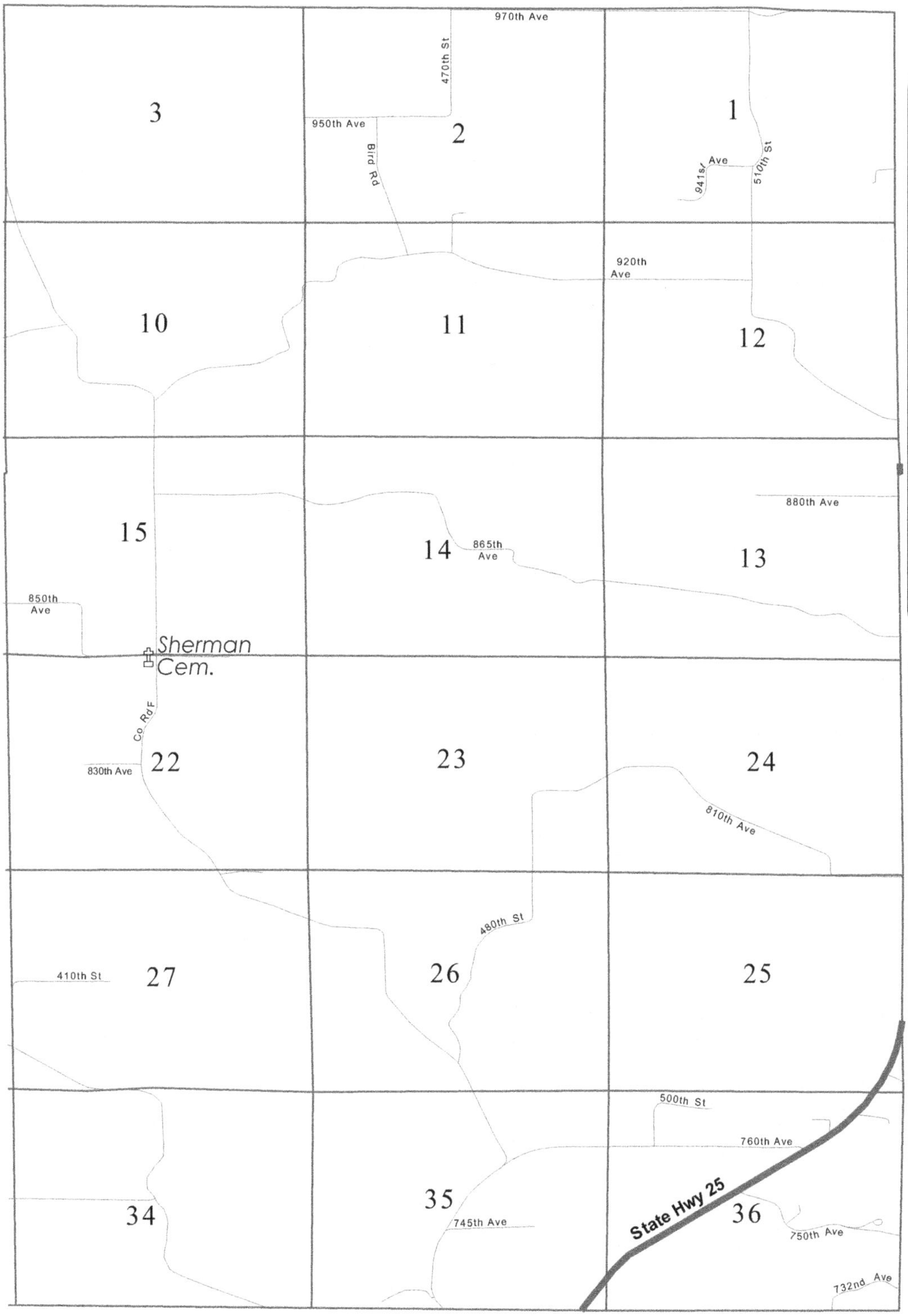

Helpful Hints

1. This road map has a number of uses, but primarily it is to help you: a) find the present location of land owned by your ancestors (at least the general area), b) find cemeteries and city-centers, and c) estimate the route/roads used by Census-takers & tax-assessors.
2. If you plan to travel to Dunn County to locate cemeteries or land parcels, please pick up a modern travel map for the area before you do. Mapping old land parcels on modern maps is not as exact a science as you might think. Just the slightest variations in public land survey coordinates, estimates of parcel boundaries, or road-map deviations can greatly alter a map's representation of how a road either does or doesn't cross a particular parcel of land.

Legend

- Section Lines
- Interstates
- Highways
- Other Roads
- Cities/Towns
- Cemeteries

Scale: Section = 1 mile X 1 mile
(generally, with some exceptions)

Historical Map

T29-N R13-W
4th PM - 1831 MN/WI Meridian

Map Group 10

Cities & Towns

None

Cemeteries

Sherman Cemetery

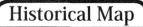

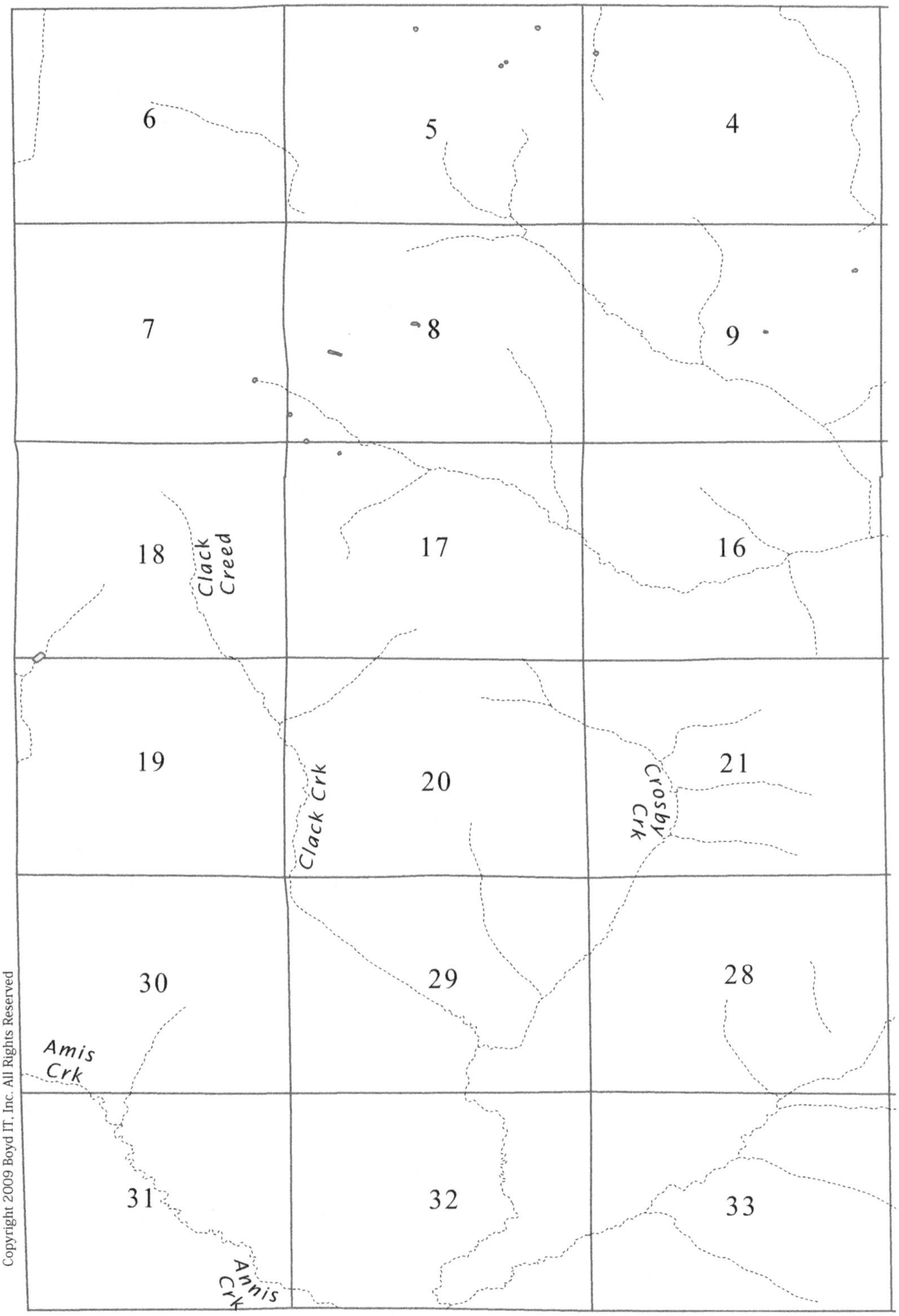

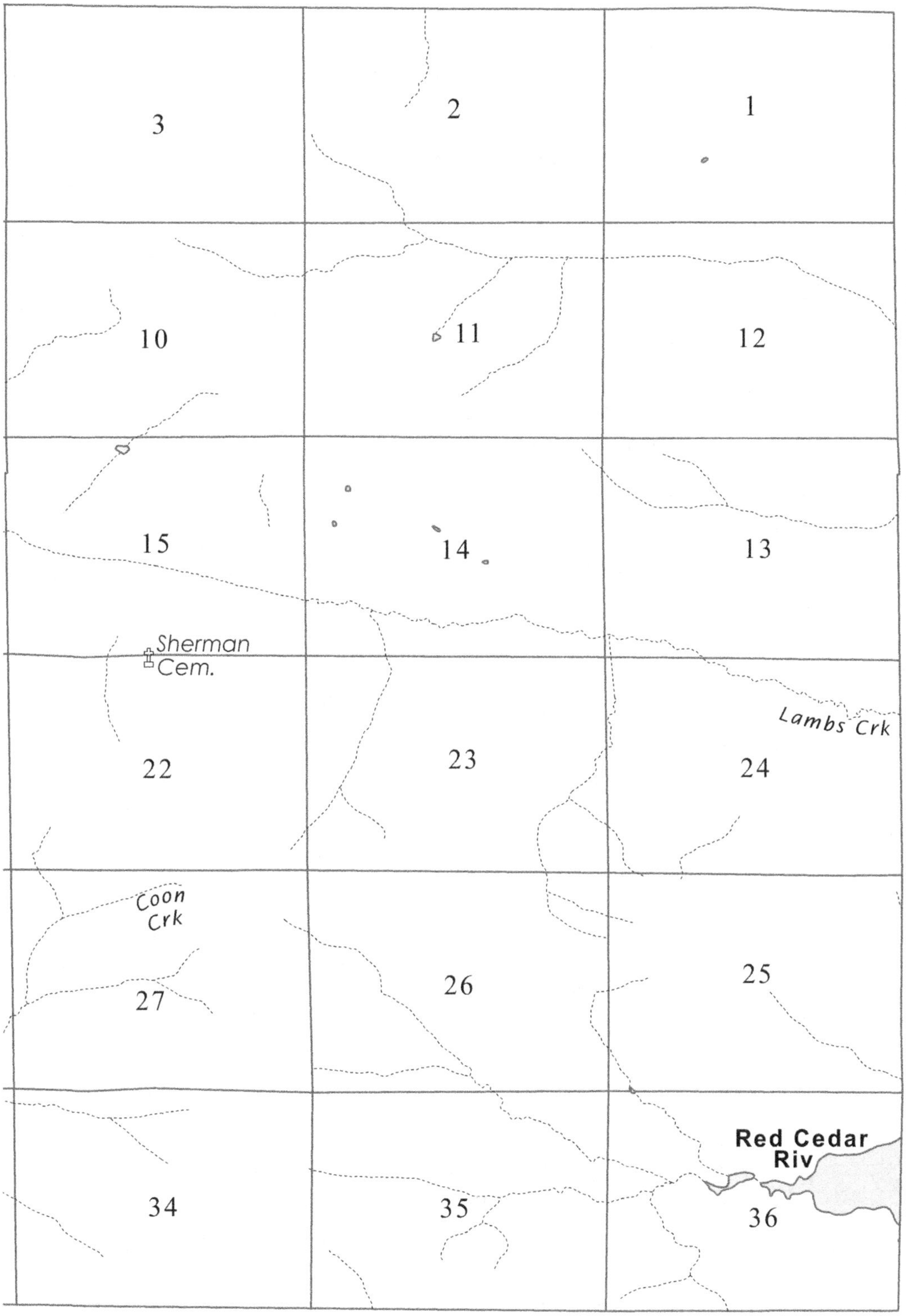

Helpful Hints

1. This Map takes a different look at the same Congressional Township displayed in the preceding two maps. It presents features that can help you better envision the historical development of the area: a) Water-bodies (lakes & ponds), b) Water-courses (rivers, streams, etc.), c) Railroads, d) City/town center-points (where they were oftentimes located when first settled), and e) Cemeteries.
2. Using this "Historical" map in tandem with this Township's Patent Map and Road Map, may lead you to some interesting discoveries. You will often find roads, towns, cemeteries, and waterways are named after nearby landowners: sometimes those names will be the ones you are researching. See how many of these research gems you can find here in Dunn County.

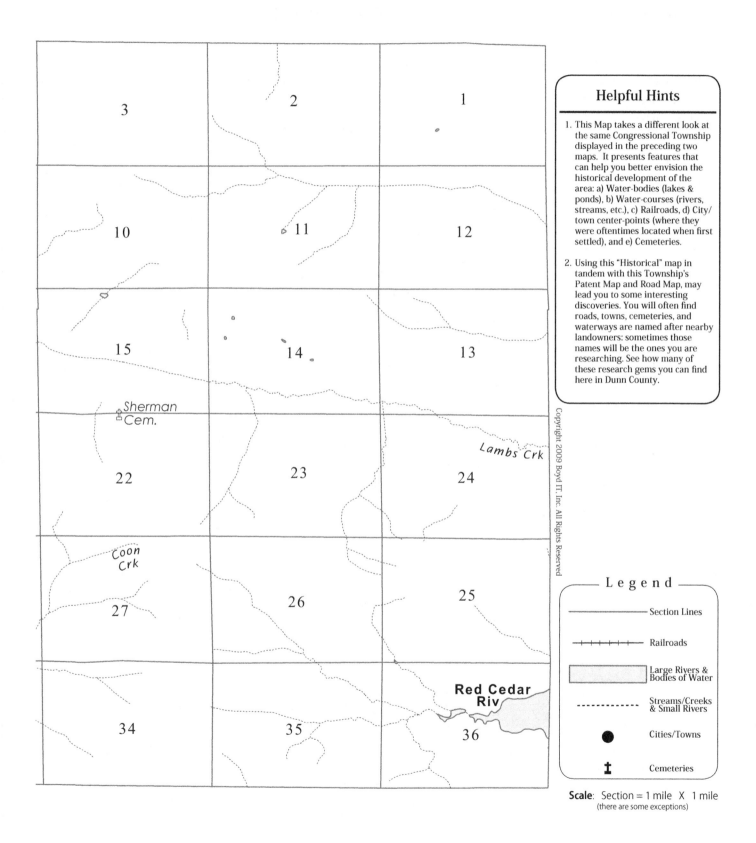

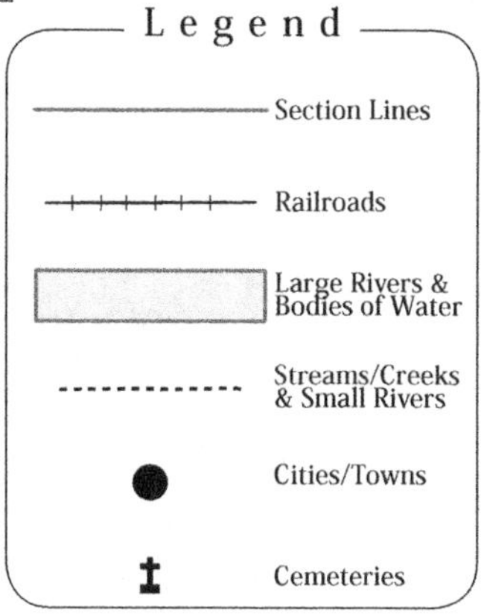
Legend
Section Lines
Railroads
Large Rivers & Bodies of Water
Streams/Creeks & Small Rivers
Cities/Towns
Cemeteries

Scale: Section = 1 mile X 1 mile
(there are some exceptions)

Map Group 11: Index to Land Patents

Township 29-North Range 12-West (4th PM - 1831 MN/WI)

After you locate an individual in this Index, take note of the Section and Section Part then proceed to the Land Patent map on the pages immediately following. You should have no difficulty locating the corresponding parcel of land.

The "For More Info" Column will lead you to more information about the underlying Patents. See the *Legend* at right, and the "How to Use this Book" chapter, for more information.

LEGEND

"For More Info . . . " column

A = Authority (Legislative Act, See Appendix "A")
B = Block or Lot (location in Section unknown)
C = Cancelled Patent
F = Fractional Section
G = Group (Multi-Patentee Patent, see Appendix "C")
V = Overlaps another Parcel
R = Re-Issued (Parcel patented more than once)

(A & G items require you to look in the Appendixes referred to above. All other Letter-designations followed by a number require you to locate line-items in this index that possess the ID number found after the letter).

ID	Individual in Patent	Sec.	Sec. Part	Date Issued	Other Counties	For More Info . . .
1821	AUKNEY, Eugene	8	W½SW	1880-09-01		A6
1860	BAKER, Lemuel	2	S½SE	1882-04-10		A6
1861	" "	2	S½SW	1882-04-10		A6
1884	BARNARD, George M	24	NE	1861-02-01		A5 G26
1884	BARNARD, Susan L	24	NE	1861-02-01		A5 G26
1870	BATCHELDER, P B	6	NENW	1884-01-15		A6 F
1855	BEALE, Mary E	25	SE	1860-10-01		A5 G343
1838	BEATTIE, James	8	W½NW	1880-11-01		A6
1877	BLODGETT, Sarah	30	NENW	1889-02-16		A6
1878	" "	30	NWNE	1889-02-16		A6
1884	BRADFORD, Lucinda	24	NE	1861-02-01		A5 G26
1896	BREEZEE, William H	14	8	1906-06-30		A6
1897	" "	14	9	1906-06-30		A6
1800	BRYANT, Jemima	20	8	1860-10-01		A5 G276
1801	" "	20	9	1860-10-01		A5 G276
1832	BUCKLEY, Henry L	18	SENW	1935-08-13		A2
1829	BUTTERFIELD, George A	6	W½NW	1873-09-20		A6
1839	CHURCH, James	18	SW	1860-08-01		A5
1859	COMPANY, Knapp Stout And	20	10	1885-07-27		A2
1865	CONE, Nancy E	36	S½NE	1898-02-09		A6 G83
1865	CONE, Simon C	36	S½NE	1898-02-09		A6 G83
1809	COOK, Charles	36	W½SE	1881-02-10		A6
1856	COOMBS, Joseph	8	SESW	1882-04-10		A6
1857	" "	8	SWSE	1882-04-10		A6
1875	DAVIS, Sarah A	4	SESW	1875-05-10		A2
1876	" "	4	SWSE	1875-05-10		A2
1811	DOWNER, Chester	25	NW	1860-07-16		A5 G113
1822	EATON, Eugene	10	E½SE	1891-11-09		A6
1879	EYTCHESON, Spencer T	2	S½NE	1882-04-10		A6
1880	" "	2	S½NW	1882-04-10		A6
1891	EYTCHESON, W J	2	N½SE	1880-09-01		A6
1892	" "	2	N½SW	1880-09-01		A6
1793	FERGUSON, Amsterd G	12	1	1860-08-20		A6
1794	" "	12	2	1860-08-20		A6
1810	FINEOUT, Charles E	30	W½NW	1882-06-01		A6 F
1873	FRENCH, S B	34	SESE	1873-06-20		A2
1847	HALVORSON, Jens	10	N½NE	1880-11-01		A6
1824	HANKE, Ferdinand	36	W½NW	1883-02-10		A6
1862	HARRINGTON, Mary	4	3	1904-08-26		A6 G180 F
1889	HARRINGTON, W C	18	SE	1871-04-20		A6 R1890
1889	" "	18	SE	1871-04-20		A6 C R1890
1890	" "	18	SE	1871-04-20		A6 R1889
1890	" "	18	SE	1871-04-20		A6 C R1889
1899	HARRINGTON, William W	10	W½NW	1880-05-15		A6
1900	" "	10	W½SW	1880-05-15		A6
1802	HARRISON, Joseph	27	N½NE	1860-10-01		A5 G277

ID	Individual in Patent	Sec.	Sec. Part	Date Issued	Other Counties	For More Info . . .
1871	HAYNES, Richmon W	2	N½NE	1883-02-10		A6 F
1872	" "	2	N½NW	1883-02-10		A6 F
1842	HILL, Charles	15	3	1864-02-01		A2 G255
1842	HILL, John	15	3	1864-02-01		A2 G255
1833	HUTCHINSON, Herbert C	4	NWSE	1882-05-10		A6
1818	IVERSON, Engebret	14	6	1883-02-10		A6
1819	" "	14	7	1883-02-10		A6
1820	" "	14	NWNW	1883-02-10		A6
1834	JOHNSON, Ingebor	4	E½SE	1882-06-01		A6
1835	" "	4	SENE	1882-06-01		A6
1836	" "	4	NENE	1883-07-10		A6 G207 F
1836	JOHNSON, Peter	4	NENE	1883-07-10		A6 G207 F
1805	KOHN, August	36	E½SW	1880-05-15		A6
1887	LEACH, Thomas A	12	E½NW	1879-10-01		A6
1888	" "	12	N½NE	1879-10-01		A6
1826	LOUSTED, Frederick	36	E½NW	1880-09-01		A6
1813	LOWERY, Edward	36	N½NE	1883-02-10		A6
1843	LOWRY, James	13	3	1872-09-25		A6
1844	" "	13	E½SE	1872-09-25		A6
1845	" "	13	SWSE	1872-09-25		A6
1804	MALHUS, Arnold	4	1	1956-07-02		A1 G248
1863	MARTIN, Mary J	12	3	1883-07-10		A6
1864	" "	12	SESE	1883-07-10		A6
1803	MATHEWS, Andrew T	14	NESW	1882-03-30		A2
1840	MATTHEWS, Andrew T	14	2	1866-09-01		A5 G256
1841	" "	14	3	1866-09-01		A5 G256
1842	MATTHEWS, James E	15	3	1864-02-01		A2 G255
1840	" "	14	2	1866-09-01		A5 G256
1841	" "	14	3	1866-09-01		A5 G256
1846	MCELWAIN, James	14	4	1878-06-01		A2
1812	MCLENNAN, Duncan	26	SESE	1882-09-30		A2
1885	MOE, Sylvester	4	N½NW	1880-09-01		A6 F
1886	" "	4	W½NE	1880-09-01		A6 F
1795	MOORE, Andrew	20	1	1860-06-01		A2
1796	" "	20	2	1860-06-01		A2
1797	" "	20	6	1860-10-01		A5
1798	" "	20	7	1860-10-01		A5
1800	" "	20	8	1860-10-01		A5 G276
1801	" "	20	9	1860-10-01		A5 G276
1799	" "	24	SE	1860-10-01		A5
1802	" "	27	N½NE	1860-10-01		A5 G277
1792	MORGAN, Alphonzo	18	N½NE	1882-06-01		A6
1808	MORGAN, Avery	18	S½NE	1882-06-30		A6
1898	MORGAN, William	6	S½SE	1883-07-10		A6
1866	NEWELL, Noah	28	S½	1855-12-15		A2
1867	" "	32	SE	1855-12-15		A2
1868	" "	33	NE	1855-12-15		A2
1814	NEWHALL, Elbridge G	32	NE	1855-12-15		A2
1908	NEWHALL, Wright	33	NW	1855-12-15		A2
1893	NEWMAN, Washington	10	E½NW	1877-02-20		A6
1894	" "	10	S½NE	1877-02-20		A6
1811	NYE, Clarissa	25	NW	1860-07-16		A5 G113
1862	OLESON, Mary	4	3	1904-08-26		A6 G180 F
1874	PADDLEFORD, Samuel T	18	W½NW	1873-04-01		A6
1854	PAINE, Mary A	19	NE	1860-10-01		A5 G344
1806	PRIRCE, Augustus H	10	E½SW	1877-07-02		A6
1807	" "	10	W½SE	1877-07-02		A6
1848	RITTENHOUSE, John B	17	NWSW	1860-10-01		A5
1849	" "	17	S½SW	1860-10-01		A5
1850	" "	19	E½SW	1860-10-01		A5
1854	" "	19	NE	1860-10-01		A5 G344
1851	" "	19	W½SE	1860-10-01		A5
1852	" "	20	NWNW	1860-10-01		A5
1855	" "	25	SE	1860-10-01		A5 G343
1853	" "	25	NE	1862-03-10		A5 G345
1823	ROSWELL, Eugene	12	W½NW	1882-04-10		A6
1804	SCHROEDER, Lawrence	4	1	1956-07-02		A1 G248
1830	SOPER, George C	20	SWNW	1881-02-10		A6
1831	" "	20	W½SW	1881-02-10		A6
1895	SUCKOW, Wilhelm	36	W½SW	1881-02-10		A6
1815	THUE, Elling P	4	2	1882-04-10		A6
1816	" "	4	NESW	1882-04-10		A6
1817	" "	4	S½NW	1882-04-10		A6

ID	Individual in Patent	Sec.	Sec. Part	Date Issued	Other Counties	For More Info . . .
1837	WEIMAN, J C	6	SENW	1874-05-06		A2
1858	WIEMAN, Julius C	8	E½SE	1872-10-01		A6
1827	WIEMANN, Frederick	8	NESW	1874-04-01		A6
1828	" "	8	NWSE	1874-04-01		A6
1853	WILSON, Elizabeth A	25	NE	1862-03-10		A5 G345
1904	WILSON, William	30	5	1859-12-10		A2
1901	" "	19	NW	1860-07-16		A5
1902	" "	30	3	1860-07-16		A5
1903	" "	30	4	1860-07-16		A5
1905	" "	30	SENW	1860-07-16		A5
1906	" "	30	SWNE	1860-07-16		A5
1907	" "	30	W½SW	1860-07-16		A5
1881	WISCONSIN, State Of	16		1941-08-16		A3
1882	WOOD, Stephen S	12	N½SE	1878-06-24		A6
1883	" "	12	S½NE	1878-06-24		A6
1884	WYMAN, Asa	24	NE	1861-02-01		A5 G26
1869	YAPLE, Oscar	21	1	1859-12-10		A2
1825	ZUEHLKE, Ferdinand	36	E½SE	1893-03-27		A6

Patent Map

T29-N R12-W
4th PM - 1831 MN/WI Meridian

Map Group 11

Township Statistics

Parcels Mapped	:	117
Number of Patents	:	82
Number of Individuals	:	82
Patentees Identified	:	73
Number of Surnames	:	70
Multi-Patentee Parcels	:	15
Oldest Patent Date	:	12/15/1855
Most Recent Patent	:	7/2/1956
Block/Lot Parcels	:	26
Parcels Re - Issued	:	1
Parcels that Overlap	:	0
Cities and Towns	:	2
Cemeteries	:	0

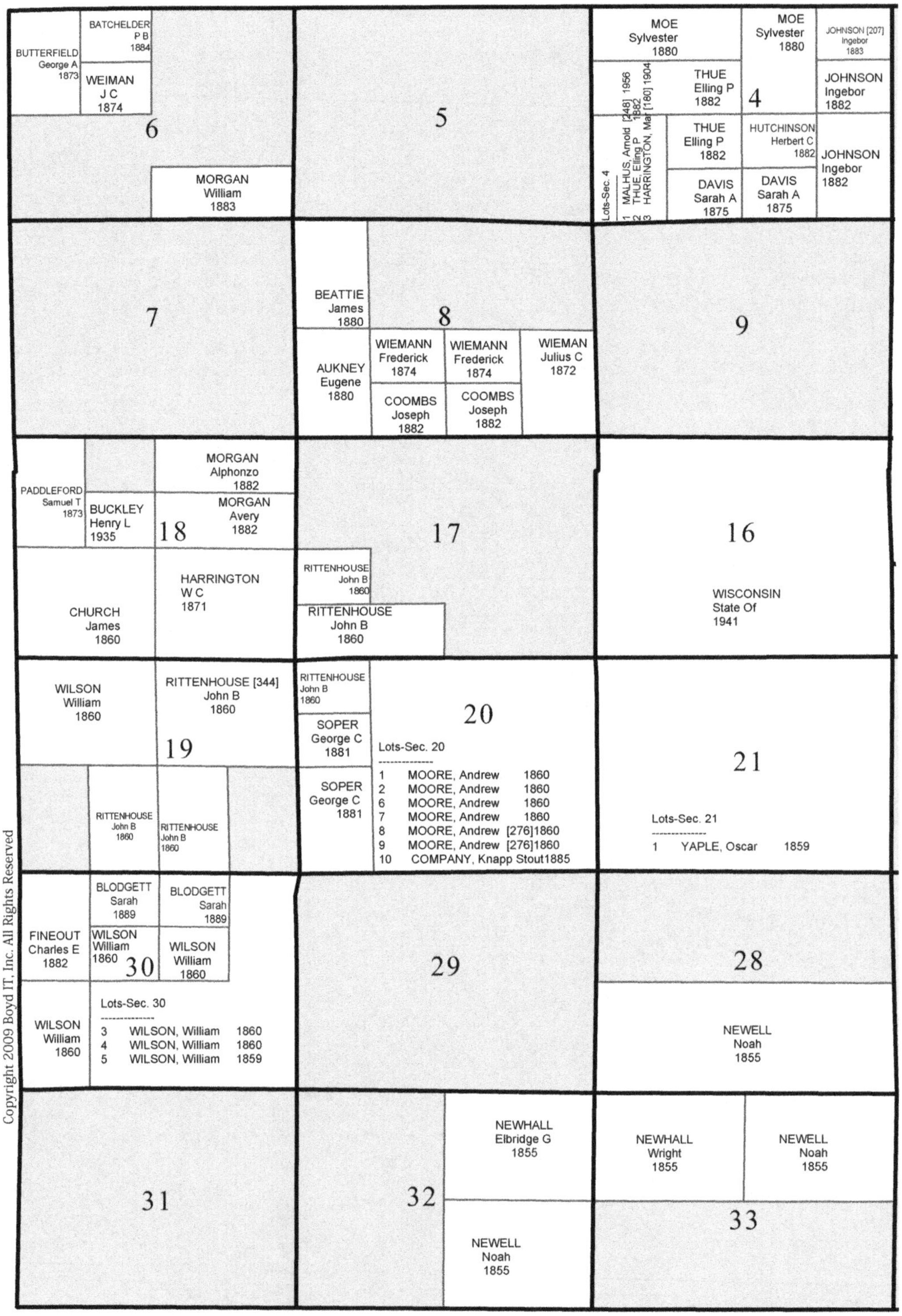

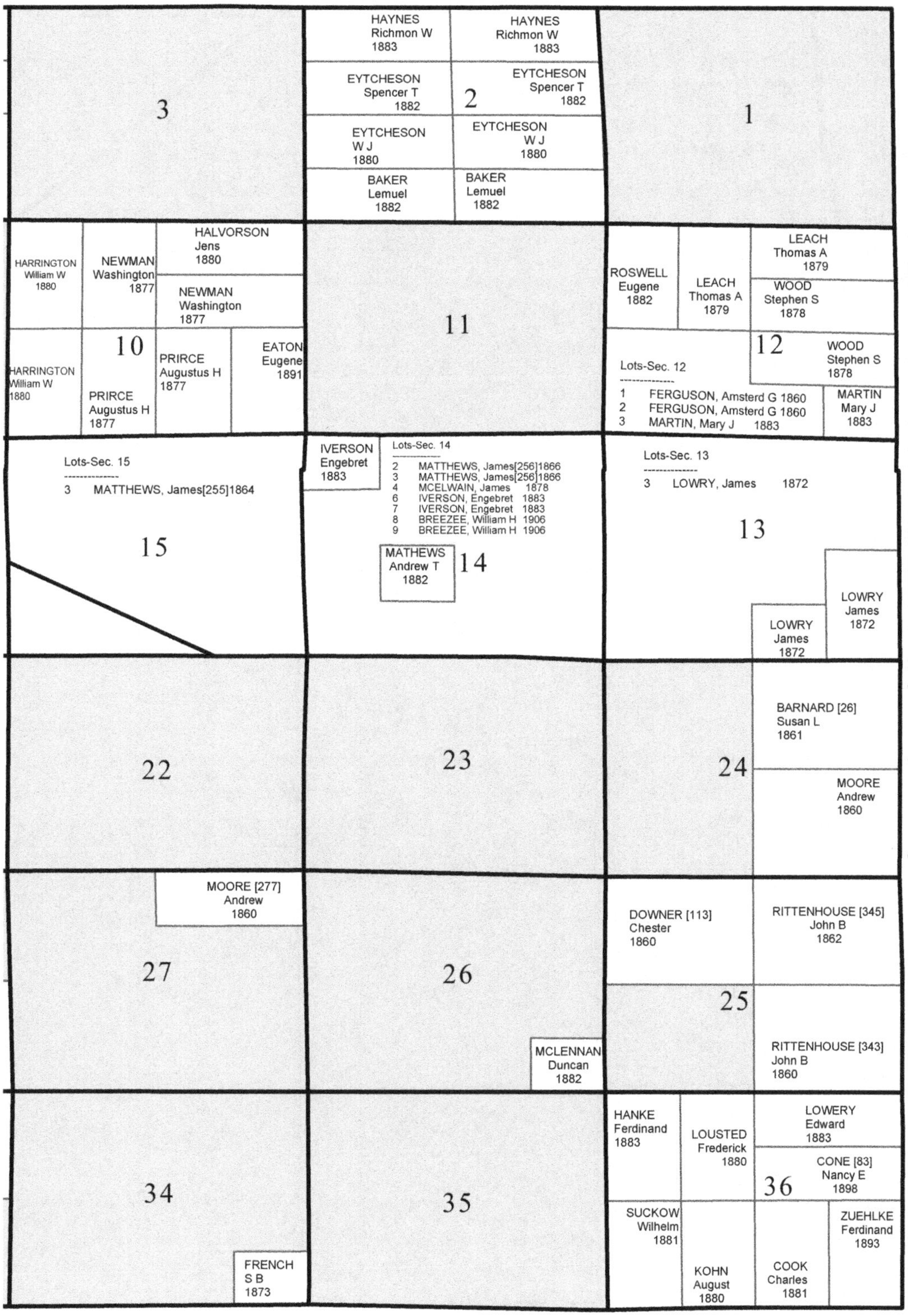
3
HAYNES Richmon W 1883
HAYNES Richmon W 1883
EYTCHESON Spencer T 1882
2
EYTCHESON Spencer T 1882
EYTCHESON W J 1880
EYTCHESON W J 1880
BAKER Lemuel 1882
BAKER Lemuel 1882
1
HARRINGTON William W 1880
NEWMAN Washington 1877
HALVORSON Jens 1880
NEWMAN Washington 1877
10
HARRINGTON William W 1880
PRIRCE Augustus H 1877
PRIRCE Augustus H 1877
EATON Eugene 1891
11
ROSWELL Eugene 1882
LEACH Thomas A 1879
LEACH Thomas A 1879
WOOD Stephen S 1878
12
WOOD Stephen S 1878
Lots-Sec. 12
1 FERGUSON, Amsterd G 1860
2 FERGUSON, Amsterd G 1860
3 MARTIN, Mary J 1883
MARTIN Mary J 1883
Lots-Sec. 15
3 MATTHEWS, James[255]1864
15
IVERSON Engebret 1883
Lots-Sec. 14
2 MATTHEWS, James[256]1866
3 MATTHEWS, James[256]1866
4 MCELWAIN, James 1878
6 IVERSON, Engebret 1883
7 IVERSON, Engebret 1883
8 BREEZEE, William H 1906
9 BREEZEE, William H 1906
MATHEWS Andrew T 1882
14
Lots-Sec. 13
3 LOWRY, James 1872
13
LOWRY James 1872
LOWRY James 1872
22
23
24
BARNARD [26] Susan L 1861
MOORE Andrew 1860
MOORE [277] Andrew 1860
27
26
DOWNER [113] Chester 1860
RITTENHOUSE [345] John B 1862
25
MCLENNAN Duncan 1882
RITTENHOUSE [343] John B 1860
34
35
HANKE Ferdinand 1883
LOUSTED Frederick 1880
LOWERY Edward 1883
CONE [83] Nancy E 1898
36
SUCKOW Wilhelm 1881
ZUEHLKE Ferdinand 1893
FRENCH S B 1873
KOHN August 1880
COOK Charles 1881

Helpful Hints

1. This Map's INDEX can be found on the preceding pages.
2. Refer to Map "C" to see where this Township lies within Dunn County, Wisconsin.
3. Numbers within square brackets [ ] denote a multi-patentee land parcel (multi-owner). Refer to Appendix "C" for a full list of members in this group.
4. Areas that look to be crowded with Patentees usually indicate multiple sales of the same parcel (Re-issues) or Overlapping parcels. See this Township's Index for an explanation of these and other circumstances that might explain "odd" groupings of Patentees on this map.

Legend

———	Patent Boundary
▬▬▬	Section Boundary
(shaded)	No Patents Found (or Outside County)
1., 2., 3., ...	Lot Numbers (when beside a name)
[ ]	Group Number (see Appendix "C")

Scale: Section = 1 mile X 1 mile (generally, with some exceptions)

Road Map

T29-N R12-W
4th PM - 1831 MN/WI Meridian

Map Group 11

Cities & Towns

Norton
Tainter Lake

Cemeteries

None

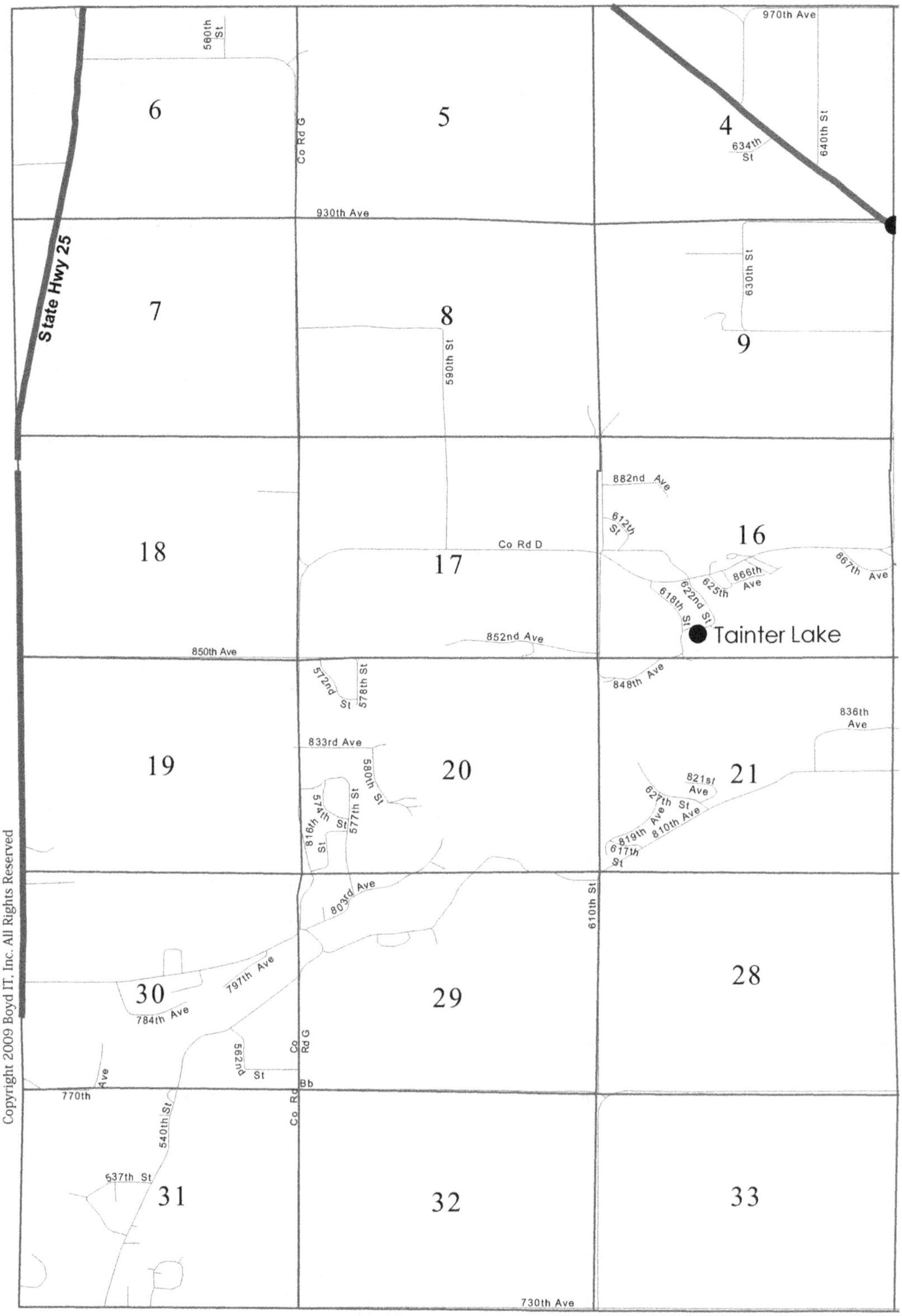

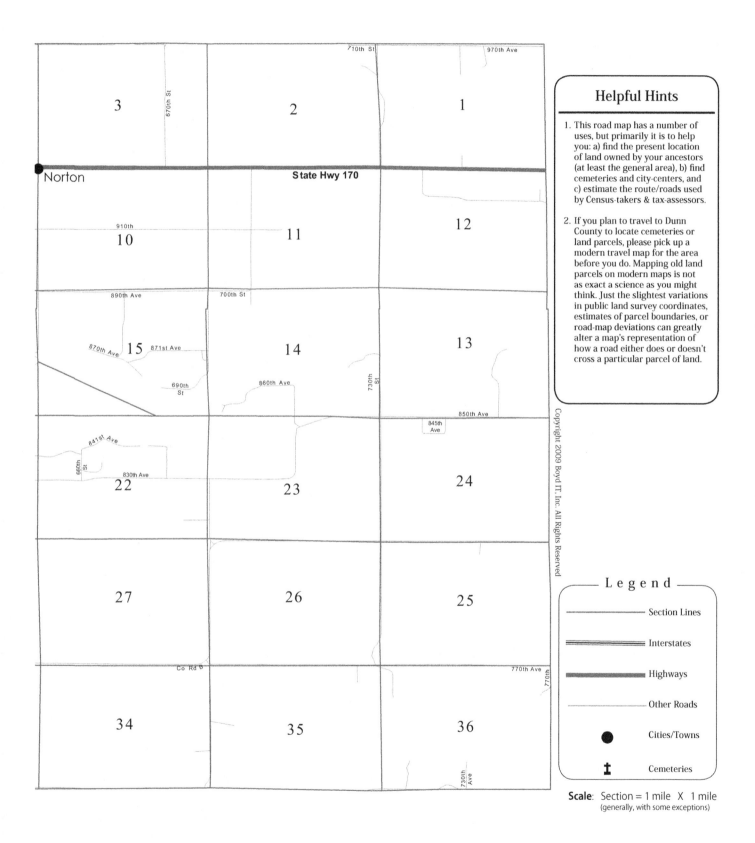

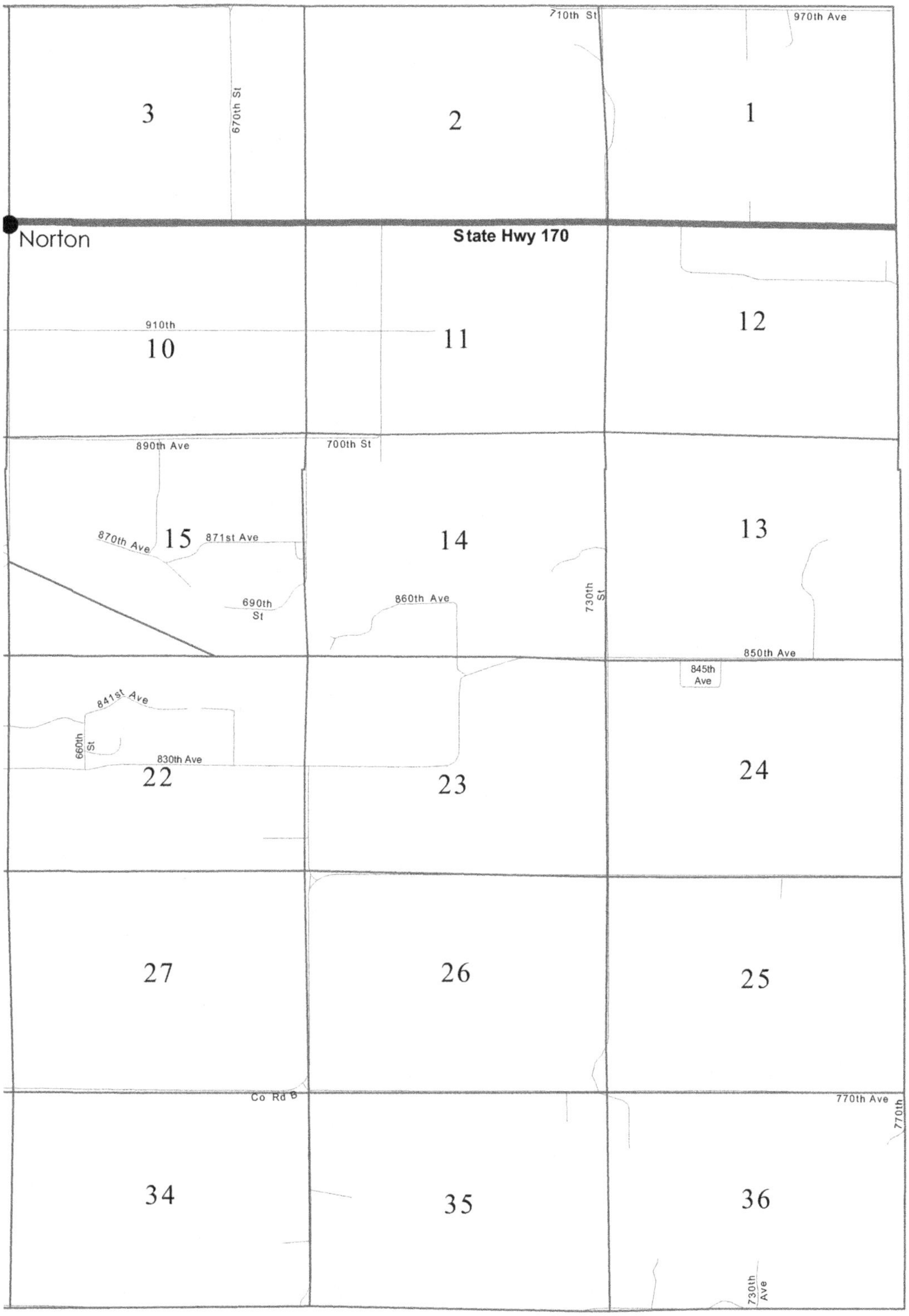

3
670th St
2
710th St
1
970th Ave
Norton
State Hwy 170
910th
10
11
12
890th Ave
700th St
870th Ave
15
871st Ave
14
13
690th St
860th Ave
730th St
850th Ave
845th Ave
841st Ave
660th St
830th Ave
22
23
24
27
26
25
Co Rd B
770th Ave
770th
34
35
36
730th Ave

Helpful Hints

1. This road map has a number of uses, but primarily it is to help you: a) find the present location of land owned by your ancestors (at least the general area), b) find cemeteries and city-centers, and c) estimate the route/roads used by Census-takers & tax-assessors.

2. If you plan to travel to Dunn County to locate cemeteries or land parcels, please pick up a modern travel map for the area before you do. Mapping old land parcels on modern maps is not as exact a science as you might think. Just the slightest variations in public land survey coordinates, estimates of parcel boundaries, or road-map deviations can greatly alter a map's representation of how a road either does or doesn't cross a particular parcel of land.

Legend

- Section Lines
- Interstates
- Highways
- Other Roads
- Cities/Towns
- Cemeteries

Scale: Section = 1 mile X 1 mile
(generally, with some exceptions)

Historical Map

T29-N R12-W
4th PM - 1831 MN/WI Meridian

Map Group 11

Cities & Towns

Norton
Tainter Lake

Cemeteries

None

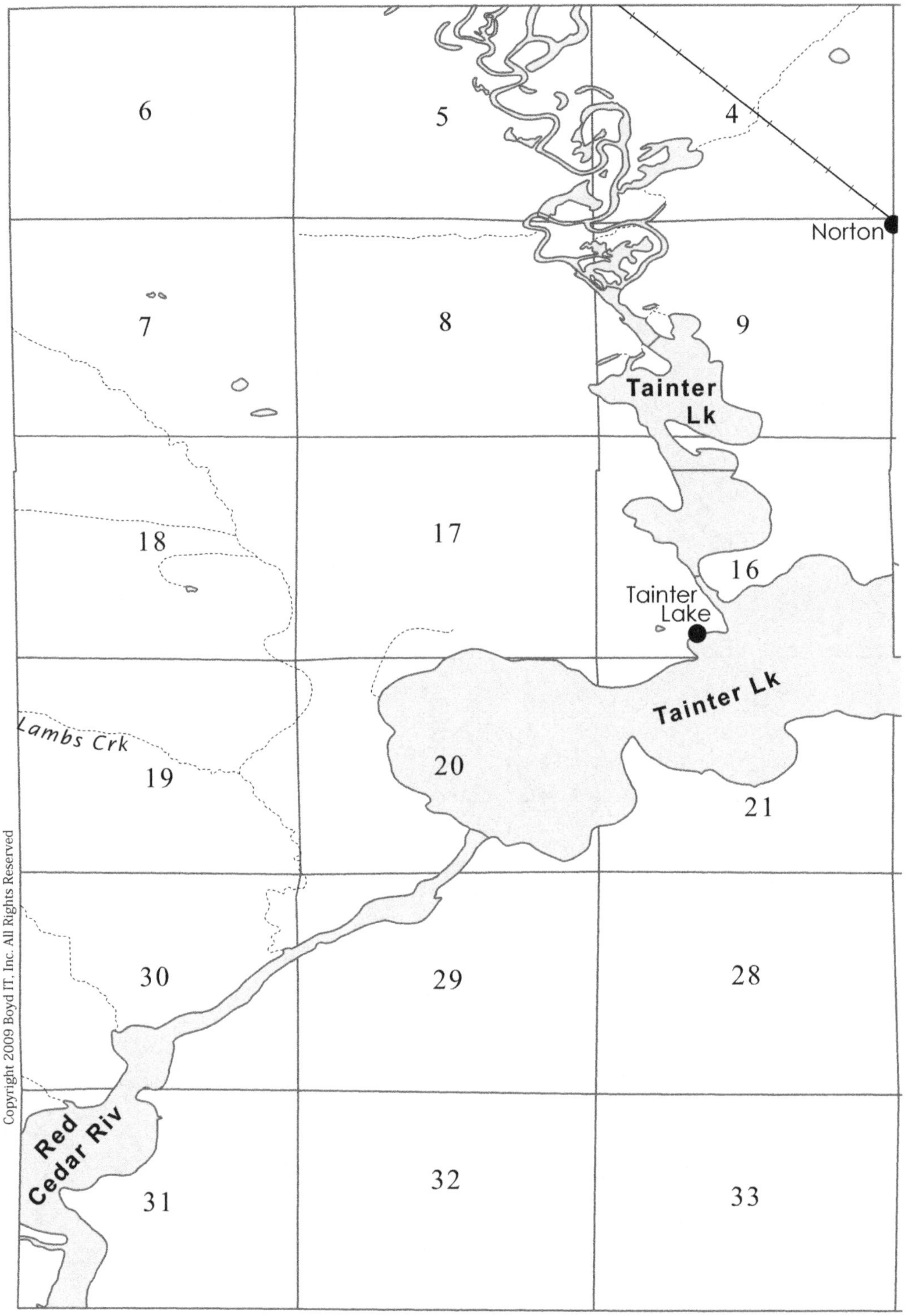
6
5
4
Norton
7
8
9
Tainter Lk
18
17
16
Tainter Lake
Lambs Crk
19
20
Tainter Lk
21
30
29
28
Red Cedar Riv
31
32
33

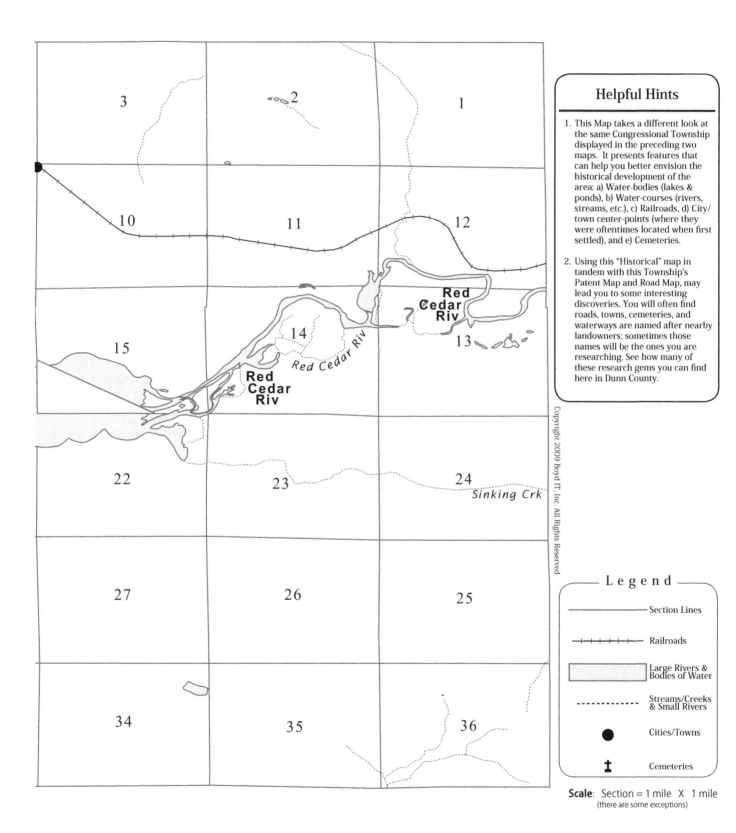

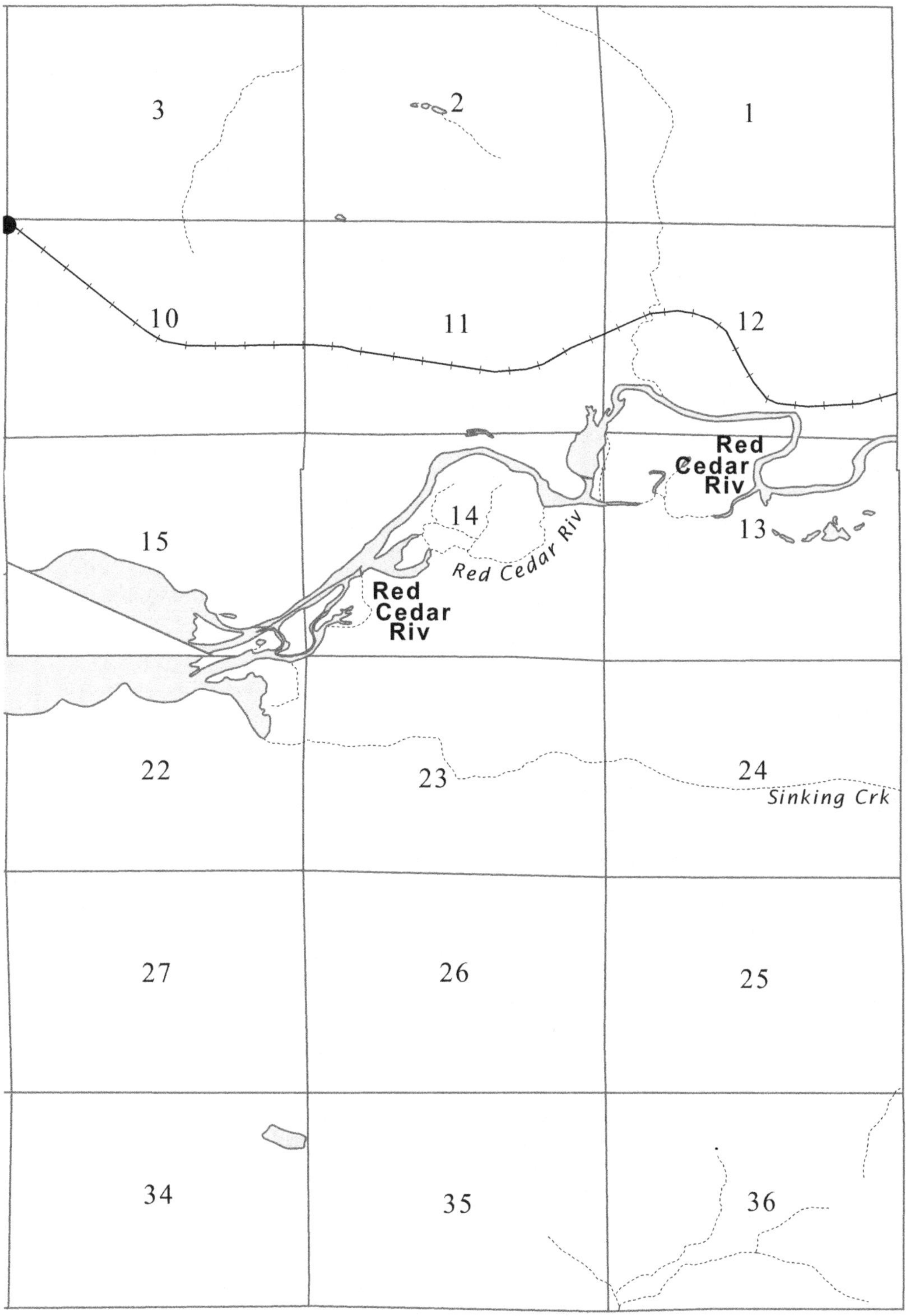
3
2
1
10
11
12
Red
Cedar
Riv
14
15
13
Red Cedar Riv
Red
Cedar
Riv
22
23
24
Sinking Crk
27
26
25
34
35
36

Helpful Hints

1. This Map takes a different look at the same Congressional Township displayed in the preceding two maps. It presents features that can help you better envision the historical development of the area: a) Water-bodies (lakes & ponds), b) Water-courses (rivers, streams, etc.), c) Railroads, d) City/town center-points (where they were oftentimes located when first settled), and e) Cemeteries.

2. Using this "Historical" map in tandem with this Township's Patent Map and Road Map, may lead you to some interesting discoveries. You will often find roads, towns, cemeteries, and waterways are named after nearby landowners: sometimes those names will be the ones you are researching. See how many of these research gems you can find here in Dunn County.

Legend

- Section Lines
- Railroads
- Large Rivers & Bodies of Water
- Streams/Creeks & Small Rivers
- Cities/Towns
- Cemeteries

Scale: Section = 1 mile X 1 mile
(there are some exceptions)

Map Group 12: Index to Land Patents

Township 29-North Range 11-West (4th PM - 1831 MN/WI)

After you locate an individual in this Index, take note of the Section and Section Part then proceed to the Land Patent map on the pages immediately following. You should have no difficulty locating the corresponding parcel of land.

The "For More Info" Column will lead you to more information about the underlying Patents. See the *Legend* at right, and the "How to Use this Book" chapter, for more information.

LEGEND

"For More Info . . . " column

A = Authority (Legislative Act, See Appendix "A")
B = Block or Lot (location in Section unknown)
C = Cancelled Patent
F = Fractional Section
G = Group (Multi-Patentee Patent, see Appendix "C")
V = Overlaps another Parcel
R = Re-Issued (Parcel patented more than once)

(A & G items require you to look in the Appendixes referred to above. All other Letter-designations followed by a number require you to locate line-items in this index that possess the ID number found after the letter).

ID	Individual in Patent	Sec.	Sec. Part	Date Issued	Other Counties	For More Info . . .
1922	AAMOT, Andrew E	34	SENW	1878-06-13		A6
1923	" "	34	SWNE	1878-06-13		A6
1920	" "	34	NWNE	1885-01-30		A6
1921	" "	34	SENE	1885-01-30		A6
1919	ANDERSEN, Andrew	28	NE	1889-04-13		A6 R2084
1912	ANDERSON, Anders	2	NW	1873-01-10		A6
1996	ANDERSON, Gustav	34	N½NW	1882-08-25		A6
1997	" "	34	SWNW	1883-02-20		A6
2082	ANDERSON, Peter	14	E½NW	1875-08-10		A6
2083	" "	14	N½SW	1875-08-10		A6
2062	ARNESON, Ole	6	W½NW	1882-04-10		A6
2063	" "	6	W½SW	1882-04-10		A6
1981	ATWOOD, George	9	SE	1860-08-01		A5 G14
1982	" "	9	SW	1860-08-01		A5 G13
1953	BALDWIN, Cyrenius	17	SWSE	1860-07-03		A7 G20
1954	" "	17	E½NE	1860-08-01		A5 G18
1956	" "	17	E½SE	1860-08-01		A5 G19
1955	" "	17	NWNE	1860-08-01		A5 G18
1957	" "	17	NWSE	1860-08-01		A5 G19
1960	BALDWIN, Daniel C	8	N½SE	1893-02-28		A6
1961	" "	8	SESE	1893-02-28		A6
2079	BARUM, Peder H	26	N½SE	1877-05-15		A6
2078	" "	26	E½NE	1885-10-22		A6
2023	BAXTER, John A	4	E½SW	1873-01-10		A6
2024	" "	9	E½NW	1873-01-10		A6
2013	BELL, James C	12	SW	1861-12-20		A5
1983	BENAVIDES, Pabla	3	W½NW	1861-12-20		A5 G181
1984	" "	4	E½NE	1861-12-20		A5 G181
2093	BERNTZON, S	22	NWNE	1866-10-10		A2
2098	BERNTZON, Staale	21	NE	1869-12-10		A6
1925	BRAATEN, Andrew G	32	S½NE	1888-10-05		A6
1924	" "	32	N½SE	1891-12-26		A6
1985	BRAATEN, Gulbrand H	32	N½SW	1886-08-10		A6 V2066
1986	" "	32	S½NW	1886-08-10		A6
2052	BRONSTAD, Kirsta	34	W½SE	1874-12-30		A6 G50 C R2002
2051	" "	34	E½SW	1875-07-30		A6 G50
2017	BULL, Henry	17	NW	1860-08-01		A5 G254
1933	CHASE, Barton W	1	SWNW	1865-07-01		A2
1910	CLARK, Albert J	18	S½SE	1880-10-01		A6
1911	" "	18	SESW	1880-10-01		A6
1909	CLOSS, Abraham	19	SWSW	1861-04-01		A5
2049	COLE, Charles C	10	NW	1860-08-01		A5 G116
2048	" "	10	SW	1860-08-01		A5 G115
2074	COLE, Omar	19	NESE	1861-09-10		A5 G82
2075	" "	19	SENE	1861-09-10		A5 G82
2076	" "	20	NWSW	1861-09-10		A5 G82

ID	Individual in Patent	Sec.	Sec. Part	Date Issued	Other Counties	For More Info . . .
2077	COLE, Omar (Cont'd)	20	SWNW	1861-09-10		A5 G82
2090	COLE, Rufus C	20	E½SW	1861-09-10		A5
2091	" "	20	SENW	1861-09-10		A5
2092	" "	29	NENW	1861-09-10		A5
2116	CUTCHEON, O M	1	N½SE	1860-08-03		A5 G242
2117	" "	1	NESW	1860-08-03		A5 G242
2107	DAHL, Tobias	1	N½NW	1873-12-15		A6 G97
2056	DARNELL, Martha	3	SW	1860-08-01		A5 G100
2056	DECKER, Permelia	3	SW	1860-08-01		A5 G100
2087	DORR, Robert L	12	NWSE	1861-12-20		A5 G112
2088	" "	12	S½NE	1861-12-20		A5 G112
2089	" "	12	SENW	1861-12-20		A5 G112
2050	DREW, Joseph P	30	W½SW	1878-06-01		A6
2049	DUNKLEE, John William	10	NW	1860-08-01		A5 G116
2048	" "	10	SW	1860-08-01		A5 G115
2074	DYER, Wayne B	19	NESE	1861-09-10		A5 G82
2075	" "	19	SENE	1861-09-10		A5 G82
2076	" "	20	NWSW	1861-09-10		A5 G82
2077	" "	20	SWNW	1861-09-10		A5 G82
1958	EATON, D C	4	E½NW	1869-12-10		A6
1959	" "	4	W½NE	1869-12-10		A6
2111	FELLOWS, William H	35	SESE	1862-08-20		A5 G440
2112	" "	36	S½SW	1862-08-20		A5 G440
1944	FIELDSTAD, Casper O	22	SE	1873-01-10		A6
2065	FJELDSTED, Ole C	22	S½NW	1877-03-01		A6
2064	" "	22	NWSW	1879-09-04		A2
2066	" "	32	E½SW	1895-10-09		A6 V2061, 1985
2020	FORSLID, Jens O	24	NESW	1885-07-13		A6
2021	" "	24	S½SW	1885-07-13		A6
2022	" "	24	SENW	1885-07-13		A6
1931	FOSLID, Arnt I	24	SENE	1884-01-15		A2
1930	" "	24	SE	1885-07-13		A6
2025	FOSLID, John	26	SWNE	1907-11-08		A6
1954	GAGE, Lovina	17	E½NE	1860-08-01		A5 G18
1955	" "	17	NWNE	1860-08-01		A5 G18
1954	GAGE, Myron W	17	E½NE	1860-08-01		A5 G18
1955	" "	17	NWNE	1860-08-01		A5 G18
1947	GILBERTSEN, Chrest	28	N½SE	1885-01-30		A6
2067	GULAKSON, Ole	22	E½NE	1884-09-20		A6
2068	" "	22	SWNE	1884-09-20		A6
1998	GUNDERSON, Hans	2	W½SW	1882-05-10		A6
1994	GUNNUFSEN, Gunnuf	12	E½SE	1873-05-15		A6
1995	" "	12	SWSE	1873-05-15		A6
2060	HALVERSEN, Nils	32	S½SE	1884-09-15		A6
2061	" "	32	S½SW	1884-09-15		A6 V2066
1948	HANSEN, Christian	34	W½SW	1891-07-27		A6
2000	HANSON, Hans R	36	NWNW	1913-12-02		A6
2002	HANSON, Harold	34	W½SE	1884-09-15		A6 R2052
2001	" "	34	E½SE	1892-04-16		A6
2052	HANSON, Peter	34	W½SE	1874-12-30		A6 G50 C R2002
2051	" "	34	E½SW	1875-07-30		A6 G50
1983	HARSH, George	3	W½NW	1861-12-20		A5 G181
1984	" "	4	E½NE	1861-12-20		A5 G181
2027	HILL, John	18	NESW	1873-12-15		A6
2028	" "	18	SENW	1873-12-15		A6
2029	" "	18	W½SW	1873-12-15		A6
2030	" "	20	SWSW	1878-11-05		A2
1982	HOOKS, Charles	9	SW	1860-08-01		A5 G13
2007	HOWARD, Henry R	36	N½SW	1883-05-05		A6
2009	" "	36	NWSE	1883-05-05		A6
2011	" "	36	SWNW	1883-05-05		A6
2006	" "	36	N½NE	1888-10-05		A6
2008	" "	36	NENW	1888-10-05		A6
2010	" "	36	SWNE	1888-10-05		A6
2016	INFINGER, Rebecca	8	SW	1860-08-01		A5 G253
2080	INGEBRETSEN, Peder	2	NWSE	1884-09-20		A6
2081	" "	2	W½NE	1884-09-20		A6
1949	ISRAELSON, Christian	10	SE	1870-05-20		A6
1987	ISRAELSON, Gunder	22	N½NW	1882-05-10		A6
1932	JACOBSON, B C	2	NENE	1870-05-20		A6
2031	JACOBSON, John	34	NENE	1901-02-27		A6
2069	JACOBSON, Ole	14	W½NW	1890-05-14		A6
2039	JOHNS, John M	4	W½NW	1888-10-05		A6

ID	Individual in Patent	Sec.	Sec. Part	Date Issued	Other Counties	For More Info . . .
2040	JOHNS, John M (Cont'd)	4	W½SW	1888-10-05		A6
2034	JOHNSON, John	35	S½SW	1870-10-20		A6
2032	" "	24	NWSW	1892-08-08		A6
2033	" "	24	W½NW	1892-08-08		A6
1988	KINNEY, Gunder	1	N½NE	1873-12-15		A6
1951	KNAPP, Christiana	15	SENW	1860-08-01		A5
1952	" "	15	W½NW	1860-08-01		A5
1950	" "	15	NENW	1861-07-10		A4
1973	KNAPP, David P	30	SWNW	1871-09-01		A6
1972	" "	30	SWNE	1872-04-01		A2
1971	" "	30	NWSE	1879-09-04		A2
1969	" "	30	E½NW	1883-05-05		A5
1970	" "	30	NWNW	1883-05-05		A5
2101	KNAPP, Susan P	15	SW	1860-08-01		A5
1979	KNUDSEN, Esten	22	SWSW	1895-06-24		A6
2084	KNUDSEN, Peter	28	NE	1892-08-27		A6 R1919
2085	" "	28	S½SW	1892-08-27		A6
2086	" "	28	SENW	1892-08-27		A6
2055	KNUDTSON, Lewis	28	S½SE	1874-12-30		A6
2113	LA FORGE, WILLIAM D	8	NE	1883-08-01		A6
2108	LAFORGE, Walter B	6	E½SE	1888-10-05		A6
2109	" "	6	SENE	1888-10-05		A6
2110	" "	6	SWSE	1888-10-05		A6
1989	LANGBERG, Gunder	6	NWSE	1889-06-20		A6
1990	" "	6	SENW	1889-06-20		A6
1991	" "	6	SWNE	1889-06-20		A6
1915	LARSEN, Andreas	14	S½SW	1878-06-13		A6
1916	" "	14	W½SE	1878-06-13		A6
2018	LARSON, James	12	NWNE	1865-07-01		A2
2048	LEAVENWORTH, George Henry	10	SW	1860-08-01		A5 G115
2035	LEONARD, John	19	NWSE	1862-04-01		A2
2036	" "	19	S½NW	1862-04-01		A2
2037	" "	19	SWNE	1862-04-01		A2
2116	LITTLE, William	1	N½SE	1860-08-03		A5 G242
2117	" "	1	NESW	1860-08-03		A5 G242
2114	" "	1	SENW	1860-08-03		A5
2115	" "	1	SWNE	1860-08-03		A5
2019	LOWERY, James	20	S½SE	1883-09-10		A6
2038	LOWERY, John	30	E½SW	1884-09-20		A6
1927	MATHEWS, Andrew T	18	E½NE	1862-04-01		A2
1928	" "	18	NWNE	1870-05-02		A6
1929	" "	7	SESE	1870-05-02		A6
2017	MATHEWS, James E	17	NW	1860-08-01		A5 G254
2016	" "	8	SW	1860-08-01		A5 G253
2014	" "	18	N½SE	1863-04-20		A5
2015	" "	18	SWNE	1863-04-20		A5
2057	MCDONALD, James P	13	NWNW	1860-08-03		A5 G259
2058	" "	14	NENE	1860-08-03		A5 G259
2059	" "	14	W½NE	1860-08-03		A5 G259
2057	MCDONALD, Mary E	13	NWNW	1860-08-03		A5 G259
2058	" "	14	NENE	1860-08-03		A5 G259
2059	" "	14	W½NE	1860-08-03		A5 G259
2057	MCDONALD, Nancy	13	NWNW	1860-08-03		A5 G259
2058	" "	14	NENE	1860-08-03		A5 G259
2059	" "	14	W½NE	1860-08-03		A5 G259
2118	MCELWAINE, William	19	N½NE	1861-05-15		A5
2119	" "	19	N½NW	1861-05-15		A5
1966	MONTEITH, David	29	NWSW	1861-12-20		A5
1967	" "	29	W½NW	1861-12-20		A5
1964	" "	19	SESE	1862-04-01		A2
1968	" "	8	SWSE	1862-04-01		A2
1962	" "	19	E½SW	1869-09-01		A6
1963	" "	19	NWSW	1869-09-01		A6
1965	" "	19	SWSE	1869-09-01		A6
2017	NEWCOMB, Sylvia	17	NW	1860-08-01		A5 G254
1977	NILSEN, Ellen	2	NESE	1878-11-05		A6 G282
1978	" "	2	SENE	1878-11-05		A6 G282
1977	NILSEN, Nils	2	NESE	1878-11-05		A6 G282
1978	" "	2	SENE	1878-11-05		A6 G282
1926	OLESEN, Andrew	10	NE	1873-12-15		A6
2070	OLESEN, Oliver	26	SESW	1878-06-13		A6
2071	" "	26	SWSE	1878-06-13		A6
1938	OLESON, Bertha	6	NENW	1871-09-15		A6 G289

ID	Individual in Patent	Sec.	Sec. Part	Date Issued	Other Counties	For More Info . . .
1939	OLESON, Bertha (Cont'd)	6	NWNE	1871-09-15		A6 G289
1938	OLESON, Forger	6	NENW	1871-09-15		A6 G289
1939	" "	6	NWNE	1871-09-15		A6 G289
2072	OLESON, Oliver	26	SESE	1884-01-15		A6
2073	" "	26	SWSW	1884-01-15		A6
1941	OLSEN, Carl O	26	E½NW	1888-10-05		A6
1942	" "	26	NWNE	1888-10-05		A6
1943	" "	26	NWNW	1888-10-05		A6
2003	OLSON, Helge	11	N½NW	1870-05-20		A6
2004	" "	11	NWSW	1870-05-20		A6
2005	" "	11	SWNW	1870-05-20		A6
2041	OLSON, John	24	NENE	1880-04-30		A6
2042	" "	24	NENW	1880-04-30		A6
2043	" "	24	W½NE	1880-04-30		A6
2044	PAUL, John	20	N½NW	1884-01-15		A6
2045	" "	20	NWNE	1884-01-15		A6
2049	PELT, Jonathan	10	NW	1860-08-01		A5 G116
1940	PETERSON, Brent	32	N½NW	1877-04-25		A6
2107	PETERSON, Nelson T	1	N½NW	1873-12-15		A6 G97
1980	PHELPS, Frank	8	NW	1880-04-30		A6
1945	POOLER, Charles	18	NENW	1898-06-10		A6 F
1946	" "	18	W½NW	1898-06-10		A6 F
1974	POOLER, Dwight	9	NE	1873-01-10		A6
2097	POOLER, Silas	4	SE	1869-12-10		A6
1934	RUNNING, Bergitta	1	S½SE	1873-12-15		A6 G349
1935	" "	1	SESW	1873-12-15		A6 G349
1934	RUNNING, Ole A	1	S½SE	1873-12-15		A6 G349
1935	" "	1	SESW	1873-12-15		A6 G349
2102	RUNNING, Thomas	12	NENE	1884-09-30		A2
1956	SANGER, S S	17	E½SE	1860-08-01		A5 G19
1957	" "	17	NWSE	1860-08-01		A5 G19
2111	SEEDS, Carey S S	35	SESE	1862-08-20		A5 G440
2112	" "	36	S½SW	1862-08-20		A5 G440
1992	SEMMINGSON, Gunder	14	E½SE	1877-03-01		A6
1993	" "	14	SENE	1877-03-01		A6
1975	SOLBERG, Edward	36	NESE	1873-05-15		A6
1976	" "	36	SENE	1873-05-15		A6
1999	SOLBERG, Hans P	36	S½SE	1873-01-10		A6
1917	SOLI, Andreas O	26	N½SW	1891-12-26		A6
1918	" "	26	SWNW	1891-12-26		A6
2094	STAPLES, Samuel	28	N½NW	1890-07-21		A6
2095	" "	28	NWSW	1890-07-21		A6
2096	" "	28	SWNW	1890-07-21		A6
1953	STEENBARGER, Elizabeth	17	SWSE	1860-07-03		A7 G20
2053	STINGLUFF, Levi	6	SESW	1865-07-01		A2
2054	STROUD, Levi	36	SENW	1912-05-13		A6
2046	STUDLEY, John	20	NENE	1873-01-10		A6
2047	" "	21	NWNW	1873-01-10		A6
2104	STUDLEY, Thomas	20	NWSE	1875-08-10		A6
2106	" "	20	SWNE	1875-08-10		A6
2103	" "	20	NESE	1884-09-15		A6
2105	" "	20	SENE	1884-09-15		A6
1936	SYVERSEN, Bersven	2	E½SW	1869-09-01		A6
1937	" "	2	S½SE	1869-09-01		A6
1982	TAYLOR, Gracey	9	SW	1860-08-01		A5 G13
2026	TAYLOR, John H	6	NENE	1885-03-16		A2
1913	TEIGENSKAU, Andor	3	E½NW	1873-12-15		A6
1914	" "	3	W½NE	1873-12-15		A6
2012	TRONSEN, Jacob	30	S½SE	1878-06-01		A6
2049	VAN PELT, ELLEN	10	NW	1860-08-01		A5 G116
2049	VAN PELT, LARKIN	10	NW	1860-08-01		A5 G116
2087	VAUGHAN, Deborah	12	NWSE	1861-12-20		A5 G112
2088	" "	12	S½NE	1861-12-20		A5 G112
2089	" "	12	SENW	1861-12-20		A5 G112
1981	WALKER, Elizabeth	9	SE	1860-08-01		A5 G14
1981	WALKER, Joseph H	9	SE	1860-08-01		A5 G14
2120	WIGHT, William	11	E½NE	1860-08-03		A5
2099	WISCONSIN, State Of	16		1941-08-16		A3
2111	WOODWARD, William A	35	SESE	1862-08-20		A5 G440
2112	" "	36	S½SW	1862-08-20		A5 G440
2100	WOODWORTH, Stephen	32	NWNE	1885-01-30		A6
2121	WRIGHT, William	12	NENW	1861-12-20		A5
2122	" "	12	W½NW	1861-12-20		A5

Patent Map

T29-N R11-W
4th PM - 1831 MN/WI Meridian

Map Group 12

Township Statistics

Parcels Mapped	:	214
Number of Patents	:	136
Number of Individuals	:	137
Patentees Identified	:	114
Number of Surnames	:	101
Multi-Patentee Parcels	:	37
Oldest Patent Date	:	7/3/1860
Most Recent Patent	:	8/16/1941
Block/Lot Parcels	:	0
Parcels Re - Issued	:	2
Parcels that Overlap	:	3
Cities and Towns	:	1
Cemeteries	:	3

Section 6: ARNESON Ole 1882; OLESON [289] Bertha 1871; OLESON [289] Bertha 1871; TAYLOR John H 1885; LANGBERG Gunder 1889; LANGBERG Gunder 1889; LAFORGE Walter B 1888; ARNESON Ole 1882; LANGBERG Gunder 1889; STINGLUFF Levi 1865; LAFORGE Walter B 1888; LAFORGE Walter B 1888

Section 5 (empty)

Section 4: EATON D C 1869; HARSH [181] George 1861; JOHNS John M 1888; EATON D C 1869; JOHNS John M 1888; BAXTER John A 1873; POOLER Silas 1869

Section 7 (empty)

Section 8: PHELPS Frank 1880; FORGE William D La 1883; MATHEWS [253] James E 1860; MATHEWS Andrew T 1870; MONTEITH David 1862; BALDWIN Daniel C 1893; BALDWIN Daniel C 1893

Section 9: BAXTER John A 1873; POOLER Dwight 1873; ATWOOD [13] George 1860; ATWOOD [14] George 1860

Section 18: POOLER Charles 1898; POOLER Charles 1898; MATHEWS Andrew T 1870; MATHEWS Andrew T 1862; HILL John 1873; MATHEWS James E 1863; HILL John 1873; MATHEWS James E 1863; HILL John 1873; CLARK Albert J 1880; CLARK Albert J 1880

Section 17: MATHEWS [254] James E 1860; BALDWIN [18] Cyrenius 1860; BALDWIN [18] Cyrenius 1860; BALDWIN [19] Cyrenius 1860; BALDWIN [19] Cyrenius 1860; BALDWIN [20] Cyrenius 1860

Section 16: WISCONSIN State Of 1941

Section 19: MCELWAINE William 1861; MCELWAINE William 1861; LEONARD John 1862; LEONARD John 1862; COLE [82] Omar 1861; MONTEITH David 1869; LEONARD John 1862; COLE [82] Omar 1861; CLOSS Abraham 1861; MONTEITH David 1869; MONTEITH David 1869; MONTEITH David 1862

Section 20: PAUL John 1884; PAUL John 1884; STUDLEY John 1873; COLE [82] Omar 1861; COLE Rufus C 1861; STUDLEY Thomas 1875; STUDLEY Thomas 1884; COLE [82] Omar 1861; STUDLEY Thomas 1875; STUDLEY Thomas 1884; HILL John 1878; COLE Rufus C 1861; LOWERY James 1883

Section 21: STUDLEY John 1873; BERNTZON Staale 1869

Section 30: KNAPP David P 1883; KNAPP David P 1883; KNAPP David P 1871; KNAPP David P 1872; DREW Joseph P 1878; KNAPP David P 1879; LOWERY John 1884; TRONSEN Jacob 1878

Section 29: COLE Rufus C 1861; MONTEITH David 1861; MONTEITH David 1861

Section 28: STAPLES Samuel 1890; ANDERSEN Andrew 1889; STAPLES Samuel 1890; KNUDSEN Peter 1892; KNUDSEN Peter 1892; STAPLES Samuel 1890; GILBERTSEN Chrest 1885; KNUDSEN Peter 1892; KNUDTSON Lewis 1874

Section 31 (empty)

Section 32: PETERSON Brent 1877; WOODWORTH Stephen 1885; BRAATEN Gulbrand H 1886; BRAATEN Andrew G 1888; BRAATEN Gulbrand H 1886; FJELDSTED Ole C 1895; BRAATEN Andrew G 1891; HALVERSEN Nils 1884; HALVERSEN Nils 1884

Section 33 (empty)

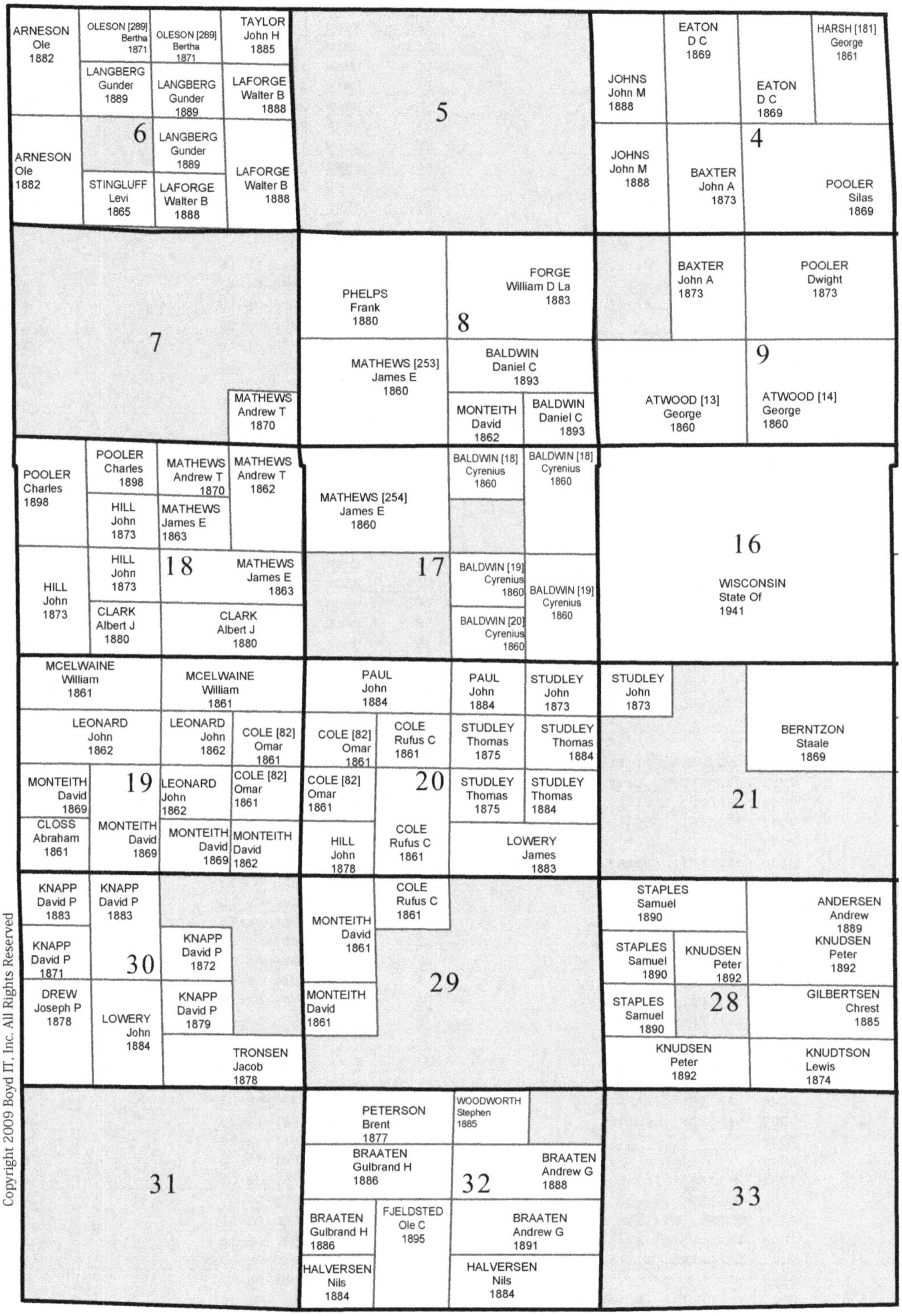

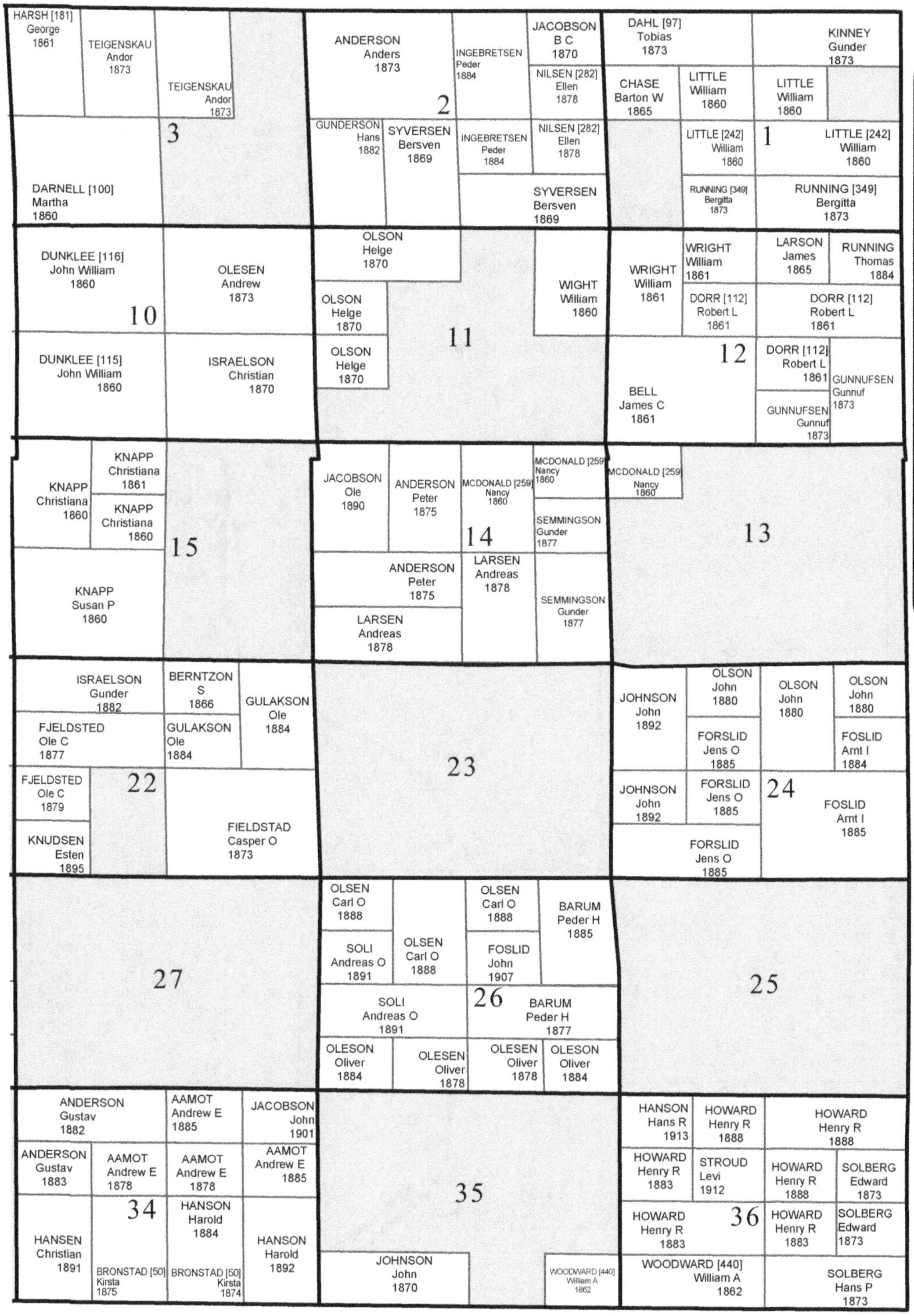
HARSH [181] George 1861
TEIGENSKAU Andor 1873
TEIGENSKAU Andor 1873
3
DARNELL [100] Martha 1860
ANDERSON Anders 1873
INGEBRETSEN Peder 1884
JACOBSON B C 1870
NILSEN [282] Ellen 1878
2
GUNDERSON Hans 1882
SYVERSEN Bersven 1869
INGEBRETSEN Peder 1884
NILSEN [282] Ellen 1878
SYVERSEN Bersven 1869
DAHL [97] Tobias 1873
KINNEY Gunder 1873
CHASE Barton W 1865
LITTLE William 1860
LITTLE William 1860
LITTLE [242] William 1860
1
LITTLE [242] William 1860
RUNNING [349] Bergitta 1873
RUNNING [349] Bergitta 1873
DUNKLEE [116] John William 1860
OLESEN Andrew 1873
10
DUNKLEE [115] John William 1860
ISRAELSON Christian 1870
OLSON Helge 1870
OLSON Helge 1870
OLSON Helge 1870
11
WIGHT William 1860
WRIGHT William 1861
WRIGHT William 1861
LARSON James 1865
RUNNING Thomas 1884
DORR [112] Robert L 1861
DORR [112] Robert L 1861
12
DORR [112] Robert L 1861
BELL James C 1861
GUNNUFSEN Gunnuf 1873
GUNNUFSEN Gunnuf 1873
KNAPP Christiana 1861
KNAPP Christiana 1860
KNAPP Christiana 1860
15
KNAPP Susan P 1860
JACOBSON Ole 1890
ANDERSON Peter 1875
MCDONALD [259] Nancy 1860
MCDONALD [259] Nancy 1860
SEMMINGSON Gunder 1877
14
ANDERSON Peter 1875
LARSEN Andreas 1878
LARSEN Andreas 1878
SEMMINGSON Gunder 1877
MCDONALD [259] Nancy 1860
13
ISRAELSON Gunder 1882
BERNTZON S 1866
GULAKSON Ole 1884
FJELDSTED Ole C 1877
GULAKSON Ole 1884
FJELDSTED Ole C 1879
22
KNUDSEN Esten 1895
FIELDSTAD Casper O 1873
23
JOHNSON John 1892
OLSON John 1880
OLSON John 1880
OLSON John 1880
FORSLID Jens O 1885
FOSLID Arnt I 1884
JOHNSON John 1892
FORSLID Jens O 1885
24
FOSLID Arnt I 1885
FORSLID Jens O 1885
27
OLSEN Carl O 1888
OLSEN Carl O 1888
BARUM Peder H 1885
SOLI Andreas O 1891
OLSEN Carl O 1888
FOSLID John 1907
26
SOLI Andreas O 1891
BARUM Peder H 1877
OLESON Oliver 1884
OLESEN Oliver 1878
OLESEN Oliver 1878
OLESON Oliver 1884
25
ANDERSON Gustav 1882
AAMOT Andrew E 1885
JACOBSON John 1901
ANDERSON Gustav 1883
AAMOT Andrew E 1878
AAMOT Andrew E 1878
AAMOT Andrew E 1885
34
HANSON Harold 1884
HANSEN Christian 1891
BRONSTAD [50] Kirsta 1875
BRONSTAD [50] Kirsta 1874
HANSON Harold 1892
35
JOHNSON John 1870
WOODWARD [440] William A 1862
HANSON Hans R 1913
HOWARD Henry R 1888
HOWARD Henry R 1888
HOWARD Henry R 1883
STROUD Levi 1912
HOWARD Henry R 1888
SOLBERG Edward 1873
HOWARD Henry R 1883
36
HOWARD Henry R 1883
SOLBERG Edward 1873
WOODWARD [440] William A 1862
SOLBERG Hans P 1873

Helpful Hints

1. This Map's INDEX can be found on the preceding pages.
2. Refer to Map "C" to see where this Township lies within Dunn County, Wisconsin.
3. Numbers within square brackets [ ] denote a multi-patentee land parcel (multi-owner). Refer to Appendix "C" for a full list of members in this group.
4. Areas that look to be crowded with Patentees usually indicate multiple sales of the same parcel (Re-issues) or Overlapping parcels. See this Township's Index for an explanation of these and other circumstances that might explain "odd" groupings of Patentees on this map.

Legend

Patent Boundary

Section Boundary

No Patents Found (or Outside County)

1., 2., 3., ... Lot Numbers (when beside a name)

[ ] Group Number (see Appendix "C")

Scale: Section = 1 mile X 1 mile (generally, with some exceptions)

Road Map

T29-N R11-W
4th PM - 1831 MN/WI Meridian

Map Group 12

Cities & Towns

Colfax

Cemeteries

Evergreen Cemetery
Hill Grove Cemetery
Lower Running Valley Cemetery

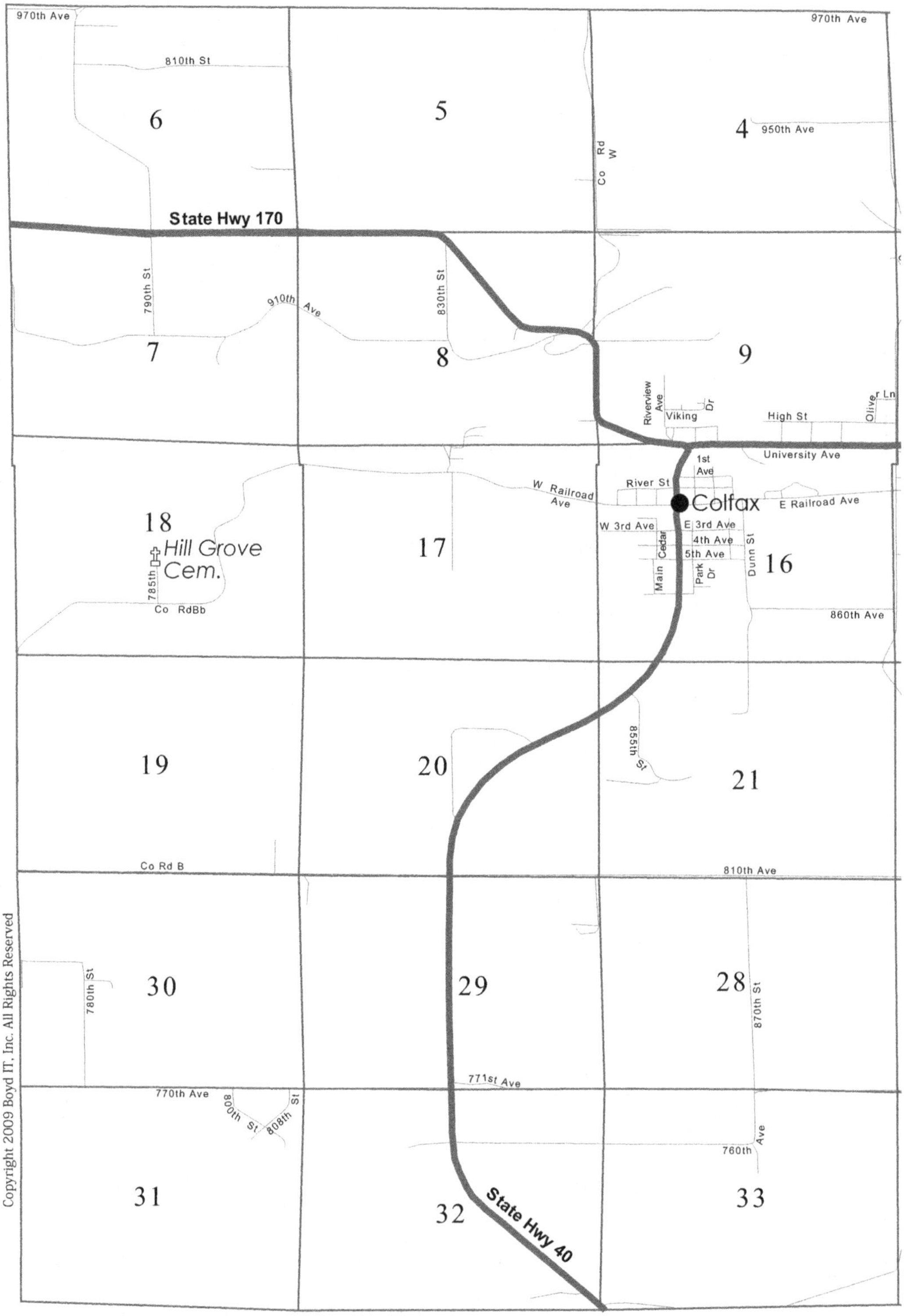

970th Ave
810th St
6
5
4
950th Ave
Co Rd W
State Hwy 170
790th St
910th Ave
830th St
7
8
9
Riverview Ave
Viking
Dr
High St
Olive
r Ln
University Ave
1st Ave
River St
W Railroad Ave
Colfax
E Railroad Ave
18
Hill Grove Cem.
17
W 3rd Ave
E 3rd Ave
4th Ave
5th Ave
Cedar
Main
Park Dr
Dunn St
16
785th
Co RdBb
860th Ave
19
20
855th St
21
Co Rd B
810th Ave
30
780th St
29
28
870th St
770th Ave
800th St
808th St
771st Ave
760th Ave
31
32
State Hwy 40
33

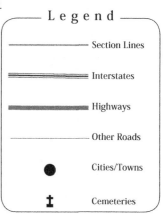

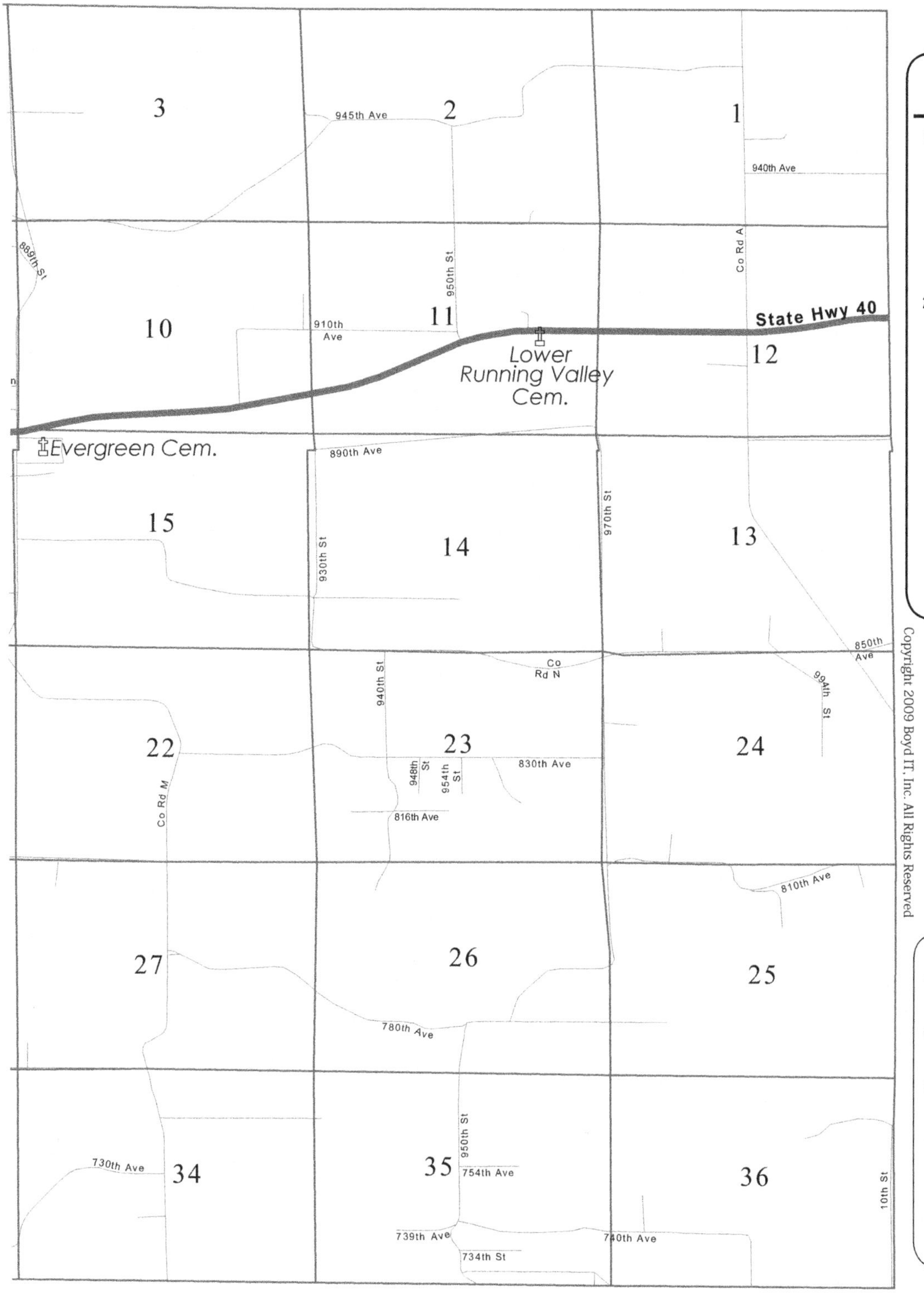

Helpful Hints

1. This road map has a number of uses, but primarily it is to help you: a) find the present location of land owned by your ancestors (at least the general area), b) find cemeteries and city-centers, and c) estimate the route/roads used by Census-takers & tax-assessors.
2. If you plan to travel to Dunn County to locate cemeteries or land parcels, please pick up a modern travel map for the area before you do. Mapping old land parcels on modern maps is not as exact a science as you might think. Just the slightest variations in public land survey coordinates, estimates of parcel boundaries, or road-map deviations can greatly alter a map's representation of how a road either does or doesn't cross a particular parcel of land.

Legend

- Section Lines
- Interstates
- Highways
- Other Roads
- Cities/Towns
- Cemeteries

Scale: Section = 1 mile X 1 mile
(generally, with some exceptions)

Historical Map

T29-N R11-W
4th PM - 1831 MN/WI Meridian

Map Group 12

Cities & Towns

Colfax

Cemeteries

Evergreen Cemetery
Hill Grove Cemetery
Lower Running Valley Cemetery

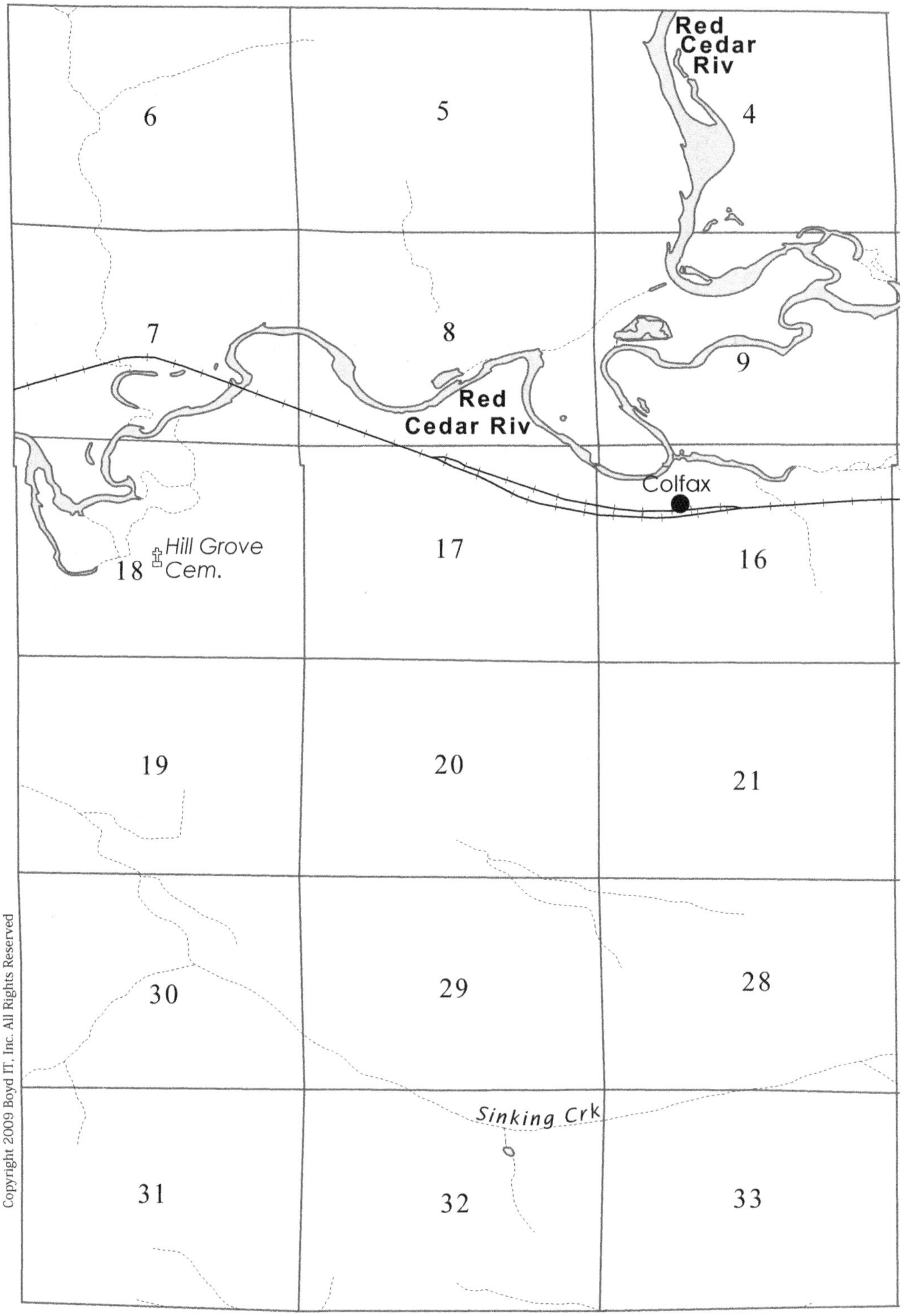

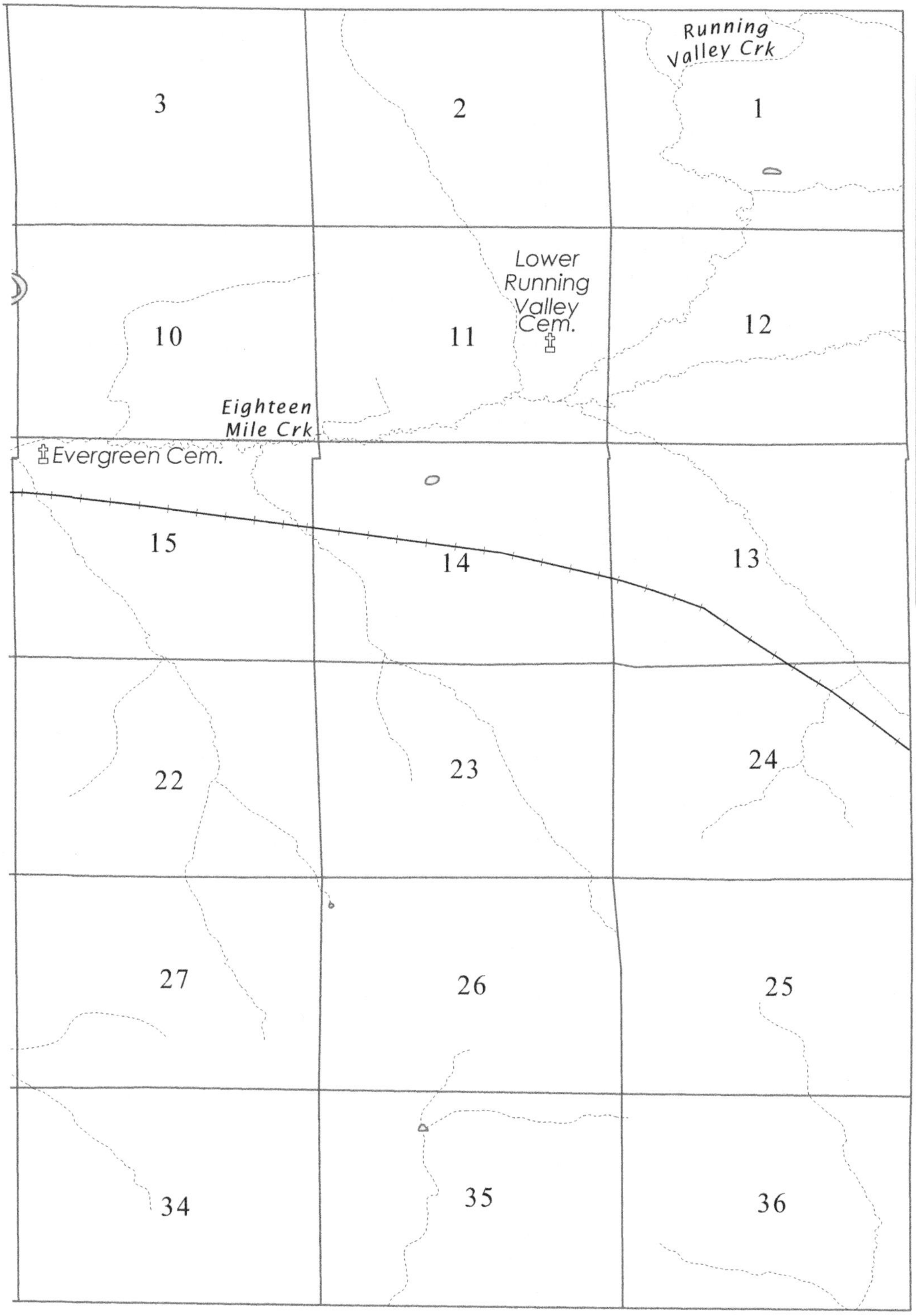
Running Valley Crk
3
2
1
10
11
12
Lower Running Valley Cem.
Eighteen Mile Crk
Evergreen Cem.
15
14
13
22
23
24
27
26
25
34
35
36

Helpful Hints

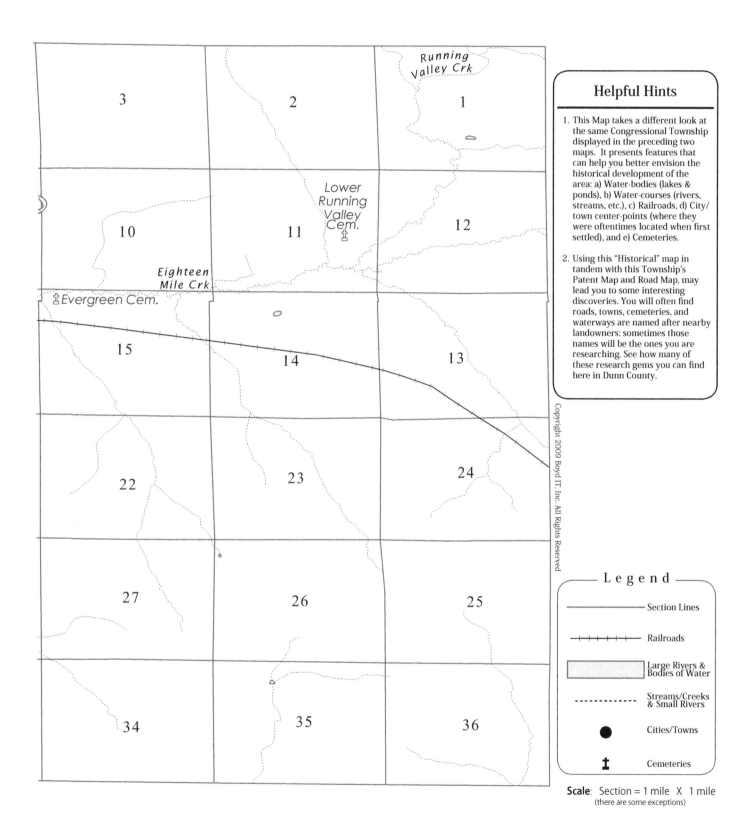

1. This Map takes a different look at the same Congressional Township displayed in the preceding two maps. It presents features that can help you better envision the historical development of the area: a) Water-bodies (lakes & ponds), b) Water-courses (rivers, streams, etc.), c) Railroads, d) City/town center-points (where they were oftentimes located when first settled), and e) Cemeteries.

2. Using this "Historical" map in tandem with this Township's Patent Map and Road Map, may lead you to some interesting discoveries. You will often find roads, towns, cemeteries, and waterways are named after nearby landowners: sometimes those names will be the ones you are researching. See how many of these research gems you can find here in Dunn County.

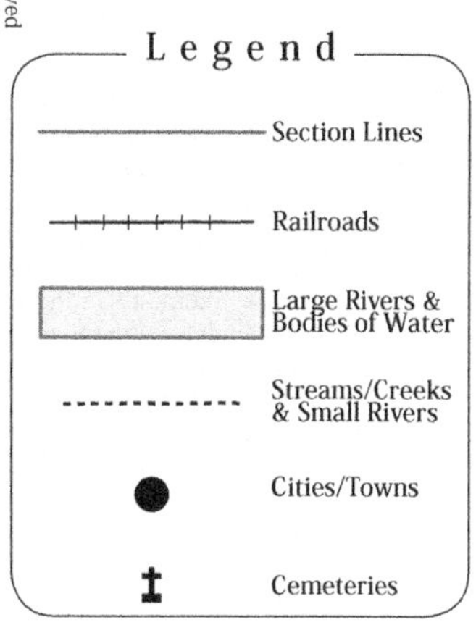
Legend
Section Lines
Railroads
Large Rivers & Bodies of Water
Streams/Creeks & Small Rivers
Cities/Towns
Cemeteries

Scale: Section = 1 mile X 1 mile
(there are some exceptions)

Map Group 13: Index to Land Patents

Township 28-North Range 14-West (4th PM - 1831 MN/WI)

After you locate an individual in this Index, take note of the Section and Section Part then proceed to the Land Patent map on the pages immediately following. You should have no difficulty locating the corresponding parcel of land.

The "For More Info" Column will lead you to more information about the underlying Patents. See the *Legend* at right, and the "How to Use this Book" chapter, for more information.

LEGEND

"For More Info . . . " column

A = Authority (Legislative Act, See Appendix "A")
B = Block or Lot (location in Section unknown)
C = Cancelled Patent
F = Fractional Section
G = Group (Multi-Patentee Patent, see Appendix "C")
V = Overlaps another Parcel
R = Re-Issued (Parcel patented more than once)

(A & G items require you to look in the Appendixes referred to above. All other Letter-designations followed by a number require you to locate line-items in this index that possess the ID number found after the letter).

ID	Individual in Patent	Sec.	Sec. Part	Date Issued	Other Counties	For More Info . . .
2162	AMICK, Samuel	36	N½NW	1880-06-30		A6
2137	AUSTIN, Frank M	34	N½SE	1872-09-25		A6
2138	" "	34	S½NE	1872-09-25		A6
2159	AUSTIN, Orson	34	NWSW	1872-09-25		A6
2160	" "	34	SENW	1872-09-25		A6
2161	" "	34	W½NW	1872-09-25		A6
2142	BARNARD, George M	36	SW	1862-03-10		A5 G22
2141	" "	36	S½NW	1862-07-01		A2
2139	BLODGETT, Franklin	34	S½SE	1873-05-20		A6
2130	BRIGHT, David S	32	N½SW	1873-01-10		A6
2151	BRIGHT, John	32	S½NW	1873-04-01		A6
2128	CLARK, Charles T	32	N½NE	1871-11-20		A6
2129	" "	32	SENE	1871-11-20		A6
2144	DANIELS, Henry	34	S½SW	1875-11-20		A6
2135	DUFFEY, Frank	30	N½SW	1874-11-10		A6
2136	" "	30	W½NE	1874-11-10		A6
2152	EARGOOD, John C	32	SWNE	1875-01-15		A6
2168	FARNHAM, Betsey	36	SE	1866-08-01		A5 G378
2140	FAUCHTER, Frederick	24	NENE	1881-02-10		A6
2123	FOSTER, Andrew R	28	N½SW	1882-04-10		A6
2143	FOSTER, George N	28	S½SW	1880-05-15		A6
2146	FREESTONE, Jacob	32	E½SE	1871-11-20		A6
2153	GIBSON, Mary A	32	S½SW	1880-09-01		A6
2155	GIBSON, Moses S	20	SESE	1857-04-01		A2
2156	GILBERT, Oliver	26	NENW	1855-12-15		A2
2158	" "	27	N½NW	1855-12-15		A2
2157	" "	27	N½NE	1857-04-01		A2
2132	HALL, Ella W	30	E½NE	1872-10-15		A2
2163	HARRIS, Seth F	32	N½NW	1872-10-01		A6
2124	JARGER, August	2	W½SW	1862-04-10		A2 C
2134	KELLEY, Francis	32	W½SE	1871-11-20		A6
2142	LARRABEE, Phebe	36	SW	1862-03-10		A5 G22
2165	MANLEY, Thomas	30	S½NW	1872-02-14		A2
2166	MCMAHON, Thomas	30	S½SW	1873-12-20		A6 F
2145	MCMANNAS, Hugh	30	E½SE	1873-12-20		A6
2154	MCMANUS, Michael	30	N½NW	1877-02-20		A6
2169	OBERLANDER, Xavier	24	SESE	1866-09-01		A2
2133	PEASE, Flavius E	36	NE	1871-03-10		A6
2149	PROPHET, James	12	SENW	1861-12-05		A5 C
2150	" "	12	SWNE	1861-12-05		A5 C
2127	REED, Charles A	34	NESW	1866-02-15		A2
2125	" "	34	N½NE	1871-11-20		A6
2126	" "	34	NENW	1871-11-20		A6
2147	ROTH, Jacob	24	NESE	1855-12-15		A2
2148	" "	24	SENE	1855-12-15		A2
2131	SIMONS, Edward	26	NWNW	1873-12-20		A6

ID	Individual in Patent	Sec.	Sec. Part	Date Issued	Other Counties	For More Info . . .
2168	STEVENS, Wilson	36	SE	1866-08-01		A5 G378
2167	WHITEFORD, William	30	W½SE	1873-01-10		A6
2164	WISCONSIN, State Of	16		1941-08-16		A3

Patent Map

T28-N R14-W
4th PM - 1831 MN/WI Meridian

Map Group 13

Township Statistics

Parcels Mapped :	47
Number of Patents :	39
Number of Individuals :	37
Patentees Identified :	36
Number of Surnames :	33
Multi-Patentee Parcels :	2
Oldest Patent Date :	12/15/1855
Most Recent Patent :	8/16/1941
Block/Lot Parcels :	0
Parcels Re - Issued :	0
Parcels that Overlap :	0
Cities and Towns :	1
Cemeteries :	2

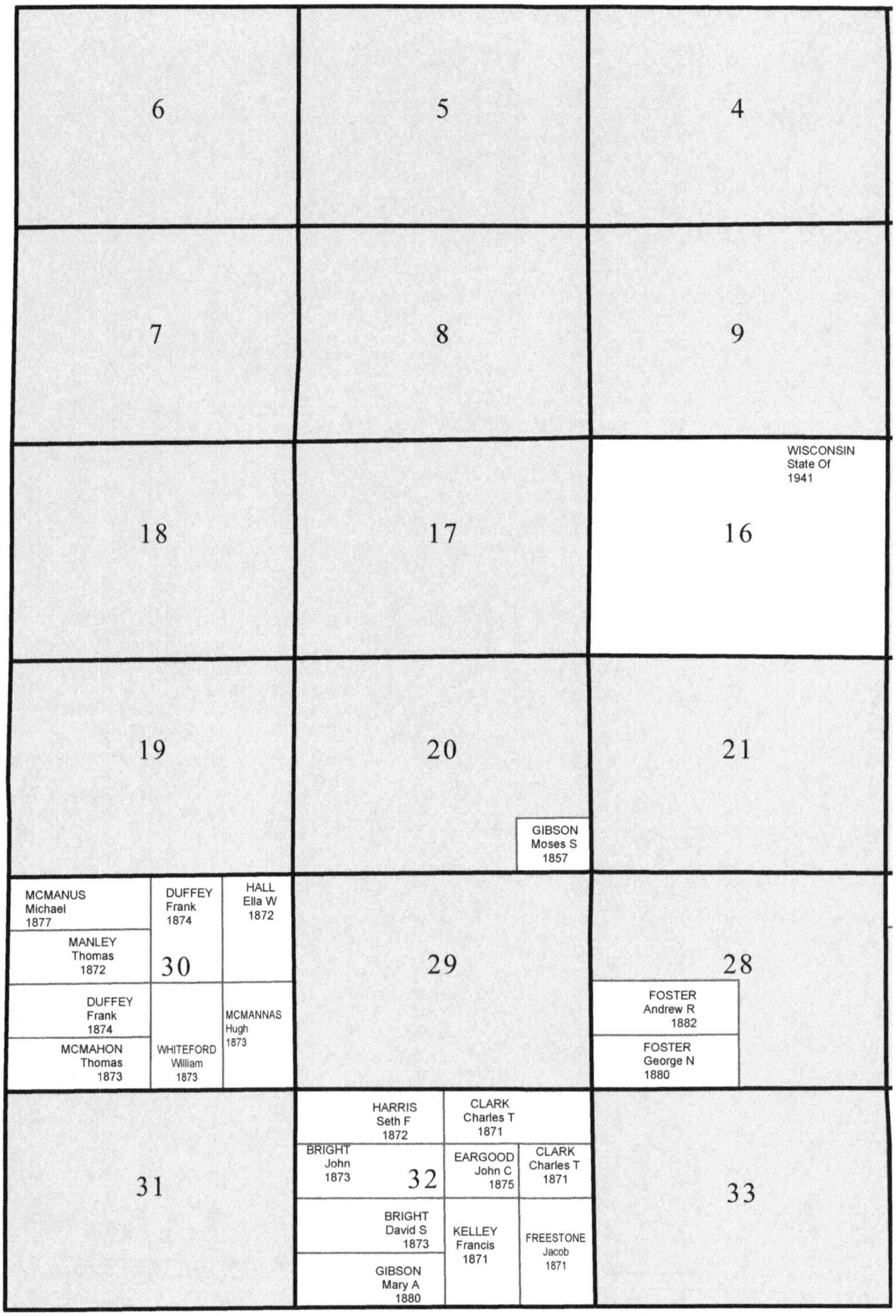

6
5
4
7
8
9
WISCONSIN State Of 1941
18
17
16
19
20
21
GIBSON Moses S 1857
MCMANUS Michael 1877
DUFFEY Frank 1874
HALL Ella W 1872
MANLEY Thomas 1872
30
29
28
DUFFEY Frank 1874
MCMANNAS Hugh 1873
FOSTER Andrew R 1882
MCMAHON Thomas 1873
WHITEFORD William 1873
FOSTER George N 1880
HARRIS Seth F 1872
CLARK Charles T 1871
BRIGHT John 1873
32
EARGOOD John C 1875
CLARK Charles T 1871
31
33
BRIGHT David S 1873
KELLEY Francis 1871
FREESTONE Jacob 1871
GIBSON Mary A 1880

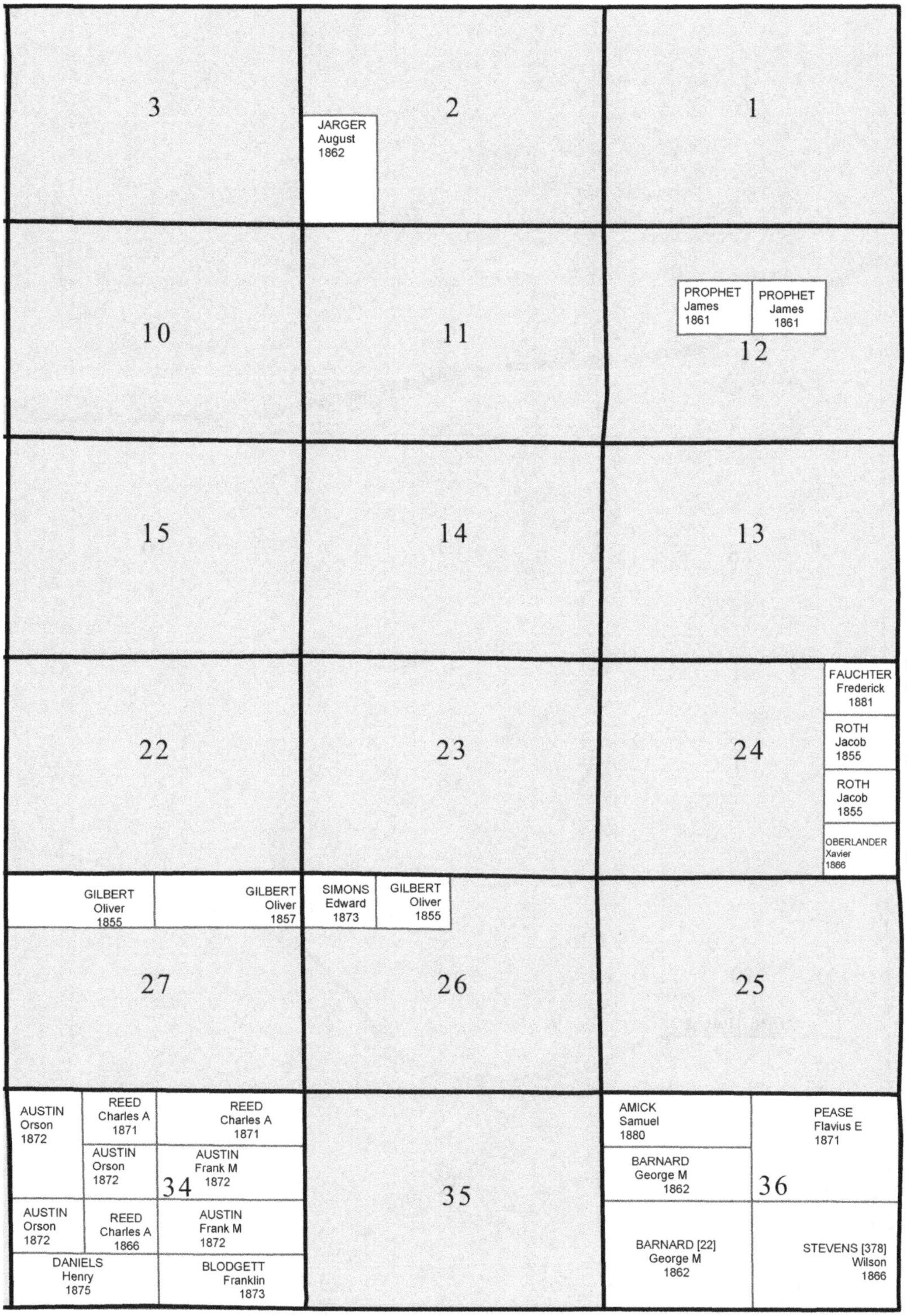
3
2
1
JARGER August 1862
10
11
12
PROPHET James 1861
PROPHET James 1861
15
14
13
22
23
24
FAUCHTER Frederick 1881
ROTH Jacob 1855
ROTH Jacob 1855
OBERLANDER Xavier 1866
GILBERT Oliver 1855
GILBERT Oliver 1857
SIMONS Edward 1873
GILBERT Oliver 1855
27
26
25
AUSTIN Orson 1872
REED Charles A 1871
REED Charles A 1871
AUSTIN Orson 1872
AUSTIN Frank M 1872
34
AUSTIN Orson 1872
REED Charles A 1866
AUSTIN Frank M 1872
DANIELS Henry 1875
BLODGETT Franklin 1873
35
AMICK Samuel 1880
PEASE Flavius E 1871
BARNARD George M 1862
36
BARNARD [22] George M 1862
STEVENS [378] Wilson 1866

Helpful Hints

1. This Map's INDEX can be found on the preceding pages.
2. Refer to Map "C" to see where this Township lies within Dunn County, Wisconsin.
3. Numbers within square brackets [ ] denote a multi-patentee land parcel (multi-owner). Refer to Appendix "C" for a full list of members in this group.
4. Areas that look to be crowded with Patentees usually indicate multiple sales of the same parcel (Re-issues) or Overlapping parcels. See this Township's Index for an explanation of these and other circumstances that might explain "odd" groupings of Patentees on this map.

Legend

Patent Boundary

Section Boundary

No Patents Found (or Outside County)

1., 2., 3., ... Lot Numbers (when beside a name)

[ ] Group Number (see Appendix "C")

Scale: Section = 1 mile X 1 mile (generally, with some exceptions)

Road Map

T28-N R14-W
4th PM - 1831 MN/WI Meridian

Map Group 13

Cities & Towns

Hatchville

Cemeteries

Lucas Cemetery
Teegarden Cemetery

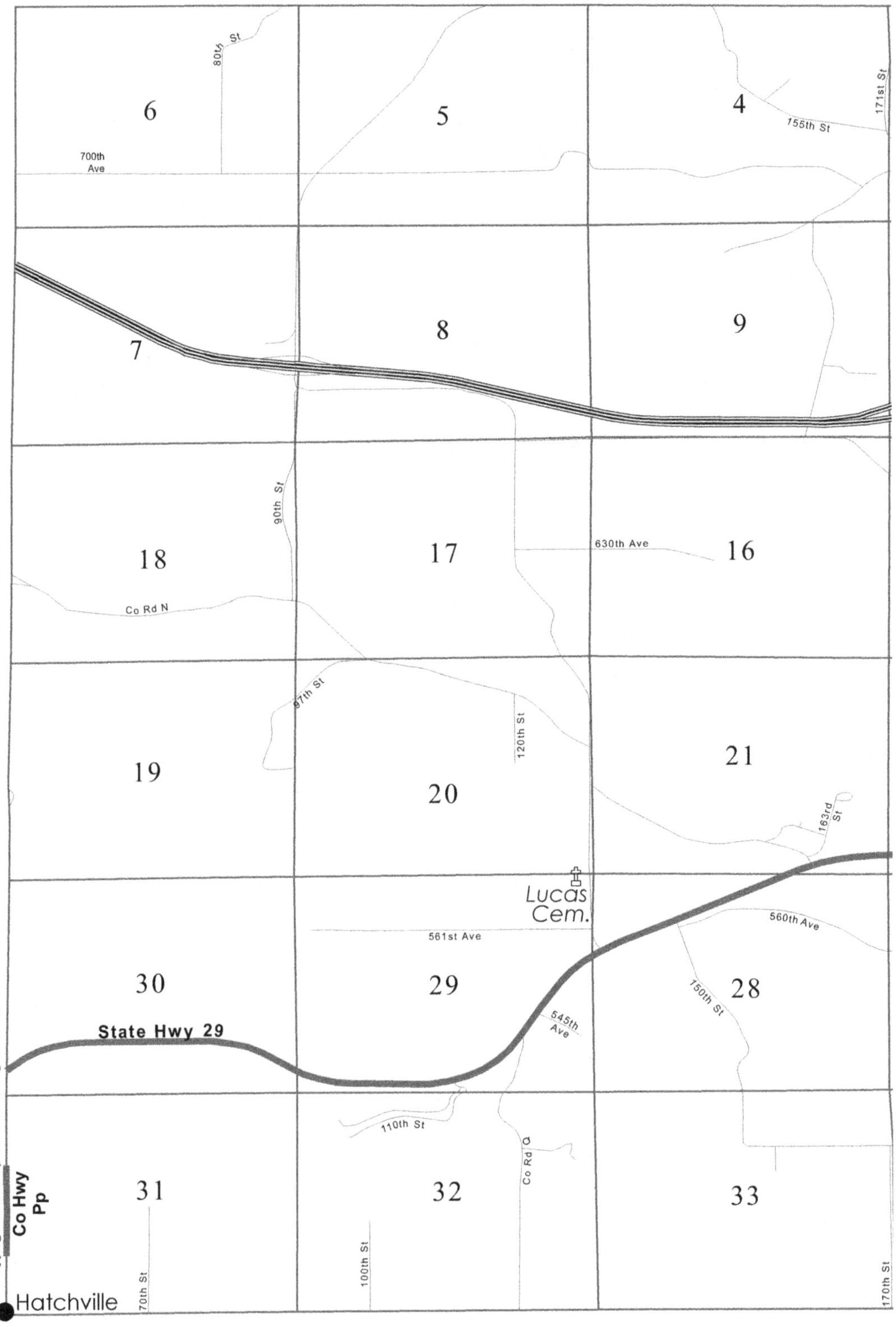

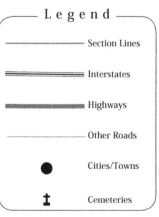

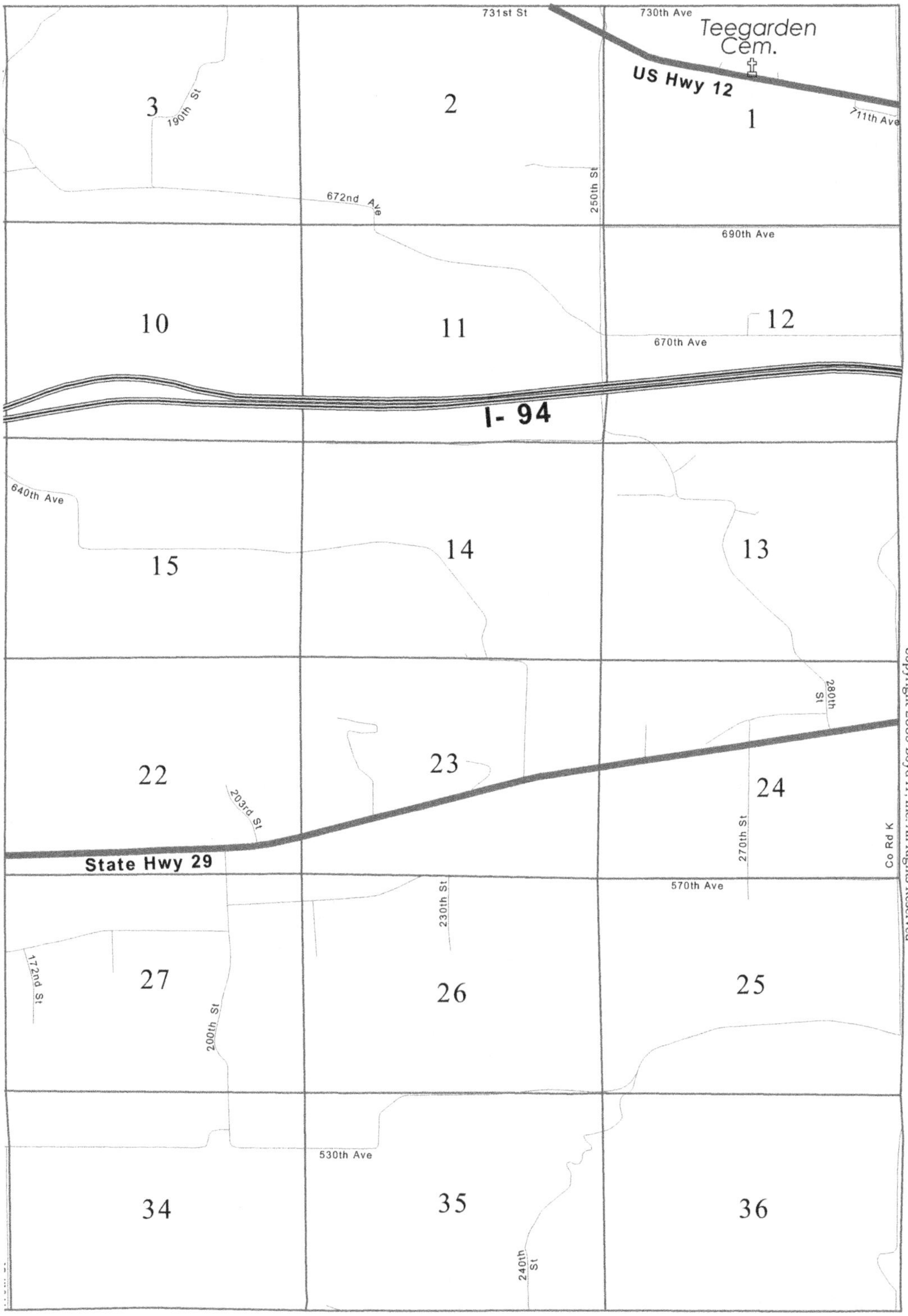
731st St
730th Ave
Teegarden Cem.
US Hwy 12
711th Ave
3
190th St
2
1
672nd Ave
250th St
690th Ave
10
11
12
670th Ave
I- 94
640th Ave
15
14
13
280th St
22
23
24
203rd St
270th St
Co Rd K
State Hwy 29
230th St
570th Ave
172nd St
27
26
25
200th St
530th Ave
34
35
36
240th St

Helpful Hints

1. This road map has a number of uses, but primarily it is to help you: a) find the present location of land owned by your ancestors (at least the general area), b) find cemeteries and city-centers, and c) estimate the route/roads used by Census-takers & tax-assessors.
2. If you plan to travel to Dunn County to locate cemeteries or land parcels, please pick up a modern travel map for the area before you do. Mapping old land parcels on modern maps is not as exact a science as you might think. Just the slightest variations in public land survey coordinates, estimates of parcel boundaries, or road-map deviations can greatly alter a map's representation of how a road either does or doesn't cross a particular parcel of land.

Legend

- Section Lines
- Interstates
- Highways
- Other Roads
- Cities/Towns
- Cemeteries

Scale: Section = 1 mile X 1 mile
(generally, with some exceptions)

Historical Map

T28-N R14-W
4th PM - 1831 MN/WI Meridian

Map Group 13

Cities & Towns

Hatchville

Cemeteries

Lucas Cemetery
Teegarden Cemetery

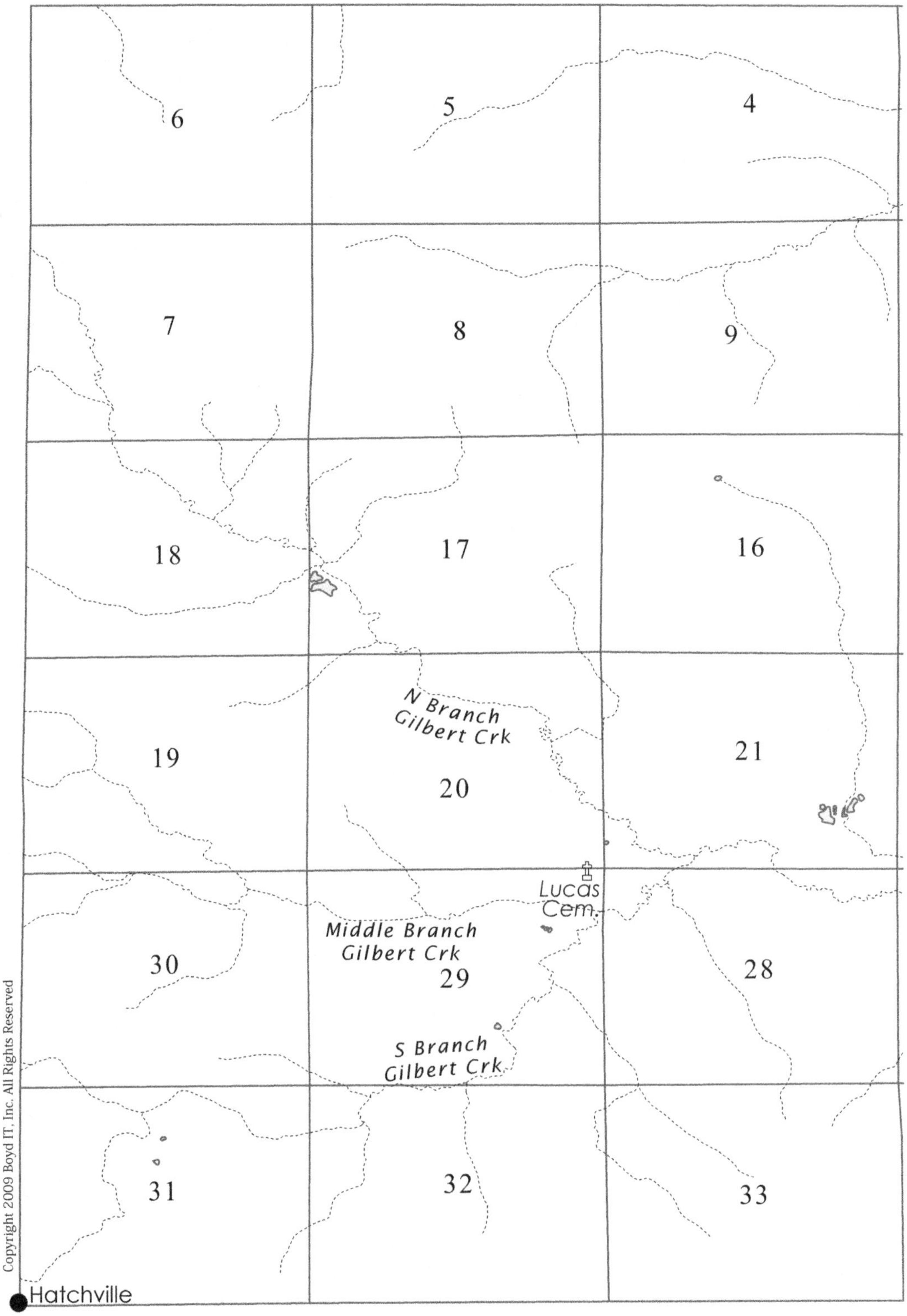
6
5
4
7
8
9
18
17
16
19
N Branch Gilbert Crk
20
21
Lucas Cem.
30
Middle Branch Gilbert Crk
29
28
S Branch Gilbert Crk
31
32
33
Hatchville

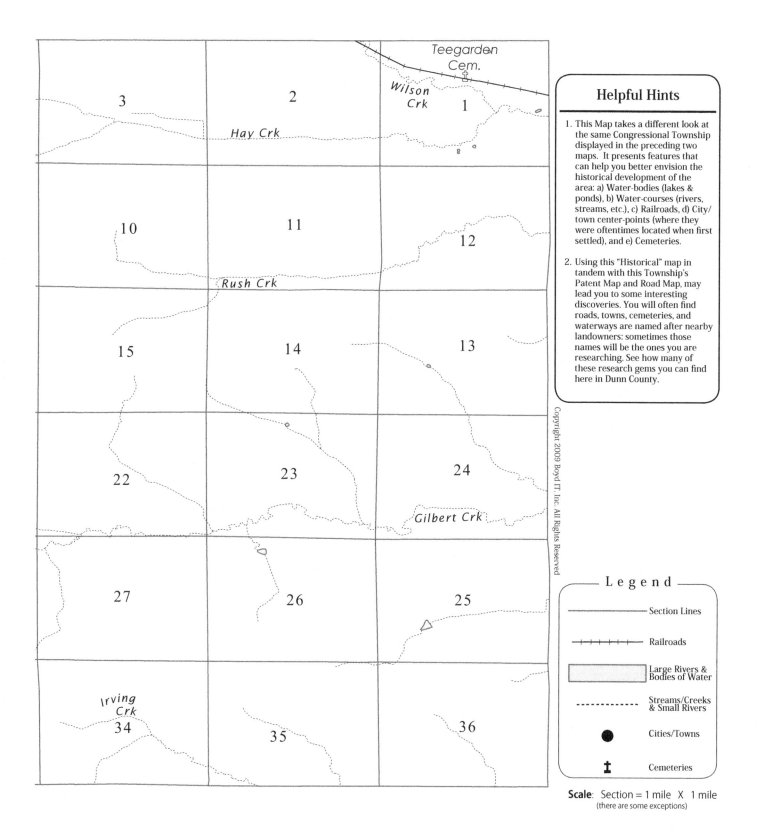

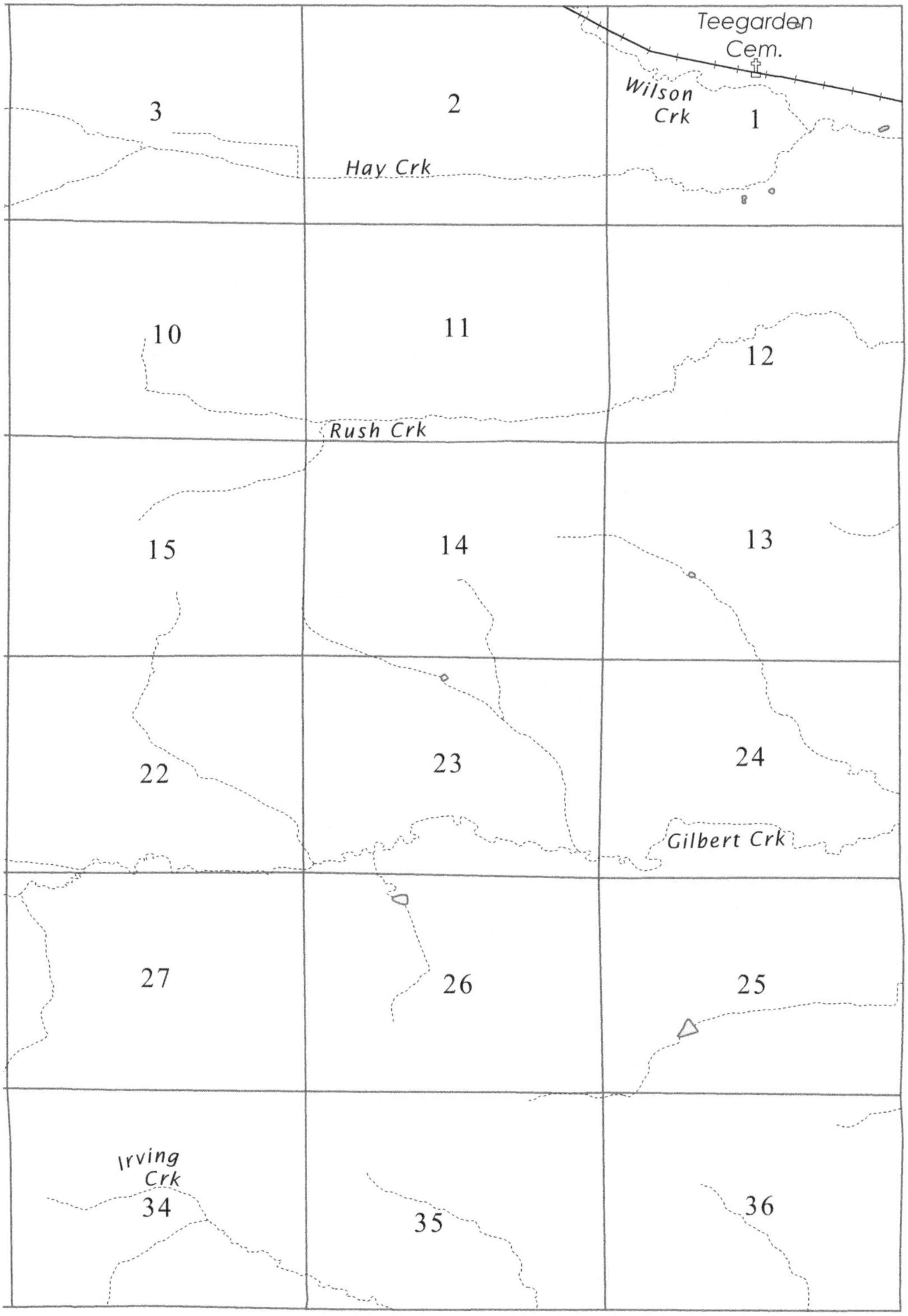
Teegarden
Cem.
Wilson
Crk
Hay Crk
Rush Crk
Gilbert Crk
Irving
Crk
3
2
1
10
11
12
15
14
13
22
23
24
27
26
25
34
35
36

Helpful Hints

1. This Map takes a different look at the same Congressional Township displayed in the preceding two maps. It presents features that can help you better envision the historical development of the area: a) Water-bodies (lakes & ponds), b) Water-courses (rivers, streams, etc.), c) Railroads, d) City/town center-points (where they were oftentimes located when first settled), and e) Cemeteries.

2. Using this "Historical" map in tandem with this Township's Patent Map and Road Map, may lead you to some interesting discoveries. You will often find roads, towns, cemeteries, and waterways are named after nearby landowners: sometimes those names will be the ones you are researching. See how many of these research gems you can find here in Dunn County.

Legend

- Section Lines
- Railroads
- Large Rivers & Bodies of Water
- Streams/Creeks & Small Rivers
- Cities/Towns
- Cemeteries

Scale: Section = 1 mile X 1 mile
(there are some exceptions)

Map Group 14: Index to Land Patents

Township 28-North Range 13-West (4th PM - 1831 MN/WI)

After you locate an individual in this Index, take note of the Section and Section Part then proceed to the Land Patent map on the pages immediately following. You should have no difficulty locating the corresponding parcel of land.

The "For More Info" Column will lead you to more information about the underlying Patents. See the *Legend* at right, and the "How to Use this Book" chapter, for more information.

LEGEND

"For More Info . . . " column

A = Authority (Legislative Act, See Appendix "A")
B = Block or Lot (location in Section unknown)
C = Cancelled Patent
F = Fractional Section
G = Group (Multi-Patentee Patent, see Appendix "C")
V = Overlaps another Parcel
R = Re-Issued (Parcel patented more than once)

(A & G items require you to look in the Appendixes referred to above. All other Letter-designations followed by a number require you to locate line-items in this index that possess the ID number found after the letter).

ID	Individual in Patent	Sec.	Sec. Part	Date Issued	Other Counties	For More Info . . .
2171	ALDEN, Philander M	4	N½NE	1863-05-20		A5 G380
2172	" "	4	SENE	1863-05-20		A5 G380
2186	ANDREWS, Charles	2	SW	1869-09-01		A6
2181	ANDREWS, John	10	NW	1863-05-20		A5 G360
2280	BANKS, Maria	24	E½SW	1862-01-07		A5 G220
2281	" "	24	N½SE	1862-01-07		A5 G220
2294	BARTON, John W	2	S½SE	1867-07-15		A2
2179	BIGFORD, Andrew J	32	SE	1870-06-10		A6
2348	BORLAND, William	36	SE	1860-02-01		A5
2188	BOYNTON, Jesse	10	SW	1863-05-20		A5 G52
2171	BRUNK, Maria	4	N½NE	1863-05-20		A5 G380
2172	" "	4	SENE	1863-05-20		A5 G380
2188	BUCKLEY, Clemson B	10	SW	1863-05-20		A5 G52
2328	BUNT, William A	36	SENE	1862-03-10		A5 G135
2329	" "	36	W½NE	1862-03-10		A5 G135
2308	BURCH, Roswell	12	N½NW	1874-07-15		A6
2173	BURGERT, Adam S	32	S½NW	1873-04-01		A6
2222	BURN, Jacob R	18	NW	1871-03-10		A6 F
2325	CHANCE, Levi	30	N½NE	1862-09-01		A7 G137
2204	CHURCH, Frederick R	14	E½NW	1862-11-20		A5 G73
2205	" "	14	W½NE	1862-11-20		A5 G73
2225	COLOMY, Sarah	35	E½SW	1857-10-30		A5 G166
2226	" "	35	SWSE	1857-10-30		A5 G166
2361	CRIPPEN, Sophronia	22	N½SW	1862-11-20		A5 G425
2362	" "	22	S½NW	1862-11-20		A5 G425
2189	DARLING, David D	4	SWNE	1866-09-01		A2
2188	DAVIS, John Almon	10	SW	1863-05-20		A5 G52
2188	DAVIS, Samuel R	10	SW	1863-05-20		A5 G52
2180	DEPEW, Andrew J	10	NE	1894-09-01		A6
2176	DREXLER, Albert	8	E½NW	1873-09-20		A6
2215	EATON, Henry	12	NE	1860-10-01		A5 V2231
2338	EVENSON, Siver	32	N½NW	1874-11-10		A6
2235	EVERNAN, John	19	NWSE	1855-12-15		A2
2236	" "	19	SWNE	1855-12-15		A2
2306	EVERNAN, Peter	20	NWSW	1855-12-15		A2
2307	" "	20	SWNW	1855-12-15		A2
2237	FORD, John	28	NW	1871-03-10		A6
2219	FRENCH, J S	18	NWNE	1869-01-01		A2
2316	FRENCH, Samuel B	13	NWNW	1857-04-01		A2
2315	" "	13	E½NW	1857-10-30		A5
2317	" "	13	SWNW	1857-10-30		A5
2314	" "	12	1	1859-12-10		A2
2326	" "	25	SESW	1861-12-05		A5 G142
2327	" "	25	W½SW	1861-12-05		A5 G142
2324	" "	36	NW	1861-12-05		A5
2318	" "	14	SW	1862-03-10		A5

ID	Individual in Patent	Sec.	Sec. Part	Date Issued	Other Counties	For More Info . . .
2328	FRENCH, Samuel B (Cont'd)	36	SENE	1862-03-10		A5 G135
2329	" "	36	W½NE	1862-03-10		A5 G135
2325	" "	30	N½NE	1862-09-01		A7 G137
2319	" "	22	N½NW	1862-11-20		A5 R2320
2321	" "	22	W½NE	1862-11-20		A5 R2322
2185	" "	4	SE	1862-12-01		A5 G386
2320	" "	22	N½NW	1863-02-04		A5 R2319
2322	" "	22	W½NE	1863-02-04		A5 R2321
2323	" "	36	NENE	1866-07-18		A2
2238	GAREHART, John	20	N½NW	1859-12-10		A2
2239	" "	20	SENW	1859-12-10		A2
2240	" "	28	NWSE	1859-12-10		A2
2241	" "	27	N½SW	1860-02-01		A5 G147
2242	" "	28	NESE	1860-02-01		A5 G147
2232	GEBHART, John B	8	E½SE	1872-09-25		A6
2233	" "	8	NWSE	1872-09-25		A6
2234	" "	8	SENE	1872-09-25		A6
2282	GERMAN, Mary E	14	NWSE	1862-03-10		A5 G221
2283	" "	14	S½SE	1862-03-10		A5 G221
2330	GILBERT, Oliver	27	1	1852-08-02		A2 G154
2331	" "	27	6	1852-08-02		A2 G154
2332	" "	34	N½NW	1852-08-02		A2 G154
2304	" "	27	SWSW	1855-12-15		A2
2303	" "	27	SESW	1857-04-01		A2
2330	GILBERT, Samuel	27	1	1852-08-02		A2 G154
2331	" "	27	6	1852-08-02		A2 G154
2332	" "	34	N½NW	1852-08-02		A2 G154
2223	GRAY, James B	35	E½NW	1857-10-30		A5
2225	" "	35	E½SW	1857-10-30		A5 G166
2224	" "	35	NWNE	1857-10-30		A5
2226	" "	35	SWSE	1857-10-30		A5 G166
2353	HALL, William S	34	8	1865-05-05		A2
2214	HALVORSEN, Halvor	14	W½NW	1873-04-01		A6
2349	HARBIT, William	12	S½NW	1877-07-02		A6
2284	HARMS, John	19	NESE	1855-12-15		A2
2285	" "	19	SENE	1855-12-15		A2
2177	HARROLD, Anderson	6	E½NE	1871-03-10		A6
2178	" "	6	E½SE	1871-03-10		A6
2227	HAVERLAND, James	20	S½SW	1874-11-10		A6
2333	HAVERLAND, Samuel H	30	W½SW	1875-11-20		A6 F
2340	HAVERLAND, Thomas B	30	S½NE	1873-04-01		A6
2187	HAVILAND, Charles H	30	E½SW	1874-11-10		A6
2220	HOUSE, Jacob	2	NW	1870-06-10		A6 F
2334	INGLE, Samuel	8	W½NW	1871-04-20		A6
2335	" "	8	W½SW	1871-04-20		A6
2213	JOHNSON, Gilbert	8	W½NE	1873-04-01		A6
2286	JOHNSON, John	2	N½SE	1869-01-01		A2
2301	JOHNSON, Ole	4	E½SW	1872-09-25		A6
2302	" "	4	NWSW	1872-09-25		A6
2287	KELLEY, John	18	SESW	1869-10-20		A6
2288	" "	18	SWSE	1869-10-20		A6
2289	" "	18	W½SW	1869-10-20		A6
2296	KERR, Nancy	30	NW	1864-09-15		A5 G441 F
2290	KIMBALL, John	12	SW	1864-09-15		A5
2190	KNAPP, David P	3	NENE	1862-03-10		A5 C
2244	KNAPP, John H	25	N½SE	1854-07-05		A7
2245	" "	27	3	1854-07-05		A7
2246	" "	27	4	1854-07-05		A7
2243	" "	24	7	1854-10-02		A2
2247	" "	27	5	1855-01-09		A4
2248	" "	13	5	1855-12-15		A2 G224
2249	" "	13	6	1855-12-15		A2 G224
2250	" "	13	7	1855-12-15		A2 G224
2251	" "	13	8	1855-12-15		A2 G224
2269	" "	22	SESE	1855-12-15		A2 G219
2252	" "	22	SWSE	1855-12-15		A2 G224
2253	" "	23	3	1855-12-15		A2 G224
2271	" "	23	SWSW	1855-12-15		A2 G219
2254	" "	24	5	1855-12-15		A2 G224
2255	" "	24	6	1855-12-15		A2 G224
2256	" "	24	S½SE	1855-12-15		A2 G224
2257	" "	25	NW	1855-12-15		A2 G224
2274	" "	26	NE	1855-12-15		A2 G219

ID	Individual in Patent	Sec.	Sec. Part	Date Issued	Other Counties	For More Info . . .
2258	KNAPP, John H (Cont'd)	26	NESW	1855-12-15		A2 G224
2259	" "	26	NWSE	1855-12-15		A2 G224
2260	" "	34	1	1855-12-15		A2 G224
2261	" "	34	2	1855-12-15		A2 G224
2262	" "	34	3	1855-12-15		A2 G224
2276	" "	34	4	1855-12-15		A2 G219
2277	" "	34	5	1855-12-15		A2 G219
2263	" "	12	2	1857-04-01		A2 G219
2264	" "	12	N½SE	1857-04-01		A2 G219
2265	" "	13	NESW	1857-04-01		A2 G219
2266	" "	13	SWSW	1857-04-01		A2 G219
2270	" "	23	N½NE	1857-04-01		A2 G219
2273	" "	24	SWNE	1857-04-01		A2 G219
2275	" "	27	NWNE	1857-04-01		A2 G219
2267	" "	22	E½NE	1861-12-05		A5 G219
2268	" "	22	N½SE	1861-12-05		A5 G219
2280	" "	24	E½SW	1862-01-07		A5 G220
2281	" "	24	N½SE	1862-01-07		A5 G220
2282	" "	14	NWSE	1862-03-10		A5 G221
2283	" "	14	S½SE	1862-03-10		A5 G221
2272	" "	24	E½NE	1862-04-10		A2 G219
2278	" "	14	E½NE	1864-09-15		A5 G223
2279	" "	14	NESE	1864-09-15		A5 G223
2292	KNOPPS, John	20	NWSE	1863-04-20		A5
2293	" "	20	S½SE	1863-04-20		A5
2291	" "	20	NWNE	1865-05-05		A2
2241	LANDRUM, Nancy	27	N½SW	1860-02-01		A5 G147
2242	" "	28	NESE	1860-02-01		A5 G147
2297	LIVERSON, Nels	32	W½NE	1873-04-01		A6
2199	MACK, Lydia	1	SWNW	1856-04-15		A7 G279
2209	MARK, George	20	NESW	1855-12-15		A2
2218	MARKHAM, Hiram J	10	SE	1870-05-20		A6
2188	MCGINNIS, Beaulah	10	SW	1863-05-20		A5 G52
2203	MERCIER, Fred	6	W½SW	1873-04-01		A6 F
2221	MILLER, Jacob	28	NE	1870-05-20		A6
2295	MOONEY, Jonas C	2	NE	1869-09-01		A6 F
2201	MORGAN, Evan J	35	W½NW	1855-12-15		A2
2202	" "	35	W½SW	1855-12-15		A2
2200	" "	34	E½SE	1859-05-02		A2
2358	MOUNTCASTLE, Mary A	36	E½SW	1860-07-16		A5 G426
2359	" "	36	NWSW	1860-07-16		A5 G426
2300	NEWELL, Noah	1	NE	1855-12-15		A2
2197	NEWHALL, Elbridge G	1	N½NW	1855-12-15		A2
2199	" "	1	SWNW	1856-04-15		A7 G279
2198	" "	1	SENW	1859-12-10		A2
2311	OFLANEGAN, Sally S	20	E½NE	1862-07-15		A5
2312	" "	20	NESE	1862-07-15		A5
2313	" "	20	SWNE	1862-07-15		A5
2298	OLSON, Nels S	34	6	1872-09-25		A6
2299	" "	34	7	1872-09-25		A6
2182	OMDOLL, Andrew	18	E½SE	1861-12-05		A5
2183	" "	18	NESW	1861-12-05		A5
2184	" "	18	NWSE	1861-12-05		A5
2309	PARK, S Halsey	18	NENE	1864-09-15		A5 G296
2310	" "	18	S½NE	1864-09-15		A5 G296
2193	POLLY, Edward B	6	NWSE	1866-01-05		A7
2194	" "	6	SWNE	1866-01-05		A7
2191	" "	6	NENW	1866-04-20		A5
2192	" "	6	NWNE	1866-04-20		A5
2210	PRATT, George	28	SW	1871-03-10		A6
2228	PROPHET, James	6	NESW	1870-06-10		A6
2229	" "	6	SENW	1870-06-10		A6
2230	" "	6	W½NW	1870-06-10		A6 F
2309	PRUITT, John W	18	NENE	1864-09-15		A5 G296
2310	" "	18	S½NE	1864-09-15		A5 G296
2350	RENDELSBACHER, William	19	NESW	1855-12-15		A2
2351	" "	19	W½NW	1855-12-15		A2 F
2352	" "	19	W½SW	1855-12-15		A2 F
2305	RICE, Orilla M	1	NWSE	1859-05-02		A2
2337	RUNNION, Sarah	32	E½NE	1873-01-10		A6
2278	SALESBURY, Jane	14	E½NE	1864-09-15		A5 G223
2279	" "	14	NESE	1864-09-15		A5 G223
2216	SEABERT, Henry	8	E½SW	1871-03-10		A6

ID	Individual in Patent	Sec.	Sec. Part	Date Issued	Other Counties	For More Info . . .
2217	SEABERT, Henry (Cont'd)	8	SWSE	1871-03-10		A6
2181	SHEPARD, Luther G	10	NW	1863-05-20		A5 G360
2336	SHERBURN, Andrew M	1	S½SE	1859-05-02		A2 G359
2336	SHERBURN, Samuel W	1	S½SE	1859-05-02		A2 G359
2181	SHERBURNE, Andrew M	10	NW	1863-05-20		A5 G360
2174	SIEFERT, Adam	6	SESW	1872-09-02		A2
2175	" "	6	SWSE	1872-09-02		A2
2170	SMITH, Enoch	4	NW	1863-05-20		A5 G383
2195	SPRAGUE, Edwin R	1	NESE	1859-05-02		A2
2196	" "	1	NESW	1859-05-02		A2
2171	STILES, Aaron K	4	N½NE	1863-05-20		A5 G380
2170	" "	4	NW	1863-05-20		A5 G383
2172	" "	4	SENE	1863-05-20		A5 G380
2248	STOUT, Henry L	13	5	1855-12-15		A2 G224
2249	" "	13	6	1855-12-15		A2 G224
2250	" "	13	7	1855-12-15		A2 G224
2251	" "	13	8	1855-12-15		A2 G224
2269	" "	22	SESE	1855-12-15		A2 G219
2252	" "	22	SWSE	1855-12-15		A2 G224
2253	" "	23	3	1855-12-15		A2 G224
2271	" "	23	SWSW	1855-12-15		A2 G219
2254	" "	24	5	1855-12-15		A2 G224
2255	" "	24	6	1855-12-15		A2 G224
2256	" "	24	S½SE	1855-12-15		A2 G224
2257	" "	25	NW	1855-12-15		A2 G224
2274	" "	26	NE	1855-12-15		A2 G219
2258	" "	26	NESW	1855-12-15		A2 G224
2259	" "	26	NWSE	1855-12-15		A2 G224
2260	" "	34	1	1855-12-15		A2 G224
2261	" "	34	2	1855-12-15		A2 G224
2262	" "	34	3	1855-12-15		A2 G224
2276	" "	34	4	1855-12-15		A2 G219
2277	" "	34	5	1855-12-15		A2 G219
2263	" "	12	2	1857-04-01		A2 G219
2264	" "	12	N½SE	1857-04-01		A2 G219
2265	" "	13	NESW	1857-04-01		A2 G219
2266	" "	13	SWSW	1857-04-01		A2 G219
2270	" "	23	N½NE	1857-04-01		A2 G219
2273	" "	24	SWNE	1857-04-01		A2 G219
2275	" "	27	NWNE	1857-04-01		A2 G219
2267	" "	22	E½NE	1861-12-05		A5 G219
2268	" "	22	N½SE	1861-12-05		A5 G219
2280	" "	24	E½SW	1862-01-07		A5 G220
2281	" "	24	N½SE	1862-01-07		A5 G220
2282	" "	14	NWSE	1862-03-10		A5 G221
2283	" "	14	S½SE	1862-03-10		A5 G221
2272	" "	24	E½NE	1862-04-10		A2 G219
2278	" "	14	E½NE	1864-09-15		A5 G223
2279	" "	14	NESE	1864-09-15		A5 G223
2360	STROTHER, Sally	28	S½SE	1860-07-16		A5 G427
2185	SUKOW, August	4	SE	1862-12-01		A5 G386
2326	SWEET, Mary	25	SESW	1861-12-05		A5 G142
2327	" "	25	W½SW	1861-12-05		A5 G142
2248	TAINTER, Andrew	13	5	1855-12-15		A2 G224
2249	" "	13	6	1855-12-15		A2 G224
2250	" "	13	7	1855-12-15		A2 G224
2251	" "	13	8	1855-12-15		A2 G224
2269	" "	22	SESE	1855-12-15		A2 G219
2252	" "	22	SWSE	1855-12-15		A2 G224
2253	" "	23	3	1855-12-15		A2 G224
2271	" "	23	SWSW	1855-12-15		A2 G219
2254	" "	24	5	1855-12-15		A2 G224
2255	" "	24	6	1855-12-15		A2 G224
2256	" "	24	S½SE	1855-12-15		A2 G224
2257	" "	25	NW	1855-12-15		A2 G224
2274	" "	26	NE	1855-12-15		A2 G219
2258	" "	26	NESW	1855-12-15		A2 G224
2259	" "	26	NWSE	1855-12-15		A2 G224
2260	" "	34	1	1855-12-15		A2 G224
2261	" "	34	2	1855-12-15		A2 G224
2262	" "	34	3	1855-12-15		A2 G224
2276	" "	34	4	1855-12-15		A2 G219
2277	" "	34	5	1855-12-15		A2 G219

ID	Individual in Patent	Sec.	Sec. Part	Date Issued	Other Counties	For More Info . . .
2263	TAINTER, Andrew (Cont'd)	12	2	1857-04-01		A2 G219
2264	" "	12	N½SE	1857-04-01		A2 G219
2265	" "	13	NESW	1857-04-01		A2 G219
2266	" "	13	SWSW	1857-04-01		A2 G219
2270	" "	23	N½NE	1857-04-01		A2 G219
2273	" "	24	SWNE	1857-04-01		A2 G219
2275	" "	27	NWNE	1857-04-01		A2 G219
2267	" "	22	E½NE	1861-12-05		A5 G219
2268	" "	22	N½SE	1861-12-05		A5 G219
2280	" "	24	E½SW	1862-01-07		A5 G220
2281	" "	24	N½SE	1862-01-07		A5 G220
2282	" "	14	NWSE	1862-03-10		A5 G221
2283	" "	14	S½SE	1862-03-10		A5 G221
2272	" "	24	E½NE	1862-04-10		A2 G219
2278	" "	14	E½NE	1864-09-15		A5 G223
2279	" "	14	NESE	1864-09-15		A5 G223
2211	TAYLOR, George W	30	SE	1865-05-06		A5
2204	VAN RIPER, MARGARET	14	E½NW	1862-11-20		A5 G73
2205	" "	14	W½NE	1862-11-20		A5 G73
2231	WHALEY, Jeremiah M	12	NENE	1855-12-15		A2 V2215
2212	WHITE, George W	32	SW	1871-03-10		A6
2206	WICHSER, Frederick	35	NENE	1855-12-15		A2
2207	" "	35	NWSE	1855-12-15		A2
2208	WICHSER, Fredoline	35	S½NE	1855-12-15		A2
2248	WILSON, Thomas B	13	5	1855-12-15		A2 G224
2249	" "	13	6	1855-12-15		A2 G224
2250	" "	13	7	1855-12-15		A2 G224
2251	" "	13	8	1855-12-15		A2 G224
2341	" "	22	S½SW	1855-12-15		A2
2269	" "	22	SESE	1855-12-15		A2 G219
2252	" "	22	SWSE	1855-12-15		A2 G224
2253	" "	23	3	1855-12-15		A2 G224
2271	" "	23	SWSW	1855-12-15		A2 G219
2254	" "	24	5	1855-12-15		A2 G224
2255	" "	24	6	1855-12-15		A2 G224
2256	" "	24	S½SE	1855-12-15		A2 G224
2342	" "	25	NESW	1855-12-15		A2
2257	" "	25	NW	1855-12-15		A2 G224
2274	" "	26	NE	1855-12-15		A2 G219
2343	" "	26	NESE	1855-12-15		A2
2258	" "	26	NESW	1855-12-15		A2 G224
2259	" "	26	NWSE	1855-12-15		A2 G224
2344	" "	26	S½SE	1855-12-15		A2
2345	" "	26	SESW	1855-12-15		A2
2346	" "	26	W½SW	1855-12-15		A2
2260	" "	34	1	1855-12-15		A2 G224
2261	" "	34	2	1855-12-15		A2 G224
2262	" "	34	3	1855-12-15		A2 G224
2276	" "	34	4	1855-12-15		A2 G219
2277	" "	34	5	1855-12-15		A2 G219
2347	" "	35	NESE	1855-12-15		A2
2263	" "	12	2	1857-04-01		A2 G219
2264	" "	12	N½SE	1857-04-01		A2 G219
2265	" "	13	NESW	1857-04-01		A2 G219
2266	" "	13	SWSW	1857-04-01		A2 G219
2270	" "	23	N½NE	1857-04-01		A2 G219
2273	" "	24	SWNE	1857-04-01		A2 G219
2275	" "	27	NWNE	1857-04-01		A2 G219
2267	" "	22	E½NE	1861-12-05		A5 G219
2268	" "	22	N½SE	1861-12-05		A5 G219
2280	" "	24	E½SW	1862-01-07		A5 G220
2281	" "	24	N½SE	1862-01-07		A5 G220
2282	" "	14	NWSE	1862-03-10		A5 G221
2283	" "	14	S½SE	1862-03-10		A5 G221
2272	" "	24	E½NE	1862-04-10		A2 G219
2278	" "	14	E½NE	1864-09-15		A5 G223
2279	" "	14	NESE	1864-09-15		A5 G223
2354	WILSON, William	26	1	1855-04-19		A2
2355	" "	26	2	1855-04-19		A2
2356	" "	26	3	1855-04-19		A2
2357	" "	34	SWSE	1859-12-10		A2
2360	" "	28	S½SE	1860-07-16		A5 G427
2358	" "	36	E½SW	1860-07-16		A5 G426

ID	Individual in Patent	Sec.	Sec. Part	Date Issued	Other Counties	For More Info . . .
2359	WILSON, William (Cont'd)	36	NWSW	1860-07-16		A5 G426
2361	" "	22	N½SW	1862-11-20		A5 G425
2362	" "	22	S½NW	1862-11-20		A5 G425
2339	WISCONSIN, State Of	16		1941-08-16		A3
2296	WRIGHT, Marshall M	30	NW	1864-09-15		A5 G441 F

Patent Map

T28-N R13-W
4th PM - 1831 MN/WI Meridian

Map Group 14

Township Statistics

Parcels Mapped	:	193
Number of Patents	:	130
Number of Individuals	:	105
Patentees Identified	:	93
Number of Surnames	:	92
Multi-Patentee Parcels	:	66
Oldest Patent Date	:	8/2/1852
Most Recent Patent	:	8/16/1941
Block/Lot Parcels	:	26
Parcels Re - Issued	:	2
Parcels that Overlap	:	2
Cities and Towns	:	4
Cemeteries	:	8

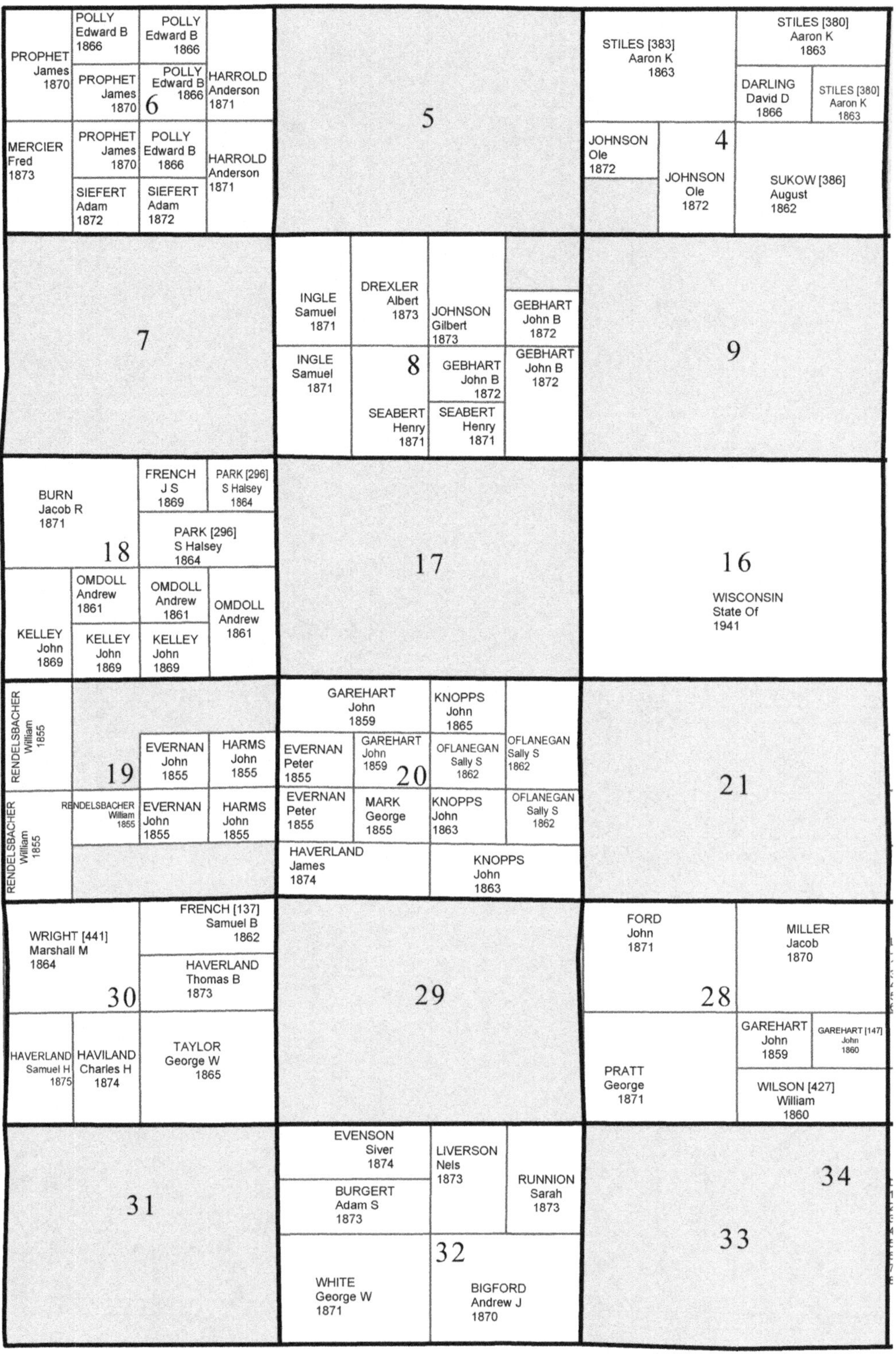
POLLY Edward B 1866
POLLY Edward B 1866
PROPHET James 1870
PROPHET James 1870
POLLY Edward B 1866
HARROLD Anderson 1871
6
MERCIER Fred 1873
PROPHET James 1870
POLLY Edward B 1866
HARROLD Anderson 1871
SIEFERT Adam 1872
SIEFERT Adam 1872
5
STILES [383] Aaron K 1863
STILES [380] Aaron K 1863
DARLING David D 1866
STILES [380] Aaron K 1863
JOHNSON Ole 1872
4
JOHNSON Ole 1872
SUKOW [386] August 1862
7
INGLE Samuel 1871
DREXLER Albert 1873
JOHNSON Gilbert 1873
GEBHART John B 1872
INGLE Samuel 1871
8
GEBHART John B 1872
GEBHART John B 1872
SEABERT Henry 1871
SEABERT Henry 1871
9
BURN Jacob R 1871
FRENCH J S 1869
PARK [296] S Halsey 1864
PARK [296] S Halsey 1864
18
OMDOLL Andrew 1861
OMDOLL Andrew 1861
OMDOLL Andrew 1861
KELLEY John 1869
KELLEY John 1869
KELLEY John 1869
17
16
WISCONSIN State Of 1941
RENDELSBACHER William 1855
EVERNAN John 1855
HARMS John 1855
19
RENDELSBACHER William 1855
EVERNAN John 1855
HARMS John 1855
RENDELSBACHER William 1855
GAREHART John 1859
KNOPPS John 1865
EVERNAN Peter 1855
GAREHART John 1859
20
OFLANEGAN Sally S 1862
OFLANEGAN Sally S 1862
EVERNAN Peter 1855
MARK George 1855
KNOPPS John 1863
OFLANEGAN Sally S 1862
HAVERLAND James 1874
KNOPPS John 1863
21
WRIGHT [441] Marshall M 1864
FRENCH [137] Samuel B 1862
HAVERLAND Thomas B 1873
30
HAVERLAND Samuel H 1875
HAVILAND Charles H 1874
TAYLOR George W 1865
29
FORD John 1871
MILLER Jacob 1870
28
GAREHART John 1859
GAREHART [147] John 1860
PRATT George 1871
WILSON [427] William 1860
31
EVENSON Siver 1874
LIVERSON Nels 1873
BURGERT Adam S 1873
RUNNION Sarah 1873
32
WHITE George W 1871
BIGFORD Andrew J 1870
34
33

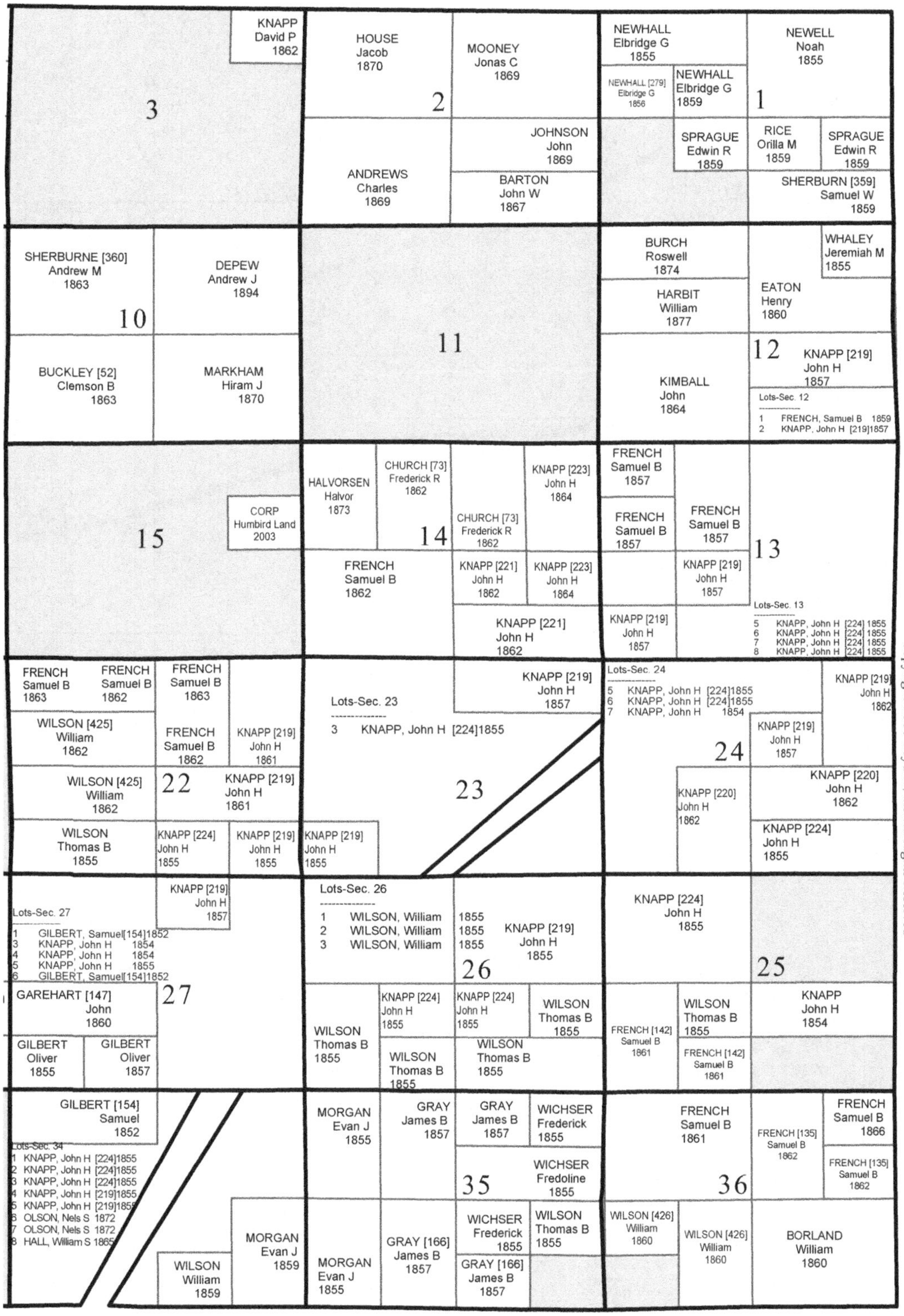
KNAPP David P 1862
3
HOUSE Jacob 1870
MOONEY Jonas C 1869
2
ANDREWS Charles 1869
JOHNSON John 1869
BARTON John W 1867
NEWHALL Elbridge G 1855
NEWELL Noah 1855
NEWHALL [279] Elbridge G 1856
NEWHALL Elbridge G 1859
1
SPRAGUE Edwin R 1859
RICE Orilla M 1859
SPRAGUE Edwin R 1859
SHERBURN [359] Samuel W 1859
SHERBURNE [360] Andrew M 1863
DEPEW Andrew J 1894
10
BUCKLEY [52] Clemson B 1863
MARKHAM Hiram J 1870
11
BURCH Roswell 1874
WHALEY Jeremiah M 1855
HARBIT William 1877
EATON Henry 1860
12
KNAPP [219] John H 1857
KIMBALL John 1864
Lots-Sec. 12
1 FRENCH, Samuel B 1859
2 KNAPP, John H [219]1857
15
CORP Humbird Land 2003
HALVORSEN Halvor 1873
CHURCH [73] Frederick R 1862
CHURCH [73] Frederick R 1862
KNAPP [223] John H 1864
14
FRENCH Samuel B 1862
KNAPP [221] John H 1862
KNAPP [223] John H 1864
KNAPP [221] John H 1862
FRENCH Samuel B 1857
FRENCH Samuel B 1857
FRENCH Samuel B 1857
13
KNAPP [219] John H 1857
KNAPP [219] John H 1857
Lots-Sec. 13
5 KNAPP, John H [224] 1855
6 KNAPP, John H [224] 1855
7 KNAPP, John H [224] 1855
8 KNAPP, John H [224] 1855
FRENCH Samuel B 1863
FRENCH Samuel B 1862
FRENCH Samuel B 1863
WILSON [425] William 1862
FRENCH Samuel B 1862
KNAPP [219] John H 1861
WILSON [425] William 1862
22
KNAPP [219] John H 1861
WILSON Thomas B 1855
KNAPP [224] John H 1855
KNAPP [219] John H 1855
KNAPP [219] John H 1855
Lots-Sec. 23
3 KNAPP, John H [224]1855
KNAPP [219] John H 1857
23
Lots-Sec. 24
5 KNAPP, John H [224]1855
6 KNAPP, John H [224]1855
7 KNAPP, John H 1854
KNAPP [219] John H 1862
KNAPP [219] John H 1857
24
KNAPP [220] John H 1862
KNAPP [220] John H 1862
KNAPP [224] John H 1855
KNAPP [219] John H 1857
Lots-Sec. 27
1 GILBERT, Samuel[154]1852
3 KNAPP, John H 1854
4 KNAPP, John H 1854
5 KNAPP, John H 1855
6 GILBERT, Samuel[154]1852
GAREHART [147] John 1860
27
GILBERT Oliver 1855
GILBERT Oliver 1857
Lots-Sec. 26
1 WILSON, William 1855
2 WILSON, William 1855
3 WILSON, William 1855
KNAPP [219] John H 1855
26
KNAPP [224] John H 1855
25
WILSON Thomas B 1855
KNAPP [224] John H 1855
KNAPP [224] John H 1855
WILSON Thomas B 1855
WILSON Thomas B 1855
WILSON Thomas B 1855
FRENCH [142] Samuel B 1861
WILSON Thomas B 1855
FRENCH [142] Samuel B 1861
KNAPP John H 1854
GILBERT [154] Samuel 1852
Lots-Sec. 34
1 KNAPP, John H [224]1855
2 KNAPP, John H [224]1855
3 KNAPP, John H [224]1855
4 KNAPP, John H [219]1855
5 KNAPP, John H [219]1855
6 OLSON, Nels S 1872
7 OLSON, Nels S 1872
8 HALL, William S 1865
MORGAN Evan J 1855
GRAY James B 1857
GRAY James B 1857
WICHSER Frederick 1855
FRENCH Samuel B 1861
FRENCH Samuel B 1866
FRENCH [135] Samuel B 1862
FRENCH [135] Samuel B 1862
WICHSER Fredoline 1855
35
36
WILSON William 1859
MORGAN Evan J 1859
MORGAN Evan J 1855
GRAY [166] James B 1857
WICHSER Frederick 1855
WILSON Thomas B 1855
GRAY [166] James B 1857
WILSON [426] William 1860
WILSON [426] William 1860
BORLAND William 1860

Helpful Hints

1. This Map's INDEX can be found on the preceding pages.
2. Refer to Map "C" to see where this Township lies within Dunn County, Wisconsin.
3. Numbers within square brackets [ ] denote a multi-patentee land parcel (multi-owner). Refer to Appendix "C" for a full list of members in this group.
4. Areas that look to be crowded with Patentees usually indicate multiple sales of the same parcel (Re-issues) or Overlapping parcels. See this Township's Index for an explanation of these and other circumstances that might explain "odd" groupings of Patentees on this map.

Legend

(thin line)	Patent Boundary
(thick line)	Section Boundary
(shaded)	No Patents Found (or Outside County)
1., 2., 3., ...	Lot Numbers (when beside a name)
[ ]	Group Number (see Appendix "C")

Scale: Section = 1 mile X 1 mile (generally, with some exceptions)

Road Map

T28-N R13-W
4th PM - 1831 MN/WI Meridian

Map Group 14

Cities & Towns

- Huber Mobile Home Park
- Menominee
- Menomonie Junction
- North Menomonie

Cemeteries

- Evergreen Cemetery
- Ford Cemetery
- Halverson Cemetery
- Highland Cemetery
- Mamre Cemetery
- Ridge Road Cemetery
- Saint Josephs Cemetery
- Tramway Cemetery

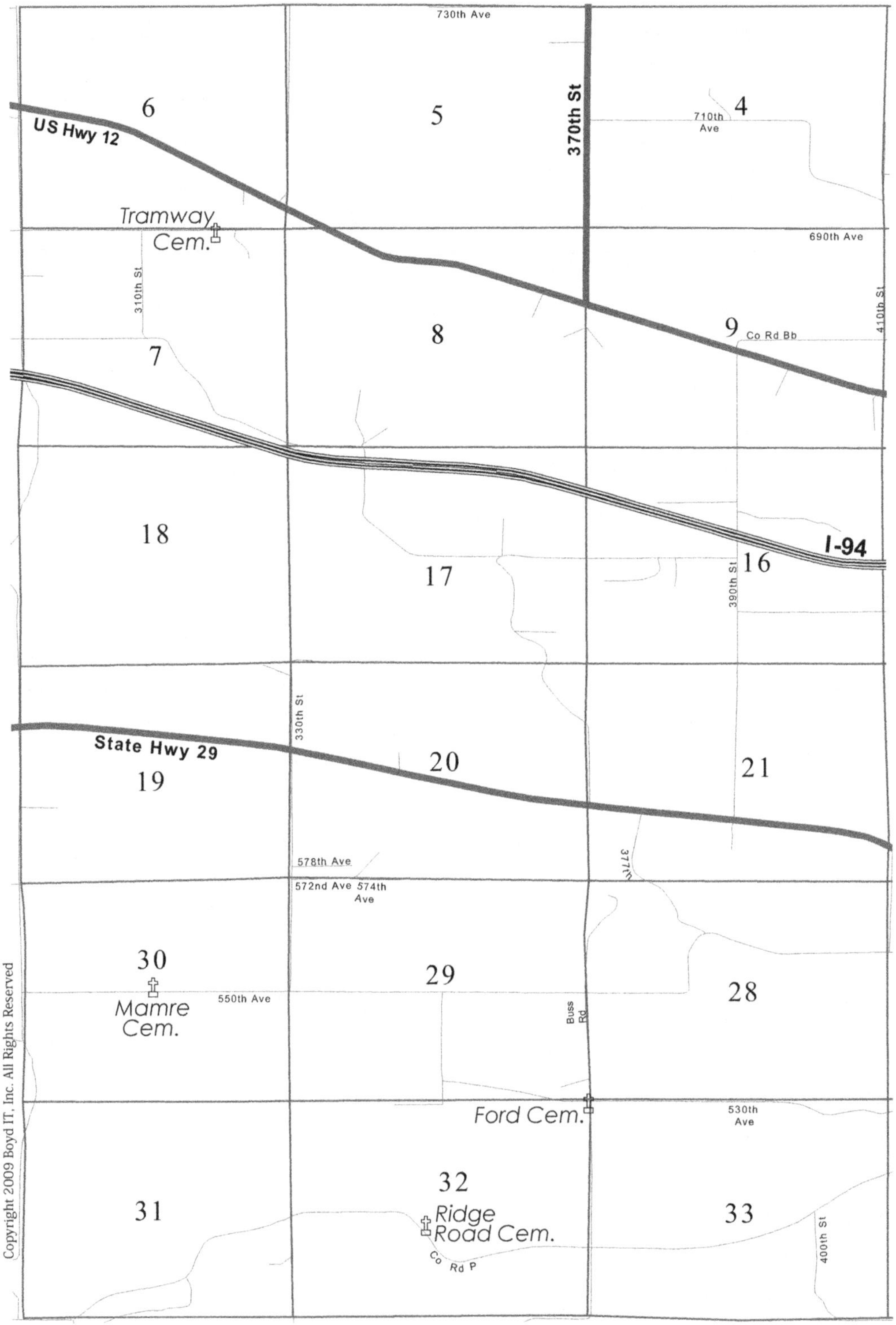
730th Ave
6
5
4
370th St
US Hwy 12
710th Ave
Tramway Cem.
690th Ave
310th St
410th St
7
8
9
Co Rd Bb
18
17
16
I-94
390th St
330th St
State Hwy 29
19
20
21
578th Ave
572nd Ave
574th Ave
30
29
28
Mamre Cem.
550th Ave
Buss Rd
Ford Cem.
530th Ave
31
32
33
Ridge Road Cem.
Co Rd P
400th St

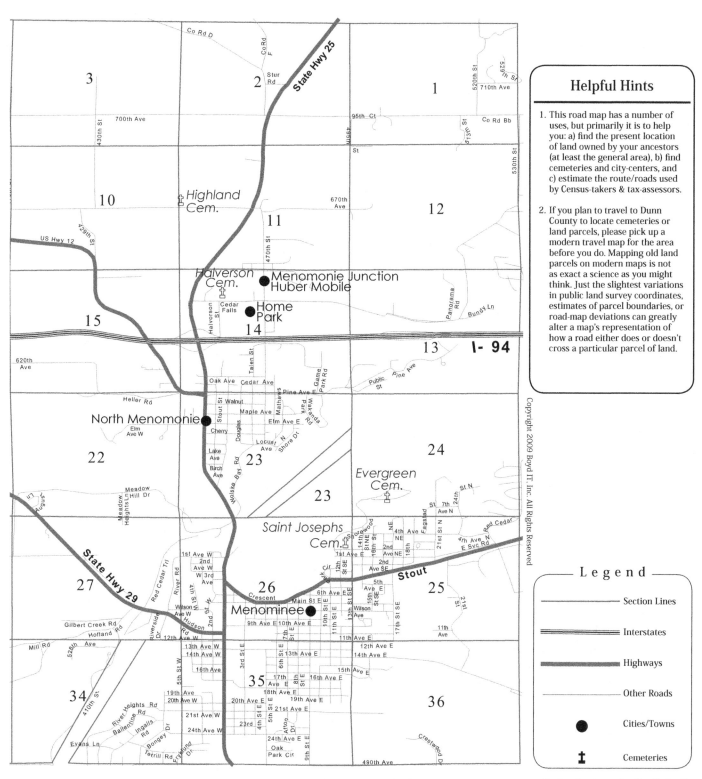

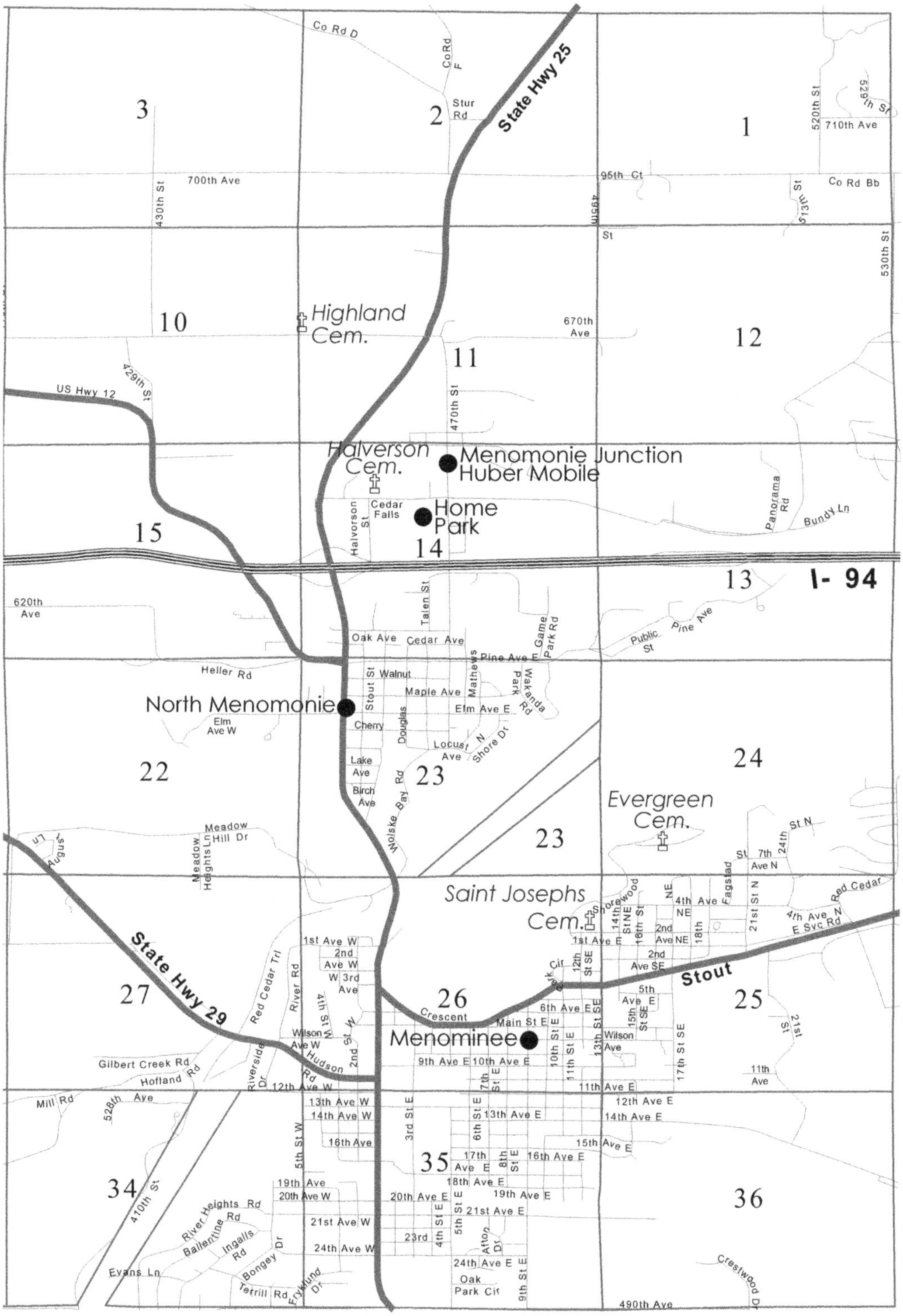

Helpful Hints

1. This road map has a number of uses, but primarily it is to help you: a) find the present location of land owned by your ancestors (at least the general area), b) find cemeteries and city-centers, and c) estimate the route/roads used by Census-takers & tax-assessors.

2. If you plan to travel to Dunn County to locate cemeteries or land parcels, please pick up a modern travel map for the area before you do. Mapping old land parcels on modern maps is not as exact a science as you might think. Just the slightest variations in public land survey coordinates, estimates of parcel boundaries, or road-map deviations can greatly alter a map's representation of how a road either does or doesn't cross a particular parcel of land.

Legend

- Section Lines
- Interstates
- Highways
- Other Roads
- Cities/Towns
- Cemeteries

Scale: Section = 1 mile X 1 mile
(generally, with some exceptions)

Historical Map

T28-N R13-W
4th PM - 1831 MN/WI Meridian

Map Group 14

Cities & Towns

Huber Mobile Home Park
Menominee
Menomonie Junction
North Menomonie

Cemeteries

Evergreen Cemetery
Ford Cemetery
Halverson Cemetery
Highland Cemetery
Mamre Cemetery
Ridge Road Cemetery
Saint Josephs Cemetery
Tramway Cemetery

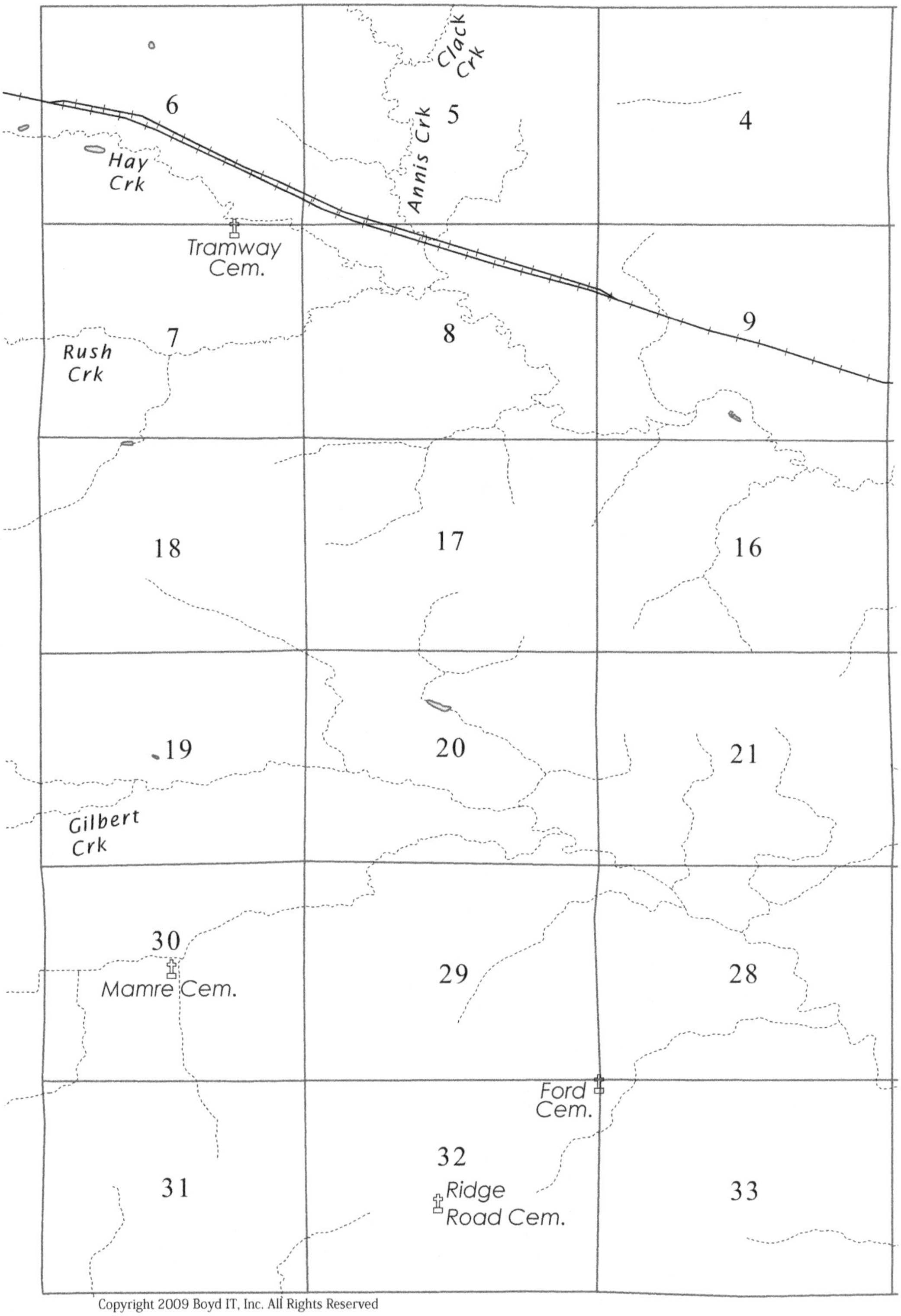

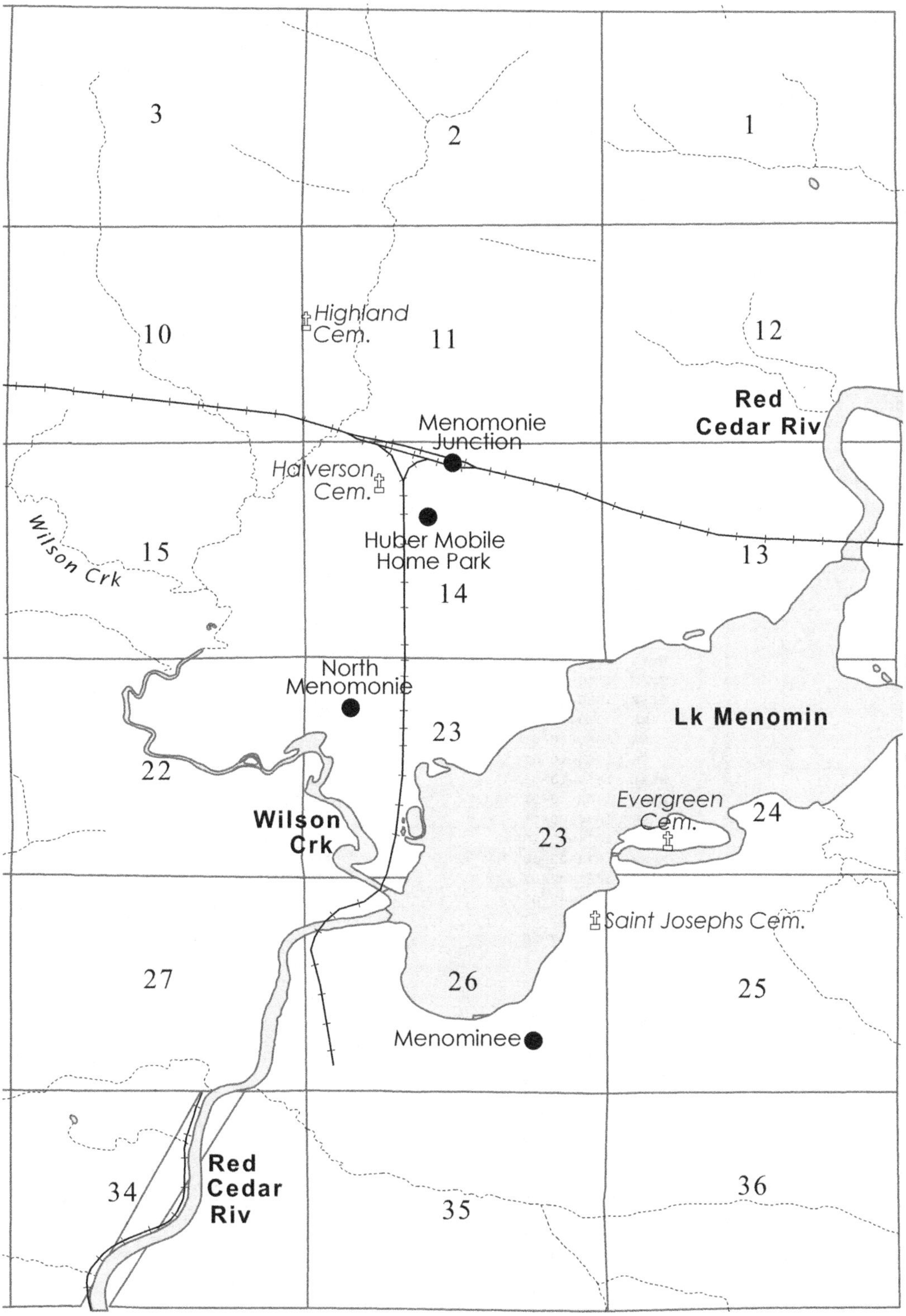

Helpful Hints

1. This Map takes a different look at the same Congressional Township displayed in the preceding two maps. It presents features that can help you better envision the historical development of the area: a) Water-bodies (lakes & ponds), b) Water-courses (rivers, streams, etc.), c) Railroads, d) City/town center-points (where they were oftentimes located when first settled), and e) Cemeteries.

2. Using this "Historical" map in tandem with this Township's Patent Map and Road Map, may lead you to some interesting discoveries. You will often find roads, towns, cemeteries, and waterways are named after nearby landowners: sometimes those names will be the ones you are researching. See how many of these research gems you can find here in Dunn County.

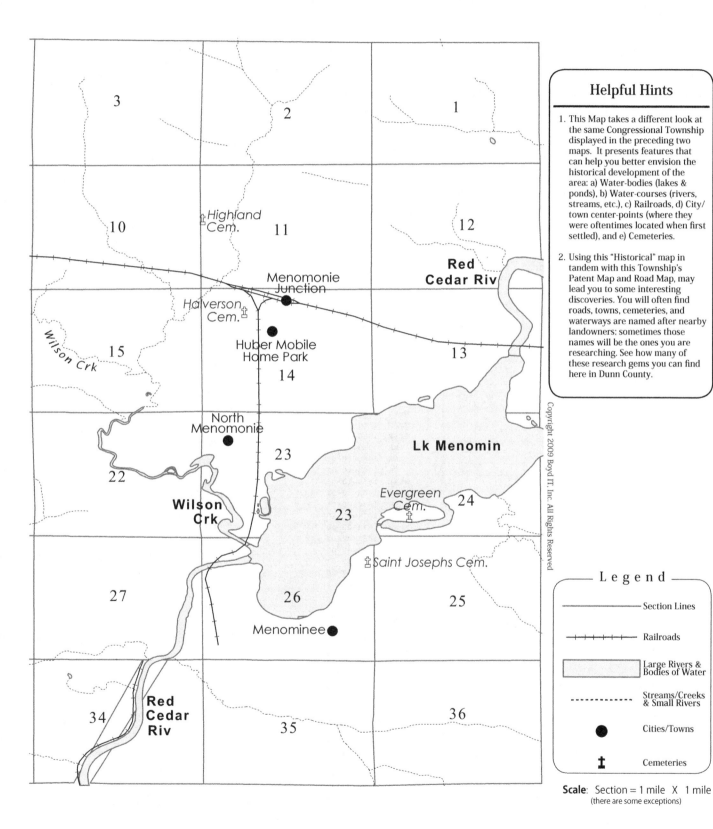

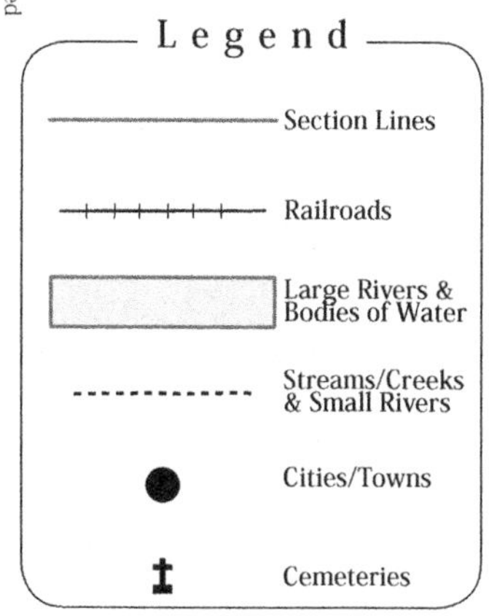
Legend
Section Lines
Railroads
Large Rivers & Bodies of Water
Streams/Creeks & Small Rivers
Cities/Towns
Cemeteries

Scale: Section = 1 mile X 1 mile
(there are some exceptions)

Map Group 15: Index to Land Patents

Township 28-North Range 12-West (4th PM - 1831 MN/WI)

After you locate an individual in this Index, take note of the Section and Section Part then proceed to the Land Patent map on the pages immediately following. You should have no difficulty locating the corresponding parcel of land.

The "For More Info" Column will lead you to more information about the underlying Patents. See the *Legend* at right, and the "How to Use this Book" chapter, for more information.

LEGEND

"For More Info . . . " column

A = Authority (Legislative Act, See Appendix "A")
B = Block or Lot (location in Section unknown)
C = Cancelled Patent
F = Fractional Section
G = Group (Multi-Patentee Patent, see Appendix "C")
V = Overlaps another Parcel
R = Re-Issued (Parcel patented more than once)

(A & G items require you to look in the Appendixes referred to above. All other Letter-designations followed by a number require you to locate line-items in this index that possess the ID number found after the letter).

ID	Individual in Patent	Sec.	Sec. Part	Date Issued	Other Counties	For More Info . . .
2536	ALDRICK, Caleb E	34	NE	1862-03-10		A5 G133
2519	ALLEN, Miriam	26	SW	1861-12-05		A5 G280
2456	ALLEN, Stillman B	17	W½SW	1857-10-30		A5 G108
2457	" "	20	NWNW	1857-10-30		A5 G108
2449	ANDERSON, James	14	NW	1861-12-05		A5 G324
2420	BABBENDORF, George	36	SESW	1865-05-05		A2
2447	BARKER, James S	14	NE	1860-10-01		A5 G21
2480	" "	23	NW	1861-09-05		A5 G401
2556	BARNARD, George M	12	NE	1861-02-01		A5 G27
2434	BARNARD, James M	1	SE	1860-10-01		A5
2446	" "	1	SW	1860-10-01		A5 G25
2435	" "	11	N½SE	1860-10-01		A5
2436	" "	11	SENE	1860-10-01		A5
2437	" "	11	SESE	1860-10-01		A5
2438	" "	2	NE	1860-10-01		A5
2439	" "	2	NW	1860-10-01		A5
2440	" "	3	SE	1860-10-01		A5
2442	" "	4	S½SE	1860-10-01		A5 G23 C R2443
2444	" "	9	E½NE	1860-10-01		A5 G23 C R2445
2441	" "	3	SW	1864-09-15		A5
2443	" "	4	S½SE	1874-03-18		A5 G23 R2442
2445	" "	9	E½NE	1874-03-18		A5 G23 R2444
2556	BARNARD, Susan L	12	NE	1861-02-01		A5 G27
2491	BARTLETT, Junius A	10	N½SE	1861-02-01		A5 G30
2492	" "	11	W½SW	1861-02-01		A5 G30
2521	BAXTER, Richard	12	NW	1862-07-15		A5 G33
2540	BEDDINGER, Sarah	27	SESW	1861-07-01		A5 G134 C
2541	" "	27	W½SW	1861-07-01		A5 G134 C
2451	BEGUHN, John	25	NWSE	1861-04-01		A7
2452	" "	25	SWSE	1861-07-01		A5 G34 C R2426
2453	" "	36	N½NE	1861-07-01		A5 G34 C R2427
2522	BENNETT, Richard	30	SW	1860-02-01		A5 G36 F
2380	BEYER, Charles	12	NESW	1870-05-20		A6
2381	" "	12	NWSE	1870-05-20		A6
2382	" "	12	S½SW	1870-05-20		A6
2561	BEYER, William	12	E½SE	1870-05-20		A6
2562	" "	12	SWSE	1870-05-20		A6
2563	BORLAND, William	24	SW	1860-10-01		A5
2521	BOUSE, Barbara	12	NW	1862-07-15		A5 G33
2504	BROWN, Michael	32	E½NW	1882-05-10		A6
2364	BRUNELLE, Alexis	19	SESE	1857-04-01		A2
2365	" "	31	NWSE	1857-04-01		A2
2448	BRUNELLE, Jane R	13	NW	1861-07-01		A5
2431	BURNHAM, Anna	11	SWSE	1860-10-01		A7 G431
2543	BURT, Samuel V	22	S½NE	1861-07-01		A5
2564	BURTON, William	15	NE	1861-02-01		A5

ID	Individual in Patent	Sec.	Sec. Part	Date Issued	Other Counties	For More Info . . .
2537	CAMERON, Christie	32	NESW	1862-07-15		A5 G136
2538	" "	32	W½SW	1862-07-15		A5 G136
2409	CHAMBERS, Ezekiel A	20	N½SE	1859-09-10		A5
2410	" "	20	S½NE	1859-09-10		A5
2424	CLACK, Henry G	15	S½SE	1861-07-01		A5
2425	" "	22	N½NE	1861-07-01		A5
2476	COLE, Melissa	34	SE	1868-01-16		A5 G278
2416	COLLINS, Betsey	23	SE	1860-10-01		A5 G169
2383	COOK, Charles	12	NWSW	1875-10-01		A2
2433	DEARY, James	28	SE	1861-07-01		A5 G104
2456	DIX, John H	17	W½SW	1857-10-30		A5 G108
2457	" "	20	NWNW	1857-10-30		A5 G108
2454	" "	29	E½NW	1857-10-30		A5
2455	" "	29	S½NE	1857-10-30		A5
2474	DYER, John L	13	S½SE	1861-07-01		A5 C
2475	" "	13	SESW	1861-07-01		A5 C
2413	ELDERD, Eliza	36	N½SW	1861-12-05		A5 G266
2414	" "	36	S½NW	1861-12-05		A5 G266
2499	EYTCHESON, Mary A	30	SWNE	1859-03-03		A7
2507	EYTCHESON, Nathan	19	NESE	1855-12-15		A2
2508	" "	19	NWSE	1855-12-15		A2
2509	" "	19	SENE	1855-12-15		A2
2510	" "	31	NESW	1857-04-01		A2
2390	FINDLEY, Edmund	18	NENW	1870-05-20		A6
2391	" "	18	NWSW	1870-05-20		A6
2392	" "	18	W½NW	1870-05-20		A6
2491	FOWLER, Mary Ann	10	N½SE	1861-02-01		A5 G30
2492	" "	11	W½SW	1861-02-01		A5 G30
2532	FRENCH, Samuel B	30	NENE	1860-06-01		A2
2526	" "	26	SWNW	1861-07-01		A5 C R2552
2527	" "	27	E½SE	1861-07-01		A5 C
2528	" "	27	NENE	1861-07-01		A5 C
2534	" "	27	NESW	1861-07-01		A5 G141 C
2529	" "	27	SENE	1861-07-01		A5 C
2540	" "	27	SESW	1861-07-01		A5 G134 C
2530	" "	27	W½NE	1861-07-01		A5 C
2535	" "	27	W½SE	1861-07-01		A5 G141 C
2541	" "	27	W½SW	1861-07-01		A5 G134 C
2539	" "	22	SE	1861-09-05		A5 G139
2481	" "	18	NESE	1861-12-05		A5 G185
2482	" "	18	SENE	1861-12-05		A5 G185
2533	" "	34	SW	1861-12-05		A5
2525	" "	22	NW	1862-03-10		A5
2536	" "	34	NE	1862-03-10		A5 G133
2531	" "	28	SW	1862-05-20		A5
2537	" "	32	NESW	1862-07-15		A5 G136
2538	" "	32	W½SW	1862-07-15		A5 G136
2523	" "	18	1	1871-06-14		A2
2524	" "	18	2	1871-06-14		A2
2375	FUNK, August	32	NESE	1877-05-15		A6
2376	" "	32	SENE	1877-05-15		A6
2408	FUNK, Ernest	32	SESE	1883-07-10		A6
2419	GRABHEIR, Gabherd	31	SWSE	1855-12-15		A2
2522	GRAY, James B	30	SW	1860-02-01		A5 G36 F
2416	GROVER, Freeman	23	SE	1860-10-01		A5 G169
2415	" "	25	NW	1860-10-01		A5
2417	" "	24	NE	1862-03-10		A5 G170
2502	HALFERTY, Mary	34	E½NW	None-NA-NA		A5 C R2512
2512	HALFORTY, Mary	34	E½NW	1862-03-05		A5 G229 R2502
2470	HANCOCK, Cynthia	5	E½SW	1860-10-01		A5 G179
2471	" "	5	SENW	1860-10-01		A5 G179
2539	HARKNESS, Margaret	22	SE	1861-09-05		A5 G139
2386	HARRINGTON, Delilah S	5	W½NW	1860-10-01		A5
2387	" "	5	W½SW	1860-10-01		A5
2468	HARRINGTON, John	5	NENW	1860-06-01		A2
2464	" "	3	NWNW	1860-10-01		A5
2466	" "	4	N½NE	1860-10-01		A5 F
2470	" "	5	E½SW	1860-10-01		A5 G179
2471	" "	5	SENW	1860-10-01		A5 G179
2465	" "	3	SWNW	1864-09-15		A5
2467	" "	4	S½NE	1864-09-15		A5
2469	" "	8	4	1873-06-20		A2
2560	HARRINGTON, Timothy	24	NW	1861-04-01		A7

ID	Individual in Patent	Sec.	Sec. Part	Date Issued	Other Counties	For More Info . . .
2511	HARRIS, Almon T	34	W½NW	1862-05-20		A5 G230
2488	HARTMAN, Joseph	30	NWSE	1870-05-20		A6
2433	HAY, Sally	28	SE	1861-07-01		A5 G104
2481	HEASLY, John W	18	NESE	1861-12-05		A5 G185
2482	" "	18	SENE	1861-12-05		A5 G185
2520	HORSTAD, Peter	10	S½SE	1860-10-01		A5
2393	HUMISTON, Edward T	4	NESE	1876-01-10		A6
2426	ISENHOOD, Henry	25	SWSE	1870-05-20		A6 R2452
2427	" "	36	N½NE	1870-05-20		A6 R2453
2506	JAMES, Frances	14	SE	1860-10-01		A5 G420
2411	KELLEY, Francis	2	NESE	1874-04-01		A6
2566	KENT, William	9	NW	1861-07-01		A5 G215
2373	KIDDER, Asa	32	NENE	1864-09-15		A5
2374	" "	32	W½NE	1864-09-15		A5
2473	KIMBALL, John	8	NW	1862-05-20		A5 F
2472	" "	8	2SW	1862-07-01		A2
2458	KNAPP, John H	19	NESW	1854-07-05		A7
2460	" "	30	NENW	1854-07-05		A7
2459	" "	19	SWSW	1854-10-02		A2
2461	" "	30	NWNW	1854-10-02		A2
2462	" "	30	S½NW	1855-12-15		A2 G224
2463	" "	30	NWNE	1857-04-01		A2 G219
2512	KRAMER, Nicholas	34	E½NW	1862-03-05		A5 G229 R2502
2511	" "	34	W½NW	1862-05-20		A5 G230
2404	KUNCLER, Frederick	4	W½SW	1860-10-01		A5 G419
2565	LANDON, William H	8	1SW	1862-01-20		A4 G235
2565	LAUDON, William H	8	1SW	1862-01-20		A4 G235
2567	LENTZ, William	25	SW	1860-10-01		A5
2423	LUND, Hans	26	NE	1860-10-01		A5
2417	LYON, Frances B	24	NE	1862-03-10		A5 G170
2550	MCKAHAN, Sarah	26	N½NW	1862-01-07		A5
2551	" "	26	SENW	1862-01-07		A5
2552	" "	26	SWNW	1867-07-15		A2 R2526
2553	MCKAHUN, Sarah	23	SW	1860-10-01		A5 G261
2503	MCMURRY, Mary Catherine	10	E½NE	1861-07-01		A5 G394
2503	MCMURRY, William	10	E½NE	1861-07-01		A5 G394
2363	MESSENGER, A J	14	NWSW	1867-07-15		A2
2412	MIESTER, Frank	25	SESE	1862-11-15		A2
2413	MIESTER, Franz	36	N½SW	1861-12-05		A5 G266
2414	" "	36	S½NW	1861-12-05		A5 G266
2553	MILLER, Jane	23	SW	1860-10-01		A5 G261
2377	MOSTELLER, Battus	20	SESW	1857-04-01		A2
2476	MOYES, John	34	SE	1868-01-16		A5 G278
2449	MURK, Michael Peterson	14	NW	1861-12-05		A5 G324
2513	NEWELL, Noah	17	NE	1855-12-15		A2
2514	" "	21	6	1855-12-15		A2
2515	" "	21	SESW	1855-12-15		A2
2516	" "	21	W½SW	1855-12-15		A2
2517	" "	28	NW	1855-12-15		A2
2518	" "	8	E½	1855-12-15		A2
2397	NEWHALL, Elbridge G	21	7	1855-12-15		A2
2398	" "	21	8	1855-12-15		A2
2399	" "	21	SESE	1855-12-15		A2
2400	" "	27	NW	1855-12-15		A2
2401	" "	5	SE	1855-12-15		A2
2573	NEWHALL, Wright	17	E½SW	1855-12-15		A2
2574	" "	17	SE	1855-12-15		A2
2575	" "	22	SW	1855-12-15		A2
2576	" "	28	NE	1855-12-15		A2
2577	" "	9	SW	1855-12-15		A2
2519	NEWSOM, Parnelle G	26	SW	1861-12-05		A5 G280
2428	NICHOLS, Henry	4	SESW	1866-09-01		A2
2500	NOWLEN, Mary Ann	14	NESW	1861-07-01		A5
2501	" "	14	S½SW	1861-07-01		A5
2542	NOYES, Samuel B	10	N½SW	1859-05-02		A2
2557	OBRIEN, Thomas	2	NESW	1861-01-21		A2
2558	" "	2	SESW	1861-02-01		A5 G284
2559	" "	2	W½SE	1861-02-01		A5 G284
2483	OLMSTEAD, Maria T	11	E½NW	1861-02-01		A5 G442
2484	" "	11	W½NE	1861-02-01		A5 G442
2477	PACHL, John	11	E½SW	1874-03-18		A5
2452	PALMER, Phebe	25	SWSE	1861-07-01		A5 G34 C R2426
2453	" "	36	N½NE	1861-07-01		A5 G34 C R2427

ID	Individual in Patent	Sec.	Sec. Part	Date Issued	Other Counties	For More Info . . .
2534	PAYNE, Betsy	27	NESW	1861-07-01		A5 G141 C
2535	" "	27	W½SE	1861-07-01		A5 G141 C
2568	PHILLIPS, William	25	NE	1883-10-20		A5
2429	PHILPOTT, Henry	30	SENE	1860-06-01		A2
2447	POWERS, Emma	14	NE	1860-10-01		A5 G21
2569	PRETY, William	2	W½SW	1864-09-15		A5 G313
2554	PROPHET, James	32	W½SE	1862-12-01		A5 G366
2389	RAIMER, Douglas	32	SESW	1879-10-01		A6
2478	REINCKE, John	36	NWNW	1871-08-25		A6
2449	REYMERT, Jenny D	14	NW	1861-12-05		A5 G324
2489	REYMOND, Joseph	30	E½SE	1865-05-06		A5
2490	" "	30	SWSE	1865-05-06		A5
2385	RIPLEY, Christopher G	13	NE	1857-10-30		A5
2485	RITER, Joseph D	6	2	1852-08-02		A2
2486	" "	6	6	1852-08-02		A2
2487	" "	6	7	1852-08-02		A2
2450	RITTENHOUSE, John B	10	NW	1860-10-01		A5
2497	ROWE, Irena	18	S½SE	1862-05-20		A5 G358
2498	" "	18	S½SW	1862-05-20		A5 G358
2379	RURICHT, Carl	25	NESE	1866-02-15		A2
2430	SCHELHAD, Henry	36	S½NE	1870-05-20		A6
2519	SEXTON, Thomas W	26	SW	1861-12-05		A5 G280
2493	SHEPARD, Luther G	18	NESW	1862-05-20		A5
2494	" "	18	NWSE	1862-05-20		A5
2495	" "	18	SENW	1862-05-20		A5
2496	" "	18	SWNE	1862-05-20		A5
2497	SHEPHARD, Luther G	18	S½SE	1862-05-20		A5 G358
2498	" "	18	S½SW	1862-05-20		A5 G358
2371	SHERBURNE, Andrew	9	N½SE	1857-04-01		A2
2372	" "	9	W½NE	1861-07-01		A5
2366	SHERBURNE, Andrew M	10	SESW	1855-12-15		A2
2368	" "	15	N½NW	1855-12-15		A2
2369	" "	9	SESE	1855-12-15		A2
2367	" "	10	SWSW	1857-04-01		A2
2370	" "	9	SWSE	1857-04-01		A2
2544	SHERBURNE, Samuel W	15	S½NW	1855-12-15		A2
2549	" "	5	W½NE	1855-12-15		A2 F
2548	" "	5	E½NE	1857-04-01		A2
2545	" "	20	N½NE	1860-03-01		A2
2546	" "	20	NENW	1860-03-01		A2
2547	" "	21	5	1860-03-01		A2
2432	SHUMAKER, Jacob	15	N½SE	1861-07-01		A5 G377
2566	SICKLES, Sarah	9	NW	1861-07-01		A5 G215
2556	SMITH, Mary	12	NE	1861-02-01		A5 G27
2554	SMITH, Sheldon	32	W½SE	1862-12-01		A5 G366
2378	SPAFFORD, C C	36	SE	1862-07-15		A5 G374
2394	SPRAGUE, Edwin R	19	N½SW	1859-05-02		A2 F
2395	" "	19	NENE	1859-05-02		A2 F
2396	" "	19	W½NE	1859-05-02		A2 F
2432	SPRAGUE, James B	15	N½SE	1861-07-01		A5 G377
2479	STEWART, John	24	SE	1862-01-07		A5
2462	STOUT, Henry L	30	S½NW	1855-12-15		A2 G224
2463	" "	30	NWNE	1857-04-01		A2 G219
2405	SWEENY, Eliza Ann	26	SE	1860-10-01		A5
2462	TAINTER, Andrew	30	S½NW	1855-12-15		A2 G224
2463	" "	30	NWNE	1857-04-01		A2 G219
2503	THIBODO, Maxime	10	E½NE	1861-07-01		A5 G394
2449	TOLASON, Jonas	14	NW	1861-12-05		A5 G324
2447	TRASHER, John	14	NE	1860-10-01		A5 G21
2480	" "	23	NW	1861-09-05		A5 G401
2384	TYLER, Charles	36	SWSW	1869-10-20		A6
2418	URSINUS, Friedrick	32	W½NW	1862-04-10		A2
2558	VOORIS, Amy	2	SESW	1861-02-01		A5 G284
2559	" "	2	W½SE	1861-02-01		A5 G284
2388	WAGNER, Dominick	10	W½NE	1861-07-01		A5
2442	WALKER, Sarah	4	S½SE	1860-10-01		A5 G23 C R2443
2444	" "	9	E½NE	1860-10-01		A5 G23 C R2445
2443	" "	4	S½SE	1874-03-18		A5 G23 R2442
2445	" "	9	E½NE	1874-03-18		A5 G23 R2444
2402	WATKINS, Eli G	4	NESW	1862-04-10		A2
2403	" "	4	NWSE	1862-04-10		A2
2569	WHEELER, Augustus C	2	W½SW	1864-09-15		A5 G313
2421	WHINERY, George	19	SWSE	1857-04-01		A2

ID	Individual in Patent	Sec.	Sec. Part	Date Issued	Other Counties	For More Info . . .
2422	WHINERY, George (Cont'd)	20	SWSW	1857-04-01		A2
2404	WHITE, Elias A	4	W½SW	1860-10-01		A5 G419
2506	WHITE, Miles	14	SE	1860-10-01		A5 G420
2505	" "	4	NW	1861-09-05		A5
2378	WILLIAMSON, Harriet	36	SE	1862-07-15		A5 G374
2406	WILSON, Eliza T	20	N½SW	1855-12-15		A2
2407	" "	20	S½NW	1855-12-15		A2
2462	WILSON, Thomas B	30	S½NW	1855-12-15		A2 G224
2463	" "	30	NWNE	1857-04-01		A2 G219
2571	WILSON, William	20	S½SE	1859-05-02		A2
2572	" "	29	N½NE	1859-05-02		A2
2570	" "	13	N½SE	1862-04-10		A2
2555	WISCONSIN, State Of	16		1941-08-16		A3
2431	WOODMAN, Horatio	11	SWSE	1860-10-01		A7 G431
2446	WOODWARD, Susannah	1	SW	1860-10-01		A5 G25
2449	YOUNG, Francis	14	NW	1861-12-05		A5 G324
2483	ZIMERMAN, John	11	E½NW	1861-02-01		A5 G442
2484	" "	11	W½NE	1861-02-01		A5 G442

Patent Map

T28-N R12-W
4th PM - 1831 MN/WI Meridian

Map Group 15

Township Statistics

Parcels Mapped	:	215
Number of Patents	:	157
Number of Individuals	:	148
Patentees Identified	:	118
Number of Surnames	:	129
Multi-Patentee Parcels	:	57
Oldest Patent Date	:	8/2/1852
Most Recent Patent	:	8/16/1941
Block/Lot Parcels	:	12
Parcels Re - Issued	:	6
Parcels that Overlap	:	0
Cities and Towns	:	2
Cemeteries	:	2

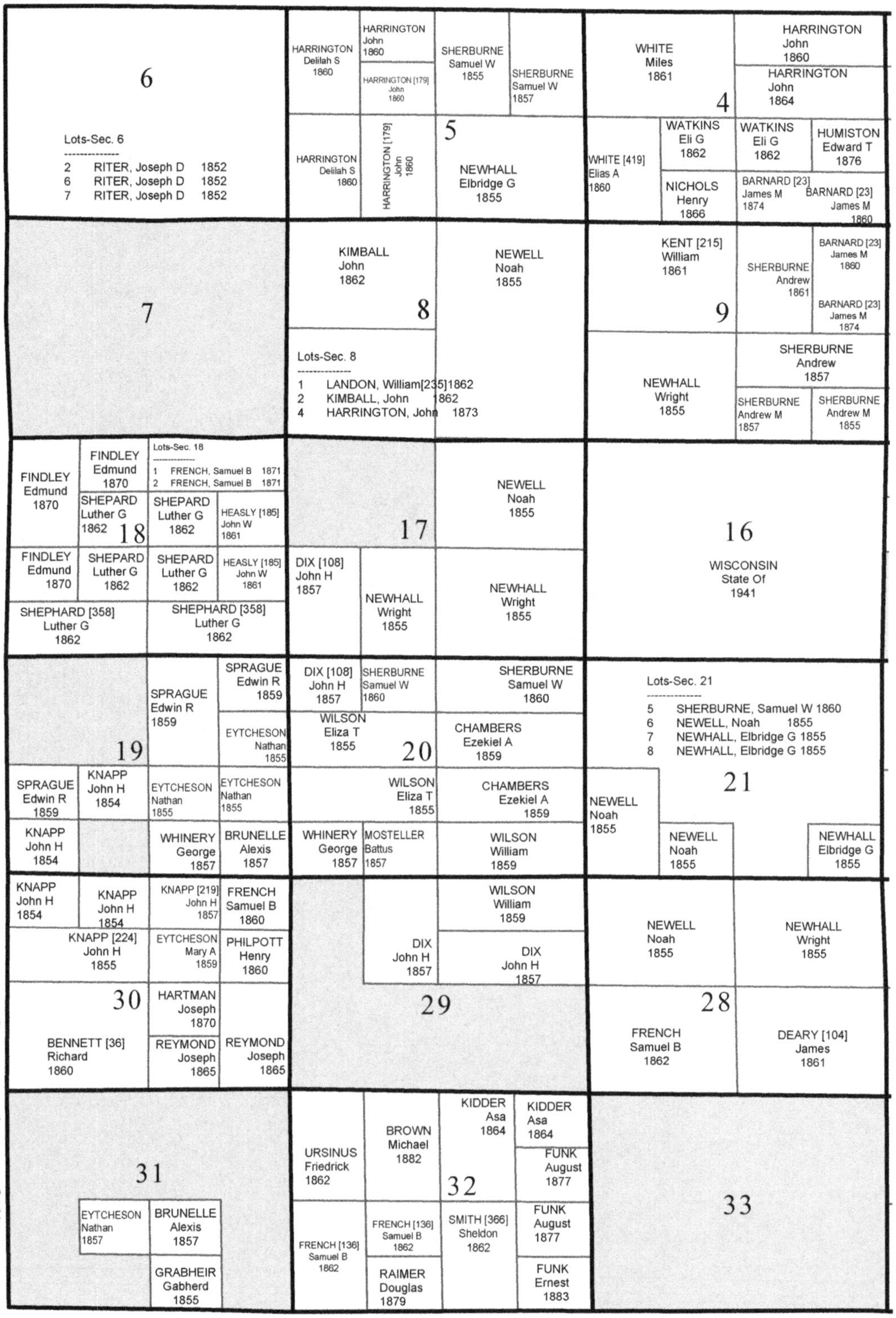
6
Lots-Sec. 6
2 RITER, Joseph D 1852
6 RITER, Joseph D 1852
7 RITER, Joseph D 1852
HARRINGTON Delilah S 1860
HARRINGTON John 1860
HARRINGTON [179] John 1860
SHERBURNE Samuel W 1855
SHERBURNE Samuel W 1857
HARRINGTON Delilah S 1860
HARRINGTON [179] John 1860
5
NEWHALL Elbridge G 1855
WHITE Miles 1861
4
HARRINGTON John 1860
HARRINGTON John 1864
WHITE [419] Elias A 1860
WATKINS Eli G 1862
NICHOLS Henry 1866
WATKINS Eli G 1862
HUMISTON Edward T 1876
BARNARD [23] James M 1874
BARNARD [23] James M 1860
7
KIMBALL John 1862
8
NEWELL Noah 1855
Lots-Sec. 8
1 LANDON, William[235]1862
2 KIMBALL, John 1862
4 HARRINGTON, John 1873
KENT [215] William 1861
9
SHERBURNE Andrew 1861
BARNARD [23] James M 1860
BARNARD [23] James M 1874
NEWHALL Wright 1855
SHERBURNE Andrew 1857
SHERBURNE Andrew M 1857
SHERBURNE Andrew M 1855
FINDLEY Edmund 1870
FINDLEY Edmund 1870
Lots-Sec. 18
1 FRENCH, Samuel B 1871
2 FRENCH, Samuel B 1871
SHEPARD Luther G 1862
18
SHEPARD Luther G 1862
HEASLY [185] John W 1861
FINDLEY Edmund 1870
SHEPARD Luther G 1862
SHEPARD Luther G 1862
HEASLY [185] John W 1861
SHEPHARD [358] Luther G 1862
SHEPHARD [358] Luther G 1862
17
NEWELL Noah 1855
DIX [108] John H 1857
NEWHALL Wright 1855
NEWHALL Wright 1855
16
WISCONSIN State Of 1941
19
SPRAGUE Edwin R 1859
SPRAGUE Edwin R 1859
EYTCHESON Nathan 1855
SPRAGUE Edwin R 1859
KNAPP John H 1854
EYTCHESON Nathan 1855
EYTCHESON Nathan 1855
KNAPP John H 1854
WHINERY George 1857
BRUNELLE Alexis 1857
DIX [108] John H 1857
SHERBURNE Samuel W 1860
SHERBURNE Samuel W 1860
WILSON Eliza T 1855
20
CHAMBERS Ezekiel A 1859
WILSON Eliza T 1855
CHAMBERS Ezekiel A 1859
WHINERY George 1857
MOSTELLER Battus 1857
WILSON William 1859
Lots-Sec. 21
5 SHERBURNE, Samuel W 1860
6 NEWELL, Noah 1855
7 NEWHALL, Elbridge G 1855
8 NEWHALL, Elbridge G 1855
21
NEWELL Noah 1855
NEWELL Noah 1855
NEWHALL Elbridge G 1855
KNAPP John H 1854
KNAPP John H 1854
KNAPP [219] John H 1857
FRENCH Samuel B 1860
KNAPP [224] John H 1855
EYTCHESON Mary A 1859
PHILPOTT Henry 1860
30
BENNETT [36] Richard 1860
HARTMAN Joseph 1870
REYMOND Joseph 1865
REYMOND Joseph 1865
WILSON William 1859
DIX John H 1857
DIX John H 1857
29
NEWELL Noah 1855
NEWHALL Wright 1855
28
FRENCH Samuel B 1862
DEARY [104] James 1861
31
EYTCHESON Nathan 1857
BRUNELLE Alexis 1857
GRABHEIR Gabherd 1855
URSINUS Friedrick 1862
BROWN Michael 1882
KIDDER Asa 1864
KIDDER Asa 1864
FUNK August 1877
32
FRENCH [136] Samuel B 1862
FRENCH [136] Samuel B 1862
SMITH [366] Sheldon 1862
FUNK August 1877
RAIMER Douglas 1879
FUNK Ernest 1883
33

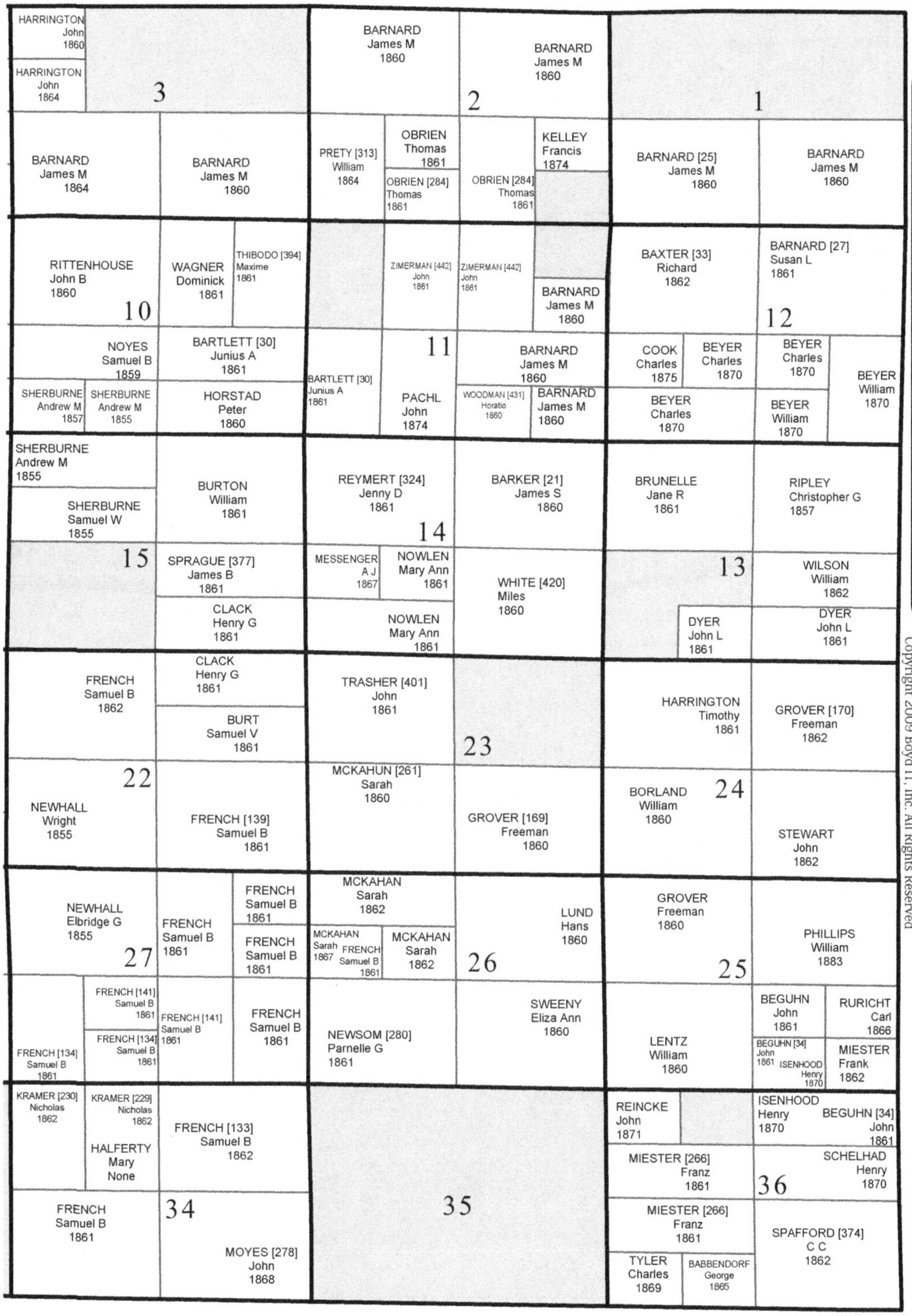
HARRINGTON John 1860
HARRINGTON John 1864
3
BARNARD James M 1864
BARNARD James M 1860
BARNARD James M 1860
BARNARD James M 1860
2
PRETY [313] William 1864
OBRIEN Thomas 1861
OBRIEN [284] Thomas 1861
OBRIEN [284] Thomas 1861
KELLEY Francis 1874
1
BARNARD [25] James M 1860
BARNARD James M 1860
RITTENHOUSE John B 1860
10
WAGNER Dominick 1861
THIBODO [394] Maxime 1861
ZIMERMAN [442] John 1861
ZIMERMAN [442] John 1861
BARNARD James M 1860
BAXTER [33] Richard 1862
BARNARD [27] Susan L 1861
12
NOYES Samuel B 1859
BARTLETT [30] Junius A 1861
11
BARNARD James M 1860
COOK Charles 1875
BEYER Charles 1870
BEYER Charles 1870
BEYER William 1870
SHERBURNE Andrew M 1857
SHERBURNE Andrew M 1855
HORSTAD Peter 1860
BARTLETT [30] Junius A 1861
PACHL John 1874
WOODMAN [431] Horatio 1860
BARNARD James M 1860
BEYER Charles 1870
BEYER William 1870
SHERBURNE Andrew M 1855
SHERBURNE Samuel W 1855
BURTON William 1861
REYMERT [324] Jenny D 1861
14
BARKER [21] James S 1860
BRUNELLE Jane R 1861
RIPLEY Christopher G 1857
15
SPRAGUE [377] James B 1861
MESSENGER A J 1867
NOWLEN Mary Ann 1861
WHITE [420] Miles 1860
13
WILSON William 1862
CLACK Henry G 1861
NOWLEN Mary Ann 1861
DYER John L 1861
DYER John L 1861
FRENCH Samuel B 1862
CLACK Henry G 1861
BURT Samuel V 1861
TRASHER [401] John 1861
23
HARRINGTON Timothy 1861
GROVER [170] Freeman 1862
22
NEWHALL Wright 1855
FRENCH [139] Samuel B 1861
MCKAHUN [261] Sarah 1860
GROVER [169] Freeman 1860
BORLAND William 1860
24
STEWART John 1862
NEWHALL Elbridge G 1855
27
FRENCH Samuel B 1861
FRENCH Samuel B 1861
FRENCH Samuel B 1861
MCKAHAN Sarah 1862
MCKAHAN Sarah 1867
FRENCH Samuel B 1861
MCKAHAN Sarah 1862
26
LUND Hans 1860
GROVER Freeman 1860
25
PHILLIPS William 1883
FRENCH [141] Samuel B 1861
FRENCH [141] Samuel B 1861
FRENCH [134] Samuel B 1861
FRENCH [134] Samuel B 1861
FRENCH Samuel B 1861
NEWSOM [280] Parnelle G 1861
SWEENY Eliza Ann 1860
LENTZ William 1860
BEGUHN John 1861
RURICHT Carl 1866
BEGUHN [34] John 1861
ISENHOOD Henry 1870
MIESTER Frank 1862
KRAMER [230] Nicholas 1862
KRAMER [229] Nicholas 1862
HALFERTY Mary None
FRENCH [133] Samuel B 1862
REINCKE John 1871
ISENHOOD Henry 1870
BEGUHN [34] John 1861
MIESTER [266] Franz 1861
SCHELHAD Henry 1870
36
FRENCH Samuel B 1861
34
35
MOYES [278] John 1868
MIESTER [266] Franz 1861
SPAFFORD [374] C C 1862
TYLER Charles 1869
BABBENDORF George 1865

Helpful Hints

1. This Map's INDEX can be found on the preceding pages.
2. Refer to Map "C" to see where this Township lies within Dunn County, Wisconsin.
3. Numbers within square brackets [ ] denote a multi-patentee land parcel (multi-owner). Refer to Appendix "C" for a full list of members in this group.
4. Areas that look to be crowded with Patentees usually indicate multiple sales of the same parcel (Re-issues) or Overlapping parcels. See this Township's Index for an explanation of these and other circumstances that might explain "odd" groupings of Patentees on this map.

Legend

- Patent Boundary
- Section Boundary
- No Patents Found (or Outside County)
- 1., 2., 3., ... Lot Numbers (when beside a name)
- [ ] Group Number (see Appendix "C")

Scale: Section = 1 mile X 1 mile (generally, with some exceptions)

Road Map

T28-N R12-W
4th PM - 1831 MN/WI Meridian

Map Group 15

Cities & Towns

Cedar Falls
Rusk

Cemeteries

Cedar Falls Cemetery
Potters Field Cemetery

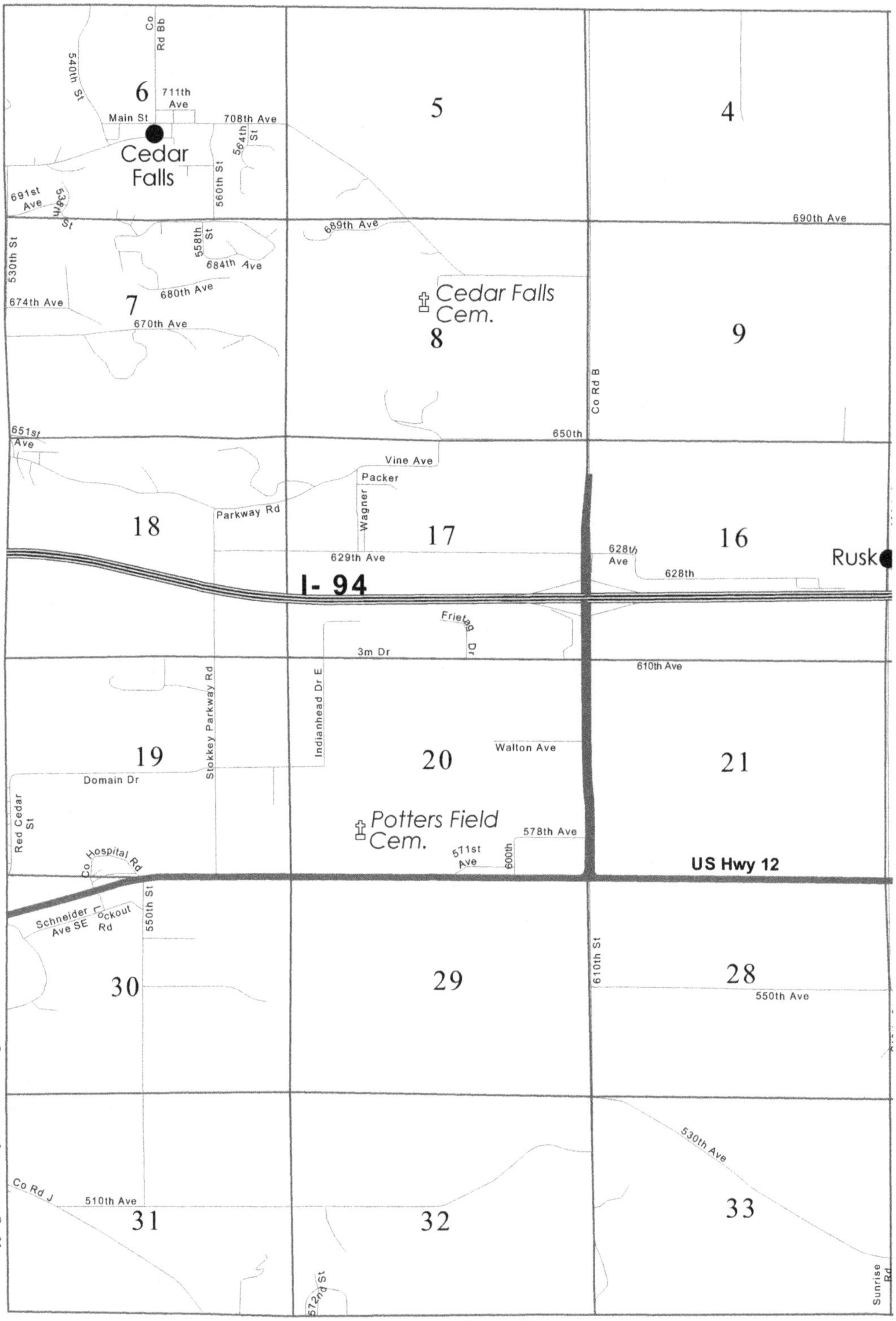

6
5
4
Co Rd Bb
540th St
711th Ave
Main St
708th Ave
564th St
Cedar Falls
560th St
691st Ave
538th St
690th Ave
689th Ave
530th St
558th St
684th Ave
680th Ave
674th Ave
7
670th Ave
Cedar Falls Cem.
8
9
Co Rd B
651st Ave
650th
Vine Ave
Packer
Wagner
Parkway Rd
18
17
16
628th Ave
628th
Rusk
629th Ave
I- 94
Frietag Dr
3m Dr
610th Ave
Stokkey Parkway Rd
Indianhead Dr E
19
20
21
Walton Ave
Domain Dr
Red Cedar St
Potters Field Cem.
578th Ave
Co Hospital Rd
571st Ave
600th
US Hwy 12
Schneider Ave SE
Lockout Rd
550th St
610th St
30
29
28
550th Ave
530th Ave
Co Rd J
510th Ave
31
32
33
572nd St
Sunrise Rd

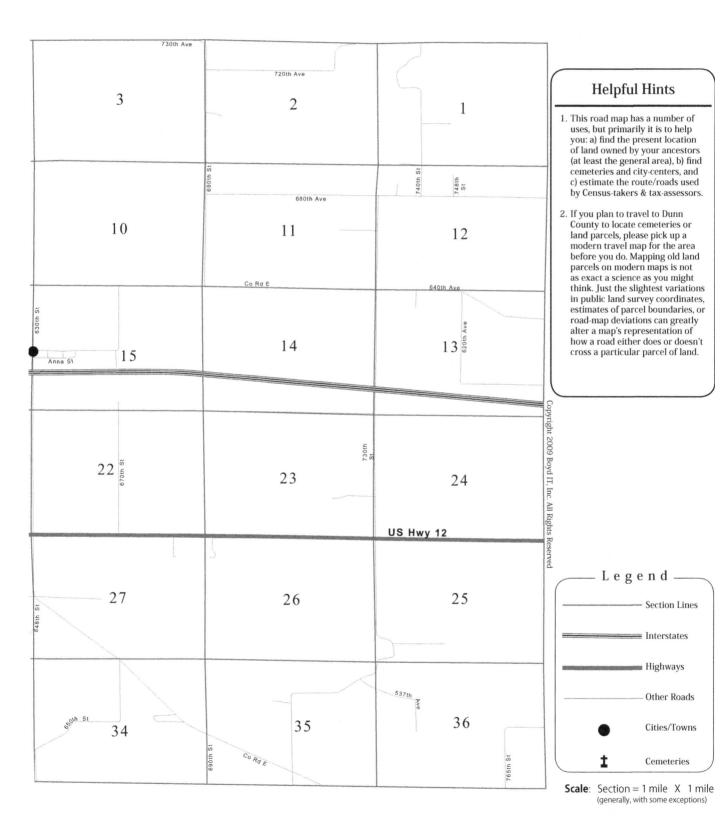

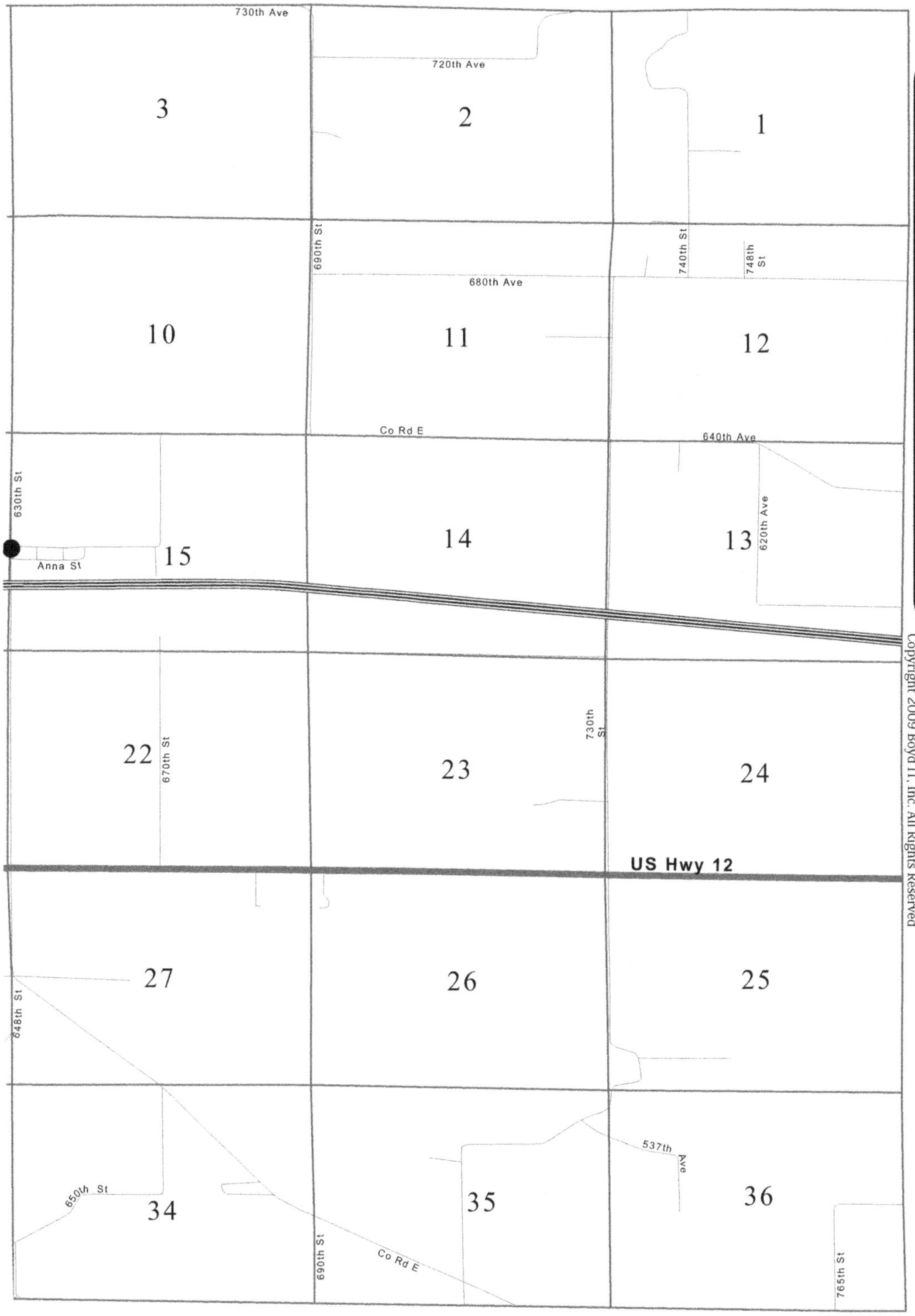

Helpful Hints

1. This road map has a number of uses, but primarily it is to help you: a) find the present location of land owned by your ancestors (at least the general area), b) find cemeteries and city-centers, and c) estimate the route/roads used by Census-takers & tax-assessors.
2. If you plan to travel to Dunn County to locate cemeteries or land parcels, please pick up a modern travel map for the area before you do. Mapping old land parcels on modern maps is not as exact a science as you might think. Just the slightest variations in public land survey coordinates, estimates of parcel boundaries, or road-map deviations can greatly alter a map's representation of how a road either does or doesn't cross a particular parcel of land.

Legend

- Section Lines
- Interstates
- Highways
- Other Roads
- Cities/Towns
- Cemeteries

Scale: Section = 1 mile X 1 mile
(generally, with some exceptions)

Historical Map

T28-N R12-W
4th PM - 1831 MN/WI Meridian

Map Group 15

Cities & Towns

Cedar Falls
Rusk

Cemeteries

Cedar Falls Cemetery
Potters Field Cemetery

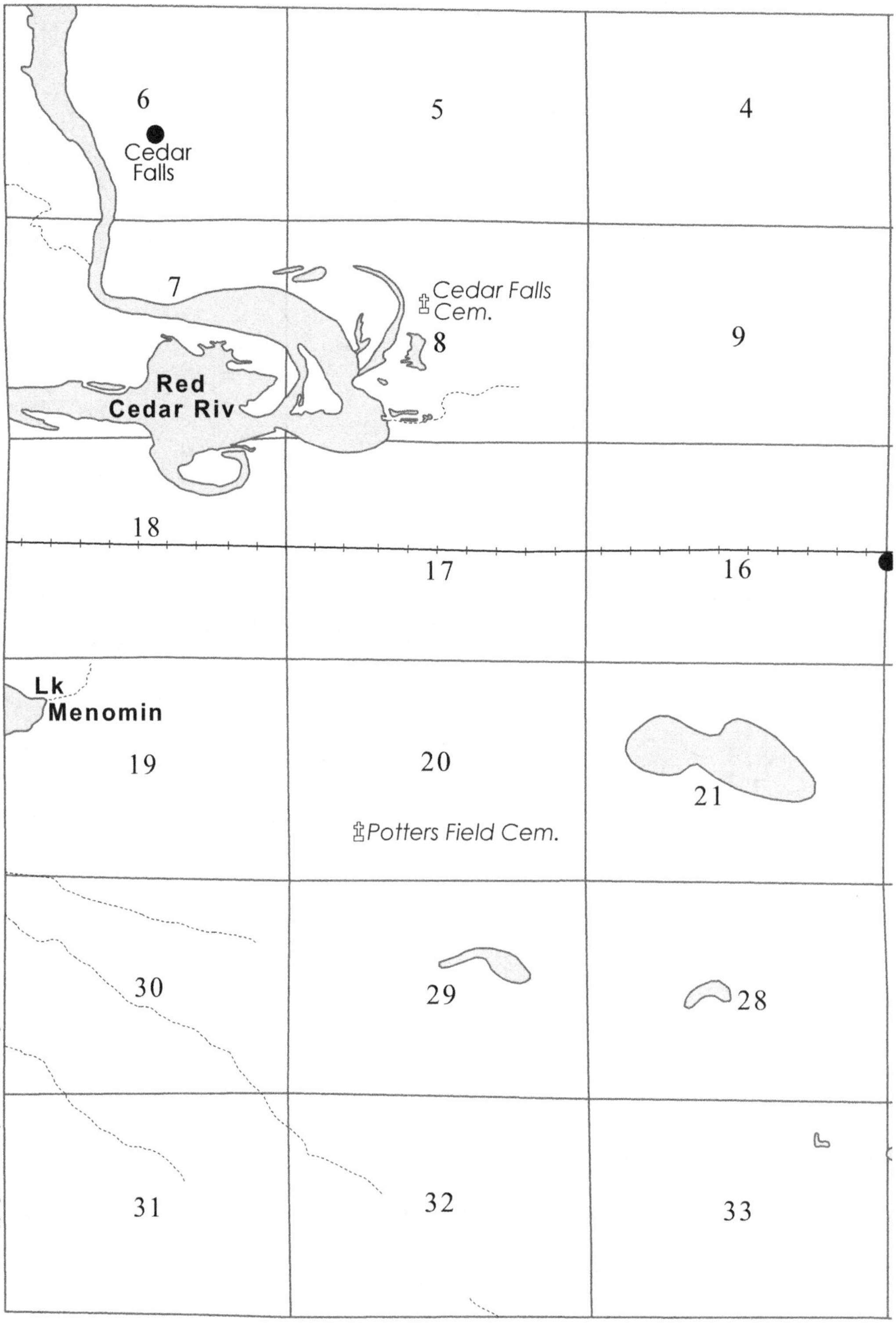

6
Cedar Falls
5
4
7
Cedar Falls Cem.
8
9
Red Cedar Riv
18
17
16
Lk Menomin
19
20
21
Potters Field Cem.
30
29
28
31
32
33

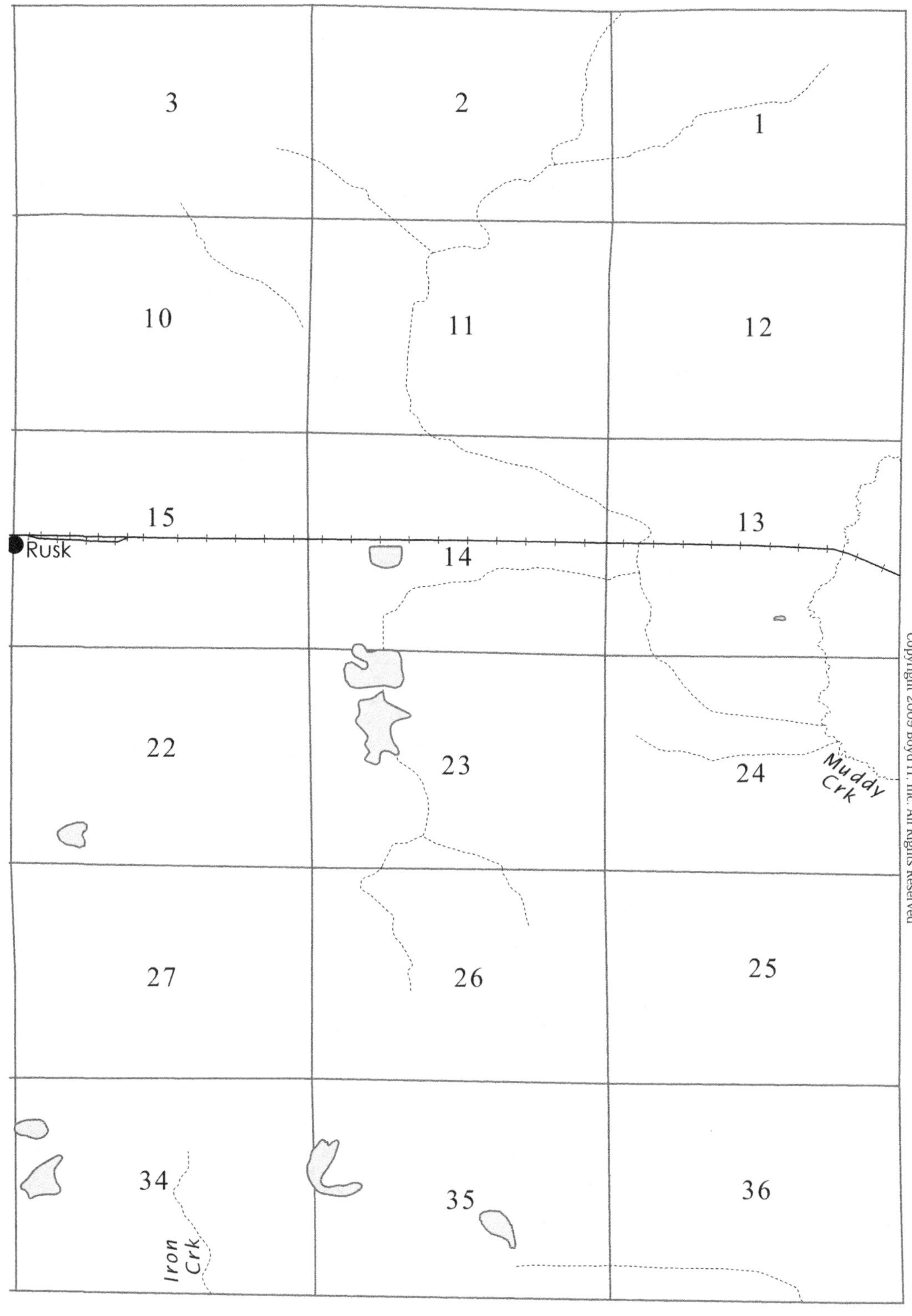
3
2
1
10
11
12
15
13
Rusk
14
22
23
24
Muddy Crk
27
26
25
34
35
36
Iron Crk

Helpful Hints

1. This Map takes a different look at the same Congressional Township displayed in the preceding two maps. It presents features that can help you better envision the historical development of the area: a) Water-bodies (lakes & ponds), b) Water-courses (rivers, streams, etc.), c) Railroads, d) City/town center-points (where they were oftentimes located when first settled), and e) Cemeteries.

2. Using this "Historical" map in tandem with this Township's Patent Map and Road Map, may lead you to some interesting discoveries. You will often find roads, towns, cemeteries, and waterways are named after nearby landowners: sometimes those names will be the ones you are researching. See how many of these research gems you can find here in Dunn County.

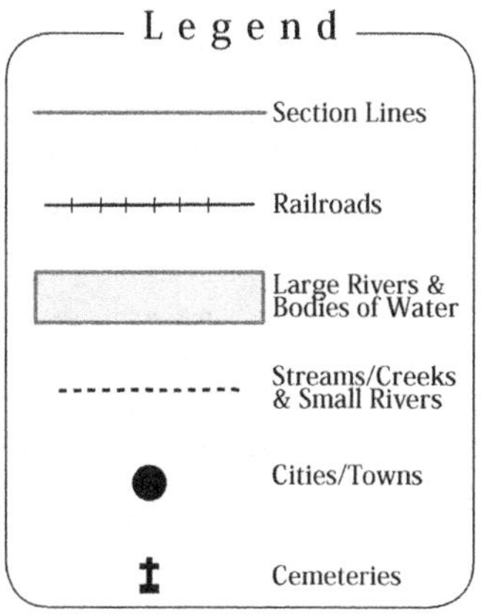
Legend
Section Lines
Railroads
Large Rivers & Bodies of Water
Streams/Creeks & Small Rivers
Cities/Towns
Cemeteries

Scale: Section = 1 mile X 1 mile
(there are some exceptions)

Map Group 16: Index to Land Patents

Township 28-North Range 11-West (4th PM - 1831 MN/WI)

After you locate an individual in this Index, take note of the Section and Section Part then proceed to the Land Patent map on the pages immediately following. You should have no difficulty locating the corresponding parcel of land.

The "For More Info" Column will lead you to more information about the underlying Patents. See the *Legend* at right, and the "How to Use this Book" chapter, for more information.

LEGEND

"For More Info . . . " column

- A = Authority (Legislative Act, See Appendix "A")
- B = Block or Lot (location in Section unknown)
- C = Cancelled Patent
- F = Fractional Section
- G = Group (Multi-Patentee Patent, see Appendix "C")
- V = Overlaps another Parcel
- R = Re-Issued (Parcel patented more than once)

(A & G items require you to look in the Appendixes referred to above. All other Letter-designations followed by a number require you to locate line-items in this index that possess the ID number found after the letter).

ID	Individual in Patent	Sec.	Sec. Part	Date Issued	Other Counties	For More Info . . .
2579	ALFARO, Isidora	25	SE	1860-11-20		A5 G391
2604	AMBLE, Axel	10	W½SE	1901-02-27		A6
2679	AMORY, James	35	SENE	1860-09-10		A5 C R2720
2680	" "	36	W½NW	1860-09-10		A5 C R2777
2599	ANDERSON, Arne	8	E½NW	1881-09-09		A6
2648	ANDERSON, Gilbert	24	NW	1865-10-20		A5 G9
2676	ANDERSON, Jacob	27	SWSW	1862-08-20		A5
2677	" "	28	E½SE	1862-08-20		A5
2678	" "	33	NENE	1862-08-20		A5
2681	ANDERSON, James	2	NWSE	1862-04-01		A2
2721	ANDERSON, Kirsti	12	NESW	1870-10-20		A6
2722	ANDERSON, Lars	26	NWSW	1877-04-25		A6
2730	ANDERSON, Lewis	26	S½SW	1862-02-05		A5
2761	ANDERSON, Petter H	4	N½SW	1882-04-10		A6
2762	" "	4	W½SE	1882-04-10		A6
2582	ARNESON, Amund	12	NWSW	1870-10-20		A6
2660	BALCOM, Henry	28	SESW	1863-04-20		A5 G17
2661	" "	28	SWNW	1863-04-20		A5 G17
2662	" "	28	W½SW	1863-04-20		A5 G17
2717	BEGUHN, Joseph	31	SESW	1861-04-01		A5
2718	" "	31	SWNW	1861-04-01		A5
2719	" "	31	W½SW	1861-04-01		A5
2750	BEGUHN, Mary	31	NESE	1865-11-10		A2
2641	BENTSEN, Even	29	E½SE	1862-04-01		A2
2644	BEYER, Frederick	6	W½SE	1865-07-01		A2
2589	BONNEY, Andrew H	30	SW	1860-08-01		A5
2580	BRAINARD, C R	28	E½NE	1860-11-20		A5 G205
2581	" "	28	NWNE	1860-11-20		A5 G205
2744	BRAYNARD, Augustus S	35	NW	1860-08-01		A5 G245
2607	BRONN, Berot D	31	SWSE	1865-07-01		A2
2682	BURNES, James	33	S½SE	1860-02-01		A5 G54
2689	BURNES, John	34	E½SW	1859-12-10		A2
2690	" "	34	NWSE	1859-12-10		A2
2691	" "	34	SWSW	1859-12-10		A2
2744	BURNETT, John M	35	NW	1860-08-01		A5 G245
2777	BUSSCHENDORF, William	36	W½NW	1861-07-01		A5 R2680
2778	" "	36	W½SW	1861-07-01		A5
2672	CARLETON, Ingalls	22	SW	1861-04-01		A5 G398
2774	CARTWRIGHT, William A	26	SWNW	1899-06-28		A6
2647	CHAPMAN, George B	21	SENE	1861-09-05		A2
2675	CHRISTENSEN, Ingebarg S	14	NWNW	1861-01-18		A2
2653	CHRISTIANSON, Gustave H	4	NW	1885-10-22		A6
2620	CHRISTOFFER, Christian	27	NE	1860-09-10		A5
2619	" "	23	NENW	1861-01-18		A2
2621	CHRISTOFFERSEN, Christian	25	NWSW	1862-04-01		A2
2622	" "	25	SWNW	1862-04-01		A2

ID	Individual in Patent	Sec.	Sec. Part	Date Issued	Other Counties	For More Info . . .
2605	CHRISTOPHERSEN, Bernt	14	NESW	1863-05-20		A7 G72
2606	CHRISTOPHERSON, Bernt	27	E½NW	1861-01-18		A2
2655	CHRISTOPHERSON, Hans	19	N½NW	1870-05-20		A6 C
2656	" "	19	NWSW	1870-05-20		A6 C
2610	CLARK, Robert	9	NWNW	1862-08-20		A5 G371
2611	" "	9	S½NW	1862-08-20		A5 G371
2638	DAHLEN, Edward O	24	NE	1862-08-20		A5
2637	DARRIN, Martha	35	SE	1860-11-20		A5 G124 C R2643
2720	DENSMORE, Joseph W	35	SENE	1881-09-09		A6 R2679
2631	DODGE, Darius	17	N½NW	1861-04-01		A5
2632	" "	17	SWNW	1861-04-01		A5
2760	ENGEBRETSON, Ole	24	N½SE	1873-05-15		A6
2682	ETHEREDGE, Margaret	33	S½SE	1860-02-01		A5 G54
2637	EVANS, Edward	35	SE	1860-11-20		A5 G124 C R2643
2594	EVENS, Anne	11	E½NW	1860-11-20		A5 G126
2595	" "	11	SWNW	1860-11-20		A5 G126
2648	FOOTE, Alpheus H	24	NW	1865-10-20		A5 G9
2726	GILBRANSON, John	21	NWNW	1869-12-10		A6 G155
2726	GILBRANSON, Laurina	21	NWNW	1869-12-10		A6 G155
2723	GRANT, John W	28	SENW	1861-01-18		A2 G210
2724	" "	28	NESW	1861-04-01		A5 G211
2725	" "	28	W½SE	1861-04-01		A5 G211
2578	HALVORSEN, Aksel L	10	SW	1892-04-20		A6
2673	HALVORSEN, Hogbart	4	E½SE	1891-11-16		A6
2674	" "	4	S½NE	1891-11-16		A6
2639	HAMILTON, Susannah	14	W½SE	1862-08-20		A5 G369
2640	" "	23	NWNE	1862-08-20		A5 G369
2584	HANSON, Anders	14	SENE	1883-03-01		A2
2740	HANSON, Hans	1	NWNW	1873-01-10		A6 G174
2654	HANSON, Hans A	10	N½NW	1876-12-30		A6
2693	HANSON, John	28	SWNE	1883-09-10		A6
2740	HANSON, Maria	1	NWNW	1873-01-10		A6 G174
2596	HINTGEN, Anton	6	N½NW	1893-12-19		A6 F
2597	" "	6	NWSW	1893-12-19		A6 F
2598	" "	6	SWNW	1893-12-19		A6 F
2766	HOLBROOK, Ruth M	35	SW	1860-08-01		A5 G192
2745	HOWE, Martin	22	NESE	1860-09-10		A5
2746	" "	22	S½SE	1860-09-10		A5
2748	HOWE, Martin L	22	NWSE	1873-01-10		A6
2583	JENSEN, Amund	12	W½NW	1878-11-05		A6
2623	JOHANNESSEN, Christian	2	SESW	1874-12-30		A6
2624	" "	2	SWSE	1874-12-30		A6
2625	" "	2	SWSW	1892-08-01		A6
2747	JOHNSEN, Martin	3	SESW	1861-09-05		A2
2580	JOHNSON, Alfred	28	E½NE	1860-11-20		A5 G205
2581	" "	28	NWNE	1860-11-20		A5 G205
2626	JOHNSON, Christian	4	S½SW	1882-04-10		A6
2649	JOHNSON, Gilbert	12	N½NE	1877-03-01		A6
2695	JOHNSON, John	9	SWNE	1862-04-01		A2
2694	" "	2	NWNW	1870-10-20		A6
2700	JOHNSON, John W	2	NWSW	1870-05-20		A6
2701	" "	2	SWNW	1870-05-20		A6
2702	" "	3	NESE	1870-05-20		A6
2703	" "	3	SENE	1870-05-20		A6
2735	JOHNSON, Louis	12	SENW	1877-03-01		A6
2736	" "	12	SWNE	1877-03-01		A6
2734	" "	12	NENW	1879-09-04		A2
2627	JOHNSON, Lydia	32	S½SW	1860-08-01		A5 G365
2757	JOHNSON, Nils	12	SE	1870-07-25		A6
2723	JONSEN, Lars	28	SENW	1861-01-18		A2 G210
2724	JONSON, Lars	28	NESW	1861-04-01		A5 G211
2725	" "	28	W½SE	1861-04-01		A5 G211
2669	KELKENBERG, Henry	22	NWNW	1876-08-15		A6
2610	KENT, George L	9	NWNW	1862-08-20		A5 G371
2611	" "	9	S½NW	1862-08-20		A5 G371
2782	KRAUS, William	26	NESW	1884-09-15		A6
2783	" "	26	SENW	1884-09-15		A6
2764	LABEREE, Rufus	6	SENW	1883-10-20		A6
2765	" "	6	SWNE	1883-10-20		A6
2613	LAMPMAN, Caroline	18	N½SE	1860-07-02		A2
2614	LAMPMAN, Caspar	18	SENE	1860-07-02		A2
2755	LANGDAL, Miles	11	NESW	1859-05-02		A2
2756	LANGDELL, Niles	11	W½SW	1859-05-02		A2

ID	Individual in Patent	Sec.	Sec. Part	Date Issued	Other Counties	For More Info . . .
2650	LARSEN, Gilbert	24	N½SW	1870-05-02		A6
2642	LEE, Frank	23	SWSE	1900-11-12		A6
2696	LIPPEL, John	27	S½SE	1860-02-01		A5
2697	" "	34	E½NE	1860-02-01		A5
2610	LOWBER, Edward J	9	NWNW	1862-08-20		A5 G371
2611	" "	9	S½NW	1862-08-20		A5 G371
2744	LYMAN, Maria T	35	NW	1860-08-01		A5 G245
2705	MANSFIELD, John W	13	N½SE	1860-08-01		A5
2706	" "	13	NESW	1860-08-01		A5
2707	" "	13	S½SE	1860-08-01		A5
2708	" "	13	SESW	1860-08-01		A5
2714	" "	11	SESW	1860-08-03		A5 G250
2704	" "	13	N½NW	1860-08-03		A5
2709	" "	14	NENE	1860-08-03		A5
2715	" "	14	NENW	1860-08-03		A5 G250
2716	" "	14	NWNE	1860-08-03		A5 G250
2712	" "	1	S½NW	1861-12-20		A5 G249
2713	" "	2	E½NE	1861-12-20		A5 G249
2710	" "	23	NESW	1861-12-20		A5
2711	" "	23	W½SW	1861-12-20		A5
2772	MARSHALL, Mary	13	SWSW	1862-01-10		A5 G290
2773	" "	14	E½SE	1862-01-10		A5 G290
2618	MAVES, Charles	6	SWSW	1888-11-24		A2
2753	MCDONALD, Michael	36	NESE	1883-03-01		A2
2781	MCGREW, Mary	21	E½SE	1860-08-01		A5 G320
2590	MOOR, Andrew	11	SESE	1860-08-01		A5 G275
2591	" "	11	W½SE	1860-08-01		A5 G275
2592	MOORE, Andrew	11	NESE	1860-11-20		A5
2593	" "	11	S½NE	1860-11-20		A5
2741	MOORE, Maria	26	SESE	1860-09-10		A5
2742	" "	35	NENE	1860-09-10		A5
2743	" "	35	W½NE	1860-09-10		A5
2590	MUMER, Jacob	11	SESE	1860-08-01		A5 G275
2591	" "	11	W½SE	1860-08-01		A5 G275
2684	NELSON, James	1	NWSW	1870-09-10		A6
2685	" "	11	NENE	1870-09-10		A6
2686	" "	2	E½SE	1870-09-10		A6
2698	NELSON, John	12	SENE	1873-12-15		A6
2659	NIELSEN, Henrik	27	NESE	1873-12-15		A6
2731	NOREM, Louis H	24	S½SE	1870-05-20		A6
2732	" "	25	NENW	1870-05-20		A6
2733	" "	25	NWNE	1870-05-20		A6
2692	NORTON, John G	26	NWNW	1875-08-10		A6
2651	OLESON, Gulbrand	23	S½NW	1863-04-20		A5
2772	OLESON, Tosten	13	SWSW	1862-01-10		A5 G290
2773	" "	14	E½SE	1862-01-10		A5 G290
2663	OLSON, Henry C	2	NWNE	1892-06-06		A6
2766	PARKER, Abigail	35	SW	1860-08-01		A5 G192
2633	PARKER, Deforest N	18	NESW	1860-08-01		A5 G297
2634	" "	18	W½SW	1860-08-01		A5 G297
2749	PEDERSEN, Martin	4	N½NE	1879-12-15		A6
2683	PENNOYER, Margaret L	36	E½SW	1860-09-10		A5 G370
2744	POST, Charles	35	NW	1860-08-01		A5 G245
2667	PUTNAM, Henry C	36	SESE	1860-09-10		A5
2668	" "	36	W½SE	1860-09-10		A5
2664	" "	23	E½NE	1861-05-15		A5
2665	" "	23	NESE	1861-05-15		A5
2666	" "	23	SWNE	1861-05-15		A5
2780	REED, William H	22	NENW	1860-07-02		A2
2781	" "	21	E½SE	1860-08-01		A5 G320
2779	" "	21	W½SE	1860-08-01		A5
2784	REKLEAN, William	8	NWNW	1888-10-05		A6
2652	ROBBE, Gunder	23	NWSE	1890-01-31		A6
2635	ROLEFF, Edmund	18	NENW	1869-12-10		A6
2636	" "	18	W½NW	1869-12-10		A6
2643	SCHIEBE, Frank	35	SE	1861-07-01		A5 R2637
2594	SEAMAN, Abigail	11	E½NW	1860-11-20		A5 G126
2595	" "	11	SWNW	1860-11-20		A5 G126
2769	SEVERSON, Torkel	2	E½NW	1870-09-10		A6
2770	" "	2	NESW	1870-09-10		A6
2771	" "	2	SWNE	1870-09-10		A6
2601	SHAW, William G	18	N½NE	1861-04-01		A5 G395
2602	" "	18	SENW	1861-04-01		A5 G395

ID	Individual in Patent	Sec.	Sec. Part	Date Issued	Other Counties	For More Info . . .
2603	SHAW, William G (Cont'd)	18	SWNE	1861-04-01		A5 G395
2670	SIEDENBERG, Henry	26	W½NE	1877-07-02		A6
2671	" "	26	W½SE	1877-07-02		A6
2699	SIPPEL, John P	32	NWSW	1879-09-04		A2
2627	SLYE, D A	32	S½SW	1860-08-01		A5 G365
2612	SOMMERKORN, Carl	8	S½SE	1875-03-01		A6
2585	SORENSEN, Anders	14	SENW	1879-12-15		A6
2586	" "	14	SWNE	1879-12-15		A6
2639	SORENSEN, Egebret	14	W½SE	1862-08-20		A5 G369
2640	" "	23	NWNE	1862-08-20		A5 G369
2587	SORENSON, Andreas	17	S½SE	1873-01-10		A6
2588	" "	20	NENE	1873-01-10		A6
2639	SORENSON, Engebret	14	W½SE	1862-08-20		A5 G369
2640	" "	23	NWNE	1862-08-20		A5 G369
2683	SOUTHGATE, James E L	36	E½SW	1860-09-10		A5 G370
2610	SPAFFORD, C C	9	NWNW	1862-08-20		A5 G371
2611	" "	9	S½NW	1862-08-20		A5 G371
2609	" "	30	W½NW	1863-02-25		A7
2608	" "	29	NE	1863-04-20		A5
2616	SPAFFORD, Charles C	34	E½SE	1861-12-20		A5 G376
2617	" "	34	SWSE	1861-12-20		A5 G376
2615	" "	12	S½SW	1862-04-01		A2
2660	SPOONER, Hannah	28	SESW	1863-04-20		A5 G17
2661	" "	28	SWNW	1863-04-20		A5 G17
2662	" "	28	W½SW	1863-04-20		A5 G17
2728	STANLEY, Lemuel C	13	N½NE	1860-08-03		A5
2729	" "	13	SWNE	1860-08-03		A5
2712	STEBBINS, Marilla L	1	S½NW	1861-12-20		A5 G249
2713	" "	2	E½NE	1861-12-20		A5 G249
2579	TAYLOR, Alexander	25	SE	1860-11-20		A5 G391
2601	THOMPSON, Austin	18	N½NE	1861-04-01		A5 G395
2602	" "	18	SENW	1861-04-01		A5 G395
2603	" "	18	SWNE	1861-04-01		A5 G395
2687	THOMPSON, James	26	NENW	1884-09-15		A6
2688	TILLESEN, Jens	20	SESE	1871-09-01		A6
2600	TILLESON, Arne	28	NENW	1883-02-10		A6
2658	TILLESON, Harald T	22	SWNW	1861-09-05		A2
2657	TILLESON, Harald T E	10	E½SE	1860-10-10		A5
2672	TILLESON, Herald T E	22	SW	1861-04-01		A5 G398
2737	TILLESON, Ludwig	21	E½SW	1870-07-25		A6
2738	" "	21	SWSW	1870-07-25		A6
2739	" "	28	NWNW	1870-07-25		A6
2768	TILLESON, Tille E	22	SENW	1875-03-01		A6
2727	TOLEFSON, Leif	10	E½NE	1905-12-30		A6
2758	TWEITEN, Olav T	10	S½NW	1891-12-26		A6
2759	" "	10	W½NE	1891-12-26		A6
2714	VAIL, Mary	11	SESW	1860-08-03		A5 G250
2715	" "	14	NENW	1860-08-03		A5 G250
2716	" "	14	NWNE	1860-08-03		A5 G250
2616	VAUGHAN, Eunice	34	E½SE	1861-12-20		A5 G376
2617	" "	34	SWSE	1861-12-20		A5 G376
2754	WEBERT, Michael	24	S½SW	1877-04-25		A6
2763	WEILLER, Phillip	6	N½NE	1877-06-04		A6
2605	WICKS, Charles	14	NESW	1863-05-20		A7 G72
2785	WILSON, William	8	NWNE	1875-03-05		A2
2767	WISCONSIN, State Of	16		1941-08-16		A3
2628	WOOD, Daniel H	25	NWNW	1862-08-20		A5
2629	" "	26	E½NE	1862-08-20		A5
2630	" "	26	NESE	1862-08-20		A5
2751	WOODWARD, Mary N	27	E½SW	1861-04-01		A5 G435
2752	" "	27	NWSE	1861-04-01		A5 G435
2775	WOODWARD, William A	1	NENW	1861-07-01		A5
2776	" "	1	W½NE	1861-07-01		A5
2633	WRIGHT, Jemima	18	NESW	1860-08-01		A5 G297
2634	" "	18	W½SW	1860-08-01		A5 G297
2751	YEAMAN, Hester A	27	E½SW	1861-04-01		A5 G435
2752	" "	27	NWSE	1861-04-01		A5 G435
2645	YOKES, Frederick	6	E½SW	1871-09-15		A6
2646	" "	7	N½NW	1871-09-15		A6

Patent Map

T28-N R11-W
4th PM - 1831 MN/WI Meridian

Map Group 16

Township Statistics

Parcels Mapped	:	208
Number of Patents	:	139
Number of Individuals	:	156
Patentees Identified	:	129
Number of Surnames	:	117
Multi-Patentee Parcels	:	45
Oldest Patent Date	:	5/2/1859
Most Recent Patent	:	8/16/1941
Block/Lot Parcels	:	0
Parcels Re - Issued	:	3
Parcels that Overlap	:	0
Cities and Towns	:	1
Cemeteries	:	1

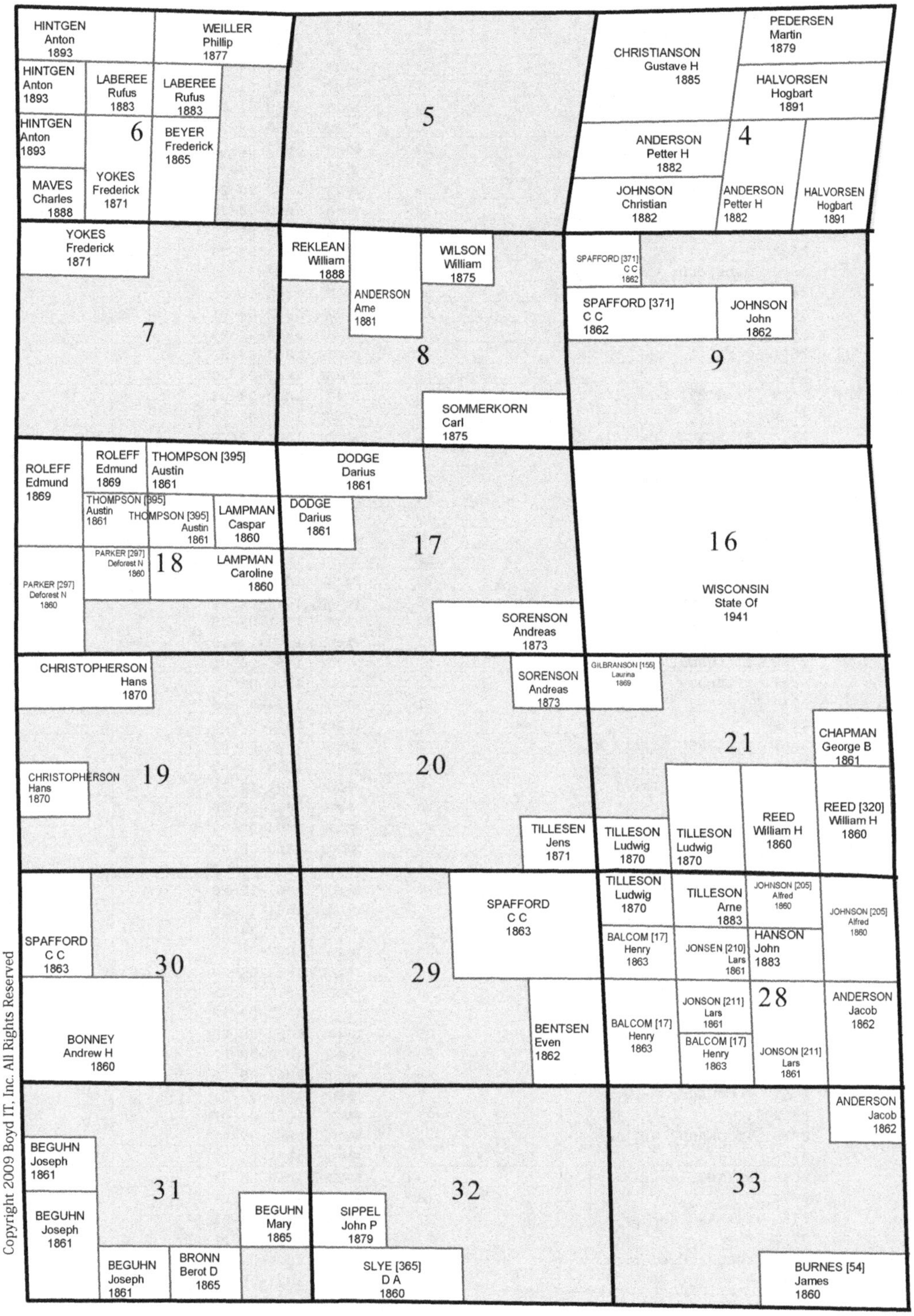

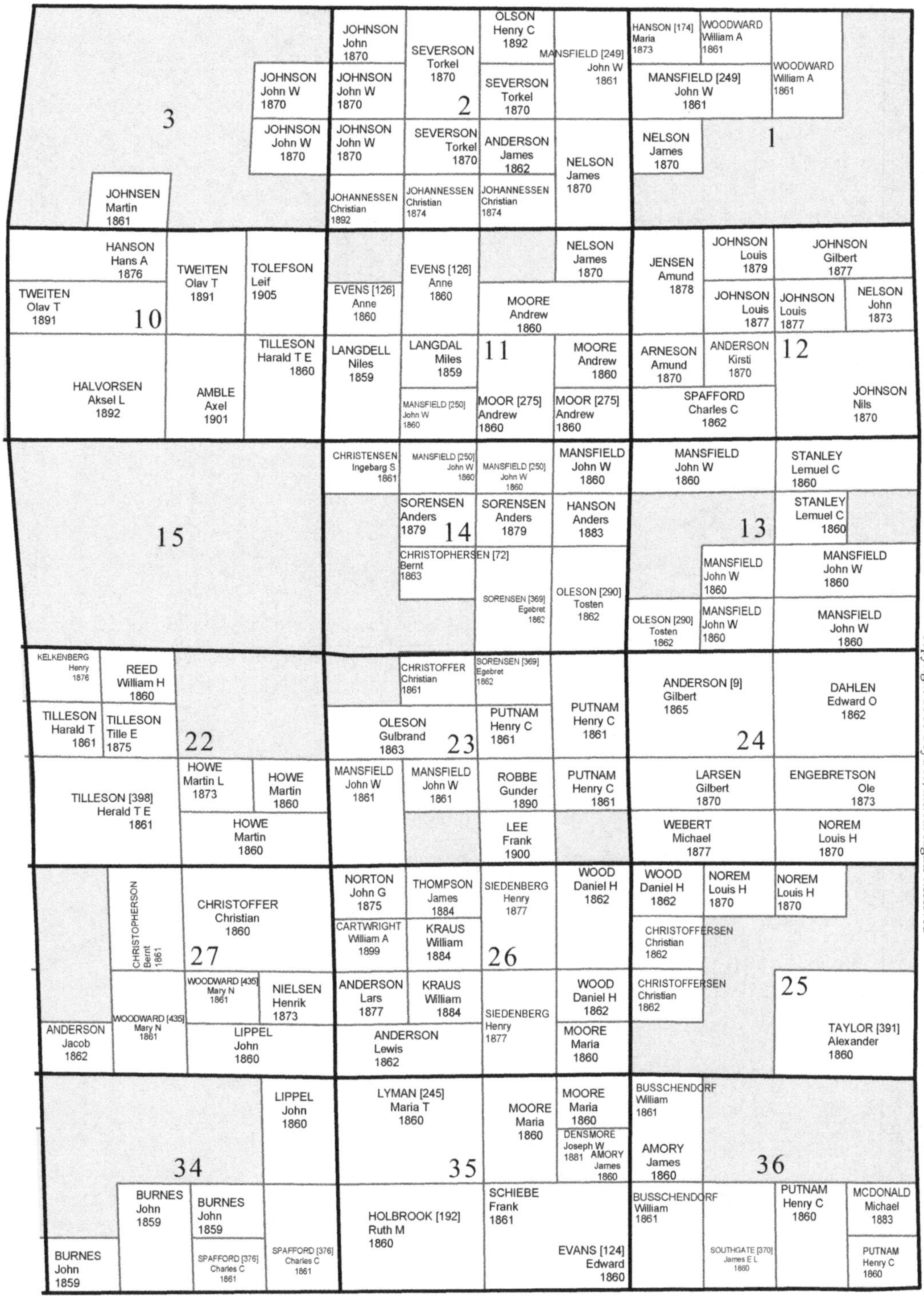
3
JOHNSON John W 1870
JOHNSON John W 1870
JOHNSEN Martin 1861
JOHNSON John 1870
JOHNSON John W 1870
JOHNSON John W 1870
JOHANNESSEN Christian 1892
SEVERSON Torkel 1870
SEVERSON Torkel 1870
JOHANNESSEN Christian 1874
2
OLSON Henry C 1892
SEVERSON Torkel 1870
ANDERSON James 1862
JOHANNESSEN Christian 1874
MANSFIELD [249] John W 1861
NELSON James 1870
HANSON [174] Maria 1873
WOODWARD William A 1861
WOODWARD William A 1861
MANSFIELD [249] John W 1861
NELSON James 1870
1
HANSON Hans A 1876
TWEITEN Olav T 1891
TWEITEN Olav T 1891
TOLEFSON Leif 1905
10
HALVORSEN Aksel L 1892
AMBLE Axel 1901
TILLESON Harald T E 1860
EVENS [126] Anne 1860
EVENS [126] Anne 1860
LANGDELL Niles 1859
LANGDAL Miles 1859
11
MANSFIELD [250] John W 1860
NELSON James 1870
MOORE Andrew 1860
MOORE Andrew 1860
MOOR [275] Andrew 1860
MOOR [275] Andrew 1860
JENSEN Amund 1878
JOHNSON Louis 1879
JOHNSON Gilbert 1877
JOHNSON Louis 1877
JOHNSON Louis 1877
NELSON John 1873
ARNESON Amund 1870
ANDERSON Kirsti 1870
12
SPAFFORD Charles C 1862
JOHNSON Nils 1870
15
CHRISTENSEN Ingebarg S 1861
MANSFIELD [250] John W 1860
MANSFIELD [250] John W 1860
MANSFIELD John W 1860
SORENSEN Anders 1879
14
SORENSEN Anders 1879
HANSON Anders 1883
CHRISTOPHERSEN [72] Bernt 1863
SORENSEN [369] Egebret 1862
OLESON [290] Tosten 1862
MANSFIELD John W 1860
STANLEY Lemuel C 1860
STANLEY Lemuel C 1860
13
MANSFIELD John W 1860
MANSFIELD John W 1860
OLESON [290] Tosten 1862
MANSFIELD John W 1860
MANSFIELD John W 1860
KELKENBERG Henry 1876
REED William H 1860
TILLESON Harald T 1861
TILLESON Tille E 1875
22
TILLESON [398] Herald T E 1861
HOWE Martin L 1873
HOWE Martin 1860
HOWE Martin 1860
CHRISTOFFER Christian 1861
SORENSEN [369] Egebret 1862
OLESON Gulbrand 1863
23
PUTNAM Henry C 1861
PUTNAM Henry C 1861
MANSFIELD John W 1861
MANSFIELD John W 1861
ROBBE Gunder 1890
PUTNAM Henry C 1861
LEE Frank 1900
ANDERSON [9] Gilbert 1865
DAHLEN Edward O 1862
24
LARSEN Gilbert 1870
ENGEBRETSON Ole 1873
WEBERT Michael 1877
NOREM Louis H 1870
CHRISTOPHERSON Bernt 1861
CHRISTOFFER Christian 1860
27
WOODWARD [435] Mary N 1861
NIELSEN Henrik 1873
WOODWARD [435] Mary N 1861
ANDERSON Jacob 1862
LIPPEL John 1860
NORTON John G 1875
THOMPSON James 1884
SIEDENBERG Henry 1877
WOOD Daniel H 1862
CARTWRIGHT William A 1899
KRAUS William 1884
26
ANDERSON Lars 1877
KRAUS William 1884
SIEDENBERG Henry 1877
WOOD Daniel H 1862
ANDERSON Lewis 1862
MOORE Maria 1860
WOOD Daniel H 1862
NOREM Louis H 1870
NOREM Louis H 1870
CHRISTOFFERSEN Christian 1862
CHRISTOFFERSEN Christian 1862
25
TAYLOR [391] Alexander 1860
LIPPEL John 1860
34
BURNES John 1859
BURNES John 1859
BURNES John 1859
SPAFFORD [376] Charles C 1861
SPAFFORD [376] Charles C 1861
LYMAN [245] Maria T 1860
MOORE Maria 1860
MOORE Maria 1860
DENSMORE Joseph W 1881
AMORY James 1860
35
HOLBROOK [192] Ruth M 1860
SCHIEBE Frank 1861
EVANS [124] Edward 1860
BUSSCHENDORF William 1861
AMORY James 1860
36
BUSSCHENDORF William 1861
SOUTHGATE [370] James E L 1860
PUTNAM Henry C 1860
MCDONALD Michael 1883
PUTNAM Henry C 1860

Helpful Hints

1. This Map's INDEX can be found on the preceding pages.
2. Refer to Map "C" to see where this Township lies within Dunn County, Wisconsin.
3. Numbers within square brackets [ ] denote a multi-patentee land parcel (multi-owner). Refer to Appendix "C" for a full list of members in this group.
4. Areas that look to be crowded with Patentees usually indicate multiple sales of the same parcel (Re-issues) or Overlapping parcels. See this Township's Index for an explanation of these and other circumstances that might explain "odd" groupings of Patentees on this map.

Legend

Patent Boundary

Section Boundary

No Patents Found (or Outside County)

1., 2., 3., ... Lot Numbers (when beside a name)

[ ] Group Number (see Appendix "C")

Scale: Section = 1 mile X 1 mile (generally, with some exceptions)

Road Map

T28-N R11-W
4th PM - 1831 MN/WI Meridian

Map Group 16

Cities & Towns
Elk Mound

Cemeteries
Evergreen Cemetery

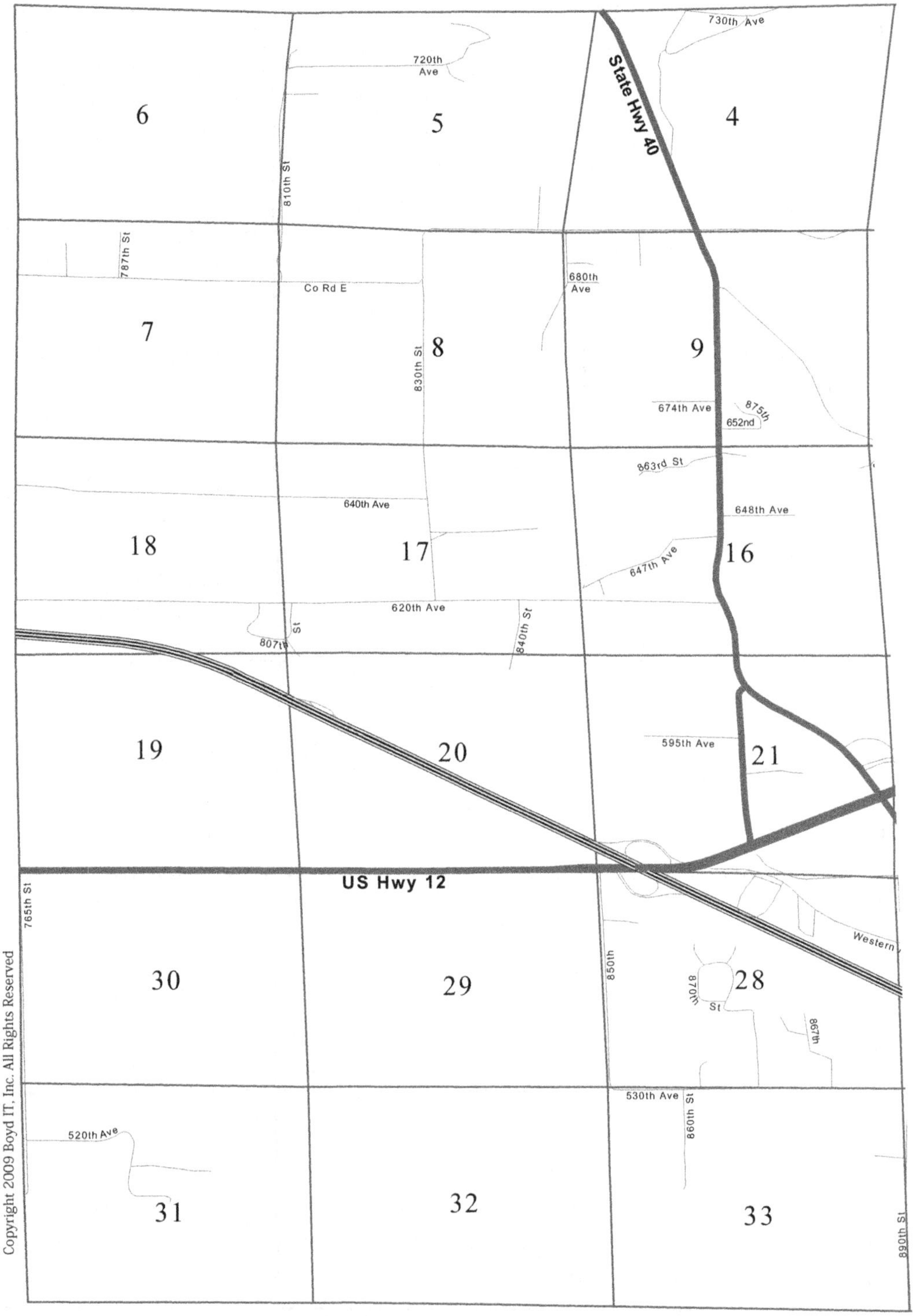

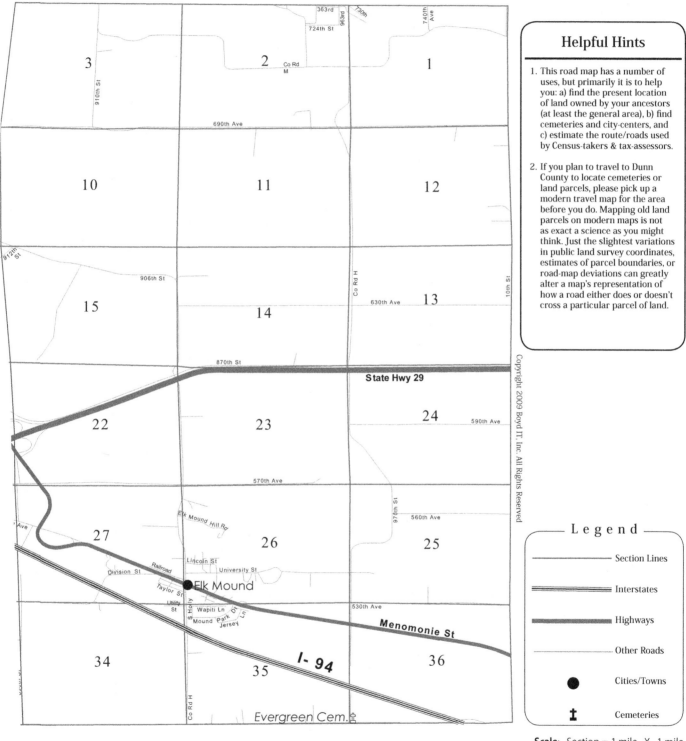

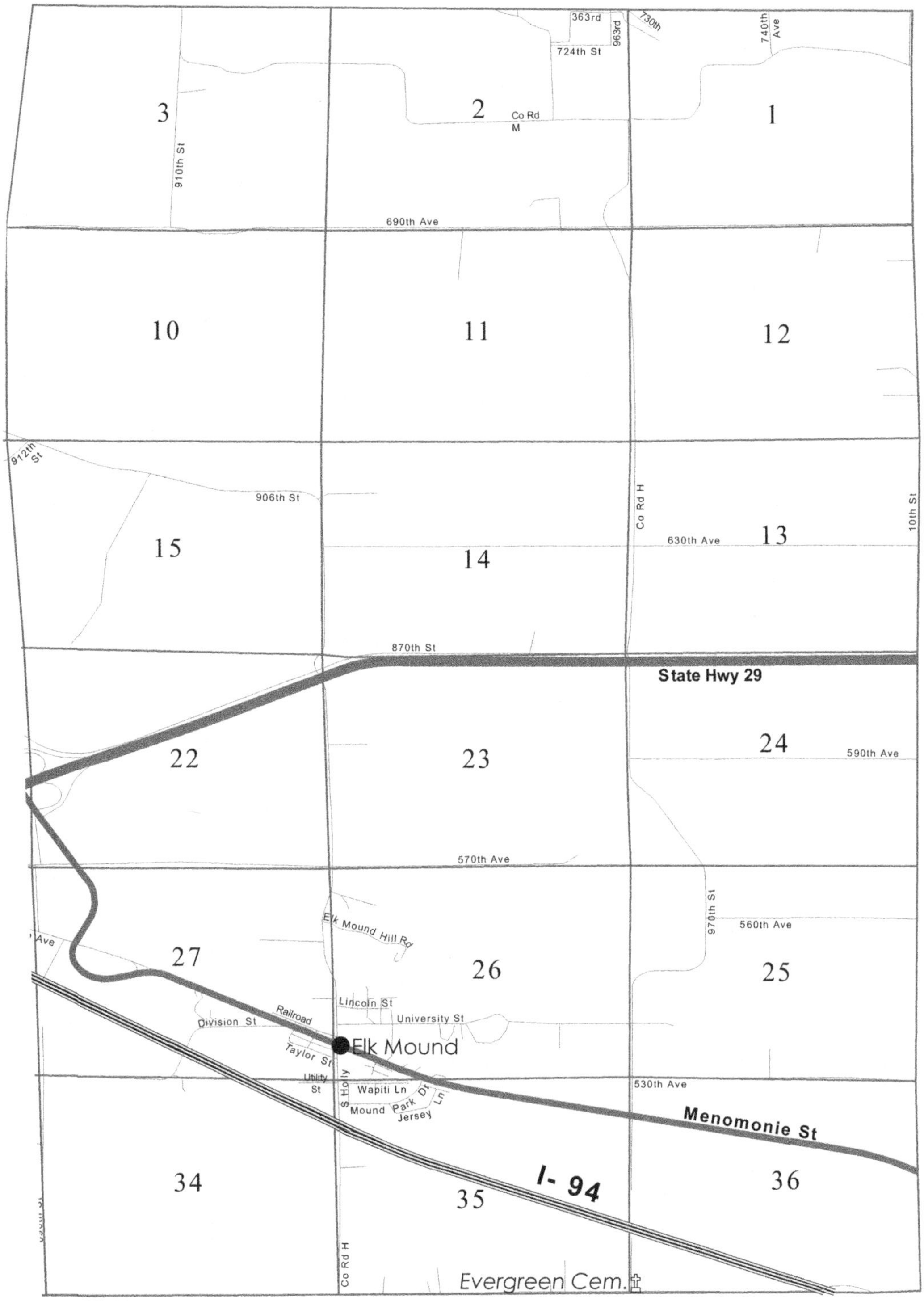

Helpful Hints

1. This road map has a number of uses, but primarily it is to help you: a) find the present location of land owned by your ancestors (at least the general area), b) find cemeteries and city-centers, and c) estimate the route/roads used by Census-takers & tax-assessors.
2. If you plan to travel to Dunn County to locate cemeteries or land parcels, please pick up a modern travel map for the area before you do. Mapping old land parcels on modern maps is not as exact a science as you might think. Just the slightest variations in public land survey coordinates, estimates of parcel boundaries, or road-map deviations can greatly alter a map's representation of how a road either does or doesn't cross a particular parcel of land.

Legend

- Section Lines
- Interstates
- Highways
- Other Roads
- Cities/Towns
- Cemeteries

Scale: Section = 1 mile X 1 mile
(generally, with some exceptions)

Historical Map

T28-N R11-W
4th PM - 1831 MN/WI Meridian

Map Group 16

Cities & Towns
Elk Mound

Cemeteries
Evergreen Cemetery

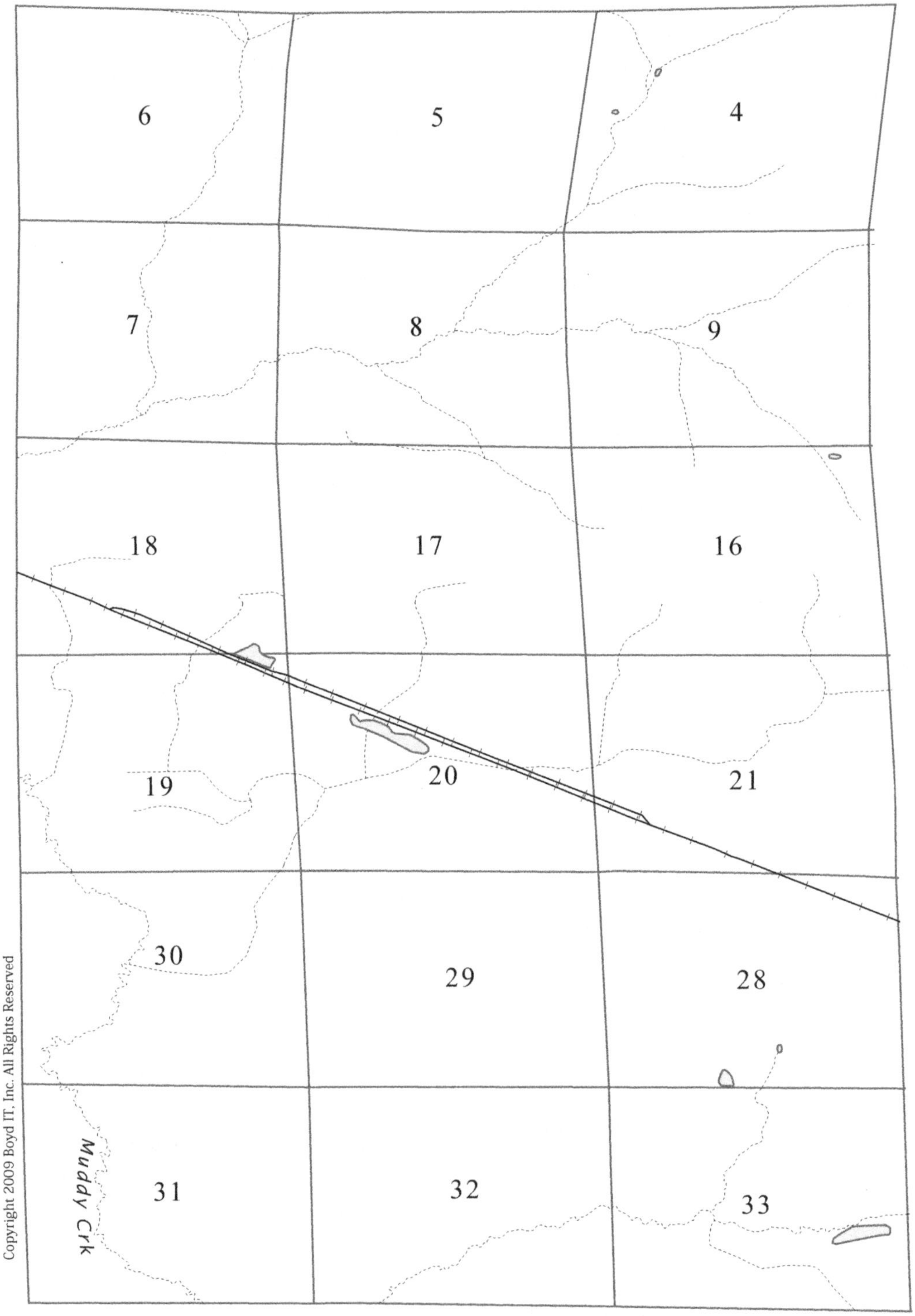

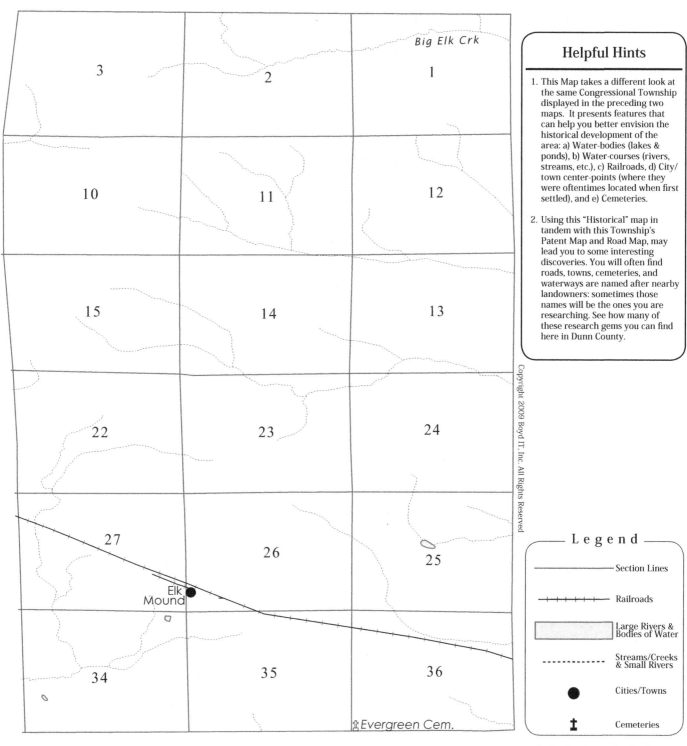

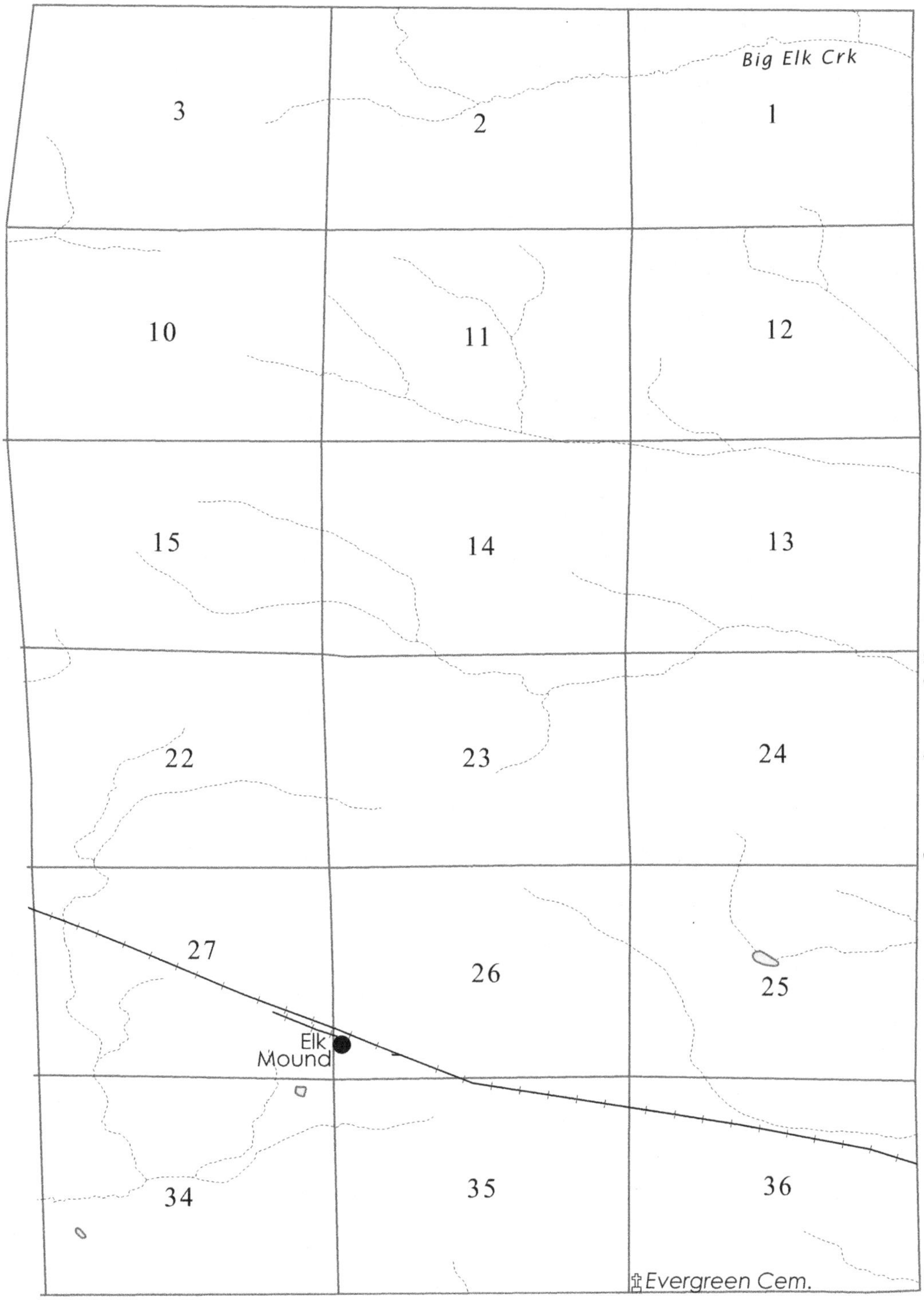

Helpful Hints

1. This Map takes a different look at the same Congressional Township displayed in the preceding two maps. It presents features that can help you better envision the historical development of the area: a) Water-bodies (lakes & ponds), b) Water-courses (rivers, streams, etc.), c) Railroads, d) City/town center-points (where they were oftentimes located when first settled), and e) Cemeteries.
2. Using this "Historical" map in tandem with this Township's Patent Map and Road Map, may lead you to some interesting discoveries. You will often find roads, towns, cemeteries, and waterways are named after nearby landowners: sometimes those names will be the ones you are researching. See how many of these research gems you can find here in Dunn County.

Legend

- Section Lines
- Railroads
- Large Rivers & Bodies of Water
- Streams/Creeks & Small Rivers
- Cities/Towns
- Cemeteries

Scale: Section = 1 mile X 1 mile
(there are some exceptions)

Map Group 17: Index to Land Patents

Township 27-North Range 14-West (4th PM - 1831 MN/WI)

After you locate an individual in this Index, take note of the Section and Section Part then proceed to the Land Patent map on the pages immediately following. You should have no difficulty locating the corresponding parcel of land.

The "For More Info" Column will lead you to more information about the underlying Patents. See the *Legend* at right, and the "How to Use this Book" chapter, for more information.

LEGEND

"For More Info . . . " column

A = Authority (Legislative Act, See Appendix "A")
B = Block or Lot (location in Section unknown)
C = Cancelled Patent
F = Fractional Section
G = Group (Multi-Patentee Patent, see Appendix "C")
V = Overlaps another Parcel
R = Re-Issued (Parcel patented more than once)

(A & G items require you to look in the Appendixes referred to above. All other Letter-designations followed by a number require you to locate line-items in this index that possess the ID number found after the letter).

ID	Individual in Patent	Sec.	Sec. Part	Date Issued	Other Counties	For More Info . . .
2806	CARSON, William	36	SENW	1852-08-02		A2 G62
2804	" "	25	SESW	1854-10-02		A2 G62
2805	" "	25	SWSE	1854-10-02		A2 G62
2807	" "	36	W½NE	1854-10-02		A2 G62
2808	" "	35	NESE	1855-12-15		A2 G65
2809	" "	36	W½SE	1855-12-15		A2 G65
2801	CUMMINGS, Robert D	32	E½SE	1889-07-20		A6
2796	DECKER, John H	14	NENW	1880-09-01		A6
2797	" "	14	NWNE	1880-09-01		A6
2808	DOWNS, Burrage B	35	NESE	1855-12-15		A2 G65
2809	" "	36	W½SE	1855-12-15		A2 G65
2806	EATON, Henry	36	SENW	1852-08-02		A2 G62
2804	" "	25	SESW	1854-10-02		A2 G62
2805	" "	25	SWSE	1854-10-02		A2 G62
2807	" "	36	W½NE	1854-10-02		A2 G62
2808	" "	35	NESE	1855-12-15		A2 G65
2809	" "	36	W½SE	1855-12-15		A2 G65
2795	FULLER, Heman	34	N½NW	1870-09-10		A6
2810	HOLMAN, William W	36	SW	1852-08-02		A2
2788	JOHNSON, Charles D	36	E½SE	1870-09-10		A6
2791	MCCARTNEY, Daniel	7	NENW	1857-04-01		A2
2786	MCCARTY, Adam	36	E½NE	1870-09-10		A6
2793	MOORE, Ephraim	33	S½NW	1852-08-02		A2
2794	" "	33	SWNE	1852-08-02		A2
2792	MORGAN, Edwin	32	N½NE	1873-09-20		A6
2789	PHILLIPS, Charles L	32	W½SE	1878-11-05		A2
2800	POST, Richard K	32	N½SW	1880-05-15		A6
2808	RAND, Eldridge D	35	NESE	1855-12-15		A2 G65
2809	" "	36	W½SE	1855-12-15		A2 G65
2790	TAPLIN, Chester D	32	S½NE	1878-06-24		A6
2799	TAPLIN, Lorenzo D	32	N½NW	1875-01-15		A6 G390
2798	" "	32	S½NW	1880-09-01		A6
2799	TAPLIN, Philena	32	N½NW	1875-01-15		A6 G390
2787	UTTER, Charles C	32	S½SW	1882-05-10		A6
2803	WEBSTER, Sylvester M	36	NENW	1872-09-02		A2
2802	WISCONSIN, State Of	16		1941-08-16		A3

Patent Map

T27-N R14-W
4th PM - 1831 MN/WI Meridian

Map Group 17

Township Statistics

Parcels Mapped :	25
Number of Patents :	20
Number of Individuals :	21
Patentees Identified :	19
Number of Surnames :	19
Multi-Patentee Parcels :	7
Oldest Patent Date :	8/2/1852
Most Recent Patent :	8/16/1941
Block/Lot Parcels :	0
Parcels Re - Issued :	0
Parcels that Overlap :	0
Cities and Towns :	2
Cemeteries :	1

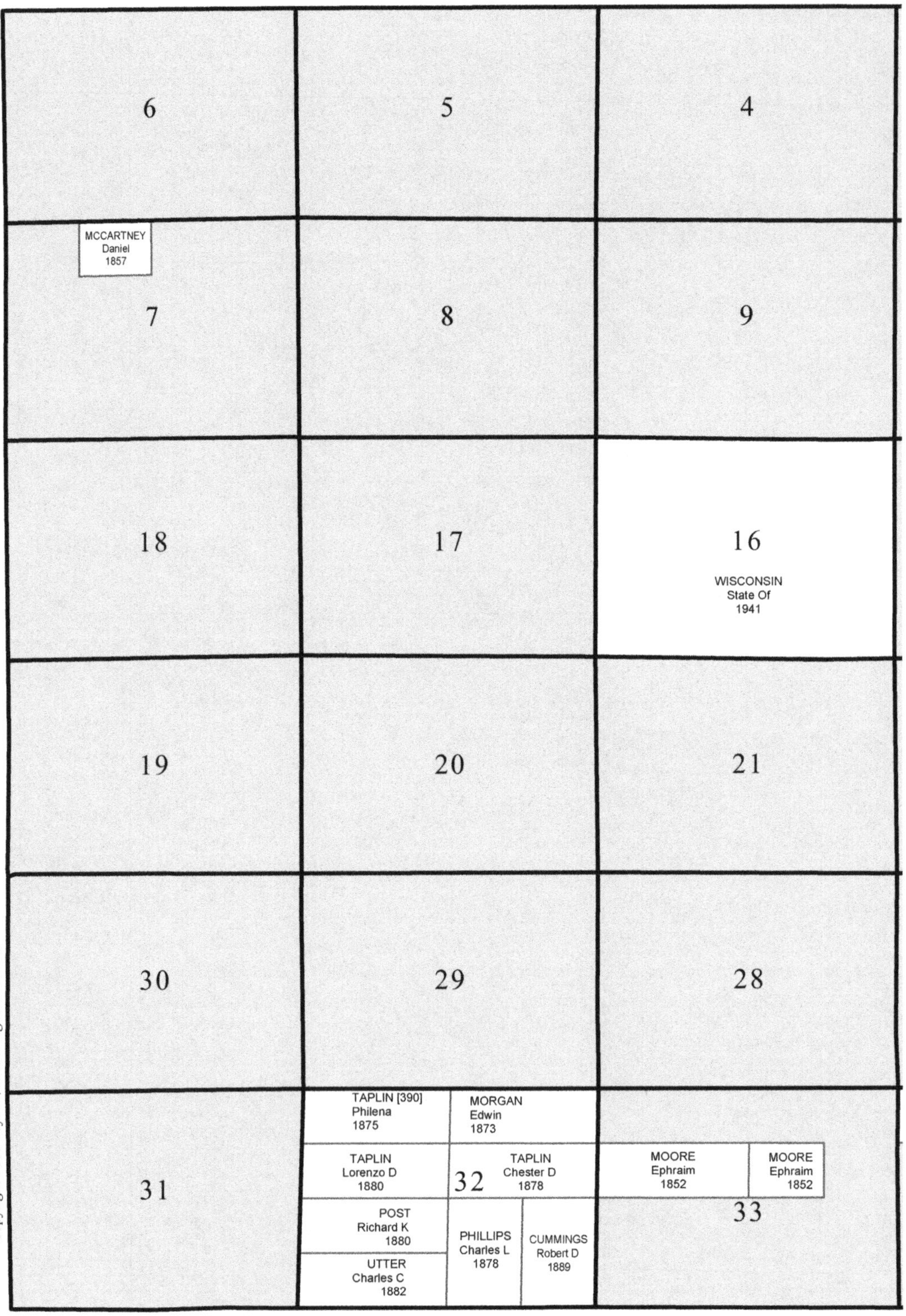
6
5
4
MCCARTNEY Daniel 1857
7
8
9
18
17
16
WISCONSIN State Of 1941
19
20
21
30
29
28
31
TAPLIN [390] Philena 1875
MORGAN Edwin 1873
TAPLIN Lorenzo D 1880
TAPLIN Chester D 1878
32
POST Richard K 1880
UTTER Charles C 1882
PHILLIPS Charles L 1878
CUMMINGS Robert D 1889
MOORE Ephraim 1852
MOORE Ephraim 1852
33

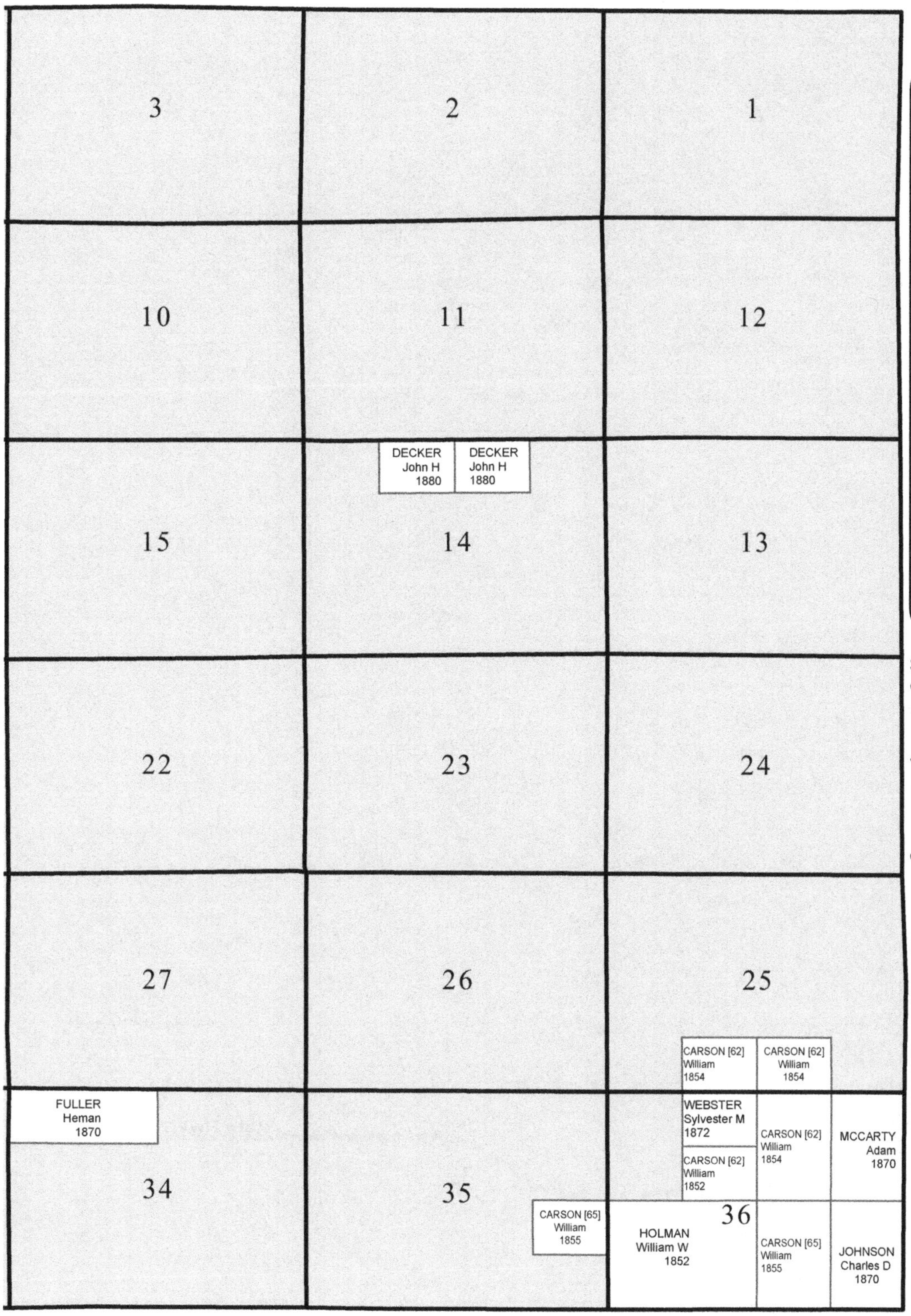
3
2
1
10
11
12
DECKER
John H
1880
DECKER
John H
1880
15
14
13
22
23
24
27
26
25
CARSON [62]
William
1854
CARSON [62]
William
1854
FULLER
Heman
1870
WEBSTER
Sylvester M
1872
CARSON [62]
William
1854
MCCARTY
Adam
1870
CARSON [62]
William
1852
34
35
CARSON [65]
William
1855
36
HOLMAN
William W
1852
CARSON [65]
William
1855
JOHNSON
Charles D
1870

Helpful Hints

1. This Map's INDEX can be found on the preceding pages.
2. Refer to Map "C" to see where this Township lies within Dunn County, Wisconsin.
3. Numbers within square brackets [ ] denote a multi-patentee land parcel (multi-owner). Refer to Appendix "C" for a full list of members in this group.
4. Areas that look to be crowded with Patentees usually indicate multiple sales of the same parcel (Re-issues) or Overlapping parcels. See this Township's Index for an explanation of these and other circumstances that might explain "odd" groupings of Patentees on this map.

Legend

Patent Boundary

Section Boundary

No Patents Found (or Outside County)

1., 2., 3., ... Lot Numbers (when beside a name)

[ ] Group Number (see Appendix "C")

Scale: Section = 1 mile X 1 mile (generally, with some exceptions)

Road Map

T27-N R14-W
4th PM - 1831 MN/WI Meridian

Map Group 17

Cities & Towns
Comfort
Weston

Cemeteries
Lower Weston Cemetery

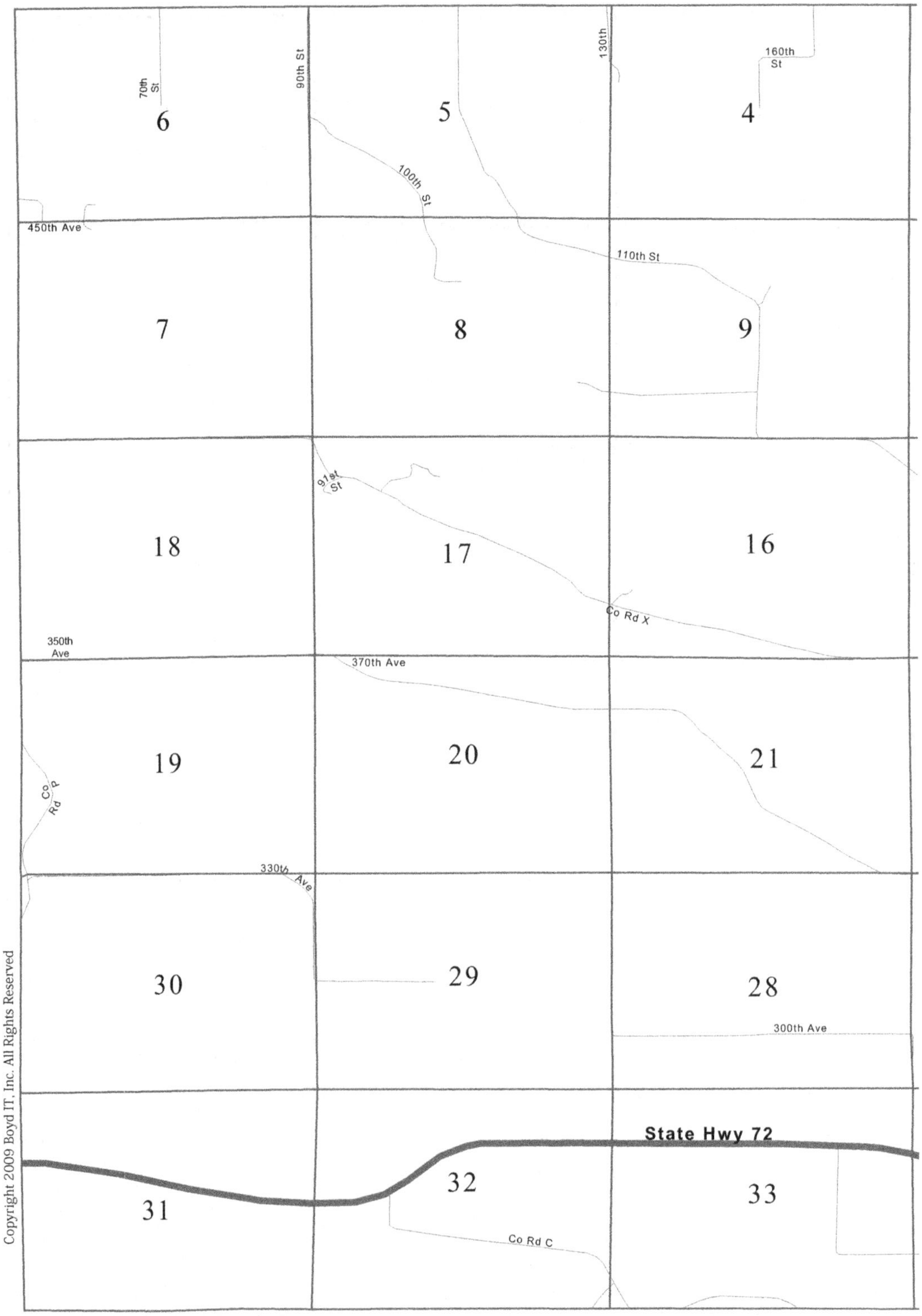

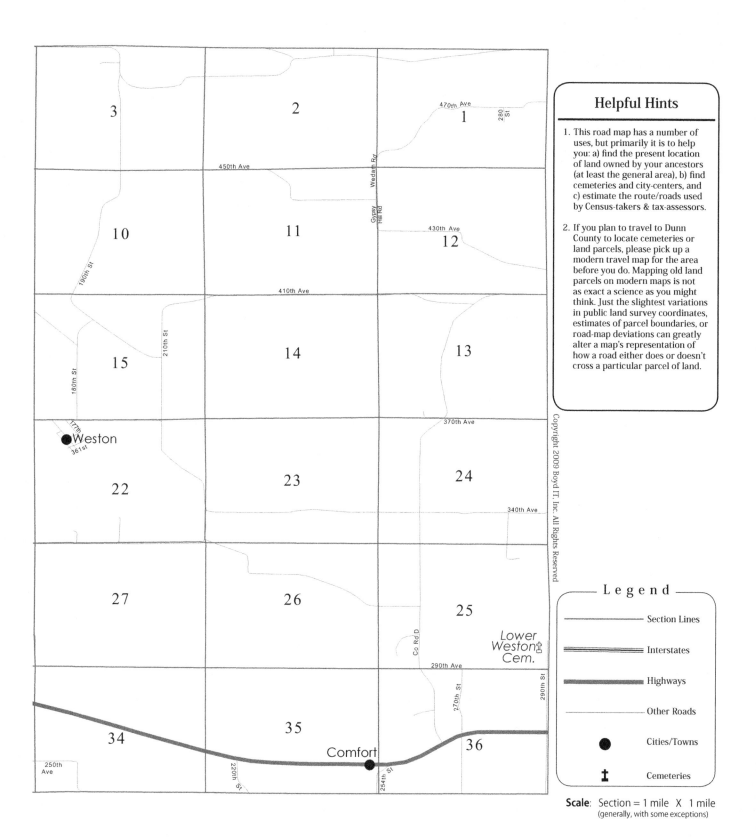

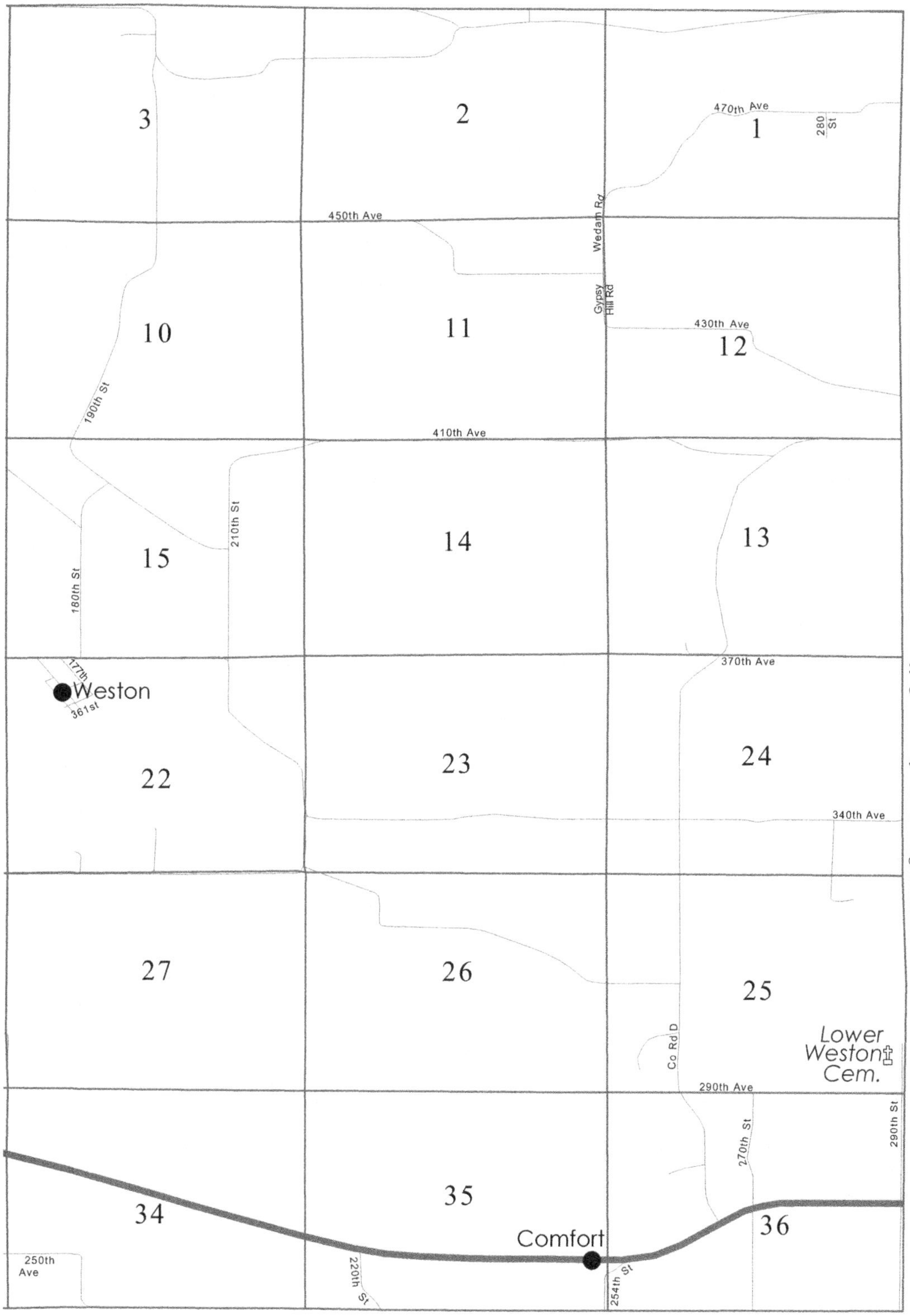

Helpful Hints

1. This road map has a number of uses, but primarily it is to help you: a) find the present location of land owned by your ancestors (at least the general area), b) find cemeteries and city-centers, and c) estimate the route/roads used by Census-takers & tax-assessors.
2. If you plan to travel to Dunn County to locate cemeteries or land parcels, please pick up a modern travel map for the area before you do. Mapping old land parcels on modern maps is not as exact a science as you might think. Just the slightest variations in public land survey coordinates, estimates of parcel boundaries, or road-map deviations can greatly alter a map's representation of how a road either does or doesn't cross a particular parcel of land.

Legend

- Section Lines
- Interstates
- Highways
- Other Roads
- Cities/Towns
- Cemeteries

Scale: Section = 1 mile X 1 mile
(generally, with some exceptions)

Historical Map

T27-N R14-W
4th PM - 1831 MN/WI Meridian

Map Group 17

Cities & Towns

Comfort
Weston

Cemeteries

Lower Weston Cemetery

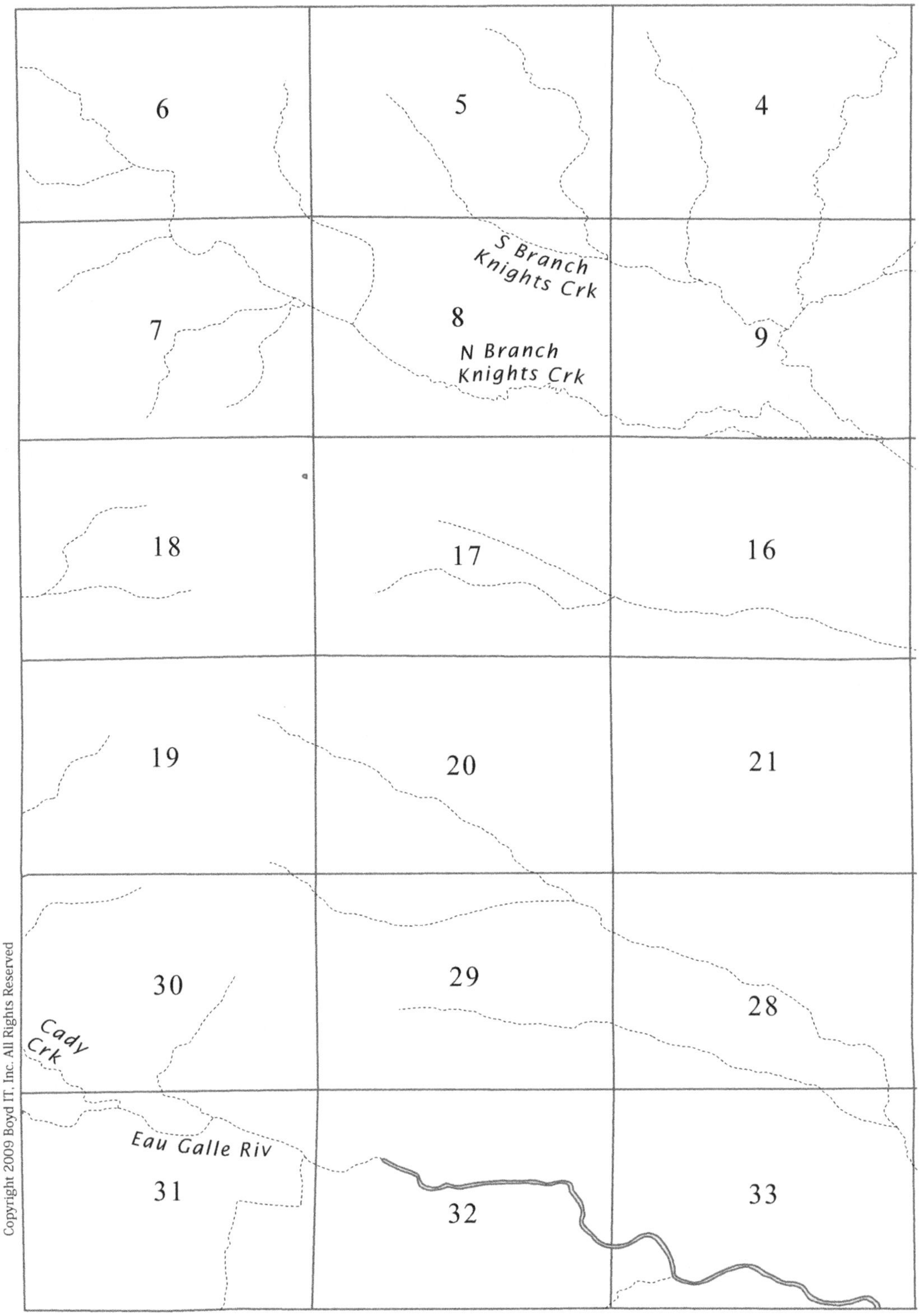

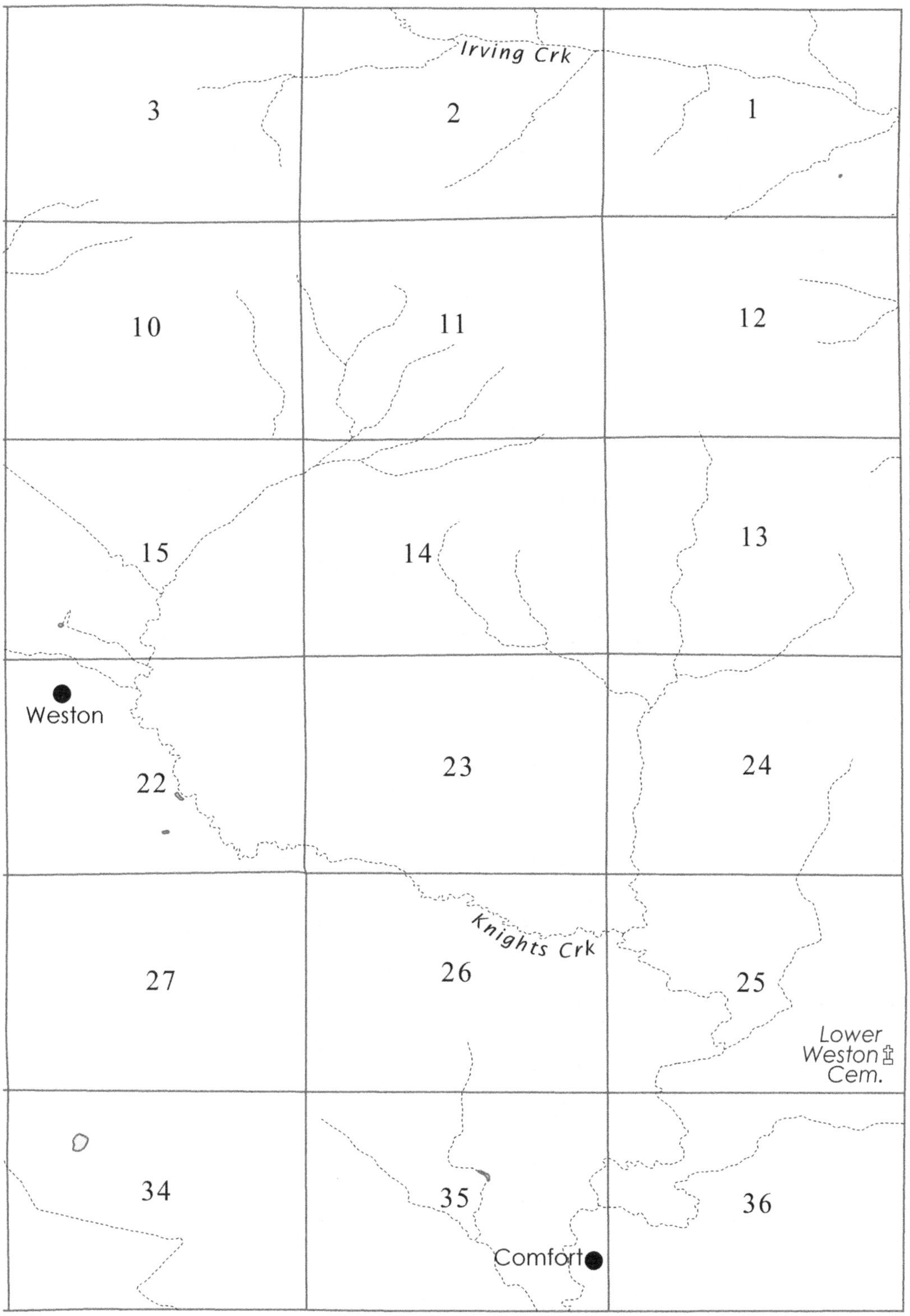
Irving Crk
3
2
1
10
11
12
15
14
13
Weston
22
23
24
Knights Crk
27
26
25
Lower Weston Cem.
34
35
36
Comfort

Helpful Hints

1. This Map takes a different look at the same Congressional Township displayed in the preceding two maps. It presents features that can help you better envision the historical development of the area: a) Water-bodies (lakes & ponds), b) Water-courses (rivers, streams, etc.), c) Railroads, d) City/town center-points (where they were oftentimes located when first settled), and e) Cemeteries.
2. Using this "Historical" map in tandem with this Township's Patent Map and Road Map, may lead you to some interesting discoveries. You will often find roads, towns, cemeteries, and waterways are named after nearby landowners: sometimes those names will be the ones you are researching. See how many of these research gems you can find here in Dunn County.

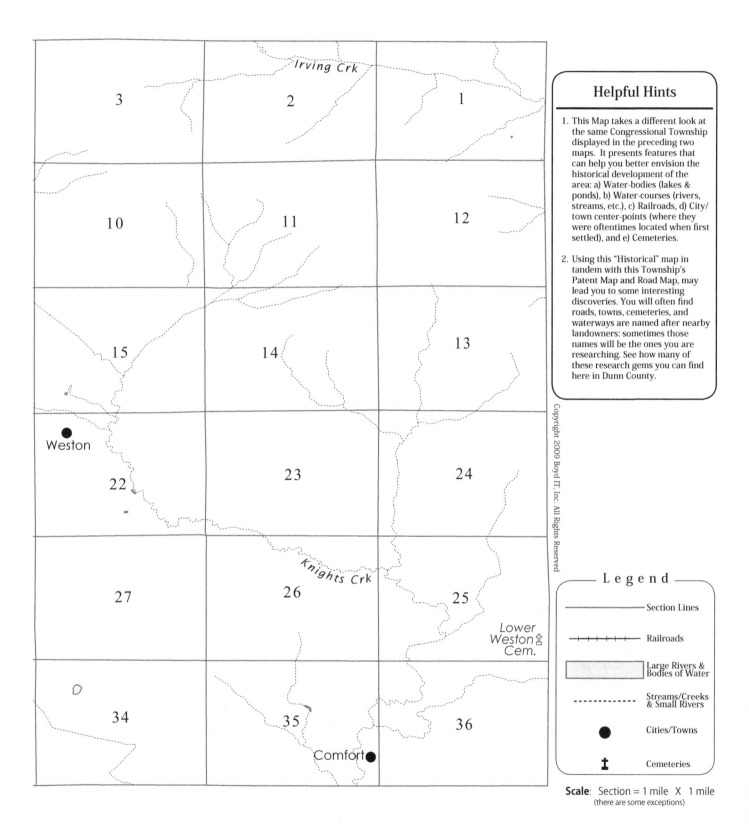

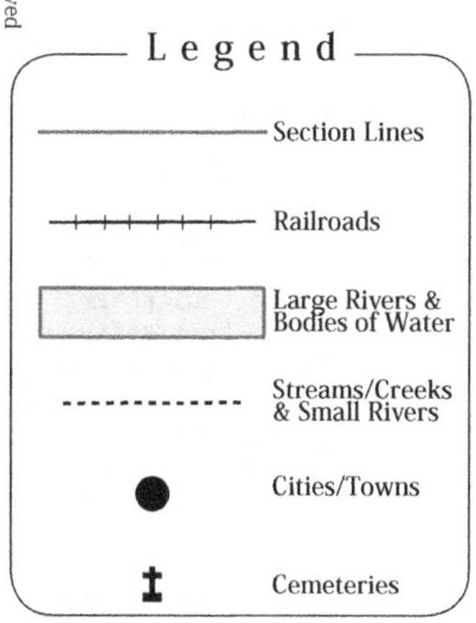
Legend
Section Lines
Railroads
Large Rivers & Bodies of Water
Streams/Creeks & Small Rivers
Cities/Towns
Cemeteries

Scale: Section = 1 mile X 1 mile
(there are some exceptions)

Map Group 18: Index to Land Patents

Township 27-North Range 13-West (4th PM - 1831 MN/WI)

After you locate an individual in this Index, take note of the Section and Section Part then proceed to the Land Patent map on the pages immediately following. You should have no difficulty locating the corresponding parcel of land.

The "For More Info" Column will lead you to more information about the underlying Patents. See the *Legend* at right, and the "How to Use this Book" chapter, for more information.

LEGEND

"For More Info . . . " column

A = Authority (Legislative Act, See Appendix "A")
B = Block or Lot (location in Section unknown)
C = Cancelled Patent
F = Fractional Section
G = Group (Multi-Patentee Patent, see Appendix "C")
V = Overlaps another Parcel
R = Re-Issued (Parcel patented more than once)

(A & G items require you to look in the Appendixes referred to above. All other Letter-designations followed by a number require you to locate line-items in this index that possess the ID number found after the letter).

ID	Individual in Patent	Sec.	Sec. Part	Date Issued	Other Counties	For More Info . . .
2972	ASLAKSEN, Swen	8	SESE	1879-10-01		A6
2824	AVERY, Beriah	24	NWSE	1855-12-15		A2
2825	" "	24	S½SE	1855-12-15		A2
2918	BANNISTER, Norton W	6	SE	1870-05-20		A6
2831	BECKWITH, Chauncey	23	S½SE	1855-12-15		A2
2832	" "	23	SESW	1855-12-15		A2
2834	" "	26	E½NW	1855-12-15		A2
2835	" "	26	NE	1855-12-15		A2
2833	" "	23	W½SW	1857-04-01		A2
2836	" "	27	NWSW	1859-05-02		A2
2837	" "	36	NENW	1859-05-02		A2
2950	BEDDINGER, Sarah	2	E½SE	1862-02-05		A5 G134
2951	" "	2	SWSE	1862-02-05		A5 G134
2827	BELLACH, Caroline	4	NE	1864-09-15		A5 G35 F
2817	BILLINGS, Andrew	35	2	1859-09-01		A5
2818	" "	35	W½NW	1859-09-01		A5
2912	BIRD, Mary A	18	W½SE	1871-04-05		A2
2917	BIRD, Nathaniel R	18	E½SE	1871-08-25		A6
2815	BISHOP, Amos	30	E½SE	1869-10-20		A6
2930	BISHOP, Potter	32	W½NW	1872-10-01		A6
2955	BLACK, Samuel	10	1	1878-06-24		A6
2847	BLANK, Edward	22	N½NE	1861-12-05		A5
2848	" "	22	NESE	1861-12-05		A5
2849	" "	22	SENE	1861-12-05		A5
2838	BOLLE, Christian	30	E½SW	1869-10-20		A6
2982	BONNEVALD, William	30	W½NW	1872-10-01		A6 F
2880	BOWDISH, Isaac B	27	SENE	1859-05-02		A2
2812	BRIGGS, Abram	4	NW	1870-05-20		A6 F
2830	BROVEN, Charley	20	E½SE	1874-11-10		A6
2813	BRUNELLE, Alexis J	14	SW	1862-03-10		A5
2814	" "	14	NW	1864-09-15		A5 G51
2864	BUSE, Fritze	20	E½NE	1872-09-02		A2
2929	CANFIELD, Philo	14	SE	1862-09-01		A7 G59
2841	CHICKERING, Daniel W	32	E½SE	1870-09-10		A6
2856	CHRISTIANSON, Ever	24	NW	1861-07-01		A5 G71
2821	CLEMENS, Benjamin	6	N½NE	1866-02-15		A2 F
2822	" "	6	SENE	1866-02-15		A2 F
2948	COLE, Patty	26	SE	1862-05-20		A5 G138
2903	CORMICAN, John W	18	N½NE	1873-01-10		A6
2933	CREASER, Robert	34	6	1870-06-01		A2
2956	CRIST, Samuel	6	E½SW	1873-05-20		A6 F
2884	DAVIS, James C	34	2	1855-12-15		A2
2828	DEAN, Charles	20	NWSE	1873-04-01		A6
2829	" "	20	SWNE	1873-04-01		A6
2966	DEXTER, Charles E	12	N½NW	1862-03-10		A5 G354
2980	" "	14	NENE	1862-07-15		A5 G216

ID	Individual in Patent	Sec.	Sec. Part	Date Issued	Other Counties	For More Info . . .
2981	DEXTER, Charles E (Cont'd)	14	S½NE	1862-07-15		A5 G216
2859	DICKEY, Eleanor	10	NE	1861-12-05		A5 G238
2983	DOANE, Samuel H	24	SW	1862-01-25		A5 G125
2929	DOOLITTLE, James R	14	SE	1862-09-01		A7 G59
2915	DOOLITTLE, Naomi	22	8	1866-02-15		A2
2929	DOOLITTLE, Ormus	14	SE	1862-09-01		A7 G59
2826	DOWNS, Burrage B	34	7	1865-05-05		A2
2916	DRAKE, Nathaniel	6	SWNE	1865-05-05		A2
2881	DREWS, Jacob	6	SENW	1875-08-10		A6
2827	DYKINS, Mary	4	NE	1864-09-15		A5 G35 F
2819	EATON, Arthur H	18	NESW	1876-04-01		A6
2820	" "	18	W½SW	1876-04-01		A6 F
2816	ERIKSON, Andreas	12	NWNE	1893-05-06		A6
2983	EVANS, William	24	SW	1862-01-25		A5 G125
2811	EVELAND, Abraham W	28	NWNE	1874-11-10		A6
2984	FAIRCHILD, William	20	NENW	1873-01-10		A6
2985	" "	20	NWNE	1873-01-10		A6
2862	FISCHER, Fritz	2	N½NE	1860-07-16		A5
2863	" "	2	SENE	1860-07-16		A5
2976	FITZGERALD, Thomas	27	NESE	1857-04-01		A2
2977	" "	34	1	1857-04-01		A2
2940	FRENCH, Samuel B	35	3	1857-04-01		A2
2941	" "	35	4	1857-04-01		A2
2942	" "	36	E½SW	1857-10-30		A5
2944	" "	36	NWSW	1857-10-30		A5
2937	" "	2	NESW	1861-09-05		A5
2938	" "	2	NWSE	1861-09-05		A5
2939	" "	2	SENW	1861-09-05		A5
2949	" "	2	S½SW	1861-12-05		A5 G144
2950	" "	2	E½SE	1862-02-05		A5 G134
2951	" "	2	SWSE	1862-02-05		A5 G134
2947	" "	12	SE	1862-03-10		A5 G143
2945	" "	36	SESE	1862-03-10		A5 G140
2946	" "	36	W½SE	1862-03-10		A5 G140
2952	" "	2	N½NW	1862-05-20		A5 G145
2953	" "	2	NWSW	1862-05-20		A5 G145
2954	" "	2	SWNW	1862-05-20		A5 G145
2948	" "	26	SE	1862-05-20		A5 G138
2943	" "	36	NE	1862-07-15		A5
2935	" "	10	N½SE	1862-11-20		A5
2936	" "	10	SESE	1862-11-20		A5
2885	GALLAWAY, James	2	SWNE	1857-04-01		A2
2882	GARRETT, Jacob	6	NENW	1867-07-15		A2 F
2994	GIBERSON, Ziba	35	NESW	1859-12-10		A2
2995	" "	35	SENW	1859-12-10		A2
2919	GILBERT, Oliver	3	E½NE	1859-05-02		A2 F
2986	GILBERT, William P	27	1	1860-02-01		A5
2987	" "	27	2	1860-02-01		A5
2914	GREEN, Minnie	14	NWNE	1877-09-26		A6
2920	HARPER, Oliver S	34	W½SW	1872-10-01		A6
2850	HENEGAN, Edward E	34	NESW	1869-09-01		A6
2851	" "	34	SENW	1869-09-01		A6
2928	HERRON, Philip	24	NESE	1871-11-20		A6
2886	HORNER, Joel	8	N½SE	1865-05-05		A2
2945	HUGHES, Fanny	36	SESE	1862-03-10		A5 G140
2946	" "	36	W½SE	1862-03-10		A5 G140
2814	HULL, David Smith	14	NW	1864-09-15		A5 G51
2889	HYNS, John	34	4	1855-12-15		A2
2890	" "	34	SESW	1855-12-15		A2
2866	IRVINE, George K	10	3	1854-07-05		A7
2869	" "	9	NESE	1854-10-02		A2
2865	" "	10	2	1855-12-15		A2
2867	" "	15	1	1855-12-15		A2
2868	" "	15	2	1855-12-15		A2
2870	" "	10	4	1863-05-20		A5 G199
2871	" "	10	5	1863-05-20		A5 G199
2872	" "	10	6	1863-05-20		A5 G199
2877	KELLOGG, Harvey D	12	S½NW	1862-07-15		A5
2980	KEY, Mary A R	14	NENE	1862-07-15		A5 G216
2981	" "	14	S½NE	1862-07-15		A5 G216
2840	KING, Daniel	32	N½SW	1871-08-25		A6
2856	KINGMAN, Phebe	24	NW	1861-07-01		A5 G71
2980	KITTELSEN, Tosten	14	NENE	1862-07-15		A5 G216

ID	Individual in Patent	Sec.	Sec. Part	Date Issued	Other Counties	For More Info . . .
2981	KITTELSEN, Tosten (Cont'd)	14	S½NE	1862-07-15		A5 G216
2887	KNAPP, John H	3	5	1855-12-15		A2 G219
2888	" "	3	6	1855-12-15		A2 G219
2909	LAMMER, Leonhard	8	E½NW	1875-08-10		A6
2852	LARKHAM, Edwin F	4	SW	1870-05-20		A6
2859	LECLERCQ, Francis L	10	NE	1861-12-05		A5 G238
2922	LITTLE, James	28	SESW	1855-12-15		A2 G241
2922	LITTLE, Peter	28	SESW	1855-12-15		A2 G241
2904	LOWE, Joseph	30	W½SW	1873-04-01		A6 F
2860	MACKEY, Frederick	26	SW	1862-07-15		A5
2861	" "	28	S½NW	1864-09-15		A5
2934	MACKEY, Robert	28	NENW	1865-05-05		A2
2969	MERRILL, Silas N	32	W½NE	1870-09-10		A6
2921	MURRAY, Patrick	36	NESE	1900-09-07		A6
2967	NELSON, Samson	12	E½NE	1864-09-15		A5 G350
2968	" "	12	SWNE	1864-09-15		A5 G350
2964	OLSON, Sarah	20	NESW	1877-02-20		A6 G291
2965	" "	20	SENW	1877-02-20		A6 G291
2923	OTTUM, Peter	28	NWNW	1869-08-05		A2
2814	PEET, Martha	14	NW	1864-09-15		A5 G51
2876	PERRY, George W	32	W½SE	1873-12-20		A6
2913	PONTOW, Michael	6	W½NW	1875-08-10		A6 F
2870	PORTER, Margaret	10	4	1863-05-20		A5 G199
2871	" "	10	5	1863-05-20		A5 G199
2872	" "	10	6	1863-05-20		A5 G199
2925	RICE, Peter	30	W½SE	1869-10-20		A6
2857	RICHARDS, Fordges	22	3	1857-04-01		A2
2858	" "	22	4	1857-04-01		A2
2910	ROWE, Luther T	6	W½SW	1873-05-20		A6 F
2967	SAMPSON, Sigbert	12	E½NE	1864-09-15		A5 G350
2968	" "	12	SWNE	1864-09-15		A5 G350
2839	SANDERSON, Clark	28	NWSW	1873-04-01		A6
2964	SANDERSON, Harrison	20	NESW	1877-02-20		A6 G291
2965	" "	20	SENW	1877-02-20		A6 G291
2964	SANDERSON, Sarah	20	NESW	1877-02-20		A6 G291
2965	" "	20	SENW	1877-02-20		A6 G291
2978	SAVILLE, Thomas W	32	E½NE	1872-09-02		A2
2901	SCANLAN, John	8	SWSE	1866-02-15		A2
2897	" "	22	5	1873-05-20		A6
2898	" "	22	6	1873-05-20		A6
2899	" "	22	7	1873-05-20		A6
2900	" "	22	SWNE	1873-05-20		A6
2883	SCHAMBERGER, Jacob	18	E½NW	1879-10-01		A6
2966	SEVERSON, Sever	12	N½NW	1862-03-10		A5 G354
2970	SHAFER, Simon	32	S½SW	1869-09-01		A6
2859	SHEPHARD, John G	10	NE	1861-12-05		A5 G238
2963	SHERLOCK, Samuel	30	W½NE	1876-01-10		A6
2988	SINGERHAUS, William	8	SESW	1870-06-10		A2
2989	SINGERHOUSE, William	8	W½NW	1872-10-01		A6
2873	SMITH, George	27	3	1855-12-15		A2
2874	" "	27	4	1855-12-15		A2
2875	" "	27	SWSW	1855-12-15		A2
2908	SMITH, Leonard B	28	E½NE	1873-12-20		A6
2924	SNYDER, Peter R	18	SESW	1871-06-14		A2
2907	STEINMAN, Joseph V	18	W½NW	1876-01-10		A6 F
2926	STOCKMAN, Peter	8	NESW	1866-02-15		A2
2927	" "	8	W½SW	1871-08-25		A6
2887	STOUT, Henry L	3	5	1855-12-15		A2 G219
2888	" "	3	6	1855-12-15		A2 G219
2842	STRATTON, David	30	E½NW	1873-05-20		A6
2906	STRATTON, Joseph	30	E½NE	1873-01-10		A6
2905	" "	18	S½NE	1875-01-15		A6
2853	SWISHER, Anthony	28	E½SE	1871-04-20		A6 G389
2853	SWISHER, Elizabeth	28	E½SE	1871-04-20		A6 G389
2896	SWISHER, John M	28	SWSE	1872-09-25		A6
2961	SWISHER, Samuel R	28	NWSE	1871-04-20		A6
2962	" "	28	SWNE	1871-04-20		A6
2990	SWISHER, William	34	W½NW	1872-09-25		A6
2887	TAINTER, Andrew	3	5	1855-12-15		A2 G219
2888	" "	3	6	1855-12-15		A2 G219
2991	THANE, William	35	SESE	1857-04-01		A2
2992	" "	36	SWSW	1857-04-01		A2
2843	THOMPSON, Ebenezer	34	3	1855-12-15		A2

ID	Individual in Patent	Sec.	Sec. Part	Date Issued	Other Counties	For More Info . . .
2844	THOMPSON, Ebenezer (Cont'd)	34	5	1855-12-15		A2
2845	" "	34	8	1855-12-15		A2
2846	" "	4	SE	1870-05-20		A6
2823	THORN, Benjamin S	10	7	1878-06-24		A6
2902	VAN VETCHTEN, JOHN	26	W½NW	1862-11-20		A5
2931	VARNEY, Reuben C	22	1	1872-10-01		A6
2932	" "	22	2	1872-10-01		A6
2854	WAIT, Emory W	20	SESW	1870-09-10		A6
2855	" "	20	SWSE	1870-09-10		A6
2960	WALKER, Samuel H	36	NWNW	1855-12-15		A2
2958	" "	35	NENW	1855-12-18		A2
2959	" "	35	NWNE	1855-12-18		A2
2957	" "	35	NENE	1857-04-01		A2
2979	WALLACE, Thompson	32	E½NW	1870-09-10		A6
2947	WARREN, Marvin	12	SE	1862-03-10		A5 G143
2947	WEST, Margarette	12	SE	1862-03-10		A5 G143
2879	WESTON, Horatio N	27	NENE	1855-12-15		A2
2878	" "	22	SESE	1866-02-15		A2
2949	WHEELER, Payton	2	S½SW	1861-12-05		A5 G144
2952	WILSON, Susan	2	N½NW	1862-05-20		A5 G145
2953	" "	2	NWSW	1862-05-20		A5 G145
2954	" "	2	SWNW	1862-05-20		A5 G145
2887	WILSON, Thomas B	3	5	1855-12-15		A2 G219
2888	" "	3	6	1855-12-15		A2 G219
2973	" "	35	N½SE	1859-05-02		A2
2974	" "	35	S½NE	1859-05-02		A2
2975	" "	36	S½NW	1859-05-02		A2
2993	WILSON, William	24	NE	1862-07-15		A5
2971	WISCONSIN, State Of	16		1941-08-16		A3
2911	WRIGHT, Marshall M	12	SW	1862-01-25		A5
2891	YOUNG, John L	15	3	1855-12-15		A2
2892	" "	15	4	1855-12-15		A2
2893	" "	28	NESW	1855-12-15		A2
2894	" "	28	SWSW	1855-12-15		A2
2895	" "	33	NWNW	1855-12-15		A2

Patent Map

T27-N R13-W
4th PM - 1831 MN/WI Meridian

Map Group 18

Township Statistics

Parcels Mapped	:	185
Number of Patents	:	138
Number of Individuals	:	133
Patentees Identified	:	115
Number of Surnames	:	116
Multi-Patentee Parcels	:	30
Oldest Patent Date	:	7/5/1854
Most Recent Patent	:	8/16/1941
Block/Lot Parcels	:	36
Parcels Re - Issued	:	0
Parcels that Overlap	:	0
Cities and Towns	:	2
Cemeteries	:	6

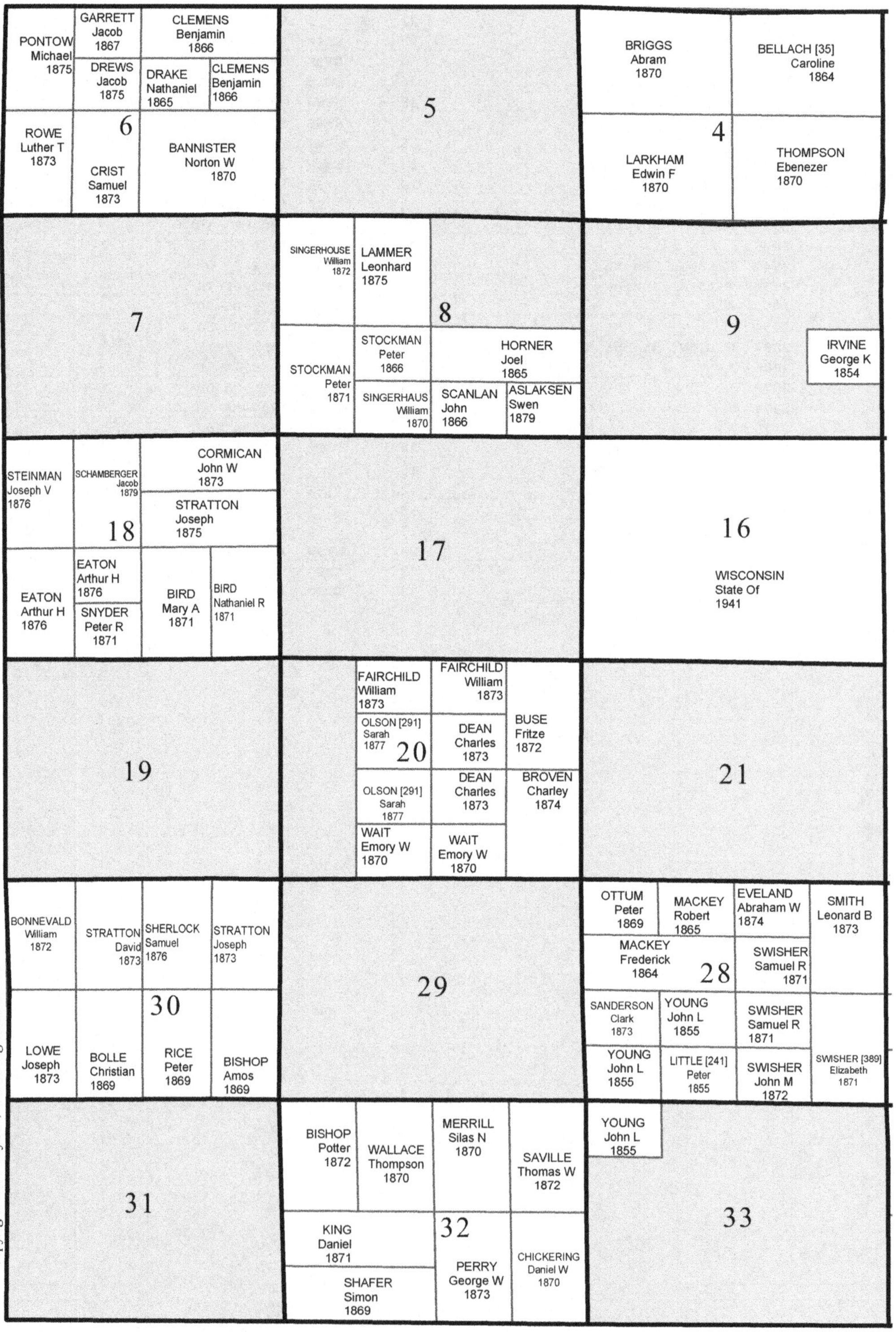
PONTOW Michael 1875
GARRETT Jacob 1867
CLEMENS Benjamin 1866
DREWS Jacob 1875
DRAKE Nathaniel 1865
CLEMENS Benjamin 1866
ROWE Luther T 1873
6
CRIST Samuel 1873
BANNISTER Norton W 1870
5
BRIGGS Abram 1870
BELLACH [35] Caroline 1864
4
LARKHAM Edwin F 1870
THOMPSON Ebenezer 1870
7
SINGERHOUSE William 1872
LAMMER Leonhard 1875
8
STOCKMAN Peter 1866
HORNER Joel 1865
STOCKMAN Peter 1871
SINGERHAUS William 1870
SCANLAN John 1866
ASLAKSEN Swen 1879
9
IRVINE George K 1854
STEINMAN Joseph V 1876
SCHAMBERGER Jacob 1879
CORMICAN John W 1873
STRATTON Joseph 1875
18
EATON Arthur H 1876
EATON Arthur H 1876
SNYDER Peter R 1871
BIRD Mary A 1871
BIRD Nathaniel R 1871
17
16
WISCONSIN State Of 1941
19
FAIRCHILD William 1873
FAIRCHILD William 1873
OLSON [291] Sarah 1877
20
DEAN Charles 1873
BUSE Fritze 1872
OLSON [291] Sarah 1877
DEAN Charles 1873
BROVEN Charley 1874
WAIT Emory W 1870
WAIT Emory W 1870
21
BONNEVALD William 1872
STRATTON David 1873
SHERLOCK Samuel 1876
STRATTON Joseph 1873
30
LOWE Joseph 1873
BOLLE Christian 1869
RICE Peter 1869
BISHOP Amos 1869
29
OTTUM Peter 1869
MACKEY Robert 1865
EVELAND Abraham W 1874
SMITH Leonard B 1873
MACKEY Frederick 1864
28
SWISHER Samuel R 1871
SANDERSON Clark 1873
YOUNG John L 1855
SWISHER Samuel R 1871
YOUNG John L 1855
LITTLE [241] Peter 1855
SWISHER John M 1872
SWISHER [389] Elizabeth 1871
31
BISHOP Potter 1872
WALLACE Thompson 1870
MERRILL Silas N 1870
SAVILLE Thomas W 1872
KING Daniel 1871
32
SHAFER Simon 1869
PERRY George W 1873
CHICKERING Daniel W 1870
YOUNG John L 1855
33

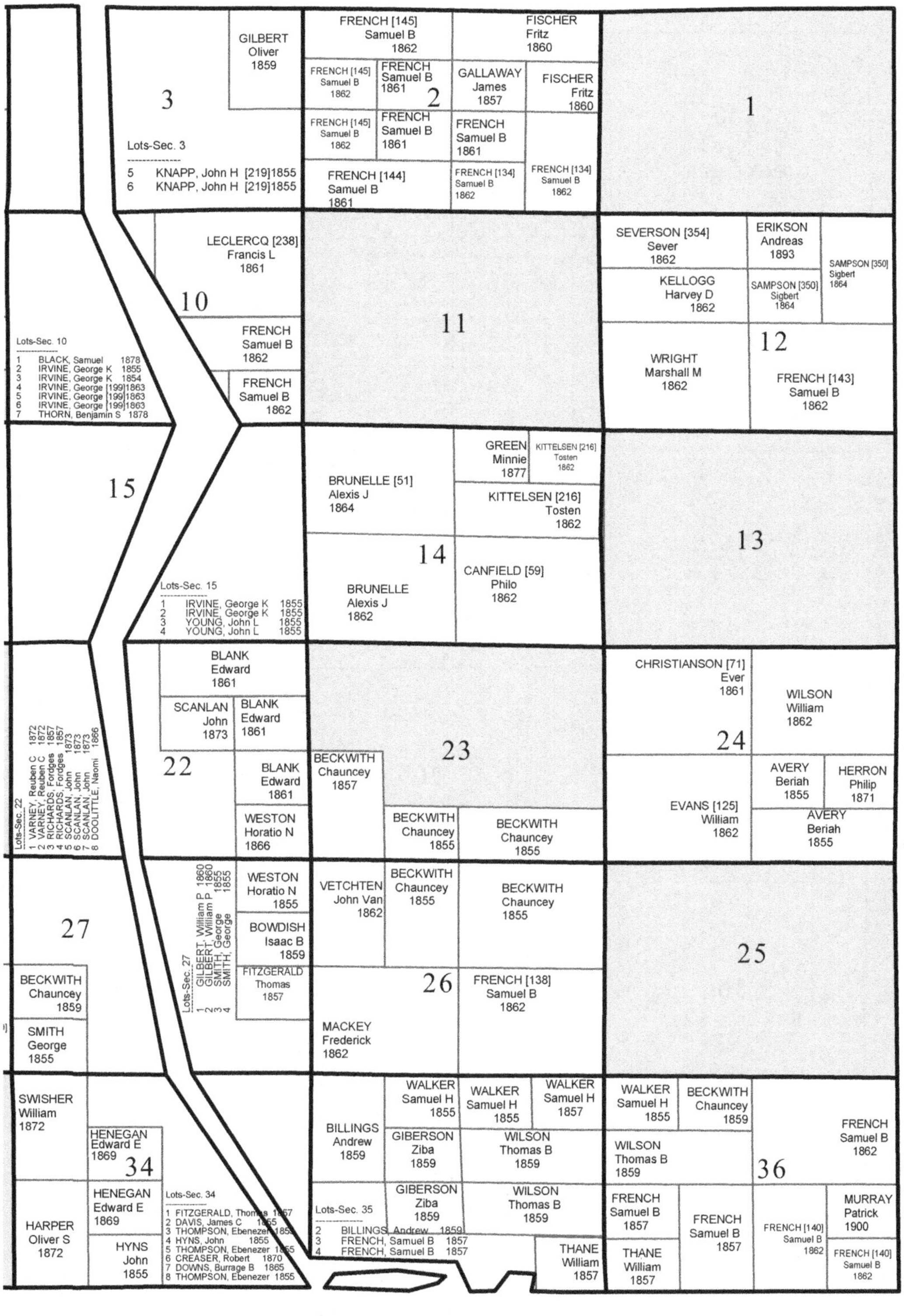

Helpful Hints

1. This Map's INDEX can be found on the preceding pages.
2. Refer to Map "C" to see where this Township lies within Dunn County, Wisconsin.
3. Numbers within square brackets [ ] denote a multi-patentee land parcel (multi-owner). Refer to Appendix "C" for a full list of members in this group.
4. Areas that look to be crowded with Patentees usually indicate multiple sales of the same parcel (Re-issues) or Overlapping parcels. See this Township's Index for an explanation of these and other circumstances that might explain "odd" groupings of Patentees on this map.

Legend

(thin line)	Patent Boundary
(thick line)	Section Boundary
(shaded)	No Patents Found (or Outside County)
1., 2., 3., ...	Lot Numbers (when beside a name)
[ ]	Group Number (see Appendix "C")

Scale: Section = 1 mile X 1 mile
(generally, with some exceptions)

Road Map

T27-N R13-W
4th PM - 1831 MN/WI Meridian

Map Group 18

Cities & Towns

Downsville
Irvington

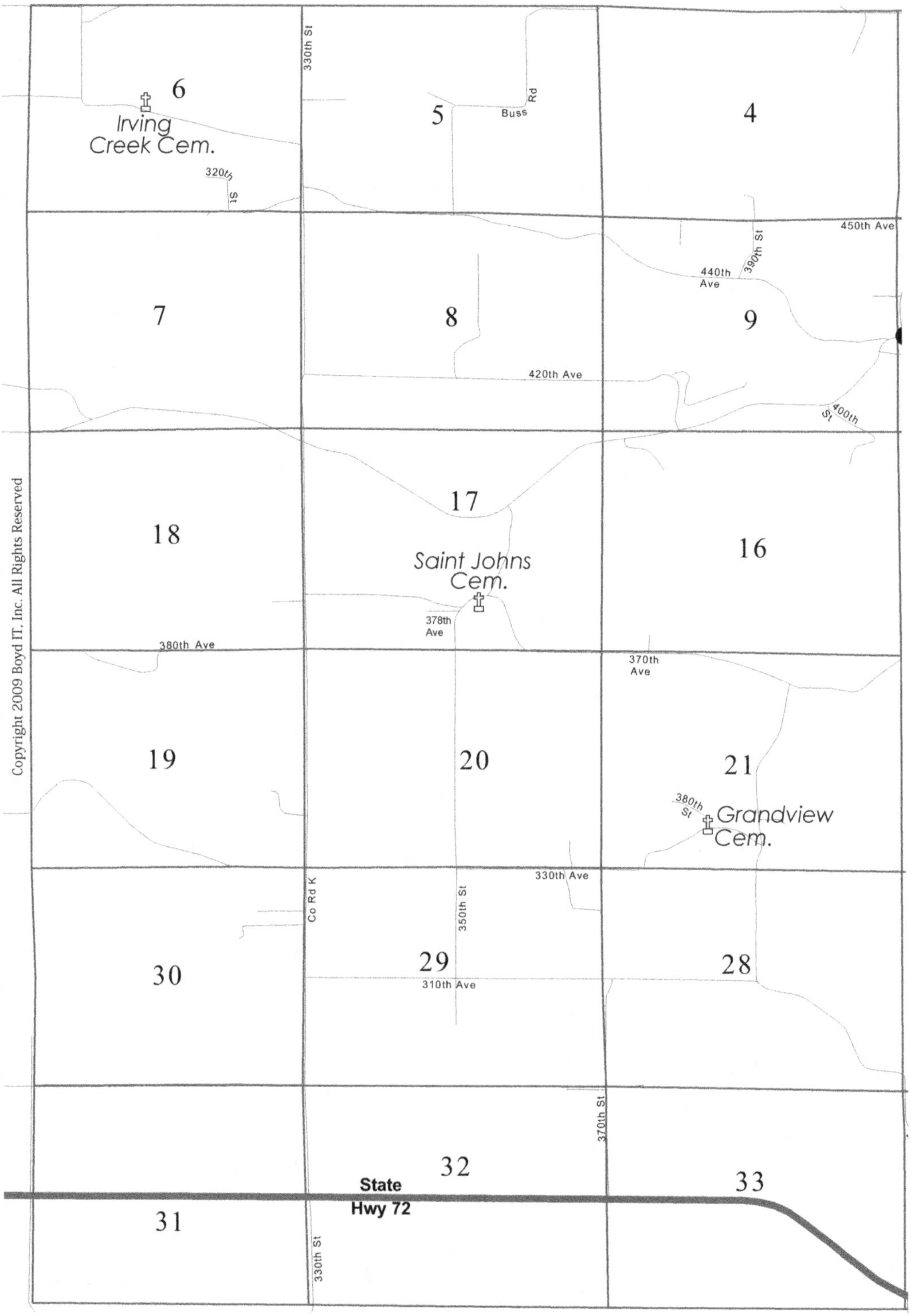

Cemeteries

Grandview Cemetery
Irving Creek Cemetery
Peace Cemetery
Riverview Cemetery
Saint Johns Cemetery
Saint Pauls Cemetery

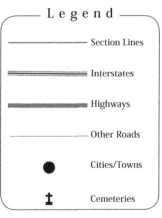

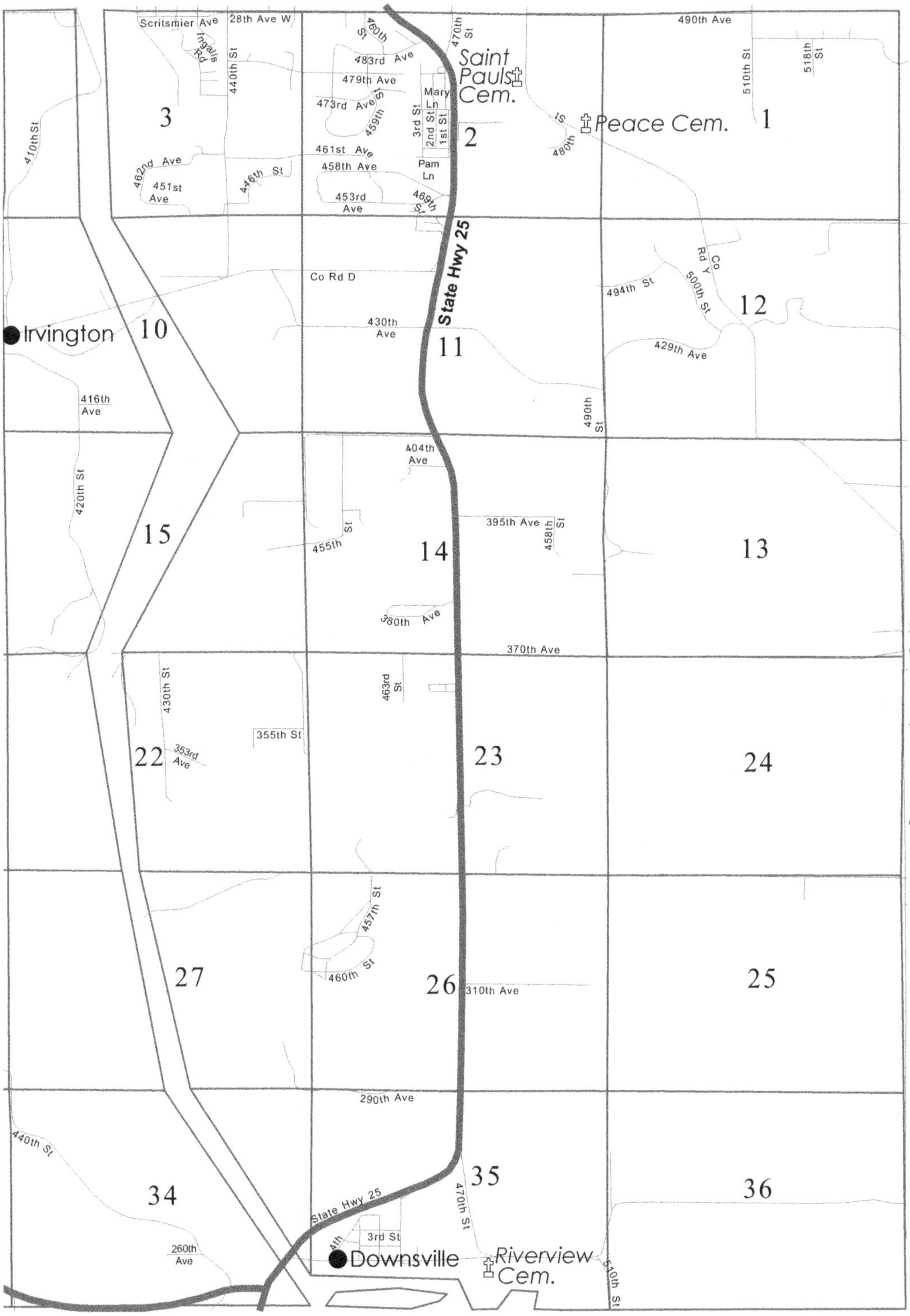

Helpful Hints

1. This road map has a number of uses, but primarily it is to help you: a) find the present location of land owned by your ancestors (at least the general area), b) find cemeteries and city-centers, and c) estimate the route/roads used by Census-takers & tax-assessors.
2. If you plan to travel to Dunn County to locate cemeteries or land parcels, please pick up a modern travel map for the area before you do. Mapping old land parcels on modern maps is not as exact a science as you might think. Just the slightest variations in public land survey coordinates, estimates of parcel boundaries, or road-map deviations can greatly alter a map's representation of how a road either does or doesn't cross a particular parcel of land.

Legend

- Section Lines
- Interstates
- Highways
- Other Roads
- Cities/Towns
- Cemeteries

Scale: Section = 1 mile X 1 mile
(generally, with some exceptions)

Historical Map

T27-N R13-W
4th PM - 1831 MN/WI Meridian

Map Group 18

Cities & Towns

Downsville
Irvington

Cemeteries

Grandview Cemetery
Irving Creek Cemetery
Peace Cemetery
Riverview Cemetery
Saint Johns Cemetery
Saint Pauls Cemetery

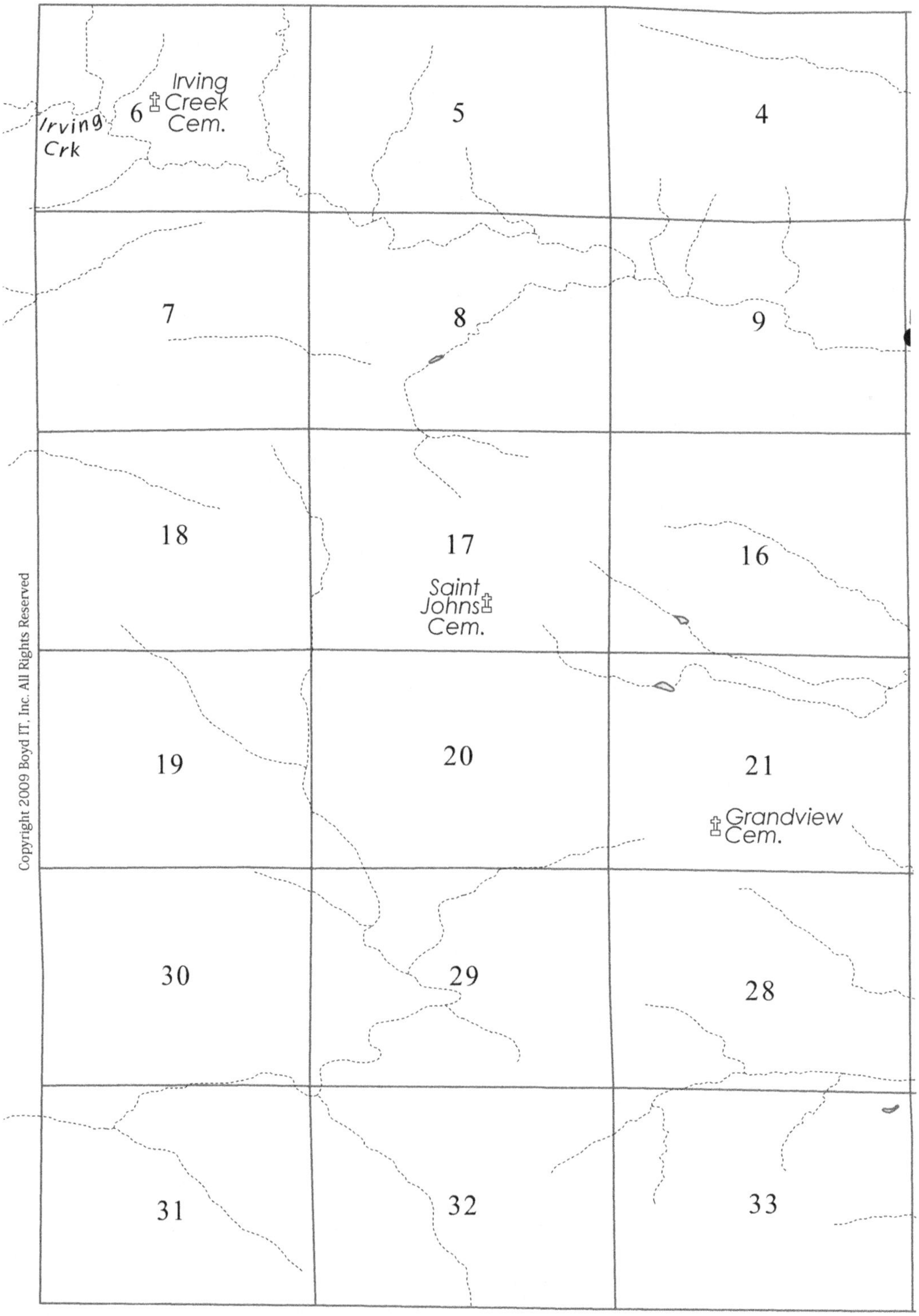

Irving Crk
6
Irving Creek Cem.
5
4
7
8
9
18
17
16
Saint Johns Cem.
19
20
21
Grandview Cem.
30
29
28
31
32
33

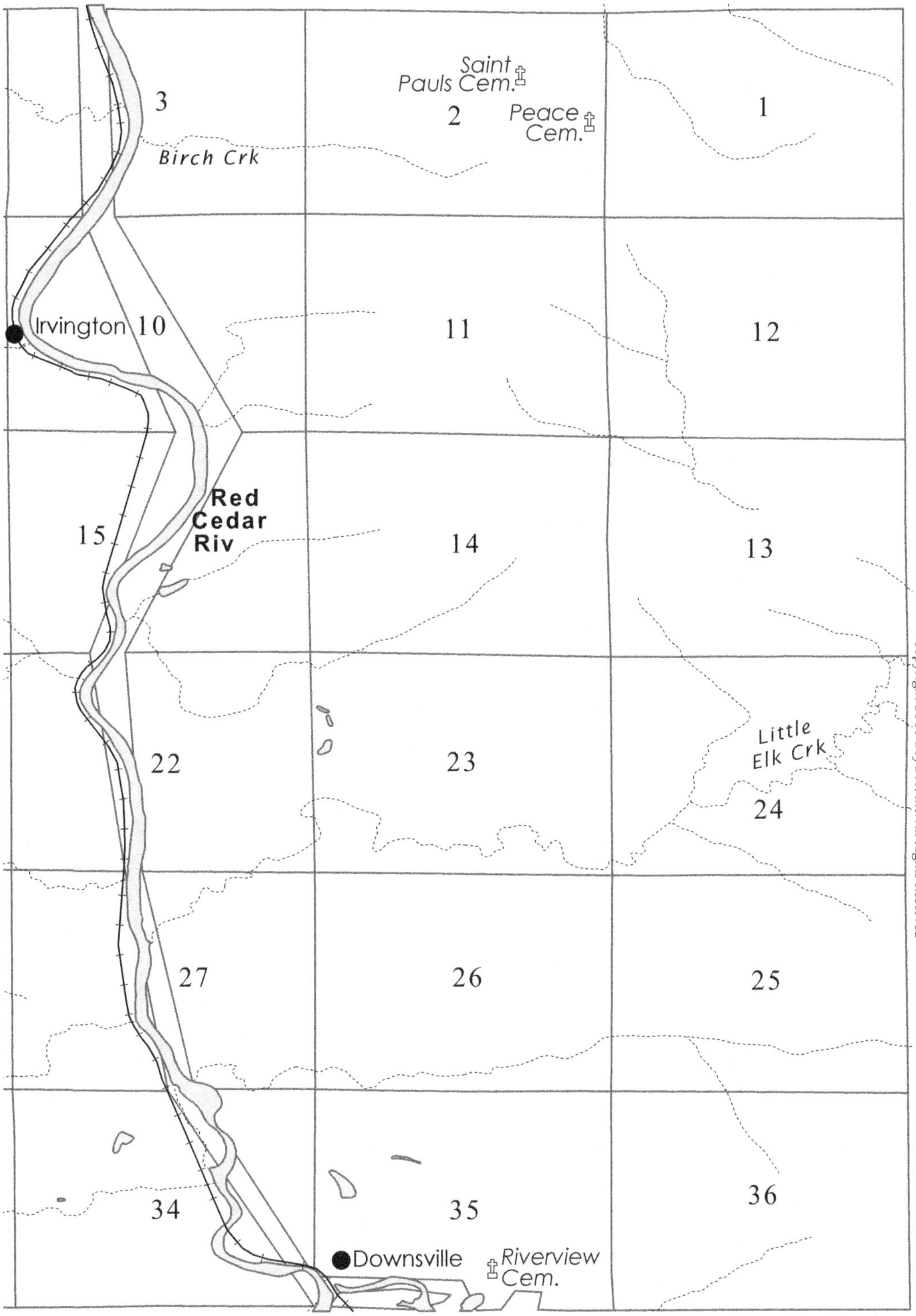
Saint Pauls Cem.
Peace Cem.
Birch Crk
Irvington
Red Cedar Riv
Little Elk Crk
Downsville
Riverview Cem.
1
2
3
10
11
12
13
14
15
22
23
24
25
26
27
34
35
36

Helpful Hints

1. This Map takes a different look at the same Congressional Township displayed in the preceding two maps. It presents features that can help you better envision the historical development of the area: a) Water-bodies (lakes & ponds), b) Water-courses (rivers, streams, etc.), c) Railroads, d) City/town center-points (where they were oftentimes located when first settled), and e) Cemeteries.
2. Using this "Historical" map in tandem with this Township's Patent Map and Road Map, may lead you to some interesting discoveries. You will often find roads, towns, cemeteries, and waterways are named after nearby landowners: sometimes those names will be the ones you are researching. See how many of these research gems you can find here in Dunn County.

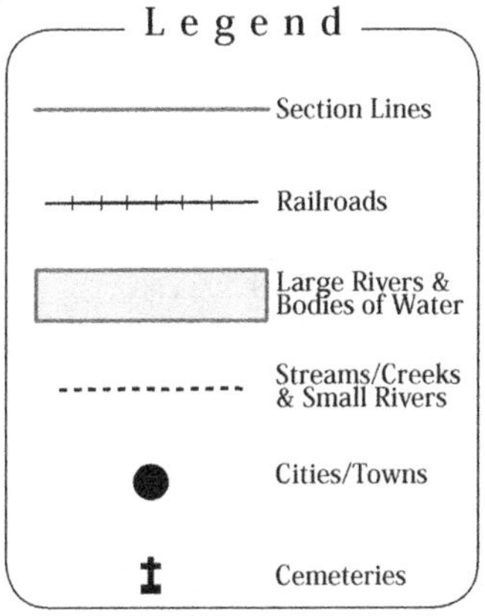
Legend
Section Lines
Railroads
Large Rivers & Bodies of Water
Streams/Creeks & Small Rivers
Cities/Towns
Cemeteries

Scale: Section = 1 mile X 1 mile
(there are some exceptions)

Map Group 19: Index to Land Patents

Township 27-North Range 12-West (4th PM - 1831 MN/WI)

After you locate an individual in this Index, take note of the Section and Section Part then proceed to the Land Patent map on the pages immediately following. You should have no difficulty locating the corresponding parcel of land.

The "For More Info" Column will lead you to more information about the underlying Patents. See the *Legend* at right, and the "How to Use this Book" chapter, for more information.

LEGEND

"For More Info . . . " column

A = Authority (Legislative Act, See Appendix "A")
B = Block or Lot (location in Section unknown)
C = Cancelled Patent
F = Fractional Section
G = Group (Multi-Patentee Patent, see Appendix "C")
V = Overlaps another Parcel
R = Re-Issued (Parcel patented more than once)

(A & G items require you to look in the Appendixes referred to above. All other Letter-designations followed by a number require you to locate line-items in this index that possess the ID number found after the letter).

ID	Individual in Patent	Sec.	Sec. Part	Date Issued	Other Counties	For More Info . . .
3031	AH-KE-NE-BOI-WE,	4	NE	1864-09-15		A5 G107 F
3111	ALLEN, Pardee	36	SW	1860-10-01		A5 G4
3049	ANDERSON, Gilbert	20	NWNW	1884-10-04		A2
3030	ATWOOD, Lois	28	NW	1864-09-15		A5 G105
3065	BARNARD, James M	3	SW	1860-10-01		A5 C
3005	BECKWITH, Chancey	30	E½NW	1859-12-20		A2
3008	BECKWITH, Chauncey	32	NESW	1859-12-20		A2
3009	" "	32	NWSE	1859-12-20		A2
3078	BENNETT, Deborah L	2	E½SW	1861-02-01		A5 G177
3079	" "	2	W½SE	1861-02-01		A5 G177
2997	BILLINGS, Andrew	32	E½NW	1859-09-01		A5
2998	" "	32	NWNW	1859-09-01		A5
3111	BISHOP, Mary	36	SW	1860-10-01		A5 G4
3131	BLAIR, Thomas	30	W½NW	1855-12-15		A2 G41
3013	BLOOM, Christopher	10	N½NE	1869-10-20		A2
3023	BLUM, Dorothea	2	SWSW	1863-05-15		A2
3034	BROWN, Eugene H	32	SWNW	1893-10-31		A6
3114	CANFIELD, Philo	8	SENW	1862-05-20		A5
3115	" "	8	W½NE	1862-05-20		A5
3113	" "	26	W½SE	1862-07-01		A2
3131	CASSADY, William	30	W½NW	1855-12-15		A2 G41
3075	CURRAN, John	18	W½NW	1860-07-16		A5
3074	DALRIMPLE, John A	24	SE	1861-12-05		A5 G98
3002	DARLINTON, Carey A	1	E½NE	1860-02-01		A5 F
3032	DAVIS, Elias	14	W½SE	1872-10-01		A6
3024	DE WOLF, EDWARD	36	S½NE	1892-05-04		A6
3118	DEXTER, Charles E	20	E½NW	1863-04-20		A5 G146
3119	" "	20	SWNW	1863-04-20		A5 G146
3025	DEXTER, Edward	20	NE	1864-09-15		A5
3026	" "	20	SE	1864-09-15		A5
3029	" "	22	NE	1864-09-15		A5 G106
3030	" "	28	NW	1864-09-15		A5 G105
3028	" "	28	SW	1864-09-15		A5
3031	" "	4	NE	1864-09-15		A5 G107 F
3027	" "	22	SW	1865-05-06		A5
3121	EIDE, Samson Nielson	8	E½NE	1862-07-15		A5 G121
3122	" "	8	E½SE	1862-07-15		A5 G121
3060	EMENS, Isaac	18	E½NW	1859-09-01		A5 G122
3109	ENNERSEN, Nels	18	E½NE	1860-02-01		A5
3110	" "	18	W½NE	1860-02-01		A5
3050	ERICKSEN, Hans	30	NWSE	1884-01-15		A6
3051	" "	30	SWNE	1884-01-15		A6
2996	ERICKSON, Anders	32	W½NE	1876-01-10		A6
3121	FLANDERS, Ann	8	E½NE	1862-07-15		A5 G121
3122	" "	8	E½SE	1862-07-15		A5 G121
3074	FLOOD, John O	24	SE	1861-12-05		A5 G98

ID	Individual in Patent	Sec.	Sec. Part	Date Issued	Other Counties	For More Info . . .
3000	FOWLER, Bartholomew	28	NE	1869-10-20		A6
3123	FRENCH, Samuel B	34	N½NE	1862-03-10		A5
3124	" "	34	NENW	1862-03-10		A5
3125	" "	34	S½NE	1862-03-10		A5 G141
3126	" "	34	SENW	1862-03-10		A5 G141
3062	FULLER, James	26	NENW	1870-06-10		A6
3063	" "	26	NWNE	1870-06-10		A6
3064	" "	26	W½NW	1870-06-10		A6
3118	FULLER, S W	20	E½NW	1863-04-20		A5 G146
3119	" "	20	SWNW	1863-04-20		A5 G146
3112	GALLAGER, Patrick	4	NENW	1885-08-20		A6 F
3081	GAUVIN, John J	25	NENE	1857-04-01		A2
3129	GAUVIN, Theodore	25	SE	1864-09-15		A5
3108	GIBSON, Moses S	2	E½NW	1859-05-02		A2
3076	GIFFORD, John	14	E½SW	1880-05-15		A6
3048	GOERCKE, Ernest	35	SW	1864-09-15		A5 G294
3048	GOERCKE, Louisa Jane	35	SW	1864-09-15		A5 G294
3141	GOERCKE, William	26	E½SE	1861-07-01		A5 G159
3039	GRABHEIR, Gabherd	6	N½NE	1855-12-15		A2 F
3061	GRAY, James B	1	W½NW	1859-05-02		A2
3035	HAERLE, Frederick	10	NESW	1861-09-05		A5 G176
3036	" "	10	NWSE	1861-09-05		A5 G176
3037	" "	10	SENW	1861-09-05		A5 G176
3038	" "	10	SWNE	1861-09-05		A5 G176
3080	HAGEN, Elizabeth	14	NE	1864-09-15		A5 G188
3029	HAMMOND, Georgia Ann E	22	NE	1864-09-15		A5 G106
3137	HANSEN, Torger	30	N½NE	1862-07-15		A5 G173
3138	" "	30	SENE	1862-07-15		A5 G173
3077	HANSON, John	20	SW	1869-09-01		A6
3011	HARLE, Christian	12	S½SW	1862-03-10		A5
3078	HARLE, Friedrich	2	E½SW	1861-02-01		A5 G177
3079	" "	2	W½SE	1861-02-01		A5 G177
3099	HARLE, Ludwig	12	N½SW	1861-02-01		A5 G175
3100	" "	12	S½NW	1861-02-01		A5 G175
3035	HARLEY, Frederick	10	NESW	1861-09-05		A5 G176
3036	" "	10	NWSE	1861-09-05		A5 G176
3037	" "	10	SENW	1861-09-05		A5 G176
3038	" "	10	SWNE	1861-09-05		A5 G176
3099	HARLEY, Louis	12	N½SW	1861-02-01		A5 G175
3100	" "	12	S½NW	1861-02-01		A5 G175
3078	HARM, John	2	E½SW	1861-02-01		A5 G177
3079	" "	2	W½SE	1861-02-01		A5 G177
3056	HARNISH, Henry	14	NW	1864-09-15		A5
3035	HARRISON, Rachel	10	NESW	1861-09-05		A5 G176
3036	" "	10	NWSE	1861-09-05		A5 G176
3037	" "	10	SENW	1861-09-05		A5 G176
3038	" "	10	SWNE	1861-09-05		A5 G176
3089	HEBERLIG, John S	18	SW	1855-12-15		A2 F
3134	HENRIKSON, Thore	18	SE	1862-03-10		A5
3135	" "	8	NENW	1862-03-10		A5
3136	" "	8	W½NW	1862-03-10		A5
3080	HINTZ, John	14	NE	1864-09-15		A5 G188
3018	HOGUELAND, William B	10	E½SE	1861-12-05		A5 G362
3019	" "	10	SENE	1861-12-05		A5 G362
3073	JOHANESON, Johanes	28	SE	1869-09-01		A6
3006	JOHNSON, Charles	22	NENW	1869-09-01		A6
3007	" "	22	W½NW	1869-09-01		A6
3082	JOHNSON, John	8	N½SW	1862-01-25		A5
3083	" "	8	NWSE	1862-01-25		A5
3084	KEHL, John	6	S½NE	1862-04-10		A2
3085	KIRKLAND, John	4	SWSW	1873-09-20		A6
3071	LASH, Jeremiah	36	E½NW	1861-06-01		A7
3072	" "	36	N½NE	1861-06-01		A7
3139	LEE, Margaret	12	SE	1862-03-10		A5 G437
3142	LENTZ, William	2	SESE	1869-10-20		A6
3021	LEONARD, Alfred B	6	SE	1862-05-20		A5 G430
3086	LINK, John	12	N½NW	1861-01-21		A2
3004	LUCAS, Carroll	13	SWSE	1855-12-15		A2 G244
3060	MASONER, Mary	18	E½NW	1859-09-01		A5 G122
3133	MASSEY, Thomas	32	SWSE	1859-05-02		A2
3143	MASSEY, William	32	E½SE	1859-05-02		A2
3031	MEE-CHIT-E-NEE,	4	NE	1864-09-15		A5 G107 F
3141	MEREDETH, John L	26	E½SE	1861-07-01		A5 G159

ID	Individual in Patent	Sec.	Sec. Part	Date Issued	Other Counties	For More Info . . .
3137	MORSE, Hiram	30	N½NE	1862-07-15		A5 G173
3138	" "	30	SENE	1862-07-15		A5 G173
3098	MORTON, Lucius	24	SENW	1860-10-01		A2
3040	MULKS, George	1	E½NW	1859-05-02		A2
3041	" "	1	W½NE	1859-05-02		A2
3042	" "	1	W½SE	1859-05-02		A2
3043	" "	2	E½NE	1860-02-01		A5
3044	" "	2	NESE	1860-02-01		A5
3087	OLSON, John	4	SENW	1861-12-05		A5
3088	" "	4	W½NW	1861-12-05		A5
3120	OLSON, Salve	8	SWSE	1883-02-10		A6
3048	ORDEMAN, Gerhard	35	SW	1864-09-15		A5 G294
3045	ORDEMANN, Gerhard H	26	NESW	1859-12-10		A2
3047	" "	26	S½SW	1859-12-10		A2
3046	" "	26	NWSW	1870-05-20		A6
3106	OWEN, Moses	13	SESE	1855-12-15		A2
3107	" "	24	SWNE	1855-12-15		A2
3117	PARKER, Rodger	14	E½SE	1870-06-10		A6
3125	PAYNE, Betsy	34	S½NE	1862-03-10		A5 G141
3126	" "	34	SENW	1862-03-10		A5 G141
3018	PROSSER, Lewis	10	E½SE	1861-12-05		A5 G362
3019	" "	10	SENE	1861-12-05		A5 G362
3130	RACKWITZ, Theodore	22	SENW	1896-08-24		A6
3012	REINECKE, Christian	10	NWSW	1867-07-15		A2
3010	REINKE, Christ	10	SWNW	1869-07-01		A7 G321
3010	REINKE, Joachim	10	SWNW	1869-07-01		A7 G321
3004	REMINGTON, Barlow	13	SWSE	1855-12-15		A2 G244
3057	REYNOLDS, Henry	32	SENE	1859-12-10		A2
3058	" "	34	E½SW	1860-07-16		A5
3059	" "	34	NWSW	1860-07-16		A5
3116	RIDER, Ralph	30	SWSE	1862-07-01		A2
3014	RIPLEY, Christopher G	22	NESE	1857-10-30		A5
3015	" "	22	W½SE	1857-10-30		A5
3022	RITTER, Daniel	1	E½SE	1859-05-02		A2
3118	RUE, Christiana	20	E½NW	1863-04-20		A5 G146
3119	" "	20	SWNW	1863-04-20		A5 G146
3052	RUMSEY, Harvey S	36	NESE	1862-11-15		A2
3053	" "	36	SESE	1863-05-15		A2
3054	RUMSEY, Harvey T	36	W½SE	1863-04-20		A5
3003	SCHAEFER, Carl	10	SWSW	1879-11-10		A6
3101	SCHAEFER, Magdalena	10	SESW	1862-04-10		A2
3102	" "	10	SWSE	1862-04-10		A2
3127	SEVERSON, Sever	8	S½SW	1862-03-10		A5 G355
3121	" "	8	E½NE	1862-07-15		A5 G121
3122	" "	8	E½SE	1862-07-15		A5 G121
3018	SIPPEL, Conrad	10	E½SE	1861-12-05		A5 G362
3019	" "	10	SENE	1861-12-05		A5 G362
3090	SOLIE, John	30	SESE	1901-06-08		A6
3001	SPAFFORD, C C	30	SW	1862-11-20		A5
3096	STANLEY, Lemuel C	24	N½NW	1863-04-20		A5
3097	" "	24	SWNW	1863-04-20		A5
3091	STEPHENS, John	12	NE	1861-07-01		A5
2999	TAINTER, Andrew	6	NW	1862-05-20		A5
3137	TAYLOR, Hiram	30	N½NE	1862-07-15		A5 G173
3138	" "	30	SENE	1862-07-15		A5 G173
3092	TAYLOR, Joseph N	32	SESW	1859-09-01		A5
3093	" "	32	W½SW	1859-09-01		A5
3094	" "	33	NESW	1859-09-01		A5
3095	" "	33	W½SW	1859-09-01		A5
3140	THOMAS, William F	2	NWSW	1869-10-20		A6
3069	TRASK, James W	33	SESW	1858-02-20		A7
3066	" "	24	E½NE	1859-09-01		A5
3067	" "	24	NWNE	1859-09-01		A5
3068	" "	24	SW	1862-03-10		A5
3016	TUBBS, Christopher	22	SESE	1855-12-15		A2
3017	" "	27	NESW	1855-12-15		A2
3031	WA-KE-MA-WET,	4	NE	1864-09-15		A5 G107 F
3070	WATERSTON, James	14	W½SW	1878-11-30		A6
3033	WIGGINS, Elijah	34	SWSW	1855-12-15		A2
3055	WIGGINS, Henry B	35	S½NE	1855-12-15		A2
3144	WILSON, William	2	W½NE	1859-05-02		A2
3145	" "	2	W½NW	1859-05-02		A2
3146	" "	3	E½NE	1859-05-02		A2

ID	Individual in Patent	Sec.	Sec. Part	Date Issued	Other Counties	For More Info . . .
3147	WILSON, William (Cont'd)	6	SW	1862-07-15		A5
3128	WISCONSIN, State Of	16		1941-08-16		A3
3020	WOOD, Daniel H	36	W½NW	1862-04-10		A2
3021	" "	6	SE	1862-05-20		A5 G430
3127	WOODHULL, Calvin	8	S½SW	1862-03-10		A5 G355
3103	WOODWARD, Mary N	26	NENE	1862-03-10		A5
3104	" "	26	S½NE	1862-03-10		A5
3105	" "	26	SENW	1862-03-10		A5
3139	WOODWARD, William A	12	SE	1862-03-10		A5 G437
3132	YOUNG, Thomas L	34	W½NW	1874-04-01		A6

Patent Map

T27-N R12-W
4th PM - 1831 MN/WI Meridian

Map Group 19

Township Statistics

Parcels Mapped	152
Number of Patents	117
Number of Individuals	125
Patentees Identified	99
Number of Surnames	107
Multi-Patentee Parcels	33
Oldest Patent Date	12/15/1855
Most Recent Patent	8/16/1941
Block/Lot Parcels	0
Parcels Re - Issued	0
Parcels that Overlap	0
Cities and Towns	0
Cemeteries	5

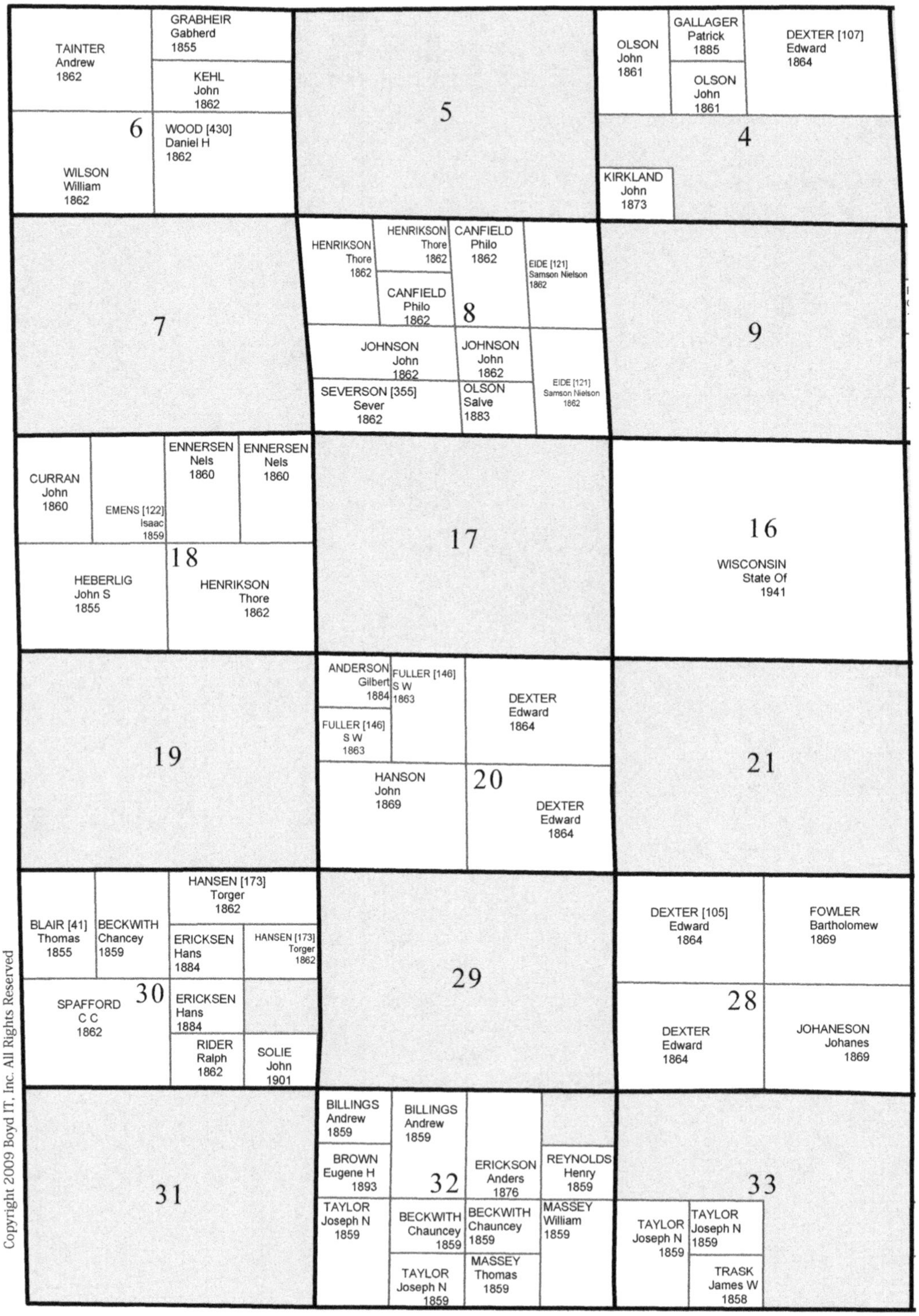

TAINTER Andrew 1862
GRABHEIR Gabherd 1855
KEHL John 1862
6
WOOD [430] Daniel H 1862
WILSON William 1862
5
OLSON John 1861
GALLAGER Patrick 1885
OLSON John 1861
DEXTER [107] Edward 1864
4
KIRKLAND John 1873
7
HENRIKSON Thore 1862
HENRIKSON Thore 1862
CANFIELD Philo 1862
EIDE [121] Samson Nielson 1862
CANFIELD Philo 1862
8
JOHNSON John 1862
JOHNSON John 1862
SEVERSON [355] Sever 1862
OLSON Salve 1883
EIDE [121] Samson Nielson 1862
9
CURRAN John 1860
EMENS [122] Isaac 1859
ENNERSEN Nels 1860
ENNERSEN Nels 1860
18
HEBERLIG John S 1855
HENRIKSON Thore 1862
17
16
WISCONSIN State Of 1941
19
ANDERSON Gilbert 1884
FULLER [146] S W 1863
FULLER [146] S W 1863
DEXTER Edward 1864
HANSON John 1869
20
DEXTER Edward 1864
21
BLAIR [41] Thomas 1855
BECKWITH Chancey 1859
HANSEN [173] Torger 1862
ERICKSEN Hans 1884
HANSEN [173] Torger 1862
SPAFFORD C C 1862
30
ERICKSEN Hans 1884
RIDER Ralph 1862
SOLIE John 1901
29
DEXTER [105] Edward 1864
FOWLER Bartholomew 1869
28
DEXTER Edward 1864
JOHANESON Johanes 1869
31
BILLINGS Andrew 1859
BILLINGS Andrew 1859
BROWN Eugene H 1893
32
ERICKSON Anders 1876
REYNOLDS Henry 1859
TAYLOR Joseph N 1859
BECKWITH Chauncey 1859
BECKWITH Chauncey 1859
MASSEY William 1859
MASSEY Thomas 1859
TAYLOR Joseph N 1859
33
TAYLOR Joseph N 1859
TAYLOR Joseph N 1859
TRASK James W 1858

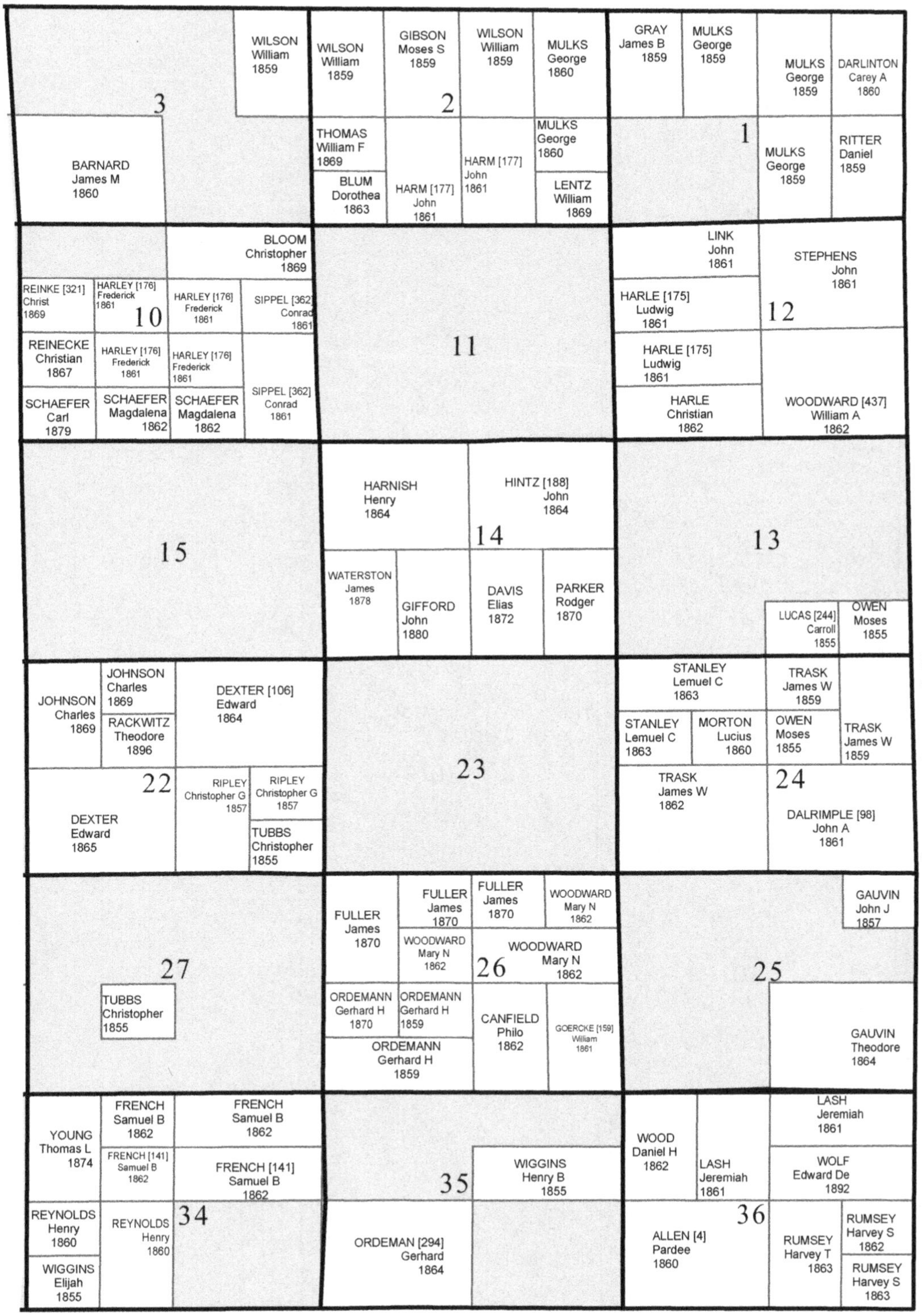
WILSON William 1859
3
BARNARD James M 1860
WILSON William 1859
GIBSON Moses S 1859
WILSON William 1859
MULKS George 1860
2
THOMAS William F 1869
BLUM Dorothea 1863
HARM [177] John 1861
HARM [177] John 1861
MULKS George 1860
LENTZ William 1869
GRAY James B 1859
MULKS George 1859
MULKS George 1859
DARLINTON Carey A 1860
1
MULKS George 1859
RITTER Daniel 1859
BLOOM Christopher 1869
REINKE [321] Christ 1869
HARLEY [176] Frederick 1861
10
HARLEY [176] Frederick 1861
SIPPEL [362] Conrad 1861
REINECKE Christian 1867
HARLEY [176] Frederick 1861
HARLEY [176] Frederick 1861
SIPPEL [362] Conrad 1861
SCHAEFER Carl 1879
SCHAEFER Magdalena 1862
SCHAEFER Magdalena 1862
11
LINK John 1861
STEPHENS John 1861
HARLE [175] Ludwig 1861
12
HARLE [175] Ludwig 1861
HARLE Christian 1862
WOODWARD [437] William A 1862
15
HARNISH Henry 1864
HINTZ [188] John 1864
14
WATERSTON James 1878
GIFFORD John 1880
DAVIS Elias 1872
PARKER Rodger 1870
13
LUCAS [244] Carroll 1855
OWEN Moses 1855
JOHNSON Charles 1869
JOHNSON Charles 1869
RACKWITZ Theodore 1896
DEXTER [106] Edward 1864
22
RIPLEY Christopher G 1857
RIPLEY Christopher G 1857
DEXTER Edward 1865
TUBBS Christopher 1855
23
STANLEY Lemuel C 1863
TRASK James W 1859
STANLEY Lemuel C 1863
MORTON Lucius 1860
OWEN Moses 1855
TRASK James W 1859
TRASK James W 1862
24
DALRIMPLE [98] John A 1861
27
TUBBS Christopher 1855
FULLER James 1870
FULLER James 1870
FULLER James 1870
WOODWARD Mary N 1862
WOODWARD Mary N 1862
WOODWARD Mary N 1862
26
ORDEMANN Gerhard H 1870
ORDEMANN Gerhard H 1859
ORDEMANN Gerhard H 1859
CANFIELD Philo 1862
GOERCKE [159] William 1861
GAUVIN John J 1857
25
GAUVIN Theodore 1864
YOUNG Thomas L 1874
FRENCH Samuel B 1862
FRENCH [141] Samuel B 1862
FRENCH Samuel B 1862
FRENCH [141] Samuel B 1862
REYNOLDS Henry 1860
REYNOLDS Henry 1860
34
WIGGINS Elijah 1855
WIGGINS Henry B 1855
35
ORDEMAN [294] Gerhard 1864
WOOD Daniel H 1862
LASH Jeremiah 1861
LASH Jeremiah 1861
WOLF Edward De 1892
36
ALLEN [4] Pardee 1860
RUMSEY Harvey T 1863
RUMSEY Harvey S 1862
RUMSEY Harvey S 1863

Helpful Hints

1. This Map's INDEX can be found on the preceding pages.
2. Refer to Map "C" to see where this Township lies within Dunn County, Wisconsin.
3. Numbers within square brackets [ ] denote a multi-patentee land parcel (multi-owner). Refer to Appendix "C" for a full list of members in this group.
4. Areas that look to be crowded with Patentees usually indicate multiple sales of the same parcel (Re-issues) or Overlapping parcels. See this Township's Index for an explanation of these and other circumstances that might explain "odd" groupings of Patentees on this map.

Legend

Patent Boundary

Section Boundary

No Patents Found (or Outside County)

1., 2., 3., ... Lot Numbers (when beside a name)

[ ] Group Number (see Appendix "C")

Scale: Section = 1 mile X 1 mile (generally, with some exceptions)

Road Map

T27-N R12-W
4th PM - 1831 MN/WI Meridian

Map Group 19

Cities & Towns

None

Cemeteries

Forest Center Cemetery
Froens Cemetery
Iron Creek Cemetery
Little Elk Creek Cemetery
Saint John Cemetery

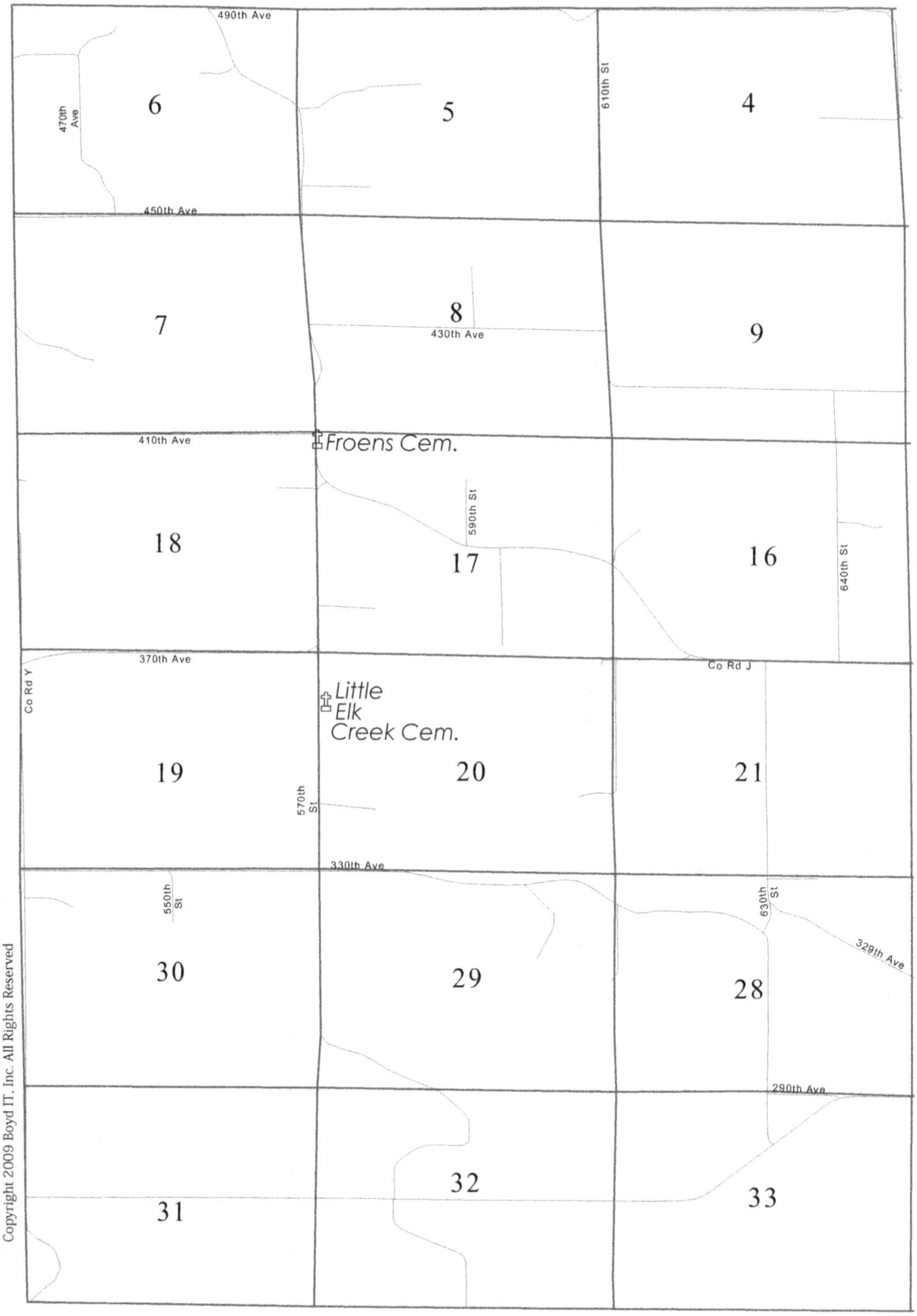

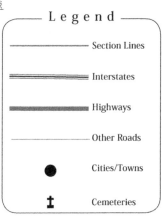

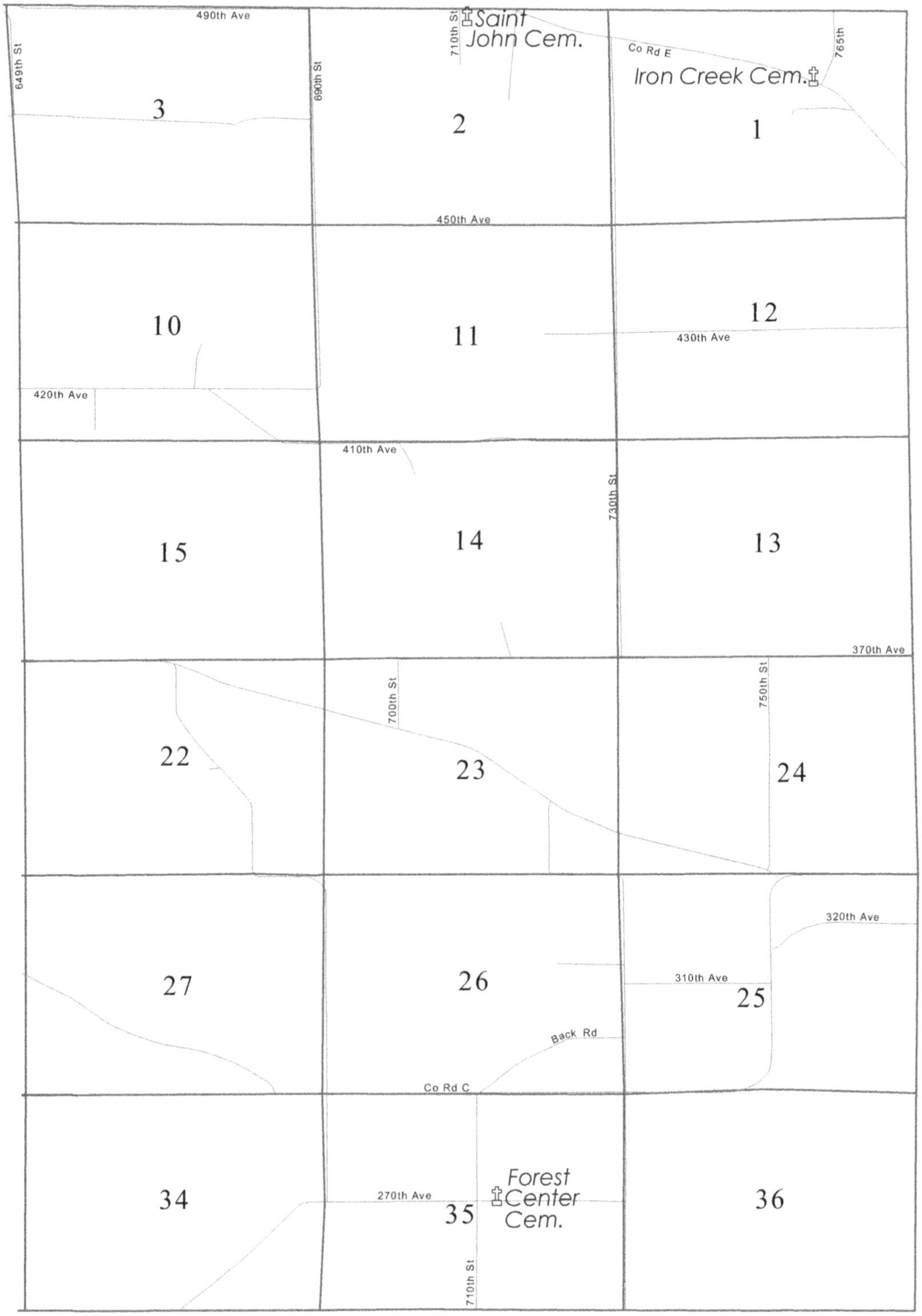

Helpful Hints

1. This road map has a number of uses, but primarily it is to help you: a) find the present location of land owned by your ancestors (at least the general area), b) find cemeteries and city-centers, and c) estimate the route/roads used by Census-takers & tax-assessors.

2. If you plan to travel to Dunn County to locate cemeteries or land parcels, please pick up a modern travel map for the area before you do. Mapping old land parcels on modern maps is not as exact a science as you might think. Just the slightest variations in public land survey coordinates, estimates of parcel boundaries, or road-map deviations can greatly alter a map's representation of how a road either does or doesn't cross a particular parcel of land.

Legend

- Section Lines
- Interstates
- Highways
- Other Roads
- Cities/Towns
- Cemeteries

Scale: Section = 1 mile X 1 mile
(generally, with some exceptions)

Historical Map

T27-N R12-W
4th PM - 1831 MN/WI Meridian

Map Group 19

Cities & Towns

None

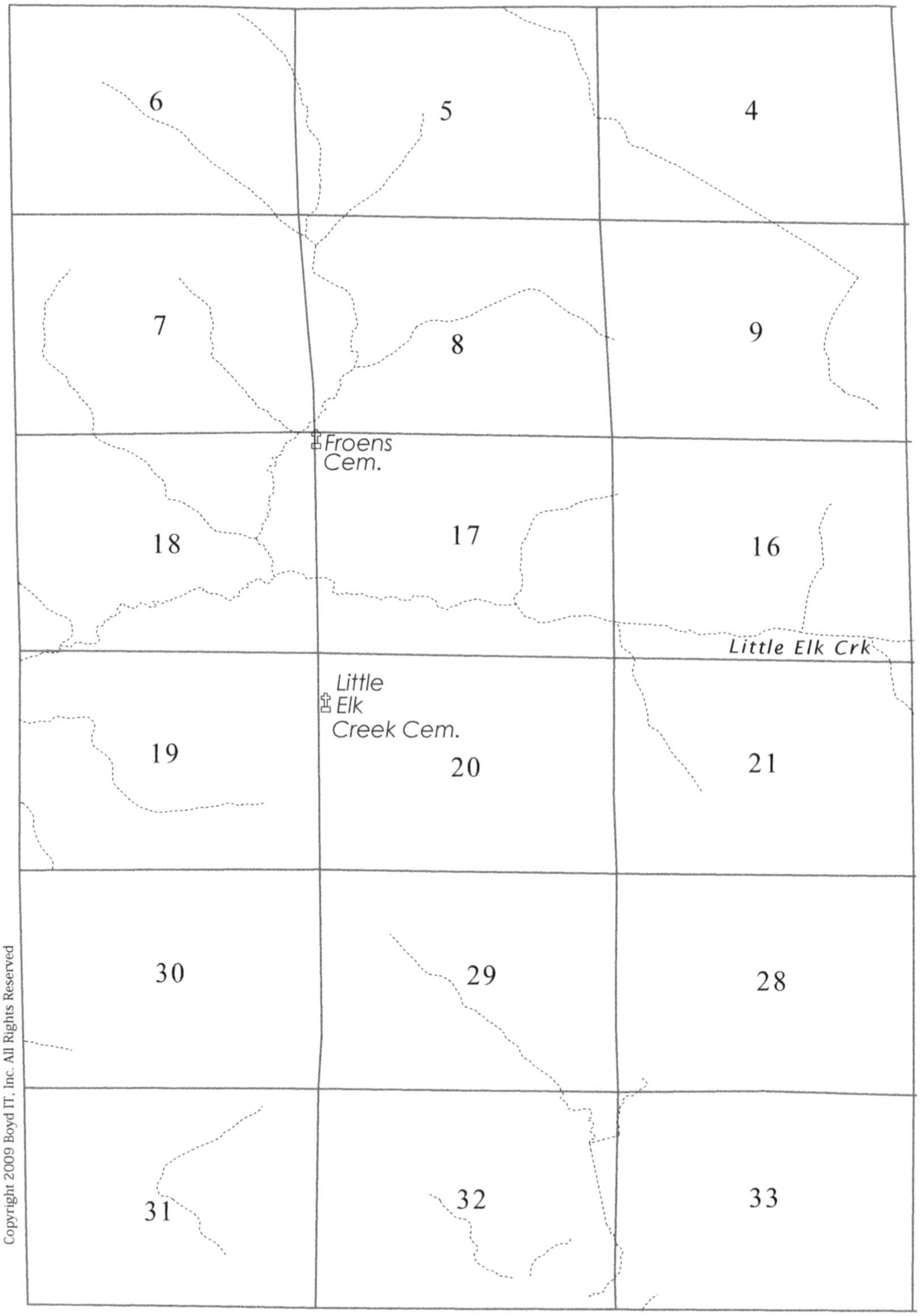

Cemeteries

- Forest Center Cemetery
- Froens Cemetery
- Iron Creek Cemetery
- Little Elk Creek Cemetery
- Saint John Cemetery

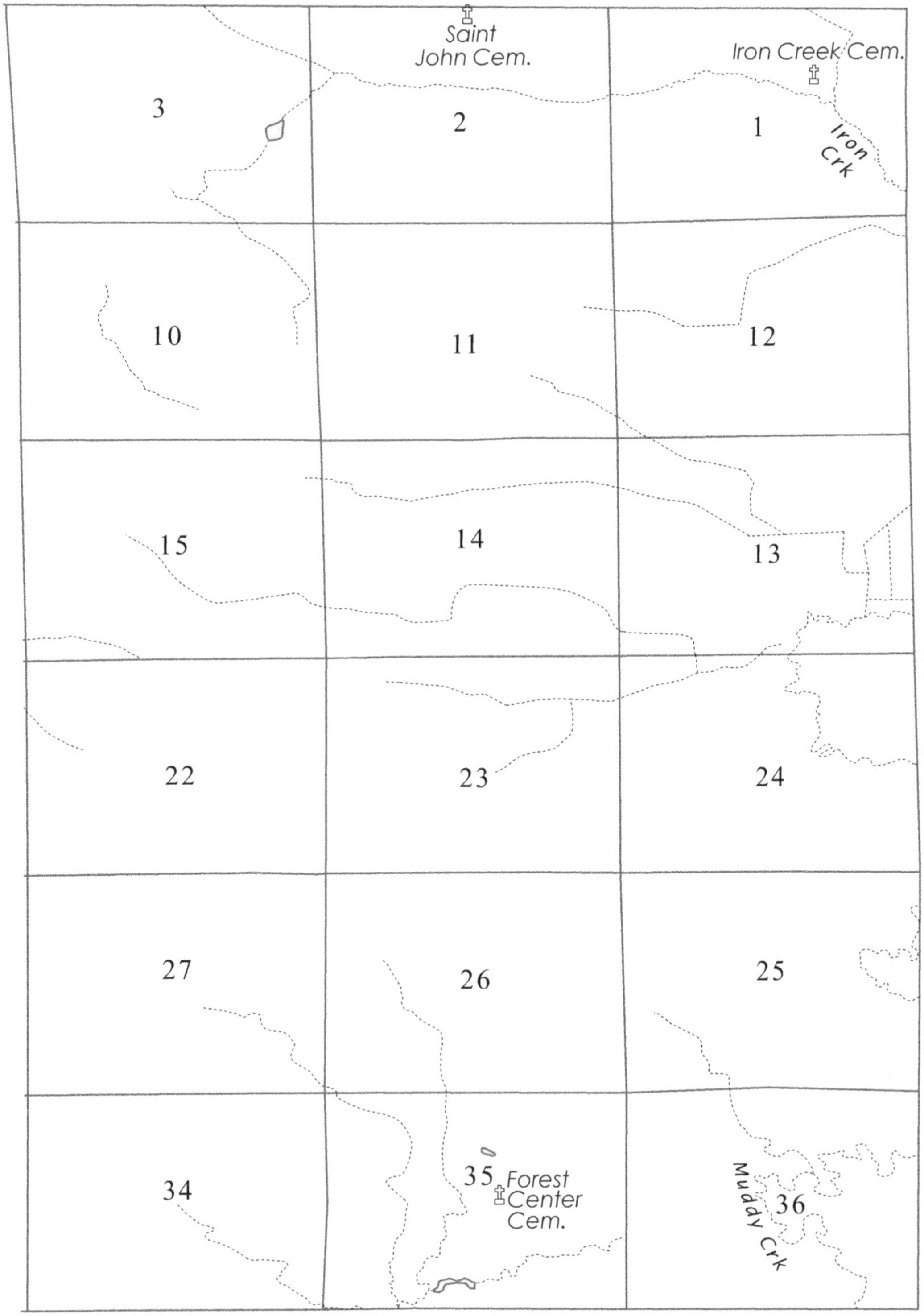
Saint
John Cem.
Iron Creek Cem.
3
2
1
Iron
Crk
10
11
12
15
14
13
22
23
24
27
26
25
34
35
Forest
Center
Cem.
Muddy Crk
36

Helpful Hints

1. This Map takes a different look at the same Congressional Township displayed in the preceding two maps. It presents features that can help you better envision the historical development of the area: a) Water-bodies (lakes & ponds), b) Water-courses (rivers, streams, etc.), c) Railroads, d) City/town center-points (where they were oftentimes located when first settled), and e) Cemeteries.
2. Using this "Historical" map in tandem with this Township's Patent Map and Road Map, may lead you to some interesting discoveries. You will often find roads, towns, cemeteries, and waterways are named after nearby landowners: sometimes those names will be the ones you are researching. See how many of these research gems you can find here in Dunn County.

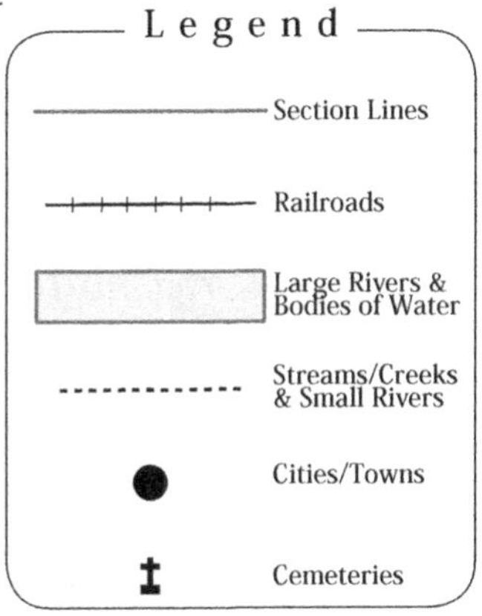
Legend
Section Lines
Railroads
Large Rivers & Bodies of Water
Streams/Creeks & Small Rivers
Cities/Towns
Cemeteries

Scale: Section = 1 mile X 1 mile
(there are some exceptions)

Map Group 20: Index to Land Patents

Township 27-North Range 11-West (4th PM - 1831 MN/WI)

After you locate an individual in this Index, take note of the Section and Section Part then proceed to the Land Patent map on the pages immediately following. You should have no difficulty locating the corresponding parcel of land.

The "For More Info" Column will lead you to more information about the underlying Patents. See the *Legend* at right, and the "How to Use this Book" chapter, for more information.

LEGEND

"For More Info . . . " column

A = Authority (Legislative Act, See Appendix "A")
B = Block or Lot (location in Section unknown)
C = Cancelled Patent
F = Fractional Section
G = Group (Multi-Patentee Patent, see Appendix "C")
V = Overlaps another Parcel
R = Re-Issued (Parcel patented more than once)

(A & G items require you to look in the Appendixes referred to above. All other Letter-designations followed by a number require you to locate line-items in this index that possess the ID number found after the letter).

ID	Individual in Patent	Sec.	Sec. Part	Date Issued	Other Counties	For More Info . . .
3336	ALLEN, Pardee F	28	W½NE	1880-10-01		A6
3335	ANDERSON, Lutilia	17	S½SE	1860-09-10		A5 G281
3357	ARMSTRONG, Adolphus	20	N½SW	1862-07-10		A5 G422
3270	AUSSMAN, John	11	S½NE	1860-09-10		A5 G15
3271	" "	12	S½NW	1860-09-10		A5 G15
3327	AUSSMAN, Nicholas	11	N½SE	1860-09-10		A5
3328	" "	12	N½SW	1860-09-10		A5
3261	AZRO, D	12	NE	1860-09-10		A5 G346
3182	BAGG, Charles	12	SE	1869-09-01		A6
3381	BARNES, Polly	13	E½SW	1861-07-01		A5 G436
3382	" "	13	SENW	1861-07-01		A5 G436
3184	BEADLE, Robert	32	2	1863-04-20		A5 G375
3185	" "	32	S½SE	1863-04-20		A5 G375
3332	BELDEN, Ozro H	3	NWSW	1859-05-02		A2
3334	" "	4	NWSE	1859-05-02		A2
3333	" "	34	E½SE	1860-02-01		A5
3355	BLODGETT, Silas	19	E½NW	1865-10-20		A5 G42
3356	" "	19	N½SW	1865-10-20		A5 G42
3391	BRAYNARD, Thomas L	15	N½NW	1860-09-10		A5 G239
3214	BRENNAN, Hannah	34	E½NE	1859-09-01		A5
3155	BROWN, Amanda M	13	SWNE	1860-10-10		A5
3156	" "	13	W½SE	1860-10-10		A5
3367	BURDETT, Stephen C	33	E½SE	1859-09-01		A5 G53
3363	" "	33	NENE	1859-09-01		A5
3368	" "	33	SENE	1859-09-01		A5 G53
3364	" "	33	SWNW	1859-09-01		A5
3365	" "	33	W½NE	1859-09-01		A5
3366	" "	33	W½SW	1859-09-01		A5
3369	BURDETT, Stephen O	34	N½SW	1859-09-01		A5
3370	" "	34	SWNW	1859-09-01		A5
3192	BURGESS, Charles W	14	NWSW	1874-04-10		A6
3248	BURNS, Lydia	24	SWNE	1858-02-20		A7 G432
3148	BURT, John	17	S½SW	1863-04-20		A5 G403
3355	BURY, William A	19	E½NW	1865-10-20		A5 G42
3356	" "	19	N½SW	1865-10-20		A5 G42
3349	CADY, Samuel M	9	E½NE	1860-10-10		A5 G55
3350	" "	9	SWNE	1860-10-10		A5 G55
3249	CAMPBELL, Hugh	17	N½SW	1860-09-10		A5
3250	" "	17	S½NW	1860-09-10		A5
3371	CANFIELD, Stephen R	11	E½SW	1869-12-10		A6
3189	CAREY, Dilane	27	SENE	1859-09-01		A5 G171
3190	" "	27	W½NE	1859-09-01		A5 G171
3236	CARRINGTON, Henry K	32	NW	1883-09-10		A6
3279	CHAMBERS, Polly	24	N½SW	1857-10-30		A5 G109
3280	" "	24	NWSE	1857-10-30		A5 G109
3178	CHASE, Barton W	14	NE	1860-09-10		A5

ID	Individual in Patent	Sec.	Sec. Part	Date Issued	Other Counties	For More Info . . .
3323	CORWITH, Nathan	24	NWNE	1859-05-02		A2
3321	COUN, Hannah	24	NESE	1859-09-01		A5 G152
3322	" "	24	SENE	1859-09-01		A5 G152
3384	CRANSTON, William H	33	E½NW	1859-09-01		A5
3385	" "	33	NWNW	1859-09-01		A5
3148	CREGO, Lester B	17	S½SW	1863-04-20		A5 G403
3259	CROSSMAN, James E	11	W½SW	1869-09-01		A6
3154	CURTIS, Almon A	28	NW	1869-09-01		A6
3208	CURTIS, George A	28	E½NE	1883-02-20		A6
3326	CURTIS, Nelson	29	NE	1861-12-20		A5
3347	DAVIS, Dorothy	3	SE	1860-02-01		A5 G316
3346	DEGRAW, Elizabeth	26	NW	1860-09-10		A5 G315
3346	DEGRAW, James L	26	NW	1860-09-10		A5 G315
3186	DEXTER, Charles E	8	W½NW	1855-12-15		A2
3235	DICKSON, Henry	15	NWNE	1885-10-22		A6
3279	DIX, John H	24	N½SW	1857-10-30		A5 G109
3280	" "	24	NWSE	1857-10-30		A5 G109
3273	" "	24	S½SW	1857-10-30		A5
3274	" "	24	SWSE	1857-10-30		A5
3275	" "	25	SWNE	1857-10-30		A5
3276	" "	25	W½SE	1857-10-30		A5
3277	" "	30	S½SW	1857-10-30		A5
3278	" "	30	SWSE	1857-10-30		A5
3281	" "	4	SW	1857-10-30		A5 G110 V3241
3215	DODGE, Harrison	5	SWSW	1855-12-15		A2 C R3216, 3217
3222	" "	6	SW	1855-12-15		A2 C
3223	" "	6	W½SE	1855-12-15		A2 C R3224, 3225
3216	" "	5	SWSW	1861-01-21		A2 R3215, 3217
3218	" "	6	E½SW	1861-01-21		A2 R3219
3220	" "	6	SESE	1861-01-21		A2 R3221
3224	" "	6	W½SE	1861-01-21		A2 R3223, 3225
3217	" "	5	SWSW	1862-11-15		A2 R3215, 3216
3219	" "	6	E½SW	1862-11-15		A2 R3218
3221	" "	6	SESE	1862-11-15		A2 R3220
3225	" "	6	W½SE	1862-11-15		A2 R3223, 3224
3386	DORRY, William H	22	E½SE	1884-01-15		A6
3399	DORRY, William W	32	N½SE	1875-08-10		A6
3400	" "	32	N½SW	1875-08-10		A6
3251	DRURY, Isaac L	35	SWNW	1857-04-01		A2
3252	" "	36	5	1859-05-02		A2
3253	" "	36	W½SW	1859-05-02		A2
3281	EATON, Sarah	4	SW	1857-10-30		A5 G110 V3241
3227	FARNHAM, Hatten A	18	W½NW	1860-03-01		A2 F
3226	" "	17	N½NW	1860-03-07		A2
3282	FOWLER, John H	7	E½SE	1856-04-01		A2
3362	FRION, Sarah	20	SE	1861-04-01		A5 G385
3209	FULLER, George E	9	NWNE	1890-05-14		A6
3285	GAUVIN, John J	30	W½NW	1855-04-19		A2
3284	" "	30	E½NW	1855-12-15		A2
3319	GIBSON, Moses S	25	NWNE	1854-10-02		A2
3320	" "	7	NW	1854-10-02		A2
3317	" "	18	E½SW	1855-12-15		A2
3318	" "	18	NE	1857-10-30		A5
3321	" "	24	NESE	1859-09-01		A5 G152
3322	" "	24	SENE	1859-09-01		A5 G152
3191	GLEASON, Charles R	10	NW	1860-11-20		A5
3258	GRAY, James B	6	W½NE	1858-02-20		A7 G167 F
3358	GRIFFIN, Simeon R	10	SE	1860-09-10		A5
3359	" "	14	E½SW	1860-09-10		A5
3360	" "	14	SWSW	1860-09-10		A5
3187	HAIGHT, Charles	23	SENW	1859-09-01		A5
3188	" "	23	W½NW	1859-09-01		A5
3189	" "	27	SENE	1859-09-01		A5 G171
3190	" "	27	W½NE	1859-09-01		A5 G171
3206	HARLY, Frederick	2	NWSW	1875-07-13		A6
3262	HARRINGTON, James	36	3	1857-04-01		A2
3263	" "	36	4	1857-04-01		A2
3266	HARRINGTON, Jeremiah	36	SWNW	1863-10-15		A2
3313	HASHMAN, Matthias	20	SWSW	1860-09-10		A5
3314	" "	29	SENW	1860-09-10		A5
3315	" "	29	W½NW	1860-09-10		A5
3298	HOLCOMB, Philanda	20	NW	1860-09-10		A5 G421
3330	HOYT, Otis	7	NE	1855-12-15		A2

ID	Individual in Patent	Sec.	Sec. Part	Date Issued	Other Counties	For More Info . . .
3331	HOYT, Otis (Cont'd)	8	SW	1855-12-15		A2
3210	HUFFTLE, George	36	1	1880-04-30		A6
3211	" "	36	2	1880-04-30		A6
3207	HULL, Friend H	3	NW	1869-09-01		A6
3387	HUTCHISON, Elizabeth	15	E½NE	1861-04-01		A5 G234
3388	" "	15	SWNE	1861-04-01		A5 G234
3246	INGERSOLL, Charles	33	E½SW	1859-09-01		A5 G434
3247	" "	33	W½SE	1859-09-01		A5 G434
3286	JERMAN, John	36	N½NW	1880-04-30		A6
3348	JERMAN, Sally	26	S½SE	1876-05-15		A6
3183	JOHNSON, Charles C	32	W½NE	1882-05-10		A6
3287	KIMBALL, John	2	NW	1860-11-20		A5
3288	" "	22	NW	1863-04-20		A5
3270	KOBB, Angelina	11	S½NE	1860-09-10		A5 G15
3271	" "	12	S½NW	1860-09-10		A5 G15
3159	LACY, Catharine	14	W½SE	1860-08-03		A5 G274
3387	LANDON, William H	15	E½NE	1861-04-01		A5 G234
3388	" "	15	SWNE	1861-04-01		A5 G234
3243	LANE, Austin	3	NE	1862-08-20		A5 G363
3202	LANGDELL, Elzaphan	23	SWNE	1860-07-02		A2
3196	LEE, David	15	NWSW	1873-01-10		A6
3339	LEE, Rachael	14	NW	1869-09-01		A6
3391	LEE, William J	15	N½NW	1860-09-10		A5 G239
3390	" "	15	SWNW	1861-01-18		A2
3389	" "	15	SENW	1862-10-01		A2
3179	LESURE, Bertha	24	W½NW	1855-12-15		A2
3149	LIVINGSTON, Ahira	11	NW	1860-09-10		A5
3201	LUCAS, Elizabeth	24	E½NW	1855-12-15		A2
3291	MANSFIELD, John W	1	N½SE	1857-10-30		A5
3292	" "	1	SWSE	1857-10-30		A5
3293	" "	13	N½NE	1857-10-30		A5
3294	" "	23	E½NE	1859-09-01		A5
3295	" "	23	NWNE	1859-09-01		A5
3272	MCADOO, Elizabeth	2	NE	1861-04-01		A5 G347
3204	MCNELIS, Francis	27	N½SE	1855-12-15		A2
3205	MCNELLIS, Francis	35	NWNW	1855-12-15		A2
3165	MINER, Asher W	10	NWSW	1860-09-10		A5 C
3166	" "	9	E½SE	1860-09-10		A5 C R3167
3168	" "	9	NWSE	1860-09-10		A5 C R3169
3167	" "	9	E½SE	1862-08-20		A5 R3166
3169	" "	9	NWSE	1862-08-20		A5 R3168
3170	" "	9	SENW	1862-08-20		A5
3157	MOOR, Andrew	36	6	1860-08-01		A5
3158	" "	36	7	1860-08-01		A5
3159	" "	14	W½SE	1860-08-03		A5 G274
3283	MOORE, John H	10	SW	1861-07-01		A5
3184	MOREHOUSE, Stephen	32	2	1863-04-20		A5 G375
3185	" "	32	S½SE	1863-04-20		A5 G375
3213	MULKS, George	7	W½SE	1857-04-01		A2
3212	" "	7	E½SW	1859-09-01		A5
3153	NAMEJUNAS, Alfred	32	1	1956-06-25		A1
3377	NEVIN, Elizabeth	25	SWNW	1860-11-20		A5 G438
3378	" "	26	S½NE	1860-11-20		A5 G438
3335	NICHOLS, Paige F	17	S½SE	1860-09-10		A5 G281
3383	NOIS, William E	9	3	1861-01-18		A2
3329	OVITT, Norman A	15	N½SE	1870-10-20		A6
3242	OWEN, Henry	30	S½NE	1855-12-15		A2
3316	OWEN, Moses H	30	N½NE	1855-12-15		A2
3373	OWEN, Wesley	30	N½SW	1855-12-15		A2 F
3392	PATTEN, William	27	SESW	1859-05-02		A2
3393	" "	34	NENW	1859-05-02		A2
3233	PEARSON, Sally S	1	NESW	1860-09-10		A5 G314
3234	" "	1	W½SW	1860-09-10		A5 G314
3289	PEISCH, John	1	NW	1864-05-02		A5 G298
3351	PENNOCK, Samuel M	21	NE	1861-09-10		A5 G300
3233	PUTNAM, Henry C	1	NESW	1860-09-10		A5 G314
3234	" "	1	W½SW	1860-09-10		A5 G314
3229	" "	2	E½SW	1860-11-20		A5
3230	" "	2	SWSW	1860-11-20		A5
3377	" "	25	SWNW	1860-11-20		A5 G438
3378	" "	26	S½NE	1860-11-20		A5 G438
3231	" "	9	NENW	1861-04-01		A5
3232	" "	9	W½NW	1861-04-01		A5

ID	Individual in Patent	Sec.	Sec. Part	Date Issued	Other Counties	For More Info . . .
3379	PUTNAN, Henry C	25	NWNW	1860-11-20		A5 G439
3380	" "	26	N½NE	1860-11-20		A5 G439
3302	RAMSEY, Leroy	13	SESE	1854-10-02		A2
3301	" "	13	NESE	1855-12-15		A2
3303	" "	24	NENE	1855-12-15		A2
3346	RANDALL, Roswell S	26	NW	1860-09-10		A5 G315
3272	RANDELL, Addis E	2	NE	1861-04-01		A5 G347
3347	RANNEY, Rufus P	3	SE	1860-02-01		A5 G316
3150	REICHARD, William	5	NWSE	1860-10-10		A5 G392
3151	" "	5	S½SE	1860-10-10		A5 G392
3152	" "	5	SESW	1860-10-10		A5 G392
3175	REMINGTON, Barlow	8	1	1856-04-01		A2
3176	" "	8	NESE	1856-04-01		A2
3177	" "	8	W½SE	1856-04-01		A2
3172	" "	17	1	1860-03-07		A2
3173	" "	17	2	1860-03-07		A2
3174	" "	17	W½NE	1860-03-07		A2
3305	REMINGTON, Margaret	13	W½SW	1855-12-15		A2
3306	" "	14	E½SE	1855-12-15		A2
3307	REPINE, Margaret	5	NESE	1881-09-09		A6 G323
3307	REPINE, Michael	5	NESE	1881-09-09		A6 G323
3367	RICKER, Catharine	33	E½SE	1859-09-01		A5 G53
3368	" "	33	SENE	1859-09-01		A5 G53
3193	RIPLEY, Christopher G	6	NW	1857-10-30		A5 F
3171	RITTER, Austin	15	S½SE	1861-04-01		A5
3194	RITTER, Daniel	6	W½SW	1859-05-02		A2
3372	RITTER, Thiletus H	15	S½SW	1862-04-01		A2
3289	ROBERTS, James H	1	NW	1864-05-02		A5 G298
3394	ROBISON, William	23	E½SE	1860-10-10		A5
3395	" "	23	NWSE	1860-10-10		A5
3340	ROCK, Reuben A	11	N½NE	1860-09-10		A5
3341	" "	12	N½NW	1860-09-10		A5
3261	RORK, James E	12	NE	1860-09-10		A5 G346
3260	" "	1	SESW	1865-07-01		A2
3272	ROSE, John C	2	NE	1861-04-01		A5 G347
3337	RUMRILL, Pliny	11	S½SE	1860-09-10		A5 G348
3338	" "	12	S½SW	1860-09-10		A5 G348
3396	SCHAAF, William	2	SE	1861-05-15		A5 R3312
3148	SEYMOUR, Betsey E	17	S½SW	1863-04-20		A5 G403
3254	SHERMAN, J Sidney	1	SESE	1860-10-01		A7
3342	SHIELDS, Robert	23	NENW	1860-10-01		A7 C R3343
3344	SHIELLS, Robert	34	S½SW	1859-09-01		A5
3345	" "	34	SWSE	1859-09-01		A5
3343	" "	23	NENW	1861-10-28		A7 R3342
3243	SIPPEL, Henry	3	NE	1862-08-20		A5 G363
3290	SIPPLE, John	17	N½SE	1865-10-20		A5 G364
3324	SKEEL, Nathan	4	NW	1869-09-01		A6
3335	SKINNER, Francis R	17	S½SE	1860-09-10		A5 G281
3353	" "	20	E½NE	1860-09-10		A5 G414
3354	" "	20	NWNE	1860-09-10		A5 G414
3397	SKINNER, William	4	NE	1869-09-01		A6
3269	SLICK, John A	35	E½NW	1857-04-01		A2
3267	" "	27	W½SW	1859-09-01		A5
3268	" "	34	NWNW	1859-09-01		A5
3261	SLY, A B	12	NE	1860-09-10		A5 G346
3355	SMITH, Elijah R	19	E½NW	1865-10-20		A5 G42
3356	" "	19	N½SW	1865-10-20		A5 G42
3184	SMITH, Horace G	32	2	1863-04-20		A5 G375
3185	" "	32	S½SE	1863-04-20		A5 G375
3184	SPAFFORD, Charles C	32	2	1863-04-20		A5 G375
3185	" "	32	S½SE	1863-04-20		A5 G375
3351	SPALDING, Celinda W	21	NE	1861-09-10		A5 G300
3351	SPALDING, William A	21	NE	1861-09-10		A5 G300
3362	STONE, Stephen B	20	SE	1861-04-01		A5 G385
3164	SWISHER, Anthony	22	W½SE	1866-06-01		A7
3163	" "	22	SW	1866-08-01		A5
3160	TAINTER, Andrew	24	SESE	1860-03-01		A2
3161	" "	25	E½NE	1860-03-01		A2
3162	" "	25	NESE	1860-03-01		A2
3398	TANTON, William	7	SWSW	1859-12-10		A2 F
3150	TAYLOR, Alexander	5	NWSE	1860-10-10		A5 G392
3151	" "	5	S½SE	1860-10-10		A5 G392
3152	" "	5	SESW	1860-10-10		A5 G392

ID	Individual in Patent	Sec.	Sec. Part	Date Issued	Other Counties	For More Info . . .
3258	TAYLOR, Mary	6	W½NE	1858-02-20		A7 G167 F
3337	TEEL, Mary Ann M J	11	S½SE	1860-09-10		A5 G348
3338	" "	12	S½SW	1860-09-10		A5 G348
3195	THOMPSON, David A	26	S½SW	1882-04-10		A6
3304	THOMPSON, Lorenzo C	26	N½SW	1882-04-10		A6
3264	TRASK, James W	34	SENW	1859-09-01		A5
3265	" "	34	W½NE	1859-09-01		A5
3148	TUBBS, A J	17	S½SW	1863-04-20		A5 G403
3180	TUBBS, C C	19	E½SE	1861-04-01		A5
3181	" "	19	SWSE	1861-04-01		A5
3255	TUBBS, Jackson	18	NENW	1855-12-15		A2
3308	TUBBS, Martin	18	SE	1855-12-15		A2
3309	" "	18	SWSW	1855-12-15		A2
3296	VIBBERTS, Joseph S	8	E½NW	1857-04-01		A2 G407
3297	" "	8	NE	1857-04-01		A2 G407
3325	WARE, Nathaniel	18	SENW	1855-12-15		A2
3296	" "	8	E½NW	1857-04-01		A2 G407
3297	" "	8	NE	1857-04-01		A2 G407
3353	WEBB, Seth	20	E½NE	1860-09-10		A5 G414
3354	" "	20	NWNE	1860-09-10		A5 G414
3352	" "	20	SWNE	1860-10-01		A7
3239	WHITE, Henry K	34	NWSE	1859-05-02		A2
3237	" "	3	E½SW	1860-02-01		A5
3238	" "	3	SWSW	1860-02-01		A5
3240	" "	4	E½SE	1860-02-01		A5
3241	" "	4	SWSW	1860-02-01		A5 V3281
3299	WHITELEY, Joshua	21	W½	1855-12-15		A2
3300	" "	9	1	1855-12-15		A2
3310	WHITELEY, Mary J	27	NW	1857-04-01		A2
3198	WIGGINS, Elijah	18	NWSW	1855-12-15		A2
3199	" "	19	NE	1860-03-07		A2
3200	" "	19	NWSE	1860-03-07		A2
3228	WIGGINS, Henry B	19	S½SW	1865-07-01		A2
3298	WIGGINS, Joseph W	20	NW	1860-09-10		A5 G421
3357	WIGGINS, Silas T	20	N½SW	1862-07-10		A5 G422
3197	WILLIAMS, Edward B	26	N½SE	1877-03-01		A6
3290	WILLIAMS, Elizabeth	17	N½SE	1865-10-20		A5 G364
3256	WILLIAMS, Jacob L	30	N½SE	1857-10-30		A5
3257	" "	30	SESE	1857-10-30		A5
3349	WILLIAMS, Maria	9	E½NE	1860-10-10		A5 G55
3350	" "	9	SWNE	1860-10-10		A5 G55
3361	WISCONSIN, State Of	16		1941-08-16		A3 F
3245	WOODMAN, Horatio	7	NWSW	1857-04-01		A2
3248	" "	24	SWNE	1858-02-20		A7 G432
3244	" "	25	SESE	1858-02-20		A7
3246	" "	33	E½SW	1859-09-01		A5 G434
3247	" "	33	W½SE	1859-09-01		A5 G434
3311	WOODWARD, Mary N	10	NE	1860-10-10		A5
3312	" "	2	SE	1860-10-10		A5 C R3396
3379	WOODWARD, William A	25	NWNW	1860-11-20		A5 G439
3377	" "	25	SWNW	1860-11-20		A5 G438
3380	" "	26	N½NE	1860-11-20		A5 G439
3378	" "	26	S½NE	1860-11-20		A5 G438
3374	" "	1	NE	1861-04-01		A5
3381	" "	13	E½SW	1861-07-01		A5 G436
3375	" "	13	N½NW	1861-07-01		A5
3382	" "	13	SENW	1861-07-01		A5 G436
3376	" "	13	SWNW	1861-07-01		A5
3203	YOUNG, Eugene B	32	E½NE	1883-09-10		A6

Patent Map

T27-N R11-W
4th PM - 1831 MN/WI Meridian

Map Group 20

Township Statistics

Parcels Mapped	:	253
Number of Patents	:	179
Number of Individuals	:	174
Patentees Identified	:	144
Number of Surnames	:	142
Multi-Patentee Parcels	:	56
Oldest Patent Date	:	10/2/1854
Most Recent Patent	:	6/25/1956
Block/Lot Parcels	:	14
Parcels Re - Issued	:	8
Parcels that Overlap	:	2
Cities and Towns	:	1
Cemeteries	:	4

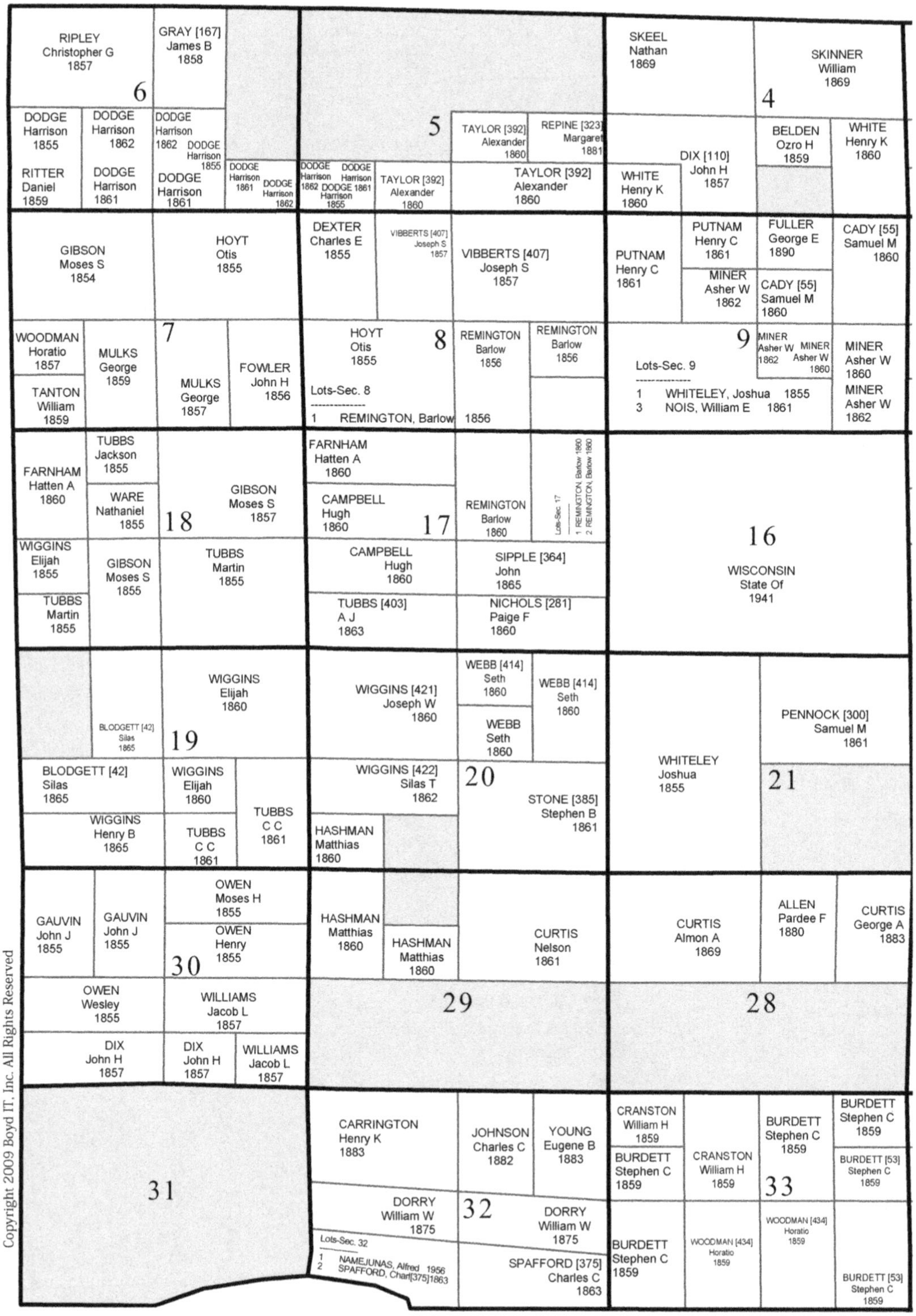

RIPLEY Christopher G 1857
GRAY [167] James B 1858
6
DODGE Harrison 1855
DODGE Harrison 1862
DODGE Harrison 1862
DODGE Harrison 1855
RITTER Daniel 1859
DODGE Harrison 1861
DODGE Harrison 1861
5
TAYLOR [392] Alexander 1860
REPINE [323] Margaret 1881
TAYLOR [392] Alexander 1860
TAYLOR [392] Alexander 1860
SKEEL Nathan 1869
SKINNER William 1869
4
BELDEN Ozro H 1859
WHITE Henry K 1860
DIX [110] John H 1857
WHITE Henry K 1860
GIBSON Moses S 1854
HOYT Otis 1855
DEXTER Charles E 1855
VIBBERTS [407] Joseph S 1857
VIBBERTS [407] Joseph S 1857
PUTNAM Henry C 1861
PUTNAM Henry C 1861
FULLER George E 1890
CADY [55] Samuel M 1860
MINER Asher W 1862
CADY [55] Samuel M 1860
WOODMAN Horatio 1857
MULKS George 1859
7
MULKS George 1857
FOWLER John H 1856
TANTON William 1859
HOYT Otis 1855
8
Lots-Sec. 8
1 REMINGTON, Barlow 1856
REMINGTON Barlow 1856
REMINGTON Barlow 1856
9
Lots-Sec. 9
1 WHITELEY, Joshua 1855
3 NOIS, William E 1861
MINER Asher W 1862
MINER Asher W 1860
MINER Asher W 1860
MINER Asher W 1862
TUBBS Jackson 1855
FARNHAM Hatten A 1860
WARE Nathaniel 1855
18
GIBSON Moses S 1857
FARNHAM Hatten A 1860
CAMPBELL Hugh 1860
17
REMINGTON Barlow 1860
Lots-Sec. 17
1 REMINGTON, Barlow 1860
2 REMINGTON, Barlow 1860
16
WISCONSIN State Of 1941
WIGGINS Elijah 1855
GIBSON Moses S 1855
TUBBS Martin 1855
CAMPBELL Hugh 1860
SIPPLE [364] John 1865
TUBBS Martin 1855
TUBBS [403] A J 1863
NICHOLS [281] Paige F 1860
BLODGETT [42] Silas 1865
WIGGINS Elijah 1860
19
WIGGINS [421] Joseph W 1860
WEBB [414] Seth 1860
WEBB [414] Seth 1860
WEBB Seth 1860
PENNOCK [300] Samuel M 1861
WHITELEY Joshua 1855
BLODGETT [42] Silas 1865
WIGGINS Elijah 1860
TUBBS C C 1861
WIGGINS [422] Silas T 1862
20
STONE [385] Stephen B 1861
21
WIGGINS Henry B 1865
TUBBS C C 1861
HASHMAN Matthias 1860
GAUVIN John J 1855
GAUVIN John J 1855
OWEN Moses H 1855
OWEN Henry 1855
30
HASHMAN Matthias 1860
HASHMAN Matthias 1860
CURTIS Nelson 1861
CURTIS Almon A 1869
ALLEN Pardee F 1880
CURTIS George A 1883
OWEN Wesley 1855
WILLIAMS Jacob L 1857
29
28
DIX John H 1857
DIX John H 1857
WILLIAMS Jacob L 1857
31
CARRINGTON Henry K 1883
JOHNSON Charles C 1882
YOUNG Eugene B 1883
CRANSTON William H 1859
BURDETT Stephen C 1859
BURDETT Stephen C 1859
BURDETT Stephen C 1859
CRANSTON William H 1859
BURDETT [53] Stephen C 1859
33
DORRY William W 1875
32
DORRY William W 1875
WOODMAN [434] Horatio 1859
Lots-Sec. 32
1 NAMEJUNAS, Alfred 1956
2 SPAFFORD, Charl[375]1863
SPAFFORD [375] Charles C 1863
BURDETT Stephen C 1859
WOODMAN [434] Horatio 1859
BURDETT [53] Stephen C 1859

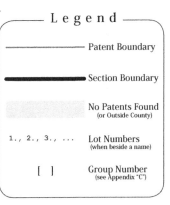

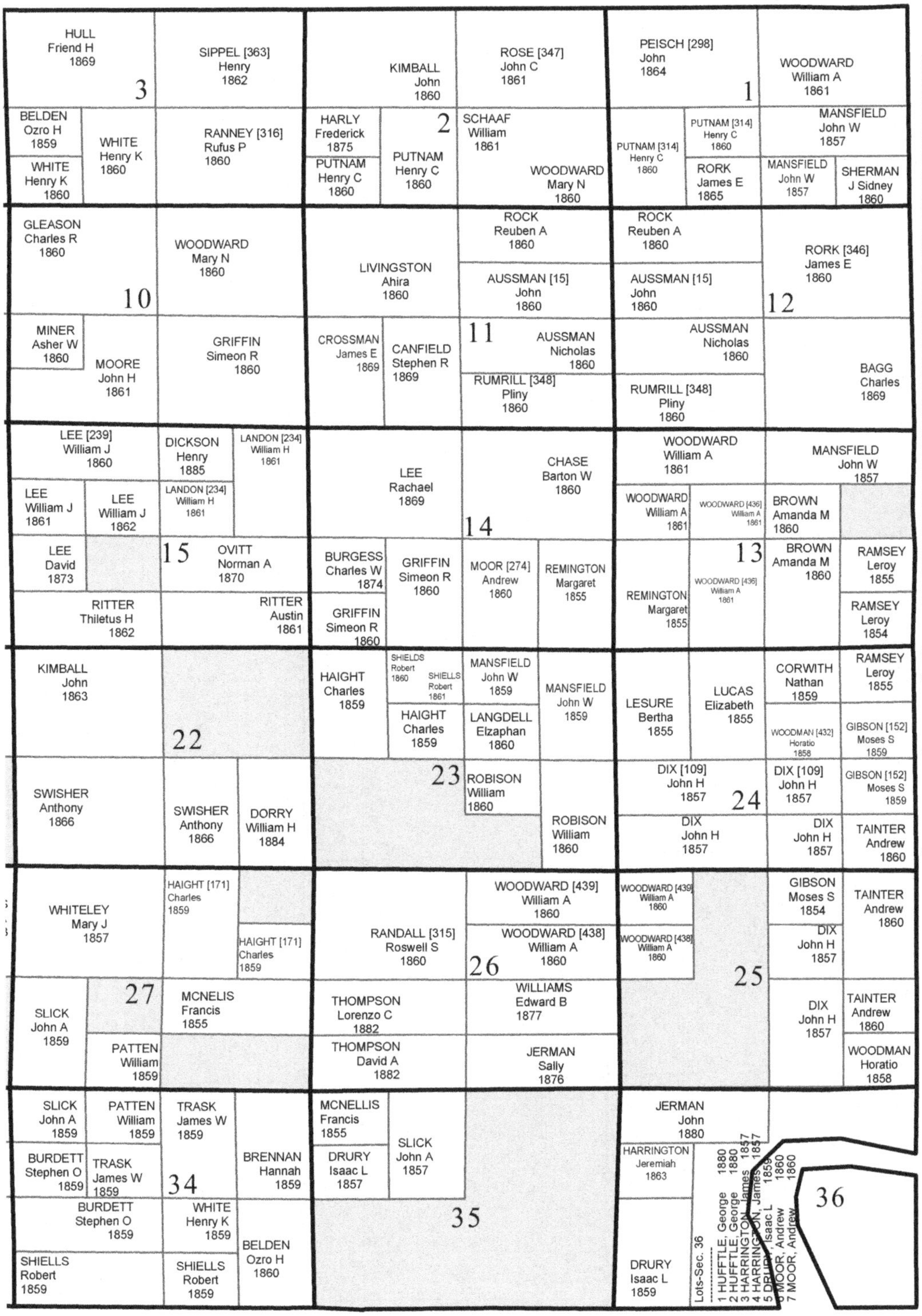
HULL Friend H 1869
3
SIPPEL [363] Henry 1862
KIMBALL John 1860
ROSE [347] John C 1861
PEISCH [298] John 1864
1
WOODWARD William A 1861
BELDEN Ozro H 1859
WHITE Henry K 1860
WHITE Henry K 1860
RANNEY [316] Rufus P 1860
HARLY Frederick 1875
2
PUTNAM Henry C 1860
PUTNAM Henry C 1860
SCHAAF William 1861
WOODWARD Mary N 1860
PUTNAM [314] Henry C 1860
PUTNAM [314] Henry C 1860
RORK James E 1865
MANSFIELD John W 1857
MANSFIELD John W 1857
SHERMAN J Sidney 1860
GLEASON Charles R 1860
WOODWARD Mary N 1860
10
LIVINGSTON Ahira 1860
ROCK Reuben A 1860
AUSSMAN [15] John 1860
ROCK Reuben A 1860
AUSSMAN [15] John 1860
RORK [346] James E 1860
12
MINER Asher W 1860
MOORE John H 1861
GRIFFIN Simeon R 1860
CROSSMAN James E 1869
CANFIELD Stephen R 1869
11
AUSSMAN Nicholas 1860
RUMRILL [348] Pliny 1860
AUSSMAN Nicholas 1860
RUMRILL [348] Pliny 1860
BAGG Charles 1869
LEE [239] William J 1860
DICKSON Henry 1885
LANDON [234] William H 1861
LEE William J 1861
LEE William J 1862
LANDON [234] William H 1861
LEE Rachael 1869
CHASE Barton W 1860
14
WOODWARD William A 1861
MANSFIELD John W 1857
WOODWARD William A 1861
WOODWARD [436] William A 1861
BROWN Amanda M 1860
LEE David 1873
15
OVITT Norman A 1870
BURGESS Charles W 1874
GRIFFIN Simeon R 1860
MOOR [274] Andrew 1860
REMINGTON Margaret 1855
REMINGTON Margaret 1855
13
WOODWARD [436] William A 1861
BROWN Amanda M 1860
RAMSEY Leroy 1855
RITTER Thiletus H 1862
RITTER Austin 1861
GRIFFIN Simeon R 1860
RAMSEY Leroy 1854
KIMBALL John 1863
22
HAIGHT Charles 1859
SHIELDS Robert 1860
SHIELLS Robert 1861
MANSFIELD John W 1859
HAIGHT Charles 1859
LANGDELL Elzaphan 1860
MANSFIELD John W 1859
LESURE Bertha 1855
LUCAS Elizabeth 1855
CORWITH Nathan 1859
RAMSEY Leroy 1855
WOODMAN [432] Horatio 1858
GIBSON [152] Moses S 1859
SWISHER Anthony 1866
SWISHER Anthony 1866
DORRY William H 1884
23
ROBISON William 1860
ROBISON William 1860
DIX [109] John H 1857
24
DIX [109] John H 1857
GIBSON [152] Moses S 1859
DIX John H 1857
DIX John H 1857
TAINTER Andrew 1860
WHITELEY Mary J 1857
HAIGHT [171] Charles 1859
HAIGHT [171] Charles 1859
RANDALL [315] Roswell S 1860
WOODWARD [439] William A 1860
WOODWARD [438] William A 1860
26
WOODWARD [439] William A 1860
WOODWARD [438] William A 1860
GIBSON Moses S 1854
TAINTER Andrew 1860
DIX John H 1857
25
SLICK John A 1859
27
MCNELIS Francis 1855
PATTEN William 1859
THOMPSON Lorenzo C 1882
THOMPSON David A 1882
WILLIAMS Edward B 1877
JERMAN Sally 1876
DIX John H 1857
TAINTER Andrew 1860
WOODMAN Horatio 1858
SLICK John A 1859
PATTEN William 1859
TRASK James W 1859
BURDETT Stephen O 1859
TRASK James W 1859
34
BRENNAN Hannah 1859
MCNELLIS Francis 1855
SLICK John A 1857
DRURY Isaac L 1857
35
JERMAN John 1880
HARRINGTON Jeremiah 1863
DRURY Isaac L 1859
Lots-Sec. 36
1 HUFFTLE, George 1880
2 HUFFTLE, George 1880
3 HARRINGTON, James 1857
4 HARRINGTON, James 1857
5 DRURY, Isaac L 1859
6 MOOR, Andrew 1860
7 MOOR, Andrew 1860
36
BURDETT Stephen O 1859
WHITE Henry K 1859
BELDEN Ozro H 1860
SHIELLS Robert 1859
SHIELLS Robert 1859

Helpful Hints

1. This Map's INDEX can be found on the preceding pages.
2. Refer to Map "C" to see where this Township lies within Dunn County, Wisconsin.
3. Numbers within square brackets [ ] denote a multi-patentee land parcel (multi-owner). Refer to Appendix "C" for a full list of members in this group.
4. Areas that look to be crowded with Patentees usually indicate multiple sales of the same parcel (Re-issues) or Overlapping parcels. See this Township's Index for an explanation of these and other circumstances that might explain "odd" groupings of Patentees on this map.

Legend

- Patent Boundary
- Section Boundary
- No Patents Found (or Outside County)
- 1., 2., 3., ... Lot Numbers (when beside a name)
- [ ] Group Number (see Appendix "C")

Scale: Section = 1 mile X 1 mile (generally, with some exceptions)

Road Map

T27-N R11-W
4th PM - 1831 MN/WI Meridian

Map Group 20

Cities & Towns

Falls City

Cemeteries

Falls City Cemetery
Saint Joseph Cemetery
Spring Brook Cemetery
Waneka Cemetery

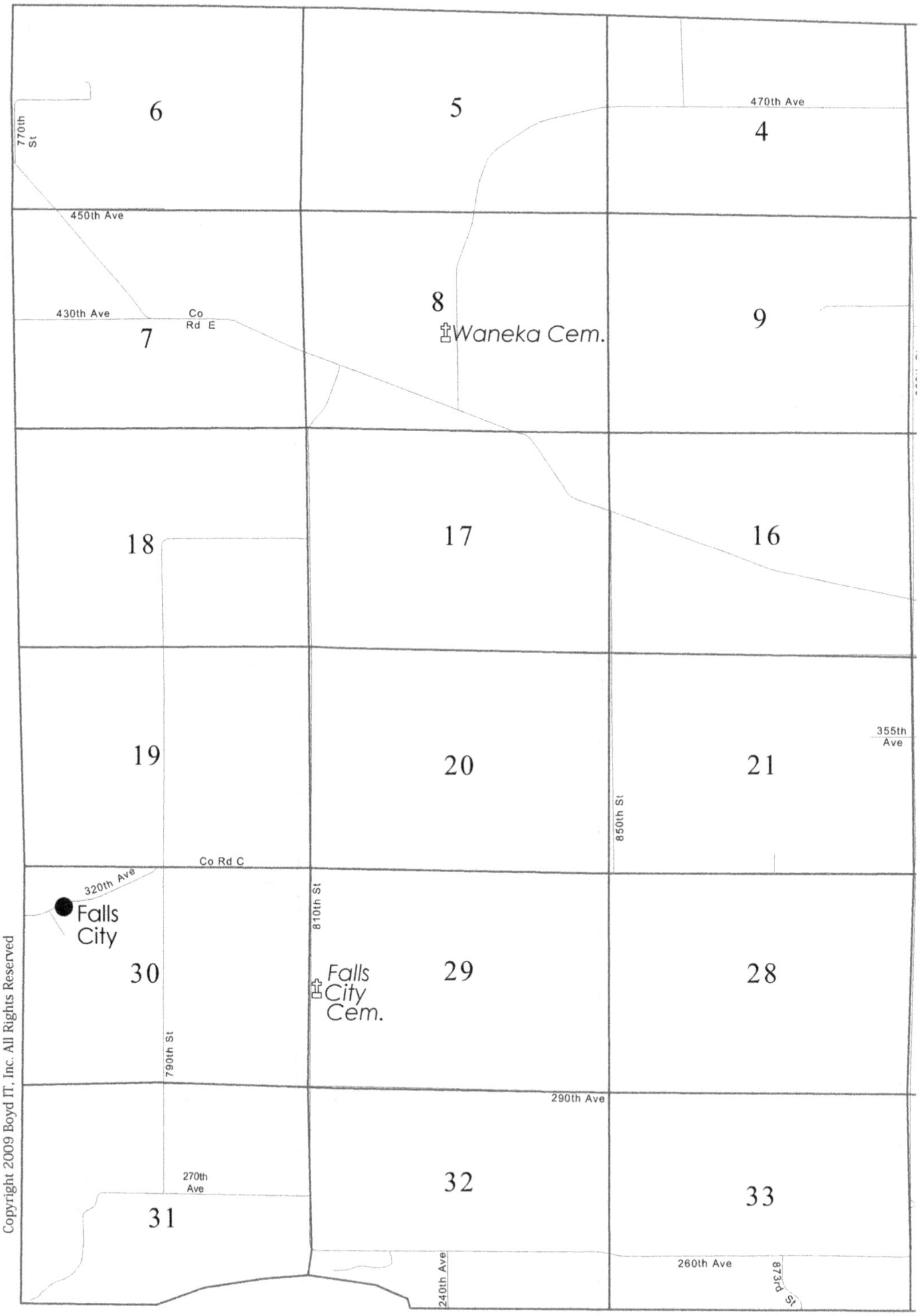

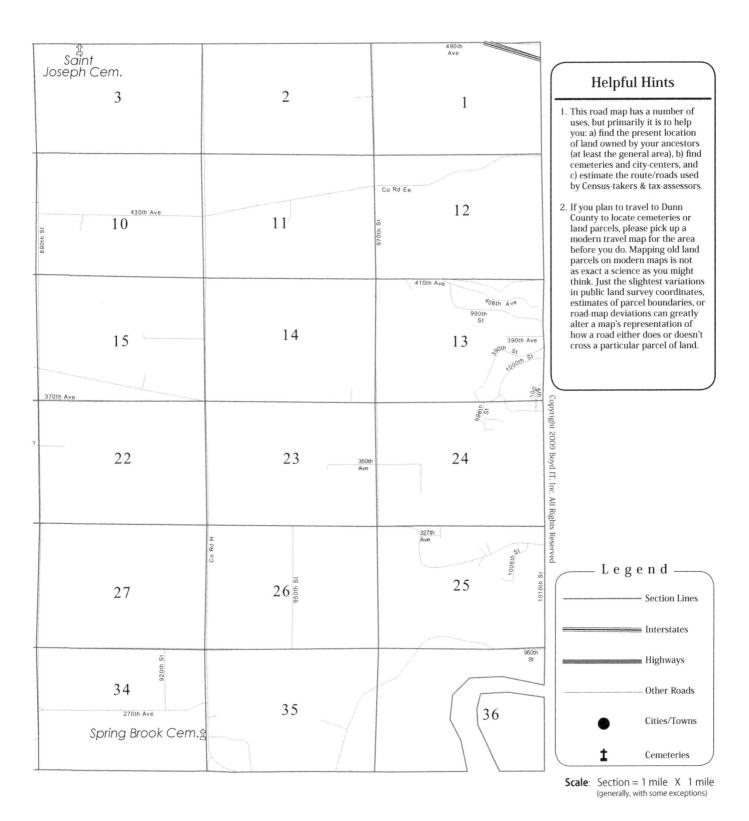

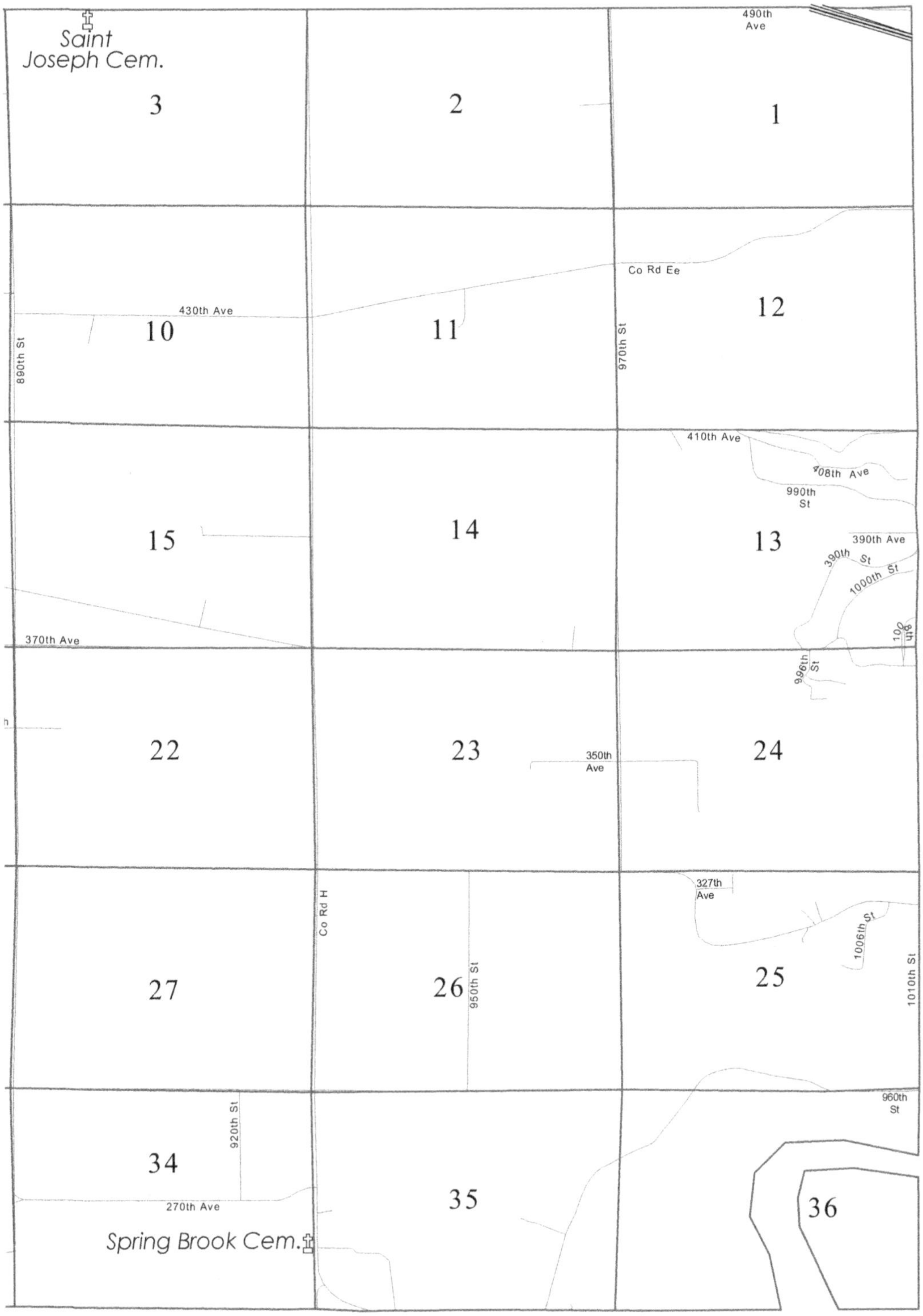

Helpful Hints

1. This road map has a number of uses, but primarily it is to help you: a) find the present location of land owned by your ancestors (at least the general area), b) find cemeteries and city-centers, and c) estimate the route/roads used by Census-takers & tax-assessors.
2. If you plan to travel to Dunn County to locate cemeteries or land parcels, please pick up a modern travel map for the area before you do. Mapping old land parcels on modern maps is not as exact a science as you might think. Just the slightest variations in public land survey coordinates, estimates of parcel boundaries, or road-map deviations can greatly alter a map's representation of how a road either does or doesn't cross a particular parcel of land.

Legend

- Section Lines
- Interstates
- Highways
- Other Roads
- Cities/Towns
- Cemeteries

Scale: Section = 1 mile X 1 mile
(generally, with some exceptions)

Historical Map

T27-N R11-W
4th PM - 1831 MN/WI Meridian

Map Group 20

Cities & Towns

Falls City

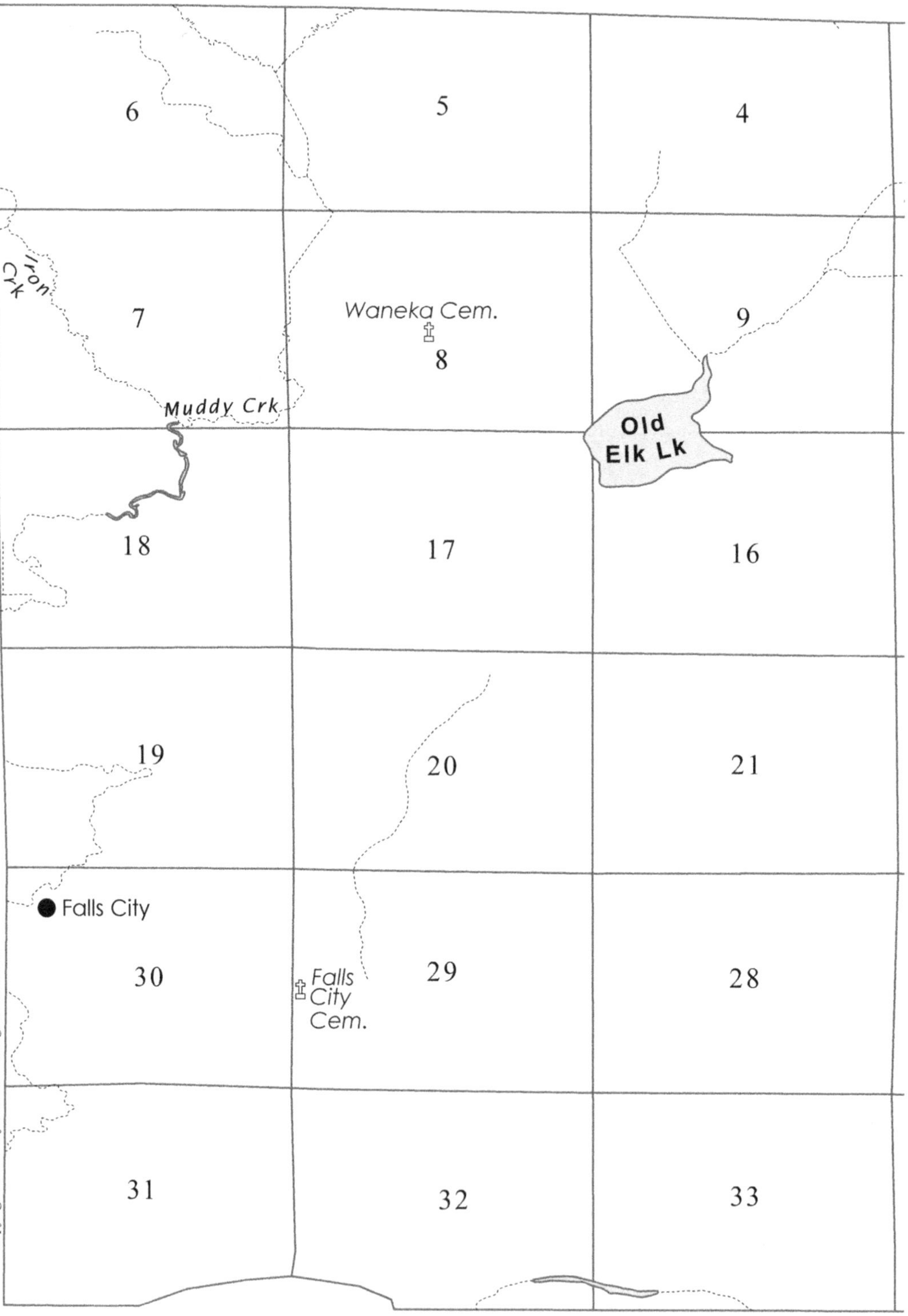
6
5
4
7
Iron Crk
Waneka Cem.
8
9
Muddy Crk
Old Elk Lk
18
17
16
19
20
21
Falls City
30
Falls City Cem.
29
28
31
32
33

Cemeteries

Falls City Cemetery
Saint Joseph Cemetery
Spring Brook Cemetery
Waneka Cemetery

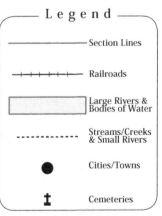

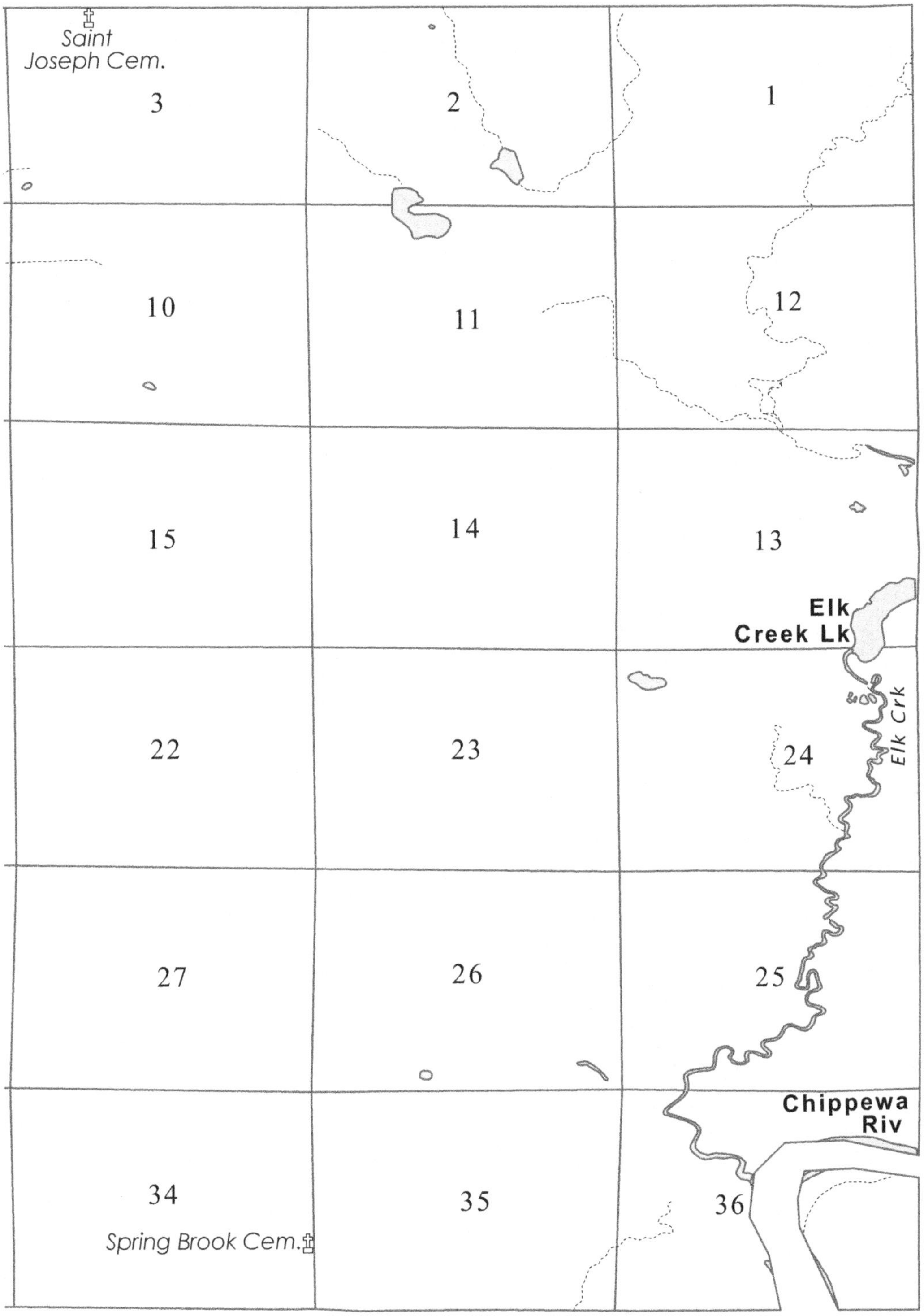
Saint
Joseph Cem.
3
2
1
10
11
12
15
14
13
Elk
Creek Lk
22
23
24
Elk Crk
27
26
25
Chippewa
Riv
34
35
36
Spring Brook Cem.

Helpful Hints

1. This Map takes a different look at the same Congressional Township displayed in the preceding two maps. It presents features that can help you better envision the historical development of the area: a) Water-bodies (lakes & ponds), b) Water-courses (rivers, streams, etc.), c) Railroads, d) City/town center-points (where they were oftentimes located when first settled), and e) Cemeteries.
2. Using this "Historical" map in tandem with this Township's Patent Map and Road Map, may lead you to some interesting discoveries. You will often find roads, towns, cemeteries, and waterways are named after nearby landowners: sometimes those names will be the ones you are researching. See how many of these research gems you can find here in Dunn County.

Legend

- Section Lines
- Railroads
- Large Rivers & Bodies of Water
- Streams/Creeks & Small Rivers
- Cities/Towns
- Cemeteries

Scale: Section = 1 mile X 1 mile
(there are some exceptions)

Map Group 21: Index to Land Patents

Township 26-North Range 14-West (4th PM - 1831 MN/WI)

After you locate an individual in this Index, take note of the Section and Section Part then proceed to the Land Patent map on the pages immediately following. You should have no difficulty locating the corresponding parcel of land.

The "For More Info" Column will lead you to more information about the underlying Patents. See the *Legend* at right, and the "How to Use this Book" chapter, for more information.

LEGEND

"For More Info . . . " column

A = Authority (Legislative Act, See Appendix "A")
B = Block or Lot (location in Section unknown)
C = Cancelled Patent
F = Fractional Section
G = Group (Multi-Patentee Patent, see Appendix "C")
V = Overlaps another Parcel
R = Re-Issued (Parcel patented more than once)

(A & G items require you to look in the Appendixes referred to above. All other Letter-designations followed by a number require you to locate line-items in this index that possess the ID number found after the letter).

ID	Individual in Patent	Sec.	Sec. Part	Date Issued	Other Counties	For More Info . . .
3432	AUSTIN, Charles C	10	E½NE	1872-10-01		A6
3558	BAILEY, Roderick	8	SESW	1869-10-20		A6
3559	" "	8	SWSE	1869-10-20		A6
3544	BAKER, R J	18	E½SE	1875-04-01		A6
3545	" "	18	SENE	1875-04-01		A6
3451	BENNETT, George W	2	SENE	1889-02-16		A6
3452	" "	2	W½NE	1889-02-16		A6
3457	BENTON, Harrison	12	S½NW	1878-11-30		A6
3458	" "	12	W½SW	1878-11-30		A6
3561	BERGEMANN, Siegesmund	22	S½SE	1857-04-01		A2
3562	" "	22	SESW	1857-04-01		A2
3563	" "	23	S½SW	1857-04-01		A2
3564	" "	26	N½NW	1857-04-01		A2
3565	" "	27	N½NE	1857-04-01		A2
3566	" "	27	NENW	1857-04-01		A2
3577	BERGEMANN, Wilhelm	22	N½SE	1859-12-10		A2
3578	" "	22	S½NE	1859-12-10		A2
3523	BINDINGER, Joseph	22	SENW	1859-05-02		A2
3524	" "	22	W½NW	1859-05-02		A2
3521	BISHOP, Johnathan	2	E½SE	1880-09-01		A6
3583	BLAIR, William	28	SESW	1875-04-01		A6
3584	" "	28	SWSE	1875-04-01		A6
3575	BOA, Thomas P	32	N½NW	1883-07-10		A6
3455	BOCK, Gustaf	4	E½NW	1884-09-20		A6 F
3425	BORCHERT, August	10	S½NW	1873-05-20		A6
3463	BOYINGTON, Hiram	21	W½NE	1860-02-01		A5 G47
3439	BOYLE, Daniel	36	SWSW	1873-04-01		A6
3467	BRANCH, Isaac B	12	NWSE	1883-02-10		A6
3468	" "	12	SWNE	1883-02-10		A6
3612	" "	12	S½SE	1885-01-30		A6 G48
3612	BRANCH, Willie M	12	S½SE	1885-01-30		A6 G48
3403	BROWN, Adolphus	8	E½SE	1872-09-25		A6
3405	BROWN, Albert	30	E½SE	1873-12-20		A6 V3426
3484	BROWNLEE, James W	6	W½NE	1874-07-15		A6
3483	" "	4	E½SW	1875-01-15		A6
3574	BROWNLEE, Thomas	6	E½NW	1873-12-20		A6
3453	BRYANT, George W	2	NENE	1900-02-24		A6
3434	BUCHANAN, Christopher	20	NENE	1860-02-01		A5
3435	" "	20	W½NE	1860-02-01		A5
3422	BURDICK, Ashbell W	12	NESE	1875-01-15		A6
3423	" "	12	SENE	1875-01-15		A6
3424	BURDICK, Ashbill W	12	NENE	1890-03-29		A6
3440	BUXTON, Nancy	35	W½SE	1860-03-10		A5 G264
3536	CALLAGHAN, Michael	23	SE	1859-05-02		A2
3406	CAPEN, Albert J	21	N½NW	1860-03-10		A5
3407	" "	21	SENW	1860-03-10		A5

ID	Individual in Patent	Sec.	Sec. Part	Date Issued	Other Counties	For More Info . . .
3474	CARLISLE, James	36	NWSW	1857-04-02		A2
3589	CARSON, William	36	NE	1855-06-15		A2 G64
3590	" "	22	NENW	1855-12-15		A2 G65
3591	" "	22	NWNE	1855-12-15		A2 G65
3592	" "	25	NESE	1855-12-15		A2 G65
3593	" "	25	SW	1855-12-15		A2 G65
3594	" "	25	W½SE	1855-12-15		A2 G65
3588	" "	25	SESE	1859-05-02		A2
3447	CASCADEN, George	24	W½SE	1857-04-01		A2
3554	CLINE, Robert E	32	W½SE	1874-04-01		A6
3401	COCKBURN, Adam W	34	SWSE	1873-04-01		A6
3486	CRANDAL, Jason W	4	W½SW	1875-01-15		A6
3487	CULLMAN, John A	21	SW	1859-12-10		A2
3442	DAVISON, Ellen J	30	W½SE	1880-09-01		A6 G102 V3426
3442	DAVISON, Joseph	30	W½SE	1880-09-01		A6 G102 V3426
3414	DE LONG, ANGELINE M	20	W½NW	1873-04-01		A6 G103
3488	DE LONG, JOHN	28	S½NE	1873-12-20		A6
3415	DEFREES, Anthony	13	E½NW	1857-04-01		A2
3416	" "	13	SENE	1857-04-01		A2
3417	" "	13	SW	1857-04-01		A2
3599	DELONG, William	26	W½SW	1859-05-02		A2
3598	" "	26	E½SW	1859-12-10		A2
3552	DICKSON, Robert	34	NWNE	1859-12-10		A2
3551	" "	34	E½NE	1860-02-01		A5
3553	" "	34	SWNE	1860-02-01		A5
3589	DOWNS, Burrage B	36	NE	1855-06-15		A2 G64
3590	" "	22	NENW	1855-12-15		A2 G65
3591	" "	22	NWNE	1855-12-15		A2 G65
3592	" "	25	NESE	1855-12-15		A2 G65
3593	" "	25	SW	1855-12-15		A2 G65
3594	" "	25	W½SE	1855-12-15		A2 G65
3589	DOWNS, Eben	36	NE	1855-06-15		A2 G64
3589	EATON, Henry	36	NE	1855-06-15		A2 G64
3590	" "	22	NENW	1855-12-15		A2 G65
3591	" "	22	NWNE	1855-12-15		A2 G65
3592	" "	25	NESE	1855-12-15		A2 G65
3593	" "	25	SW	1855-12-15		A2 G65
3594	" "	25	W½SE	1855-12-15		A2 G65
3543	FEAZEL, Pleasant	2	W½SW	1873-04-01		A6
3542	" "	2	E½SW	1882-04-10		A6
3430	FITCH, C M	32	E½SE	1872-09-25		A6
3576	FITCH, Victor	20	S½SW	1870-06-10		A6
3600	FLETCHER, William	15	NWSW	1854-10-02		A2
3601	" "	15	SWNW	1854-10-02		A2
3581	FLETCHER, William A	15	NESE	1859-05-02		A2
3582	" "	15	SENE	1859-05-02		A2
3489	FORA, John	12	NWNW	1911-12-07		A6
3560	FRENCH, Samuel B	22	NESW	1861-01-21		A2
3567	GORDON, Sofronia	4	S½NE	1884-09-20		A6
3448	GREEN, George	24	NE	1860-02-01		A5 G168
3477	GRUMPRY, James	28	W½SW	1876-12-30		A6
3529	HANSEN, Lauritz	32	N½SW	1879-10-01		A6
3479	HOBBS, James M	32	S½SW	1874-07-15		A6
3496	HODGDON, John	11	E½NE	1859-09-01		A5
3497	" "	11	E½NW	1859-09-01		A5
3498	" "	11	E½SE	1859-09-01		A5
3499	" "	11	E½SW	1859-09-01		A5
3500	" "	11	NWNE	1859-09-01		A5
3501	" "	11	NWSW	1859-09-01		A5
3502	" "	11	SWNE	1859-09-01		A5
3503	" "	11	SWSE	1859-09-01		A5
3504	" "	11	SWSW	1859-09-01		A5
3505	" "	11	W½NW	1859-09-01		A5
3506	" "	13	E½SE	1859-09-01		A5
3507	" "	13	NENE	1859-09-01		A5
3508	" "	13	NWSE	1859-09-01		A5
3509	" "	13	W½NE	1859-09-01		A5
3510	" "	13	W½NW	1859-09-01		A5
3579	HOLBROOK, Willard F	26	SENE	1854-10-02		A2
3580	" "	26	SWNE	1855-12-15		A2
3414	HOYT, John	20	W½NW	1873-04-01		A6 G103
3440	HUDSPETH, Henry S	35	W½SE	1860-03-10		A5 G264
3421	HUGHS, Arthusa	12	E½SW	1883-02-10		A6

ID	Individual in Patent	Sec.	Sec. Part	Date Issued	Other Counties	For More Info . . .
3463	HUSH, Elizabeth	21	W½NE	1860-02-01		A5 G47
3456	JENSON, Hans	32	W½NE	1874-04-01		A6
3478	JUNOR, James	34	S½SW	1876-01-10		A6
3493	KELLY, John H	28	W½NW	1880-05-15		A6
3525	KENNEDY, Joseph	13	SWSE	1857-04-02		A2
3527	KERNES, Laurence	30	NENW	1889-02-16		A6
3528	" "	30	NWNE	1889-02-16		A6
3530	KERNES, Lawrence	30	SENW	1876-01-10		A6
3531	" "	30	SWNE	1876-01-10		A6 V3429
3464	KIMBALL, Hiram H	10	N½NW	1877-02-20		A6
3465	" "	10	W½NE	1877-02-20		A6
3570	KIRK, Thales	15	S½SE	1860-02-01		A5
3571	" "	22	NENE	1860-02-01		A5
3555	KITE, Robert F	8	NENE	1869-08-05		A2
3556	" "	8	NWNE	1872-09-25		A6
3557	" "	8	S½NE	1872-09-25		A6
3459	KRANSZ, Henry	6	W½SW	1873-04-01		A6 F
3441	LAMPHARE, Elisha	35	E½SE	1857-04-02		A2
3460	LANE, Henry	30	E½NE	1879-11-10		A6 V3429
3449	LAWRENCE, Sarah	25	NW	1860-03-10		A5 G247
3511	LAYNE, John	28	E½NW	1872-09-25		A6
3418	LEMON, Anthony	25	N½NE	1857-04-01		A2
3449	MAGILTON, George	25	NW	1860-03-10		A5 G247
3538	MANNING, Nathaniel W	25	S½NE	1856-06-16		A7
3481	MARTIN, James	34	NWSE	1869-10-20		A2
3480	" "	34	NESE	1873-04-01		A6
3517	MAYBEE, John	22	W½SW	1859-12-10		A2
3603	MCGILTON, William	26	N½NE	1860-03-10		A5
3466	MCGINNIS, Judith	35	E½SW	1859-09-01		A5 G303
3440	MCROBERT, Edward	35	W½SE	1860-03-10		A5 G264
3541	MELLEN, Peter P	18	N½NE	1869-10-20		A6
3512	MILLS, John M	26	SE	1857-04-01		A2
3513	" "	35	NE	1857-04-01		A2
3514	" "	36	E½SW	1857-04-01		A2
3515	" "	36	NW	1857-04-01		A2
3516	" "	36	SE	1857-04-01		A2
3491	MOODY, Benjamin Franklin	21	NESE	1865-10-10		A5 G273
3492	" "	21	W½SE	1865-10-10		A5 G273
3490	MOODY, John G	21	SESE	1866-02-15		A2
3491	MOODY, John Gilman	21	NESE	1865-10-10		A5 G273
3492	" "	21	W½SE	1865-10-10		A5 G273
3475	MORTON, James D	6	W½SE	1872-09-25		A6
3494	MORTON, John H	6	E½SW	1872-09-25		A6
3586	MORTON, William C	8	NWNW	1867-07-15		A2
3585	" "	8	E½NW	1872-09-25		A6
3587	" "	8	SWNW	1872-12-10		A2
3537	MULHERON, Morris	30	S½SW	1873-04-01		A6
3540	MURPHY, Patrick	34	SESE	1870-09-10		A2
3518	NELSON, John	32	E½NE	1874-04-01		A6
3595	OSMER, William D	18	NENW	1877-06-04		A6 F
3596	" "	18	W½NW	1877-06-04		A6 F
3431	OTIS, Cary	32	S½NW	1882-05-10		A6
3448	PALMER, Mercy S	24	NE	1860-02-01		A5 G168
3404	PEASE, Albert A	30	W½NW	1876-12-30		A6
3408	PETTIS, Albert M	8	N½SW	1875-01-15		A6
3409	" "	8	NWSE	1875-01-15		A6
3410	" "	8	SWSW	1875-01-15		A6
3466	PHELPS, Ira W	35	E½SW	1859-09-01		A5 G303
3450	PHILLIPS, George	4	N½NE	1880-09-01		A6 F
3526	PIRKL, Joseph	34	N½SW	1871-04-20		A6
3476	RAMSEY, James E	6	E½NE	1875-01-15		A6 F
3602	RAMSEY, William H	6	E½SE	1876-03-10		A6
3590	RAND, Eldridge D	22	NENW	1855-12-15		A2 G65
3591	" "	22	NWNE	1855-12-15		A2 G65
3592	" "	25	NESE	1855-12-15		A2 G65
3593	" "	25	SW	1855-12-15		A2 G65
3594	" "	25	W½SE	1855-12-15		A2 G65
3482	RANDS, James	34	S½NW	1859-05-02		A2
3547	RAUENBUEHLER, Richard	24	NW	1860-03-10		A5
3604	ROBERTS, William	35	NWSW	1859-05-02		A2
3605	" "	35	S½NW	1859-05-02		A2
3519	ROSEYCRANCE, John	4	W½NW	1862-04-10		A2 F
3461	ROSSON, Daniel P	23	N½SW	1860-02-01		A5 G353

ID	Individual in Patent	Sec.	Sec. Part	Date Issued	Other Counties	For More Info . . .
3462	ROSSON, Daniel P (Cont'd)	23	SWNW	1860-02-01		A5 G353
3548	SCHAFNER, Richard	10	SESW	1870-09-10		A2
3549	" "	10	SWSW	1886-01-20		A2
3426	SCHMITT, Bernard	30	N½SE	1857-04-01		A2 V3405, 3442
3427	" "	30	N½SW	1857-04-01		A2 F R3420
3428	" "	30	NW	1857-04-01		A2 F
3429	" "	30	S½NE	1857-04-01		A2 V3531, 3460
3438	SCHROETER, Christopher	7	NENW	1859-12-10		A2
3436	" "	17	S½NE	1860-02-01		A5
3437	" "	17	SENW	1860-02-01		A5
3433	SCOTT, Charles H	2	W½NW	1880-09-01		A6 F
3461	SENG, Herman	23	N½SW	1860-02-01		A5 G353
3462	" "	23	SWNW	1860-02-01		A5 G353
3520	SHAFFER, John	6	W½NW	1871-03-15		A6
3550	SHAFFNER, Richard	10	N½SW	1873-05-20		A6
3419	SINTZ, Anton	28	N½NE	1870-06-10		A6
3445	SLAGEL, Francis M	28	NESW	1880-09-01		A6
3446	" "	28	NWSE	1880-09-01		A6
3411	SLAGLE, Alonzo	18	E½SW	1878-06-24		A6
3495	SLAGLE, John H	18	W½SW	1873-12-20		A6 F
3532	SLAGLE, Leander	18	SENW	1873-12-20		A6
3533	" "	18	SWNE	1873-12-20		A6
3443	SMITH, Ephraim	26	S½NW	1869-09-01		A6
3485	SMITH, James W	28	E½SE	1880-09-01		A6
3569	SMITH, Sylvester	20	E½NW	1869-09-01		A6
3539	SWIGER, Nelson J	21	E½NE	1859-12-10		A2
3535	THOMPSON, Merrill C	18	W½SE	1873-12-20		A6
3606	THOMPSON, William	10	SWSE	1860-03-07		A2
3607	" "	10	E½SE	1860-03-10		A5 G397
3608	" "	10	NWSE	1860-03-10		A5 G397
3610	VOEGT, William	14	SWSW	1857-04-01		A2
3609	" "	14	E½SW	1857-10-30		A5
3611	WADE, William	2	W½SE	1873-04-01		A6
3402	WAINZIRL, Adolph	24	SW	1857-04-01		A2
3597	WATSON, William D	2	E½NW	1882-04-10		A6 F
3412	WEBER, Andrew	14	NWSW	1857-04-01		A2
3413	" "	14	W½NW	1857-10-30		A5
3472	WEBER, Jacob	23	E½NW	1859-05-02		A2
3473	" "	23	NWNW	1859-05-02		A2
3469	" "	14	E½NW	1859-12-20		A2
3470	" "	14	NE	1859-12-20		A2
3471	" "	14	SE	1859-12-20		A2
3454	WESTERMEYER, George	34	N½NW	1874-04-01		A6
3607	WILLIAMS, John H	10	E½SE	1860-03-10		A5 G397
3608	" "	10	NWSE	1860-03-10		A5 G397
3444	WILSON, Eugene M	31	N½NE	1860-03-07		A2
3522	WILSON, Jonathan	24	E½SE	1872-10-01		A6
3546	WILSON, Ralph	20	S½SE	1875-04-01		A6
3572	WILSON, Thomas B	12	NENW	1872-09-02		A2
3573	" "	12	NWNE	1872-09-02		A2
3568	WISCONSIN, State Of	16		1941-08-16		A3
3420	WOODS, Arthur	30	N½SW	1876-12-30		A6 F R3427
3534	ZIBBLE, Lewis D	4	SE	1876-05-15		A6

Patent Map

T26-N R14-W
4th PM - 1831 MN/WI Meridian

Map Group 21

Township Statistics

Parcels Mapped	:	212
Number of Patents	:	157
Number of Individuals	:	145
Patentees Identified	:	133
Number of Surnames	:	120
Multi-Patentee Parcels	:	20
Oldest Patent Date	:	10/2/1854
Most Recent Patent	:	8/16/1941
Block/Lot Parcels	:	0
Parcels Re - Issued	:	1
Parcels that Overlap	:	6
Cities and Towns	:	0
Cemeteries	:	2

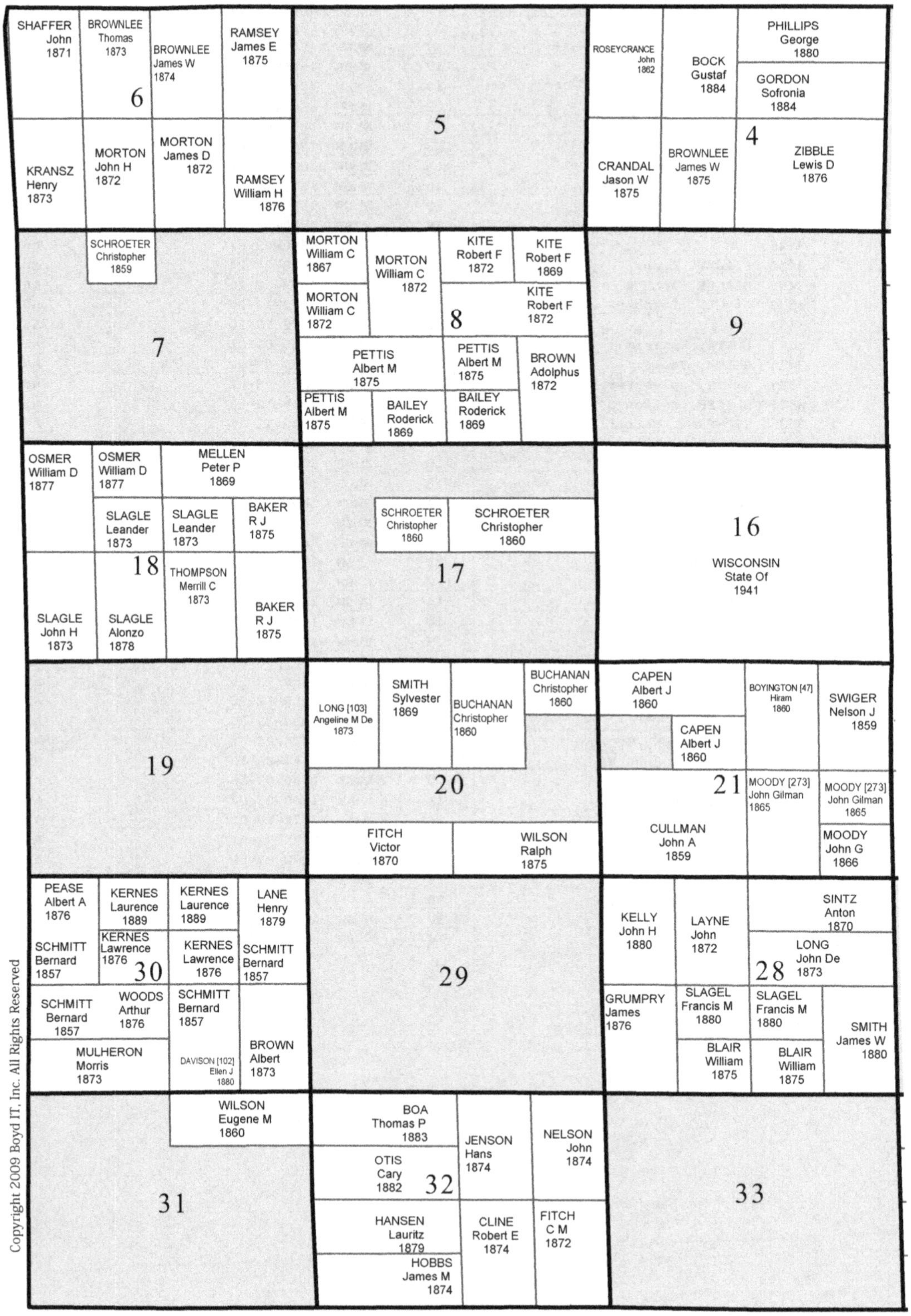

SHAFFER John 1871
BROWNLEE Thomas 1873
BROWNLEE James W 1874
RAMSEY James E 1875
6
KRANSZ Henry 1873
MORTON John H 1872
MORTON James D 1872
RAMSEY William H 1876
5
ROSEYCRANCE John 1862
BOCK Gustaf 1884
PHILLIPS George 1880
GORDON Sofronia 1884
CRANDAL Jason W 1875
BROWNLEE James W 1875
4
ZIBBLE Lewis D 1876
SCHROETER Christopher 1859
7
MORTON William C 1867
MORTON William C 1872
MORTON William C 1872
KITE Robert F 1872
KITE Robert F 1869
KITE Robert F 1872
8
PETTIS Albert M 1875
PETTIS Albert M 1875
BROWN Adolphus 1872
PETTIS Albert M 1875
BAILEY Roderick 1869
BAILEY Roderick 1869
9
OSMER William D 1877
OSMER William D 1877
MELLEN Peter P 1869
SLAGLE Leander 1873
SLAGLE Leander 1873
BAKER R J 1875
18
THOMPSON Merrill C 1873
SLAGLE John H 1873
SLAGLE Alonzo 1878
BAKER R J 1875
SCHROETER Christopher 1860
SCHROETER Christopher 1860
17
16
WISCONSIN State Of 1941
19
LONG [103] Angeline M De 1873
SMITH Sylvester 1869
BUCHANAN Christopher 1860
BUCHANAN Christopher 1860
20
FITCH Victor 1870
WILSON Ralph 1875
CAPEN Albert J 1860
CAPEN Albert J 1860
BOYINGTON [47] Hiram 1860
SWIGER Nelson J 1859
21
MOODY [273] John Gilman 1865
MOODY [273] John Gilman 1865
CULLMAN John A 1859
MOODY John G 1866
PEASE Albert A 1876
KERNES Laurence 1889
KERNES Laurence 1889
LANE Henry 1879
SCHMITT Bernard 1857
KERNES Lawrence 1876
30
KERNES Lawrence 1876
SCHMITT Bernard 1857
SCHMITT Bernard 1857
WOODS Arthur 1876
SCHMITT Bernard 1857
MULHERON Morris 1873
DAVISON [102] Ellen J 1880
BROWN Albert 1873
29
KELLY John H 1880
LAYNE John 1872
SINTZ Anton 1870
LONG John De 1873
28
GRUMPRY James 1876
SLAGEL Francis M 1880
SLAGEL Francis M 1880
SMITH James W 1880
BLAIR William 1875
BLAIR William 1875
WILSON Eugene M 1860
31
BOA Thomas P 1883
OTIS Cary 1882
32
JENSON Hans 1874
NELSON John 1874
HANSEN Lauritz 1879
HOBBS James M 1874
CLINE Robert E 1874
FITCH C M 1872
33

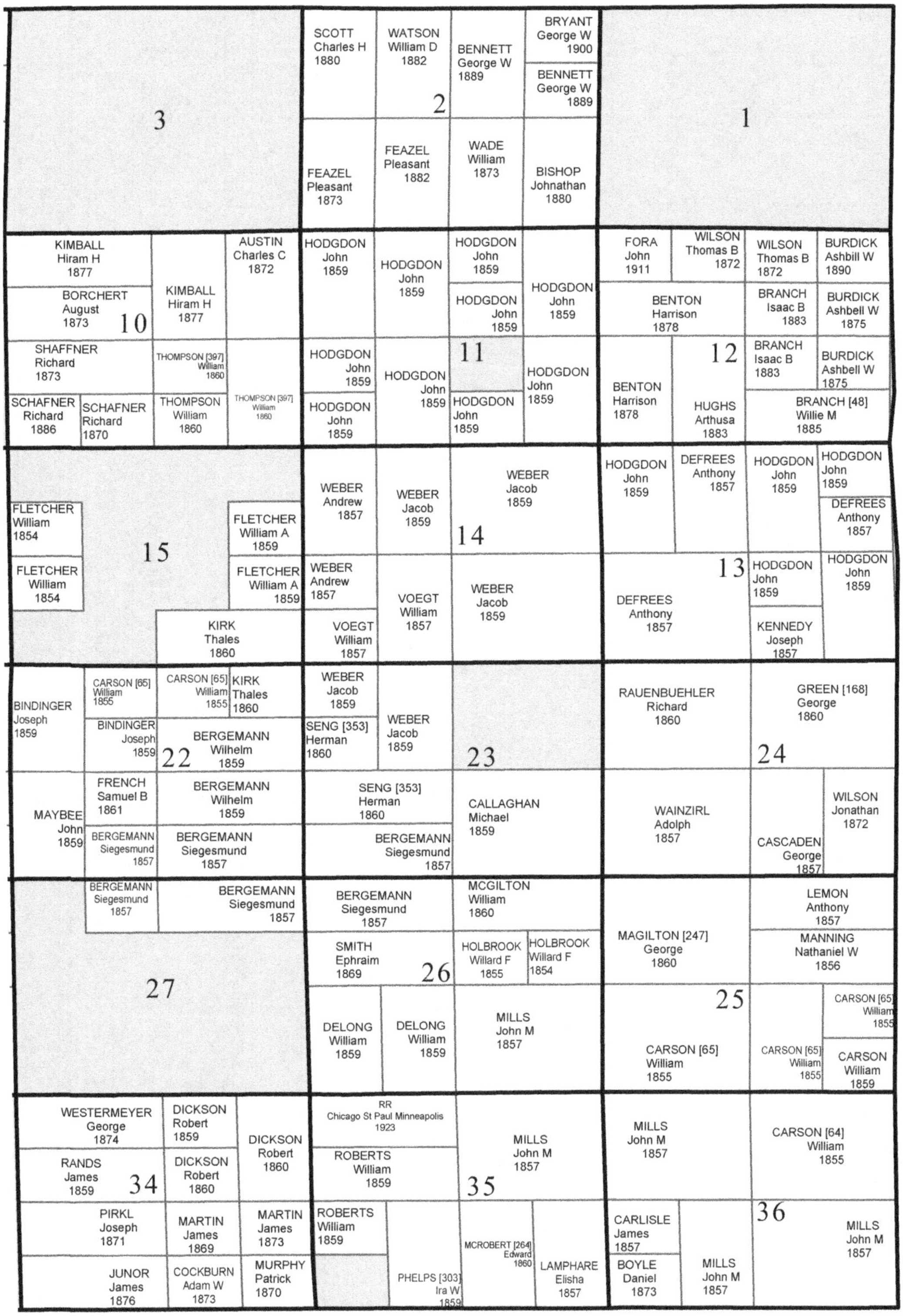
3
SCOTT Charles H 1880
WATSON William D 1882
BENNETT George W 1889
BRYANT George W 1900
BENNETT George W 1889
2
1
FEAZEL Pleasant 1873
FEAZEL Pleasant 1882
WADE William 1873
BISHOP Johnathan 1880
KIMBALL Hiram H 1877
AUSTIN Charles C 1872
BORCHERT August 1873
KIMBALL Hiram H 1877
10
SHAFFNER Richard 1873
THOMPSON [397] William 1860
SCHAFNER Richard 1886
SCHAFNER Richard 1870
THOMPSON William 1860
THOMPSON [397] William 1860
HODGDON John 1859
HODGDON John 1859
HODGDON John 1859
HODGDON John 1859
HODGDON John 1859
HODGDON John 1859
11
HODGDON John 1859
HODGDON John 1859
HODGDON John 1859
HODGDON John 1859
FORA John 1911
WILSON Thomas B 1872
WILSON Thomas B 1872
BURDICK Ashbill W 1890
BENTON Harrison 1878
BRANCH Isaac B 1883
BURDICK Ashbell W 1875
12
BRANCH Isaac B 1883
BURDICK Ashbell W 1875
BENTON Harrison 1878
HUGHS Arthusa 1883
BRANCH [48] Willie M 1885
FLETCHER William 1854
FLETCHER William A 1859
15
FLETCHER William 1854
FLETCHER William A 1859
KIRK Thales 1860
WEBER Andrew 1857
WEBER Jacob 1859
WEBER Jacob 1859
14
WEBER Andrew 1857
VOEGT William 1857
WEBER Jacob 1859
VOEGT William 1857
HODGDON John 1859
DEFREES Anthony 1857
HODGDON John 1859
HODGDON John 1859
DEFREES Anthony 1857
13
HODGDON John 1859
HODGDON John 1859
DEFREES Anthony 1857
KENNEDY Joseph 1857
BINDINGER Joseph 1859
CARSON [65] William 1855
CARSON [65] William 1855
KIRK Thales 1860
BINDINGER Joseph 1859
22
BERGEMANN Wilhelm 1859
FRENCH Samuel B 1861
BERGEMANN Wilhelm 1859
MAYBEE John 1859
BERGEMANN Siegesmund 1857
BERGEMANN Siegesmund 1857
WEBER Jacob 1859
SENG [353] Herman 1860
WEBER Jacob 1859
23
SENG [353] Herman 1860
CALLAGHAN Michael 1859
BERGEMANN Siegesmund 1857
RAUENBUEHLER Richard 1860
GREEN [168] George 1860
24
WAINZIRL Adolph 1857
WILSON Jonathan 1872
CASCADEN George 1857
BERGEMANN Siegesmund 1857
BERGEMANN Siegesmund 1857
27
BERGEMANN Siegesmund 1857
MCGILTON William 1860
SMITH Ephraim 1869
26
HOLBROOK Willard F 1855
HOLBROOK Willard F 1854
DELONG William 1859
DELONG William 1859
MILLS John M 1857
LEMON Anthony 1857
MAGILTON [247] George 1860
MANNING Nathaniel W 1856
25
CARSON [65] William 1855
CARSON [65] William 1855
CARSON [65] William 1855
CARSON William 1859
WESTERMEYER George 1874
DICKSON Robert 1859
DICKSON Robert 1860
RANDS James 1859
DICKSON Robert 1860
34
PIRKL Joseph 1871
MARTIN James 1869
MARTIN James 1873
JUNOR James 1876
COCKBURN Adam W 1873
MURPHY Patrick 1870
RR Chicago St Paul Minneapolis 1923
ROBERTS William 1859
MILLS John M 1857
35
ROBERTS William 1859
MCROBERT [264] Edward 1860
PHELPS [303] Ira W 1859
LAMPHARE Elisha 1857
MILLS John M 1857
CARSON [64] William 1855
CARLISLE James 1857
36
MILLS John M 1857
BOYLE Daniel 1873
MILLS John M 1857

Helpful Hints

1. This Map's INDEX can be found on the preceding pages.
2. Refer to Map "C" to see where this Township lies within Dunn County, Wisconsin.
3. Numbers within square brackets [ ] denote a multi-patentee land parcel (multi-owner). Refer to Appendix "C" for a full list of members in this group.
4. Areas that look to be crowded with Patentees usually indicate multiple sales of the same parcel (Re-issues) or Overlapping parcels. See this Township's Index for an explanation of these and other circumstances that might explain "odd" groupings of Patentees on this map.

Legend

- Patent Boundary
- Section Boundary
- No Patents Found (or Outside County)
- 1., 2., 3., ... Lot Numbers (when beside a name)
- [ ] Group Number (see Appendix "C")

Scale: Section = 1 mile X 1 mile (generally, with some exceptions)

Road Map

T26-N R14-W
4th PM - 1831 MN/WI Meridian

Map Group 21

Cities & Towns

None

Cemeteries

Saint Henrys Cemetery
Weber Valley Cemetery

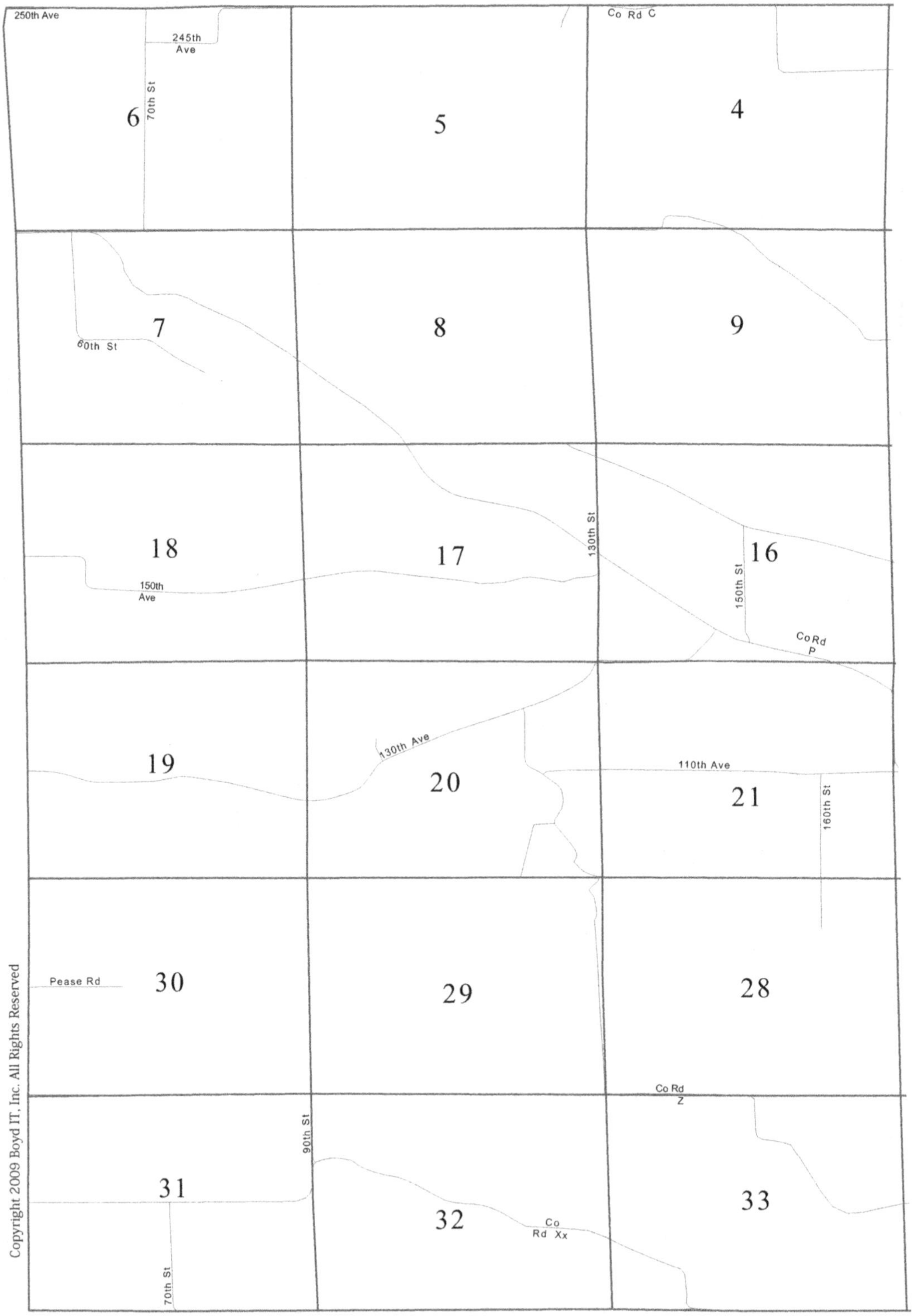

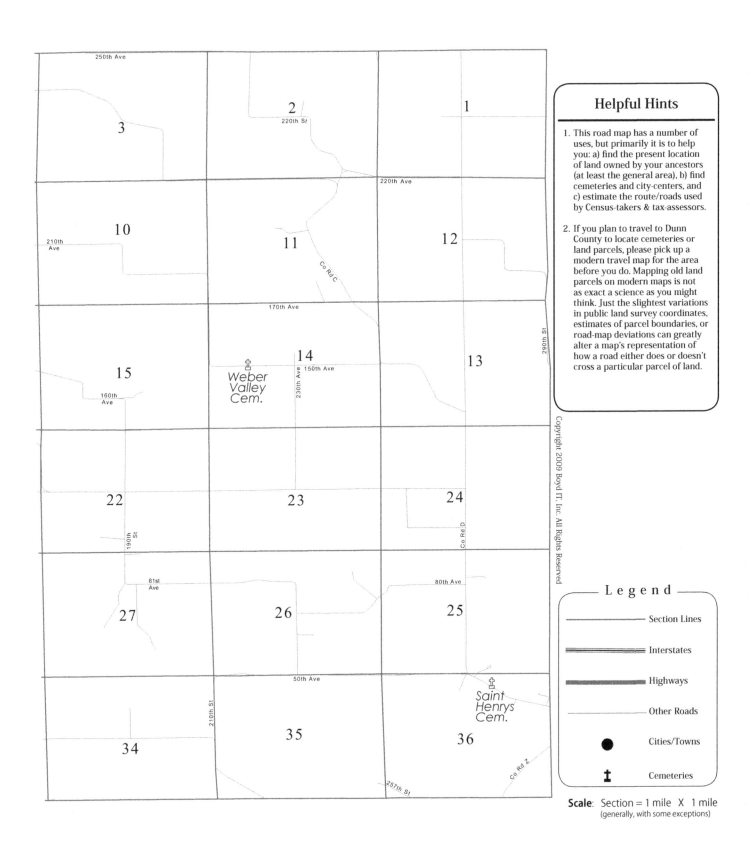

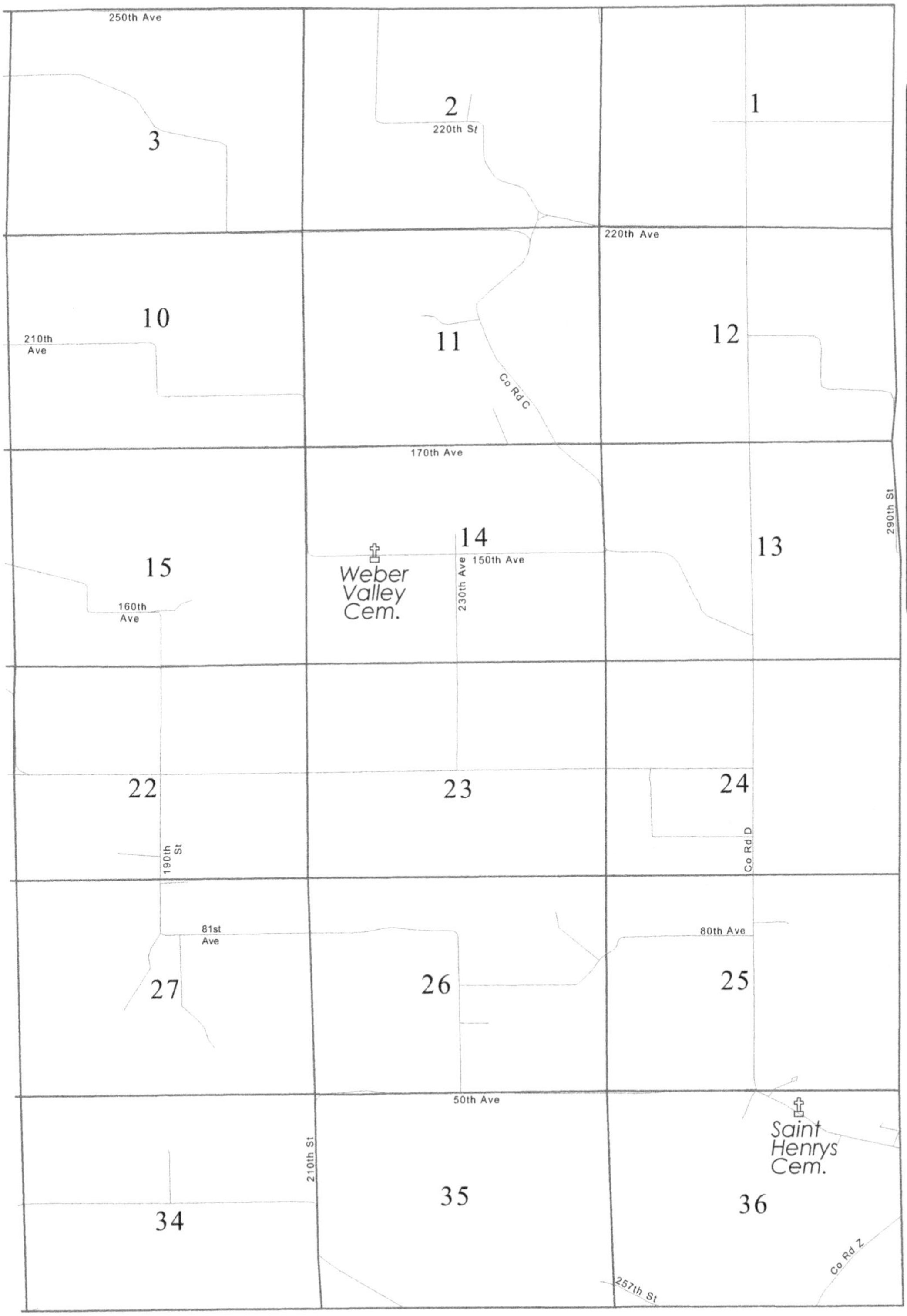

Helpful Hints

1. This road map has a number of uses, but primarily it is to help you: a) find the present location of land owned by your ancestors (at least the general area), b) find cemeteries and city-centers, and c) estimate the route/roads used by Census-takers & tax-assessors.

2. If you plan to travel to Dunn County to locate cemeteries or land parcels, please pick up a modern travel map for the area before you do. Mapping old land parcels on modern maps is not as exact a science as you might think. Just the slightest variations in public land survey coordinates, estimates of parcel boundaries, or road-map deviations can greatly alter a map's representation of how a road either does or doesn't cross a particular parcel of land.

Legend

- Section Lines
- Interstates
- Highways
- Other Roads
- Cities/Towns
- Cemeteries

Scale: Section = 1 mile X 1 mile
(generally, with some exceptions)

Historical Map

T26-N R14-W
4th PM - 1831 MN/WI Meridian

Map Group 21

Cities & Towns

None

Cemeteries

Saint Henrys Cemetery
Weber Valley Cemetery

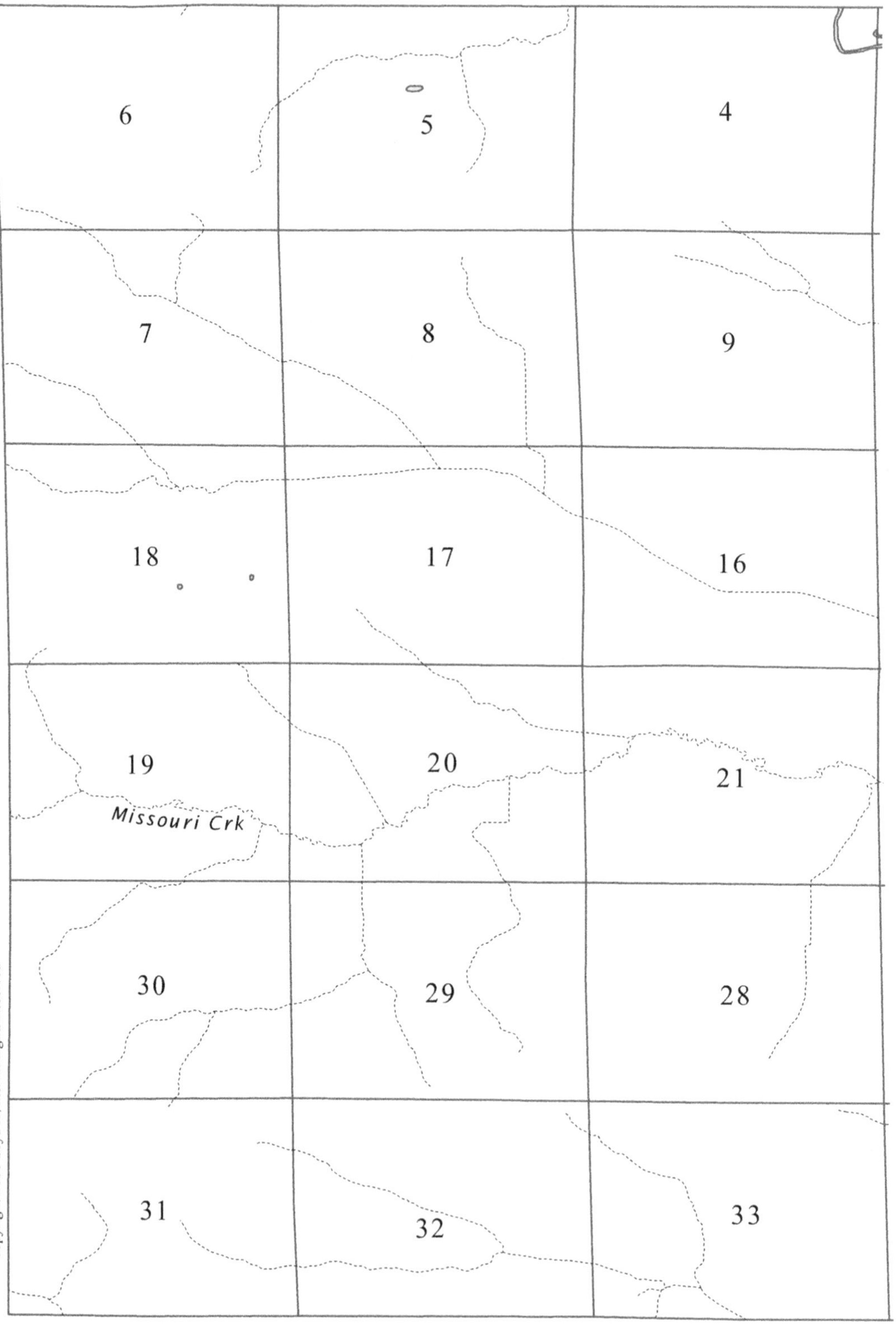

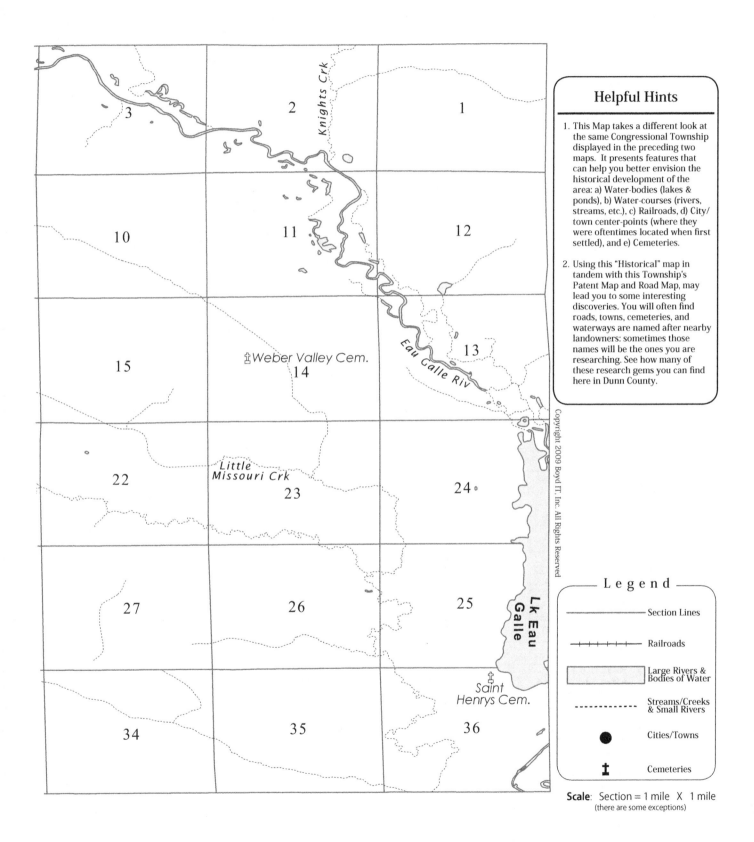

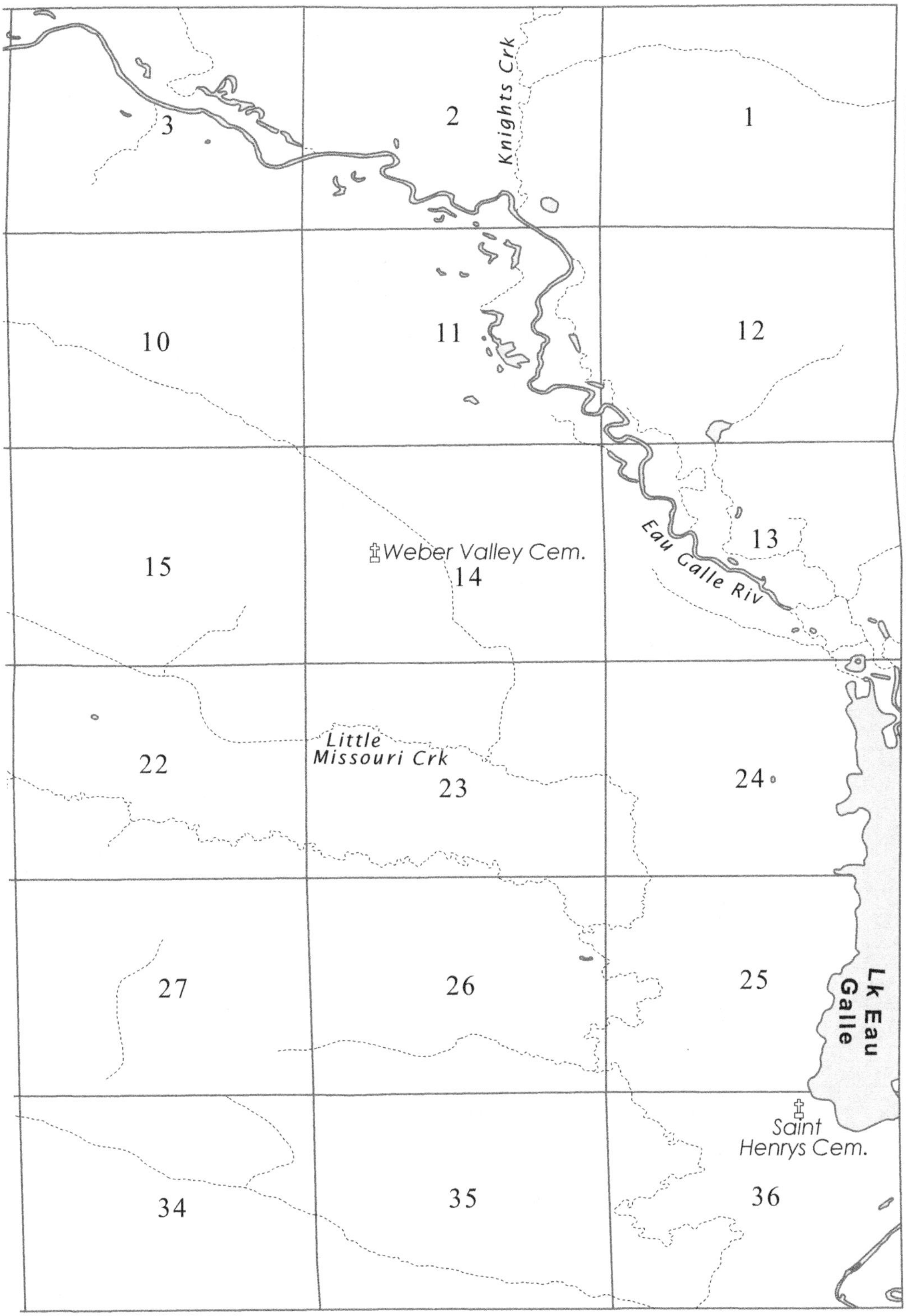

Helpful Hints

1. This Map takes a different look at the same Congressional Township displayed in the preceding two maps. It presents features that can help you better envision the historical development of the area: a) Water-bodies (lakes & ponds), b) Water-courses (rivers, streams, etc.), c) Railroads, d) City/town center-points (where they were oftentimes located when first settled), and e) Cemeteries.

2. Using this "Historical" map in tandem with this Township's Patent Map and Road Map, may lead you to some interesting discoveries. You will often find roads, towns, cemeteries, and waterways are named after nearby landowners: sometimes those names will be the ones you are researching. See how many of these research gems you can find here in Dunn County.

Legend

- Section Lines
- Railroads
- Large Rivers & Bodies of Water
- Streams/Creeks & Small Rivers
- Cities/Towns
- Cemeteries

Scale: Section = 1 mile X 1 mile
(there are some exceptions)

Map Group 22: Index to Land Patents

Township 26-North Range 13-West (4th PM - 1831 MN/WI)

After you locate an individual in this Index, take note of the Section and Section Part then proceed to the Land Patent map on the pages immediately following. You should have no difficulty locating the corresponding parcel of land.

The "For More Info" Column will lead you to more information about the underlying Patents. See the *Legend* at right, and the "How to Use this Book" chapter, for more information.

LEGEND

"For More Info . . . " column

A = Authority (Legislative Act, See Appendix "A")
B = Block or Lot (location in Section unknown)
C = Cancelled Patent
F = Fractional Section
G = Group (Multi-Patentee Patent, see Appendix "C")
V = Overlaps another Parcel
R = Re-Issued (Parcel patented more than once)

(A & G items require you to look in the Appendixes referred to above. All other Letter-designations followed by a number require you to locate line-items in this index that possess the ID number found after the letter).

ID	Individual in Patent	Sec.	Sec. Part	Date Issued	Other Counties	For More Info . . .
3866	ACKLEY, William J	15	NWSE	1860-02-01		A5
3867	" "	15	SENW	1860-02-01		A5
3868	" "	15	SWNE	1860-02-01		A5
3710	ADAMS, Isaac	4	W½NW	1873-05-20		A6 F
3729	AIKEN, John A	29	NW	1860-02-01		A5 G3
3841	ALLEN, Benjamin	23	SE	1855-06-15		A2 G129
3662	AMES, Benjamin K	18	W½SW	1855-12-15		A2 F
3663	AMES, Benjamin R	19	W½NW	1855-12-15		A2 F
3685	AMES, Franklin	34	SESE	1855-12-15		A2
3716	AMES, James F	27	N½SW	1855-12-15		A2
3717	" "	27	NWSE	1855-12-15		A2
3718	" "	27	S½NW	1855-12-15		A2
3719	" "	27	SWNE	1855-12-15		A2
3723	" "	33	NENE	1855-12-15		A2
3720	" "	27	SWSW	1856-06-03		A7
3715	" "	21	SWSE	1859-05-02		A2
3721	" "	28	SENE	1859-05-02		A2
3722	" "	28	W½NE	1859-05-02		A2
3768	AMES, Leonard	34	NWSE	1863-05-15		A2
3664	ANDERSON, Carlos	10	E½SE	1879-10-01		A6
3726	BARNARD, James M	21	E½NW	1860-10-01		A5
3727	" "	21	N½NE	1860-10-01		A5
3688	BASKIN, George	8	NWSW	1875-03-10		A2
3689	" "	8	SWSW	1890-03-29		A6
3690	BASKINS, George	8	E½SW	1869-09-01		A6
3824	BECKWITH, Seth S	15	NENW	1860-02-01		A5
3825	" "	15	W½NW	1860-02-01		A5
3698	BENTON, Heman A	20	E½NE	1876-12-30		A6
3789	BILLINGS, Charles	18	W½NW	1875-01-15		A6 G40 F
3789	BILLINGS, Mary	18	W½NW	1875-01-15		A6 G40 F
3684	BIRKEL, Frank J	18	NENE	1874-07-15		A6
3686	BOHN, Friedrick	6	SENW	1874-11-10		A6
3687	" "	6	SWNE	1874-11-10		A6
3673	BOWERS, Cyrus W	34	E½SW	1875-12-20		A6
3865	BOYLE, William H	34	NWNE	1878-11-30		A6
3699	BRAKER, Henry	6	E½NE	1873-12-20		A6
3786	BRECK, Martin B	12	NWSW	1860-10-01		A5
3787	" "	12	W½NW	1860-10-01		A5
3666	BRIDGHAM, Charles	30	NE	1859-12-20		A2
3709	BRIGHT, Hyda C	6	N½SE	1877-02-20		A6
3847	CANTRELL, William	2	3	1866-08-01		A5 G60
3848	" "	2	4	1866-08-01		A5 G60
3853	CARSON, William	28	SW	1855-04-19		A2 G63
3854	" "	29	SE	1855-04-19		A2 G63
3855	" "	32	NESE	1855-04-19		A2 G63
3856	" "	32	SENE	1855-04-19		A2 G63

ID	Individual in Patent	Sec.	Sec. Part	Date Issued	Other Counties	For More Info . . .
3857	CARSON, William (Cont'd)	33	NENW	1855-04-19		A2 G63
3858	" "	33	NWSW	1855-04-19		A2 G63
3859	" "	33	W½NE	1855-04-19		A2 G63
3860	" "	33	W½NW	1855-04-19		A2 G63
3851	" "	31	E½SE	1855-12-15		A2
3852	" "	32	W½SW	1855-12-15		A2
3862	" "	33	NWSE	1857-04-01		A2 G66
3849	" "	28	E½NW	1859-05-02		A2
3850	" "	30	W½SW	1860-10-01		A5 F
3861	" "	31	W½SW	1861-09-14		A2 G65 F
3757	CAVANAGH, John J	22	W½SW	1862-03-10		A5 G67
3697	CLAPP, Harvey S	26	NWSE	1862-01-20		A4 C
3642	COBURN, Amos	25	E½NW	1855-12-15		A2 G79
3643	COLBURN, Amos	24	1	1852-08-02		A2
3644	" "	24	6	1852-08-02		A2
3645	" "	24	7	1852-08-02		A2
3648	" "	25	NESW	1855-06-15		A2 G80
3649	" "	25	NWSE	1855-06-15		A2 G80
3650	" "	25	W½NE	1855-06-15		A2 G80
3646	" "	24	NWSW	1859-06-15		A2 G80
3647	" "	24	SESW	1859-06-15		A2 G80
3704	COPELAND, Howard	25	NWNW	1860-02-01		A5
3707	" "	26	E½NW	1860-02-01		A5 G86
3705	" "	26	E½SW	1860-02-01		A5
3706	" "	26	N½NE	1860-02-01		A5
3708	" "	26	SWNE	1860-02-01		A5 G86
3682	COVELL, Erastus M	6	N½NW	1873-04-01		A6 F
3621	CROPSEY, Alfred	29	SW	1857-04-01		A2
3762	CROSBY, John O	34	SWSW	1855-12-15		A2
3731	CUNNINGHAM, John	4	N½SE	1870-09-10		A6
3803	CUNNINGHAM, Richard	4	S½SE	1876-12-30		A6
3782	CURTIS, Jennett	12	E½SW	1860-02-01		A5 G262
3783	" "	12	SENW	1860-02-01		A5 G262
3784	" "	12	SWSW	1860-02-01		A5 G262
3652	DEFREES, Anthony	18	E½SW	1857-04-01		A2
3653	" "	18	NWSE	1857-04-01		A2
3654	" "	18	S½SE	1857-04-01		A2
3655	" "	18	SENW	1857-04-01		A2
3656	" "	18	SWNE	1857-04-01		A2
3657	" "	19	E½NW	1857-04-01		A2
3658	" "	19	N½SE	1857-04-01		A2
3659	" "	19	NE	1857-04-01		A2
3660	" "	19	NESW	1857-04-01		A2
3774	DELONG, Lias	30	E½SW	1859-12-10		A2
3667	DOEKENDORFF, Charles	24	E½NE	1859-05-02		A2
3668	" "	24	NWNE	1859-05-02		A2
3853	DOWNS, Burage B	28	SW	1855-04-19		A2 G63
3854	" "	29	SE	1855-04-19		A2 G63
3855	" "	32	NESE	1855-04-19		A2 G63
3856	" "	32	SENE	1855-04-19		A2 G63
3857	" "	33	NENW	1855-04-19		A2 G63
3858	" "	33	NWSW	1855-04-19		A2 G63
3859	" "	33	W½NE	1855-04-19		A2 G63
3860	" "	33	W½NW	1855-04-19		A2 G63
3862	DOWNS, Burrage B	33	NWSE	1857-04-01		A2 G66
3861	" "	31	W½SW	1861-09-14		A2 G65 F
3853	DOWNS, Eben	28	SW	1855-04-19		A2 G63
3854	" "	29	SE	1855-04-19		A2 G63
3855	" "	32	NESE	1855-04-19		A2 G63
3856	" "	32	SENE	1855-04-19		A2 G63
3857	" "	33	NENW	1855-04-19		A2 G63
3858	" "	33	NWSW	1855-04-19		A2 G63
3859	" "	33	W½NE	1855-04-19		A2 G63
3860	" "	33	W½NW	1855-04-19		A2 G63
3772	DRAKE, Levi P	15	SESW	1859-05-02		A2
3769	" "	15	E½NE	1860-02-01		A5
3770	" "	15	E½SE	1860-02-01		A5
3771	" "	15	NWNE	1860-02-01		A5
3773	" "	15	SWSE	1860-02-01		A5
3640	" "	19	S½SE	1860-02-01		A5 G299
3641	" "	20	SWSW	1860-02-01		A5 G299
3636	" "	21	E½SW	1860-02-01		A5 G165
3638	" "	21	NESE	1860-02-01		A5 G164

ID	Individual in Patent	Sec.	Sec. Part	Date Issued	Other Counties	For More Info . . .
3637	DRAKE, Levi P (Cont'd)	21	NWSE	1860-02-01		A5 G165
3639	" "	21	S½NE	1860-02-01		A5 G164
3729	" "	29	NW	1860-02-01		A5 G3
3730	EARGOOD, John C	14	NWSW	1891-11-03		A2
3676	EATON, Delos W	6	NWNE	1882-06-30		A6 F
3700	EATON, Henry	31	NW	1852-08-02		A2
3853	" "	28	SW	1855-04-19		A2 G63
3854	" "	29	SE	1855-04-19		A2 G63
3855	" "	32	NESE	1855-04-19		A2 G63
3856	" "	32	SENE	1855-04-19		A2 G63
3857	" "	33	NENW	1855-04-19		A2 G63
3858	" "	33	NWSW	1855-04-19		A2 G63
3859	" "	33	W½NE	1855-04-19		A2 G63
3860	" "	33	W½NW	1855-04-19		A2 G63
3862	" "	33	NWSE	1857-04-01		A2 G66
3861	" "	31	W½SW	1861-09-14		A2 G65 F
3808	FALTENBERY, Rodolph	10	S½NW	1883-07-10		A6
3681	FAYERWEATHER, David C	4	SENW	1871-04-20		A6 G128
3681	FAYERWEATHER, Eliza	4	SENW	1871-04-20		A6 G128
3864	FHUHRER, William	10	W½SE	1870-06-10		A6
3841	FIELDS, Truman	23	SE	1855-06-15		A2 G129
3648	FISK, James D	25	NESW	1855-06-15		A2 G80
3649	" "	25	NWSE	1855-06-15		A2 G80
3650	" "	25	W½NE	1855-06-15		A2 G80
3642	" "	25	E½NW	1855-12-15		A2 G79
3646	" "	24	NWSW	1859-06-15		A2 G80
3647	" "	24	SESW	1859-06-15		A2 G80
3781	FITCH, Lyman	31	E½SW	1866-04-20		A5 G131
3777	" "	34	E½NW	1871-06-14		A2
3778	" "	34	NWNW	1871-06-14		A2
3780	" "	34	SWNE	1871-06-14		A2
3779	" "	34	SENE	1894-09-28		A6
3671	FRANK, Charlie	10	N½NW	1898-04-25		A6
3810	FRENCH, Samuel B	12	SESE	1857-10-30		A5
3811	" "	12	W½SE	1857-10-30		A5
3775	FUHLROTT, Louis	25	SWSE	1859-12-10		A2
3776	" "	36	1	1859-12-10		A2
3732	GANE, John	33	NESW	1854-07-05		A7
3733	" "	33	SENW	1854-07-05		A7
3834	GARDNER, Thomas B	19	W½SW	1859-12-20		A2
3835	" "	30	SENW	1912-11-11		A2
3796	GENTRY, William E	32	E½NW	1860-10-01		A5 G178
3797	" "	32	SWNW	1860-10-01		A5 G178
3794	GIBSON, Moses S	34	NENE	1857-04-01		A2
3792	" "	27	S½SE	1859-09-01		A5
3793	" "	27	SESW	1859-09-01		A5
3796	GLENN, Thomas M	32	E½NW	1860-10-01		A5 G178
3797	" "	32	SWNW	1860-10-01		A5 G178
3734	GOBEL, John	35	1	1860-03-10		A5 G157
3735	" "	35	NENE	1860-03-10		A5 G157
3736	" "	36	3	1860-03-10		A5 G157
3629	GOSS, Alfred	27	NESE	1858-02-20		A7
3630	" "	30	NENW	1858-02-20		A7
3622	" "	10	S½SW	1860-02-01		A5
3623	" "	15	NESW	1860-02-01		A5
3624	" "	15	W½SW	1860-02-01		A5
3625	" "	17	E½NW	1860-02-01		A5
3626	" "	17	N½SW	1860-02-01		A5
3627	" "	20	NWSW	1860-02-01		A5
3631	" "	20	S½SE	1860-02-01		A5 G162
3628	" "	20	W½NW	1860-02-01		A5
3633	" "	26	W½NW	1860-02-01		A5 G161
3634	" "	26	W½SW	1860-02-01		A5 G161
3632	" "	29	NWNE	1860-02-01		A5 G162
3788	GRANGER, Martin	6	W½SW	1883-07-10		A6 F
3636	GRAY, Almon D	21	E½SW	1860-02-01		A5 G165
3638	" "	21	NESE	1860-02-01		A5 G164
3637	" "	21	NWSE	1860-02-01		A5 G165
3639	" "	21	S½NE	1860-02-01		A5 G164
3683	GREEN, Erastus T	4	S½SW	1879-11-10		A6
3618	GRIPPEN, Alexander W	17	SWNW	1860-02-01		A5
3619	" "	18	NESE	1860-02-01		A5
3620	" "	18	SENE	1860-02-01		A5

ID	Individual in Patent	Sec.	Sec. Part	Date Issued	Other Counties	For More Info . . .
3694	HANNEMEYER, George	14	SWNW	1865-05-05		A2
3796	HARRIGAN, Patrick	32	E½NW	1860-10-01		A5 G178
3797	" "	32	SWNW	1860-10-01		A5 G178
3795	" "	32	NWNW	1860-10-03		A7
3674	HARTKOPP, Daniel	10	8	1857-04-01		A2
3675	" "	3	2	1857-04-01		A2
3711	HERMANN, Jacob	11	7	1874-05-06		A2
3712	" "	11	8	1874-05-06		A2
3713	" "	11	SWNW	1874-05-06		A2
3636	HOBBS, James H	21	E½SW	1860-02-01		A5 G165
3637	" "	21	NWSE	1860-02-01		A5 G165
3822	HOLBROOK, Schuyler	33	SWSW	1855-12-15		A2
3823	" "	34	NESE	1857-04-01		A2
3821	" "	33	SESW	1859-05-02		A2
3842	HOLBROOK, Willard F	33	NESE	1857-04-01		A2
3843	" "	33	SENE	1857-04-01		A2
3844	" "	34	NWSW	1857-04-01		A2
3845	" "	34	SWNW	1857-04-01		A2
3827	HOLMAN, Squire	32	NENE	1854-10-02		A2
3828	" "	32	NWNE	1854-10-02		A2
3665	HUG, Casper	10	N½SW	1870-06-10		A6
3701	HUMPHREY, Horace	8	NW	1859-05-02		A2 G195
3702	" "	8	S½NE	1859-05-02		A2 G195
3701	HUMPHREY, Riley	8	NW	1859-05-02		A2 G195
3702	" "	8	S½NE	1859-05-02		A2 G195
3847	JOHNSTON, Margaret M	2	3	1866-08-01		A5 G60
3848	" "	2	4	1866-08-01		A5 G60
3874	JORDAN, Hannah	21	SESE	1859-09-10		A5 G368
3875	" "	27	N½NW	1859-09-10		A5 G368
3876	" "	28	NENE	1859-09-10		A5 G368
3725	KEEFE, James	25	SWNW	1860-03-07		A2
3758	KENT, John	31	W½SE	1859-05-02		A2
3714	KIRSCHER, Jacob L	6	S½SE	1883-02-10		A6
3740	KNAPP, John H	24	2	1854-07-05		A7
3756	" "	24	5	1854-07-05		A7 G217
3737	" "	13	1	1854-10-02		A2
3738	" "	13	2	1854-10-02		A2
3739	" "	13	3	1854-10-02		A2
3741	" "	24	3	1854-10-02		A2
3742	" "	24	4	1854-10-02		A2
3743	" "	24	8	1855-12-15		A2
3744	" "	11	1	1857-04-01		A2 G219
3745	" "	11	10	1857-04-01		A2 G219
3746	" "	11	11	1857-04-01		A2 G219
3747	" "	11	2	1857-04-01		A2 G219
3748	" "	11	3	1857-04-01		A2 G219
3749	" "	11	9	1857-04-01		A2 G219
3750	" "	14	3	1857-04-01		A2 G219
3751	" "	14	4	1857-04-01		A2 G219
3752	" "	14	5	1857-04-01		A2 G219
3753	" "	14	6	1857-04-01		A2 G219
3754	" "	2	6	1862-04-10		A2 G219
3755	" "	2	7	1862-04-10		A2 G219
3815	KYLE, Samuel	1	S½SW	1855-12-15		A2
3820	" "	2	SE	1855-12-15		A2
3818	" "	2	1	1859-05-02		A2
3819	" "	2	2	1859-05-02		A2
3816	" "	11	5	1860-03-01		A2
3817	" "	11	6	1860-03-01		A2
3800	LARSON, Peter	20	W½NE	1876-08-23		A6
3661	LEMON, Anthony	32	S½SE	1856-06-16		A7
3804	LOW, Richard F	12	NESE	1857-04-01		A2
3805	" "	12	S½NE	1857-04-01		A2
3759	MACAULAY, John	2	5	1855-12-15		A2
3760	" "	2	SWNE	1855-12-15		A2
3806	MACAULEY, Robert	36	2	1859-09-10		A5
3807	" "	36	N½NW	1859-09-10		A5
3728	MALONEY, James	22	NW	1861-07-01		A5
3847	MANLEY, Reuben	2	3	1866-08-01		A5 G60
3848	" "	2	4	1866-08-01		A5 G60
3801	MANS, Fritz	34	SWSE	1866-10-10		A2 G351
3846	MARR, William B	8	N½NE	1859-05-02		A2
3761	MCAULEY, John	2	E½NE	1856-04-01		A2

ID	Individual in Patent	Sec.	Sec. Part	Date Issued	Other Counties	For More Info . . .
3871	MCBRIDE, Mary	4	NENE	1860-02-01		A5 G367
3872	" "	4	S½NE	1860-02-01		A5 G367
3651	MCCORKLE, Andrew	25	E½NE	1857-10-30		A5 G258
3782	MCLAIN, Malcolm	12	E½SW	1860-02-01		A5 G262
3783	" "	12	SENW	1860-02-01		A5 G262
3784	" "	12	SWSW	1860-02-01		A5 G262
3799	MCMILLAN, Anna	23	E½SW	1911-10-26		A7 G318
3799	MCMILLAN, Daniel A	23	E½SW	1911-10-26		A7 G318
3799	MCMILLAN, Elizabeth	23	E½SW	1911-10-26		A7 G318
3799	MCMILLAN, Martha H	23	E½SW	1911-10-26		A7 G318
3799	MCMILLAN, Mary Ann	23	E½SW	1911-10-26		A7 G318
3799	MCMILLAN, Nancy	23	E½SW	1911-10-26		A7 G318
3799	MCMILLAN, Rachael F	23	E½SW	1911-10-26		A7 G318
3799	MCMILLAN, Robert T	23	E½SW	1911-10-26		A7 G318
3799	MCMILLAN, William L	23	E½SW	1911-10-26		A7 G318
3757	MONTGOMERY, Margery	22	W½SW	1862-03-10		A5 G67
3830	MORFEY, Stephen	12	NENE	1884-01-15		A2
3677	MORRISON, Dorilus	14	1	1854-10-02		A2
3678	" "	14	2	1854-10-02		A2
3679	" "	14	8	1854-10-02		A2
3840	MYERS, Tinkey C	20	E½SW	1874-07-15		A6
3791	NULPH, Moses	8	N½SE	1876-08-23		A6
3757	NYE, William H	22	W½SW	1862-03-10		A5 G67
3633	PAINE, Rachel	26	W½NW	1860-02-01		A5 G161
3634	" "	26	W½SW	1860-02-01		A5 G161
3640	PENNOCK, Ames C	19	S½SE	1860-02-01		A5 G299
3641	" "	20	SWSW	1860-02-01		A5 G299
3767	PICKERING, Joseph	6	E½SW	1882-06-01		A6
3734	POTE, Lovell	35	1	1860-03-10		A5 G157
3735	" "	35	NENE	1860-03-10		A5 G157
3736	" "	36	3	1860-03-10		A5 G157
3756	POTETE, Isabella	24	5	1854-07-05		A7 G217
3651	PYE, Sarah	25	E½NE	1857-10-30		A5 G258
3861	RAND, Eldridge D	31	W½SW	1861-09-14		A2 G65 F
3862	RAND, Eldrige D	33	NWSE	1857-04-01		A2 G66
3799	RAYBURN, Patrick	23	E½SW	1911-10-26		A7 G318
3798	" "	23	W½SW	1911-10-26		A5 G319
3781	REYNOLDS, John L	31	E½SW	1866-04-20		A5 G131
3672	RIPLEY, Christopher Gore	31	NE	1859-09-01		A5
3869	RISS, William	3	NW	1860-02-01		A5
3631	SANGER, Elizabeth	20	S½SE	1860-02-01		A5 G162
3632	" "	29	NWNE	1860-02-01		A5 G162
3801	SCHECKEL, Philip	34	SWSE	1866-10-10		A2 G351
3763	SCHMITT, John P	20	N½SE	1894-03-20		A6
3670	SEGUR, Charles W	28	W½NW	1873-09-20		A6
3696	SEILER, Gottlieb	10	S½NE	1896-02-29		A6
3669	SMITH, Charles	23	NE	1860-10-01		A5
3764	SMITH, John	14	NENE	1873-12-20		A6
3870	SMITH, William	4	NWNE	1859-12-10		A2
3871	" "	4	NENE	1860-02-01		A5 G367
3872	" "	4	S½NE	1860-02-01		A5 G367
3874	SNELL, Zachariah	21	SESE	1859-09-10		A5 G368
3875	" "	27	N½NW	1859-09-10		A5 G368
3876	" "	28	NENE	1859-09-10		A5 G368
3707	SPALDING, Mary	26	E½NW	1860-02-01		A5 G86
3708	" "	26	SWNE	1860-02-01		A5 G86
3691	STARKWEATHER, George F	26	E½SE	1859-09-01		A5
3692	" "	26	SWSE	1859-09-01		A5
3693	" "	35	2	1859-09-01		A5
3798	STINSON, Sarah Ann	23	W½SW	1911-10-26		A5 G319
3744	STOUT, Henry L	11	1	1857-04-01		A2 G219
3745	" "	11	10	1857-04-01		A2 G219
3746	" "	11	11	1857-04-01		A2 G219
3747	" "	11	2	1857-04-01		A2 G219
3748	" "	11	3	1857-04-01		A2 G219
3749	" "	11	9	1857-04-01		A2 G219
3750	" "	14	3	1857-04-01		A2 G219
3751	" "	14	4	1857-04-01		A2 G219
3752	" "	14	5	1857-04-01		A2 G219
3753	" "	14	6	1857-04-01		A2 G219
3754	" "	2	6	1862-04-10		A2 G219
3755	" "	2	7	1862-04-10		A2 G219
3873	SUNDERLIN, William	10	N½NE	1869-09-01		A6

ID	Individual in Patent	Sec.	Sec. Part	Date Issued	Other Counties	For More Info . . .
3744	TAINTER, Andrew	11	1	1857-04-01		A2 G219
3745	" "	11	10	1857-04-01		A2 G219
3746	" "	11	11	1857-04-01		A2 G219
3747	" "	11	2	1857-04-01		A2 G219
3748	" "	11	3	1857-04-01		A2 G219
3749	" "	11	9	1857-04-01		A2 G219
3750	" "	14	3	1857-04-01		A2 G219
3751	" "	14	4	1857-04-01		A2 G219
3752	" "	14	5	1857-04-01		A2 G219
3753	" "	14	6	1857-04-01		A2 G219
3754	" "	2	6	1862-04-10		A2 G219
3755	" "	2	7	1862-04-10		A2 G219
3680	THOMPSON, Ebenezer	3	1	1855-12-15		A2
3809	THOMPSON, Royal	30	SE	1860-02-01		A5
3831	TIBBETTS, Stephen	2	9	1857-04-01		A2
3832	" "	3	SE	1860-02-01		A5
3635	TIMMERMAN, Alfred	20	E½NW	1873-05-20		A6
3617	TOTMAN, Alexander	28	SE	1860-02-01		A5
3785	TURNER, Manoah	8	S½SE	1876-12-30		A6
3826	TURNER, Sion	4	NENW	1880-09-01		A6 F
3695	VAN ALLEN, GEORGE	4	N½SW	1882-04-10		A6
3613	VASEY, Aaron	1	NE	1857-04-01		A2
3614	" "	6	SWNW	1857-04-01		A2
3863	WADE, William E	5	SE	1859-05-02		A2
3813	WALKER, Samuel H	1	N½SW	1855-12-15		A2
3814	" "	1	NW	1855-12-15		A2
3812	WASHBURNE, Samuel B	27	E½NE	1859-09-01		A5
3615	WEBB, Albert	18	NENW	1880-09-01		A6
3616	" "	18	NWNE	1880-09-01		A6
3724	WEBB, James K	32	E½SW	1862-12-01		A5
3802	WELCH, Pliney	30	W½NW	1884-01-15		A6
3766	WILLEY, John	33	SESE	1855-12-15		A2
3837	WILSON, Thomas B	12	NENW	1855-12-15		A2
3838	" "	12	NWNE	1855-12-15		A2
3839	" "	24	SWSW	1855-12-15		A2
3744	" "	11	1	1857-04-01		A2 G219
3745	" "	11	10	1857-04-01		A2 G219
3746	" "	11	11	1857-04-01		A2 G219
3747	" "	11	2	1857-04-01		A2 G219
3748	" "	11	3	1857-04-01		A2 G219
3749	" "	11	9	1857-04-01		A2 G219
3750	" "	14	3	1857-04-01		A2 G219
3751	" "	14	4	1857-04-01		A2 G219
3752	" "	14	5	1857-04-01		A2 G219
3753	" "	14	6	1857-04-01		A2 G219
3836	" "	1	SE	1857-10-30		A5
3754	" "	2	6	1862-04-10		A2 G219
3755	" "	2	7	1862-04-10		A2 G219
3829	WISCONSIN, State Of	16		1941-08-16		A3
3765	WOODHOUSE, John V	23	NW	1861-10-05		A5
3703	WOODMAN, Horatio	25	SESW	1858-02-20		A7
3790	WOODWARD, Mary N	25	E½SE	1857-10-30		A5
3833	WOODWORTH, Stephen	22	E½SW	1870-06-10		A6

Patent Map

T26-N R13-W
4th PM - 1831 MN/WI Meridian

Map Group 22

Township Statistics

Parcels Mapped :	264
Number of Patents :	173
Number of Individuals :	164
Patentees Identified :	138
Number of Surnames :	138
Multi-Patentee Parcels :	68
Oldest Patent Date :	8/2/1852
Most Recent Patent :	8/16/1941
Block/Lot Parcels :	44
Parcels Re - Issued :	0
Parcels that Overlap :	0
Cities and Towns :	3
Cemeteries :	4

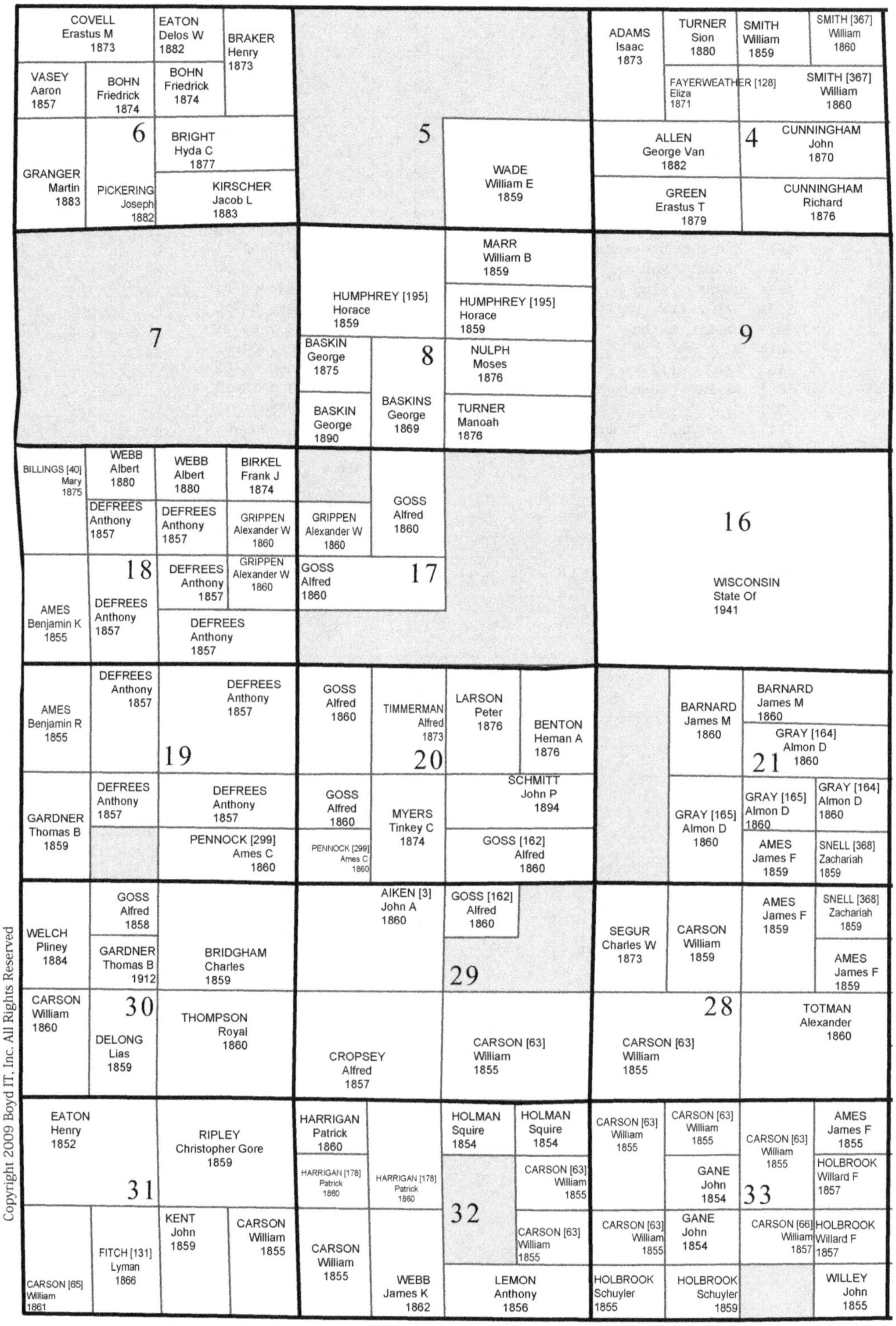

COVELL Erastus M 1873
EATON Delos W 1882
BRAKER Henry 1873
VASEY Aaron 1857
BOHN Friedrick 1874
BOHN Friedrick 1874
6
BRIGHT Hyda C 1877
GRANGER Martin 1883
PICKERING Joseph 1882
KIRSCHER Jacob L 1883
5
WADE William E 1859
ADAMS Isaac 1873
TURNER Sion 1880
SMITH William 1859
SMITH [367] William 1860
FAYERWEATHER [128] Eliza 1871
SMITH [367] William 1860
ALLEN George Van 1882
4
CUNNINGHAM John 1870
GREEN Erastus T 1879
CUNNINGHAM Richard 1876
7
MARR William B 1859
HUMPHREY [195] Horace 1859
HUMPHREY [195] Horace 1859
BASKIN George 1875
8
NULPH Moses 1876
BASKIN George 1890
BASKINS George 1869
TURNER Manoah 1876
9
BILLINGS [40] Mary 1875
WEBB Albert 1880
WEBB Albert 1880
BIRKEL Frank J 1874
DEFREES Anthony 1857
DEFREES Anthony 1857
GRIPPEN Alexander W 1860
GRIPPEN Alexander W 1860
GOSS Alfred 1860
16
18
DEFREES Anthony 1857
GRIPPEN Alexander W 1860
GOSS Alfred 1860
17
WISCONSIN State Of 1941
AMES Benjamin K 1855
DEFREES Anthony 1857
DEFREES Anthony 1857
DEFREES Anthony 1857
AMES Benjamin R 1855
DEFREES Anthony 1857
19
GOSS Alfred 1860
TIMMERMAN Alfred 1873
20
LARSON Peter 1876
BENTON Heman A 1876
BARNARD James M 1860
BARNARD James M 1860
GRAY [164] Almon D 1860
21
GARDNER Thomas B 1859
DEFREES Anthony 1857
DEFREES Anthony 1857
PENNOCK [299] Ames C 1860
GOSS Alfred 1860
PENNOCK [299] Ames C 1860
MYERS Tinkey C 1874
SCHMITT John P 1894
GOSS [162] Alfred 1860
GRAY [165] Almon D 1860
GRAY [165] Almon D 1860
GRAY [164] Almon D 1860
AMES James F 1859
SNELL [368] Zachariah 1859
WELCH Pliney 1884
GOSS Alfred 1858
GARDNER Thomas B 1912
BRIDGHAM Charles 1859
AIKEN [3] John A 1860
GOSS [162] Alfred 1860
29
SEGUR Charles W 1873
CARSON William 1859
AMES James F 1859
SNELL [368] Zachariah 1859
AMES James F 1859
CARSON William 1860
30
DELONG Lias 1859
THOMPSON Royal 1860
CROPSEY Alfred 1857
CARSON [63] William 1855
28
CARSON [63] William 1855
TOTMAN Alexander 1860
EATON Henry 1852
RIPLEY Christopher Gore 1859
31
HARRIGAN Patrick 1860
HARRIGAN [178] Patrick 1860
HARRIGAN [178] Patrick 1860
HOLMAN Squire 1854
HOLMAN Squire 1854
CARSON [63] William 1855
32
CARSON [63] William 1855
CARSON [63] William 1855
CARSON [63] William 1855
CARSON [63] William 1855
AMES James F 1855
GANE John 1854
33
HOLBROOK Willard F 1857
KENT John 1859
CARSON William 1855
FITCH [131] Lyman 1866
CARSON [65] William 1861
CARSON William 1855
WEBB James K 1862
LEMON Anthony 1856
CARSON [63] William 1855
GANE John 1854
CARSON [66] William 1857
HOLBROOK Willard F 1857
HOLBROOK Schuyler 1855
HOLBROOK Schuyler 1859
WILLEY John 1855

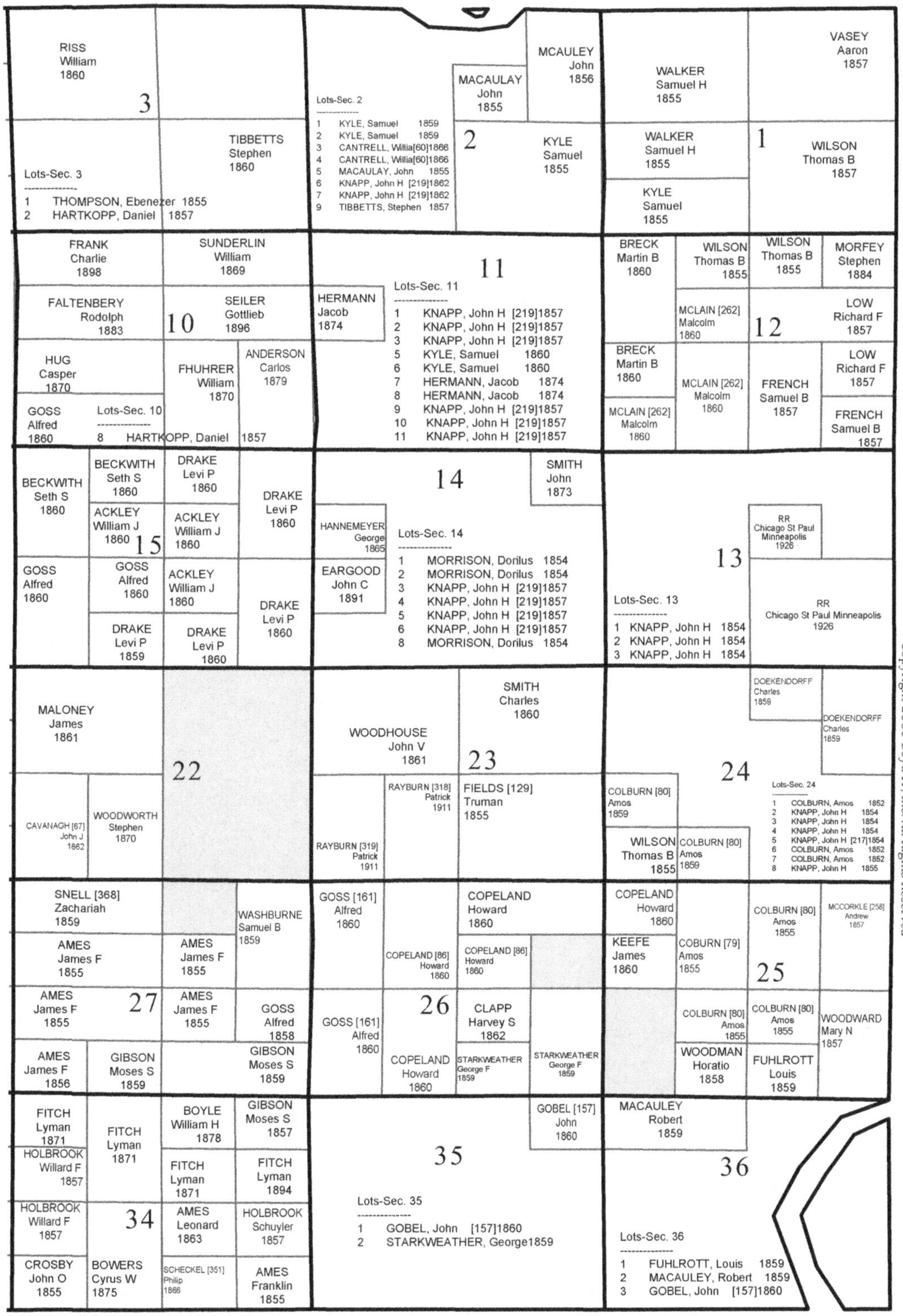

RISS William 1860
3
TIBBETTS Stephen 1860
Lots-Sec. 3
1 THOMPSON, Ebenezer 1855
2 HARTKOPP, Daniel 1857
MACAULAY John 1855
MCAULEY John 1856
Lots-Sec. 2
1 KYLE, Samuel 1859
2 KYLE, Samuel 1859
3 CANTRELL, Willia[60]1866
4 CANTRELL, Willia[60]1866
5 MACAULAY, John 1855
6 KNAPP, John H [219]1862
7 KNAPP, John H [219]1862
9 TIBBETTS, Stephen 1857
2
KYLE Samuel 1855
WALKER Samuel H 1855
VASEY Aaron 1857
WALKER Samuel H 1855
1
WILSON Thomas B 1857
KYLE Samuel 1855
FRANK Charlie 1898
SUNDERLIN William 1869
FALTENBERY Rodolph 1883
SEILER Gottlieb 1896
10
HUG Casper 1870
FHUHRER William 1870
ANDERSON Carlos 1879
GOSS Alfred 1860
Lots-Sec. 10
8 HARTKOPP, Daniel 1857
11
HERMANN Jacob 1874
Lots-Sec. 11
1 KNAPP, John H [219]1857
2 KNAPP, John H [219]1857
3 KNAPP, John H [219]1857
5 KYLE, Samuel 1860
6 KYLE, Samuel 1860
7 HERMANN, Jacob 1874
8 HERMANN, Jacob 1874
9 KNAPP, John H [219]1857
10 KNAPP, John H [219]1857
11 KNAPP, John H [219]1857
BRECK Martin B 1860
WILSON Thomas B 1855
WILSON Thomas B 1855
MORFEY Stephen 1884
MCLAIN [262] Malcolm 1860
12
LOW Richard F 1857
BRECK Martin B 1860
MCLAIN [262] Malcolm 1860
FRENCH Samuel B 1857
LOW Richard F 1857
MCLAIN [262] Malcolm 1860
FRENCH Samuel B 1857
BECKWITH Seth S 1860
BECKWITH Seth S 1860
DRAKE Levi P 1860
DRAKE Levi P 1860
ACKLEY William J 1860
ACKLEY William J 1860
15
GOSS Alfred 1860
GOSS Alfred 1860
ACKLEY William J 1860
DRAKE Levi P 1860
DRAKE Levi P 1859
DRAKE Levi P 1860
14
SMITH John 1873
HANNEMEYER George 1865
Lots-Sec. 14
EARGOOD John C 1891
1 MORRISON, Dorilus 1854
2 MORRISON, Dorilus 1854
3 KNAPP, John H [219]1857
4 KNAPP, John H [219]1857
5 KNAPP, John H [219]1857
6 KNAPP, John H [219]1857
8 MORRISON, Dorilus 1854
RR Chicago St Paul Minneapolis 1926
13
Lots-Sec. 13
1 KNAPP, John H 1854
2 KNAPP, John H 1854
3 KNAPP, John H 1854
RR Chicago St Paul Minneapolis 1926
MALONEY James 1861
22
CAVANAGH [67] John J 1862
WOODWORTH Stephen 1870
WOODHOUSE John V 1861
SMITH Charles 1860
23
RAYBURN [318] Patrick 1911
FIELDS [129] Truman 1855
RAYBURN [319] Patrick 1911
DOEKENDORFF Charles 1859
DOEKENDORFF Charles 1859
24
COLBURN [80] Amos 1859
WILSON Thomas B 1855
COLBURN [80] Amos 1859
Lots-Sec. 24
1 COLBURN, Amos 1852
2 KNAPP, John H 1854
3 KNAPP, John H 1854
4 KNAPP, John H 1854
5 KNAPP, John H [217]1854
6 COLBURN, Amos 1852
7 COLBURN, Amos 1852
8 KNAPP, John H 1855
SNELL [368] Zachariah 1859
WASHBURNE Samuel B 1859
AMES James F 1855
AMES James F 1855
AMES James F 1855
27
AMES James F 1855
GOSS Alfred 1858
AMES James F 1856
GIBSON Moses S 1859
GIBSON Moses S 1859
GOSS [161] Alfred 1860
COPELAND Howard 1860
COPELAND [86] Howard 1860
COPELAND [86] Howard 1860
26
CLAPP Harvey S 1862
GOSS [161] Alfred 1860
COPELAND Howard 1860
STARKWEATHER George F 1859
STARKWEATHER George F 1859
COPELAND Howard 1860
KEEFE James 1860
COBURN [79] Amos 1855
COLBURN [80] Amos 1855
MCCORKLE [258] Andrew 1857
25
COLBURN [80] Amos 1855
COLBURN [80] Amos 1855
WOODWARD Mary N 1857
WOODMAN Horatio 1858
FUHLROTT Louis 1859
FITCH Lyman 1871
FITCH Lyman 1871
BOYLE William H 1878
GIBSON Moses S 1857
HOLBROOK Willard F 1857
FITCH Lyman 1871
FITCH Lyman 1894
HOLBROOK Willard F 1857
34
AMES Leonard 1863
HOLBROOK Schuyler 1857
CROSBY John O 1855
BOWERS Cyrus W 1875
SCHECKEL [351] Philip 1866
AMES Franklin 1855
GOBEL [157] John 1860
35
Lots-Sec. 35
1 GOBEL, John [157]1860
2 STARKWEATHER, George1859
MACAULEY Robert 1859
36
Lots-Sec. 36
1 FUHLROTT, Louis 1859
2 MACAULEY, Robert 1859
3 GOBEL, John [157]1860

Helpful Hints

1. This Map's INDEX can be found on the preceding pages.
2. Refer to Map "C" to see where this Township lies within Dunn County, Wisconsin.
3. Numbers within square brackets [ ] denote a multi-patentee land parcel (multi-owner). Refer to Appendix "C" for a full list of members in this group.
4. Areas that look to be crowded with Patentees usually indicate multiple sales of the same parcel (Re-issues) or Overlapping parcels. See this Township's Index for an explanation of these and other circumstances that might explain "odd" groupings of Patentees on this map.

Legend

- Patent Boundary
- Section Boundary
- No Patents Found (or Outside County)
- 1., 2., 3., ... Lot Numbers (when beside a name)
- [ ] Group Number (see Appendix "C")

Scale: Section = 1 mile X 1 mile (generally, with some exceptions)

Road Map

T26-N R13-W
4th PM - 1831 MN/WI Meridian

Map Group 22

Cities & Towns

- Dunnville
- Eau Galle
- Welch Point (historical)

Cemeteries

- Clearview Cemetery
- Evergreen Cemetery
- Pownell Cemetery
- Rosehill Cemetery

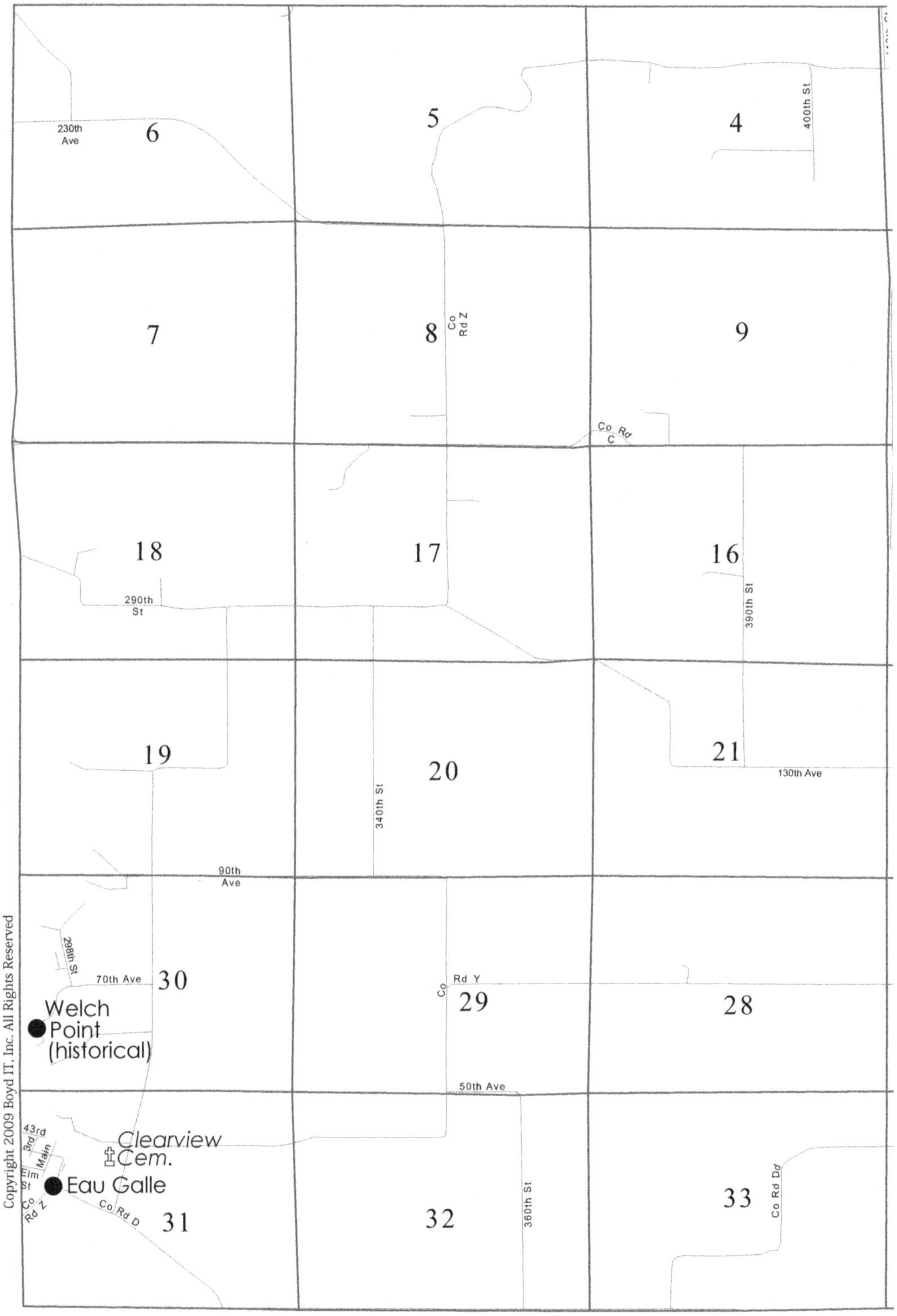

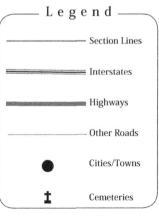

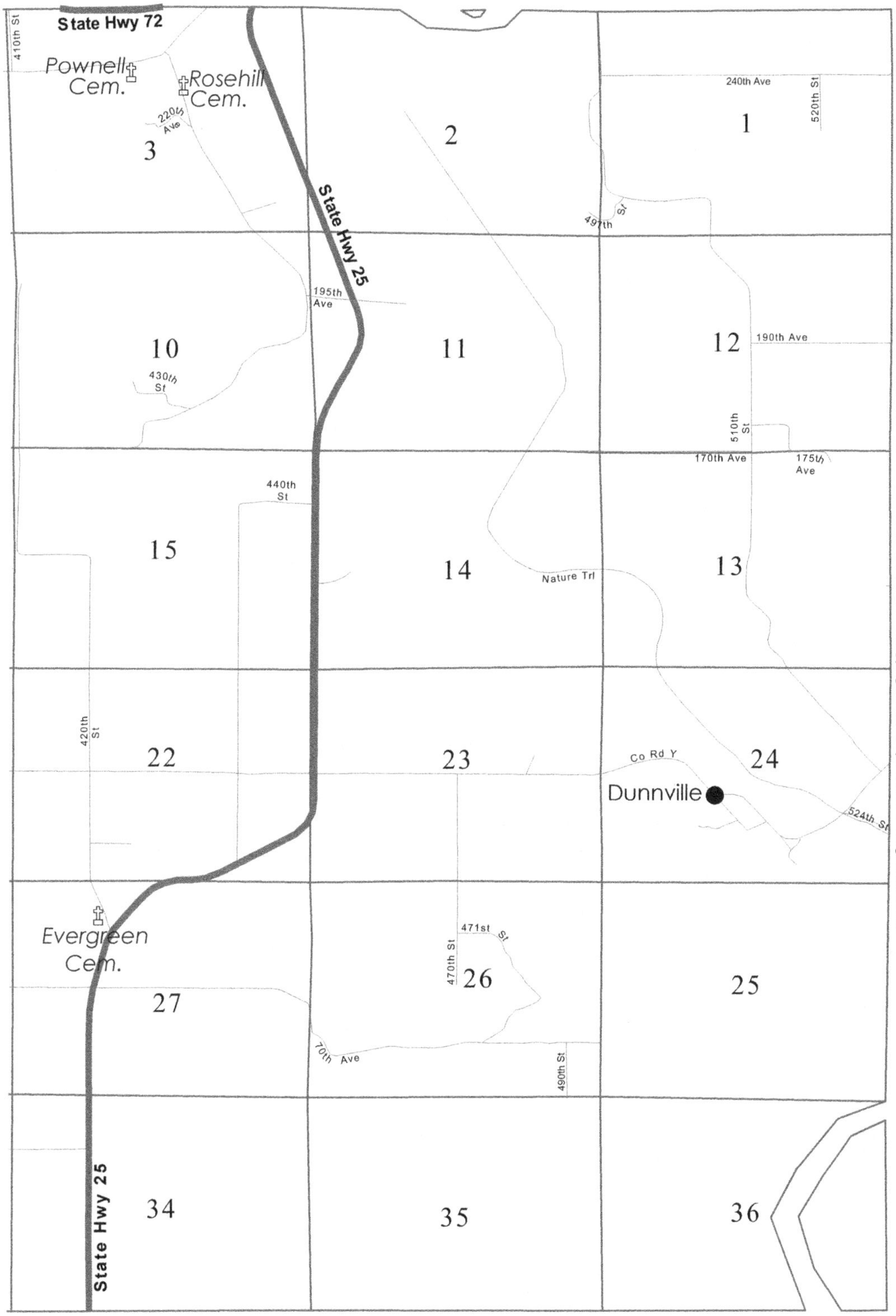
410th St
State Hwy 72
Pownell Cem.
Rosehill Cem.
220th Ave
3
2
1
240th Ave
520th St
State Hwy 25
497th St
195th Ave
10
11
12
190th Ave
430th St
510th St
170th Ave
175th Ave
440th St
15
14
Nature Trl
13
420th St
22
23
Co Rd Y
24
Dunnville
524th St
Evergreen Cem.
471st St
470th St
26
27
25
70th Ave
490th St
34
35
36
State Hwy 25

Helpful Hints

1. This road map has a number of uses, but primarily it is to help you: a) find the present location of land owned by your ancestors (at least the general area), b) find cemeteries and city-centers, and c) estimate the route/roads used by Census-takers & tax-assessors.
2. If you plan to travel to Dunn County to locate cemeteries or land parcels, please pick up a modern travel map for the area before you do. Mapping old land parcels on modern maps is not as exact a science as you might think. Just the slightest variations in public land survey coordinates, estimates of parcel boundaries, or road-map deviations can greatly alter a map's representation of how a road either does or doesn't cross a particular parcel of land.

Legend

- Section Lines
- Interstates
- Highways
- Other Roads
- Cities/Towns
- Cemeteries

Scale: Section = 1 mile X 1 mile
(generally, with some exceptions)

Historical Map

T26-N R13-W
4th PM - 1831 MN/WI Meridian

Map Group 22

Cities & Towns

Dunnville
Eau Galle
Welch Point (historical)

Cemeteries

Clearview Cemetery
Evergreen Cemetery
Pownell Cemetery
Rosehill Cemetery

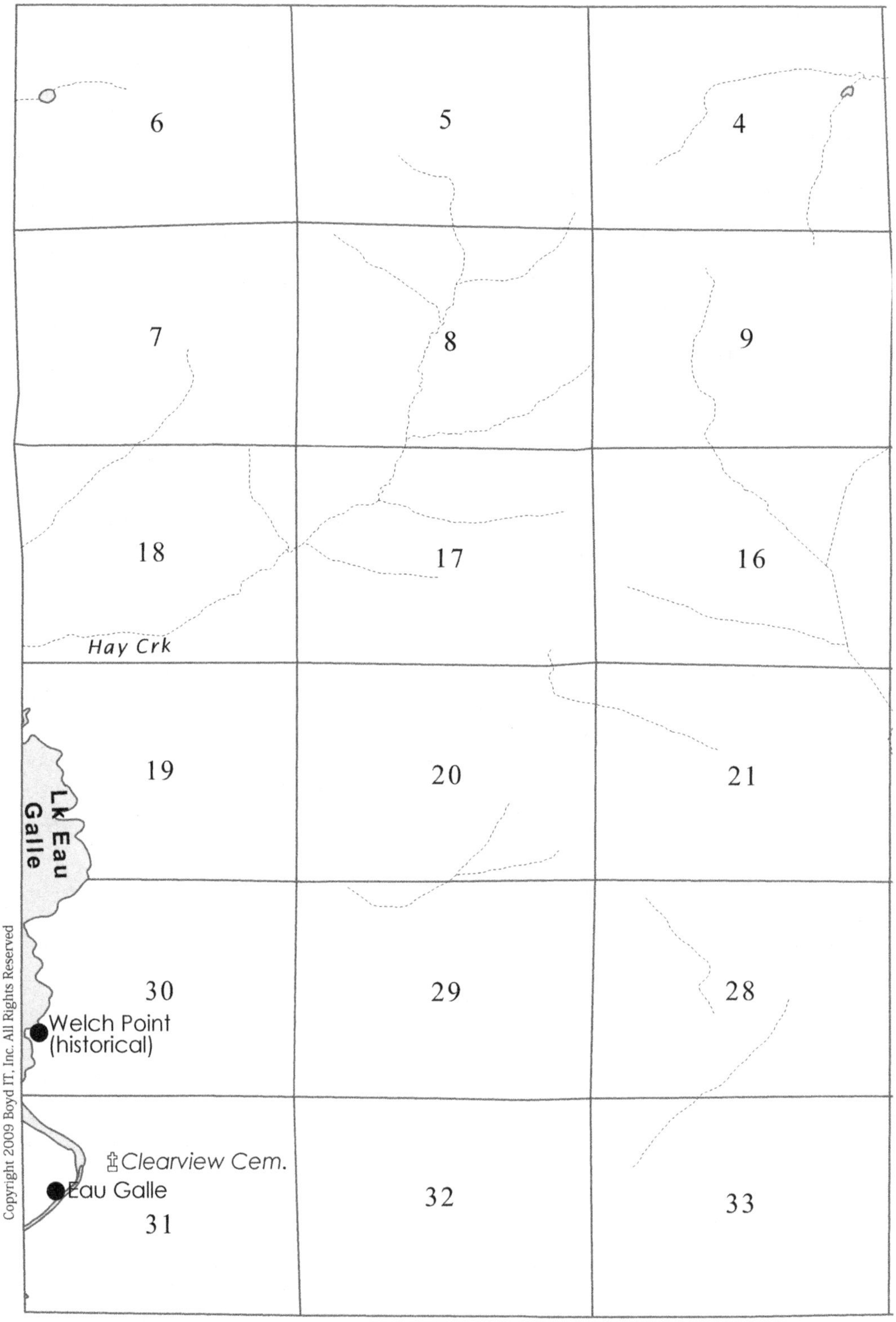

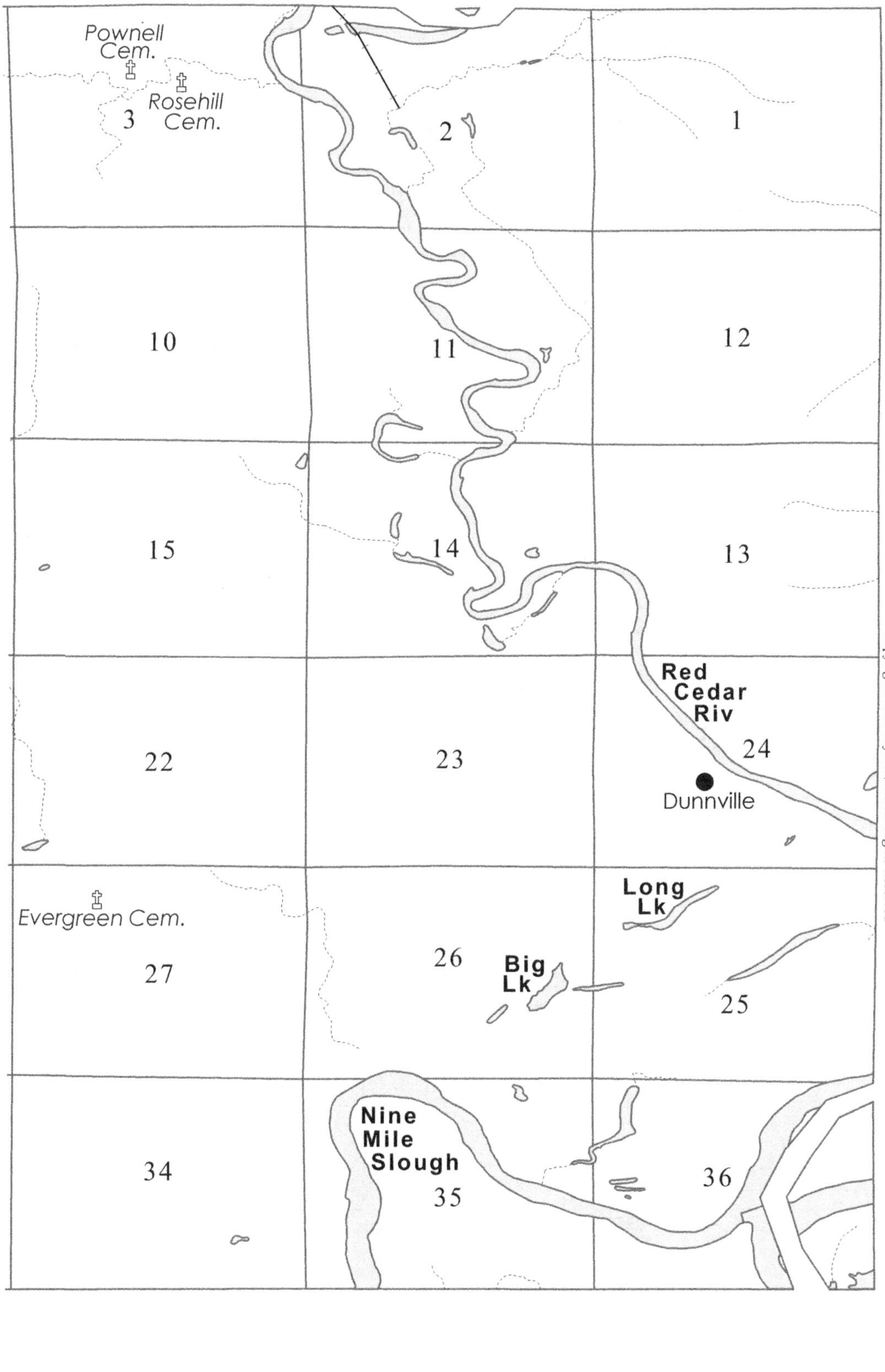
Pownell Cem.
Rosehill Cem.
3
2
1
10
11
12
15
14
13
Red Cedar Riv
22
23
24
Dunnville
Evergreen Cem.
27
26
Long Lk
Big Lk
25
34
Nine Mile Slough
35
36

Helpful Hints

1. This Map takes a different look at the same Congressional Township displayed in the preceding two maps. It presents features that can help you better envision the historical development of the area: a) Water-bodies (lakes & ponds), b) Water-courses (rivers, streams, etc.), c) Railroads, d) City/town center-points (where they were oftentimes located when first settled), and e) Cemeteries.

2. Using this "Historical" map in tandem with this Township's Patent Map and Road Map, may lead you to some interesting discoveries. You will often find roads, towns, cemeteries, and waterways are named after nearby landowners: sometimes those names will be the ones you are researching. See how many of these research gems you can find here in Dunn County.

Legend

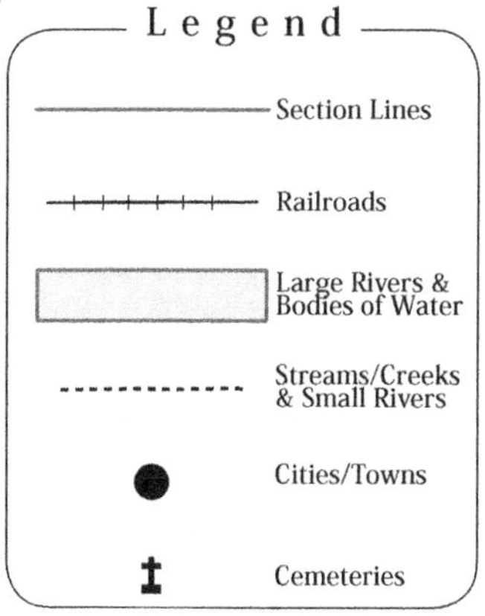
Section Lines
Railroads
Large Rivers & Bodies of Water
Streams/Creeks & Small Rivers
Cities/Towns
Cemeteries

Scale: Section = 1 mile X 1 mile
(there are some exceptions)

Map Group 23: Index to Land Patents

Township 26-North Range 12-West (4th PM - 1831 MN/WI)

After you locate an individual in this Index, take note of the Section and Section Part then proceed to the Land Patent map on the pages immediately following. You should have no difficulty locating the corresponding parcel of land.

The "For More Info" Column will lead you to more information about the underlying Patents. See the *Legend* at right, and the "How to Use this Book" chapter, for more information.

LEGEND

"For More Info . . . " column

A = Authority (Legislative Act, See Appendix "A")
B = Block or Lot (location in Section unknown)
C = Cancelled Patent
F = Fractional Section
G = Group (Multi-Patentee Patent, see Appendix "C")
V = Overlaps another Parcel
R = Re-Issued (Parcel patented more than once)

(A & G items require you to look in the Appendixes referred to above. All other Letter-designations followed by a number require you to locate line-items in this index that possess the ID number found after the letter).

ID	Individual in Patent	Sec.	Sec. Part	Date Issued	Other Counties	For More Info . . .
4174	ACKLEY, William J	10	5	1859-05-02		A2
4177	" "	10	6	1860-02-01		A5 G1
4178	" "	10	NWSW	1860-02-01		A5 G1
4175	" "	10	SWSW	1860-02-01		A5
4176	" "	9	E½SE	1860-02-01		A5
4129	ANDERSON, Robert	36	N½NW	1858-08-10		A2
4051	AUSTIN, Kesiah	28	NWSW	1858-06-16		A5 G189
4052	" "	28	W½NW	1858-06-16		A5 G189
4113	BAILEY, Ozias	17	E½SW	1860-02-01		A5
4114	" "	17	NE	1860-02-01		A5
4115	" "	17	NWSW	1860-02-01		A5
4014	BARNE, James R	27	E½NE	1858-05-03		A5 G28
4015	" "	27	SWNE	1858-05-03		A5 G28
3999	BARNUM, Israel	6	NWSE	1859-12-10		A2
4000	" "	18	E½SE	1860-07-16		A5 G29
4001	" "	18	SENE	1860-07-16		A5 G29
4170	BATES, William F	27	NWSW	1858-03-01		A5
4171	" "	27	SWNW	1858-03-01		A5
4172	" "	28	S½NE	1858-03-01		A5
3991	BENNET, Deborah	33	E½NW	1858-05-03		A5 G90
3992	" "	33	SWNW	1858-05-03		A5 G90
3896	BENNETT, Harriet	20	NESW	1859-09-01		A5 G38
3897	" "	20	W½SW	1859-09-01		A5 G38
4135	BETTS, Smith Burton	31	NENE	1858-06-16		A5
4136	" "	31	W½NE	1858-06-16		A5
3888	BILLIILNGS, Andrew	19	SESE	1859-09-01		A5 G37
3889	" "	19	W½SE	1859-09-01		A5 G37 R3913
3890	BILLINGS, Andrew	19	E½NW	1859-09-01		A5
3891	" "	19	NWNW	1859-09-01		A5 F
3892	" "	20	E½NE	1859-09-01		A5
3898	" "	20	E½NW	1859-09-01		A5 G39
3896	" "	20	NESW	1859-09-01		A5 G38
3893	" "	20	NWNE	1859-09-01		A5
3899	" "	20	NWNW	1859-09-01		A5 G39
3897	" "	20	W½SW	1859-09-01		A5 G38
3894	" "	5	SWNE	1859-09-01		A5
3895	" "	5	W½SE	1859-09-01		A5
4127	BISHOP, Richard	6	SW	1859-05-02		A2
4093	BOOTH, Lucius	25	E½SW	1858-03-01		A5 G45
4094	" "	25	SWSW	1858-03-01		A5 G45
4095	BOOTH, Lucius S	25	NENW	1857-10-30		A7
4097	" "	25	SENW	1858-03-01		A5
4098	" "	25	W½NW	1858-03-01		A5
4096	" "	25	NWSW	1858-08-10		A2
3918	BOWMAN, Mildred B	30	5	1858-06-16		A5 G312
3919	" "	30	6	1858-06-16		A5 G312

ID	Individual in Patent	Sec.	Sec. Part	Date Issued	Other Counties	For More Info . . .
3920	BOWMAN, Mildred B (Cont'd)	30	7	1858-06-16		A5 G312
3921	" "	31	3	1858-06-16		A5 G312
4156	BRENNAN, Hannah	5	W½NW	1858-02-20		A7 G49 F
4156	BRENNAN, Timothy	5	W½NW	1858-02-20		A7 G49 F
4068	BULLOCK, Loretta	1	SESE	1858-06-16		A5 G295
4069	" "	12	E½NE	1858-06-16		A5 G295
4010	CAMPBELL, James H	22	E½SE	1858-06-16		A5 G57
4011	" "	22	SENE	1858-06-16		A5 G57
3930	CARPENTER, Charles Z	34	E½SE	1875-07-30		A6
4018	CHASE, Sarah	5	E½NW	1859-09-01		A5 G402 F
3963	CHENEY, Hazen	3	S½NE	1859-09-01		A5 G70
3964	" "	3	SENW	1859-09-01		A5 G70
3965	" "	8	E½SE	1859-09-01		A5 G69
3966	" "	8	SENE	1859-09-01		A5 G69
4023	CLEAVELAND, Lucinda P	11	1	1859-09-01		A5 G428
4024	" "	12	5	1859-09-01		A5 G428
4025	" "	12	6	1859-09-01		A5 G428
4026	" "	2	7	1859-09-01		A5 G428
3987	CLINTON, Albert T	33	E½NE	1858-05-03		A5 G91
3991	" "	33	E½NW	1858-05-03		A5 G90
3990	" "	33	SWNE	1858-05-03		A5 G91
3992	" "	33	SWNW	1858-05-03		A5 G90
3988	" "	33	NWNE	1858-08-10		A2 G91
3989	" "	33	NWNW	1858-08-10		A2 G91
3949	COLE, George W	22	N½SW	1874-11-20		A6
3993	COLE, Ira	24	NENW	1858-08-10		A2
3994	" "	24	SENW	1859-09-01		A5 G81
3995	" "	24	W½NW	1859-09-01		A5 G81
3985	COPELAND, Howard	18	SWNE	1860-02-01		A5
3986	" "	18	W½SE	1860-02-01		A5
3967	CORWITH, Henry	26	SE	1858-05-03		A5 G87
3968	" "	32	SW	1858-05-03		A5 G88
3883	COUZENS, Abigail	4	SW	1860-02-01		A5 G193
4159	CRAGIN, Trueworthy G	13	S½SW	1858-04-03		A5
4160	" "	14	S½SE	1858-04-03		A5
3987	CRAMER, Howard	33	E½NE	1858-05-03		A5 G91
3991	" "	33	E½NW	1858-05-03		A5 G90
3990	" "	33	SWNE	1858-05-03		A5 G91
3992	" "	33	SWNW	1858-05-03		A5 G90
3988	" "	33	NWNE	1858-08-10		A2 G91
3989	" "	33	NWNW	1858-08-10		A2 G91
3922	CRANDALL, Betsey A	36	S½NW	1871-12-15		A6 G92
3922	CRANDALL, William E	36	S½NW	1871-12-15		A6 G92
4116	CRATSENBERG, Peter	24	NESW	1858-08-10		A2
4117	" "	24	S½SW	1858-08-10		A2
4165	CREASER, William	6	NW	1859-05-02		A2
4061	CUMMINGS, John W	2	1	1860-02-01		A5 G95
4062	" "	2	2	1860-02-01		A5 G95
4063	" "	2	NWNE	1860-02-01		A5 G95
4014	CURTISS, Gertrude	27	E½NE	1858-05-03		A5 G28
4015	" "	27	SWNE	1858-05-03		A5 G28
3927	DARLINTON, Carey A	18	E½SW	1860-02-01		A5 G99
3928	" "	18	SENW	1860-02-01		A5 G99
3925	" "	18	W½NW	1860-02-01		A5 F
3926	" "	18	W½SW	1860-02-01		A5 F
4109	DOWD, Orson	23	NESW	1858-05-03		A5
4110	" "	23	NWSW	1858-05-03		A5
4111	" "	23	S½NW	1858-05-03		A5
4112	" "	23	S½SW	1858-05-03		A5
4138	DUNN, Elizabeth	10	N½SW	1915-11-03		A5 G361 C
4076	EDWARDS, Julius	25	NESE	1858-03-01		A5 C R4077
4078	" "	25	NWSE	1858-03-01		A5
4080	" "	25	S½SW	1858-03-01		A5 C
4081	" "	25	W½NE	1858-03-01		A5
4082	" "	35	NESW	1858-05-01		A5
4083	" "	35	NWSE	1858-05-01		A5
4074	" "	21	SENE	1858-05-03		A5
4075	" "	22	S½NW	1858-05-03		A5
4077	" "	25	NESE	1971-04-14		A5 R4076
4079	" "	25	S½SE	1971-04-14		A5
4086	EDWARDS, Julius L	13	SENW	1858-03-01		A5
4087	" "	13	W½NW	1858-03-01		A5
4084	" "	12	3	1858-08-10		A2

ID	Individual in Patent	Sec.	Sec. Part	Date Issued	Other Counties	For More Info . . .
4085	EDWARDS, Julius L (Cont'd)	13	NENW	1858-08-10		A2
4088	" "	14	NENE	1858-08-10		A2
4139	EDWARDS, Theodore B	27	SWSW	1859-09-01		A5 G120
4140	" "	34	NWNW	1859-09-01		A5 G120
3898	ELDERT, Mary	20	E½NW	1859-09-01		A5 G39
3899	" "	20	NWNW	1859-09-01		A5 G39
3996	EMENS, Isaac	19	N½NE	1859-09-01		A5
3932	EVANS, David	27	SESE	1858-08-10		A2
3933	" "	33	N½SE	1859-07-01		A2
3969	EWER, Henry	25	E½NE	1858-08-10		A2
3970	EWERS, Henry	36	W½NE	1858-08-10		A2
4168	FALES, William E	14	NWSE	1860-07-03		A7
4166	" "	14	NESE	1860-08-01		A5
4167	" "	14	NWNE	1860-08-01		A5
4169	" "	14	S½NE	1860-08-01		A5
3967	FEEKS, Mary Ann	26	SE	1858-05-03		A5 G87
4177	FILLEY, Hannah	10	6	1860-02-01		A5 G1
4178	" "	10	NWSW	1860-02-01		A5 G1
3906	FLAGLER, Arthur B	35	NENW	1858-06-16		A5
3907	" "	35	SENW	1858-06-16		A5
3908	" "	35	W½NE	1858-06-16		A5
3909	" "	35	W½NW	1858-06-16		A5
4032	FLEMING, Sarah	1	SESW	1858-06-16		A5 G429
4033	" "	12	NENW	1858-06-16		A5 G429
3958	FORGERSON, Hans	24	NE	1860-04-02		A2
4034	FOX, John	31	SENE	1858-06-16		A5
4035	" "	32	S½NW	1858-06-16		A5
4133	FRENCH, Samuel B	2	3	1863-06-01		A2
3971	GEORGE, Henry	4	N½SE	1859-09-01		A5 G148
3972	GODFREY, Henry	28	S½SW	1858-05-03		A5
3973	" "	29	SESE	1858-05-03		A5
3974	" "	33	N½SW	1858-08-10		A2
4173	GOERCKE, William	2	4	1860-10-01		A2
4060	GOSS, John S	24	NWSW	1884-03-15		A6
3880	GRAY, Adam	15	E½NE	1858-05-03		A5 G163
3881	" "	15	SWNE	1858-05-03		A5 G163
3880	GRAY, Nancy	15	E½NE	1858-05-03		A5 G163
3881	" "	15	SWNE	1858-05-03		A5 G163
4141	GREEN, Ambrose	34	E½NW	1859-09-01		A5 G271
4142	" "	34	SWNW	1859-09-01		A5 G271
3982	HALSTEAD, Phila	8	NENE	1860-07-16		A5 G325
3983	" "	8	NWSE	1860-07-16		A5 G325
3984	" "	8	W½NE	1860-07-16		A5 G325
3913	HANCHETT, Asel M	19	W½SE	1858-08-10		A2 R3889
4092	HILL, Lovinia	34	NENE	1867-09-10		A2
4107	HILL, Orrin	2	5	1861-09-05		A2
4108	" "	2	NWSW	1861-09-05		A2
4128	HILL, Richard	34	NWNE	1872-09-06		A2
4143	HILL, Theodore	10	W½NW	1860-02-01		A5
4144	" "	3	E½SW	1860-02-01		A5
4145	" "	3	NWSE	1860-02-01		A5
4146	" "	9	SENE	1860-02-01		A5
4147	" "	10	7	1862-02-05		A5 G187
4148	" "	10	8	1862-02-05		A5 G187
4149	" "	3	2	1862-02-05		A5 G187
4089	HOADLEY, Lester S	21	6	1858-08-10		A2
4044	HODGDON, John	29	N½SE	1858-03-01		A5
4045	" "	29	S½SW	1858-03-01		A5
4046	" "	30	SESE	1858-03-01		A5
4040	" "	14	E½SW	1858-06-16		A5
4041	" "	14	W½SW	1858-06-16		A5
4042	" "	23	NENW	1858-06-16		A5
4043	" "	23	NWNW	1858-06-16		A5
4053	" "	28	E½NW	1858-06-16		A5 G190
4054	" "	28	NESW	1858-06-16		A5 G190
4051	" "	28	NWSW	1858-06-16		A5 G189
4052	" "	28	W½NW	1858-06-16		A5 G189
4047	" "	31	SE	1858-06-16		A5
4048	" "	32	N½NW	1858-06-16		A5
4049	" "	32	NWNE	1858-06-16		A5
4050	" "	36	SW	1858-06-16		A5
4055	HOLVORSON, John	29	SWSE	1857-10-30		A2
3942	HOPKINS, Ervin	27	E½SW	1858-05-03		A5

ID	Individual in Patent	Sec.	Sec. Part	Date Issued	Other Counties	For More Info . . .
3943	HOPKINS, Ervin (Cont'd)	27	SENW	1858-05-03		A5
3883	HORSTMANN, Adolph	4	SW	1860-02-01		A5 G193
3923	HORTWICK, Dorotha	29	2	1859-09-01		A5 G260
3924	" "	29	NWNW	1859-09-01		A5 G260
4061	HOUSER, Frances	2	1	1860-02-01		A5 G95
4062	" "	2	2	1860-02-01		A5 G95
4063	" "	2	NWNE	1860-02-01		A5 G95
3878	HUBBARD, Abijah A	24	SESE	1858-03-01		A5
3879	" "	24	W½SE	1858-03-01		A5
3877	" "	24	NESE	1858-08-10		A2
3955	HUBBARD, Hamilton W	21	SESE	1858-06-16		A5 G194
3956	" "	27	NWNW	1858-06-16		A5 G194
3957	" "	28	NENE	1858-06-16		A5 G194
3951	" "	21	7	1858-08-10		A2
3952	" "	21	NENE	1858-08-10		A2
3953	" "	22	S½SW	1858-08-10		A2
3954	" "	27	NENW	1858-08-10		A2
3929	HUNT, Charles	27	SWSE	1858-08-10		A2
3965	HUNT, Mehitable	8	E½SE	1859-09-01		A5 G69
3966	" "	8	SENE	1859-09-01		A5 G69
4151	JONES, George B	9	E½NW	1860-02-01		A5 G240
4152	" "	9	NWNW	1860-02-01		A5 G240
3941	JOYCE, Elisha E	34	S½NE	1888-04-26		A6
4059	KELLEY, John	20	SWNW	1874-05-06		A2
4036	KNAPP, John H	19	1	1855-12-15		A2 G219
4037	" "	19	2	1855-12-15		A2 G219
4038	" "	19	SESW	1855-12-15		A2 G219
4039	" "	30	10	1855-12-15		A2 G219
3950	KNAPP, Martha	32	S½SE	1858-05-01		A5 G270
4118	LARSON, Peter	20	1	1858-08-10		A2
4119	" "	21	4	1858-08-10		A2
3918	LATHROP, William H	30	5	1858-06-16		A5 G312
3919	" "	30	6	1858-06-16		A5 G312
3920	" "	30	7	1858-06-16		A5 G312
3921	" "	31	3	1858-06-16		A5 G312
4150	LEWIS, Theodore	9	SWNW	1859-12-10		A2
4151	" "	9	E½NW	1860-02-01		A5 G240
4152	" "	9	NWNW	1860-02-01		A5 G240
3905	LIBBEY, Artemus	36	SE	1859-09-01		A5
4013	LOCKE, James	26	NE	1859-07-01		A2
3937	LOCKWOOD, Edwin	21	5	1858-08-10		A2
3938	" "	21	SWSE	1858-08-10		A2
3939	" "	22	W½SE	1858-08-10		A2
3940	" "	28	NWNE	1858-08-10		A2
4072	LOTT, Williampie	7	NESW	1859-09-01		A5 G393
4073	" "	7	W½SW	1859-09-01		A5 G393
3914	LUCAS, Carol	1	1	1855-12-15		A2 G322
3915	" "	1	2	1855-12-15		A2 G322
3916	" "	1	NWNE	1855-12-15		A2 G322
3997	LYTLE, George	13	E½SE	1858-04-03		A5 G246
3998	" "	13	SENE	1858-04-03		A5 G246
3997	LYTLE, Isabella E	13	E½SE	1858-04-03		A5 G246
3998	" "	13	SENE	1858-04-03		A5 G246
4130	MACAULEY, Robert	20	2	1859-05-02		A2
4131	" "	20	3	1859-05-02		A2
4132	" "	29	1	1859-05-02		A2
3955	MARSHALL, Loruhama	21	SESE	1858-06-16		A5 G194
3956	" "	27	NWNW	1858-06-16		A5 G194
3957	" "	28	NENE	1858-06-16		A5 G194
4157	MARSTON, Stephen	13	NENE	1860-08-01		A5 G292
4158	" "	13	W½NE	1860-08-01		A5 G292
3997	MARTIN, Susan	13	E½SE	1858-04-03		A5 G246
3998	" "	13	SENE	1858-04-03		A5 G246
3945	MASSEE, George	6	N½NE	1857-04-01		A2 F
3946	" "	8	N½SW	1857-04-01		A2
3947	" "	8	NW	1857-04-01		A2
4155	MASSEY, Thomas	5	N½NE	1859-05-02		A2
4179	MASSEY, William	17	N½NW	1859-05-02		A2
4180	" "	8	SESW	1859-05-02		A2
4070	MATHERS, Joseph H	30	3	1859-09-01		A5 G252
4071	" "	30	SWNW	1859-09-01		A5 G252
3900	MCCORKLE, Andrew	30	1	1857-04-01		A2
3901	" "	4	NENE	1859-09-01		A5

ID	Individual in Patent	Sec.	Sec. Part	Date Issued	Other Counties	For More Info . . .
3902	MCCORKLE, Andrew (Cont'd)	4	S½NE	1859-09-01		A5
3903	" "	4	SENW	1859-09-01		A5 G257
3904	" "	4	W½NW	1859-09-01		A5 G257
3923	MCGEOGH, Bridget	29	2	1859-09-01		A5 G260
3924	" "	29	NWNW	1859-09-01		A5 G260
3888	MONFORT, Elizabeth	19	SESE	1859-09-01		A5 G37
3889	" "	19	W½SE	1859-09-01		A5 G37 R3913
3950	MONTAGUE, Giles R	32	S½SE	1858-05-01		A5 G270
4141	MONTAGUE, Theodore G	34	E½NW	1859-09-01		A5 G271
4142	" "	34	SWNW	1859-09-01		A5 G271
3934	MORRISON, Dorilus	30	2	1855-06-15		A2
3935	" "	30	4	1855-06-15		A2
3936	" "	30	9	1855-06-15		A2
4003	MOYER, James A	36	SENE	1879-11-25		A6
4053	MURPHY, Lucinda J	28	E½NW	1858-06-16		A5 G190
4054	" "	28	NESW	1858-06-16		A5 G190
4090	NEWMAN, Lorenzo	23	S½SE	1858-08-10		A2
4091	" "	26	NESW	1858-08-10		A2
4020	NEWVILLE, Jeremiah	33	S½SW	1858-01-15		A2
3903	NICHOLS, Sally	4	SENW	1859-09-01		A5 G257
3904	" "	4	W½NW	1859-09-01		A5 G257
3886	OLSON, Anders	26	NW	1857-10-30		A2
3887	" "	26	NWSW	1857-10-30		A2
4157	OLSON, Torger	13	NENE	1860-08-01		A5 G292
4158	" "	13	W½NE	1860-08-01		A5 G292
3994	ONDERDONK, Catharine	24	SENW	1859-09-01		A5 G81
3995	" "	24	W½NW	1859-09-01		A5 G81
4147	PAGE, Nancy	10	7	1862-02-05		A5 G187
4148	" "	10	8	1862-02-05		A5 G187
4149	" "	3	2	1862-02-05		A5 G187
4068	PALEN, Joseph G	1	SESE	1858-06-16		A5 G295
4069	" "	12	E½NE	1858-06-16		A5 G295
4065	" "	12	4	1858-08-18		A5
4067	" "	12	W½SE	1858-08-18		A5
4064	" "	1	SWSE	1859-09-01		A5
4066	" "	12	W½NE	1859-09-01		A5
3948	PIERCE, George S	15	SW	1859-07-01		A2
3968	PIERSON, Sarah L	32	SW	1858-05-03		A5 G88
3918	PRESTON, Bennett S	30	5	1858-06-16		A5 G312
3919	" "	30	6	1858-06-16		A5 G312
3920	" "	30	7	1858-06-16		A5 G312
3921	" "	31	3	1858-06-16		A5 G312
3927	PRICKETT, Lucinda E	18	E½SW	1860-02-01		A5 G99
3928	" "	18	SENW	1860-02-01		A5 G99
3914	REMINGTON, Barlow	1	1	1855-12-15		A2 G322
3915	" "	1	2	1855-12-15		A2 G322
3916	" "	1	NWNE	1855-12-15		A2 G322
3980	REYNOLDS, Henry	4	NENW	1859-12-10		A2
3981	" "	8	SWSE	1859-12-10		A2
3982	" "	8	NENE	1860-07-16		A5 G325
3983	" "	8	NWSE	1860-07-16		A5 G325
3984	" "	8	W½NE	1860-07-16		A5 G325
4004	RORK, James E	23	E½NE	1858-05-03		A5
4007	" "	23	SWNE	1858-05-03		A5
4005	" "	23	N½SE	1858-08-10		A2
4006	" "	23	NWNE	1858-08-10		A2
4008	" "	26	S½SW	1858-08-10		A2
4009	" "	36	NENE	1858-08-10		A2
3963	SAXTON, Ebenezer M	3	S½NE	1859-09-01		A5 G70
3964	" "	3	SENW	1859-09-01		A5 G70
3965	" "	8	E½SE	1859-09-01		A5 G69
3966	" "	8	SENE	1859-09-01		A5 G69
4120	SECOR, Peter	31	E½SW	1860-02-10		A5
4121	" "	31	NWSW	1860-02-10		A5
4106	SEVALDSON, Ole	12	E½SE	1873-07-10		A6
4070	SEXTON, Ebenezer M	30	3	1859-09-01		A5 G252
4071	" "	30	SWNW	1859-09-01		A5 G252
3971	" "	4	N½SE	1859-09-01		A5 G148
4000	SHANKLIN, Martha	18	E½SE	1860-07-16		A5 G29
4001	" "	18	SENE	1860-07-16		A5 G29
4056	SHAW, John J	10	3	1872-10-01		A6
4057	" "	10	4	1872-10-01		A6
4058	" "	10	SESE	1872-10-01		A6

ID	Individual in Patent	Sec.	Sec. Part	Date Issued	Other Counties	For More Info . . .
4138	SHERMAN, Thaddeus	10	N½SW	1915-11-03		A5 G361 C
4010	SHIPMAN, Elender	22	E½SE	1858-06-16		A5 G57
4011	" "	22	SENE	1858-06-16		A5 G57
4093	SHUGERT, Sarah	25	E½SW	1858-03-01		A5 G45
4094	" "	25	SWSW	1858-03-01		A5 G45
3911	SMEAD, Asa	34	SESW	1858-05-03		A5
3912	" "	34	W½SW	1858-05-03		A5
3910	" "	34	NESW	1858-08-10		A2
3917	SMITH, Benjamin	7	NWSE	1857-04-01		A2
4104	SMITH, Mary	7	E½SE	1857-04-01		A2
4105	" "	8	SWSW	1857-04-01		A2
4123	STEARNS, Phineas S	29	NESW	1858-01-15		A2
4124	" "	32	N½SE	1858-01-15		A2
4125	" "	32	NENE	1858-01-15		A2
4126	" "	32	S½NE	1858-01-15		A2
4139	STEEL, Charlotte	27	SWSW	1859-09-01		A5 G120
4140	" "	34	NWNW	1859-09-01		A5 G120
3882	STEVENS, Adna	15	S½SE	1858-08-10		A2
4012	STEVENS, James L	22	N½NW	1872-10-01		A6
4019	STEVENS, Jason	22	N½NE	1858-08-10		A2
4162	STEVENS, Walter	14	NW	1858-08-10		A2
3975	STEVES, Henry H	6	NESE	1857-04-01		A2
3976	" "	6	S½NE	1857-04-01		A2
3977	" "	6	S½SE	1857-04-01		A2
3978	" "	7	N½NE	1857-04-01		A2 F
3979	" "	7	NW	1857-04-01		A2 F
4036	STOUT, Henry L	19	1	1855-12-15		A2 G219
4037	" "	19	2	1855-12-15		A2 G219
4038	" "	19	SESW	1855-12-15		A2 G219
4039	" "	30	10	1855-12-15		A2 G219
4036	TAINTER, Andrew	19	1	1855-12-15		A2 G219
4037	" "	19	2	1855-12-15		A2 G219
4038	" "	19	SESW	1855-12-15		A2 G219
4039	" "	30	10	1855-12-15		A2 G219
4072	TAYLOR, Joseph N	7	NESW	1859-09-01		A5 G393
4073	" "	7	W½SW	1859-09-01		A5 G393
3963	TOBEY, Lucy	3	S½NE	1859-09-01		A5 G70
3964	" "	3	SENW	1859-09-01		A5 G70
3959	TORGERSON, Hans	13	N½SW	1857-10-30		A2
4018	TRASK, James W	5	E½NW	1859-09-01		A5 G402 F
3931	TUBBS, Christopher C	3	NENW	1855-12-15		A2 F
4099	TUBBS, Martin	3	SWNW	1857-04-01		A2
3944	TUTTLE, George M	33	S½SE	1857-10-30		A7
3960	TUTTLE, Harvey	2	E½NW	1860-02-01		A5 F
3961	" "	2	SWNW	1860-02-01		A5 F
3962	TUTTLE, Harvy	2	NWNW	1859-12-10		A2
4016	VASEY, James	5	SENE	1857-04-01		A2
4017	" "	5	SW	1857-04-01		A2
4122	VROMAN, Peter	28	SE	1858-03-01		A5
4134	WALKER, Samuel H	5	E½SE	1857-04-01		A2
4014	WELLS, Thomas O	27	E½NE	1858-05-03		A5 G28
4015	" "	27	SWNE	1858-05-03		A5 G28
4002	WHEELER, Jacob	34	W½SE	1878-12-30		A6
4161	WIGGINS, Truman	4	NWNE	1855-12-15		A2
4163	WILKINS, Warren	11	2	1858-08-10		A2
4164	" "	12	2	1858-08-10		A2
4153	WILSON, Thomas B	1	NENE	1855-12-15		A2
4036	" "	19	1	1855-12-15		A2 G219
4037	" "	19	2	1855-12-15		A2 G219
4038	" "	19	SESW	1855-12-15		A2 G219
4039	" "	30	10	1855-12-15		A2 G219
4154	" "	7	S½NE	1857-04-01		A2
4023	WILSTACH, John A	11	1	1859-09-01		A5 G428
4024	" "	12	5	1859-09-01		A5 G428
4025	" "	12	6	1859-09-01		A5 G428
4026	" "	2	7	1859-09-01		A5 G428
4021	" "	1	6	1860-02-07		A5 R4028
4022	" "	1	7	1860-02-07		A5 R4029
4027	WILSTACK, John A	1	5	1858-06-16		A5 F
4032	" "	1	SESW	1858-06-16		A5 G429
4030	" "	1	W½SW	1858-06-16		A5
4033	" "	12	NENW	1858-06-16		A5 G429
4031	" "	2	6	1858-06-16		A5 F

ID	Individual in Patent	Sec.	Sec. Part	Date Issued	Other Counties	For More Info . . .
4028	WILSTACK, John A (Cont'd)	1	6	1859-09-01		A5 C F R4021
4029	" "	1	7	1859-09-01		A5 C F R4022
4137	WISCONSIN, State Of	16		1941-08-16		A3 F
4100	WOODWARD, Mary N	3	N½NE	1857-10-30		A5
4101	" "	3	W½SW	1857-10-30		A5
4102	" "	4	S½SE	1857-10-30		A5
4103	" "	9	W½NE	1857-10-30		A5
4181	WYLIE, William	18	N½NE	1859-12-20		A2
4182	" "	18	NENW	1859-12-20		A2
3884	ZIELIE, Alexander	30	8	1878-06-24		A6
3885	" "	30	NENE	1878-06-24		A6

Patent Map

T26-N R12-W
4th PM - 1831 MN/WI Meridian

Map Group 23

Township Statistics

Parcels Mapped	:	306
Number of Patents	:	191
Number of Individuals	:	171
Patentees Identified	:	141
Number of Surnames	:	147
Multi-Patentee Parcels	:	94
Oldest Patent Date	:	6/15/1855
Most Recent Patent	:	4/14/1971
Block/Lot Parcels	:	50
Parcels Re - Issued	:	4
Parcels that Overlap	:	0
Cities and Towns	:	3
Cemeteries	:	2

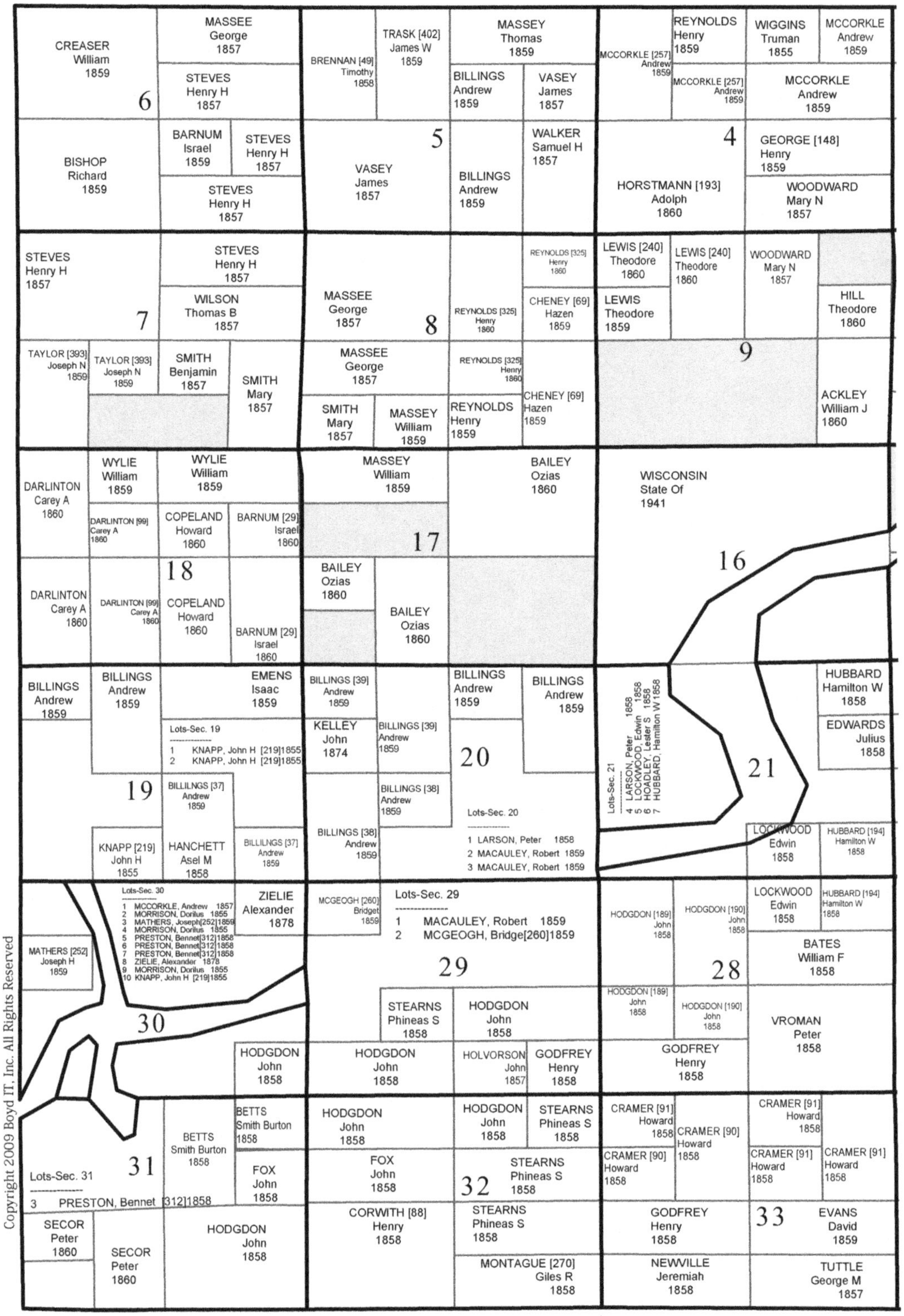

CREASER William 1859
MASSEE George 1857
STEVES Henry H 1857
6
BISHOP Richard 1859
BARNUM Israel 1859
STEVES Henry H 1857
STEVES Henry H 1857
BRENNAN [49] Timothy 1858
TRASK [402] James W 1859
MASSEY Thomas 1859
BILLINGS Andrew 1859
VASEY James 1857
5
VASEY James 1857
BILLINGS Andrew 1859
WALKER Samuel H 1857
MCCORKLE [257] Andrew 1859
REYNOLDS Henry 1859
WIGGINS Truman 1855
MCCORKLE Andrew 1859
MCCORKLE [257] Andrew 1859
MCCORKLE Andrew 1859
4
HORSTMANN [193] Adolph 1860
GEORGE [148] Henry 1859
WOODWARD Mary N 1857
STEVES Henry H 1857
STEVES Henry H 1857
WILSON Thomas B 1857
7
TAYLOR [393] Joseph N 1859
TAYLOR [393] Joseph N 1859
SMITH Benjamin 1857
SMITH Mary 1857
MASSEE George 1857
8
REYNOLDS [325] Henry 1860
REYNOLDS [325] Henry 1860
CHENEY [69] Hazen 1859
MASSEE George 1857
REYNOLDS [325] Henry 1860
CHENEY [69] Hazen 1859
SMITH Mary 1857
MASSEY William 1859
REYNOLDS Henry 1859
LEWIS [240] Theodore 1860
LEWIS [240] Theodore 1860
WOODWARD Mary N 1857
HILL Theodore 1860
LEWIS Theodore 1859
9
ACKLEY William J 1860
DARLINTON Carey A 1860
WYLIE William 1859
WYLIE William 1859
DARLINTON [99] Carey A 1860
COPELAND Howard 1860
BARNUM [29] Israel 1860
18
DARLINTON Carey A 1860
DARLINTON [99] Carey A 1860
COPELAND Howard 1860
BARNUM [29] Israel 1860
MASSEY William 1859
BAILEY Ozias 1860
17
BAILEY Ozias 1860
BAILEY Ozias 1860
WISCONSIN State Of 1941
16
BILLINGS Andrew 1859
BILLINGS Andrew 1859
EMENS Isaac 1859
Lots-Sec. 19
1 KNAPP, John H [219]1855
2 KNAPP, John H [219]1855
19
BILLILNGS [37] Andrew 1859
KNAPP [219] John H 1855
HANCHETT Asel M 1858
BILLILNGS [37] Andrew 1859
BILLINGS [39] Andrew 1859
BILLINGS Andrew 1859
BILLINGS Andrew 1859
KELLEY John 1874
BILLINGS [39] Andrew 1859
20
BILLINGS [38] Andrew 1859
BILLINGS [38] Andrew 1859
Lots-Sec. 20
1 LARSON, Peter 1858
2 MACAULEY, Robert 1859
3 MACAULEY, Robert 1859
Lots-Sec. 21
4 LARSON, Peter 1858
5 LOCKWOOD, Edwin 1858
6 HOADLEY, Lester S 1858
7 HUBBARD, Hamilton W 1858
21
HUBBARD Hamilton W 1858
EDWARDS Julius 1858
LOCKWOOD Edwin 1858
HUBBARD [194] Hamilton W 1858
Lots-Sec. 30
1 MCCORKLE, Andrew 1857
2 MORRISON, Dorilus 1855
3 MATHERS, Joseph[252]1859
4 MORRISON, Dorilus 1855
5 PRESTON, Bennet[312]1858
6 PRESTON, Bennet[312]1858
7 PRESTON, Bennet[312]1858
8 ZIELIE, Alexander 1878
9 MORRISON, Dorilus 1855
10 KNAPP, John H [219]1855
ZIELIE Alexander 1878
MATHERS [252] Joseph H 1859
30
HODGDON John 1858
MCGEOGH [260] Bridget 1859
Lots-Sec. 29
1 MACAULEY, Robert 1859
2 MCGEOGH, Bridge[260]1859
29
STEARNS Phineas S 1858
HODGDON John 1858
HODGDON John 1858
HOLVORSON John 1857
GODFREY Henry 1858
LOCKWOOD Edwin 1858
HUBBARD [194] Hamilton W 1858
HODGDON [189] John 1858
HODGDON [190] John 1858
BATES William F 1858
28
HODGDON [189] John 1858
HODGDON [190] John 1858
VROMAN Peter 1858
GODFREY Henry 1858
BETTS Smith Burton 1858
BETTS Smith Burton 1858
31
Lots-Sec. 31
3 PRESTON, Bennet [312]1858
FOX John 1858
SECOR Peter 1860
SECOR Peter 1860
HODGDON John 1858
HODGDON John 1858
HODGDON John 1858
STEARNS Phineas S 1858
FOX John 1858
STEARNS Phineas S 1858
32
CORWITH [88] Henry 1858
STEARNS Phineas S 1858
MONTAGUE [270] Giles R 1858
CRAMER [91] Howard 1858
CRAMER [90] Howard 1858
CRAMER [91] Howard 1858
CRAMER [90] Howard 1858
CRAMER [91] Howard 1858
CRAMER [91] Howard 1858
GODFREY Henry 1858
33
EVANS David 1859
NEWVILLE Jeremiah 1858
TUTTLE George M 1857

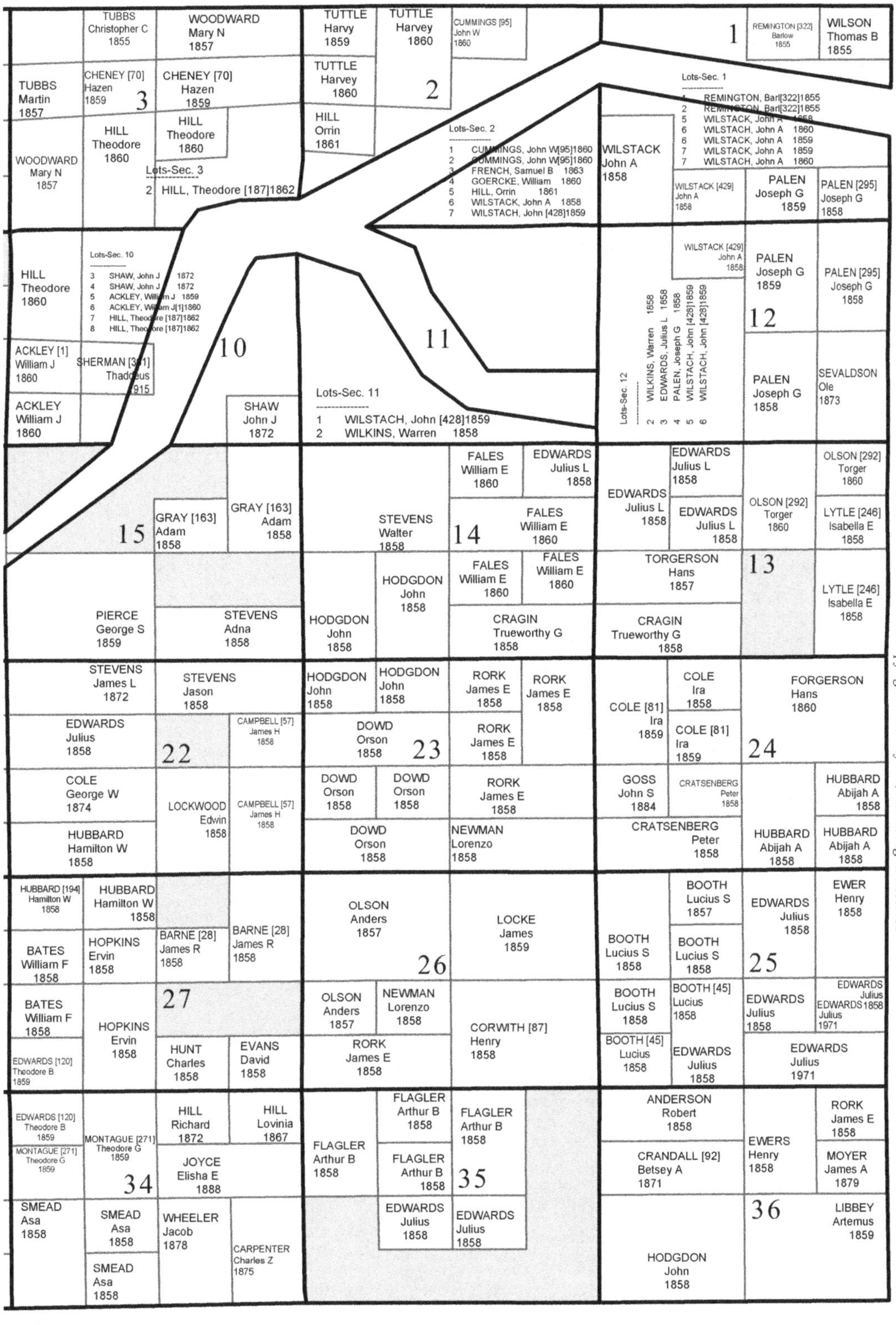

Helpful Hints

1. This Map's INDEX can be found on the preceding pages.
2. Refer to Map "C" to see where this Township lies within Dunn County, Wisconsin.
3. Numbers within square brackets [ ] denote a multi-patentee land parcel (multi-owner). Refer to Appendix "C" for a full list of members in this group.
4. Areas that look to be crowded with Patentees usually indicate multiple sales of the same parcel (Re-issues) or Overlapping parcels. See this Township's Index for an explanation of these and other circumstances that might explain "odd" groupings of Patentees on this map.

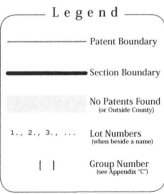

Legend

———	Patent Boundary
▬▬▬	Section Boundary
(shaded)	No Patents Found (or Outside County)
1., 2., 3., ...	Lot Numbers (when beside a name)
[ ]	Group Number (see Appendix "C")

Scale: Section = 1 mile X 1 mile (generally, with some exceptions)

Road Map

T26-N R12-W
4th PM - 1831 MN/WI Meridian

Map Group 23

Cities & Towns

Meridean
Old Tyrone (historical)
Red Cedar

Cemeteries

Peru Cemetery
Pleasant Valley Cemetery

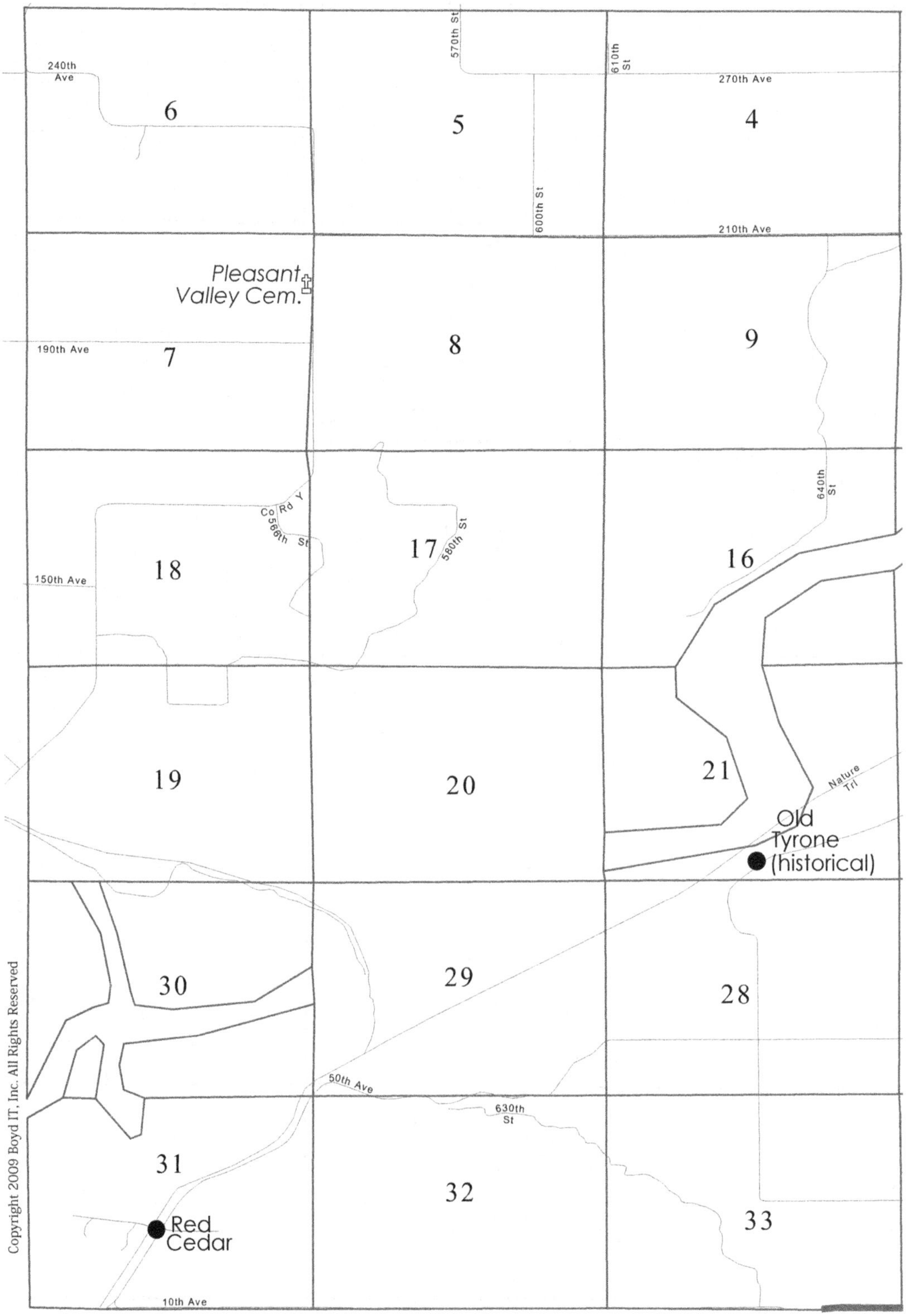

240th Ave
570th St
610th St
270th Ave
6
5
4
600th St
210th Ave
Pleasant Valley Cem.
190th Ave
7
8
9
640th St
Co Rd Y
566th St
580th St
150th Ave
18
17
16
19
20
21
Nature Trl
Old Tyrone (historical)
30
29
28
50th Ave
630th St
31
32
33
Red Cedar
10th Ave

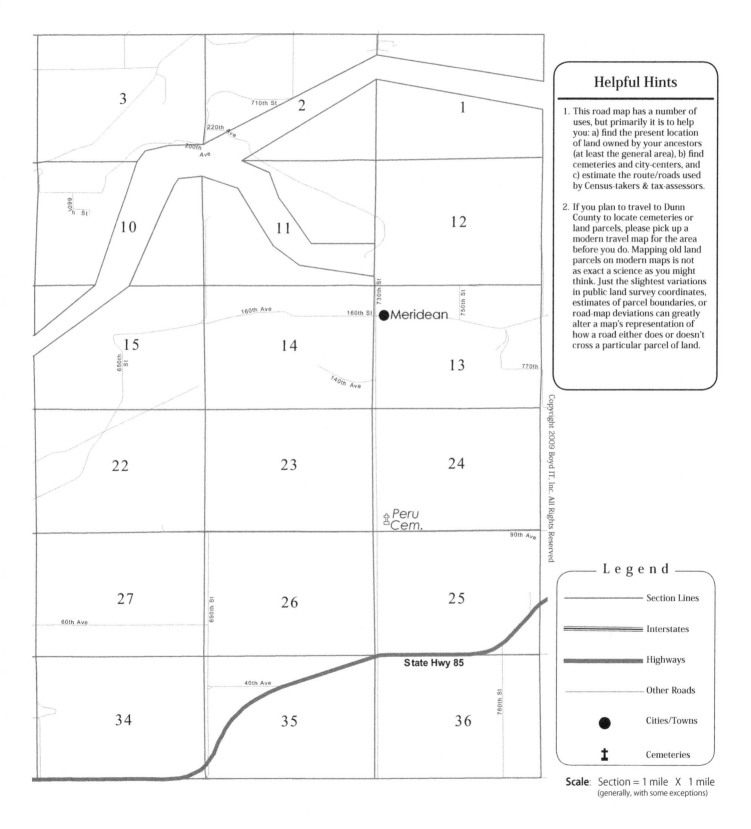

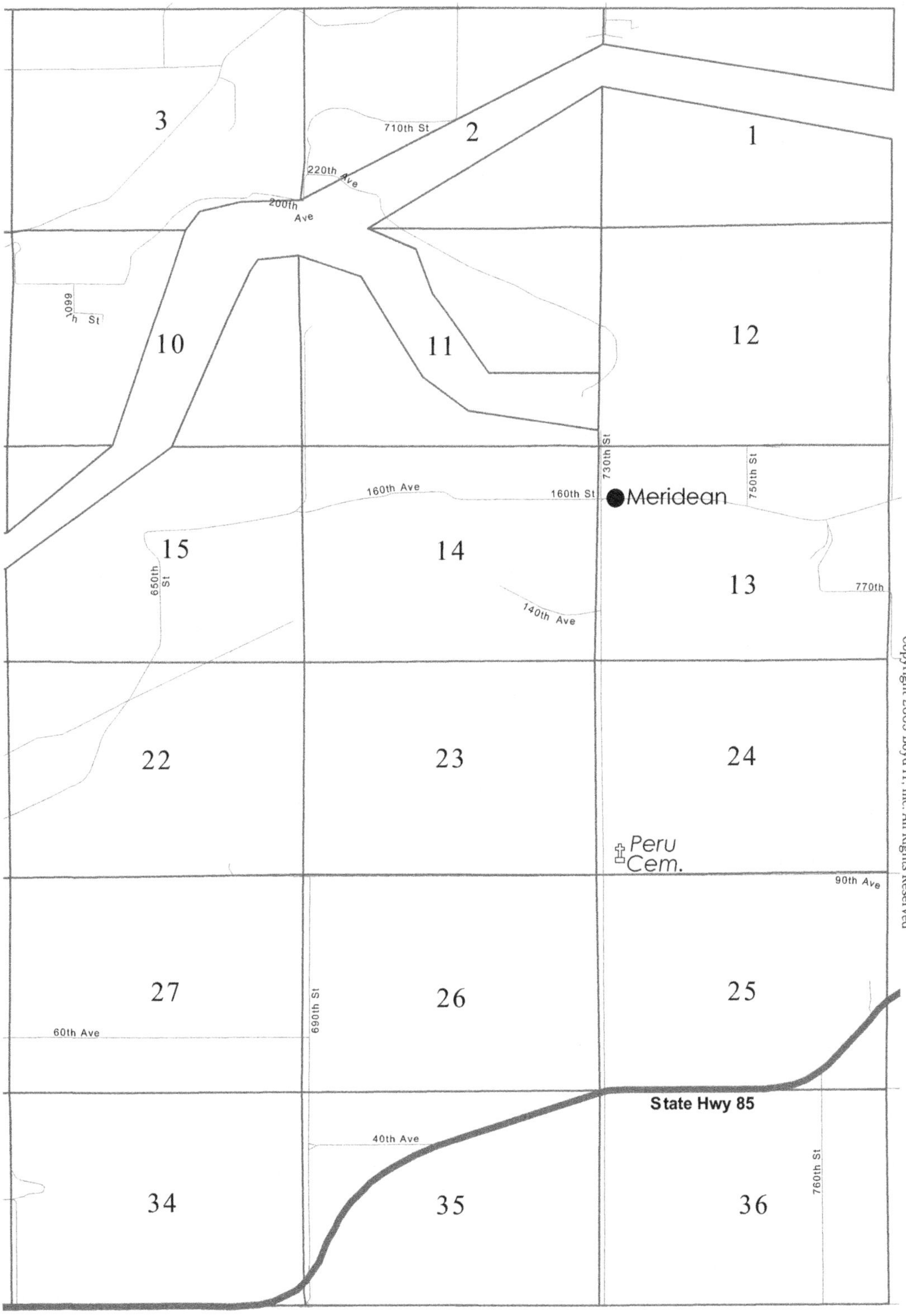

Helpful Hints

1. This road map has a number of uses, but primarily it is to help you: a) find the present location of land owned by your ancestors (at least the general area), b) find cemeteries and city-centers, and c) estimate the route/roads used by Census-takers & tax-assessors.

2. If you plan to travel to Dunn County to locate cemeteries or land parcels, please pick up a modern travel map for the area before you do. Mapping old land parcels on modern maps is not as exact a science as you might think. Just the slightest variations in public land survey coordinates, estimates of parcel boundaries, or road-map deviations can greatly alter a map's representation of how a road either does or doesn't cross a particular parcel of land.

Legend

- Section Lines
- Interstates
- Highways
- Other Roads
- Cities/Towns
- Cemeteries

Scale: Section = 1 mile X 1 mile
(generally, with some exceptions)

Historical Map

T26-N R12-W
4th PM - 1831 MN/WI Meridian

Map Group 23

Cities & Towns

Meridean
Old Tyrone (historical)
Red Cedar

Cemeteries

Peru Cemetery
Pleasant Valley Cemetery

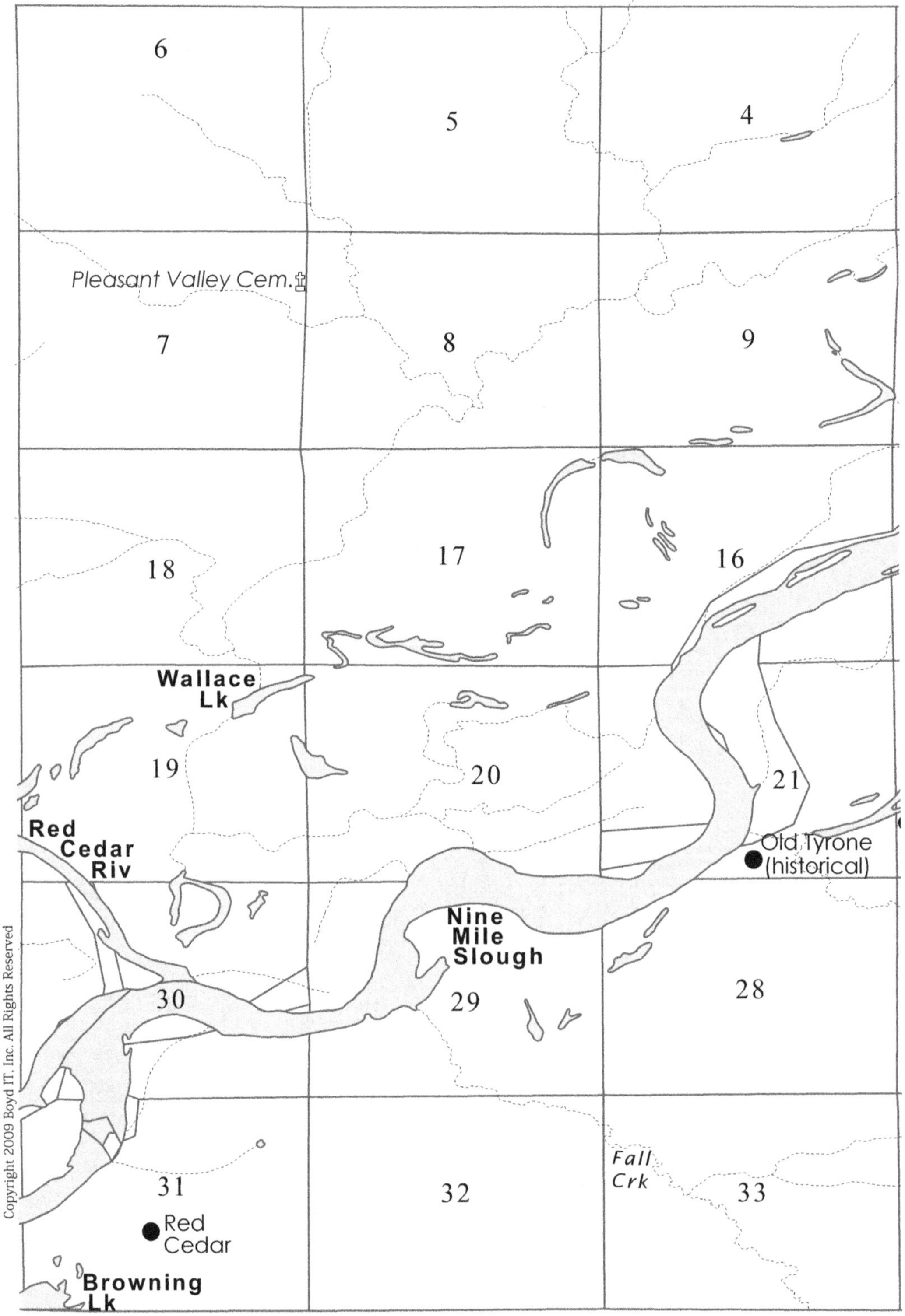

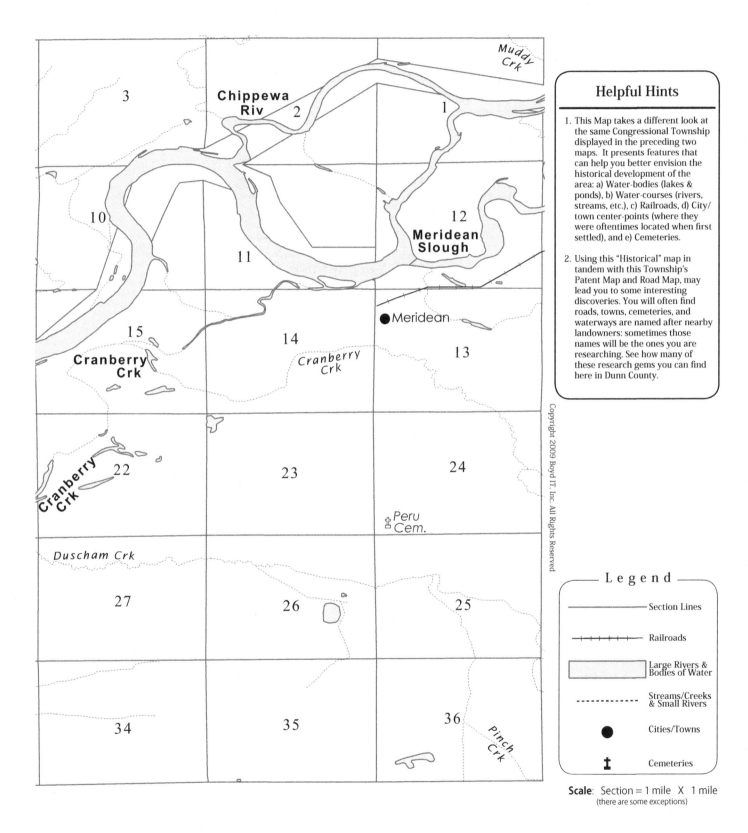

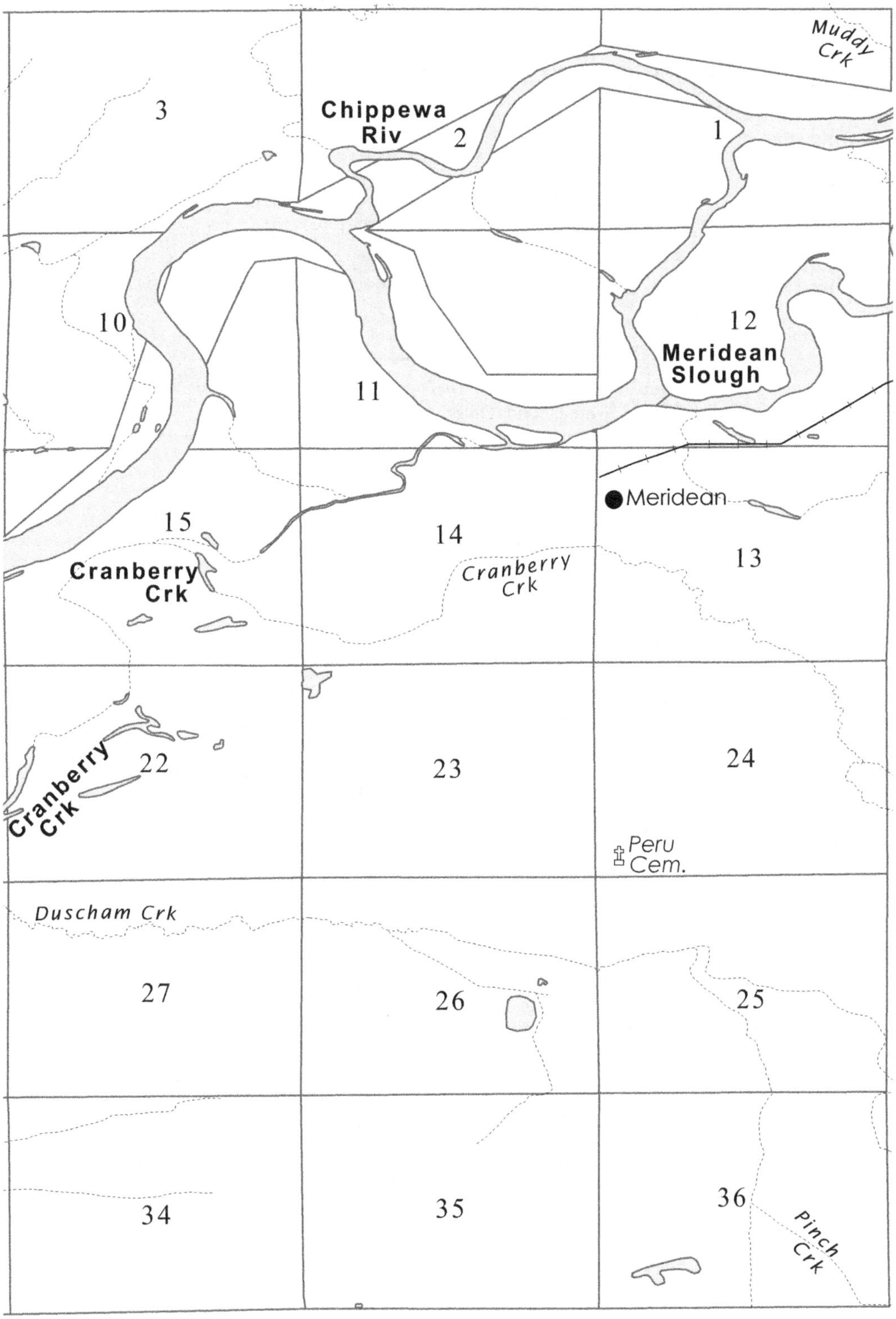
Muddy Crk
3
Chippewa Riv
2
1
10
12
Meridean Slough
11
Meridean
15
14
13
Cranberry Crk
Cranberry Crk
22
23
24
Cranberry Crk
Peru Cem.
Duscham Crk
27
26
25
34
35
36
Pinch Crk

Helpful Hints

1. This Map takes a different look at the same Congressional Township displayed in the preceding two maps. It presents features that can help you better envision the historical development of the area: a) Water-bodies (lakes & ponds), b) Water-courses (rivers, streams, etc.), c) Railroads, d) City/town center-points (where they were oftentimes located when first settled), and e) Cemeteries.
2. Using this "Historical" map in tandem with this Township's Patent Map and Road Map, may lead you to some interesting discoveries. You will often find roads, towns, cemeteries, and waterways are named after nearby landowners: sometimes those names will be the ones you are researching. See how many of these research gems you can find here in Dunn County.

Legend

- Section Lines
- Railroads
- Large Rivers & Bodies of Water
- Streams/Creeks & Small Rivers
- Cities/Towns
- Cemeteries

Scale: Section = 1 mile X 1 mile
(there are some exceptions)

Map Group 24: Index to Land Patents

Township 26-North Range 11-West (4th PM - 1831 MN/WI)

After you locate an individual in this Index, take note of the Section and Section Part then proceed to the Land Patent map on the pages immediately following. You should have no difficulty locating the corresponding parcel of land.

The "For More Info" Column will lead you to more information about the underlying Patents. See the *Legend* at right, and the "How to Use this Book" chapter, for more information.

LEGEND

"For More Info . . . " column

A = Authority (Legislative Act, See Appendix "A")
B = Block or Lot (location in Section unknown)
C = Cancelled Patent
F = Fractional Section
G = Group (Multi-Patentee Patent, see Appendix "C")
V = Overlaps another Parcel
R = Re-Issued (Parcel patented more than once)

(A & G items require you to look in the Appendixes referred to above. All other Letter-designations followed by a number require you to locate line-items in this index that possess the ID number found after the letter).

ID	Individual in Patent	Sec.	Sec. Part	Date Issued	Other Counties	For More Info . . .
4397	ADAMS, Luther	14	S½NE	1858-03-01		A5 G2
4429	ALBURTUS, Samuel	3	SW	1859-09-01		A5
4297	ALDERMAN, George	2	1	1861-04-01		A5
4298	" "	2	2	1861-04-01		A5
4299	" "	2	SWNW	1861-04-01		A5
4489	ALLEN, William W	4	N½NE	1860-08-03		A5 G5
4490	" "	4	N½NW	1860-08-03		A5 G5
4418	AMORY, Peter B	24	NWSE	1860-10-01		A7
4199	ANDERSON, Annie M	26	S½SE	1893-08-28		A6 G408
4415	ANDERSON, Ole	12	E½NE	1861-12-05		A5 G11 R4227
4416	" "	12	NWNE	1861-12-05		A5 G11 V4463
4305	ARNOLD, Henry	22	NWNW	1890-05-14		A6
4200	AVERY, Beriah	2	NWNE	1859-05-02		A2
4212	BABCOCK, Charles F	32	E½NE	1858-08-10		A2
4213	" "	32	NWNE	1858-08-10		A2
4224	BABCOCK, Charles T	28	NW	1858-08-10		A2 V4477
4309	BABCOCK, Henry C	25	S½SE	1858-05-03		A5 G16
4307	" "	36	E½NE	1858-05-03		A5
4308	" "	36	NWNE	1858-05-03		A5
4306	" "	25	SESW	1858-08-10		A2
4309	BASFORD, Aurelin	25	S½SE	1858-05-03		A5 G16
4240	BEEMAN, Daniel	11	SE	1859-07-01		A2
4188	BENNETT, Albert B	32	E½SE	1862-04-01		A2
4415	BISSINGER, H	12	E½NE	1861-12-05		A5 G11 R4227
4416	" "	12	NWNE	1861-12-05		A5 G11 V4463
4205	BOLLES, Charles	1	W½NW	1857-04-01		A2 F
4207	" "	2	4	1857-04-01		A2 F
4209	" "	2	E½NE	1857-04-01		A2 F
4335	" "	23	SWNW	1858-01-15		A2 G68
4202	" "	1	10	1858-08-10		A2
4203	" "	1	8	1858-08-10		A2
4204	" "	1	9	1858-08-10		A2
4206	" "	10	10	1858-08-10		A2
4208	" "	2	5	1858-08-10		A2
4401	BOLLES, Martha	2	3	1859-12-20		A2
4254	BOOKS, David	28	W½SW	1883-08-01		A6
4193	BRILL, Albert S	26	NW	1858-01-15		A2
4194	" "	32	NWSW	1858-08-10		A2
4195	" "	32	SWNW	1858-08-10		A2
4283	BROWN, Ephraim	11	5	1858-08-10		A2
4282	" "	10	4	1859-05-02		A2
4289	BRUSH, Daniel	29	SWNW	1858-04-03		A5 G183
4290	" "	29	W½SW	1858-04-03		A5 G183
4349	BURNS, John	25	NW	1858-08-10		A2
4239	BUTTER, Albert C	36	SE	1861-05-15		A5 G233
4210	CAIN, Charles E	17	SESW	1858-08-10		A2

ID	Individual in Patent	Sec.	Sec. Part	Date Issued	Other Counties	For More Info . . .
4211	CAIN, Charles E (Cont'd)	20	NENW	1858-08-10		A2
4381	CAMP, Joseph W	13	SESW	1858-03-01		A5 G56
4382	" "	13	W½SW	1858-03-01		A5 G56
4380	" "	14	N½NE	1858-03-01		A5
4339	CAMPBELL, James H	6	4	1858-06-16		A5 G58
4340	" "	6	5	1858-06-16		A5 G58
4341	" "	6	SENE	1858-06-16		A5 G58
4350	CANEY, John	10	1	1857-04-02		A2
4351	" "	10	2	1857-04-02		A2
4300	CARPENTER, George H	9	5	1858-05-03		A5
4301	" "	9	S½SW	1858-05-03		A5
4243	CHAMBERLIN, George H	22	NWNE	1857-10-30		A2 G417
4244	" "	22	S½NE	1857-10-30		A2 G417
4245	" "	36	N½SW	1857-10-30		A2 G417
4246	" "	36	S½NW	1857-10-30		A2 G417
4335	CHASE, Isaac P	23	SWNW	1858-01-15		A2 G68
4357	CLAIR, John G	30	SENE	1858-03-01		A5
4358	" "	30	W½NE	1858-03-01		A5
4356	" "	30	NENE	1858-08-10		A2
4236	CLARK, Chester R	19	SESE	1858-03-01		A5 G74
4237	" "	19	W½SE	1858-03-01		A5 G74
4233	" "	19	NESE	1858-08-10		A2
4234	" "	19	NESW	1858-08-10		A2
4235	" "	8	7	1858-08-10		A2
4473	CLEAVE, William A	31	N½NW	1858-05-03		A5
4189	CONE, Albert	11	2	1926-01-25		A5
4190	" "	11	3	1926-01-25		A5
4191	" "	2	7	1926-01-25		A5
4479	COON, William F	29	E½SE	1858-06-16		A5 G84
4480	" "	29	SWSE	1858-06-16		A5 G84
4478	" "	29	NWSE	1858-08-10		A2
4198	COONS, Andrew J	17	N½NW	1858-11-10		A7 G85
4310	CORWITH, Henry	31	S½SE	1858-05-03		A5
4311	" "	31	SW	1858-05-03		A5 G89
4413	CORWITH, Nathan	21	SESE	1858-04-03		A5
4414	" "	28	E½NE	1858-04-03		A5
4304	CRAMER, Harriet	26	W½NE	1858-08-10		A2
4405	CRANDALL, Elizabeth	13	NWSE	1861-12-20		A5 G226
4406	" "	13	W½NE	1861-12-20		A5 G226
4405	CRANDALL, John S	13	NWSE	1861-12-20		A5 G226
4406	" "	13	W½NE	1861-12-20		A5 G226
4278	CUMMINGS, Enoch L	11	4	1860-02-10		A5
4279	" "	11	SESW	1860-02-10		A5
4474	CURTIS, William	25	SWSW	1857-10-30		A2
4475	" "	36	N½NW	1857-10-30		A2
4314	DANTIN, Henry G	18	S½SW	1858-05-03		A5 V4183, 4247
4345	DAY, Jesse	23	N½SW	1858-01-15		A2
4192	DOWNER, Albert	1	2	1859-05-02		A2
4229	DOWNER, Chester	35	NESW	1858-03-01		A5
4230	" "	35	NWSE	1858-03-01		A5
4231	" "	35	SENW	1858-03-01		A5
4232	" "	35	SWNE	1858-03-01		A5
4227	" "	12	E½NE	1858-04-03		A5 R4415
4228	" "	12	E½SE	1858-04-03		A5
4415	DOXTER, Charles E	12	E½NE	1861-12-05		A5 G11 R4227
4416	" "	12	NWNE	1861-12-05		A5 G11 V4463
4261	DRINKWINE, Docter F	32	SENW	1888-10-05		A6
4262	" "	32	SWNE	1888-10-05		A6
4421	EATON, Ralph H	13	NESW	1858-06-16		A5
4422	" "	13	SENW	1858-06-16		A5
4424	" "	19	NE	1858-06-16		A5
4420	" "	13	N½NW	1863-05-30		A5
4423	" "	13	SWNW	1863-05-30		A5
4388	EDWARDS, Julius	21	SWSE	1858-05-01		A5 G117
4389	" "	28	W½NE	1858-05-01		A5 G117
4383	" "	24	NWNE	1858-08-10		A2
4385	" "	32	SWSW	1858-08-10		A2
4384	" "	26	SESW	1862-07-15		A5
4386	" "	35	NENW	1862-07-15		A5
4387	" "	35	NWNE	1862-07-15		A5
4390	EDWARDS, Julius L	25	NENE	1858-01-15		A5
4392	" "	25	W½NE	1858-01-15		A5
4391	" "	25	SENE	1858-08-10		A2

ID	Individual in Patent	Sec.	Sec. Part	Date Issued	Other Counties	For More Info . . .
4444	EDWARDS, Theodore B	22	E½SW	1858-01-15		A5
4446	" "	22	SESE	1858-01-15		A2
4447	" "	22	SWSW	1858-01-15		A5
4448	" "	26	NESW	1858-01-15		A5
4449	" "	26	W½SW	1858-01-15		A5
4457	" "	30	SESE	1858-04-03		A5 G118
4458	" "	31	N½NE	1858-04-03		A5 G118
4438	" "	17	E½NE	1858-05-03		A5
4439	" "	17	NESE	1858-05-03		A5
4442	" "	17	SWNE	1858-05-03		A5
4443	" "	17	W½SE	1858-05-03		A5
4451	" "	30	E½NW	1858-06-16		A5
4440	" "	17	NWNE	1858-08-10		A2
4441	" "	17	SESE	1858-08-10		A2
4445	" "	22	NWSW	1858-08-10		A2
4450	" "	27	NWNW	1858-08-10		A2
4452	" "	30	SWSE	1858-08-10		A2
4453	" "	5	1	1858-08-10		A2
4454	" "	6	2	1860-02-10		A5 G119
4455	" "	6	3	1860-02-10		A5 G119
4456	" "	6	SWSW	1860-02-10		A5 G119
4323	ELLIS, Hurnando C	24	NENE	1858-04-03		A5
4324	" "	24	S½NE	1858-04-03		A5
4255	ELTING, David S	23	S½SW	1858-01-15		A2
4256	" "	27	E½NE	1858-01-15		A5
4257	" "	27	E½NW	1858-01-15		A5
4258	" "	27	NWNE	1858-01-15		A5
4259	" "	27	SWNE	1858-01-15		A5
4260	" "	34	S½NE	1860-11-20		A5
4393	ESTIS, Leonard	1	3	1861-04-01		A7
4312	EWER, Henry	30	W½NW	1858-08-10		A2
4313	" "	31	NWSE	1858-08-10		A2
4476	FALES, William E	21	SWSW	1862-01-15		A2 V4355
4477	" "	28	NWNW	1862-01-15		A2 V4224
4388	FALKNER, Sophia	21	SWSE	1858-05-01		A5 G117
4389	" "	28	W½NE	1858-05-01		A5 G117
4372	FINCH, Joseph	12	SW	1860-02-10		A5
4396	FLINT, Levi	4	W½SE	1860-08-01		A5
4214	FORD, Charles	32	N½NW	1859-07-01		A2
4249	GIBBS, David B	18	W½SE	1858-06-16		A5 G150
4250	" "	21	N½NE	1858-06-16		A5 G151
4251	" "	21	S½NE	1858-06-16		A5 G151
4253	" "	21	S½NW	1858-06-16		A5 G149
4252	" "	31	S½NE	1858-06-16		A5 G151
4247	" "	18	E½SW	1858-11-10		A7 V4314
4248	" "	21	N½NW	1858-11-10		A7
4409	GIBSON, Moses S	9	2	1859-05-02		A2
4410	" "	5	6	1859-09-01		A5 G153
4411	" "	5	7	1859-09-01		A5 G153
4412	" "	5	NESE	1859-09-01		A5 G153 F
4407	" "	4	S½NW	1859-09-10		A5
4408	" "	5	SENE	1859-09-10		A5 F
4274	GOODRICH, Elizur T	25	N½SE	1858-05-03		A5
4275	" "	25	NESW	1858-05-03		A5
4276	" "	25	NWSW	1858-05-03		A5
4277	" "	26	N½SE	1858-05-03		A5
4215	GRAY, Charles	22	SWSE	1860-10-01		A7
4430	HARMON, Samuel	14	SWSW	1858-01-15		A2
4431	" "	15	SESE	1858-01-15		A2
4288	HAWES, Franklin B	24	NW	1858-01-15		A5
4291	" "	29	E½NW	1858-04-03		A5 G184
4292	" "	29	NWNW	1858-04-03		A5 G184
4289	" "	29	SWNW	1858-04-03		A5 G183
4290	" "	29	W½SW	1858-04-03		A5 G183
4293	HAWS, Franklin B	24	E½SW	1859-09-01		A5
4294	" "	24	SWSW	1859-09-01		A5
4410	HAYWARD, Jerusha	5	6	1859-09-01		A5 G153
4411	" "	5	7	1859-09-01		A5 G153
4412	" "	5	NESE	1859-09-01		A5 G153 F
4352	HERRON, John D	7	NW	1858-06-16		A5
4353	" "	7	2	1858-11-10		A7 G186
4354	" "	7	SWNE	1858-11-10		A7 G186
4437	HOBART, Harrison C	34	SE	1861-04-01		A5 G388

ID	Individual in Patent	Sec.	Sec. Part	Date Issued	Other Counties	For More Info . . .
4198	HODGES, Rachel	17	N½NW	1858-11-10		A7 G85
4483	HOPE, William	30	NESE	1858-08-10		A2
4484	" "	32	E½SW	1860-08-01		A5
4485	" "	32	W½SE	1860-08-01		A5
4284	HOPKINS, Ervin	8	5	1858-05-03		A5
4285	" "	8	6	1858-05-03		A5
4286	" "	8	S½SE	1858-05-03		A5
4183	HUBBARD, Abijah A	18	SWSW	1858-08-10		A2 V4314
4184	" "	19	NWNW	1858-08-10		A2
4342	HUSTED, James H	1	4	1861-04-01		A5
4343	" "	1	SENW	1861-04-01		A5
4359	HUYSSEN, Augustus	10	5	1860-08-03		A5 G201
4360	" "	10	6	1860-08-03		A5 G201
4361	" "	10	NWNE	1860-08-03		A5 G201
4217	INGERSOLL, Charles	2	N½NW	1859-09-01		A5 G198
4218	" "	3	NENE	1859-09-01		A5 G198
4370	JAMERSON, William	15	SESW	1858-05-03		A5 G251
4371	" "	15	W½SW	1858-05-03		A5 G251
4359	JERMAN, John	10	5	1860-08-03		A5 G201
4360	" "	10	6	1860-08-03		A5 G201
4361	" "	10	NWNE	1860-08-03		A5 G201
4457	JOHNSON, Nathan P	30	SESE	1858-04-03		A5 G118
4458	" "	31	N½NE	1858-04-03		A5 G118
4457	JOHNSON, Sarah B	30	SESE	1858-04-03		A5 G118
4458	" "	31	N½NE	1858-04-03		A5 G118
4437	KAH-TE-NEEW-O-HO-PAZ-SHAY-NAH-,	34	SE	1861-04-01		A5 G388
4419	KEENER, Peter	20	W½SW	1858-08-10		A2
4454	KIGHTLINGER, Peggy	6	2	1860-02-10		A5 G119
4455	" "	6	3	1860-02-10		A5 G119
4456	" "	6	SWSW	1860-02-10		A5 G119
4436	KIGWIN, Sterry S	26	E½NE	1858-06-16		A5
4362	KIMBALL, John	5	5	1859-09-01		A5
4363	" "	5	N½NE	1859-09-01		A5
4373	KIMBALL, Joseph L	18	NE	1858-05-01		A5
4405	KOPP, Matthew	13	NWSE	1861-12-20		A5 G226
4406	" "	13	W½NE	1861-12-20		A5 G226
4374	LAMB, Joseph	34	SW	1860-11-20		A5
4219	LANDON, Charles O	23	NENE	1858-08-10		A2
4220	" "	23	SENE	1858-08-10		A2
4221	" "	23	W½NE	1858-08-10		A2
4222	" "	34	NW	1860-02-10		A5 G232
4238	LANDON, Cyrus K	28	N½SE	1860-07-02		A2
4239	" "	36	SE	1861-05-15		A5 G233
4481	LATHROP, William H	7	SE	1858-06-16		A5 G237
4353	LEWIS, Catharine	7	2	1858-11-10		A7 G186
4354	" "	7	SWNE	1858-11-10		A7 G186
4355	LEWIS, John D	21	SW	1858-06-16		A5 V4476
4482	LOCKE, Alfred J	20	NE	1858-08-10		A2 G243
4482	LOCKE, William H	20	NE	1858-08-10		A2 G243
4397	LOTT, Jane	14	S½NE	1858-03-01		A5 G2
4398	LUCAS, Marcelia	6	1	1855-12-15		A2
4336	LYTLE, Isabella E	18	NWSW	1858-08-10		A2
4470	MANNING, Sarah	9	8	1858-06-16		A5 G415
4368	MARVIN, Jonathan W	15	NESW	1858-05-03		A5
4370	" "	15	SESW	1858-05-03		A5 G251
4369	" "	15	W½SE	1858-05-03		A5
4371	" "	15	W½SW	1858-05-03		A5 G251
4315	MCCART, Henry	27	NESW	1858-02-01		A2
4316	" "	27	SE	1858-02-01		A2
4287	MCCOLLUM, Francis	31	S½NW	1858-08-10		A2
4346	MEAD, Ira	22	E½NW	1858-05-03		A5 G413
4347	" "	22	SWNW	1858-05-03		A5 G413
4325	" "	5	2	1858-08-10		A2
4326	" "	5	3	1858-08-10		A2
4327	" "	5	4	1858-08-10		A2
4328	" "	6	6	1858-08-10		A2
4329	" "	6	7	1858-08-10		A2
4330	" "	6	8	1858-08-10		A2
4331	" "	7	1	1858-08-10		A2
4332	" "	8	1	1858-08-10		A2
4333	" "	8	2	1858-08-10		A2
4334	" "	8	3	1858-08-10		A2
4196	MEGGETT, Alexander	24	NWSW	1860-07-02		A2

ID	Individual in Patent	Sec.	Sec. Part	Date Issued	Other Counties	For More Info . . .
4197	MEGGETT, Alexander (Cont'd)	36	SWNE	1860-07-02		A2
4185	MOORE, Abram	20	SE	1858-08-10		A2
4187	" "	29	N½NE	1858-08-10		A2
4186	" "	23	SE	1859-07-01		A2
4296	MOORE, Frederic A	24	E½SE	1858-06-16		A5
4295	" "	20	SESW	1858-08-10		A2
4399	MOSHER, Marcus L	13	E½NE	1858-08-10		A2
4425	MOULTON, Riley	18	W½NW	1858-08-10		A2
4263	NORRISH, Edward S	14	E½SW	1858-01-15		A2 G283
4264	" "	14	NWSW	1858-01-15		A2 G283
4265	" "	14	SE	1858-01-15		A2 G283
4263	NORRISH, John	14	E½SW	1858-01-15		A2 G283
4264	" "	14	NWSW	1858-01-15		A2 G283
4265	" "	14	SE	1858-01-15		A2 G283
4364	" "	14	NW	1858-08-10		A2
4375	NORTON, Joseph	17	SWSW	1858-03-01		A5
4376	" "	18	E½SE	1858-03-01		A5
4377	" "	20	NWNW	1858-03-01		A5
4437	PE-QUAH-KO-NAH,	34	SE	1861-04-01		A5 G388
4280	PERRY, Albert	4	E½SE	1859-09-10		A5 G400
4281	" "	4	S½NE	1859-09-10		A5 G400
4434	PETERSON, Simon	18	E½NW	1870-05-02		A6
4280	PHILLIPS, Millea	4	E½SE	1859-09-10		A5 G400
4281	" "	4	S½NE	1859-09-10		A5 G400
4400	PLAISTED, Marilla B	22	NENE	1861-09-05		A2
4487	PLAISTED, William	22	N½SE	1857-03-10		A2
4486	" "	10	9	1858-01-15		A2
4488	" "	9	7	1858-01-15		A2
4236	PRESCOTT, Frances	19	SESE	1858-03-01		A5 G74
4237	" "	19	W½SE	1858-03-01		A5 G74
4365	QUIGGLE, John	15	N½NW	1858-05-03		A5
4366	" "	19	NWSW	1858-05-03		A5
4367	" "	19	S½SW	1858-05-03		A5
4426	RANNEY, Rufus P	3	1	1859-09-10		A5
4427	" "	3	NESE	1859-09-10		A5
4428	" "	3	W½SE	1859-09-10		A5
4489	RAY, Dolly Ann	4	N½NE	1860-08-03		A5 G5
4490	" "	4	N½NW	1860-08-03		A5 G5
4239	REYNOLDS, Anna	36	SE	1861-05-15		A5 G233
4321	REYNOLDS, Horace R	10	S½SW	1860-09-10		A5 G326
4432	RIDDELL, Samuel	23	E½NW	1858-01-15		A5
4433	" "	23	NWNW	1858-01-15		A5
4241	ROBBINS, Daniel	13	E½SE	1858-08-10		A2
4242	" "	13	SWSE	1858-08-10		A2
4462	ROBERTS, Thomas	12	NW	1858-08-10		A2
4463	" "	12	W½NE	1858-08-10		A2 V4416
4339	ROBERTSON, Jane	6	4	1858-06-16		A5 G58
4340	" "	6	5	1858-06-16		A5 G58
4341	" "	6	SENE	1858-06-16		A5 G58
4394	ROCK, Leroy E	20	NESW	1858-05-03		A5
4395	" "	20	S½NW	1858-05-03		A5
4337	RORK, James E	29	E½SW	1858-08-10		A2
4338	" "	30	NWSE	1858-08-10		A2
4302	SELLERS, George	30	SW	1858-08-10		A2
4268	SHAFER, Elias R	8	4	1859-07-01		A2
4269	" "	9	3	1859-07-01		A2
4270	" "	9	4	1859-07-01		A2
4348	SHAFER, John B	4	SW	1859-12-10		A2
4223	SHAY, Charles	36	SESW	1903-11-10		A6
4437	SHO-CHETTES,	34	SE	1861-04-01		A5 G388
4311	SLOVER, Margaret	31	SW	1858-05-03		A5 G89
4464	SMITH, Alexander H	12	W½SE	1860-02-10		A5 G406
4321	SMITH, Margaret Ann	10	S½SW	1860-09-10		A5 G326
4339	SPENCE, Thomas	6	4	1858-06-16		A5 G58
4340	" "	6	5	1858-06-16		A5 G58
4341	" "	6	SENE	1858-06-16		A5 G58
4415	STEPPACHER, W	12	E½NE	1861-12-05		A5 G11 R4227
4416	" "	12	NWNE	1861-12-05		A5 G11 V4463
4253	STONE, Mary	21	S½NW	1858-06-16		A5 G149
4216	SWAN, Charles H	28	E½SW	1880-10-01		A6
4303	SWAN, George	24	SWSE	1896-10-16		A6
4437	SWAN, Sylvester P	34	SE	1861-04-01		A5 G388
4322	SWENSON, Howel	15	NENE	1858-08-10		A2

ID	Individual in Patent	Sec.	Sec. Part	Date Issued	Other Counties	For More Info . . .
4402	THOMAS, Mary	9	6	1858-01-15		A2
4459	TOMLINSON, Thomas A	2	6	1857-10-30		A7
4460	" "	34	N½NE	1858-05-03		A5
4461	" "	35	W½NW	1858-05-03		A5
4280	TOWNSEND, Enoch W	4	E½SE	1859-09-10		A5 G400
4281	" "	4	S½NE	1859-09-10		A5 G400
4344	TRASK, James W	3	S½NW	1859-09-01		A5
4403	UNDERHILL, John	15	S½NW	1858-05-03		A5 G404
4404	" "	15	SWNE	1858-05-03		A5 G404
4403	UNDERHILL, Mary	15	S½NW	1858-05-03		A5 G404
4404	" "	15	SWNE	1858-05-03		A5 G404
4464	VEDDER, Van Vleck	12	W½SE	1860-02-10		A5 G406
4378	VIBBERTS, Joseph S	15	NESE	1857-02-20		A2
4379	" "	15	SENE	1857-02-20		A2
4201	VIETS, Byron	11	NE	1859-07-01		A2
4479	VROOMAN, Rachel	29	E½SE	1858-06-16		A5 G84
4480	" "	29	SWSE	1858-06-16		A5 G84
4199	WAGONER, Annie M	26	S½SE	1893-08-28		A6 G408
4317	WALKER, Hiram	29	S½NE	1858-06-16		A5
4318	" "	35	SESW	1860-02-10		A5
4319	" "	35	SWSE	1860-02-10		A5
4320	" "	35	W½SW	1860-02-10		A5
4417	WALKER, Oramel	1	1	1857-04-01		A2
4222	WARD, Sybel	34	NW	1860-02-10		A5 G232
4291	WATSON, Sarah	29	E½NW	1858-04-03		A5 G184
4292	" "	29	NWNW	1858-04-03		A5 G184
4346	WATTERMAN, Joel	22	E½NW	1858-05-03		A5 G413
4347	" "	22	SWNW	1858-05-03		A5 G413
4465	WEBB, Walter	10	7	1858-06-16		A5
4466	" "	10	8	1858-06-16		A5
4467	" "	10	NWSW	1858-06-16		A5
4468	" "	17	N½SW	1858-06-16		A5
4469	" "	17	S½NW	1858-06-16		A5
4470	" "	9	8	1858-06-16		A5 G415
4243	WESTON, Daniel	22	NWNE	1857-10-30		A2 G417
4244	" "	22	S½NE	1857-10-30		A2 G417
4245	" "	36	N½SW	1857-10-30		A2 G417
4246	" "	36	S½NW	1857-10-30		A2 G417
4226	WHIPPLE, Charles	9	1	1857-04-01		A2
4225	" "	10	3	1859-05-02		A2
4249	WHITTLESEY, Elisha	18	W½SE	1858-06-16		A5 G150
4250	WHITTLESEY, Elisha	21	N½NE	1858-06-16		A5 G151
4251	" "	21	S½NE	1858-06-16		A5 G151
4252	" "	31	S½NE	1858-06-16		A5 G151
4271	" "	19	E½NW	1858-08-10		A2
4272	" "	19	SWNW	1858-08-10		A2
4273	" "	31	NESE	1883-08-10		A2
4266	WILKINS, Eli	6	E½SW	1858-08-10		A2
4267	" "	6	NWSE	1858-08-10		A2
4471	WILKINS, Warren	7	3	1858-08-10		A2
4472	" "	8	8	1858-08-10		A2
4481	WILLIFORD, Polly	7	SE	1858-06-16		A5 G237
4217	WINSLOW, Charlotte	2	N½NW	1859-09-01		A5 G198
4218	" "	3	NENE	1859-09-01		A5 G198
4435	WISCONSIN, State Of	16		1941-08-16		A3
4381	WOOD, Maria	13	SESW	1858-03-01		A5 G56
4382	" "	13	W½SW	1858-03-01		A5 G56

Patent Map

T26-N R11-W
4th PM - 1831 MN/WI Meridian

Map Group 24

Township Statistics

Parcels Mapped :	308
Number of Patents :	204
Number of Individuals :	175
Patentees Identified :	149
Number of Surnames :	150
Multi-Patentee Parcels :	70
Oldest Patent Date :	12/15/1855
Most Recent Patent :	8/16/1941
Block/Lot Parcels :	63
Parcels Re - Issued :	1
Parcels that Overlap :	9
Cities and Towns :	2
Cemeteries :	4

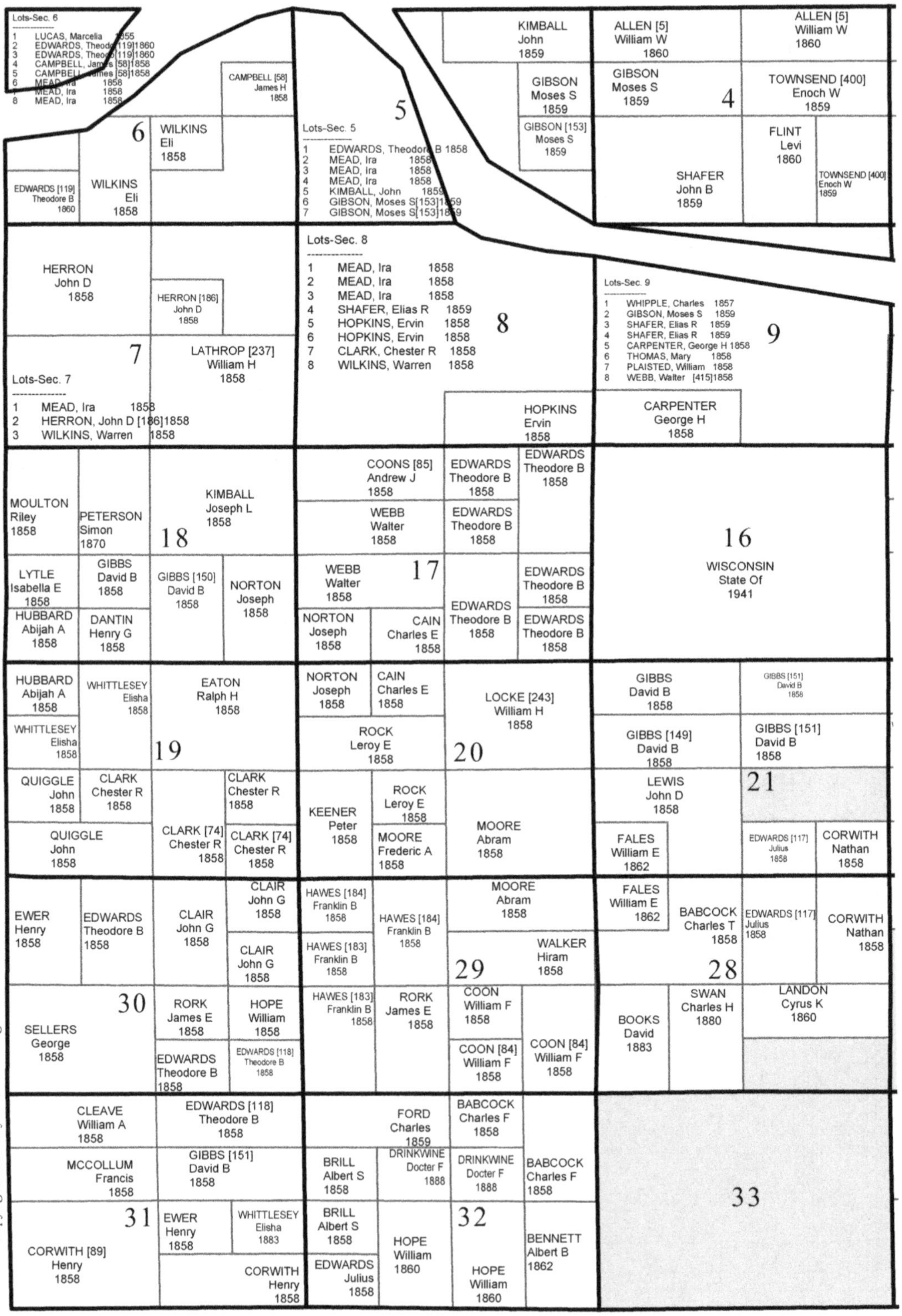

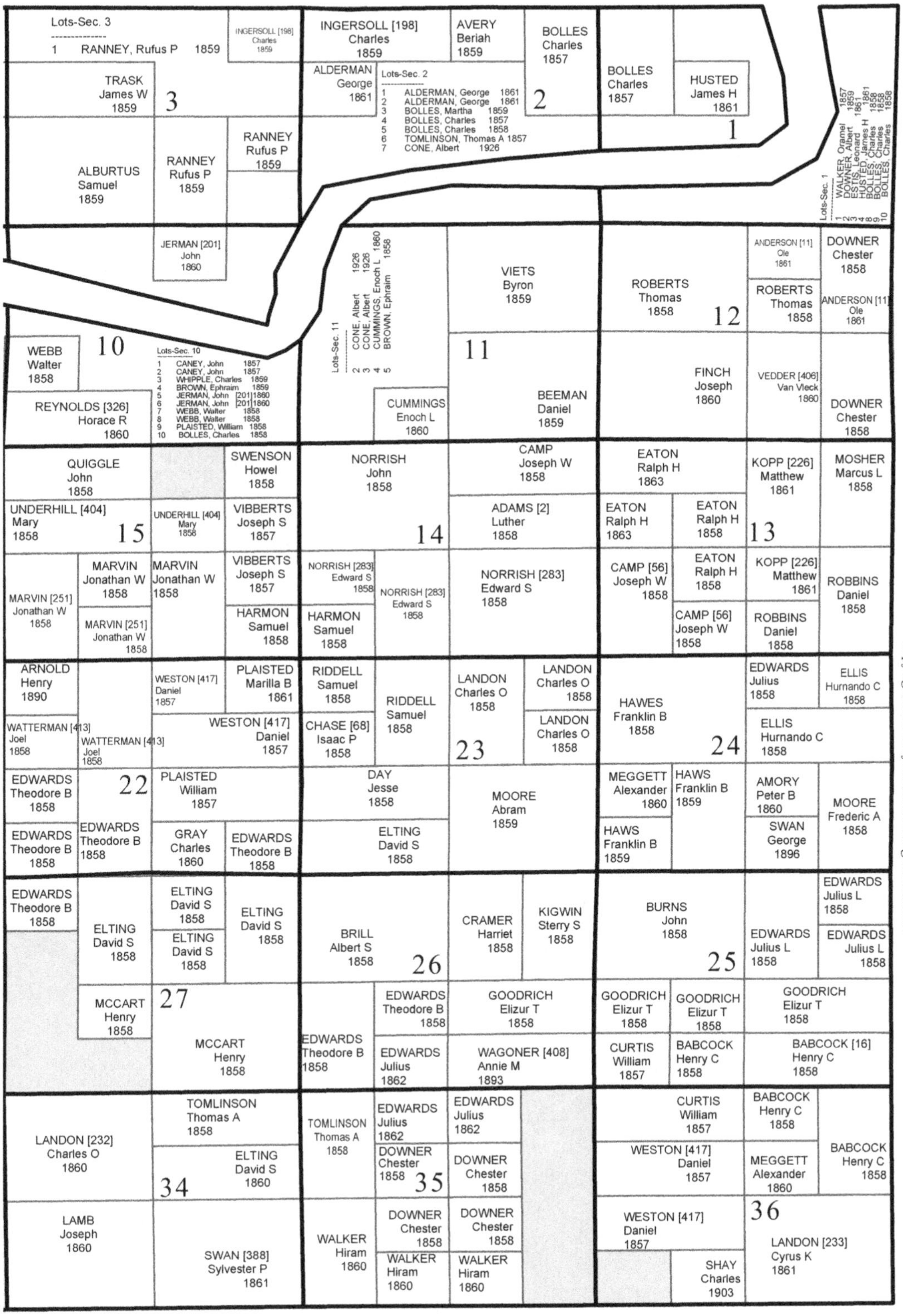

Helpful Hints

1. This Map's INDEX can be found on the preceding pages.
2. Refer to Map "C" to see where this Township lies within Dunn County, Wisconsin.
3. Numbers within square brackets [ ] denote a multi-patentee land parcel (multi-owner). Refer to Appendix "C" for a full list of members in this group.
4. Areas that look to be crowded with Patentees usually indicate multiple sales of the same parcel (Re-issues) or Overlapping parcels. See this Township's Index for an explanation of these and other circumstances that might explain "odd" groupings of Patentees on this map.

Legend

Patent Boundary

Section Boundary

No Patents Found (or Outside County)

1., 2., 3., ... Lot Numbers (when beside a name)

[ ] Group Number (see Appendix "C")

Scale: Section = 1 mile X 1 mile (generally, with some exceptions)

Road Map

T26-N R11-W
4th PM - 1831 MN/WI Meridian

Map Group 24

Cities & Towns

Caryville
Rock Falls

Cemeteries

Fossum Cemetery
Rock Creek Cemetery
Peterson Cemetery
Sand Hill Cemetery

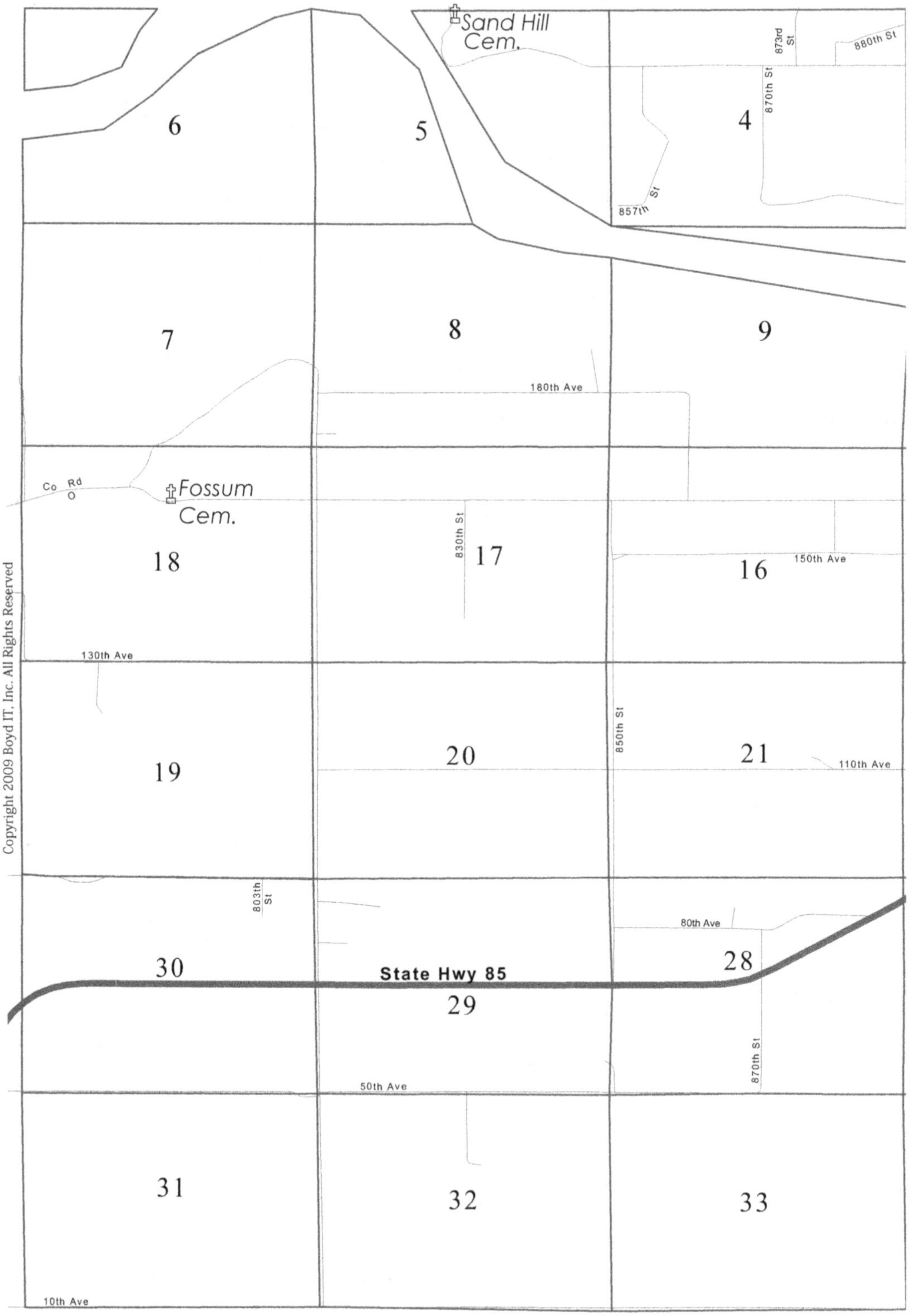

Sand Hill Cem.
873rd St
880th St
870th St
857th St
6
5
4
7
8
9
180th Ave
Co Rd O
Fossum Cem.
830th St
18
17
16
150th Ave
130th Ave
850th St
19
20
21
110th Ave
803th St
80th Ave
30
State Hwy 85
28
29
870th St
50th Ave
31
32
33
10th Ave

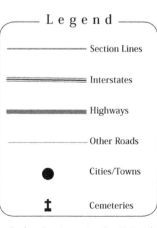

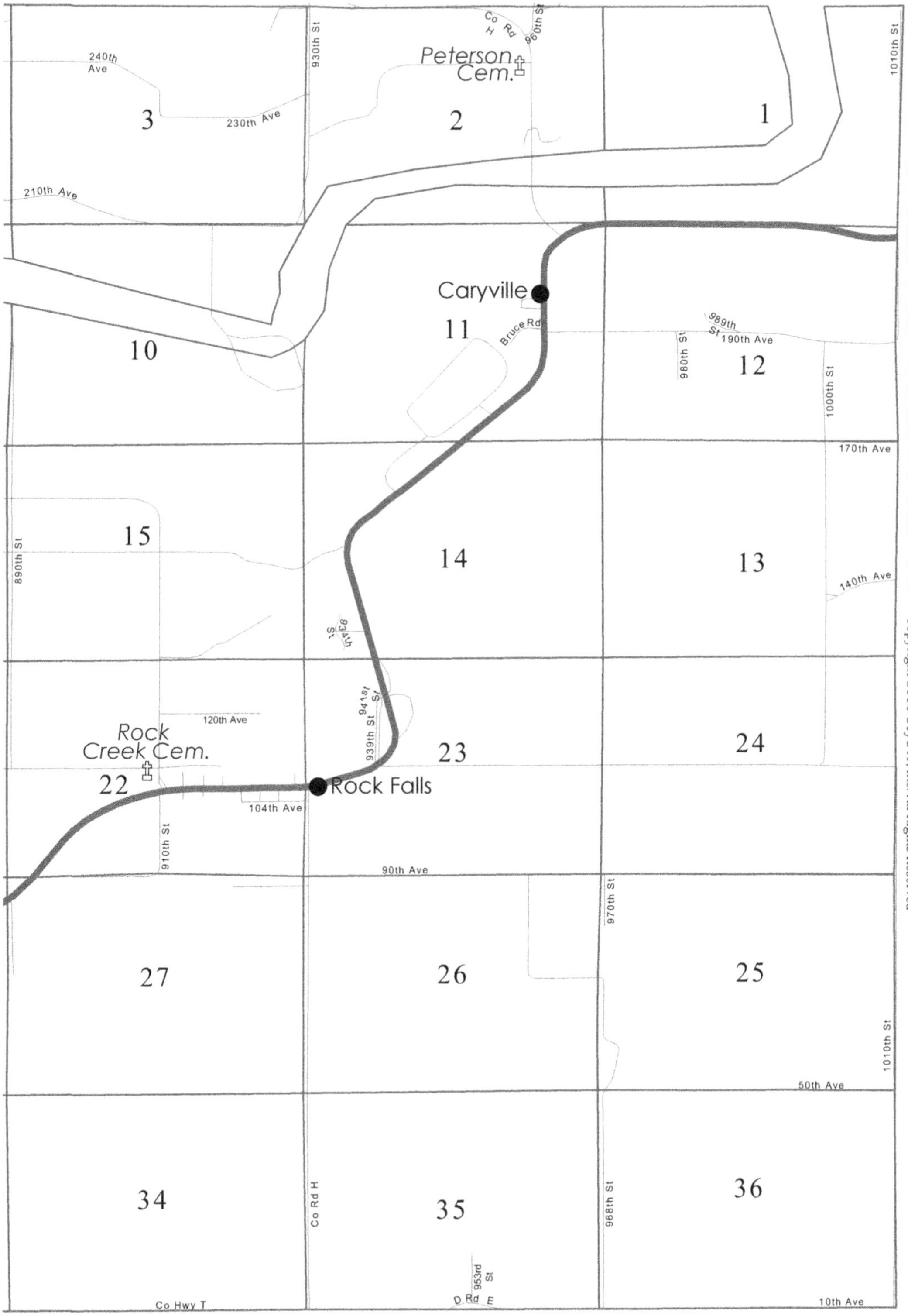
240th Ave
3
230th Ave
210th Ave
930th St
Co Rd H
960th St
Peterson Cem.
2
1
1010th St
Caryville
11
Bruce Rd
10
989th St
190th Ave
980th St
12
1000th St
170th Ave
15
890th St
14
13
140th Ave
934th St
941st St
939th St
120th Ave
Rock Creek Cem.
22
23
24
Rock Falls
104th Ave
910th St
90th Ave
970th St
27
26
25
1010th St
50th Ave
34
Co Rd H
35
968th St
36
953rd St
D Rd E
Co Hwy T
10th Ave

Helpful Hints

1. This road map has a number of uses, but primarily it is to help you: a) find the present location of land owned by your ancestors (at least the general area), b) find cemeteries and city-centers, and c) estimate the route/roads used by Census-takers & tax-assessors.
2. If you plan to travel to Dunn County to locate cemeteries or land parcels, please pick up a modern travel map for the area before you do. Mapping old land parcels on modern maps is not as exact a science as you might think. Just the slightest variations in public land survey coordinates, estimates of parcel boundaries, or road-map deviations can greatly alter a map's representation of how a road either does or doesn't cross a particular parcel of land.

Legend

- Section Lines
- Interstates
- Highways
- Other Roads
- Cities/Towns
- Cemeteries

Scale: Section = 1 mile X 1 mile
(generally, with some exceptions)

Historical Map

T26-N R11-W
4th PM - 1831 MN/WI Meridian

Map Group 24

Cities & Towns

Caryville
Rock Falls

Cemeteries

Fossum Cemetery
Rock Creek Cemetery
Peterson Cemetery
Sand Hill Cemetery

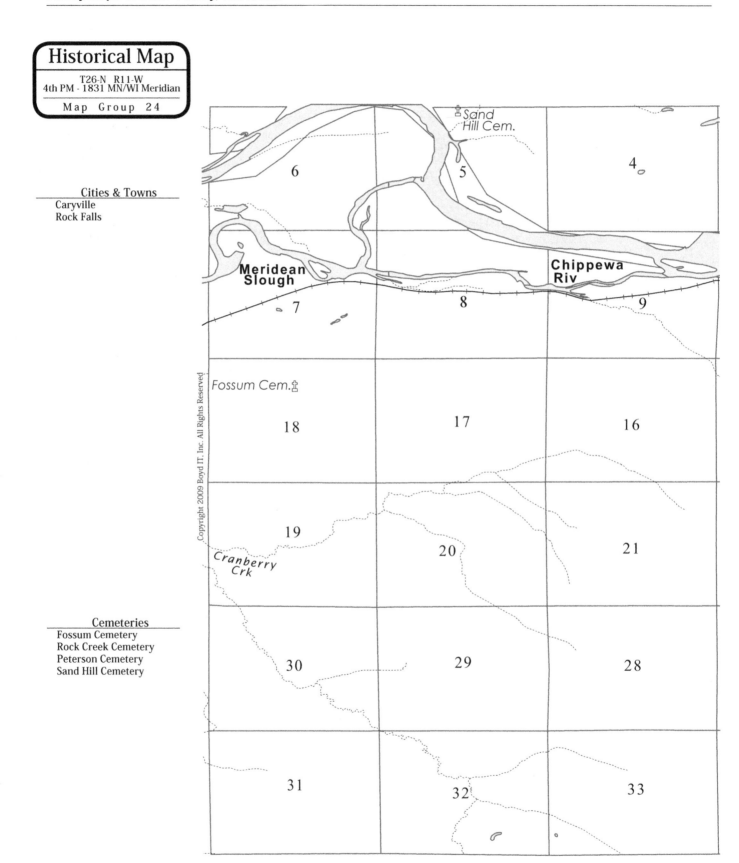

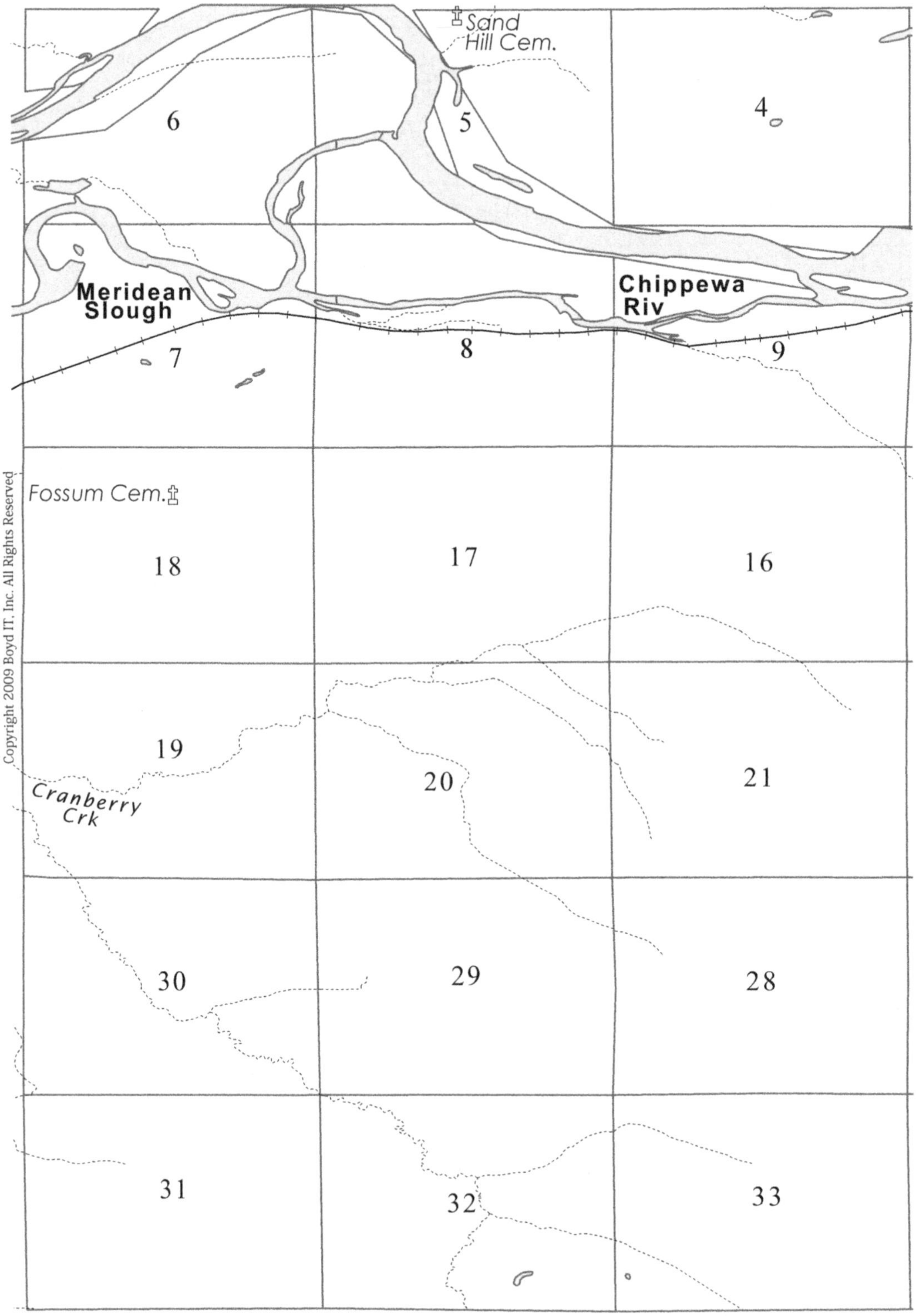

Sand Hill Cem.
6
5
4
Meridean Slough
Chippewa Riv
7
8
9
Fossum Cem.
18
17
16
19
20
21
Cranberry Crk
30
29
28
31
32
33

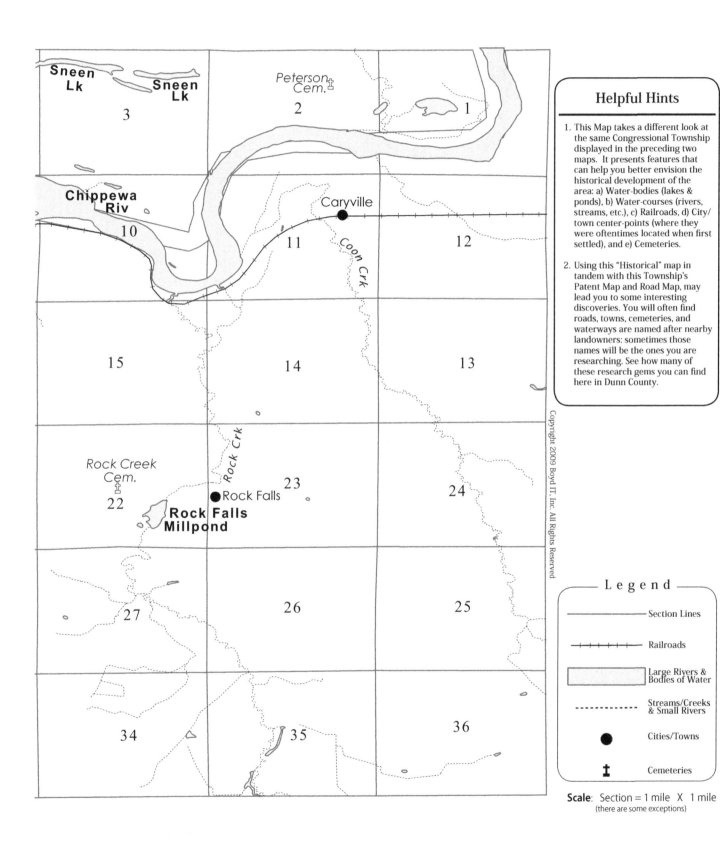

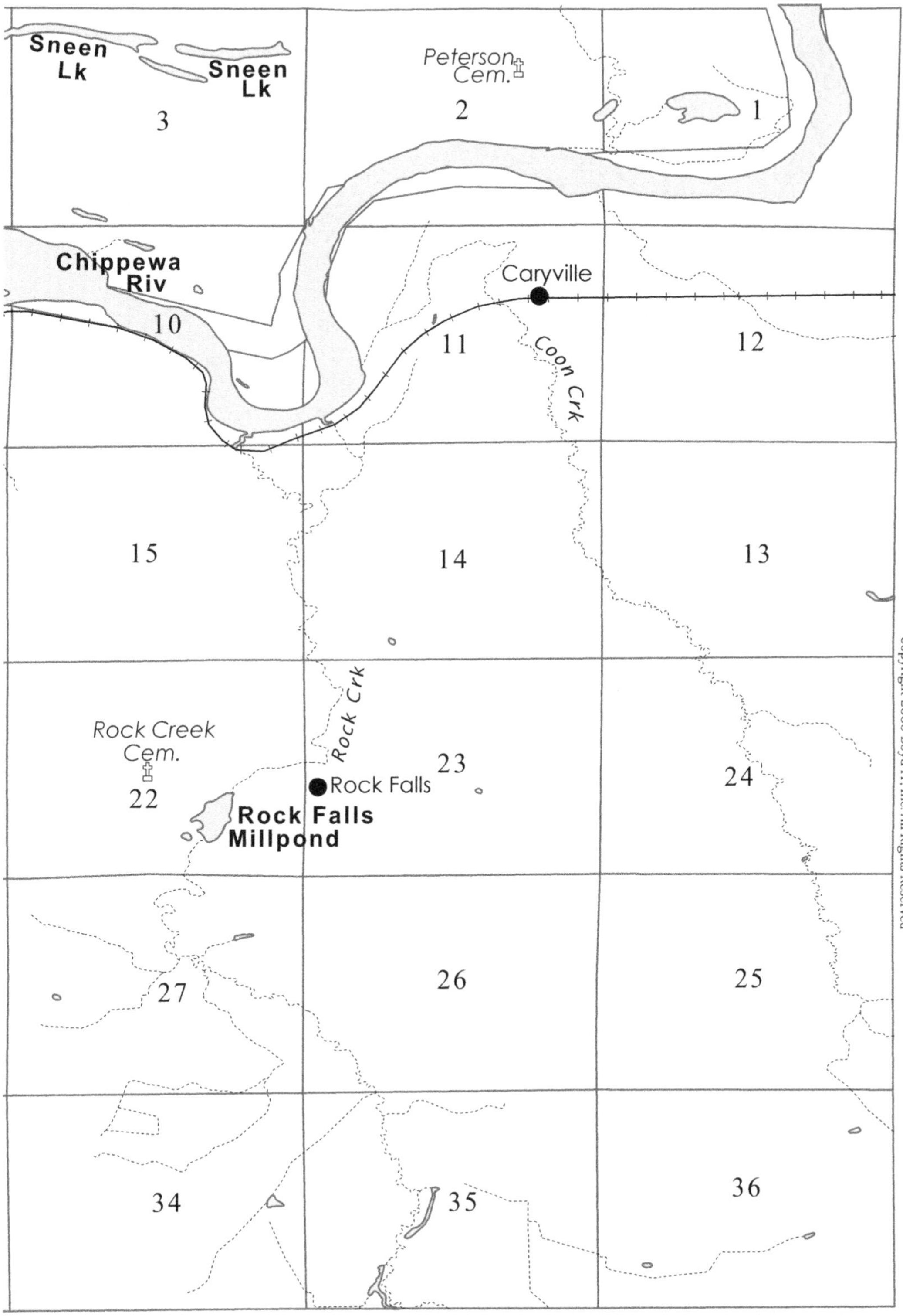
Sneen Lk
Sneen Lk
3
Peterson Cem.
2
1
Chippewa Riv
10
Caryville
11
12
Coon Crk
15
14
13
Rock Crk
Rock Creek Cem.
22
Rock Falls
23
24
Rock Falls Millpond
27
26
25
34
35
36

Helpful Hints

1. This Map takes a different look at the same Congressional Township displayed in the preceding two maps. It presents features that can help you better envision the historical development of the area: a) Water-bodies (lakes & ponds), b) Water-courses (rivers, streams, etc.), c) Railroads, d) City/town center-points (where they were oftentimes located when first settled), and e) Cemeteries.
2. Using this "Historical" map in tandem with this Township's Patent Map and Road Map, may lead you to some interesting discoveries. You will often find roads, towns, cemeteries, and waterways are named after nearby landowners: sometimes those names will be the ones you are researching. See how many of these research gems you can find here in Dunn County.

Legend

- Section Lines
- Railroads
- Large Rivers & Bodies of Water
- Streams/Creeks & Small Rivers
- Cities/Towns
- Cemeteries

Scale: Section = 1 mile X 1 mile
(there are some exceptions)

Appendices

Appendix A - Acts of Congress Authorizing the Patents Contained in this Book

The following Acts of Congress are referred to throughout the Indexes in this book. The text of the Federal Statutes referred to below can usually be found on the web. For more information on such laws, check out the publishers's web-site at www.arphax.com, go to the "Research" page, and click on the "Land-Law" link.

Ref. No.	Date and Act of Congress	Number of Parcels of Land
1	NA: Sale-Title 32 Chapter 7 (RS 2353 43 USC 672)	2
2	April 24, 1820: Sale-Cash Entry (3 Stat. 566)	1094
3	June 21, 1934: State Grant-School Sec Patent (48 Stat. 1185)	24
4	March 22, 1852: ScripWarrant Act of 1852 (10 Stat. 3)	5
5	March 3, 1855: ScripWarrant Act of 1855 (10 Stat. 701)	1328
6	May 20, 1862: Homestead EntryOriginal (12 Stat. 392)	1966
7	September 28, 1850: ScripWarrant Act of 1850 (9 Stat. 520)	71

Appendix B - Section Parts (Aliquot Parts)

The following represent the various abbreviations we have found thus far in describing the parts of a Public Land Section. Some of these are very obscure and rarely used, but we wanted to list them for just that reason. A full section is 1 square mile or 640 acres.

Section Part	Description	Acres
<none>	Full Acre (if no Section Part is listed, presumed a full Section)	640
<1-??>	A number represents a Lot Number and can be of various sizes	?
E$\frac{1}{2}$	East Half-Section	320
E$\frac{1}{2}$E$\frac{1}{2}$	East Half of East Half-Section	160
E$\frac{1}{2}$E$\frac{1}{2}$SE	East Half of East Half of Southeast Quarter-Section	40
E$\frac{1}{2}$N$\frac{1}{2}$	East Half of North Half-Section	160
E$\frac{1}{2}$NE	East Half of Northeast Quarter-Section	80
E$\frac{1}{2}$NENE	East Half of Northeast Quarter of Northeast Quarter-Section	20
E$\frac{1}{2}$NENW	East Half of Northeast Quarter of Northwest Quarter-Section	20
E$\frac{1}{2}$NESE	East Half of Northeast Quarter of Southeast Quarter-Section	20
E$\frac{1}{2}$NESW	East Half of Northeast Quarter of Southwest Quarter-Section	20
E$\frac{1}{2}$NW	East Half of Northwest Quarter-Section	80
E$\frac{1}{2}$NWNE	East Half of Northwest Quarter of Northeast Quarter-Section	20
E$\frac{1}{2}$NWNW	East Half of Northwest Quarter of Northwest Quarter-Section	20
E$\frac{1}{2}$NWSE	East Half of Northwest Quarter of Southeast Quarter-Section	20
E$\frac{1}{2}$NWSW	East Half of Northwest Quarter of Southwest Quarter-Section	20
E$\frac{1}{2}$S$\frac{1}{2}$	East Half of South Half-Section	160
E$\frac{1}{2}$SE	East Half of Southeast Quarter-Section	80
E$\frac{1}{2}$SENE	East Half of Southeast Quarter of Northeast Quarter-Section	20
E$\frac{1}{2}$SENW	East Half of Southeast Quarter of Northwest Quarter-Section	20
E$\frac{1}{2}$SESE	East Half of Southeast Quarter of Southeast Quarter-Section	20
E$\frac{1}{2}$SESW	East Half of Southeast Quarter of Southwest Quarter-Section	20
E$\frac{1}{2}$SW	East Half of Southwest Quarter-Section	80
E$\frac{1}{2}$SWNE	East Half of Southwest Quarter of Northeast Quarter-Section	20
E$\frac{1}{2}$SWNW	East Half of Southwest Quarter of Northwest Quarter-Section	20
E$\frac{1}{2}$SWSE	East Half of Southwest Quarter of Southeast Quarter-Section	20
E$\frac{1}{2}$SWSW	East Half of Southwest Quarter of Southwest Quarter-Section	20
E$\frac{1}{2}$W$\frac{1}{2}$	East Half of West Half-Section	160
N$\frac{1}{2}$	North Half-Section	320
N$\frac{1}{2}$E$\frac{1}{2}$NE	North Half of East Half of Northeast Quarter-Section	40
N$\frac{1}{2}$E$\frac{1}{2}$NW	North Half of East Half of Northwest Quarter-Section	40
N$\frac{1}{2}$E$\frac{1}{2}$SE	North Half of East Half of Southeast Quarter-Section	40
N$\frac{1}{2}$E$\frac{1}{2}$SW	North Half of East Half of Southwest Quarter-Section	40
N$\frac{1}{2}$N$\frac{1}{2}$	North Half of North Half-Section	160
N$\frac{1}{2}$NE	North Half of Northeast Quarter-Section	80
N$\frac{1}{2}$NENE	North Half of Northeast Quarter of Northeast Quarter-Section	20
N$\frac{1}{2}$NENW	North Half of Northeast Quarter of Northwest Quarter-Section	20
N$\frac{1}{2}$NESE	North Half of Northeast Quarter of Southeast Quarter-Section	20
N$\frac{1}{2}$NESW	North Half of Northeast Quarter of Southwest Quarter-Section	20
N$\frac{1}{2}$NW	North Half of Northwest Quarter-Section	80
N$\frac{1}{2}$NWNE	North Half of Northwest Quarter of Northeast Quarter-Section	20
N$\frac{1}{2}$NWNW	North Half of Northwest Quarter of Northwest Quarter-Section	20
N$\frac{1}{2}$NWSE	North Half of Northwest Quarter of Southeast Quarter-Section	20
N$\frac{1}{2}$NWSW	North Half of Northwest Quarter of Southwest Quarter-Section	20
N$\frac{1}{2}$S$\frac{1}{2}$	North Half of South Half-Section	160
N$\frac{1}{2}$SE	North Half of Southeast Quarter-Section	80
N$\frac{1}{2}$SENE	North Half of Southeast Quarter of Northeast Quarter-Section	20
N$\frac{1}{2}$SENW	North Half of Southeast Quarter of Northwest Quarter-Section	20
N$\frac{1}{2}$SESE	North Half of Southeast Quarter of Southeast Quarter-Section	20

Section Part	Description	Acres
N½SESW	North Half of Southeast Quarter of Southwest Quarter-Section	20
N½SESW	North Half of Southeast Quarter of Southwest Quarter-Section	20
N½SW	North Half of Southwest Quarter-Section	80
N½SWNE	North Half of Southwest Quarter of Northeast Quarter-Section	20
N½SWNW	North Half of Southwest Quarter of Northwest Quarter-Section	20
N½SWSE	North Half of Southwest Quarter of Southeast Quarter-Section	20
N½SWSE	North Half of Southwest Quarter of Southeast Quarter-Section	20
N½SWSW	North Half of Southwest Quarter of Southwest Quarter-Section	20
N½W½NW	North Half of West Half of Northwest Quarter-Section	40
N½W½SE	North Half of West Half of Southeast Quarter-Section	40
N½W½SW	North Half of West Half of Southwest Quarter-Section	40
NE	Northeast Quarter-Section	160
NEN½	Northeast Quarter of North Half-Section	80
NENE	Northeast Quarter of Northeast Quarter-Section	40
NENENE	Northeast Quarter of Northeast Quarter of Northeast Quarter	10
NENENW	Northeast Quarter of Northeast Quarter of Northwest Quarter	10
NENESE	Northeast Quarter of Northeast Quarter of Southeast Quarter	10
NENESW	Northeast Quarter of Northeast Quarter of Southwest Quarter	10
NENW	Northeast Quarter of Northwest Quarter-Section	40
NENWNE	Northeast Quarter of Northwest Quarter of Northeast Quarter	10
NENWNW	Northeast Quarter of Northwest Quarter of Northwest Quarter	10
NENWSE	Northeast Quarter of Northwest Quarter of Southeast Quarter	10
NENWSW	Northeast Quarter of Northwest Quarter of Southwest Quarter	10
NESE	Northeast Quarter of Southeast Quarter-Section	40
NESENE	Northeast Quarter of Southeast Quarter of Northeast Quarter	10
NESENW	Northeast Quarter of Southeast Quarter of Northwest Quarter	10
NESESE	Northeast Quarter of Southeast Quarter of Southeast Quarter	10
NESESW	Northeast Quarter of Southeast Quarter of Southwest Quarter	10
NESW	Northeast Quarter of Southwest Quarter-Section	40
NESWNE	Northeast Quarter of Southwest Quarter of Northeast Quarter	10
NESWNW	Northeast Quarter of Southwest Quarter of Northwest Quarter	10
NESWSE	Northeast Quarter of Southwest Quarter of Southeast Quarter	10
NESWSW	Northeast Quarter of Southwest Quarter of Southwest Quarter	10
NW	Northwest Quarter-Section	160
NWE½	Northwest Quarter of Eastern Half-Section	80
NWN½	Northwest Quarter of North Half-Section	80
NWNE	Northwest Quarter of Northeast Quarter-Section	40
NWNENE	Northwest Quarter of Northeast Quarter of Northeast Quarter	10
NWNENW	Northwest Quarter of Northeast Quarter of Northwest Quarter	10
NWNESE	Northwest Quarter of Northeast Quarter of Southeast Quarter	10
NWNESW	Northwest Quarter of Northeast Quarter of Southwest Quarter	10
NWNW	Northwest Quarter of Northwest Quarter-Section	40
NWNWNE	Northwest Quarter of Northwest Quarter of Northeast Quarter	10
NWNWNW	Northwest Quarter of Northwest Quarter of Northwest Quarter	10
NWNWSE	Northwest Quarter of Northwest Quarter of Southeast Quarter	10
NWNWSW	Northwest Quarter of Northwest Quarter of Southwest Quarter	10
NWSE	Northwest Quarter of Southeast Quarter-Section	40
NWSENE	Northwest Quarter of Southeast Quarter of Northeast Quarter	10
NWSENW	Northwest Quarter of Southeast Quarter of Northwest Quarter	10
NWSESE	Northwest Quarter of Southeast Quarter of Southeast Quarter	10
NWSESW	Northwest Quarter of Southeast Quarter of Southwest Quarter	10
NWSW	Northwest Quarter of Southwest Quarter-Section	40
NWSWNE	Northwest Quarter of Southwest Quarter of Northeast Quarter	10
NWSWNW	Northwest Quarter of Southwest Quarter of Northwest Quarter	10
NWSWSE	Northwest Quarter of Southwest Quarter of Southeast Quarter	10
NWSWSW	Northwest Quarter of Southwest Quarter of Southwest Quarter	10
S½	South Half-Section	320
S½E½NE	South Half of East Half of Northeast Quarter-Section	40
S½E½NW	South Half of East Half of Northwest Quarter-Section	40
S½E½SE	South Half of East Half of Southeast Quarter-Section	40

Section Part	Description	Acres
S½E½SW	South Half of East Half of Southwest Quarter-Section	40
S½N½	South Half of North Half-Section	160
S½NE	South Half of Northeast Quarter-Section	80
S½NENE	South Half of Northeast Quarter of Northeast Quarter-Section	20
S½NENW	South Half of Northeast Quarter of Northwest Quarter-Section	20
S½NESE	South Half of Northeast Quarter of Southeast Quarter-Section	20
S½NESW	South Half of Northeast Quarter of Southwest Quarter-Section	20
S½NW	South Half of Northwest Quarter-Section	80
S½NWNE	South Half of Northwest Quarter of Northeast Quarter-Section	20
S½NWNW	South Half of Northwest Quarter of Northwest Quarter-Section	20
S½NWSE	South Half of Northwest Quarter of Southeast Quarter-Section	20
S½NWSW	South Half of Northwest Quarter of Southwest Quarter-Section	20
S½S½	South Half of South Half-Section	160
S½SE	South Half of Southeast Quarter-Section	80
S½SENE	South Half of Southeast Quarter of Northeast Quarter-Section	20
S½SENW	South Half of Southeast Quarter of Northwest Quarter-Section	20
S½SESE	South Half of Southeast Quarter of Southeast Quarter-Section	20
S½SESW	South Half of Southeast Quarter of Southwest Quarter-Section	20
S½SESW	South Half of Southeast Quarter of Southwest Quarter-Section	20
S½SW	South Half of Southwest Quarter-Section	80
S½SWNE	South Half of Southwest Quarter of Northeast Quarter-Section	20
S½SWNW	South Half of Southwest Quarter of Northwest Quarter-Section	20
S½SWSE	South Half of Southwest Quarter of Southeast Quarter-Section	20
S½SWSE	South Half of Southwest Quarter of Southeast Quarter-Section	20
S½SWSW	South Half of Southwest Quarter of Southwest Quarter-Section	20
S½W½NE	South Half of West Half of Northeast Quarter-Section	40
S½W½NW	South Half of West Half of Northwest Quarter-Section	40
S½W½SE	South Half of West Half of Southeast Quarter-Section	40
S½W½SW	South Half of West Half of Southwest Quarter-Section	40
SE	Southeast Quarter Section	160
SEN½	Southeast Quarter of North Half-Section	80
SENE	Southeast Quarter of Northeast Quarter-Section	40
SENENE	Southeast Quarter of Northeast Quarter of Northeast Quarter	10
SENENW	Southeast Quarter of Northeast Quarter of Northwest Quarter	10
SENESE	Southeast Quarter of Northeast Quarter of Southeast Quarter	10
SENESW	Southeast Quarter of Northeast Quarter of Southwest Quarter	10
SENW	Southeast Quarter of Northwest Quarter-Section	40
SENWNE	Southeast Quarter of Northwest Quarter of Northeast Quarter	10
SENWNW	Southeast Quarter of Northwest Quarter of Northwest Quarter	10
SENWSE	Souteast Quarter of Northwest Quarter of Southeast Quarter	10
SENWSW	Southeast Quarter of Northwest Quarter of Southwest Quarter	10
SESE	Southeast Quarter of Southeast Quarter-Section	40
SESENE	SoutheastQuarter of Southeast Quarter of Northeast Quarter	10
SESENW	Southeast Quarter of Southeast Quarter of Northwest Quarter	10
SESESE	Southeast Quarter of Southeast Quarter of Southeast Quarter	10
SESESW	Southeast Quarter of Southeast Quarter of Southwest Quarter	10
SESW	Southeast Quarter of Southwest Quarter-Section	40
SESWNE	Southeast Quarter of Southwest Quarter of Northeast Quarter	10
SESWNW	Southeast Quarter of Southwest Quarter of Northwest Quarter	10
SESWSE	Southeast Quarter of Southwest Quarter of Southeast Quarter	10
SESWSW	Southeast Quarter of Southwest Quarter of Southwest Quarter	10
SW	Southwest Quarter-Section	160
SWNE	Southwest Quarter of Northeast Quarter-Section	40
SWNENE	Southwest Quarter of Northeast Quarter of Northeast Quarter	10
SWNENW	Southwest Quarter of Northeast Quarter of Northwest Quarter	10
SWNESE	Southwest Quarter of Northeast Quarter of Southeast Quarter	10
SWNESW	Southwest Quarter of Northeast Quarter of Southwest Quarter	10
SWNW	Southwest Quarter of Northwest Quarter-Section	40
SWNWNE	Southwest Quarter of Northwest Quarter of Northeast Quarter	10
SWNWNW	Southwest Quarter of Northwest Quarter of Northwest Quarter	10

Section Part	Description	Acres
SWNWSE	Southwest Quarter of Northwest Quarter of Southeast Quarter	10
SWNWSW	Southwest Quarter of Northwest Quarter of Southwest Quarter	10
SWSE	Southwest Quarter of Southeast Quarter-Section	40
SWSENE	Southwest Quarter of Southeast Quarter of Northeast Quarter	10
SWSENW	Southwest Quarter of Southeast Quarter of Northwest Quarter	10
SWSESE	Southwest Quarter of Southeast Quarter of Southeast Quarter	10
SWSESW	Southwest Quarter of Southeast Quarter of Southwest Quarter	10
SWSW	Southwest Quarter of Southwest Quarter-Section	40
SWSWNE	Southwest Quarter of Southwest Quarter of Northeast Quarter	10
SWSWNW	Southwest Quarter of Southwest Quarter of Northwest Quarter	10
SWSWSE	Southwest Quarter of Southwest Quarter of Southeast Quarter	10
SWSWSW	Southwest Quarter of Southwest Quarter of Southwest Quarter	10
W½	West Half-Section	320
W½E½	West Half of East Half-Section	160
W½N½	West Half of North Half-Section (same as NW)	160
W½NE	West Half of Northeast Quarter	80
W½NENE	West Half of Northeast Quarter of Northeast Quarter-Section	20
W½NENW	West Half of Northeast Quarter of Northwest Quarter-Section	20
W½NESE	West Half of Northeast Quarter of Southeast Quarter-Section	20
W½NESW	West Half of Northeast Quarter of Southwest Quarter-Section	20
W½NW	West Half of Northwest Quarter-Section	80
W½NWNE	West Half of Northwest Quarter of Northeast Quarter-Section	20
W½NWNW	West Half of Northwest Quarter of Northwest Quarter-Section	20
W½NWSE	West Half of Northwest Quarter of Southeast Quarter-Section	20
W½NWSW	West Half of Northwest Quarter of Southwest Quarter-Section	20
W½S½	West Half of South Half-Section	160
W½SE	West Half of Southeast Quarter-Section	80
W½SENE	West Half of Southeast Quarter of Northeast Quarter-Section	20
W½SENW	West Half of Southeast Quarter of Northwest Quarter-Section	20
W½SESE	West Half of Southeast Quarter of Southeast Quarter-Section	20
W½SESW	West Half of Southeast Quarter of Southwest Quarter-Section	20
W½SW	West Half of Southwest Quarter-Section	80
W½SWNE	West Half of Southwest Quarter of Northeast Quarter-Section	20
W½SWNW	West Half of Southwest Quarter of Northwest Quarter-Section	20
W½SWSE	West Half of Southwest Quarter of Southeast Quarter-Section	20
W½SWSW	West Half of Southwest Quarter of Southwest Quarter-Section	20
W½W½	West Half of West Half-Section	160

Appendix C - Multi-Patentee Groups

The following index presents groups of people who jointly received patents in Dunn County, Wisconsin. The Group Numbers are used in the Patent Maps and their Indexes so that you may then turn to this Appendix in order to identify all the members of the each buying group.

Group Number 1
ACKLEY, William J; FILLEY, Hannah

Group Number 2
ADAMS, Luther; LOTT, Jane

Group Number 3
AIKEN, John A; DRAKE, Levi P

Group Number 4
ALLEN, Pardee; BISHOP, Mary

Group Number 5
ALLEN, William W; RAY, Dolly Ann

Group Number 6
ALLISON, John; PICKARD, Mercy

Group Number 7
AMORY, James; RYDER, Ann

Group Number 8
ANDERSEN, Anne; ANDERSEN, Knud

Group Number 9
ANDERSON, Gilbert; FOOTE, Alpheus H

Group Number 10
ANDERSON, Kgreste; ANDERSON, Thorsten

Group Number 11
ANDERSON, Ole; STEPPACHER, W; BISSINGER, H; DOXTER, Charles E

Group Number 12
ANDERSON, Sarah A; ANDERSON, Jacob

Group Number 13
ATWOOD, George; TAYLOR, Gracey; HOOKS, Charles

Group Number 14
ATWOOD, George; WALKER, Elizabeth; WALKER, Joseph H

Group Number 15
AUSSMAN, John; KOBB, Angelina

Group Number 16
BABCOCK, Henry C; BASFORD, Aurelin

Group Number 17
BALCOM, Henry; SPOONER, Hannah

Group Number 18
BALDWIN, Cyrenius; GAGE, Lovina; GAGE, Myron W

Group Number 19
BALDWIN, Cyrenius; SANGER, S S

Group Number 20
BALDWIN, Cyrenius; STEENBARGER, Elizabeth

Group Number 21
BARKER, James S; TRASHER, John; POWERS, Emma

Group Number 22
BARNARD, George M; LARRABEE, Phebe

Group Number 23
BARNARD, James M; WALKER, Sarah

Group Number 24
BARNARD, James M; WILLIAMS, Mary; FOLJAMBE, Charles

Group Number 25
BARNARD, James M; WOODWARD, Susannah

Group Number 26
BARNARD, Susan L; BRADFORD, Lucinda; WYMAN, Asa; BARNARD, George M

Group Number 27
BARNARD, Susan L; SMITH, Mary; BARNARD, George M

Group Number 28
BARNE, James R; WELLS, Thomas O; CURTISS, Gertrude

Group Number 29
BARNUM, Israel; SHANKLIN, Martha

Group Number 30
BARTLETT, Junius A; FOWLER, Mary Ann

Group Number 31
BARTON, Gorham; ADAMS, Esther H

Group Number 32
BARTON, Gorham; MILES, Lucy

Group Number 33
BAXTER, Richard; BOUSE, Barbara

Group Number 34
BEGUHN, John; PALMER, Phebe

Group Number 35
BELLACH, Caroline; DYKINS, Mary

Group Number 36
BENNETT, Richard; GRAY, James B

Group Number 37
BILLILNGS, Andrew; MONFORT, Elizabeth

Group Number 38
BILLINGS, Andrew; BENNETT, Harriet

Group Number 39
BILLINGS, Andrew; ELDERT, Mary

Group Number 40
BILLINGS, Mary; BILLINGS, Charles

Group Number 41
BLAIR, Thomas; CASSADY, William

Group Number 42
BLODGETT, Silas; BURY, William A; SMITH, Elijah R

Group Number 43
BOGGESS, Jeptha; DRINKER, Joseph H; FIXICO, Tallissee; MILLER, Sam

Group Number 44
BOGGESS, Jeptha; TAYLOR, B W

Group Number 45
BOOTH, Lucius; SHUGERT, Sarah

Group Number 46
BOTTOM, John; BOTUME, John

Group Number 47
BOYINGTON, Hiram; HUSH, Elizabeth

Group Number 48
BRANCH, Willie M; BRANCH, Isaac B

Group Number 49
BRENNAN, Timothy; BRENNAN, Hannah

Group Number 50
BRONSTAD, Kirsta; HANSON, Peter

Group Number 51
BRUNELLE, Alexis J; PEET, Martha; HULL, David Smith

Group Number 52
BUCKLEY, Clemson B; DAVIS, John Almon; BOYNTON, Jesse; DAVIS, Samuel R; MCGINNIS, Beaulah

Group Number 53
BURDETT, Stephen C; RICKER, Catharine

Group Number 54
BURNES, James; ETHEREDGE, Margaret

Group Number 55
CADY, Samuel M; WILLIAMS, Maria

Group Number 56
CAMP, Joseph W; WOOD, Maria

Group Number 57
CAMPBELL, James H; SHIPMAN, Elender

Group Number 58
CAMPBELL, James H; SPENCE, Thomas; ROBERTSON, Jane

Group Number 59
CANFIELD, Philo; DOOLITTLE, Ormus; DOOLITTLE, James R

Group Number 60
CANTRELL, William; JOHNSTON, Margaret M; MANLEY, Reuben

Group Number 61
CARD, William; CARD, D P; CARD, Abel C

Group Number 62
CARSON, William; EATON, Henry

Group Number 63
CARSON, William; EATON, Henry; DOWNS, Burage B; DOWNS, Eben

Group Number 64
CARSON, William; EATON, Henry; DOWNS, Burrage B; DOWNS, Eben

Group Number 65
CARSON, William; EATON, Henry; DOWNS, Burrage B; RAND, Eldridge D

Group Number 66
CARSON, William; EATON, Henry; DOWNS, Burrage B; RAND, Eldrige D

Group Number 67
CAVANAGH, John J; MONTGOMERY, Margery; NYE, William H

Group Number 68
CHASE, Isaac P; BOLLES, Charles

Group Number 69
CHENEY, Hazen; HUNT, Mehitable; SAXTON, Ebenezer M

Group Number 70
CHENEY, Hazen; TOBEY, Lucy; SAXTON, Ebenezer M

Group Number 71
CHRISTIANSON, Ever; KINGMAN, Phebe

Group Number 72
CHRISTOPHERSEN, Bernt; WICKS, Charles

Group Number 73
CHURCH, Frederick R; VAN RIPER, MARGARET

Group Number 74
CLARK, Chester R; PRESCOTT, Frances

Group Number 75
CLARK, Hannah; CLARK, Elias

Group Number 76
CLARK, Thomas L; KNOX, Rebecca W

Group Number 77
CLARK, Thomas Lewis; TREFETHREN, Jane

Group Number 78
CLYNGENPEEL, Edward; BROWN, Martin

Group Number 79
COBURN, Amos; FISK, James D

Group Number 80
COLBURN, Amos; FISK, James D

Group Number 81
COLE, Ira; ONDERDONK, Catharine

Group Number 82
COLE, Omar; DYER, Wayne B

Group Number 83
CONE, Nancy E; CONE, Simon C

Group Number 84
COON, William F; VROOMAN, Rachel

Group Number 85
COONS, Andrew J; HODGES, Rachel

Group Number 86
COPELAND, Howard; SPALDING, Mary

Group Number 87
CORWITH, Henry; FEEKS, Mary Ann

Group Number 88
CORWITH, Henry; PIERSON, Sarah L

Group Number 89
CORWITH, Henry; SLOVER, Margaret

Group Number 90
CRAMER, Howard; BENNET, Deborah; CLINTON, Albert T

Group Number 91
CRAMER, Howard; CLINTON, Albert T

Group Number 92
CRANDALL, Betsey A; CRANDALL, William E

Group Number 93
CROSBY, Elhanan W; THAYER, Linus B; LEWELLEN, George

Group Number 94
CROSSMAN, Marcia A; CUTLER, Henry; CUTLER, Mary; CUTLER, Charles

Group Number 95
CUMMINGS, John W; HOUSER, Frances

Group Number 96
CUTTING, Sally; PAIRO, Charles W

Group Number 97
DAHL, Tobias; PETERSON, Nelson T

Group Number 98
DALRIMPLE, John A; FLOOD, John O

Group Number 99
DARLINTON, Carey A; PRICKETT, Lucinda E

Group Number 100
DARNELL, Martha; DECKER, Permelia

Group Number 101
DARROW, Amanda; CARD, Amanda D

Group Number 102
DAVISON, Ellen J; DAVISON, Joseph

Group Number 103
DE LONG, ANGELINE M; HOYT, John

Group Number 104
DEARY, James; HAY, Sally

Group Number 105
DEXTER, Edward; ATWOOD, Lois

Group Number 106
DEXTER, Edward; HAMMOND, Georgia Ann E

Group Number 107
DEXTER, Edward; WA-KE-MA-WET, ; MEE-CHIT-E-NEE, ; AH-KE-NE-BOI-WE,

Group Number 108
DIX, John H; ALLEN, Stillman B

Group Number 109
DIX, John H; CHAMBERS, Polly

Group Number 110
DIX, John H; EATON, Sarah

Group Number 111
DODGE, Samuel; LIVINGSTON, Mehitable

Group Number 112
DORR, Robert L; VAUGHAN, Deborah

Group Number 113
DOWNER, Chester; NYE, Clarissa

Group Number 114
DUELL, Charles E; DUELL, Horace M

Group Number 115
DUNKLEE, John William; LEAVENWORTH, George Henry; COLE, Charles C

Group Number 116
DUNKLEE, John William; PELT, Jonathan; VAN PELT, LARKIN; VAN PELT, ELLEN; COLE, Charles C

Group Number 117
EDWARDS, Julius; FALKNER, Sophia

Group Number 118
EDWARDS, Theodore B; JOHNSON, Sarah B; JOHNSON, Nathan P

Group Number 119
EDWARDS, Theodore B; KIGHTLINGER, Peggy

Group Number 120
EDWARDS, Theodore B; STEEL, Charlotte

Group Number 121
EIDE, Samson Nielson; FLANDERS, Ann; SEVERSON, Sever

Group Number 122
EMENS, Isaac; MASONER, Mary

Group Number 123
EMERY, Stephen; CROCKETT, Abigail

Group Number 124
EVANS, Edward; DARRIN, Martha

Group Number 125
EVANS, William; DOANE, Samuel H

Group Number 126
EVENS, Anne; SEAMAN, Abigail

Group Number 127
FAIRBANKS, John B; GALE, Betsey

Group Number 128
FAYERWEATHER, Eliza; FAYERWEATHER, David C

Group Number 129
FIELDS, Truman; ALLEN, Benjamin

Group Number 130
FINEGAN, Patrick; HAGAR, Margaret

Group Number 131
FITCH, Lyman; REYNOLDS, John L

Group Number 132
FLINT, David; VAN SLIKE, ELIZABETH

Group Number 133
FRENCH, Samuel B; ALDRICK, Caleb E

Group Number 134
FRENCH, Samuel B; BEDDINGER, Sarah

Group Number 135
FRENCH, Samuel B; BUNT, William A

Group Number 136
FRENCH, Samuel B; CAMERON, Christie

Group Number 137
FRENCH, Samuel B; CHANCE, Levi

Group Number 138
FRENCH, Samuel B; COLE, Patty

Group Number 139
FRENCH, Samuel B; HARKNESS, Margaret

Group Number 140
FRENCH, Samuel B; HUGHES, Fanny

Group Number 141
FRENCH, Samuel B; PAYNE, Betsy

Group Number 142
FRENCH, Samuel B; SWEET, Mary

Group Number 143
FRENCH, Samuel B; WEST, Margarette; WARREN, Marvin

Group Number 144
FRENCH, Samuel B; WHEELER, Payton

Group Number 145
FRENCH, Samuel B; WILSON, Susan

Group Number 146
FULLER, S W; RUE, Christiana; DEXTER, Charles E

Group Number 147
GAREHART, John; LANDRUM, Nancy

Group Number 148
GEORGE, Henry; SEXTON, Ebenezer M

Group Number 149
GIBBS, David B; STONE, Mary

Group Number 150
GIBBS, David B; WHITLLESEY, Elisha

Group Number 151
GIBBS, David B; WHITTLESEY, Elisha

Group Number 152
GIBSON, Moses S; COUN, Hannah

Group Number 153
GIBSON, Moses S; HAYWARD, Jerusha

Group Number 154
GILBERT, Samuel; GILBERT, Oliver

Group Number 155
GILBRANSON, Laurina; GILBRANSON, John

Group Number 156
GLENNY, Elizabeth A; BOND, Elizabeth A

Group Number 157
GOBEL, John; POTE, Lovell

Group Number 158
GODELL, Betsy; GODELL, John

Group Number 159
GOERCKE, William; MEREDETH, John L

Group Number 160
GOSS, Alfred; GOODRICH, Allen S

Group Number 161
GOSS, Alfred; PAINE, Rachel

Group Number 162
GOSS, Alfred; SANGER, Elizabeth

Group Number 163
GRAY, Adam; GRAY, Nancy

Group Number 164
GRAY, Almon D; DRAKE, Levi P

Group Number 165
GRAY, Almon D; HOBBS, James H; DRAKE, Levi P

Group Number 166
GRAY, James B; COLOMY, Sarah

Group Number 167
GRAY, James B; TAYLOR, Mary

Group Number 168
GREEN, George; PALMER, Mercy S

Group Number 169
GROVER, Freeman; COLLINS, Betsey

Group Number 170
GROVER, Freeman; LYON, Frances B

Group Number 171
HAIGHT, Charles; CAREY, Dilane

Group Number 172
HALVORSON, Christian; DOYLE, William

Group Number 173
HANSEN, Torger; MORSE, Hiram; TAYLOR, Hiram

Group Number 174
HANSON, Maria; HANSON, Hans

Group Number 175
HARLE, Ludwig; HARLEY, Louis

Group Number 176
HARLEY, Frederick; HAERLE, Frederick; HARRISON, Rachel

Group Number 177
HARM, John; BENNETT, Deborah L; HARLE, Friedrich

Group Number 178
HARRIGAN, Patrick; GENTRY, William E; GLENN, Thomas M

Group Number 179
HARRINGTON, John; HANCOCK, Cynthia

Group Number 180
HARRINGTON, Mary; OLESON, Mary

Group Number 181
HARSH, George; BENAVIDES, Pabla

Group Number 182
HAUGE, Berthe M; SCHULSTAD, Berthe M

Group Number 183
HAWES, Franklin B; BRUSH, Daniel

Group Number 184
HAWES, Franklin B; WATSON, Sarah

Group Number 185
HEASLY, John W; FRENCH, Samuel B

Group Number 186
HERRON, John D; LEWIS, Catharine

Group Number 187
HILL, Theodore; PAGE, Nancy

Group Number 188
HINTZ, John; HAGEN, Elizabeth

Group Number 189
HODGDON, John; AUSTIN, Kesiah

Group Number 190
HODGDON, John; MURPHY, Lucinda J

Group Number 191
HOFFMAN, Mary; KEISER, Jacob

Group Number 192
HOLBROOK, Ruth M; PARKER, Abigail

Group Number 193
HORSTMANN, Adolph; COUZENS, Abigail

Group Number 194
HUBBARD, Hamilton W; MARSHALL, Loruhama

Group Number 195
HUMPHREY, Horace; HUMPHREY, Riley

Group Number 196
HYDE, Dillon; WARD, Alice

Group Number 197
INABNIT, Eliza; INABNIT, Peter

Group Number 198
INGERSOLL, Charles; WINSLOW, Charlotte

Group Number 199
IRVINE, George K; PORTER, Margaret

Group Number 200
JACKSON, Aaron N; JACKSON, Andrew; JACKSON, Berthier M; JACKSON, Sally J

Group Number 201
JERMAN, John; HUYSSEN, Augustus

Group Number 202
JEWETT, George K; MARCH, Leonard; CHASE, Jonathan

Group Number 203
JEWETT, Samuel A; STAMPS, Sarah

Group Number 204
JEWETT, Samuel A; SUMMERS, Mary

Group Number 205
JOHNSON, Alfred; BRAINARD, C R

Group Number 206
JOHNSON, Bergith; ANDERSON, Bergith

Group Number 207
JOHNSON, Ingebor; JOHNSON, Peter

Group Number 208
JONES, Eliza Selina; THOMAS, Samuel A

Group Number 209
JONES, Isaac S; ROGERS, Betsey

Group Number 210
JONSEN, Lars; GRANT, John W

Group Number 211
JONSON, Lars; GRANT, John W

Group Number 212
KEEN, David M; BAILEY, Mary

Group Number 213
KEEN, David M; GRAY, James B

Group Number 214
KENT, Joseph D; KENT, Depusey; TAYLOR, Hiram H; BALIS, Luther

Group Number 215
KENT, William; SICKLES, Sarah

Group Number 216
KITTELSEN, Tosten; KEY, Mary A R; DEXTER, Charles E

Group Number 217
KNAPP, John H; POTETE, Isabella

Group Number 218
KNAPP, John H; STOUT, Henry L; TAINTER, Andrew; WILSON, Thomas B

Group Number 219
KNAPP, John H; STOUT, Henry L; TAINTER, Andrew; WILSON, Thomas B

Group Number 220
KNAPP, John H; STOUT, Henry L; TAINTER, Andrew; WILSON, Thomas B; BANKS, Maria

Group Number 221
KNAPP, John H; STOUT, Henry L; TAINTER, Andrew; WILSON, Thomas B; GERMAN, Mary E

Group Number 222
KNAPP, John H; STOUT, Henry L; TAINTER, Andrew; WILSON, Thomas B; GREENWEIG, Elizabeth

Group Number 223
KNAPP, John H; STOUT, Henry L; TAINTER, Andrew; WILSON, Thomas B; SALESBURY, Jane

Group Number 224
KNAPP, John H; TAINTER, Andrew; STOUT, Henry L; WILSON, Thomas B

Group Number 225
KNAPP, John H; TAINTER, J B

Group Number 226
KOPP, Matthew; CRANDALL, Elizabeth; CRANDALL, John S

Group Number 227
KOWING, Francis; CURRY, Lucy

Group Number 228
KOWING, Francis; QUARLES, Nancy

Group Number 229
KRAMER, Nicholas; HALFORTY, Mary

Group Number 230
KRAMER, Nicholas; HARRIS, Almon T

Group Number 231
KRAMPERT, Meri; SCHLUCH, Meri; SCHLUCH, Paul

Group Number 232
LANDON, Charles O; WARD, Sybel

Group Number 233
LANDON, Cyrus K; REYNOLDS, Anna; BUTTER, Albert C

Group Number 234
LANDON, William H; HUTCHISON, Elizabeth

Group Number 235
LANDON, William H; LAUDON, William H

Group Number 236
LARSON, Bertie; LARSON, John

Group Number 237
LATHROP, William H; WILLIFORD, Polly

Group Number 238
LECLERCQ, Francis L; DICKEY, Eleanor; SHEPHARD, John G

Group Number 239
LEE, William J; BRAYNARD, Thomas L

Group Number 240
LEWIS, Theodore; JONES, George B

Group Number 241
LITTLE, Peter; LITTLE, James

Group Number 242
LITTLE, William; CUTCHEON, O M

Group Number 243
LOCKE, William H; LOCKE, Alfred J

Group Number 244
LUCAS, Carroll; REMINGTON, Barlow

Group Number 245
LYMAN, Maria T; POST, Charles; BRAYNARD, Augustus S; BURNETT, John M

Group Number 246
LYTLE, Isabella E; MARTIN, Susan; LYTLE, George

Group Number 247
MAGILTON, George; LAWRENCE, Sarah

Group Number 248
MALHUS, Arnold; SCHROEDER, Lawrence

Group Number 249
MANSFIELD, John W; STEBBINS, Marilla L

Group Number 250
MANSFIELD, John W; VAIL, Mary

Group Number 251
MARVIN, Jonathan W; JAMERSON, William

Group Number 252
MATHERS, Joseph H; SEXTON, Ebenezer M

Group Number 253
MATHEWS, James E; INFINGER, Rebecca

Group Number 254
MATHEWS, James E; NEWCOMB, Sylvia; BULL, Henry

Group Number 255
MATTHEWS, James E; HILL, John; HILL, Charles

Group Number 256
MATTHEWS, James E; MATTHEWS, Andrew T

Group Number 257
MCCORKLE, Andrew; NICHOLS, Sally

Group Number 258
MCCORKLE, Andrew; PYE, Sarah

Group Number 259
MCDONALD, Nancy; MCDONALD, Mary E; MCDONALD, James P

Group Number 260
MCGEOGH, Bridget; HORTWICK, Dorotha

Group Number 261
MCKAHUN, Sarah; MILLER, Jane

Group Number 262
MCLAIN, Malcolm; CURTIS, Jennett

Group Number 263
MCPHERSON, D D; GLUTH, Louis F; BUTTERFIELD, A G; BUTTERFIELD, Mattie; DAY, Perry; MCINTYRE, Janett

Group Number 264
MCROBERT, Edward; BUXTON, Nancy; HUDSPETH, Henry S

Group Number 265
MICKELSON, Ingle; REID, Robert

Group Number 266
MIESTER, Franz; ELDERD, Eliza

Group Number 267
MILLS, Richard; CHRISTIE, Priscilla

Group Number 268
MILLS, Richard; LAMB, Jacob C; HARVEY, William R

Group Number 269
MILLS, Richard; LYMAN, Elias A

Group Number 270
MONTAGUE, Giles R; KNAPP, Martha

Group Number 271
MONTAGUE, Theodore G; GREEN, Ambrose

Group Number 272
MONTGOMERY, James; HUTCHINSON, Elizabeth

Group Number 273
MOODY, John Gilman; MOODY, Benjamin Franklin

Group Number 274
MOOR, Andrew; LACY, Catharine

Group Number 275
MOOR, Andrew; MUMER, Jacob

Group Number 276
MOORE, Andrew; BRYANT, Jemima

Group Number 277
MOORE, Andrew; HARRISON, Joseph

Group Number 278
MOYES, John; COLE, Melissa

Group Number 279
NEWHALL, Elbridge G; MACK, Lydia

Group Number 280
NEWSOM, Parnelle G; SEXTON, Thomas W; ALLEN, Miriam

Group Number 281
NICHOLS, Paige F; ANDERSON, Lutilia; SKINNER, Francis R

Group Number 282
NILSEN, Ellen; NILSEN, Nils

Group Number 283
NORRISH, Edward S; NORRISH, John

Group Number 284
OBRIEN, Thomas; VOORIS, Amy

Group Number 285
OCONNOR, Edgar; BROWN, Che-par-nee; MALINDA, ; TOEL, William

Group Number 286
OCONNOR, Edgar; CUSSETAH-MICCO, ; JOHN, ; TOEL, William

Group Number 287
OCONNOR, Edgar; KINNIARD, James; SIM-IS-HOYA, ; SUSEY, ; TOEL, William

Group Number 288
OCONNOR, Edgar; WILLOCK-HOYE, ; TOEL, William

Group Number 289
OLESON, Bertha; OLESON, Forger

Group Number 290
OLESON, Tosten; MARSHALL, Mary

Group Number 291
OLSON, Sarah; SANDERSON, Sarah; SANDERSON, Harrison

Group Number 292
OLSON, Torger; MARSTON, Stephen

Group Number 293
OMDAHL, Samuel; OMDAHLE, Samuel

Group Number 294
ORDEMAN, Gerhard; GOERCKE, Louisa Jane; GOERCKE, Ernest

Group Number 295
PALEN, Joseph G; BULLOCK, Loretta

Group Number 296
PARK, S Halsey; PRUITT, John W

Group Number 297
PARKER, Deforest N; WRIGHT, Jemima

Group Number 298
PEISCH, John; ROBERTS, James H

Group Number 299
PENNOCK, Ames C; DRAKE, Levi P

Group Number 300
PENNOCK, Samuel M; SPALDING, Celinda W; SPALDING, William A

Group Number 301
PEROT, William Henry; CORNWELL, Eliza; LIGHTBOURN, Donald S

Group Number 302
PEROT, William Henry; PUTNEY, Persis; LIGHTBOURN, Donald S

Group Number 303
PHELPS, Ira W; MCGINNIS, Judith

Group Number 304
PLANT, Henry B; ALEXANDER, Rebecca

Group Number 305
PLANT, Henry B; GILLESPIE, Fabian

Group Number 306
PLANT, Henry B; HODGES, Mary B

Group Number 307
PLATT, William H; JARCKE, Ann

Group Number 308
POISKE, Caroline; POISKE, Charles

Group Number 309
POWELL, George May; CHAPIN, George W

Group Number 310
POWELL, George May; KOLB, Susanna

Group Number 311
POWELL, George May; SERVIS, Joseph L

Group Number 312
PRESTON, Bennett S; BOWMAN, Mildred B; LATHROP, William H

Group Number 313
PRETY, William; WHEELER, Augustus C

Group Number 314
PUTNAM, Henry C; PEARSON, Sally S

Group Number 315
RANDALL, Roswell S; DEGRAW, James L; DEGRAW, Elizabeth

Group Number 316
RANNEY, Rufus P; DAVIS, Dorothy

Group Number 317
RASMUSON, Thomas; NELSON, Samuel

Group Number 318
RAYBURN, Patrick; MCMILLAN, William L; MCMILLAN, Robert T; MCMILLAN, Nancy; MCMILLAN, Elizabeth; MCMILLAN, Daniel A; MCMILLAN, Mary Ann; MCMILLAN, Martha H; MCMILLAN, Anna; MCMILLAN, Rachael F

Group Number 319
RAYBURN, Patrick; STINSON, Sarah Ann

Group Number 320
REED, William H; MCGREW, Mary

Group Number 321
REINKE, Christ; REINKE, Joachim

Group Number 322
REMINGTON, Barlow; LUCAS, Carol

Group Number 323
REPINE, Margaret; REPINE, Michael

Group Number 324
REYMERT, Jenny D; YOUNG, Francis; TOLASON, Jonas; ANDERSON, James; MURK, Michael Peterson

Group Number 325
REYNOLDS, Henry; HALSTEAD, Phila

Group Number 326
REYNOLDS, Horace R; SMITH, Margaret Ann

Group Number 327
RIGGS, George W; CO, Riggs And; ELLIOTT, John; KIECKHOEFER, A T

Group Number 328
RIGGS, George W; CO, Riggs And; KIECKHOEFER, A T; ELLIOTT, John

Group Number 329
RIGGS, George W; COBB, Sarah N; CO, Riggs And; KIECKHOEFER, A T; ELLIOTT, John

Group Number 330
RIGGS, George W; CORNISH, Susan W; CO, Riggs And; KIECKHOEFER, A T; ELLIOTT, John

Group Number 331
RIGGS, George W; GIBSON, W W; CO, Riggs And; KIECKHOEFER, A T; ELLIOTT, John

Group Number 332
RIGGS, George W; JOHNSON, Hannah; CO, Riggs And; KIECKHOEFER, A T; ELLIOTT, John

Group Number 333
RIGGS, George W; KIECKHOEFER, A T; ELLIOTT, John; CO, Riggs And

Group Number 334
RIGGS, George W; MORRISON, Elizabeth; CULBERT, James W; CO, Riggs And; KIECKHOEFER, A T; ELLIOTT, John

Group Number 335
RIGGS, George W; OLIVER, Eleanor; CO, Riggs And; KIECKHOEFER, A T; ELLIOTT, John

Group Number 336
RIGGS, George W; PREMBLE, Charles; CO, Riggs And; KIECKHOEFER, A T; ELLIOTT, John; MCLESKEY, W L; CURRY, Lucinda F; CURRY, Elizabeth; CURRY, Louisa L

Group Number 337
RIGGS, George W; SANDERS, Harriet H; CO, Riggs And; KIECKHOEFER, A T; ELLIOTT, John

Group Number 338
RIGGS, George W; TOLEDANO, Arthur G; CO, Riggs And; KIECKHOEFER, A T; ELLIOTT, John

Group Number 339
RIGGS, George W; WALKER, Robert D; CO, Riggs And; KIECKHOEFER, A T; ELLIOTT, John

Group Number 340
RIGGS, George W; WHIPPLE, William L; JENONSON, Eunice A; WHIPPLE, Adaline E; PRESTON, David; CO, Riggs And; KIECKHOEFER, A T; ELLIOTT, John

Group Number 341
RIGGS, George W; WHITEMAN, Anna; CO, Riggs And; KIECKHOEFER, A T; ELLIOTT, John

Group Number 342
RIGGS, George W; WILSON, Sally; LAINE, Lewis; CO, Riggs And; KIECKHOEFER, A T; ELLIOTT, John

Group Number 343
RITTENHOUSE, John B; BEALE, Mary E

Group Number 344
RITTENHOUSE, John B; PAINE, Mary A

Group Number 345
RITTENHOUSE, John B; WILSON, Elizabeth A

Group Number 346
RORK, James E; AZRO, D; SLY, A B

Group Number 347
ROSE, John C; MCADOO, Elizabeth; RANDELL, Addis E

Group Number 348
RUMRILL, Pliny; TEEL, Mary Ann M J

Group Number 349
RUNNING, Bergitta; RUNNING, Ole A

Group Number 350
SAMPSON, Sigbert; NELSON, Samson

Group Number 351
SCHECKEL, Philip; MANS, Fritz

Group Number 352
SEEVER, Elizabeth I; SEEVER, John W

Group Number 353
SENG, Herman; ROSSON, Daniel P

Group Number 354
SEVERSON, Sever; DEXTER, Charles E

Group Number 355
SEVERSON, Sever; WOODHULL, Calvin

Group Number 356
SHARPLES, Ellen; SHARPLES, Franklin W

Group Number 357
SHARPLES, Susan; SHARPLES, Henry

Group Number 358
SHEPHARD, Luther G; ROWE, Irena

Group Number 359
SHERBURN, Samuel W; SHERBURN, Andrew M

Group Number 360
SHERBURNE, Andrew M; SHEPARD, Luther G; ANDREWS, John

Group Number 361
SHERMAN, Thaddeus; DUNN, Elizabeth

Group Number 362
SIPPEL, Conrad; HOGUELAND, William B; PROSSER, Lewis

Group Number 363
SIPPEL, Henry; LANE, Austin

Group Number 364
SIPPLE, John; WILLIAMS, Elizabeth

Group Number 365
SLYE, D A; JOHNSON, Lydia

Group Number 366
SMITH, Sheldon; PROPHET, James

Group Number 367
SMITH, William; MCBRIDE, Mary

Group Number 368
SNELL, Zachariah; JORDAN, Hannah

Group Number 369
SORENSEN, Egebret; SORENSON, Engebret; HAMILTON, Susannah

Group Number 370
SOUTHGATE, James E L; PENNOYER, Margaret L

Group Number 371
SPAFFORD, C C; CLARK, Robert; KENT, George L; LOWBER, Edward J

Group Number 372
SPAFFORD, C C; HENRY, Catharine

Group Number 373
SPAFFORD, C C; RULE, Rebecca

Group Number 374
SPAFFORD, C C; WILLIAMSON, Harriet

Group Number 375
SPAFFORD, Charles C; BEADLE, Robert; SMITH, Horace G; MOREHOUSE, Stephen

Group Number 376
SPAFFORD, Charles C; VAUGHAN, Eunice

Group Number 377
SPRAGUE, James B; SHUMAKER, Jacob

Group Number 378
STEVENS, Wilson; FARNHAM, Betsey

Group Number 379
STILES, Aaron K; BELDING, Aretus M; GARDNER, William R

Group Number 380
STILES, Aaron K; BRUNK, Maria; ALDEN, Philander M

Group Number 381
STILES, Aaron K; MEAD, Welthy

Group Number 382
STILES, Aaron K; MUDGE, William R; CHAMBERLIN, Edwin E

Group Number 383
STILES, Aaron K; SMITH, Enoch

Group Number 384
STILES, Aaron K; STURTEVANT, Ann L

Group Number 385
STONE, Stephen B; FRION, Sarah

Group Number 386
SUKOW, August; FRENCH, Samuel B

Group Number 387
SVENUNGSON, Hage; SVENUNGSON, Torge

Group Number 388
SWAN, Sylvester P; PE-QUAH-KO-NAH, ; HOBART, Harrison C; KAH-TE-NEEW-O-HO-PAZ-SHAY-NAH-, ; SHO-CHETTES,

Group Number 389
SWISHER, Elizabeth; SWISHER, Anthony

Group Number 390
TAPLIN, Philena; TAPLIN, Lorenzo D

Group Number 391
TAYLOR, Alexander; ALFARO, Isidora

Group Number 392
TAYLOR, Alexander; REICHARD, William

Group Number 393
TAYLOR, Joseph N; LOTT, Williampie

Group Number 394
THIBODO, Maxime; MCMURRY, Mary Catherine; MCMURRY, William

Group Number 395
THOMPSON, Austin; SHAW, William G

Group Number 396
THOMPSON, Reuben; BENTON, Betsey

Group Number 397
THOMPSON, William; WILLIAMS, John H

Group Number 398
TILLESON, Herald T E; CARLETON, Ingalls

Group Number 399
TOEL, William; NARSEE, ; HARDAGE, Siah

Group Number 400
TOWNSEND, Enoch W; PHILLIPS, Millea; PERRY, Albert

Group Number 401
TRASHER, John; BARKER, James S

Group Number 402
TRASK, James W; CHASE, Sarah

Group Number 403
TUBBS, A J; SEYMOUR, Betsey E; CREGO, Lester B; BURT, John

Group Number 404
UNDERHILL, Mary; UNDERHILL, John

Group Number 405
VARBLE, Elizabeth A; RING, Elizabeth A

Group Number 406
VEDDER, Van Vleck; SMITH, Alexander H

Group Number 407
VIBBERTS, Joseph S; WARE, Nathaniel

Group Number 408
WAGONER, Annie M; ANDERSON, Annie M

Group Number 409
WARREN, Catharine; WARREN, Jacob A; MONROE, Dennis; WARREN, James; DUNCAN, J H

Group Number 410
WASHBURN, Cadwallader C; HARDING, Polly; WASHBURN, William D

Group Number 411
WASHBURN, Cadwallader C; WASHBURN, William D

Group Number 412
WASHBURN, William D; GRIZZELL, Letty

Group Number 413
WATTERMAN, Joel; MEAD, Ira

Group Number 414
WEBB, Seth; SKINNER, Francis R

Group Number 415
WEBB, Walter; MANNING, Sarah

Group Number 416
WELTON, Maria L; WELTON, Bennett H

Group Number 417
WESTON, Daniel; CHAMBERLIN, George H

Group Number 418
WETHERBY, Matilda E; WETHERBY, Leonard

Group Number 419
WHITE, Elias A; KUNCLER, Frederick

Group Number 420
WHITE, Miles; JAMES, Frances

Group Number 421
WIGGINS, Joseph W; HOLCOMB, Philanda

Group Number 422
WIGGINS, Silas T; ARMSTRONG, Adolphus

Group Number 423
WILLIAMS, John F; HAVENSTICK, Susanna

Group Number 424
WILSON, William; CRAGIN, George A

Group Number 425
WILSON, William; CRIPPEN, Sophronia

Group Number 426
WILSON, William; MOUNTCASTLE, Mary A

Group Number 427
WILSON, William; STROTHER, Sally

Group Number 428
WILSTACH, John A; CLEAVELAND, Lucinda P

Group Number 429
WILSTACK, John A; FLEMING, Sarah

Group Number 430
WOOD, Daniel H; LEONARD, Alfred B

Group Number 431
WOODMAN, Horatio; BURNHAM, Anna

Group Number 432
WOODMAN, Horatio; BURNS, Lydia

Group Number 433
WOODMAN, Horatio; CHUBBUCK, Ann M

Group Number 434
WOODMAN, Horatio; INGERSOLL, Charles

Group Number 435
WOODWARD, Mary N; YEAMAN, Hester A

Group Number 436
WOODWARD, William A; BARNES, Polly

Group Number 437
WOODWARD, William A; LEE, Margaret

Group Number 438
WOODWARD, William A; NEVIN, Elizabeth; PUTNAM, Henry C

Group Number 439
WOODWARD, William A; PUTNAN, Henry C

Group Number 440
WOODWARD, William A; SEEDS, Carey S S; FELLOWS, William H

Group Number 441
WRIGHT, Marshall M; KERR, Nancy

Group Number 442
ZIMERMAN, John; OLMSTEAD, Maria T

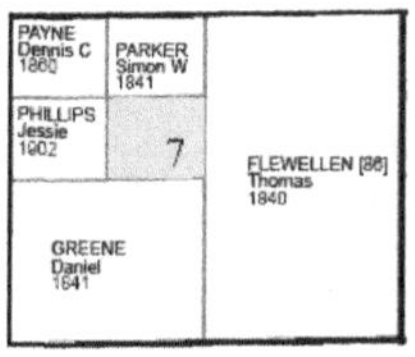

Extra! Extra! (about our Indexes)

We purposefully do not have an all-name index in the back of this volume so that our readers do not miss one of the best uses of this book: finding misspelled names among more specialized indexes.

Without repeating the text of our "How-to" chapter, we have nonetheless tried to assist our more anxious researchers by delivering a short-cut to the two county-wide Surname Indexes, the second of which will lead you to all-name indexes for each Congressional Township mapped in this volume :

Surname Index (whole county, with number of parcels mapped) ....page 18
Surname Index (township by township) ....just following

For your convenience, the "How To Use this Book" Chart on page 2 is repeated on the reverse of this page.

We should be releasing new titles every week for the foreseeable future. We urge you to write, fax, call, or email us any time for a current list of titles. Of course, our web-page will always have the most current information about current and upcoming books.

Arphax Publishing Co.
2210 Research Park Blvd.
Norman, Oklahoma 73069
(800) 681-5298 toll-free
(405) 366-6181 local
(405) 366-8184 fax
info@arphax.com

www.arphax.com

How to Use This Book - A Graphical Summary

Part I
"The Big Picture"

Map A ▸ *Counties in the State*
Map B ▸ *Surrounding Counties*
Map C ▸ *Congressional Townships (Map Groups) in the County*
Map D ▸ *Cities & Towns in the County*
Map E ▸ *Cemeteries in the County*
Surnames in the County ▸ *Number of Land-Parcels for Each Surname*
Surname/Township Index ▸ Directs you to Township Map Groups in Part II

The Surname/Township Index can direct you to any number of **Township Map Groups**

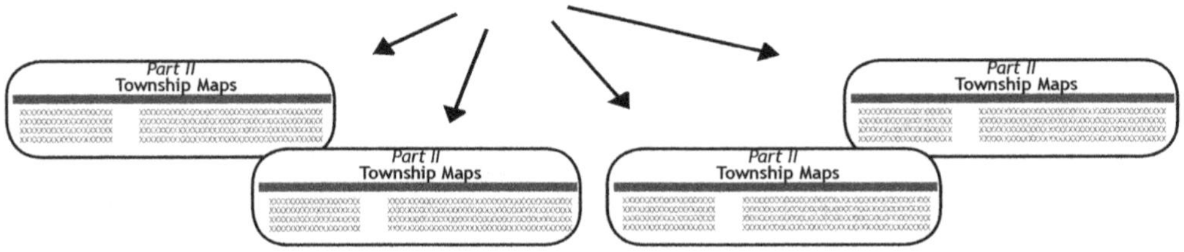

Part II
Township Map Groups
(1 for each Township in the County)

Each Township Map Group contains all four of of the following tools . . .

Land Patent Index ▸ *Every-name Index of Patents Mapped in this Township*
Land Patent Map ▸ *Map of Patents as listed in above Index*
Road Map ▸ *Map of Roads, City-centers, and Cemeteries in the Township*
Historical Map ▸ *Map of Railroads, Lakes, Rivers, Creeks, City-Centers, and Cemeteries*

Appendices

Appendix A ▸ *Congressional Authority enabling Patents within our Maps*
Appendix B ▸ *Section-Parts / Aliquot Parts (a comprehensive list)*
Appendix C ▸ *Multi-patentee Groups (Individuals within Buying Groups)*

(This page is a repeat of page 2 in the text)